Read this first!

Here's how to find the incredible wedding and special event information in *Here Comes The Guide:*

• Event Locations

Sites are organized by region and city, with illustrated descriptions and details about capacities, fees and services. To find a specific site, see the index starting on page 781.

• Event Services

We feature Northern California's best event professionals—caterers, coordinators, photographers, florists, DJs and more. To review all of them, see pages 707–778. And to find out how they qualified to be in *Here Comes The Guide,* read page 701.

• Bridal Salons

Looking for a fabulous wedding dress or bridesmaid dresses? Find some of the best salons listed on pages 794–795.

Don't forget to check out HereComesTheGuide.com!

HereComesTheGuide.com has the most up-to-date information on event sites and services, as well as lots of color photos and virtual tours. And if you have a certain type of location or event professional in mind, you'll really appreciate our amazingly useful search engine. We make it easy to find exactly what you're looking for.

Cover Photographer

Jihan Abdalla Photography

Award-winning international photographer Jihan Abdalla is so enthusiastic that she seems to live her life with an exclamation point. A self-proclaimed people person with a special knack for photography, it was only fitting that she would gravitate toward shooting weddings.

Jihan radiates such positive energy that couples are immediately at ease in front of her camera. She has a reputation for having fun with her clients and often stays in touch with them after their wedding. While she's normally unobtrusive on the job, the artist in her simply won't let her pass up a perfect moment or the right light, so she may just pull the couple aside to get the shot…and the results are usually so amazing they don't regret her taking action.

The key to Jihan's success is her ability to balance her instincts with her technical skills. "When I see an image through my camera, I know what the photo is going to look like before I take it," she says. And she's so adept at using natural lighting, she's able to capture the instant when the bride's hair is backlit by the setting sun or her face takes on a tender softness in dappled shade. At the same time, she's fascinated by personal stories, and infuses her wedding images with a documentary quality that conveys the mood, thoughts and feelings of her subjects.

Jihan is adventurous, fearless and even a bit of a "MacGyver" if necessary—she and her team have saved the day on several occasions, one time by stitching a bride into her dress at the last minute! In fact, Jihan is not just a photographer: She's attuned to the Big Picture and so aware of everything going on around her that she often steps in to help her clients, the coordinator and any other vendors so that the wedding flows smoothly.

Jihan grew up in Santa Barbara, California, but has lived in Brazil, Costa Rica, Belgium and Italy, and speaks Portuguese, Spanish and Italian. It was while documenting her global travels that she discovered photography. The craft has added a dynamic dimension to her appreciation of the world, even beyond her career. "I remember my life through photography," says Jihan. "I can look at almost any photo I have ever taken, whether it's from my own experience or one of my client's, and instantly relive everything about that moment." That's just how couples feel when looking at their Jihan Abdalla photographs: The past is suddenly present, along with the emotions that made the time so special.

A professional wedding photojournalist since 2005, Jihan's images have appeared in *Vogue Noiva* (Brazil), *Santa Barbara, Martha's Vineyard Island Weddings, The Knot, Latter Day Bride, Your Wedding Day* and *Ines del Mar Weddings.*

Jihan's zestful personality certainly comes across in our cover photo. We were drawn to this image by the energy and sparkle in the bride's expression. It's as if she has a little secret she's sharing with you, the lucky reader.

www.jihanabdalla.com

Back Cover Photos:

From Top Left: *Adobe Lodge,* photo by Tom Bracco; *San Francisco Conservatory of Flowers,* photo by Larry Kunkel; *Poppy Ridge Golf Club,* photo by Joanne Dost; *Kohl Mansion,* photo by Peter Atherton; *Edgewood Tahoe,* photo by Joanne Dost

From Bottom Left: *Branch Out,* photo by Kathleen Harrison; *Tu Photography; Le Papillon; Hyegraph Invitations & Calligraphy; Events of Distinction,* photo by Irvine Photography

What Makes Us Different?

We do most of your homework for you.

1. We actually visit the locations in *Here Comes The Guide*.

We check out 99% of our event sites in person before we include them in *The Guide*.

2. We write every location description with you in mind.

Each site description is based on our personal experience, so it's informative, accurate and often entertaining.

3. We provide real prices, along with nitty-gritty details about capacity, site services and amenities.

By the time you call or visit a location, you're a thoroughly informed consumer!

4. We prescreen all of our event professionals so you don't have to.

All of the photographers, floral designers, caterers and other vendors in our Service Directory have been **CERTIFIED BY THE GUIDE.** That means we've thoroughly checked them out, so you don't have to worry about hiring them. Every one is outstanding—we're honored to represent them.

5. We save you a ton of time.

By putting so much comprehensive information all in one place, we save you hours...days...maybe months of searching for event locations and professionals. And, you can actually do most of your planning without leaving home!

HereComesTheGuide.com has it ALL:

- ## Virtual Tours

  Most of the event sites we feature on **HereComesTheGuide.com** have virtual tours! It's *the* way to explore wedding locations on your own time (and in your pajamas).

- ## Color Photos of Hundreds of Wedding Venues and Services

  Each location and event professional has their own photo gallery. Our website also includes many locations that are so new they aren't even in this book! **HereComesTheGuide.com** has the most updated pricing info, too.

- ## CERTIFIED BY THE GUIDE Event Services

  We don't just feature any old caterer or DJ. We've carefully checked out each event professional so you don't have to!

- ## Local Bridal Shows

  Find out what events are happening near you: fab food tastings, fashion shows…. Did you have something better to do this weekend?

- ## Handpicked Bridal Salons

  You may never walk a runway, but you'll walk down the aisle as the glittering fashionista you were born to be! We've scoped out the shops that'll make it all happen.

- ## My Guide

  Log in to organize your **HereComesTheGuide.com** search results. You can save and share your favorite locations and event services (and we won't give out your email address—period).

What People Say

"I went out and spent the money on your book without hesitation. I'm so glad I did! I've gotten some great ideas and was able to create an outline for my budget. Not only did I find great reception locations in your book, but I think I found my rehearsal dinner place as well. It was a gold mine!"

—*Liz Davis*

"I went to about ten locations that are in your book and found that the site descriptions were pretty accurate. I'm amazed at how well you were able to capture the feeling of a place and put it into words."

—*Stephanie Stevensen*

"I'm in the process of helping my daughter research sites for her wedding reception and your site has been hugely helpful! **The location information is thorough and consistent, making comparing the different locations so easy.** We have found places to check out that we never would have thought of on our own. Thanks so much for all the work you must have done to put all this information together!"

—*Rebecca's Mom*

"Having recently gotten married, I have a special appreciation for *Here Comes The Guide.* It was extremely helpful during my time of planning. **The quick descriptions painted a beautiful picture of each and every location, and were very helpful in narrowing down the search by budget, criteria and location.** I feel this is a very important tool for every busy bride and still recommend it to all my engaged friends."

—*A Southern California Bride*

"I got married in August and cannot stress how much help *Here Comes The Guide* was to me. **I was often able to receive more information from your site than from my contact with the actual locations and vendors!** Especially since I was planning a Northern California wedding from Southern California, you saved me A TON of legwork."

—*Jamie Juster, Bride*

"I have finally found a website that has it all! **I'm planning my wedding from out of state and your event locations search is the best!** I've been looking for a website that has all the information in one place. Thank you!!!"

—*Sarah*

About Here Comes The Guide

"I just had to let you know how WONDERFUL your website is. I was amazed to finally find a website with REAL information. Other wedding websites just gave me names and phone numbers, and I still had to do all the research on my own. Yours gave me all the nitty-gritty stuff I needed to know to find locations and vendors. **With only two sessions at your website, my wedding was planned. Amazing!**"

—Christina R.

"I have to tell you, **I was blown away by your website. It's so beautiful and professionally done.** The detail you provide is just enough so that the browser doesn't get bogged down in minutiae. Your site is such a great resource that I've started telling everybody about it. I've seen tons of wedding sites, so I know that you've come up with something that's really different."

—Kimberly P.

"I completely love your website and look forward to the book. **This is the only resource that is so detailed on California sites, and it makes it so much easier to plan from a long distance.** *Here Comes The Guide* is the best source of information."

—Jocelyn

"**I absolutely love your new website. It's warm, feminine and has what one might call 'simple elegance.'** Great job! I refer friends to your website all the time—for weddings, showers and of course, birthdays. Keep up the fabulous work."

—Maria, Bride

"I love your site! Most other sites that I visited seemed to have a hidden agenda to steer me towards only what benefited them. **This site is non-biased and easy to use.** Thank you!"

—Elisa Parra, Bride

"Thanks for providing this invaluable resource! **I'll be using the site for corporate event planning—I don't know what I did without it!**"

—Mary, Corporate Planner

"**This is a wonderful website, with all the details that a bride looks for when she's searching for a reception location.** It's well organized and incredibly useful. I wish there were more sites like this one. THANK YOU!!!"

—Amy

We Need Your Help

- **Tell locations that you're using *Here Comes The Guide*.**

  When you call the places we feature, let the sites' representatives know that you heard about them through *The Guide*.

- **Help us keep our information current.**

  We'd appreciate it if you'd contact us with your comments, corrections, suggestions and complaints. Your feedback helps us maintain the accuracy of our information.

- **Let us know if you discover a great location that's not featured in *Here Comes The Guide*.**

  Please call or email us if you find an event site you think we should include in our book and on our website.

Hopscotch Press, Inc.
930 Carleton Street, Berkeley CA 94710
510/548-0400   fax 510/548-0144

info@HereComesTheGuide.com
www.HereComesTheGuide.com

Information Is Always Changing

Everything changes:
pricing, services, décor,
landscaping and even ownership.

We've tried to make the information in this book completely accurate, but it's not possible. Locations give us incorrect facts and figures, change ownership or management, revamp their pricing and policies and sometimes go out of business. Truth is, things can turn upside down overnight.

So how can you make sure that you're getting correct information? It's simple:

- Bring your book with you (or printouts from our website) when you hunt for locations.

- When you contact a location, show or read the information in *Here Comes The Guide* to the facility's representative to verify that it's still current.

- Get everything that's been agreed on in writing, and review it carefully before you sign any contract!

Here Comes The Guide

Twelfth Edition

Copyright © 2011–2012

Published by Hopscotch Press, Inc.

Printed in the U.S.A.

Here Comes The Guide, Northern California®

Twelfth Edition

Jan Brenner, *Co-Author/Editor-in-Chief*
Jolene Rae Harrington, *Co-Author/Editor*

Meredith Monday Schwartz, *Managing Director, Hopscotch Press, Inc.*
Sharon Carl, *Production Director*
Lisa Edd, *Managing Editor*
Denise Auerbach, *Director of Vendor Sales*
Jennifer Ahearn, *Online Media Director*
Julia Snippen, *Regional Sales Manager*
Jenna Miller, *Vendor Sales Manager*
Angela Mullan, *Sales and Production*

Lynn Broadwell, *Publisher*

Inside Illustrations: *Jon Dalton and Michael Tse*

Library of Congress Control Number: 2010937404
ISBN 9781885355171

Here Comes The Guide®

Twelfth Edition

Acknowledgments

We're able to update every edition of *Here Comes The Guide*, because we get a lot of help.

Our deepest appreciation goes to our writers, Jolene Rae Harrington (also an invaluable editor) and Laurie Turner. Without them none of our books would ever get written.

Our artist, Jon Dalton, penned all the new illustrations for this edition of *Here Comes The Guide*. Using both computer graphics and fine art skills, he transformed photographs of the facilities into the distinctive line drawings that give *The Guide* its unique style.

And as always, we are eternally grateful to our clients and our readers. Your support year in and year out keeps *Here Comes The Guide* a going concern.

Table of Contents

Really Really Important Information

Part One: Event Locations

Regional Areas and Cities

San Francisco

North Bay

Part Two: Event Services

Preface

When I graduated from college, I thought I'd never have to do another endless research project again. Boy, was I wrong. Compared to looking for a place to get married, term papers were a piece of cake. I began my quest optimistically enough, but after a couple of days of frantic and fruitless networking (my wedding date was a mere three months down the road!), the enormity of my task started to sink in. It had taken me 33 years to find the right guy, and it was beginning to look like it might take an equally long time to find the right place.

Going into high gear, I reached out and touched just about everyone I knew, along with quite a few total strangers. Friends and friends of friends didn't have any recommendations that suited our particular needs, and although wedding consultants had information, they were reluctant to part with their lists of sites unless I hired them to plan my wedding. I even called some caterers, florists and cake makers, but they were usually too busy to give me in-depth descriptions of places over the phone. Some chambers of commerce had organized wedding location lists ready to mail out; others had nothing and knew nothing.

After days of phoning, all I had was a patchwork quilt of information. I still hadn't found *the* place, and finally had to face the painful truth: there was no central resource or comprehensive, detailed list. I became anxious. With a full-time job I was hardly free to conduct an exhaustive search, and I realized that I would never be able to find out about the vast majority of interesting or unusual wedding sites, let alone thoroughly evaluate them! My frustration was exacerbated by the fact that it was August and the wedding date in October was drawing closer with each passing day.

As luck would have it, my sister mentioned that her hairdresser had gotten married on a yacht in San Francisco Bay. Hallelujah! That's it! I cried. What a great idea! I'd never even thought about a floating wedding and had no idea you could do such a thing.

We got married on a hot, sunny day behind Angel Island in San Francisco Bay. The captain performed the ceremony on the bow, and afterwards the yacht tooted its horn, the crew let loose multi-colored balloons, and a "just married" sign was thrown over the stern. As we swept past Alcatraz Island, Sausalito and the Golden Gate and Bay Bridges, our guests relaxed in the sun, enjoying drinks and hors d'oeuvres. What a wonderful day! Even my parents' friends had a great time, and wrote us after the wedding to let us know how much they'd loved their outing on the water.

Serendipity was largely responsible for making my wedding memorable, but you don't have to rely on luck. I created *Here Comes The Guide* so that others wouldn't have to experience what I went through, and I hope it makes your search for the perfect location easy and painless.

Lynn Broadwell
Publisher

Really Really Important Information

Introduction

Little did we know when we wrote *Here Comes The Guide, Northern California* in 1989 that we would receive such an overwhelming response from our readers. The first edition sold out in less than a year, and as public demand grew we hustled to get the second edition in print. Thanks to our enthusiastic readership of engaged brides, savvy party hostesses and event planners, *The Guide* continues to be a best-seller!

So what makes this book so popular?

We've done most of your homework for you.

We present comprehensive, solid information: a full description and illustration of each location, plus details about fees, capacities and services. Our wide selection of facilities includes delightful places that you might not have found on your own.

This book cuts your search time by 90%.

Instead of having to call dozens of facilities and ask the same questions over and over again, you can look up many of the answers in *The Guide*. Once you've narrowed down your list of potential sites, you can contact them to schedule an in-person visit. Not only does *The Guide* save you time, it often saves you money by letting you comparison shop!

We screen all our locations.

We personally evaluated almost every property in *Here Comes The Guide,* sending a professional writer to 99% of our sites to make sure they met our criteria. (Yes, we actually turn down locations that don't satisfy our requirements.)

All our service professionals are *Certified By The Guide.*

Our goal is to represent only the best event professionals in the industry. In order to achieve this, we thoroughly screen all of the service providers in *Here Comes The Guide.* That means you don't have to take a chance on some anonymous photographer or caterer. Every one of our vendors has been carefully checked out and *Certified By The Guide.*

Our rigorous certification process requires each vendor to submit 30 references, half wedding industry professionals and half recent brides. Then we contact each person and get their honest feedback. Only if the company gets a rave review do we accept them as a client.

(Even though we've checked out all of our professionals very carefully, we can't guarantee their performance. Here Comes The Guide is not responsible for the contract you ultimately sign with them, or for how your event goes. Our best advice is to be thorough, careful consumers and get every single thing in writing. This is what we tell our sisters and best friends, so this is what we're telling you.)

We're experienced.

We've been writing and publishing *Here Comes The Guide* since 1989. We're proud that our publication has become the essential resource for weddings—and just about any kind of event in California.

If you can't find the perfect spot or service in *Here Comes The Guide*, check out our website at HereComesTheGuide.com.

You'll have access to the *Here Comes The Guide* book online and a lot more:

- **More locations,** along with photo galleries, virtual tours and slide shows. You'll be able to tour hundreds of sites in your pajamas.

- **More services,** with lots of color photos of bouquets, cakes, dresses, you name it!

- **More tips, trends, and ideas—more inspiration!** Check out our Find Ideas section to get the skinny on all things wedding.

Navigation is a snap, and our searchable database lets you find event sites by city, type, capacity, view, etc., and event professionals by company name or service category. A special *My Guide* feature lets you save your favorites and share them with friends and family.

And check back often—we regularly update our website with event locations and services that are not featured in the book!

Understanding Our Information

Explanation of Main Headings

Each location description in *Here Comes The Guide* follows the same format. To help you understand the information presented, we've provided an explanation of the main headings in the same order as they appear.

Description

Once you've selected a geographical area and you're clear about your needs, then thoroughly review all the sites listed in your area of preference. The descriptions are written to give you a good idea of what places are like, from ambiance to physical layout. However, before reading the descriptions, you may want to check the *Capacity* and *Fees & Deposits* sections to determine which places seem to be a good fit from a size and budget perspective. If a facility is still a viable option after you've read the entire two-page editorial, mark it with a ✔ or flag it for easy reference when planning phone calls and site visits later on.

Ceremony Capacity

Standing and seated capacities are included for ceremonies since these numbers may be totally different than the corresponding numbers for receptions.

Reception Capacity

By now you should have a rough idea of how many people will be attending. If not, you may be in trouble, since many facilities want a deposit based on an estimated head count. Look at the capacity figures for each event location. Seated or sit-down capacity refers to guests seated at tables. Standing capacity refers to a function where the majority of guests are not seated, such as a champagne/hors d'oeuvres reception. Put a ✔ next to those facilities that are compatible with your guest count. If you're planning well in advance and don't have your guest list whittled down yet, then you'll just have to estimate and refine the count as the date draws near. There is a world of difference in cost and planning effort between an intimate party of 60 and a large wedding with over 200 guests. Pin down your numbers as soon as you can.

Meeting Capacity

In general, the seated capacity for meetings is listed as a range or a maximum. Sometimes, specific spaces are named along with their individual capacities. Occasionally, seating configurations are also provided: *theater-style* (auditorium row seating with chairs arranged closely together), *classroom-style* (an organized table-and-chair arrangement, usually in rows) and *conference-style* (seating around tables).

Fees and Deposits

We've tried to make the information regarding costs as accurate as possible. Where we haven't mentioned the price, it may be because the facility's fee schedule was either changing at time of publication or too complicated to fit into our format. Some facilities want the flexibility to negotiate prices, and prefer not to state them until they know exactly what kind of function you have in mind.

It's a good idea to confirm the information in *Here Comes The Guide* with the facility you're calling, just to make sure it's still valid. If you're planning far in advance, anticipate price increases by the time your function occurs. Once you're definite about your location, try to lock in your fees in a contract, protecting yourself from possible rate increases later. Make sure you ask about every service provided and are clear about all of the extras that can really add up. Facilities may charge you for tables, chairs, linens, plateware and silverware, glassware and additional hours. Don't be surprised to see tax and service charges in fixed amounts applied to the total bill if the facility provides restaurant or catering services. Although it may seem redundant to include the phrase "tax and service charges are additional" in each entry, we find that most people forget (or just don't want to accept the painful reality) that 19%–28% will be applied to the food and beverage total.

Sometimes a deposit is nonrefundable—a fact you'll definitely want to know if the deposit is a large percentage of the total bill. And even if it's refundable, you still need to read the cancellation policy thoroughly. Also make

> **Look at the information regarding fees and deposits and remember that these figures change regularly and usually in one direction—up!**

sure you understand the policies that will ensure you get your cleaning and security deposit returned in full and again, get everything in writing.

Food costs vary considerably. Carefully plan your menu with the caterer, event consultant or chef. Depending on the style of service and the type of food being served, the total food bill can vary dramatically—even if you're getting quotes from the same caterer. Expect a multicourse seated meal to be the most expensive part of your event.

Alcohol is expensive, too, and you may be restricted in what you can serve and who can serve it. A facility may not allow you to bring your own alcoholic beverages, and if it does it may limit you to wine or champagne. Many places discourage you from bringing your own (BYO) by charging an exorbitant corkage fee to remove the cork and pour. Other places have limited permits that don't allow them to serve alcohol or restrict them from serving certain kinds; some will let you or the caterer serve alcohol, others require someone with a license. Make sure you know what's allowed. Decide what your budget is for alcohol and determine what types you're able to provide. And keep in mind that the catering fees you are quoted rarely include the cost of alcohol. If you provide the alcohol, make sure you keep your purchase receipts so you can return any unopened bottles.

So how much will your event cost? Facility deposits are usually not large, but sometimes the rental fees plus food and beverage services can add up to $30,000 or more, depending on the site and number of guests. Be sure you have a sensible handle on your budget and read all the fine print before you sign any contract.

Availability

Some facilities are available 7am to 2am; others offer very limited "windows." If you'd like to save some money, consider a weekday or weeknight reception, or think about having your event in the off-season (November, or January through March). Even the most sought-after places have openings midweek and during non-peak months—and at reduced costs. Facilities want your business and are more likely to negotiate terms and prices if they have nothing else scheduled. Again, read all the fine print carefully and ✔ those facilities that have time slots that meet your needs. If the date you have in mind is already booked, it doesn't hurt to ask if someone actually confirmed that date by paying a deposit or signing a contract. If they haven't, you may be in luck.

Services/Amenities and Restrictions

Most facilities provide something in the way of services and many have limitations that may affect your function. For instance, they may not allow you to have amplified music outdoors or bring your own caterer.

We've attempted to give you a brief description of what each location has to offer and what is restricted. Because of space limitations, we've shortened words and developed a key to help you decipher our abbreviated notations. Once you're familiar with our notation style, you'll be able to read through all the data outlined at the bottom of each entry and put a ✔ next to each facility that meets your requirements.

Services/Amenities Key

CATERING
- **provided:** the facility provides catering (for a fee)
- **provided, no BYO:** the facility provides catering; you cannot bring in your own
- **preferred list:** you must select your caterer from the facility's approved list
- **provided or BYO:** the facility will provide catering or you can select an outside caterer of your own
- **BYO, licensed:** arrange for your own licensed caterer

KITCHEN FACILITIES
- **ample** or **fully equipped:** large and well-equipped with major appliances
- **moderate:** medium-sized and utilitarian
- **minimal:** small with limited equipment, may not have all the basic appliances
- **setup** or **prep only:** room for setup and food prep, but not enough space or utilities to cook food
- **n/a:** not applicable because facility provides catering

TABLES & CHAIRS
- **some provided** or **provided:** facility provides some or all of the tables and chairs
- **BYO:** make arrangements to bring your own

LINENS, SILVER, ETC.
- same as above

RESTROOMS
- **wheelchair accessible** or
- **not wheelchair accessible**

DANCE FLOOR
- **yes:** an area for dancing (hardwood floor, cement terrace, patio) is available
- **CBA, extra charge:** you can arrange for a dance floor to be brought in for a fee

BRIDE'S & GROOM'S DRESSING AREA
- **yes:** there is an area for changing
- **no:** there's no area for changing
- **limited:** smaller space not fully equipped as changing room
- **CBA:** can be arranged

PARKING
- **CBA:** can be arranged
  other descriptions are self explanatory

ACCOMMODATIONS
If overnight accommodations are available on site, the number of guestrooms is listed.
- **CBA:** the facility will arrange accommodations for you

TELEPHONE
- **restricted:** calls made on the house phone must be local, collect or charged to a credit card
- **guest phones:** private phones in guestrooms
- **house phone:** central phone used by all guests
- **emergency only:** self-explanatory

OUTDOOR NIGHT LIGHTING
- **yes:** there is adequate light to conduct your event outdoors after dark
- **access only** or **limited:** lighting is sufficient for access only

OUTDOOR COOKING FACILITIES

- **BBQ:** the facility has a barbecue on the premises
- **BBQ, CBA:** a barbecue can be arranged through the facility
- **BYO BBQ:** make arrangements for your own barbecue
- **n/a:** not applicable

CLEANUP

- **provided:** facility takes care of cleanup
- **caterer:** your caterer is responsible
- **caterer or renter:** both you and/or your caterer are responsible for cleanup

MEETING EQUIPMENT

- **full range:** facility has a full range of audiovisual equipment, including projectors, overhead screens, etc.
- **no:** no equipment is available
- **BYO:** bring your own meeting equipment
- **CBA:** equipment can be arranged
- **CBA, extra fee:** equipment can be arranged for an extra fee

VIEW

We've described what type of view is available for each facility.

- **no:** the facility has no views to speak of

OTHER

Description of any service or amenity not included in above list.

Restrictions Key

ALCOHOL

- **provided, no BYO:** the facility provides alcoholic beverages (for a fee) and does not permit you to bring your own
- **BYO:** you can bring your own alcohol
- **corkage, $/bottle:** if you bring your own alcohol, the facility charges a fee per bottle to remove the cork and pour
- **WCB only:** *(or any combination of these three letters)* only wine, champagne and beer are permitted
- **licensed server:** the server of alcohol must be licensed

SMOKING

- **allowed:** smoking is permitted throughout the facility
- **outside only:** smoking is not permitted inside the facility
- **not allowed:** smoking is not permitted anywhere on the premises
- **designated areas:** specific areas for smoking have been designated

MUSIC

Almost every facility allows acoustic music unless stated otherwise. Essentially, restrictions refer to amplified music.

- **amplified OK:** amplified music is acceptable without restriction
- **outside only:** no amplified music allowed inside
- **inside only:** no amplified music permitted outside
- **amplified OK with limits or restrictions:** amplified music is allowed but there are limits on volume, hours of play, type of instruments, etc.

WHEELCHAIR ACCESS

Accessibility is based on whether the event areas (not necessarily the restrooms) of a facility are wheelchair accessible or not.

- **yes:** the facility is accessible
- **limited:** the facility is accessible but with difficulty (there may be a step at the entrance, for example, but all of the rooms are accessible)
- **no:** the facility is not accessible

INSURANCE

Many facilities require that you purchase and show proof of some insurance coverage. The type and amount of insurance varies with the facility, and some facilities offer insurance for a minimal charge.

- **required, certificate required** or **proof of insurance required:** additional insurance is required
- **not required:** no additional insurance is required
- **may be required:** sometimes additional insurance is required

Valuable Tips

Selecting an Event Location

Before you jump into the facility descriptions in *Here Comes The Guide,* identify what kind of celebration you want and establish selection criteria early. Here are some basics:

Is Your Site Geographically Desirable?

Your first big decision is to select a location that will make geographical sense to you, your family and the majority of your guests. Most people have special events close to home or office, so there's not much to consider. But if you pick a spot out of town, you need to think about the logistics of getting everyone to your event site.

Special Considerations in Northern California

Guests may be traveling a considerable distance by car to get to your party destination. Given the Northern California freeway system and traffic congestion, you'll save them lots of time and trouble if you provide, along with the invitation, specific directions on a separate map drawn to scale. Include symbols indicating directions (north, south, etc.) and the names of the appropriate off-ramps. If you're not sure about exits, landmarks or street names, take a dry run of the route to make sure everything on your map is accurate and easy to follow. If your function occurs after dark, do the test drive at night so you can note well-lit landmarks that will prevent your guests from getting lost—both coming to your event and going home.

If you're having a Friday evening event, take commuters into account, especially if your event site is in an area that gets bumper-to-bumper traffic. Plan to have your event after 7pm when freeways are less congested.

Even if you have few constraints when picking a location, it's still worth considering the total driving time to and from your destination. When it's over two hours, an overnight stay may be necessary and you may be limited to a Saturday night event, since your nearest and dearest won't be able to spend hours on the road during the week. If you have guests arriving by plane, it's certainly helpful if there's an airport nearby, and if your co-workers, friends or family enjoy drinking, try to house them close to the event site.

There's no reason why you can't contemplate a special event in the Santa Cruz mountains or in a wine cave in Calistoga. Just remember that the further out you go, the more time it will take to choreograph your event—and you may end up having to delegate the details of party planning to someone else.

Budget

You'd think that working from a budget would be obvious, but you'd be surprised how many people, especially brides and grooms, are unrealistic about what they can afford. Part of the problem is that most people aren't very experienced with event budgeting and don't know how to estimate what locations, products and services will ultimately cost.

In the early planning stages it's a good idea to talk to a professional event planner or wedding consultant to get a sense of what's feasible and what's not. You don't have to make a big financial or time commitment to use a professional; many will assist you on an hourly basis for a nuts-and-bolts session to determine priorities and to assign costs to items on your wish list.

Part of being realistic involves some simple arithmetic. For instance, the couple who has $5,000 for 250 guests should know that $20 per guest won't go very far. Tax and gratuity combined can consume an average of 25% of the food and beverage budget (the range is generally 19% to 28%). If you subtract that 25% from $20, you have $15 left. If you also serve alcohol at $6/person, you're down to $9/person for food. That's not enough for a seated meal, let alone location rental fees, band, flowers, printed invitations, etc.

Before you make any major decisions or commit any of your funds for specific items, take a serious look at your total budget and make sure it can cover all your anticipated expenses. If it can't, it's time for some hard decisions. If you have a very large guest list and a small pocketbook, you may need to shorten the list or cut back on some of the amenities you want to include. No matter who foots the bill, be advised that doing the homework here really counts. Pin down your costs at the beginning of the planning stage and get all estimates in writing.

> **The important point is that if you know what kind of event you want and are clear about your budget, your search will be made faster and easier.**

Style

Do you know what kind of event you want? Will it be a formal or informal affair, a traditional wedding or an innovative party? Will it be held at night or during the day, indoors or outdoors? You can set the tone of your function by selecting the right location, but know what you want before you start looking at locations or the sheer number of options will be overwhelming.

Guest Count

How many people are anticipated? Many facilities request a rough estimate 60 to 90 days in advance of your function—and they'll want a deposit based on the figure you give them. A confirmed guest count or guarantee is usually required 72 hours prior to the event. It's important to know what the numbers are early on in order to plan your budget and select the right ceremony or reception spot.

It's also important to ensure that the guest count you give the facility *before* your event doesn't change *during* your event. Believe it or not, it's possible to have more people at your reception than you expected. How? Some folks who did not bother to RSVP may decide to show up anyway. In one case we know of, the parents of the bride got an additional bill for $1,200 on the event day because there were 30 "surprise" guests beyond the guest count guarantee who were wined and dined. To prevent this from happening to you—especially if you're having a large reception where it's hard to keep track of all the guests—it's a good idea to phone everyone who did *not* RSVP. Let them know as politely as possible that you will need to have their response by a given date to finalize food and beverage totals.

Seasonal Differences

Northern California, for all its (pardon the expression) faults, has got some great advantages weather-wise. Outdoor special events, ceremonies and receptions can take place throughout most of the year, and from September to November you can anticipate sunny skies and warm climes. However, when the mercury rises in inland areas, watch out. A canopy or tables with umbrellas are essential for screening the sun. In fact, you should ask each facility manager about the sun's direction and intensity with respect to the time of day and month your event will take place. Guests will be uncomfortable facing into the sun during a ceremony, and white walls and enclosed areas bounce light around and can hold in heat. If your event is scheduled for midday in July, for example, include a note on your location map to bring sunglasses, hat and sunscreen. If you also mention words like "poolside," "yacht deck" or "lawn seating" on the map, it will help guests know how to dress. In summer, you might want to consider an evening rather than a midday celebration. Not only is the air cooler, but you may also get an extra bonus—a glorious sunset.

If you're arranging an outdoor party November through April, or in the foothills or mountain areas, expect cooler weather and prepare a contingency plan. Despite our region's favorable Mediterranean climate, it has rained in May, June and July, so consider access to an inside space or a tent.

Special Requirements

Sometimes, places have strict rules and regulations. If most of your guests smoke, then pick a location that doesn't restrict smoking. If alcohol is going to be consumed, make sure it's allowed and find out if bar service needs to be licensed. If dancing and a big band are critical, then limit yourself to those locations that can accommodate them and the accompanying decibels. Do you have children, seniors or disabled guests, vegetarians or folks who want kosher food on your list? If so, you need to plan for them, too. It's essential that you identify the special factors that are important for your event before you sign a contract.

Locking in Your Event Date

Let's say it's the first day of your hunt for the perfect spot, and the second place you see is an enchanting garden that happens to be available on the date you want. You really like it but, since you've only seen two locations, you're not 100% sure that this is *the* place. No problem. You decide to keep your options open by making a tentative reservation. The site coordinator dutifully pencils your name into her schedule book and says congratulations. You say thanks, we have a few more places (like 25) to check out, but this one looks terrific. Then off you go, secure in the knowledge that if none of the other sites you visit pans out, you still have this lovely garden waiting for you.

The nightmare begins a couple of weeks or perhaps months down the road when you've finished comparison-shopping and call back the first place you liked to finalize the details. So sorry, the coordinator says. We gave away your date because a) oops, one of the other gals who works here erased your name by mistake (after all, it was only *penciled* in), b) we didn't hear back from you soon enough, or c) you never confirmed your reservation with a deposit.

For the tiniest instant you picture yourself inflicting bodily harm on the coordinator or at least slapping the facility with a lawsuit, but alas, there's really not much you can do. Whether a genuine mistake was made or the facility purposely gave your date to another, perhaps more lucrative party (this happens sometimes with hotels who'd rather book a big convention on your date than a little wedding), you're out of luck. To avoid the pain (and ensuing panic) of getting bumped, here's what we suggest: instead of just being penciled in, ask if you can write a refundable $100–250 check to hold the date for a limited time. If the person in charge is willing to do this but wants the full deposit up front (usually nonrefundable), then you'll need to decide whether you can afford to lose the entire amount if you find a more appealing location later on. Once the coordinator or sales person takes your money, you're automatically harder to bump. Make sure you get a receipt which has the event date, year, time and space(s) reserved written on it, as well as the date your tentative reservation runs out. Then, just to be on the safe side, check in with the facility weekly while you're considering other sites to prevent any possible "mistakes" from being made. When you finally do commit to a place, get a signed contract or at least a confirmation letter. If you don't receive written confirmation within a week, hound the coordinator until you get it, even if you have to drive to the sales office and stand there until they hand it over to you. And

> **If you try to pick a location before you've made basic decisions, selection will be a struggle and it will take longer to find a spot that will make you happy.**

even after you've plunked down your money and have a letter and/or contract securing your date, call the coordinator every other month to reconfirm your reservation. It pays to stay on top of this, no matter how locked in you think you are.

Parking

Parking is seldom a critical factor if you get married outside an urban area, but make sure you know how it's going to be handled if you're planning a party in a parking-challenged place like downtown San Francisco, San Jose or Berkeley.

A map is a handy supplement to any invitation, and there's usually enough room on it to indicate how and where vehicles should be parked. Depending on the location, you may want to add a note suggesting carpooling or mention that a shuttle service or valet parking is provided. If there's a fee for parking, identify the anticipated cost per car and where the entry points are to the nearest parking lots. The last thing you want are surprised and disgruntled guests who can't find a place to stash their car, or who are shocked at the $20 to $40 parking tab.

Professional Help

If you're a busy person with limited time to plan and execute a party, pick a facility that offers complete coordination services, from catering and flowers to decorations and music. Or better yet, hire a professional event or wedding consultant. Either way, you'll make your life much easier by having someone else handle the details.

Food and Alcohol Quality

Food and alcohol account for the greatest portion of an event's budget; consequently, food and beverage selections are a big deal. Given the amount of money you will spend on this category alone, you should be concerned about the type, quantity and quality of what you eat and drink. If in-house catering is provided, we suggest you sample different menu options prior to paying a facility deposit. If you'd like to see how a facility handles food setup and presentation, ask the caterer to arrange a visit to someone else's party about a half hour before it starts. It's wise to taste wines and beers in advance, and be very specific about hard alcohol selections.

Hidden Costs

This may come as a surprise, but not all services and event equipment are covered in the rental fee, and some facilities hide the *true* cost of renting their space by having a low rental fee. It's possible to get nickeled and dimed for all the extras: tables, chairs, linens, glassware, valet service and so forth. You can also end up paying more than you expected for security and cleanup. All these additional charges can really add up, so save yourself a big headache by understanding exactly what's included in the rental fee and what's not before you sign any contract.

Tips for Previewing a Location

Make Appointments.

If you liked what you read about a site in *The Guide,* then we recommend you make an appointment to see that location rather than just driving by. Sometimes an unremarkable-looking building will surprise you with a secluded garden or hidden courtyard. And sometimes the opposite is true—you'll love the stunning façade, but the interior isn't your style.

Incidentally, we've withheld the addresses of privately owned properties. Should you happen to know where any of these facilities is located, we urge you to respect the owner's or manager's privacy and make an appointment instead of stopping by.

When you do call for an appointment, don't forget to ask for specific directions, including cross streets. You can also look up the site on *HereComesTheGuide.com* and print out a detailed street map. Try to cluster your visits so that you can easily drive from one place to another without backtracking. Schedule at least 30 minutes per facility and leave ample driving time. You want to be efficient, but don't over-schedule yourself. It's best to view places when you're fresh and your judgment isn't clouded by fatigue.

Bring along *The Guide* or printed pages from the website.

We've listed the street address for each site, and our illustrations in the book often make it easier to identify the buildings you're planning to see. And if you bring the book or web pages into the facilities with you, you can double-check our information with the site representative and jot down changes.

Bring a notebook.

If there are too many changes to fit legibly in your copy of *Here Comes The Guide,* have a small notebook ready. Make sure you write down the date, time and name of the person relating the information, and then play back your understanding to the site representative to confirm that what you heard is correct. Remember to have that notebook in front of you when you review your contract, and go over in detail what you were told versus what's in the contract before you sign anything.

Bring a videocam, or a tape recorder and digital camera.

Let technology help you keep track of your visits—your likes, dislikes and any other observations. A word of caution: you'd be surprised how easy it is to confuse various sites in your mind, so make sure you keep a log of photos. And bring extra batteries, tapes, and memory cards along—whatever you need to make your gear work properly.

File everything.

Many facilities will hand you pamphlets, menus, rate charts and other materials. Develop a system for sorting and storing the information that keeps your notes, photos and handouts together, clearly labeled and easily accessible.

Bring a checkbook or credit card.

Some of the more attractive venues book a year to 18 months in advance. If you actually fall in love with a location and your date is available, plunk down a deposit to hold the date.

Working With a Location

Confirm All the Details

When you make the initial phone call, confirm that the information presented in *Here Comes The Guide* is still valid. Show or read the information in our book to the site's representative, and have him or her inform you of any changes. If there have been significant increases in fees or new restrictions that you can't live with, cross the place off your list and move on. If the facility is still a contender, request a tour.

Once you've determined that the physical elements of the place suit you, it's time to discuss details. Ask about services and amenities or fees that may not be listed in the book and make a note of them. Outline your plans to the representative and make sure that the facility can accommodate your particular needs. If you don't want to handle all the details yourself, find out what the facility is willing and able to do, and if there will be an additional cost for their assistance. Facilities often provide planning services for little or no extra charge. If other in-house services are offered, such as flowers or wedding cakes, inquire about the quality of each service provider and whether or not substitutions can be made. If you want to use your own vendors, find out if the facility will charge you an extra fee.

The Importance of Rapport

Another factor to consider is your rapport with the person(s) you're working with. Are you comfortable with them? Do they listen well and respond to your questions directly? Do they inspire trust and confidence? Are they warm and enthusiastic or cold and aloof? If you have doubts, you need to resolve them before embarking on a working relationship with these folks—no matter how wonderful the facility itself is. Discuss your feelings with them, and if you're still not completely satisfied, get references and call them. If at the end of this process you still have lingering concerns, you may want to eliminate the facility from your list even though it seems perfect in every other way.

Signing a Contract

It's easy to get emotionally attached to a location, but remember that it's not a done deal until you sign a contract. Now's the time to be businesslike and put your emotions aside. If you can't do that, get a non-emotional partner, friend or relative to help you review the small print and negotiate changes before you sign. Remember all those notes you took when you first visited the site? Compare them with what's actually written in the contract. No matter what someone told you about the availability of a dance floor, the price of pastel linens, or the ceremony arch, you can't hold the facility to it until the contract is signed. Places revise their prices and policies all the time, so assume that things may have changed since you originally saw the site or talked to a site representative.

If you're not happy with the contract, prepare to negotiate. Before your appointment with whoever has the power to alter the contract, make an itemized list, in order of importance, of the changes you want. Decide what you're willing to give up, and what you can't live without. If in the end the most important things on your list cannot be addressed to your satisfaction, this is probably not the right place for you. It's better to find another location than to stay with a facility that isn't willing to work with you.

Insurance Considerations

Nowadays, if someone gets injured at an event or something is damaged at or near the event site, it's likely that someone will be sued.

In order to protect themselves and spread the risk among all parties involved, facilities have begun to require additional insurance and/or proof of insurance from service professionals and their clients.

Event sites and service professionals (such as caterers) are very aware of their potential liability and all have coverage of one kind or another. A few years ago, less than 10% of the facilities we represent required the "renter" to obtain extra insurance coverage. Now, more than a third of our sites require it. That's a remarkable increase, and this trend will probably continue. The bottom line is that a large chunk of the properties we represent will require you, the renter, to get extra insurance.

What's funny (or not so funny) is that as more and more event sites require extra liability and/or a certificate of insurance, fewer insurance companies are willing to issue either one—even if you're covered under a homeowner's policy. At this point, insurance carriers don't want to attach extra clauses to your policy to increase coverage for a single event, and most, if not all, companies are unwilling to add the event site's name to your existing policy as an additional insured.

Don't despair. Even though it's hard to come by, you can get extra insurance for a specified period of time, and it's relatively inexpensive.

Obtaining Extra Insurance

- **The first thing to do is read your rental contract carefully.** Make sure you understand exactly *what's* required and *when* it's required. Most facilities want $1,000,000–2,000,000 in extra liability coverage. If you don't pay attention to the insurance clauses early in the game, you'll have to play catch-up at the last moment, frantically trying to locate a carrier who will issue you additional insurance. And, if you don't supply the certificate to the facility *on time,* you may run the risk of forfeiting your event site altogether.

- **The second thing is to ask your event site's representative if the site has an insurance policy through which you can purchase the required extra coverage.** If the answer is yes, then consider purchasing it—that's the easiest route (but not necessarily the best!). The facility's extra insurance coverage may not be the least expensive and it may not provide you with the best coverage. What you need to ask is: "If one of my guests or one of the professionals working at my event causes some damage to the premises or its contents, will this extra insurance cover it?" If the answer if yes, get it in writing.

- **The third thing, if the answer is no, is to find your own coverage.** We suggest you avoid the *Yellow Pages* and call:

  R.V. Nuccio & Associates, Inc. at 1-800-ENGAGED (1-800-364-2433) or www. rvnuccio.com. They specialize in insuring special events, and can send you a brochure detailing what's offered.

  Coverage starts at $95/wedding or special event; the total cost will depend on what you want. Rob Nuccio's coverage is underwritten by Fireman's Fund.

Here are some of the items a typical policy might cover:

- Cancellation or postponement due to: weather, damage to the facility, sickness, failure to show of the caterer or officiant, financial reasons—even limited change-of-heart circumstances!

- Photography or videography: failure of the professional to appear, loss of original negatives, etc.

- Lost, stolen or damaged gifts

- Lost, stolen or damaged equipment rentals

- Lost, stolen or damaged bridal gown or other special attire

- Lost, stolen or damaged jewelry

- Personal liability and additional coverage

- Medical payments for injuries incurred during the event

If you use this service, let us know whether you're happy with them. Call us. We'd love to get your feedback.

It Can't Happen To Me

Don't be lulled into the notion that an event disaster can't happen to you. It could rain when you least expect it. Or your well-intentioned aunt might melt your wedding dress while ironing out a few wrinkles. Wouldn't it be nice to know that your dress, wedding photos, equipment rentals and gifts are covered? Naturally, a New Year's Eve party or a high school prom night is riskier than a wedding, but we could tell you stories of upscale parties where something did happen and a lawsuit resulted.

So even if extra insurance is not required, you may still want to consider additional coverage, especially if alcohol is being served. *You are the best predictor of your guests' behavior.* If you plan on having a wild, wonderful event, a little additional insurance could be a good thing.

Recycling

Do Your Part!

If you're wondering why we're including a brief item about recycling in a book like *Here Comes The Guide,* it's because parties and special events often generate recyclable materials and leftover food that the bride and groom don't want to take home. Nowadays, you and the caterer can feel good by donating the excess, and recycling plastic bottles, glass, metal and paper. An added benefit is that food donations are tax deductible for either you or the caterer. And if you recycle, the cost for extra garbage containers (bins) can be reduced or eliminated.

Food donations are distributed to teenage drop-in centers, youth shelters, alcoholic treatment centers, AIDS hospices, senior centers and refugee centers throughout the region.

Your packaged food can be picked up the day of the event or brought back to the caterer's kitchen to be picked up later on. Place food in clean plastic bags, plastic containers or boxes. Perishables should be refrigerated; other recyclable materials must be separated. Food must also be edible—if dressing has been poured over a salad, for example, it won't be worth eating the next day.

To recycle, call your local recycling center to arrange a pickup. To make a donation, look online or through your phone book to find a local Food Bank or call the following organizations to make advance arrangements.

For more valuable tips about going green, read our article "It's A Nice Day for a Green Wedding" on *HereComesTheGuide.com!*

Donation Organizations

• **San Francisco**

Food Runners   415/929-1866
www.foodrunners.org

Food Bank   415/282-1900
www.sffoodbank.org

• **Berkeley**

Daily Bread Project   510/339-9811
www.breadproject.org

• **Oakland**

Alameda County
Food Bank   510/635-3663
www.accfb.org

Oakland Potluck   510/272-0414

• **Santa Cruz Area**

Second Harvest   831/722-7110
www.thefoodbank.org

• **San Mateo/Santa Clara Counties**

Second Harvest   650/610-0800
www.2ndharvest.net

• **Marin County**

Food Bank   415/833-1302
www.marinfoodbank.org

• **Sacramento**

Food Bank   916/456-1980
www.sfbs.org

Loaves & Fishes   916/446-0874
www.sacloaves.org

Questions To Ask
Locations and Event Professionals

Questions to Ask an Event Location

Here Comes The Guide is a fantastic resource to help you find the location to host your wedding, rehearsal dinner or company party. Even with all the info we provide, though, you'll need to address your specific needs with each venue you visit to come up with a winner.

The following list of questions and tips will help you navigate through your location search. Print them out and use them as a guide while you're talking with a site contact or reviewing a site information packet. Feel free to add questions that relate to your particular event (e.g. "Can my dog be the ring bearer in my ceremony?") Make sure to get everything in writing in your final contract! **Don't forget to have a notebook or your planning binder handy so that you can record answers to all these questions.**

1. What dates are available in the month I'm considering?

2. How many people can this location accommodate?

3. What is the rental fee and what is included in that price? Is there a discount for booking an off-season date or Sunday through Friday?

4. How much is the deposit, when is it due, and is it refundable? What's the payment plan for the entire bill?

5. Can I hold my ceremony here, too? Is there an additional charge? Is the ceremony site close to the reception site? Is there a bride's changing area? How much time is allocated for the rehearsal?

6. What's the cancellation policy? *NOTE: Some places will refund most of your deposit if you cancel far enough in advance (often 60 days), since there's still a chance they can rent the space. After a certain date, though, you may not be able to get a refund—at least not a full one).*

7. What's your weather contingency plan for outdoor spaces?

8. How long will I have use of the event space(s) I reserve? Is there an overtime fee if I stay longer? Is there a minimum or maximum rental time?

9. Can I move things around and decorate to suit my purposes, or do I have to leave everything as is? Are there decoration guidelines/restrictions? Can I use real candles? *TIP: Keep the existing décor in mind when planning your own decorations so that they won't clash. If your event is in December, ask what the venue's holiday décor will be.*

10. How much time will I have for décor setup? Does the venue provide assistance getting gifts or décor back to a designated car, hotel room, etc. after the event has concluded?

11. Do you provide a coat check service (especially important for winter weddings)? If not, is there an area that can be used and staffed for that purpose?

12. Is there an outdoor space where my guests can mingle, and can it be heated and/or protected from the elements if necessary? Is there a separate indoor "socializing" space?

13. Do you have an in-house caterer or a list of "preferred" caterers, or do I need to provide my own? Even if there is an in-house caterer, do I have the option of using an outside caterer instead?

14. If I hire my own caterer, are kitchen facilities available for them? *NOTE: Caterers charge extra if they have to haul in refrigerators and stoves.*

15. Are tables, chairs, plates, silverware and glassware provided, or will I have to rent them myself or get them through my caterer?

16. What is the food and beverage cost on a per/person basis? What is the service charge?

17. Can we do a food tasting prior to finalizing our menu selection? If so, is there an additional charge?

18. Can I bring in a cake from an outside cake maker or must I use a cake made on the premises? Is there a cake-cutting fee? If I use a cake made on site is the fee waived?

19. Can I bring my own wine, beer or champagne, and is there a corkage fee if I do? Can I bring in other alcohol?

20. Are you licensed to provide alcohol service? If so, is alcohol priced per person? By consumption? Are there additional charges for bar staff? Is there a bar minimum that must be met before the conclusion of the event? What is the average bar tab for the number of people attending my event? *NOTE: Some facilities (private estates and wineries in particular) aren't licensed to serve hard alcohol. You may need to get permission from the location to bring in an outside beverage catering company.*

21. Are there restrictions on what kind of music I can play, or a time by which the music must end? Can the venue accommodate a DJ or live band? *TIP: Check where the outlets are located in your*

event space, because that will help you figure out where the band can set up and where other vendors can hook up their equipment. You don't want the head table to block the only outlet in the room.

22. Is there parking on site? If so, is it complimentary? Do you offer valet parking, and what is the charge? If there is no parking on site, where will my guests park? Are cabs easily accessible from the venue? *TIP: You should have the venue keep track of the number of cars parked for your event and add the total valet gratuity to your final bill so that your guests won't have to tip.*

23. How many restrooms are there? *TIP: You should have at least 10 restrooms per 100 people.*

24. Do you offer on-site coordination? If so, what services are included and is there an additional charge for them? Will the coordinator supervise day-of? How much assistance can I get with the setup/décor?

25. What security services do you offer? Do I need to hire my own security guards, or does the site hire them or have them on staff? *TIP: In general, you should have 2 security guards for the first 100 guests and 1 more for every additional 100 guests.*

26. Does the venue have liability insurance? *NOTE: If someone gets injured during the party, you don't want to be held responsible—if the site doesn't have insurance, you'll need to get your own. For info on insurance go to www.rvnuccio.com.*

27. Can I hire my own vendors (caterer, coordinator, DJ, etc.), or must I select from a preferred vendor list? If I can bring my own, do you have a list of recommended vendors?

28. What overnight accommodations do you provide? Do you offer a discount for booking multiple rooms? Do you provide a complimentary room or upgrade for the newlyweds? What are the nearest hotels to the venue? *TIP: Some venues have partnerships with local hotels that offer a discount if you book a block of rooms.*

29. Do you have signage or other aids to direct guests to my event?

30. Do you have a recycling policy?

More Tips:

- If you really love the site, ask the venue representative to put together a proposal with all the pricing and policies—including the tax and service charge—so you have an idea of the basic cost.

- Bring a camera with you to every location you visit, and organize the photos by location name when you get home. After seeing a series of places it's easy to confuse them. Having a photographic record will help you remember what was special about each site.

- Pay attention to the venue as a whole: Check out everything, including the restrooms, the foyer, the dressing rooms, the outdoor lighting and even the kitchen. You want to be sure your vision can be realized at this location. If possible, make arrangements with the site representative to visit the venue when it's set up for a wedding.

- GET EVERYTHING IN WRITING. Your date is not officially reserved until you sign a contract and, in many cases, give a deposit—even if a site contact says you don't need to worry about it. Once you've found THE PLACE, make sure you ask what is required to get your booking locked in and then follow through on satisfying those requirements. And don't assume that just because the site coordinator said you can have 4 votive candles per table you'll get them. Before you sign a contract, read the fine print and make sure it includes everything you and the site contact agreed on. As new things are added or changed in your contract, have the updated version printed out and signed by you and the site representative. Also, document all your conversations in emails and keep your correspondence.

Questions to Ask a Wedding Photographer

You've put so much time and effort into planning your wedding you'll want every special moment captured for your photo album. But how do you know which photographer is right for you? Whether you're considering any of our *Certified By The Guide* wedding photographers or another professional, you need to do your homework.

Here are the questions you should ask those photographers who've made your short list, to ensure that the one you ultimately choose is a good fit for you and your wedding.

The Basics

1. Do you have my date available? *NOTE: Obviously, if the answer is NO and you're not willing or able to change your date, don't bother asking the rest of these questions.*

2. How far in advance do I need to book with you?

3. How long have you been in business?

4. How many weddings have you shot? Have you done many that were similar to mine in size and style?

5. How would you describe your photography style (e.g. traditional, photojournalistic, creative)? *NOTE: It's helpful to know the differences between wedding photography styles so that you can discuss your preferences with your photographer. For descriptions of the various styles, see the next page.*

6. How would you describe your working style? *NOTE: The answer should help you determine whether this is a photographer who blends into the background and shoots what unfolds naturally, or creates a more visible presence by taking charge and choreographing shots.*

7. What do you think distinguishes your work from that of other photographers?

8. Do you have a portfolio I can review? Are all of the images yours, and is the work recent?

9. What type of equipment do you use?

10. Are you shooting in digital or film format or both? *NOTE: The general consensus seems to be that either format yields excellent photos in the hands of an experienced professional, and that most people can't tell the difference between film and digital images anyway.*

11. Do you shoot in color and black & white? Both? Infrared? *NOTE: Photographers who shoot in a digital format can make black & white or sepia versions of color photos.*

12. Can I give you a list of specific shots we would like?

13. Can you put together a slideshow of the engagement session (along with other photos the couple provides) and show it during the cocktail hour? What about an "instant" slideshow of the ceremony?

14. What information do you need from me before the wedding day?

15. Have you ever worked with my florist? DJ? Coordinator, etc.? *NOTE: Great working relationships between vendors can make things go more smoothly. It's especially helpful if your videographer and photographer work well together.*

16. May I have a list of references? *NOTE: The photographer should not hesitate to provide this.*

The Shoot

17. Are you the photographer who will shoot my wedding? If so, will you have any assistants with you on that day? If not, who will be taking the pictures and can I meet them before my wedding? *NOTE: You should ask the questions on this list of whoever is going to be the primary photographer at your event, and that photographer's name should be on your contract.*

18. Do you have backup equipment? What about a backup plan if you (or my scheduled photographer) are unable to shoot my wedding for some reason?

19. If my wedding site is out of your area, do you charge a travel fee and what does that cover?

20. Are you photographing other events on the same day as mine?

21. How will you (and your assistants) be dressed? *NOTE: The photographer and his/her staff should look professional and fit in with the style of your event.*

22. Is it okay if other people take photos while you're taking photos?

23. Have you ever worked at my wedding site before? If not, do you plan to check it out in advance? *NOTE: Photographers who familiarize themselves with a location ahead of time will be prepared for any lighting issues or restrictions, and will know how best to incorporate the site's architectural elements into the photos.*

24. What time will you arrive at the site and for how long will you shoot?

25. If my event lasts longer than expected, will you stay? Is there an additional charge?

Packages, Proofs and Prints

26. What packages do you offer?

27. Can I customize a package based on my needs?

28. Do you include engagement photos in your packages?

29. What type of album designs do you offer? Do you provide any assistance in creating an album?

30. Do you provide retouching, color adjustment or other corrective services?

31. How long after the wedding will I get the proofs? Will they be viewable online? On a CD?

32. What is the ordering process?

33. How long after I order my photos/album will I get them?

34. Will you give me the negatives or the digital images, and is there a fee for that?

Contracts and Policies

35. When will I receive a written contract? *TIP: Don't book a photographer—or any vendor—who won't provide a written contract.*

36. How much of a deposit do you require and when is it due? Do you offer a payment plan?

37. What is your refund/cancellation policy?

38. Do you have liability insurance?

Questions to Ask Yourself:

1. Do I feel a connection with this photographer as well as his/her photos? Are our personalities a good match?

2. Am I comfortable with this person's work and communication style?

3. Has this photographer listened well and addressed all my concerns?

Check references. *Ask the photographer for at least 5 references, preferably of couples whose wedding was similar to yours in size and/or style. Getting feedback from several people who have actually hired the photographer in question can really help you decide if that person is right for you.*

Photography Style Glossary

Though there are no standard "dictionary definitions" of photographic styles, it's still a good idea to have an understanding of the following approaches before you interview photographers:

Traditional, Classic: The main idea behind this timeless style is to produce posed photographs for display in a portrait album. The photographer works from a "shot list," ensuring he or she covers all the elements the bride and groom have requested. To make sure every detail of the shots is perfect, the photographer and her assistants not only adjust their equipment, but also the background, the subject's body alignment, and even the attire.

Photojournalism: Originally favored by the news media, this informal, reality-based approach is the current rage in wedding photography. Rather than posing your pictures, the photographer follows you and your guests throughout the wedding day, capturing events as they unfold in order to tell the story of your wedding. The photographer has to be able to fade into the background and become "invisible" to the crowd in order to get these candid or unposed shots. Since the photojournalist does not give direction, he'll need a keen eye and a willingness to "do what it takes to get the shot."

Illustrative Photography: This style, which is often used for engagement photos, is a pleasing blend of traditional and photojournalistic, with an emphasis on composition, lighting and background. The photographer places subjects together in an interesting environment and encourages them to relax and interact. Illustrative captures some of the spontaneity of candids, while offering the technical control of posed shots.

Portraiture: Traditional photographers generally excel at the precision required in portraiture—formal, posed pictures that emphasize one or more people. Couples interested in a more edgy result may prefer Fine Art Portraiture, with its dramatic lighting, unique angles and European flavor.

High Fashion: Commercial photographers excel at creating striking, simple photographs that dramatize the subject—and, of course, her clothes! Though not a style generally included in wedding photography, you may want to choose a photographer with high fashion experience if looking artsy and glamorous while showing off your dress is important to you.

Natural Light: Rather than using a camera flash, photographers use the natural light found in a setting, usually daylight. The look is warm and, well, natural—yet the photographer must be skilled to deal with shadows and other lighting challenges.

Questions to Ask a Wedding Planner

In the first flush of joy after your engagement, you'll probably begin browsing magazines and wedding websites…and soon feel buried by a blizzard of checklists and a daunting array of decisions. That's when you and your fiancé might want to think about hiring a professional wedding planner.

Good idea. Depending on your budget and needs, you can contract:

- a full-service planner to arrange every detail

- someone to assist you only in choosing your wedding location and vendors

- a Day-of Coordinator (which really means 30 days before your wedding)

NOTE: Many locations have in-house coordinators, but make sure you're clear on exactly what level of service they provide. Venue coordinators usually just handle day-of issues and offer a list of their preferred vendors, so having your own planner may still be a great help.

Even though hiring a planner is an added cost, they often end up saving you money in the long run. And no doubt about it—the right wedding planner can definitely save you time and stress (priceless!).

Before interviewing potential wedding planners, you and your fiancé should have an idea of:

- How much money you have in your budget

- How many people you would like to invite

- Your preferred wedding date

- Your vision for your wedding *(NOTE: If you aren't sure yet don't worry—getting help with this is one of the reasons why you're hiring a wedding planner!)*

After each interview is complete, ask yourselves:

- Did we feel heard?

- Does the planner understand our vision?

- Did we get a strong sense she will work with our budget?

- Was there a good connection and did our personalities mesh well?

Listen to your gut. If an interview doesn't feel right, then maybe that person just isn't a good fit for you. Your wedding planner is the vendor you'll be spending the most time with, so it's important to pick someone who's compatible with you and your fiancé.

Now, here are THE QUESTIONS!

Getting to Know a Planner

1. Do you have our wedding date open? If so, do you anticipate any issues with the date such as weather, travel for our guests, difficulty booking a venue, etc.?

2. What made you want to be a wedding planner?

3. Describe the most challenging wedding you planned and how you handled the problems that came up.

4. How would you rate your problem-solving skills?

5. How would you rate your communication skills?

6. Are you a certified wedding planner? If so, where did you get certified? What is your educational background?

7. Are you a member of any wedding association(s)? If so, does your association require you to satisfy yearly education requirements?

8. How long have you been in business? Do you have a business license?

9. How many full-scale weddings have you planned? When was your last one?

10. How many wedding clients do you take on in a year? How many do you expect to have during the month of our wedding?

11. Is wedding planning your full-time job? If it's part-time, what is your other job?

Working With the Venue

12. Have you ever worked at the venue we've chosen?

13. If our event is outdoors, what contingency plan would you have for bad weather? (Describe an event where you had weather issues and how you resolved them.)

Hiring Other Vendors

14. Are we required to book only the vendors you recommend or do we have the freedom to hire someone even if you haven't worked with them before?

15. Do you take a commission or discount from any of the vendors you would refer us to?

16. Will you be present at all of the vendor meetings and will you assist us in reviewing all of the vendor contracts and making sure everything is in order?

17. Will you invoice us for all the vendor fees or will we need to pay each one of them ourselves?

18. For the vendors who will be on site the day of our wedding, can I provide you with checks for final payment that you will distribute to them?

19. If issues arise with the vendors before, during or after our wedding, will you handle them or are we responsible for this?

Scope of Work

20. What kind planning do you offer? Logistical only (i.e. organizational—handling things like the timeline and floor plan) or Design and Logistical (i.e. bringing a client's vision to life as well as taking care of all the organizational aspects of the wedding)?

21. If you just do logistical planning, can you refer us to a vendor who can assist us with event design? *(NOTE: Floral designers often do full event design, as do vendors who specialize in design.)*

22. Will you handle every aspect of the planning or can we do some things on our own? In other words, what parts of the planning will we be responsible for?

23. Will you be the person on site the day of our wedding or will it be another planner? How many assistants will you have?

24. In case of an emergency that prevents you from being at our wedding, who will be the backup planner? What are their qualifications?

25. What time will you arrive and depart on the day of our wedding?

26. Will you stay on site after our wedding to make sure everything has been broken down and all vendors have left the location?

27. Will you provide us with a timeline of the wedding and a floor plan of the wedding venue?

28. Do you offer different package options or is everything customized based on what we're looking for?

29. How many meetings and phone calls are included in our package?

30. Is the wedding day rehearsal included in your services?

31. Do any of your packages include planning the rehearsal dinner and/or post-wedding brunch? If not, would you provide that service and what would be the extra cost to include it in our contract?

32. Do any of your packages include honeymoon planning? If not, would you provide that service and what would be the extra cost to include it in our contract?

33. Do any of your packages include assistance with finding my wedding dress and wedding party attire? If not, would you provide that service and what would be the extra cost to include it in our contract?

Getting Down to Business

34. Once we book with you, how quickly can we expect to receive the contract?

35. After we give you our budget, will you provide us with a breakdown of how the money is going to be allocated?

36. As changes are made to our plans, will you update us with a revised estimate and updated contract?

37. How do you charge for your services? Hourly, percentage of the wedding cost, or flat rate?

38. Can you provide a detailed list of all the items included in your fee?

39. What is your payment policy? Do you accept credit cards?

40. How much of a deposit is required to book your services? When is the final payment due?

41. Are there any fees that won't be included in your proposal that we should be aware of?

42. What is your refund or cancellation policy?

43. Can you provide a list of references?

44. Can you provide us with a portfolio and/or video of weddings you have done?

Questions to Ask a Caterer

Besides your location, the food and drink for your wedding bash will probably consume the largest portion of your wedding budget. Catering costs are usually presented as "per-person" charges, sometimes abbreviated in wedding brochures as "pp" after the amount. But be aware—the per-person charge often doesn't include everything: Tax and the gratuity (sometimes called the "service charge") might be extra, and there may also be separate per-person charges for the meal, drinks, hors d'oeuvres, and even setup. So your actual per-person charge might end up being considerably more than you expect. Bring your calculator along when meeting with potential caterers to help you arrive at the real bottom line.

There's more to consider. Nowadays, many caterers offer a range of services in addition to catering. Some are actual "event producers," providing props, special effects, décor—in other words, complete event design. They might also be able to assist in finding a location, coordinating your affair, or lining up vendors. One thing a caterer can't do, however, is cook up a 5-course Beef Wellington dinner for $20 per person. When planning your menu, be realistic about what you can serve given your budget and the size of your guest list.

A lot of factors come into play when selecting a caterer, so don't be afraid to ask as many questions as you need to. You can refer to the following list, whether your potential caterer works at your event facility or you're hiring them independently.

The Basics

1. Do you have my date open?

2. How many weddings do you do per year, and how long have you been in business?

3. Have you done events at my location? *TIP: If you haven't chosen your location yet, ask the caterer if they can help you select one.*

4. Are you licensed by the state of California? Are you licensed to serve alcohol?

5. Will I need any permits for my event? If so, will you handle obtaining them?

6. Will you provide a banquet manager to coordinate the meal service or an on-site coordinator who will run the entire event?

7. Can you assist with other aspects of the wedding like selecting other vendors, event design (e.g. specialty lighting, elaborate décor, theme events, etc.)?

Food & Presentation

8. Given my budget, guest count and event style, what food choices would you recommend? Do you specialize in certain cuisines?

9. Do we have to work off a preset menu or can you create a custom menu for our event? If I have a special dish I'd like served, would you accommodate that?

10. Do you offer event packages or is everything à la carte? What exactly do your packages include?

11. Do you use all fresh produce, meat, fish, etc.? Can you source organic or sustainably farmed ingredients?

12. Can you accommodate dietary restrictions, such as kosher, vegan, etc.?

13. What décor do you provide for appetizer stations or buffet tables?

14. Do you offer package upgrades such as chocolate fountains, ice sculptures, cappuccino machines or specialty displays?

15. Can you do theme menus (e.g. barbecue, luau, etc.)? Would you also provide the décor?

16. What is the price difference between a buffet and a sit-down meal? *NOTE: Don't automatically assume that a buffet is going to be the less expensive option. Ask your caterer which type of service is more affordable for you, given the menu you're planning.*

17. How much do you charge for children's meals?

18. How much do you charge for vendor meals?

19. Do you do wedding cakes? If so, is this included in the per-person meal price or is it extra?

20. Can you show me photos of cakes you've done in the past?

21. If I decide not to serve cake, can you provide a dessert display instead?

22. If we use an outside cake designer, do you charge a cake-cutting fee?

23. Do you do food tastings and is there an extra charge for this?

24. Do you handle rental equipment such as tables, chairs, etc.?

25. What types of linens, glassware, plates and flatware do you provide? *NOTE: Some low-budget*

caterers have basic packages that use disposable dinnerware instead of the real thing, so make sure you know exactly what you'll be getting.

26. Can you provide presentation upgrades such as chair covers, lounge furniture, Chiavari chairs, etc.? What would be the additional fees?

27. What is your policy on cleanup? *TIP: Be very clear about what "cleanup" means and who's responsible for handling it—and be sure to get it in writing. We've heard many tales about caterers that left dirty dishes, trash and uneaten food behind. In most cases, when you rent a location it will be YOUR responsibility to leave the place in acceptable condition. You want to spend your wedding night with your honey, not picking up empty bottles from the lawn!*

28. If there is leftover food from my event, can we have it wrapped up for guests to take home or have it delivered to a local shelter?

Drink

29. Do you provide alcoholic beverages and bartenders? Can you accommodate specialty cocktails?

30. What brands of alcohol will be served?

31. Can we provide the alcohol and you provide the bar labor?

32. Do you charge a corkage fee if we provide our own wine or champagne?

33. How do you charge for alcoholic and non-alcoholic beverages? Per consumption or per person? Which is more cost-effective?

34. Is the champagne toast after the ceremony included in your meal packages or is it extra?

35. Will your staff serve the wine with dinner?

36. How long will alcohol be served?

37. Is coffee and tea service included with the per-person meal charge? What brands of each do you offer and do they include decaf and herbal tea options?

Business Matters

38. What is the ratio of servers to guests?

39. How will the servers be dressed?

40. How is your pricing broken down (e.g. food, bar, cake-cutting, tax, gratuity)? *NOTE: Usually tax and a service charge are tacked on to your final cost. The service charge, which can range 18–23%, is used to tip the staff. And in many states, the service charge itself is taxable.*

41. How much time do you require for setting up and breaking down my event, and are there extra fees for this?

42. If my event runs longer than contracted, what are your overtime fees?

43. What is the last date by which I can give you a final guaranteed guest count?

44. What is your payment policy? Do you accept credit cards?

45. How much of a deposit is required to hold my date? When is the final payment due?

46. Are there any fees that won't be included in the proposal that we should be aware of?

47. Once we book with you, how quickly can we expect a contract? And if we make changes to menu choices or other items, will you update us with a revised estimate and contract?

48. What is your refund or cancellation policy?

49. Can you provide a list of recent references?

Questions to Ask a Floral Designer

Floral designers do much more than just supply the bouquet! They help create the look and mood for your wedding ceremony, as well as centerpieces and other table decorations for the reception. They add the floral flourishes for the wedding party (don't forget that corsage for Grandma!), and some may even work with your cake designer to provide embellishments.

Before sitting down with a floral designer, you should already have reserved your ceremony and reception venue. That way you'll be able to discuss how much additional floral décor will be needed to either achieve a specific look at your site or complement an existing garden and/or room aesthetic.

Another must: Don't design the wedding bouquet until you've ordered your wedding dress. Since that task will hopefully be completed at least 6 months before your wedding date (hint, hint!), you should have plenty of time to work out the details of both your accessories and floral décor.

So where to start? Do a little research prior to interviewing floral artists by visiting the websites or shops of vendors you're considering. You want to know that whomever you hire can create bouquets and arrangements that suit your style. (And do explore our Brides Want to Know: Bouquet Brainstorm for more GUIDElines and inspiration.)

Once you've compiled your short list of contenders, use these questions to zero in on your final choice:

The Basics

1. Do you have my date open?

2. Have you done events at my ceremony and reception location(s) before? If not, are you familiar with the sites?

3. How long have you been in business?

4. How many weddings have you done?

5. Where did you receive your training?

6. How many other weddings or events will you schedule on the same day?

7. Will you be doing my arrangements yourself or would it be another floral designer?

8. What design styles (e.g. ikebana, traditional, modern, trendy, European, Oriental) do you work in?

9. Can you work with my budget?

10. What recommendations can you give me to maximize my budget?

11. Do you offer specific packages or is everything customized?

12. Can you provide me with 3–4 recent brides that I can contact for references?

The Flowers

13. What flowers are in season for the month I am getting married?

14. Based on my color scheme and budget, what flowers do you recommend?

15. Is there a difference in price if I use one type of flower vs. a mixed arrangement or bouquet?

16. If I request it, can you provide any organic, pesiticide-free or sustainably grown varieties? *TIP: Organic roses cost more, but last so much longer!*

17. What are the different kinds of wraps (called "collars" in florist-speak) you can do for my bouquet?

18. What about coordinating boutonnières, bridesmaid flowers, and centerpieces? Can you suggest anything special to coordinate with the theme/venue/season of my event?

19. What other décor can you provide (aisle runner, candelabras, trees, arches, votives, mirrors, etc.)? How will these items affect the overall cost?

20. If I give you a picture of a bouquet and/or arrangement that I like, can you recreate it?

21. Do you have photos or live examples of florals designed in the style I want?

22. Can you do sketches or mockups of the arrangements you've described before I sign the contract?

23. Will you work with my cake designer if I decide to add flowers to my wedding cake? If so, is there an additional setup fee for this?

24. How far in advance of the wedding will you create the bouquets and arrangements, and how are they stored?

25. Can you assist me in the preservation of my bouquet after the wedding? If not, can you recommend someone?

The Costs

26. Do you charge a delivery fee?

27. Do you have an extra charge for the setup and breakdown of the floral décor?

28. Is there an extra fee if I need you to stay throughout the ceremony to move arrangements to the reception site?

29. Are there any additional fees that have not already been taken into account?

The Contract

30. How far in advance do I need to secure your services? What is the deposit required to secure my date?

31. Will you provide me with an itemized list of all the elements we've discussed, along with prices?

32. When can I expect to receive my contract from you?

33. What is your refund policy if for some reason I need to cancel my order?

Useful Tips:

- Prior to meeting with potential floral designers, have your color scheme finalized; create a list of the kinds of flowers you like; and have some examples (pictures from magazines or photos) of the kind of bouquets and arrangements that appeal to you.

- After you've met with each floral designer ask yourself, "Did the florist answer all my questions to my satisfaction?" "Do I feel like the florist really listened and understood my vision?" "Am I comfortable with this person?"

- Once you've booked your floral designer you'll want to provide them with a picture of your dress and swatches or photos of the bridesmaids dresses and the linens you'll be using.

For more ideas, read about "Unique Bridal Bouquets," "Bouquet Options for Bridesmaids," "Beachy Boutonnières," and "Green Centerpieces" in Find Ideas: Flowers on HereComesTheGuide.com.

And don't forget to browse our Certified by The Guide Floral Designers in Northern California!

Questions to Ask a Cake Designer

Next to your dress, the cake is probably a wedding's most important icon. And whether you want a traditional multitiered confection, a miniature Statue of Liberty (hey, that's where he proposed!) or a cupcake tower, your wedding cake should reflect your personality. Use the following questions as a guide when evaluating a potential cake designer. If you're not familiar with cake terms, please see the cake glossary on page 29.

Business Matters

1. Do you have my wedding date open?

2. How many wedding cakes do you schedule on the same day? *NOTE: You want to feel comfortable that your designer is sufficiently staffed to handle the number of cakes they've scheduled to deliver and set up on your date.*

3. How do you price your cakes? By the slice? Does the cost vary depending on the design and flavors I choose?

4. What is your minimum per-person cake cost?

5. What recommendations can you give me to maximize my budget?

6. Do you have a "menu" of cakes and prices that I can take with me?

7. What are the fees for delivery and setup of the cake? Do you decorate the cake table, too?

8. What do you do if the cake gets damaged in transit to or at my reception site?

9. Do you provide or rent cake toppers, a cake-cutting knife, cake stands, etc.? What are the fees?

10. How far in advance should I order my cake?

11. How much is the deposit and when is it due?

12. When is the final payment due?

13. Are there any additional fees that I should be aware of?

14. What is your refund policy if for some reason I need to cancel my order? What if I'm not happy with the cake?

15. When can I expect to receive my contract from you?

Background Check

16. How long have you been in business?

17. How many weddings have you done?

18. Where did you receive your training?

19. Can you provide me with 3–4 recent brides that I can contact for references?

The Cake

20. If you're not familiar with cake terms, please look at the cake glossary on page 29.

21. Do you have a portfolio of your work I can view, and did you make all the cakes in it?

22. What are your specialties?

23. Can you design a custom cake to match my theme, dress or color scheme, or do I select from set designs?

24. If I provide you with a picture of what I'd like, can you recreate it? Does it cost extra for a custom design?

25. I have an old family cake recipe. Can you adapt it for my wedding cake design?

26. If I don't have a clear vision of what I would like, can you offer some design ideas based on my theme and budget?

27. What flavors and fillings do you offer?

28. What are the different ingredients you typically use? Do you offer all organic or vegan options? *TIP: Quality ingredients cost more, but the investment is worth it—the cake will taste better.*

29. Do you have cake tastings? Is there a charge?

30. Do you do both fondant and buttercream icing?

31. Are there any other icing options I should consider? Which do you recommend for my cake design?

32. Can you create sugar paste, gum paste or chocolate flowers? If I decide to have fresh flowers on my cake will you work with my florist or will you obtain and arrange the flowers yourself?

33. Will you preserve the top tier of my cake for my first wedding anniversary or do you provide a special cake for the occasion?

34. Can you make a groom's cake? Is this priced the same as my wedding cake?

35. How much in advance of the wedding is the cake actually made? Do you freeze your cakes? *NOTE: Wedding cakes usually take at least a couple of days to make.*

Useful Tips:

- Arrange a consultation with your potential cake designer in person, and do a tasting before you sign a contract. *NOTE: Not all cake tastings are complimentary.*

- Make sure your cake designer specializes in wedding cakes. A wedding cake is generally much more elaborate than a birthday cake from your local bakery. Your cake professional should have special training in constructing this type of cake.

- In general, you should order your cake 6–8 months prior to your wedding.

- You might be able to save money by choosing one overall flavor for your cake.

Wedding Cake Glossary

Icings

Buttercream: It's rich and creamy, is easily colored or flavored, and is used for fancy decorations like shells, swags, basketweaves, icing flowers, etc. Since it's made almost entirely of butter (hence the name), buttercream has a tendency to melt in extreme heat, so it's not recommended for outdoor weddings.

Fondant: Martha Stewart's favorite. This icing looks smooth and stiff and is made with gelatin and corn syrup to give it its helmet-like appearance (it's really very cool looking). It looks best when decorated with marzipan fruits, gum paste flowers, or a simple ribbon, like Martha likes to do. Although not as tasty as buttercream or ganache, fondant does not need refrigeration so it's the perfect icing to serve at your beach wedding.

Royal Icing: A mix of confectioner's sugar and milk or egg whites, royal icing is what the faces of gingerbread men are decorated with. It's white, shiny and hard, and does not need to be refrigerated. It's used for decorations like dots and latticework.

Ganache: This chocolate and heavy cream combination is very dark, and has the consistency of store-bought chocolate icing. It can be poured over cakes for a glass-like chocolate finish or used as filling (it stands up wonderfully between cake layers). Due to the ingredients, however, it's unstable—don't use it in hot or humid weather or the icing will slide right off the cake.

Whipped Cream: Delicious, but by far the most volatile, fresh whipped cream is usually not recommended for wedding cakes because they have to be out of the fridge for so long. If you really want to use it (it looks extremely white and fresh, which goes beautifully with real flowers) just keep it in the fridge until the very last second.

Decorations

Marzipan: An Italian paste made of almonds, sugar and egg whites that is molded into flowers and fruits to decorate the cake. They're usually brightly colored and very sugary. Marzipan can also be used as icing.

Gum Paste: This paste, made from gelatin, cornstarch, and sugar, produces the world's most realistic, edible fruit and flower decorations. Famous cake designers like Sylvia Weinstock are huge fans of gum paste. One nice benefit: these decorations last for centuries in storage.

Piping: Piping is ideal for icing decorations like dotted Swiss, basketweave, latticework, and shells. It comes out of a pastry bag fitted with different tips to create these different looks, which can range from simple polka dots to a layered weave that you'd swear is a wicker basket.

Pulled Sugar: If you boil sugar, water, and corn syrup it becomes malleable and the most beautiful designs can be created. Roses and bows that have been made from pulled sugar look like silk or satin—they're so smooth and shiny.

Dragees: These hard little sugar balls are painted with edible gold or silver paint, and they look truly stunning on a big ol' wedding cake.

Questions to Ask a DJ or Live Entertainment

Too often choosing the entertainment is left to the end of your overwhelming "Wedding To Do List"—but it shouldn't be. Not only does music set the appropriate mood, but a skilled Master or Mistress of Ceremonies will gracefully guide your guests from one spotlight moment to another. And practically speaking, the best performers are often booked well in advance—so shake your groove thing, or you may be stuck doing the chicken dance with Uncle Edgar.

To get you started, we've put together this list of questions that will help you evaluate a DJ, band, or other entertainer. Note that rather than interviewing a specific performer or DJ yourself, you might be dealing with an entertainment agency rep.

The Basics

1. Do you have my date open?

2. Have you done events at my ceremony and/or reception location before? If not, are you familiar with them?

3. How long have you been in business? *NOTE: If you are interviewing a live band, you'll want to ask how long the musicians have played together. However, if you work with a reputable agency, instead of booking a specific band you'll most likely be getting seasoned professionals brought together for your event. Even though all the band members may not have played together before, they're professional musicians who are able to work together and sound fantastic anyway. The key is to make sure you book the specific singer and/or bandleader that you liked in the demo. The players will take their cues from them.*

4. How many weddings have you done? How many do you do in an average weekend?

5. What sets you apart from your competition?

6. Are there any other services that you provide, such as lighting design?

7. How far in advance do I need to secure your services?

8. Can you provide me with 3–4 recent brides that I can contact for references?

Pricing and Other Business Details

9. What is your pricing? Does this include setup and breakdown between ceremony and reception locations?

10. How much is the deposit and when is it due? When is the final payment due?

11. If the event lasts longer than scheduled, what are the overtime charges?

12. What is the continuous music charge? *NOTE: For bands, bookings traditionally run for 4 hours divided into 4 sets, each lasting 45 minutes with a 15-minute break. If you want "continuous music," i.e. with band members trading breaks, there is usually an additional charge.*

13. When can I expect to receive my contract from you?

14. Are there any additional fees that could accrue that I am not taking into account, like travel expenses or charges for special musical requests? (One performer was asked to prepare an entire set of songs from *Phantom of the Opera!* Yes, he charged extra.)

15. What is your refund policy if for some reason I need to cancel or alter my date?

16. Do you carry liability insurance? *NOTE: This usually only applies to production companies that also supply lighting, effects, etc.*

17. If I hire musicians for the ceremony and want them to play at the wedding rehearsal, what is the extra charge?

The Music

18. Do you have a DVD of your music or a video from a prior wedding where you performed?

19. Can you assist me in choosing the music for my processional, recessional, father-daughter dance, etc.?

20. How extensive is your music library or song list? What genres can you cover? Can I give you a specific list of songs I want or don't want played?

21. Are we guaranteed to have the performer(s) of our choice at our event? *SEE NUMBER 3 ABOVE. As mentioned, many bands hired by an agency are made up of members who may not play together regularly. Even set bands often have substitute players. If there are specific performers (singer, harpist, guitarist, etc.) that you want, make sure that your contract includes them. Of course, illness or other circumstances may still preclude their being able to perform at your event.*

22. If the DJ or one of the band members scheduled for my event is unable to perform for some reason, do you have a backup replacement ready to go?

23. Can you provide wireless mics for the ceremony?

24. Does any of your equipment require special electrical outlets that I need to inform my wedding site about?

25. Do you bring backup equipment?

26. What kind of space or stage do you require for the DJ or band? If my site doesn't provide what you need, will you make arrangements for the stage or am I responsible for renting it? *NOTE: a band will require a specific amount of square feet per band member.*

27. How much time will you need for setup, sound check and breakdown on the day of the event?

28. What music will be provided during the breaks? *NOTE: If you have a preference, make it known. If you want them to play your home-burned CD mix, be sure to test it on their equipment first because not all CDs will play on every system.*

29. How many people will you staff for my event?

Useful Tips:

- Discuss with your site manager any restrictions that might affect your event, like noise limits, a music curfew and availability/load of electrical circuits. Also check with your facility and caterer about where and what to feed the performers.

- All professional entertainers have access to formalwear (if they don't, that's your first clue they're not professionals!) However, it is YOUR responsibility to be specific about how you expect your performers to be dressed. Any extraordinary requests (period costumes, all-white tuxes, etc.) are normally paid for by the client.

- Make notes of your general music preferences before you meet with your DJ, bandleader, etc. For example: "Classical for the ceremony, Rat Pack-era for the cocktail hour and a set of Motown during the reception." Not only will this help you determine which entertainment professionals are a good match for you, it will guide them in preparing your set list.

Can't decide between a DJ or live music? Check out our expert advice under Find Ideas: "Brides Want to Know" on HereComesTheGuide.com.

For more information on hiring a DJ or other professional, see our article "Hiring Professionals Pays Off."

Questions to Ask When Ordering Your Wedding Invitations

Letterpress, thermography, engraved, matte, jacquard, glassine... ordering invites will mean learning a few new vocabulary words (see page 34). You'll also need to learn about all the components that you might want to include in your invitation, as well as what other printed materials could be part of your wedding scenario. With so many details to consider, you'll depend on a creative wedding invitation professional to clue you in on the jargon, and guide you in choosing invites that reflect your wedding style. After all, nothing sets the tone for an event like an impeccably designed wedding invitation.

Bring this list of must-ask questions to the stationery boutique or graphic designer you're considering to ensure that no detail is left unaddressed (no pun intended).

Getting To Know Your Invitation Professional

1. How long have you been in business?

2. What is your design background? *NOTE: This may or may not involve formal training. Remember, "good taste" isn't necessarily something that can be taught!*

3. What types of printing processes do you offer and which do you specialize in? Which do you recommend for my budget and style?

4. Is your printing done in-house or do you outsource it? *NOTE: Printing is usually less expensive if it's outsourced. However, a possible benefit of in-house printing is a quicker turnaround time, which could come in especially handy if any reprinting (say, due to an error) is required.*

5. Do you offer custom invitations as well as templated styles? Is there a fee if I want to order a sample of either an existing invitation style or a custom design? If so, how much?

6. If I choose a custom wedding invitation, what are my options for color, paper type, ink and fonts? What is the word limit for the text?

7. Can I also order my table numbers, place cards, escort cards, ceremony programs, menus, etc. from you?

8. Do you offer a package or a discounted price if I order all of the invitation components at the same time? (For a complete list of what might be included, see the next page.)

9. If I want to include a picture or graphic on my save-the-date card or invitation, can you accommodate that? If so, does the image need to be saved in a specific format? Do you have photo retouching available, and if so, what is the price range? Can your photo specialist also convert color images to black & white or sepia? Is there an additional cost?

10. Are there any new styles, trends and color combinations I might consider? Which are the most popular? What kinds of handmade or artisanal paper do you offer? *NOTE: The answers to these questions will give you a sense of how creative and up-to-the-minute your invitation professional is.*

11. Can my invitations be printed on recycled paper and/or with soy-based ink?

12. Based on the paper I select and the number of pieces involved, what would it cost to mail my wedding invitation? *NOTE: If you use a non-standard sized envelope, postage may be more expensive.*

Getting Down To Business

13. Once I place my order, how long will it take to have the completed invitations delivered? Do you have rush-order available and what are the extra fees? If you are ordering from an online company, ask: What are the shipping methods available to me, and their respective costs?

14. If the invitation involves multiple pieces, can you assemble them? If so, is there an additional fee? How will the assembly affect my delivery date?

15. Do you offer an invitation addressing service? If so, what is the charge for this? What lettering style options are available? Will the lettering push back my delivery date?

16. When is payment due?

17. I will have an opportunity to sign off on my invitation proof before you send my order to print, right?

18. Once I've signed off on the proof, I expect the printed invitations to match the approved sample. If they don't (i.e. an error was made after I signed off on the proof), will my invitations be corrected and reprinted at no additional cost? How much additional time will it take to redo my order if there is a problem with it?

19. What is your refund policy if for some reason I need to cancel my order?

20. When can I expect to receive my contract from you?

21. Can you provide me with the contact information of 3–4 recent brides who I can call or email for references?

Possible Printed Invitation Components

(Don't panic...most of the extra elements are OPTIONAL!!)

- Save-the-Date cards

- Wedding Announcement

- Wedding Invitation Components:
  - Outer Envelope
  - Optional Inner Envelope
  - Invitation
  - Reception Card, if held at a different location than the ceremony
  - Directions/Map
  - Response Card & SASE

- Thank-You Cards

- Shower Thank-You Cards

- Other Invites:
  - Engagement Party
  - Shower
  - Bachelor/Bacherlorette Party
  - Rehearsal Dinner
  - After Party

- Wedding Program

- Pew Cards

- Place Cards

- Table Cards

- Menus

- Napkins, matchbooks or labels for favors

Useful Tips:

- Ordering your invitations over the phone increases the possibility of mistakes, so order in person if possible. If you order your invitations from an online company, make sure your contract states that they will correct mistakes they make for free.

- Insist on getting a proof. Have at least two other people review all your proofs before you sign off on them—it's amazing what a fresh pair of eyes will see!

- If ordering online, remember that color resolution can vary drastically between computers. The best way to guarantee the exact color you want is to ask that a sample be snail mailed to you.

- Order 20–30 extra save-the-dates and/or invitations with envelopes in case you have to add to the guest list or you make a mistake when assembling or addressing the envelopes.

- Save-the-date cards should be sent out 6–9 months prior to your wedding.

- Invitations should be sent out 6–9 weeks prior to your wedding.

- Consider working with one stationer or graphic designer for all of your printed materials. She'll guide you in making sure all of the components convey a consistent design concept. Not that they have to be identical, but as Joyce Scardina Becker observes in *Countdown to Your Perfect Wedding*, "It's like making a fashion statement: All of the accessories in your wardrobe should coordinate and fit together nicely."

- To Evite or not to Evite? For the main event, even we progressives at Here Comes The Guide come down on the side of tradition and say go with real paper and snail mail—even if your budget determines that you have to DIY. However, if your overall wedding style is relaxed and casual, then we think Evites are fine for the supporting events, such as your Bachelorette Party. We like Evite's built-in RSVP system and creative style options.

Invitations Glossary

A glossary of common printing terms.

Printing Terms

Letterpress: Letterpress printing dates back to the 14th century, and involves inking the raised surface of metal type or custom-engraved plates and then applying the inked surface against paper with a press. When used with the right paper (thick, softer paper results in a deeper impression), fonts and colors, letterpress creates an elegant product with a stamped, tactile quality. This process offers lots of options, but can cost more than other methods. Also, photographs and metallic inks generally don't work well with letterpress.

Embossing: Using a metal die, letters and images are pressed into the paper from behind, creating a raised "relief" surface, imparting added dimension to the invitation design. Usually used for large initials or borders. Ink or foil may be applied to the front of the paper so that the raised letters and images are colored.

Blind embossing: No ink or foil is applied, so the embossed (raised) image is the same color as the paper.

Thermography: This popular printing method uses heat to fuse ink and resinous powder, producing raised lettering. Though it looks almost exactly like engraved printing, thermography is much less expensive. This process will not reproduce detail as sharply as engraving will. The powder is added after the ink is applied, generally with an offset press, so the use of paper or metal offset plates affects quality here, too.

Engraving: Engraving is generally the most formal and expensive printing option. The image is etched into a metal plate, and the ink held in the etched grooves is applied to the paper with a press. The resulting raised image is comprised entirely of ink sitting on the surface of the paper. The ink applied is opaque, making it possible to print a lighter colored ink on a darker colored paper. Engraving is not the best printing choice if you have a photo or illustration that requires a screen.

Offset printing: Most printing these days is offset, which means the original image is transferred from a plate to a drum before it is applied to the paper. This process produces print that sits flat on the surface. There are many levels of quality with this method: If your printer uses paper printing plates, the job will cost less but the result may be fuzzy, inconsistent lettering. Metal plates yield much sharper, crisper type.

Digital printing: In this method the computer is linked to the printing press and the image is applied to paper or another material directly from a digital file rather than using film and/or plates. Digital is best for short-run, quick jobs. This can also be a good option if you want to use full color.

Foil stamping: Foil is applied to the front side of the paper, stamped on with a metal die. Foils can be metallic or colored, shiny or dull. They are usually very opaque, and this is a great way to print white on a dark colored paper.

Calligraphy: This is the perfected art of writing by hand. Often associated with fancy, curlicue script, calligraphy can be done in several genres and styles.

Paper Terms

Matte: A paper coating that's flat and non-reflective (no gloss).

Jacquard: Screen-printed paper that creates an illusion of layering; for example, paper that looks like it's overlaid with a swatch of lace.

Parchment paper: This paper is somewhat translucent and often a bit mottled to mimic the appearance of ancient, historical documents made out of animal skin. It's excellent for calligraphy.

Linen finish: Paper with a surface that actually mimics linen fabric. If you look closely, you see lines of texture going both horizontally and vertically on the surface.

Rice paper: Not actually made of rice, this paper is extremely thin and elegant.

Glassine: A very thin, waxy paper. Thinner than vellum (see below), its surface is slick and shiny, whereas vellum is more translucent. Glassine is best suited for envelope use, while vellum is sturdy enough to be printed on directly for invitation use.

Vellum: A heavier, finely textured, translucent paper made from wood fiber. Similar to parchment, it was originally made from the skin of a calf, lamb or baby goat and used for writing and painting during the pre-printing age.

www.HereComesTheGuide.com

You've gotta visit our website! Here's what you'll find:

- A fast and easy way to search for the perfect locations and services.
- Information about new locations that aren't in the book!
- More great wedding and special event services!
- Direct links to the event locations and services we feature.
- Tons of color photos.
- Virtual tours of most locations.
- Information about wedding fairs.
- Many of the top wedding dress salons.

Part One: Event Locations

Northern California

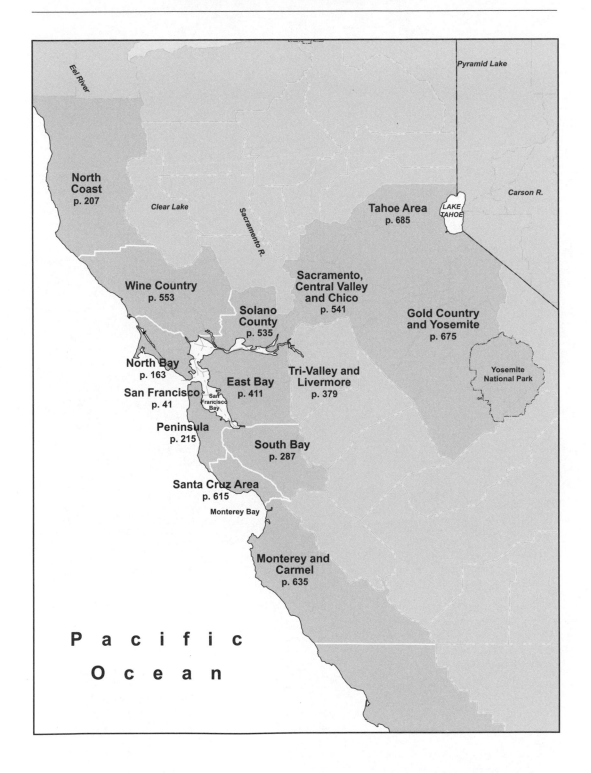

Eel River

Pyramid Lake

North Coast
p. 207

Clear Lake

Sacramento R.

Carson R.

Tahoe Area
p. 685

LAKE TAHOE

Wine Country
p. 553

Sacramento, Central Valley and Chico
p. 541

Solano County
p. 535

Gold Country and Yosemite
p. 675

North Bay
p. 163

East Bay
p. 411

Tri-Valley and Livermore
p. 379

Yosemite National Park

San Francisco
p. 41

San Francisco Bay

Peninsula
p. 215

South Bay
p. 287

Santa Cruz Area
p. 615

Monterey Bay

Monterey and Carmel
p. 635

P a c i f i c

O c e a n

San Francisco

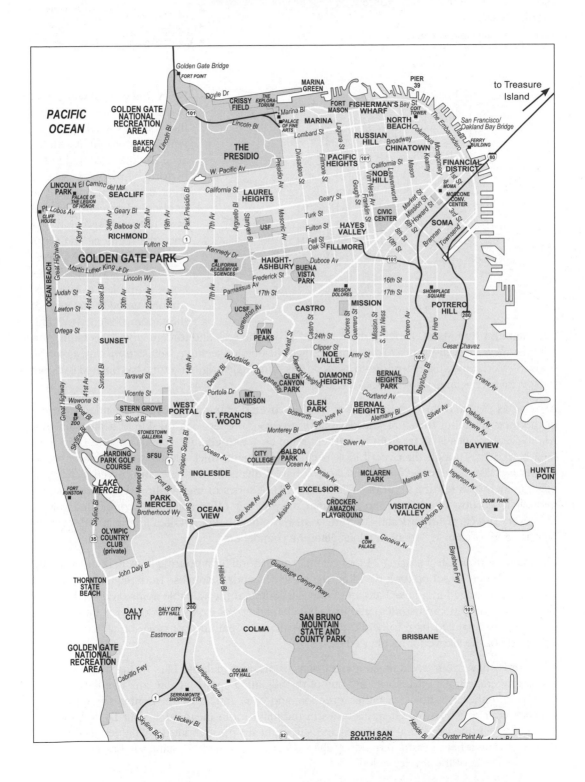

Ambiance Antiques

Event Site

550 15th Street, Suite 1, San Francisco
415/626-0145

www.theambiancevenue.com
events@ambianceantiques.com

● Rehearsal Dinners	● Corp. Events/Mtgs.
● Ceremonies	● Private Parties
● Wedding Receptions	○ Accommodations

Every once in a while you discover a place so unique that you want to tell everyone you know about it. Ambiance Antiques, located in the historic Showplace Square West, is just such a place. The red-bricked structure was built over 100 years ago, and was once the scene of The City's most talked-about VIP soirées. For the last seven years, it's housed Ambiance Antiques' sumptuous 6000-square-foot showroom, designed by luminary architect Ron Mann. Evoking the romance of bygone eras and foreign lands, this family-run antiques mecca is well-known to discerning design aficionados seeking *Architectural Digest*-worthy finds. Now, in somewhat of a return to its roots, this stunningly original setting has opened its doors for special events, film/photo shoots and weddings.

As soon as you step through the private, awning-covered entrance, you're surrounded by some of the most beautiful furniture and decorative arts you've ever seen outside of a museum. But Ambiance Antiques is as far from a stuffy museum as a 19th-century walnut armoire is from an Ikea bookcase. Though the overall look is chic and elegant, thick plaster walls, massive wood beams and distressed stone floors lend a comfortable, "lived in" aesthetic, and curved niches and graceful archways recall a luxurious Old World villa. A series of high-ceilinged open rooms and multiple levels flow effortlessly into each other, a layout that offers something compelling to look at in every direction: an intricately carved Swedish cabinet; a gilded Italian mirror; a 17th-century tapestry and, of course, lots of fabulous glittering chandeliers.

The main room boasts a soaring 23-foot ceiling, with natural light pouring in from floor-to-ceiling windows. When it's set up for a wedding, the bride descends a staircase from the mezzanine and vows are exchanged in a raised alcove to one side. Some of the valuable items on display, which change periodically, can be integrated into your ceremony. For example, you may want to use an ethereal, hand-painted harp to herald the bride's dramatic entrance or place ornate columns on either side of the alcove for an altar effect.

Afterwards, have your cocktail hour right here or arrange multiple bars (using a 200-year-old mahogany credenza, perhaps?) in any one of the adjoining spaces. There are a variety of room options for either a sit-down or buffet reception, and you can choose the configuration that best matches your event vision. Great acoustics in the main room means that your DJ or band can entertain from one of several platforms and still be heard throughout the galleries. The mezzanine, featuring a faux hearth and kidney-shaped banquettes, makes a fantastic lounge area with bird's-eye views of the revelry below.

This downtown showroom is an art director and wedding planner's dream—with access to more than a million dollars worth of rare *objets d'art* and eclectic furnishings, there's no need to "dress the stage" for your event. Also, the congenial owners will move pieces around or remove them altogether to accommodate your vision. But what really sets Ambiance Antiques apart is the opportunity to host your celebration right in town, yet feel like you're time-traveling the world, enveloped by grace and beauty.

CEREMONY CAPACITY: The site holds 80 seated guests indoors.

EVENT/RECEPTION CAPACITY: The facility can accommodate 120 seated or 200 standing indoors.

MEETING CAPACITY: Meeting spaces seat 50 guests.

FEES & DEPOSITS: A $500 deposit is required to reserve your date and the balance is due 30 days prior to the event. Rental fees range $1,500–5,500 depending on the number of guests.

AVAILABILITY: Year-round, weekdays: 4pm–2am and weekends: 10am–2am.

SERVICES/AMENITIES:

Catering: select from preferred list or BYO
Kitchen Facilities: fully equipped
Tables & Chairs: some provided
Linens, Silver, etc.: CBA or BYO
Restrooms: wheelchair accessible
Dance Floor: provided
Bride's Dressing Area: CBA
Meeting Equipment: BYO

Parking: large lot, on street
Accommodations: no guestrooms
Telephone: office phone
Outdoor Night Lighting: access only
Outdoor Cooking Facilities: BBQ CBA
Cleanup: provided
View: cityscape

RESTRICTIONS:

Alcohol: BYO
Smoking: outdoors only
Music: amplified OK indoors

Wheelchair Access: yes
Insurance: liability required

Argonaut Hotel

Waterfront Hotel

495 Jefferson Street, San Francisco
415/345-5552 Catering Dept.

www.argonauthotel.com
catering@argonauthotel.com

● Rehearsal Dinners	● Corp. Events/Mtgs.
● Ceremonies	● Private Parties
● Wedding Receptions	● Accommodations

The newest property along Fisherman's Wharf—the chic and upscale Argonaut Hotel—handily dispels the myth that the wharf is a destination for tourists only. Although it shares its waterfront location with restaurants and shops, the Argonaut remains in a class by itself.

Just steps from the Maritime National Historical Park, the hotel overlooks the green stretch of the park, the bay and the numerous historic vessels docked along the water's edge. Fantastic backdrops for photos include Victoria Park, cable cars, and Aquatic Beach with Alcatraz and the Golden Gate Bridge in the distance.

The Argonaut occupies a historic brick building that was once a Del Monte fruit cannery, and thanks to the renowned Kimpton Design Group, the impressive structure has been reborn as a boutique-style hotel of the highest order. One of the most pleasing aspects of this transformation is the décor: The designers have taken their inspiration from the water and boats right outside, seamlessly linking the interior to the bay and its history. Shades of deep blue and white, lights shaped like portals, ships' wheels, and tasteful nods to maritime life show up throughout the hotel.

When it comes to weddings or other special events, the Argonaut offers four private areas for parties. Perhaps the most unusual is the San Francisco Maritime National Historical Park Museum Visitors Center on the first floor of the hotel. The public gets to enjoy the center during the day, but in the evening it can be exclusively yours. Throughout the event you and your guests are free to walk through the Visitors Center and admire the wondrous antique nautical objects and memorabilia, as well as placards explaining the history of the wharf.

For a more traditional setting, book the hotel's Golden Gate Ballroom. Here, chandeliers shaped like giant ships' compasses hang above a whimsical naval-inspired carpet of rolling waves and stars. Tawny yellow walls contribute to the warm feel of the room, and its open, unstructured layout accommodates all manner of festivities. An open-air courtyard next to the Argonaut is available for semi-private cocktail receptions.

The Blue Mermaid Chowder House and Bar presents a more casual atmosphere and is available for private parties. The restaurant continues the nautical theme and offers a full bar, an open kitchen and patio seating. Casual reception-style events and rehearsal dinners work well within its laid-back confines, and the patio can also be tented, nearly doubling the amount of indoor space.

From its vantage point at the far west edge of Fisherman's Wharf, the Argonaut stands sentinel over a sweeping, nearly panoramic bay view. If you love all things nautical, or you're simply looking for a luxurious hotel in one of San Francisco's most historic areas, the Argonaut may be just the place to celebrate.

CEREMONY CAPACITY: The Argonaut holds up to 250 seated guests both indoors and outdoors.

EVENT/RECEPTION CAPACITY: The hotel accommodates 320 seated or 450 standing guests indoors (260 with a dance floor).

MEETING CAPACITY: With over 7,000 square feet of private space, the Argonaut can accommodate groups ranging from 10–300 guests.

FEES & DEPOSITS: A $2,000 deposit is required to reserve your date and a second deposit is due 2 months prior to the event. The balance is due 3 days prior. Ceremony fees range $500–1,000. A $425 setup fee applies to all wedding receptions. Meals range $44–62/person and full wedding packages start at $94/person for dinner events and $76–79/person for lunch or events. Wedding packages include passed hors d'oeuvres, open bar during cocktail hour, plated 3-course or buffet lunch or dinner, wine offered tableside, champagne toast, cake-cutting fee, chair covers/sashes, and a suite for the bride and groom. Tax and a 21% service charge are additional.

AVAILABILITY: Daily until midnight. Early morning hours by arrangement. Closed on Thanksgiving, Christmas, and New Year's Days.

SERVICES/AMENITIES:

Catering: provided, will consider kosher and ethnic caterers
Kitchen Facilities: n/a
Tables & Chairs: provided
Linens, Silver, etc.: provided
Restrooms: wheelchair accessible
Dance Floor: provided
Bride's & Groom's Dressing Area: yes
Meeting Equipment: full range

Parking: valet or public garage
Accommodations: 252 guestrooms
Telephone: pay phones
Outdoor Night Lighting: yes
Outdoor Cooking Facilities: no
Cleanup: provided
View: SF cityscape, SF Bay and park
Other: event coordination

RESTRICTIONS:

Alcohol: provided
Smoking: outside only
Music: amplified OK indoors with volume restrictions

Wheelchair Access: yes
Insurance: not required but recommended
Other: no glitter, rice or birdseed

This is important! Tell locations you're reading HERE COMES THE GUIDE and ask if our information is still current.

45

Asian Art Museum

Museum

200 Larkin Street, San Francisco
415/581-3777
www.asianart.org/facilityrentals.htm
facilityrentals@asianart.org

- Rehearsal Dinners
- Ceremonies
- Wedding Receptions
- Corp. Events/Mtgs.
- Private Parties
- ☐ Accommodations

The historic and regal building that houses San Francisco's Asian Art Museum is as captivating as the art inside. A massive stone Beaux-Arts structure—which was built in 1917 and functioned as the city's main library for decades—stands four stories high with columns, stairs, and inscriptions completing its stately façade. Gleaming marble surfaces, beautifully carved stone arches, and antique light fixtures greet visitors in the lobby and grace the sophisticated special event spaces beyond.

The stunning transformation from book repository to museum was masterminded by Italian architect Gae Aulenti, who is perhaps best known for taking a defunct train station in Paris and turning it into the award-winning Musée D'Orsay.

Through the central archway leading off the lobby, guests encounter the opulent Grand Staircase and Loggia, which still retain an early 1900s elegance. Three flights of gently ascending travertine marble steps lead up to the Loggia, an airy arcade that overlooks the staircase and has a decorative barrel-vaulted ceiling. The glass cases that line its walls display an array of distinctive Asian ceramics, and remind us that this is indeed a museum. Some couples have married on the stairs, which look amazing when decorated with candles and flowers; with this setup, wedding attendees observe the ceremony from the Loggia above, as if gazing upon royalty. Once the service concludes, cocktails, passed champagne and hors d'oeuvres are served in the Loggia, where tall tables, candles and special linens personalize the space. During this time, your guests can explore the art galleries situated on either side of the Hall, where a world-class collection of works from China, Japan and Korea awaits.

For an elegant sit-down dinner and dancing, the adjacent Samsung Hall is equally classy. Vast and square-shaped, it continues the visual theme of columns and plenty of marble, but also boasts enormous windows crisscrossed with intricate metalwork. A huge bronze chandelier illuminates the festivities from high above. When you add linen-clad tables, mood lighting and the dulcet sounds of a string quartet, the hall feels positively palatial.

If you prefer a contemporary setting, the museum has a pair of almost identical courts on the lower level that are connected by two open hallways. Known as the North and South Courts, they were completely remodeled during the museum construction, and present a striking contrast to the historic sections of the facility. Their thoroughly modern and minimalist design features clean lines, a marble floor, and an angular ceiling of skylights nearly three stories above. Because of their considerable size, the Courts lend themselves to a wide range of event options: wedding ceremonies, sit-down dinners, buffets with food stations, and cocktail parties. You can even create a lounge atmosphere by bringing in a bar, conversational groupings of couches, and tables and chairs.

Before the festivities begin, brides who want a secluded spot in which to get ready or relax can utilize the lovely Peterson Room on the first floor. A lavish private room, it has Oriental rugs and Asian-inspired décor that's very Zen.

There are many advantages to planning an event at the Asian Art Museum, but the main one is this: No matter where you hold your celebration, you're surrounded by beauty. The building has so much style and history (not to mention its world-renowned art collection) that you don't have to add much to make your celebration dazzling.

CEREMONY, EVENT/RECEPTION & MEETING CAPACITY: The Museum accommodates a maximum of 400 seated or 1,500 standing guests, though not all in one room. Samsung Hall and the Loggia hold up to 250 seated guests (225 when including space for a dance area), and up to 350 standing. Each Court holds up to 200 seated or 250 standing guests. The Galleries may be rented with event spaces. Food and beverages are not permitted in the galleries.

Please inquire about outdoor tent options to increase maximum capacity.

FEES & DEPOSITS: A $5,000 nonrefundable deposit is required to reserve your date. The balance is due 30 days prior to event. Rental fees range $6,500–20,000 depending on space rented.

AVAILABILITY: Weddings are contracted from 5:15pm–1am (including setup, event, and load-out) year-round, except Thursday nights.

SERVICES/AMENITIES:

Catering: select from list
Kitchen Facilities: prep only
Tables & Chairs: through caterer
Linens, Silver, etc.: through caterer
Restrooms: wheelchair accessible
Dance Floor: built-in or BYO through caterer
Bride's Dressing Area: yes
Meeting Equipment: CBA, extra charge

Parking: valet or public garage
Accommodations: no guestrooms
Telephone: pay phones
Outdoor Night Lighting: yes
Outdoor Cooking Facilities: yes
Cleanup: through caterer
View: artwork
Other: in-house audiovisual

RESTRICTIONS:

Alcohol: BYO, licensed server
Smoking: outside only
Music: amplified OK

Wheelchair Access: yes
Insurance: liability required
Other: no glitter, rice or birdseed

Bently Reserve and Conference Center

Historic Bank Foyer

301 Battery Street, San Francisco
415/294-2226
www.bentlyreserve.com
vivian.perez@bentlyreserve.com

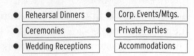

- Rehearsal Dinners
- Corp. Events/Mtgs.
- Ceremonies
- Private Parties
- Wedding Receptions
- Accommodations

We always get asked about mansions in San Francisco, and to tell you the truth, there aren't many that can accommodate large wedding receptions indoors. Although the Bently Reserve is not a mansion, it possesses the stately, elegant and understated grandeur you'd expect from a palatial estate. And it can handle quite a crowd.

Originally part of the lobby of the 1924 Bently Reserve, the event space has been fully restored and the building in which it's housed is included in the National Register of Historic Places. The Bently Reserve is a fine example of San Francisco's "banking temple" tradition and the government's penchant for monumental classical architecture during that era. Inside, you'll find one of the most dramatic staircases we've ever seen. If you'd like to make a theatrical entrance, descend the bronze and marble double stairway, which starts from two separate places and curves seamlessly down onto the gleaming marble floor below. Everywhere you look you'll see French and Italian marble (or a close facsimile). Expertly painted faux marbling has transformed the two rows of 25-foot-tall Ionic columns that flank the room into "rock-solid" architectural elements. The entry doors are solid bronze, and two original bronze chandeliers (designed by the architect) draw your eyes up to the awe-inspiring 34-foot ceiling overhead. All in all, if you have an extended guest list and are searching for a grand location in the City, you couldn't ask for a better spot.

CEREMONY CAPACITY: The main hall holds 350 seated guests. The Conference Center holds up to 70 seated guests.

EVENT/RECEPTION & MEETING CAPACITY: The Banking Hall holds 200 seated theater-style, 350 seated banquet-style or up to 650 standing guests; the Conference Center holds up to 70 guests, and has 7 separate meeting spaces.

FEES & DEPOSITS: The Banking Hall rental fee ranges $5,500–10,000 depending on the day of your event. A $1,000 refundable security deposit is payable with the signed license agreement. On-site facility security services are required and are an additional charge. The Conference Center's rental fee for special events is contingent on the time and day of the event, the size of the group, and is subject to availability.

AVAILABILITY: Sunday–Thursday, 5pm–midnight; Friday and Saturday events until 1am. Daytime events by special arrangement. Tours of the facility are by appointment only.

SERVICES/AMENITIES:

Catering: select from exclusive list
Kitchen Facilities: prep only
Tables & Chairs: caterer
Linens, Silver, etc.: caterer
Restrooms: wheelchair accessible
Dance Floor: yes
Bride's Dressing Area: yes
Meeting Equipment: full range CBA
Other: coat check room

Parking: adjacent garage, discounted on evenings and weekends
Accommodations: hotels nearby
Telephone: no
Outdoor Night Lighting: access only
Outdoor Cooking Facilities: no
Cleanup: renter
View: no

RESTRICTIONS:

Alcohol: through caterer
Smoking: outside only
Music: amplified OK indoors

Wheelchair Access: yes
Insurance: liability required
Other: no glitter or confetti

California Academy of Sciences

Museum

Golden Gate Park, 55 Music Concourse Drive, San Francisco
415/379-5868
www.calacademy.org/visit/plan_an_event/wedding/
weddings@calacademy.org

- Rehearsal Dinners
- Ceremonies
- Wedding Receptions
- Corp. Events/Mtgs.
- Private Parties
- Accommodations

There's only one place on the planet where you can get married in front of a coral reef, dine in the company of penguins, and stroll through a rainforest. We're talking about the California Academy of Sciences, San Francisco's world-renowned, eco-friendly natural history museum. Whether you're hosting a private dinner for 30, a wedding for 300 or a corporate extravaganza for 3,000, it will be as green as it is memorable.

The California Academy of Sciences building is one of the most innovative and environmentally conscious structures in the world. Not only does it house an aquarium, planetarium and rainforest, but it also has a living roof, whose undulating contours mirror the seven hills of the city and are covered with millions of plants. Hosting a wedding here is truly a once-in-a-lifetime experience. You have access to the main floor as well as the Aquarium on the lower level, and you can even pose for pictures on the roof before your family and friends arrive. Your coordinator will help you choreograph your celebration, while top Bay Area caterers create your menu—featuring organic, sustainable foods, of course.

With a dozen areas to choose from, your event can flow seamlessly from one part of the museum to another. You might serve cocktails in the elegantly columned Swamp, famously inhabited by an albino alligator, then move on to a gourmet five-course repast in the African Hall. Here you'll be flanked by 21 meticulously crafted dioramas depicting wild animals like lions, antelope, baboons, leopards and mountain gorillas in their natural settings. The best spot for the head table has to be at the end of the room, where permanently "tuxedoed" penguins frolic in the water, observing the festivities from their glassed-in habitat.

Several exhibits offer immersive and interactive activities that will engage your guests. Just add a bar and cocktail tables throughout for a unique social hour. Or serve hors d'oeuvres in the Aquarium itself—the popular "touch tidepool" provides an unusual icebreaker.

Have your ceremony here, too, and prepare to be dazzled: There's nothing like exchanging vows against a 25-foot-high backdrop of turquoise water, filled with a glimmering confetti of neon-colored fish...unless it's saying "I do" with the misty greenery of the four-story Rainforest dome behind you. If you prefer an outdoor option, the East and West Gardens are lovely during warm weather. For an intimate rehearsal dinner that's literally out of this world, reserve the Planetarium anteroom, which can be transformed into a starry galaxy by the state-of-the-art media system.

At the California Academy of Sciences the "décor" often flies, swims or grows before your very eyes. Let the museum take your guests to beautiful and amazing places they've never seen and inspire them with wonder. An event here is so much more than an event—it's an adventure.

CEREMONY CAPACITY: The site holds 280 seated guests indoors.

EVENT/RECEPTION CAPACITY: The museum accommodates 280 seated or 3,000 standing guests indoors.

MEETING CAPACITY: The facility holds 300 seated guests.

FEES & DEPOSITS: 50% of the rental fee is required to confirm your date. The balance is due 30 days prior to the event. For your wedding event, you'll have access to the entire Academy, including use of the following spaces: Rainforest, Aquarium, Swamp, Piazza, African Hall, East Pavilion, West Pavilion, Forum and Main Lobby. Also included are a Wedding Ready Room with adjoining restroom, plus additional services such as security for the museum, coat check, custodial services, and docents for the Academy living exhibits (as available). Please contact the Special Events Department for details. The all-inclusive use fee is $18,500 for up to 3,000 standing guests.

AVAILABILITY: Year-round, 7pm–midnight, every day except Thursday.

SERVICES/AMENITIES:

Catering: select from list
Kitchen Facilities: prep only
Tables & Chairs: through caterer
Linens, Silver, etc.: through caterer
Restrooms: wheelchair accessible
Dance Floor: CBA
Bride's Dressing Area: yes
Meeting Equipment: CBA

Parking: garage nearby
Accommodations: no guestrooms
Telephone: pay phone
Outdoor Night Lighting: no
Outdoor Cooking Facilities: no
Cleanup: caterer or renter
View: cityscape, park, landscaped grounds

RESTRICTIONS:

Alcohol: BYO licensed server
Smoking: not allowed
Music: amplified OK with restrictions

Wheelchair Access: yes
Insurance: liability required

Overwhelmed? Use the search criteria on www.HereComesTheGuide.com to narrow down your choices.

Cartoon Art Museum

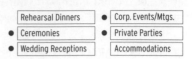

Museum

655 Mission Street, San Francisco
415/227-8666

www.cartoonart.org
rentals@cartoonart.org

Rehearsal Dinners	● Corp. Events/Mtgs.
● Ceremonies	Private Parties
● Wedding Receptions	Accommodations

Just a hop-skip from the Yerba Buena Center for the Arts, the Moscone Convention Center, SFMOMA and the San Francisco Academy of Art, in what is becoming the increasingly artsy Mission corridor, is a cool and creative event space that might still be a bit of a secret. Whether you're planning a company or social event, a zany product launch or a sophisticated, out-of-the-ordinary urban wedding reception, you don't want to overlook the Cartoon Art Museum. Affairs here aren't merely enjoyable; they are a blast.

Your experience begins in the contemporary, stainless steel and concrete lobby, where a big heart sculpture from the 2004 Hearts in San Francisco campaign greets guests warmly and a large black animation camera stand creates the perfect spot for guest photos. Or how about doing caricatures of some of the celebrants? The museum can easily recommend a talented cartoonist who can dash off keepsake sketches of guests.

Beyond the lobby, five galleries provide space for multiroom events with a flow that is totally art-astic. Galleries 1 and 2 on the left side of the museum are the largest and share a movable wall that allows for maximum event flexibility. Plan a ceremony, a sit-down affair or dinner and dancing here. The ceilings are high, the acoustics fine, and the treated concrete floors can handle plenty of action. All the lighting is on tracks and dimmers, which means it can be adjusted to make both the art and the partygoers look their best. Even the soft gray walls add a level of festivity and inspiration: They might feature artwork on loan for the rotating exhibits, or selections from the museum's permanent 5,000-piece collection of original cartoon drawings and watercolors. Possibilities include early Mickey Mouse and Superman cels, as well as turn-of-the-century comic strips like George Herriman's Krazy Kat. They even have underground comix from Robert Crumb and favorite Peanuts strips, not to mention dozens of other choices.

Galleries 4 and 5, which are situated on the left, are a bit smaller and better suited for more intimate gatherings or for food stations, cocktails and passed hors d'oeuvres. Set up bars or desert tables in one or both of the rooms. Here, too, the artwork can contribute to spirited conversation and keep guests merrily moving and mingling.

Gallery 3 in the back of the museum has a 42" flat-panel TV monitor and doors leading to Minna Street and one of the neighborhood's many large public parking structures. With easy access for caterers, it's a terrific place to stage food service or situate more elaborate food presentations and buffets.

But why limit your planning to these options? Consider an evening that progresses from one gallery to the next, entertainers who roam the entire museum, or food from a different culture in every room. Whatever your vision, the experienced museum staff—well versed in art openings and other functions—can help make it smoothly take shape.

Best of all, the Cartoon Art Museum is a nonprofit organization, so not only is a portion of your rental fee tax deductible, your use of the gallery space also helps provide for arts programs.

CEREMONY CAPACITY: The site can accommodate 120 seated guests indoors.

EVENT/RECEPTION CAPACITY: The museum holds 150 seated or 250 standing indoors.

MEETING CAPACITY: The site holds 120 seated guests.

FEES & DEPOSITS: A $500 deposit plus a refundable cleaning deposit is required to reserve your date. The balance is due 30 days prior to the event. Rental fees range $1,000–4,000. Liability insurance is required. A movable wall can be modified to open up the space for larger events for an additional fee ($100 weekdays, $200 weekends).

AVAILABILITY: Year-round, all day on Mondays, and Tuesday–Sunday, 5pm–midnight.

SERVICES/AMENITIES:

Catering: select from list
Kitchen Facilities: limited
Tables & Chairs: some provided or through caterer
Linens, Silver, etc.: through caterer or BYO
Restrooms: wheelchair accessible
Dance Floor: CBA
Bride's Dressing Area: CBA
Meeting Equipment: some provided

Parking: limited, garage nearby
Accommodations: no guestrooms
Telephone: emergency use only
Outdoor Night Lighting: access only
Outdoor Cooking Facilities: no
Cleanup: renter
View: no
Other: event coordination

RESTRICTIONS:

Alcohol: BYO
Smoking: not allowed
Music: amplified OK indoors

Wheelchair Access: yes
Insurance: liability required

Casa de la Vista

Treasure Island, San Francisco
415/274-2013, Wine Valley Catering
www.winevalleycatering.com
lynn@winevalleycatering.com

Historic Officer's Club

- Rehearsal Dinners
- Ceremonies
- Wedding Receptions
- Corp. Events/Mtgs.
- Private Parties
- Accommodations

Named "Best Place To Say 'I Do' in San Francisco" by *7x7 Magazine,* Treasure Island's Casa de la Vista has the most spectacular views of The City you're likely to find anywhere, and it offers a number of other attractions (starting with plenty of parking and flexibility) that make it well worth the visit.

Casa de la Vista has hosted all types of events. Formerly an officer's club, the newly renovated facility boasts a gloriously unobstructed view of downtown San Francisco, Alcatraz, and the Golden Gate and Bay Bridges. Celebrations are held in one large room, whose façade of windows and high, beamed ceiling give the space a light, open feeling. Windows along the back of the room look out onto a lovely courtyard, enclosed on three sides by the building. All around, mature pines, eucalyptus, palms and olive trees provide shade and a restful backdrop. Weather permitting, you can use the patio for cocktails and appetizers, or perhaps for your ceremony. *Wine Valley Catering,* the exclusive caterer for this site, can help you with all your food and beverage needs.

Just a few steps away is another ceremony possibility: the wooden chapel. This redwood-paneled sanctuary is nondenominational and minimally ornamented, aside from two stained-glass windows (one of which depicts Jesus). However, during the warmer months, you might want to take full advantage of the magnificent views by saying your vows on the Great Lawn—a sweeping expanse of grass as close to shore as you can get—or in one of several tree-sheltered areas. Not just for ceremonies, the lawn can accommodate a variety of events, from a garden reception to a corporate picnic.

For groups of up to 400, consider the adjacent Pavilion by the Bay, a new permanent tented structure that will shelter you from the elements while preserving the dramatic bay views. The Pavilion works well for grand weddings, and is also popular for fundraisers and corporate functions.

Nearby is another option for larger events: the beautiful Art Deco lobby in the historic Building One, originally built for the 1939 San Francisco World's Fair. This space is wonderful for product launch parties, fundraisers and other galas. If you'd like to reserve any of the island's event sites in combination, go right ahead—they're all within walking distance of each other.

Perfectly positioned between the East Bay and San Francisco, Treasure Island's venues balance a relaxed, pastoral feeling with the glamour of city lights. This is one place where you and your guests can meet in the middle without compromising anything.

CEREMONY, EVENT/RECEPTION & MEETING CAPACITY: Casa de la Vista holds 150 seated or 200 standing guests. The Great Lawn holds 500 seated or 750 standing.

FEES & DEPOSITS: 50% of the rental fee is required to reserve your date; the rental balance is due 30 days prior to the event. Rental fees start at $3,950 depending on the day of the event. Overtime fees may apply. Catering is provided by *Wine Valley Catering,* meals start at $65/person. Tax, alcohol, service charge, permits, linen and all needed rentals are additional.

AVAILABILITY: Year-round, daily, 6am–2am.

SERVICES/AMENITIES:

Catering: provided by *Wine Valley Catering*
Kitchen Facilities: n/a
Tables & Chairs: provided
Linens, Silver, etc.: through *Wine Valley Catering*
Restrooms: wheelchair accessible
Dance Floor: through *Wine Valley Catering*
Bride's Dressing Area: yes
Meeting Equipment: through *Wine Valley Catering*

Parking: 200-space lot, more CBA
Accommodations: no guestrooms
Telephone: none
Outdoor Night Lighting: access only
Outdoor Cooking Facilities: no
Cleanup: through *Wine Valley Catering*
View: panorama of SF Bay and skyline

RESTRICTIONS:

Alcohol: through *Wine Valley Catering*
Smoking: outside only
Music: amplified OK until 2am

Wheelchair Access: yes
Insurance: liability required
Other: no rose petals, rice, confetti, birdseed; no nails, tacks or tape

The Century Club of California
and the Julia Morgan Ballroom

Historic Women's Club

1355 Franklin Street, San Francisco
415/673-7117
www.thecenturyclubofcalifornia.org
centuryc@earthlink.net

● Rehearsal Dinners		● Corp. Events/Mtgs.	
● Ceremonies		● Private Parties	
● Wedding Receptions		Accommodations	

More than 100 years ago, when San Francisco was still in its infancy, a group of urban sophisticates banded together, forming a women's social organization called The Century Club of California. They lunched each Wednesday at one another's homes, but soon decided their club needed a special, larger place to meet. The "clubhouse" they built in 1905 was a Victorian mansion on Franklin Street, and it's been The Century Club headquarters ever since. Now the venerable establishment has opened its doors to nonmembers, making its gorgeous rooms available for weddings and other special occasions.

When you step into the expansive foyer of this historic building, you feel like you've just taken a trip back in time. Antique furniture, a handsome and ancient-looking grandfather clock, and handmade light fixtures create a warm, old-fashioned feeling. Carved, dark wood chairs—from Shakespeare's Church in England—and a rich set of Oriental rugs complete the picture.

A pair of French doors open into the Reception Room, an intimate banquet space with seafoam green carpet, white walls and a gold-toned Japanese screen covering one wall. Brides often decorate this simple, but charming, room with flowers, and host a luncheon or shower here. Two adjacent lounges offer the bride and groom ample space for getting ready or just relaxing before, during or after the ceremony.

If you're having a larger event, ascend the stairs to the second floor, passing by colorful stained-glass windows on your way. The cozy foyer on this level is shared by two grand spaces, the Drawing Room and the Auditorium. In the luxurious Old World atmosphere of the Drawing Room, couples marry in front of the monumental marble fireplace. Guests gather 'round, either standing, or sitting on the many overstuffed couches and chairs. When the ceremony concludes, friends and family enjoy cocktails and hors d'oeuvres while admiring the interesting artwork and built-in bookshelves (which also make a lovely backdrop for a tea or luncheon).

Seated dinners and buffets are held in the Auditorium, a spacious room designed by Julia Morgan with a vaulted ceiling, white walls and decorative wainscoting. Add plants, flowers, linens and candlelight, and the Auditorium takes on a magical glow. The small stage at one end accommodates a DJ or a band quite easily, and the polished wood floor is ready-made for dancing.

If the bride wants a moment or two alone, she can steal away to the "bride's room" on the third floor. Accessible via a somewhat hidden back staircase or the elevator, it's a comfortable and feminine living room that provides total privacy and has its own bathroom next door.

Standing in any of The Century Club's many rooms, the past doesn't seem distant at all. You can almost imagine the stylish club members, taking tea in front of the fireplace or fêting city luminaries in the Auditorium. Close your eyes and you might even hear the horse-drawn carriages that used to carry the ladies to and from this elegant clubhouse. Inside The Century Club, tradition, history and the beauty of a bygone era still exist, enriching every celebration that takes place here.

CEREMONY CAPACITY: Small ceremonies may be held in the Drawing Room for 40–75 guests.

EVENT/RECEPTION CAPACITY: The Century Club holds up to 170 seated or 200 standing guests.

MEETING CAPACITY: Meeting spaces accommodate up to 225 guests seated theater-style.

FEES & DEPOSITS: A $750 refundable deposit is required. The rental balance is due 15 days prior to the event. Rental fees range $700–3,500 depending on space rented and level of building access. A kitchen use fee may also apply. The Club is beautifully decorated for the holidays in December. The rental price of the Auditorium includes one free daytime rehearsal.

AVAILABILITY: Year-round, daily, 8am–midnight.

SERVICES/AMENITIES:

Catering: select from list or BYO
Kitchen Facilities: prep only
Tables & Chairs: some provided, more CBA
Linens, Silver, etc.: BYO or through caterer
Restrooms: not wheelchair accessible
Dance Floor: yes
Bride's Dressing Area: yes
Meeting Equipment: limited

Parking: public lots nearby
Accommodations: no guestrooms
Telephone: pay phone
Outdoor Night Lighting: access only
Outdoor Cooking Facilities: no
Cleanup: caterer or renter
View: no

RESTRICTIONS:

Alcohol: BYO, licensed server
Smoking: outside only
Music: amplified OK with restrictions

Wheelchair Access: limited
Insurance: liability required
Other: no rice, confetti or birdseed

The professionals in the back of this book are the best in the business. How do we know? Read page 701.

The City Club of San Francisco

Historic Club

155 Sansome Street, San Francisco
415/362-2480
www.cityclubsf.com
catering@cityclubsf.com

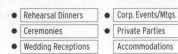

- Rehearsal Dinners
- Ceremonies
- Wedding Receptions
- Corp. Events/Mtgs.
- Private Parties

Accommodations

Just walking into the lobby of this former Stock Exchange Tower, situated in the heart of the Financial District, gives you an inkling of what's to follow. One glance at the highly polished black-and-green marble floors, black-and-white marble walls and gold ceiling and you feel instantly surrounded by glamour.

Elevators whisk you up to the 10th floor, and the entrance to The City Club itself. Here, even the elevator doors—framed in bronze and decorated in silver, bronze and brass appliqué—offer an elegant example of this facility's attention to detail. The Club (which occupies the 10th and 11th floors) features one of the most striking and exquisite Art Deco interiors we've seen, including a remarkable stairwell painted with an original 30-foot-high Diego Rivera fresco. Furnishings are original Art Deco pieces and appointments are generously clad in black marble, silver and brass. The ceiling is stunning, covered with burnished gold leaf squares. Sophisticated with just the right amount of glitz, this is an exceptional place for a wedding reception or corporate special event.

CEREMONY CAPACITY: The 10th floor (Cafe) can accommodate 220 seated or 300 standing; the 11th floor (Main Dining Room) 240 seated or 300 standing guests.

EVENT/RECEPTION & MEETING CAPACITY: For receptions, the entire Club (10th and 11th floors) may be reserved. The Club holds 20–460 seated or up to 500 for a standing reception on two floors.

FEES & DEPOSITS: For special events, the rental fee for a 5-hour block of time is $2,500 for Saturday and $2,000 for Sunday. Food and beverage minimums range $10,000–23,000. Curfew is 2am and the overtime charge is $500/hour. On weeknights, Monday–Thursday, food and beverage minimums range $6,000–12,000 and rental fees are waived. Minimums vary depending on the month and day of the event. Tax and a 21% service charge are additional. Member sponsorship is available. For business meetings, room rental fees apply with fewer than 15 guests. Additional labor fees apply for evening events.

AVAILABILITY: Year-round, Monday–Friday, 7:30am–2am. On Saturdays and Sundays, 8am–2am.

SERVICES/AMENITIES:

Catering: provided, no BYO
Kitchen Facilities: n/a
Tables & Chairs: provided, styles and quantities vary
Linens, Silver, etc.: provided
Restrooms: wheelchair accessible
Dance Floor: yes
Bride's Dressing Area: yes
Meeting Equipment: full AV services available

Parking: CBA
Accommodations: no guestrooms, affiliate club hotels
Telephone: guest phones
Outdoor Night Lighting: access only
Outdoor Cooking Facilities: no
Cleanup: provided
View: San Francisco skyline

RESTRICTIONS:

Alcohol: provided
Smoking: smoking room only
Music: amplified OK

Wheelchair Access: yes
Insurance: not required

Cliff House

1090 Point Lobos, San Francisco
415/666-4027

www.cliffhouse.com
virginia@cliffhouse.com

● Rehearsal Dinners	● Corp. Events/Mtgs.
● Ceremonies	● Private Parties
● Wedding Receptions	Accommodations

For nearly a century and a half, the Cliff House has been one of The City's most familiar and beloved landmarks. Generations of San Franciscans have brought visiting friends and relatives to this spot to show off the glorious westernmost part of the city. Drawn here by the spectacular ocean views and the waves crashing along the rocky shore, they often stopped in at the restaurant for a hot meal after a blustery walk on Ocean Beach, or to watch a particularly lovely sunset over a glass of wine.

What most people don't realize is that the Cliff House has just begun its fourth incarnation. The plain first structure, built in 1863, was succeeded by an improbably large, turreted Victorian building perched wildly far out on the Point Lobos cliff. Though it survived the 1906 earthquake, the all-wood structure burned down the following year. (Luckily, almost no one was there because it was closed for renovations!) In 1909, a simple neoclassical cement version was constructed, but over the years that building was obscured by numerous renovations and accretions. Well, that Cliff House—which is the one most of us remember—has undergone a complete restoration, and it's now more captivating than ever for a wedding or special event.

The 1909 building at the core has been uncovered and restored, and the new Sutro Wing on the north side (named for the famous public bathhouse that flourished on this site in the early 1900s) has been designed as an upscale restaurant. This clever addition's two-story windows frame the truly breathtaking views, while an opalescent floor-to-ceiling sea-glass mosaic reflects the shimmery light of the ocean and evokes the pearly inside of an abalone shell. An exhibition kitchen, which expands the open feeling, is visible from nearly everywhere in the room. Two large Italian ceramic panels, which depict ladies bathing and once hung in the Sutro Baths, have been restored and now grace the restaurant.

The completely separate Terrace Room in the 1909 section, however, is the place for weddings. All of the glories of a Pacific sunset to the west and misty Ocean Beach stretching southward can be viewed through floor-to-ceiling windows on two sides. If you hold your ceremony on the private Terrace, you'll have the beach and the Pacific as your backdrop while you face Seal Rock. Afterwards, invite your guests inside the Terrace Room for cocktails followed by dinner and dancing.

A palette of muted sand dune tones is carried through the chairs, carpet and window treatments; seven large framed mirrors run along the wall opposite the windows, brightening the room and reflecting the view. (Consider having your cake table in front of one of the mirrors.) There's often an extended dusk here—the kind you get when you're out at sea. With any luck, that lingering glow will illuminate the room all during your reception. An adjacent dedicated kitchen turns out updated classic cuisine for your private party, so there's no conflict with restaurant dining.

Come rediscover this uniquely San Franciscan treasure. Its mesmerizing clifftop location and exceptional sea (and seal!) views make it well worth the trip.

CEREMONY CAPACITY: The Terrace Deck and Terrace Room each accommodate 70 seated guests.

EVENT/RECEPTION & MEETING CAPACITY: The Terrace Room can accommodate 120 seated or 180 standing guests.

FEES & DEPOSITS: To reserve for events, a $2,000 nonrefundable deposit (which is applied towards the final bill) is required when reservations are confirmed. 75% of the estimated event total is due 5 weeks prior to the event; the balance payable at the end of the function. A guest count confirmation is due 2 weeks in advance. Food service is provided. Per person costs run $65–75 for buffets, $46–75 for seated dinners. Beverages, tax and a 20% service charge are additional.

For business meetings, a room rental fee may apply. The fee will vary depending on day of week, event duration and food and beverage total.

AVAILABILITY: Year-round, daily, 8am–1:30am. The Terrace Room is not available Sunday before 6pm or on major holidays.

SERVICES/AMENITIES:

Catering: provided, no BYO
Kitchen Facilities: n/a
Tables & Chairs: provided
Linens, Silver, etc.: provided
Restrooms: wheelchair accessible
Dance Floor: yes
Bride's Dressing Area: no
Meeting Equipment: CBA, extra charge

Parking: nearby lots
Accommodations: no guestrooms
Telephone: emergency use only
Outdoor Night Lighting: no
Outdoor Cooking Facilities: no
Cleanup: provided
View: ocean
Other: wedding and event coordination

RESTRICTIONS:

Alcohol: provided
Smoking: outdoors only
Music: amplified OK indoors

Wheelchair Access: yes
Insurance: not required

Clift

Historic Boutique Hotel

495 Geary Street, San Francisco
415/929-2302
www.clifthotel.com
lindsay.chew@morganshotelgroup.com

● Rehearsal Dinners	● Corp. Events/Mtgs.
● Ceremonies	● Private Parties
● Wedding Receptions	● Accommodations

Here is a venue so notable, it really needs no introduction. It's not *the* Clift or Clift *Hotel*; it's simply Clift. A celebrated property and landmark hotel since its commission in 1913, it was purchased and transformed in 1996 by aesthetic and cultural impresario, Ian Schrager. Schrager, best known for trendsetting night-clubs Studio 54 and Palladium and for high-profile boutique hotels like New York's Royalton and L.A.'s so-phisticated Mondrian, enlisted the formidable talents of internationally acclaimed designer Philippe Starck to update Clift in a manner that would maintain its celebrity status and add a hot new spin.

The lobby, with its soaring 25-foot ceilings, polished Italian plaster walls and Italian Pietra Serena limestone floors, is your portal to another world. Whimsical design touches—an enormous bronze chair, three times normal size; a fabulous couch with arms of curling horn—create art and an atmosphere that is innovative and striking.

The drama and innovation continue in event spaces that capture the glamour of a bygone era. White velvet curtains cover all of the walls, softening the spaces and providing an elegant back-drop for custom-etched mirrors and hanging, illuminated demilune vases of etched Murano glass. Classic banquet room furniture is given a witty signature twist: Polyurethane chairs with silver legs are slipcovered with printed etchings of Italian Renaissance chair frames. The stylish, smaller-scale meeting rooms—also draped in velvet—mix dark exotic wood furnishings with polished stainless steel and rich brown leather. All offer video conferencing, projectors and other high-tech accoutrements.

You can take your function to new heights in the sumptuous Spanish Suite on the 15th floor. Gray and silver accents, a beautiful mahogany fireplace and tented outdoor terraces with panoramic city views create a stage worthy of your VIP event. Self-contained, with its own coatroom, executive restroom and kitchen, this is a unique, star-pleasing setting that can be arranged to suit banquet or buffet, CEO, socialite, diva or not-so-blushing bride.

Catering for all events originates in Clift's restaurant, Velvet Room, a captivating place for dining, drinking and entertaining. The look is chic and dramatic, thanks to lush velvet curtains, mahogany and leather banquettes, and hand-blown Murano glass lamps. Executive Chef Ewart Wardhaugh has worked with some of the world's top chefs and cooked at notable establishments such as Raffles Singapore, the Lanesborough Hotel London and Wynn Las Vegas. His seasonal menus feature fresh ingredients that are locally grown in a sustainable, organic manner. Bounty from producers in a 100-mile radius of San Francisco finds its way into Chef Wardhaugh's culinary repertoire: Fulton Valley Organic Chicken with Creamed Corn and Forged Mushrooms; Grilled Zuckerman's Farms Asparagus with Point Reyes Blue Cheese, Poached Pheasant Egg and Marshall's Honeycomb; and Ravioli of Bellwether Farms Ricotta are just a few examples. Customized menus for your event are also available.

Once you have found Clift, you and your guests won't want to leave. So don't. Extend your brush with romance and glamour for days. Lounge in luxury in one of the hotel's tranquil ivory, gray and lavender guestrooms, rest up, get refreshed, then head down to the newly refurbished Redwood Room for a toast in Clift's gorgeous, much lauded bar.

CEREMONY CAPACITY: Clift holds up to 150 seated guests.

EVENT/RECEPTION CAPACITY: The Velvet Room seats 200, while the Velvet and Redwood Rooms combined seat 350 guests.

MEETING CAPACITY: Meeting spaces seat 8–90 guests.

FEES & DEPOSITS: 50% of the estimated event total is required to reserve your date; the balance is due 2 weeks prior to the event. Rental fees range $500–2,000 depending on space rented and day and time of event. Meals range $65–100/person. Alcohol is additional.

AVAILABILITY: Year-round, daily, anytime.

SERVICES/AMENITIES:

Catering: provided by *Velvet Room*
Kitchen Facilities: n/a
Tables & Chairs: provided
Linens, Silver, etc.: provided
Restrooms: wheelchair accessible
Dance Floor: yes
Bride's Dressing Area: yes
Meeting Equipment: video conferencing, projectors, full range CBA

Parking: valet
Accommodations: 363 guestrooms
Telephone: yes
Outdoor Night Lighting: yes
Outdoor Cooking Facilities: no
Cleanup: provided
View: San Francisco skyline
Other: event design and coordination available

RESTRICTIONS:

Alcohol: provided
Smoking: outdoors only
Music: amplified OK with restrictions

Wheelchair Access: yes
Insurance: not required

Conservatory of Flowers

Historic Conservatory

100 John F. Kennedy Drive, San Francisco
415/831-2090
www.conservatoryofflowers.org
info@conservatoryofflowers.org

● Rehearsal Dinners	● Corp. Events/Mtgs.
● Ceremonies	● Private Parties
● Wedding Receptions	Accommodations

If you're looking for a symbolic place to begin your marriage, you can't beat the Conservatory of Flowers in Golden Gate Park. This seemingly fragile, multifaceted gem of a building with a thriving, ever-growing, organic heart, has suffered fire, earthquakes and windstorms—and yet, it's still standing after 130 years.

In December 1995, a Pacific storm with 100-mile-an-hour winds shattered 40 percent of the frosty white glass panels, and damaged the framework so badly that the entire structure had to be dismantled and reassembled using a mixture of old and replacement wood beams. Luckily, a rebuilt and thoroughly revitalized Conservatory was able to reopen in the fall of 2003.

The Vestibule is the entry to the Conservatory and a lovely entrée to your event. While you're serving cocktails in this peaked roof section, take a look at the surrounding glass: It's not all white or clear, but punctuated by jewel-like insets of green, tiger lily orange, ruby and delphinium blue.

From the Vestibule, go through the Lowland Tropics, the large central gallery with the gorgeous pointed cupola housing the enormous century-old philodendron and a dense mix of other tropical plants. The cool Highland Tropics gallery contains a collection of delicate high-altitude orchids. The Aquatic Plants gallery has a water lily pond with little waterfalls and fantastic *Victoria amazonica* lily pads—the kind that grow so large they're depicted in fairy-tale books with children sitting on them.

The two galleries where you can host a celebration are Potted Plants and Special Exhibits in the western wing. Inside Potted Plants, the wooden arbor is tailor-made for exchanging vows. It's flanked by potted palms, and the vines overhead drip with star-shaped lavender flowers. Throughout this gallery are hibiscus plants with showy blooms in yellows, pinks, oranges and reds, and orchids in all the crazy variety of sizes, shapes and colors that orchids exhibit. Huge pots of Dr. Suessian, spiky-stemmed Madagascar Palms sit here, and two banks of plants with a mesmerizing diversity of leaf textures, shapes and patterns run the length of the room.

Just past Potted Plants is Special Exhibits, a large open gallery dominated by the ethereal, spun-sugar look of the Conservatory's structure. Depending on the availability of this space, ceremonies take place here among changing exhibits that always include a variety of plants.

In 2008, a new event space adjacent to the Aquatic Plants gallery was added for larger, sit-down dinner functions, events or meetings. Outdoor ceremonies and tented events for up to 300+ people can be held on the Conservatory's lawn or platform. Of course, other spots for ceremonies and photo ops are hardly lacking in Golden Gate Park.

Flower lovers will find no better place for a celebration than this Conservatory. It's a uniquely beautiful San Francisco landmark.

CEREMONY CAPACITY: The Conservatory can accommodate 150 seated guests indoors and 300 seated outdoors.

EVENT/RECEPTION & MEETING CAPACITY: The Conservatory holds up to 165 seated or 400 standing guests total. Smaller celebrations as well as larger tented events can be accommodated, call for details.

FEES & DEPOSITS: 25% of the rental fee is required to reserve your date. The balance is due 30 days prior to event date. Rental fees range $2,500–10,000 depending on space, day and length of time rented.

AVAILABILITY: Year-round, daily, 5pm–midnight. Daytime hours are available with some restrictions.

SERVICES/AMENITIES:

Catering: select from list
Kitchen Facilities: prep only
Tables & Chairs: through vendor
Linens, Silver, etc.: BYO or through caterer
Restrooms: wheelchair accessible
Dance Floor: through vendor
Bride's Dressing Area: no
Meeting Equipment: BYO or through vendor

Parking: on street
Accommodations: no guestrooms
Telephone: emergency use only
Outdoor Night Lighting: access only
Outdoor Cooking Facilities: no
Cleanup: caterer
View: landscaped grounds, Golden Gate Park

RESTRICTIONS:

Alcohol: BYO, licensed server
Smoking: not allowed
Music: amplified OK with restrictions

Wheelchair Access: yes
Insurance: liability required

Want to know WHAT TO ASK a potential location or vendor? Check out our Questions to Ask on page 17.

de Young Museum

Landmark Museum

50 Hagiwara Tea Garden Drive, Golden Gate Park, San Francisco
415/750-3683
www.famsf.org
deyoungevents@famsf.org

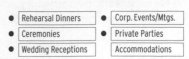

● Rehearsal Dinners		● Corp. Events/Mtgs.
● Ceremonies		● Private Parties
● Wedding Receptions		○ Accommodations

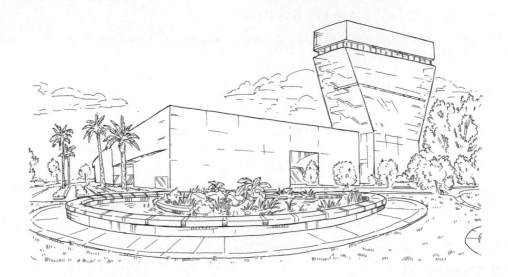

If you want your event to be as captivating as a work of art, the de Young Museum is unquestionably the right venue. Founded in 1895 and situated in the heart of San Francisco's Golden Gate Park, the museum was completely redesigned in 2005 as an ultra-cool contemporary frame for fine art and outstanding functions.

Entrance is through the courtyard installation by famed sculptor Andy Goldsworthy. Once inside, a right turn will take you to Hamon Tower—intriguing from both an architectural and events perspective. An invitingly lit lobby, featuring Italian stone floors and Ruth Asawa sculptures, seems a fitting place to greet guests with champagne before whisking them up nine stories to the Observation Floor. Here, surrounded by honey-colored wood floors and walls of glass, delighted celebrants can savor cocktails, hors d'oeuvres, music and perhaps even dance. All the while they'll be admiring an unimpeded 360-degree panorama that includes San Francisco's downtown, the Golden Gate Bridge and the sparkling Pacific, as well as aerial views of the park.

Your guests will also be impressed by the spectacular architecture of the ground floor event spaces and galleries. The walls soar two stories high in dramatic Wilsey Court, a magnificent concourse fit for an über-elegant wedding reception, dinner dance or upscale corporate affair. Designed by renowned Swiss architects Herzog & de Meuron, its inspired use of angles, openness and art gives the space a fluid vitality. A grand staircase to the upper galleries is perfect for regal entrances and photo ops. And don't forget that you can include the de Young's exciting exhibits in your event, if you choose. The adjacent Piazzoni Murals Room, with burnished Italian landscapes animating its walls, can serve as a special lounge, a separate bar and entertainment area, or an exclusive, extra-private chamber for more intimate gatherings.

But why stop here? For an artsy vibe with a whimsical twist, take your party to the de Young Café, de Young Terrace, and Barbro Osher Sculpture Garden, which can be used separately or in combination. Have your ceremony on the broad sculpture garden lawn amid playful artworks and fanciful landscaping, host cocktails on the adjacent terrace, then dine and dance in the café. One of the museum's most popular venues, it transforms to suit your mood: casual, formal, festive or even sultry. Striking touches like the colorful hand-blown lamps suspended overhead remind you that no matter where you go in the de Young art is everywhere, contributing a dynamic dimension to your celebration.

CEREMONY & MEETING CAPACITY: Indoors, spaces hold up to 400 seated guests. Outdoors, the Garden holds up to 200 seated guests for a ceremony.

EVENT/RECEPTION CAPACITY: Indoors, spaces hold up to 400 seated or 2,500 standing guests.

FEES & DEPOSITS: 50% of the rental fee is due at the time of booking. Rental fees start at $5,000 and vary depending on the space rented.

AVAILABILITY: Year-round, daily. Special events take place in a 4-hour window between 6:30pm and 1am. Daytime rental is available in limited spaces during museum hours. Overtime fees are additional.

SERVICES/AMENITIES:

Catering: preferred list
Kitchen Facilities: fully equipped
Tables & Chairs: some provided
Linens, Silver, etc.: through caterer
Restrooms: wheelchair accessible
Dance Floor: provided
Bride's & Groom's Dressing Area: no
Meeting Equipment: some provided

Parking: valet or public garage
Accommodations: no guestrooms
Telephone: pay phones
Outdoor Night Lighting: access only
Outdoor Cooking Facilities: no
Cleanup: provided
View: park, garden, pond, cityscape
Other: event coordination, AV equipment

RESTRICTIONS:

Alcohol: BYO
Smoking: not allowed
Music: amplified OK

Wheelchair Access: yes
Insurance: liability required

E&O Trading Company

Restaurant

314 Sutter Street, San Francisco
415/788-2622, Private Dining
www.eandosanfrancisco.com
events@eandosanfrancisco.com

● Rehearsal Dinners	● Corp. Events/Mtgs.
Ceremonies	● Private Parties
● Wedding Receptions	Accommodations

Inspired by the story of a legendary friendship between an English trader and an Indonesian spice merchant, this celebrated restaurant in the heart of San Francisco's Union Square district has an air of romance and adventure powerful enough to sweep anyone off their feet. A three-level space modeled after the Asian trading warehouses of a century ago, it has been featured in *Gourmet Magazine* and on the *San Francisco Chronicle's* Top Ten list. It's sure to top your list as well.

Step through the portals and into the robust world of the exotic Marketplace. A dramatic dining area featuring dark tables, plush banquettes and gleaming hardwood floors, it's a festive setting for your event, be it buffet, sit-down dinner, cocktails and hors d'oeuvres pre-dinner or dancing. Imagine a first dance, cake-cutting, announcements or an award ceremony taking place amidst the elegant sheen of this spacious chamber. Playful touches like bamboo plaiting and antique artifacts enhance the ambiance. The spectacular bar hugs one full side of the room, while large gossamer chandeliers hang from a soaring ceiling two stories overhead. The high ceiling also makes for awesome acoustics, and a discreet performance space at the front of the restaurant is the ideal spot for your entertainment, whether it's a jazz trio, DJ or emcee.

For a great view of the Marketplace and its action, ascend via stairs or elevator to the regal calm of the restaurant's open horseshoe-shaped mezzanine. Your guests can dine in style in one or all of the softly carpeted semiprivate salons. The E&O Room is subtly illumined by windows affording Sutter Street views. Chandeliers, spots, wall sconces and candles light up the North Mezzanine, where thick velvet draperies offer additional options for cordoning off the space. Ivory linens add just the right touch of formality and a creamy canvas upon which to place food every bit as tantalizing and inventive as the environment. Dinners are served family style so that guests can sample a variety of exceptional dishes. Choose from hors d'oeuvres like Steak Satay, Short Rib Sliders and Sweet Corn Fritters.

For an ultraprivate atmosphere, descend the stairs that lead from the Marketplace to the appropriately named Cinnabar Room, where guests can mingle in intimate fashion. Cozy leather and velvet seating, a spicy color scheme and dreamy lighting give it a relaxed, lounge-like feel. They also serve an excellent selection of Asian beers and specialty cocktails, too.

You get the picture; this is the place where the outlook is rosy and the company's always superb. After your celebration, there's no need to take off right away. Step out into the pulsating, stylish center of San Francisco where you can sightsee and stay overnight at some of the best hotels in the world.

CEREMONY CAPACITY: Ceremonies do not take place at this facility.

EVENT/RECEPTION CAPACITY: Private dining spaces accommodate up to 275 seated or 300 standing guests.

MEETING CAPACITY: The restaurant holds up to 200 seated guests.

FEES & DEPOSITS: 50% of the estimated event total is required to reserve your date. The balance is due at the end of the event. Meals range $35–75/person. Tax, alcohol and a 20% service charge are additional.

AVAILABILITY: Year-round, daily, 7am–midnight.

SERVICES/AMENITIES:

Catering: provided, no BYO
Kitchen Facilities: n/a
Tables & Chairs: provided
Linens, Silver, etc.: provided
Restrooms: wheelchair accessible
Dance Floor: CBA
Bride's Dressing Area: no
Meeting Equipment: some provided

Parking: public garage
Accommodations: no guestrooms
Telephone: house and office phones
Outdoor Night Lighting: no
Outdoor Cooking Facilities: no
Cleanup: provided
View: SF cityscape
Other: event coordination, on-site florals

RESTRICTIONS:

Alcohol: provided, no BYO
Smoking: outside only
Music: amplified OK indoors

Wheelchair Access: yes
Insurance: not required

Exploratorium

Landmark Museum

3601 Lyon Street, San Francisco
415/561-0311
www.exploratorium.edu/rentals
events@exploratorium.edu

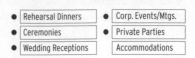

● Rehearsal Dinners	● Corp. Events/Mtgs.
● Ceremonies	● Private Parties
● Wedding Receptions	Accommodations

Few cities in America have even one world-famous landmark, so the opportunity to celebrate your big event at two of San Francisco's iconic sites—starting at the Marina District's most romantic and ending at its most inventive—seems too good to pass up.

Both venues were built for the 1915 Panama-Pacific International Exposition and designed to stimulate visitors both inside and out. The classical Palace of Fine Arts was the last building constructed for the fair, and its stunning Greco-Roman rotunda and surrounding lagoon so enamored locals and visitors alike that before the exposition even closed there was a movement to preserve it for the future. Today, the domed and colonnaded pavilion, rebuilt to its earlier glory, has become a favorite Bay Area spot for enchanting wedding ceremonies and photographs.

The original Exhibit Hall went through many incarnations over the years before debuting in 1969 as the Exploratorium. Pioneering a new, hands-on way to learn about science, art and the world around us, it became an instant hit. Here was a place where you could question, experience and learn—all while having fun. And if you've never been here, or haven't been back since some happily remembered school trip, it's still a blast!

After exchanging vows in the sylvan beauty of the rotunda (rented separately through the San Francisco Recreation and Parks Department), walk through the arched entry of the neighboring Exploratorium into a world of wonder and a cocktail reception where "interactive" means far more than just chitchat over appetizers. The Main Corridor, an enormous space with exposed industrial grids and a ceiling as high as an airplane hangar, is filled with intriguing exhibits just begging for your attention, like the 18-foot-tall tornado you can touch or the cloud rings you can send flying up into the air with a push of your hand. These and other displays and experiments, developed in-house by a combination of artists and scientists, will have guests of all ages sharing and laughing from the get-go in a way that's quite unique.

When you're ready for dinner, curtains are pulled back to reveal the Skylight Area, the main event space, which can be custom-designed to your specs. Since some of the most innovative minds in town work here, it really is a pleasure to discuss your options with the staff. Looking at photos of past events to see how they've incorporated stunning lighting accents, glowing neon drinks served in test tubes, henna tattoo artists, caricature artists, Einstein stilt walkers, and much more, can help get your own ideas flowing. You can also opt for more intimate, elegant seating arrangements and still have plenty of room for dancing plus a large raised stage for your DJ or band—flanked by two magnificent winged angels that were originally part of the 1915 exposition.

An excellent vantage for people-watching after dinner is the Mezzanine, which gives a bird's-eye view of the action below and feels like a separate lounge area. This curving, meandering aerie has lots of exhibits to keep everyone entertained. Back on the main level, the comfy McBean Theater is perfect for screening home movies or belting out karaoke tunes.

There's a joyful spirit that imbues this venue as well as a hearty appreciation for experimentation, so go ahead, get creative and let the fun begin.

CEREMONY CAPACITY: Ceremonies are held in the adjacent Palace of Fine Arts rotunda, rented separately through the San Francisco Recreation and Parks Department. Ceremonies may also be held in the 125-seat McBean Theater.

EVENT/RECEPTION CAPACITY: The facility holds 400 seated or 2,500 standing guests indoors.

MEETING CAPACITY: Meeting spaces hold 125 seated guests.

FEES & DEPOSITS: 20% of the total event cost is required to reserve your date. Half the balance is due 4 months prior and the remaining balance is due 2 months prior to the event. Rental fees start at $6,500 and vary depending on the event hours, time needed for vendor load-out and guest count.

AVAILABILITY: Year-round, daily, starting at 5:15pm.

SERVICES/AMENITIES:

Catering: select from approved list
Kitchen Facilities: prep only
Tables & Chairs: some provided, or through caterer
Linens, Silver, etc.: through caterer
Restrooms: wheelchair accessible
Dance Area: provided
Bride's Dressing Area: CBA
Meeting Equipment: CBA

Parking: large lot, on street
Accommodations: no guestrooms
Telephone: office phone
Outdoor Night Lighting: access only
Outdoor Cooking Facilities: no
Cleanup: caterer or renter
View: Palace of Fine Arts Rotunda and grounds
Other: AV equipment, access to hundreds of hands-on exhibits

RESTRICTIONS:

Alcohol: through caterer, licensed server required
Smoking: outdoors only
Music: amplified OK with restrictions

Wheelchair Access: yes
Insurance: liability required

Want to find more locations and services? Check out our informative website, www.HereComesTheGuide.com.

71

The Fairmont Hotel

Hotel

Atop Nob Hill, San Francisco
415/772-5000
www.fairmont.com/sanfrancisco
barbara.greaves@fairmont.com

● Rehearsal Dinners	● Corp. Events/Mtgs.
● Ceremonies	● Private Parties
● Wedding Receptions	● Accommodations

As the first hotel to open after the 1906 earthquake, the Fairmont San Francisco became the main gathering place and grand centerpiece of the City by the Bay. Since then, this extraordinary hotel continues to be a mecca for guests from all over the world and one of San Francisco's most treasured landmarks.

Over the last century, the Fairmont has undergone many changes, but an $85 million restoration not only brought back architect Julia Morgan's stunning turn-of-the-century interior, it added all the modern amenities you'd expect in a world-class hotel.

The lobby is now both larger and lighter in tone, and is splendidly understated with rich plum and gold hues. The original white-and-gray marble floor (lifted out slab by slab, cleaned and meticulously replaced) has been given a high sheen. The gold leaf on the 26-foot-high ceilings has been enhanced, and the ornate moldings have been cleaned and restored. Multiple pilasters and columns, painted in a *trompe l'oeil* marble finish, are highlighted with gold leaf accents. Informal clusters of period-style furniture, rich in detail with lots of tassels and trim, dot the lobby. The adjacent Laurel Court has become a warm and elegant restaurant and bar where your guests will enjoy mingling over drinks and hors d'oeuvres.

Two of the most grand and glamorous spaces in the Fairmont are the Venetian and Gold Ballrooms. Both are light and airy, with elaborately ornamented vaulted ceilings, gold leaf detailing, and crystal chandeliers. The Pavilion Room has picture windows that overlook the Fairmont's rooftop garden, a sublime spot for exchanging vows. The Crown Room, named for its spectacular location on the top floor of the Fairmont Tower, is a soothing environment in soft celadon, sage, pale violet and gold highlights. The room's most remarkable feature, however, is the view. Tall wraparound windows reveal a sweeping 270-degree panorama of the Golden Gate and Bay Bridges, Coit Tower, Alcatraz, Downtown and the Twin Peaks. The setting here is impressive enough, but if you really want to have the ultimate reception, opt for the Presidential Service: Each table has its own waiter, and everyone is served at exactly the same time.

The ultimate place to hold your event may be the 6,000-square-foot Penthouse, a palatial residence spanning the entire eighth floor of the main building following a $2 million enhancement. This extraordinary suite features a living room with a grand piano, a formal dining room that seats 50, a two-story circular library, a billiard room, a breathtaking terrace with sweeping views of the San Francisco skyline and bay, and three oversized bedrooms. When you reserve the Penthouse, you and your guests have exclusive use of it and are free to flow from one space to another throughout the celebration.

If your event is on a more intimate scale, the Fairmont has many beautiful smaller banquet rooms from which to choose. For a more casual rehearsal dinner or post-wedding gathering, the Tonga Room consistently receives awards for hosting San Francisco's best happy hour and offers exceptional Pacific Rim Asian Cuisine in a tropical setting.

This is one historic hotel that's also quite forward thinking. Their Green Weddings program includes hundreds of options from organic, locally produced foods and biodynamic wines to recyclable favors and confetti. Guestrooms are also totally up-to-date, with flat screen TVs, MP3 docking stations, Frette linens and pillow-top beds. There is no question that the Fairmont's combination of exquisite classic décor, first-rate amenities and personalized service puts this deluxe five-star hotel in a category of its own.

CEREMONY CAPACITY: Seven indoor ceremony sites accommodate 50–500 seated guests. The Roof Garden holds 150 seated.

EVENT/RECEPTION CAPACITY: The hotel's event spaces can accommodate 40–900 seated or 150–2,500 standing guests indoors.

MEETING CAPACITY: There are 19 rooms that hold 35–1,500 seated guests theater-style or 12–1,000 seated classroom-style.

FEES & DEPOSITS: A nonrefundable deposit is required when reservations are confirmed. 20% of the estimated event total is due 90 days prior to the event. An additional deposit of 60% of the estimated total is due 30 days prior, with the remaining balance due 14 days before the event. Wedding packages range $165–230/person and include service charges and sales tax. For ceremonies, a $350–12,500 fee may be charged depending on room(s) selected and extent of setup. Bride and groom receive a complimentary suite for the night of the event. Group rates for overnight guests can be arranged.

AVAILABILITY: Year-round, daily, 8am–2am.

SERVICES/AMENITIES:
Catering: provided, no BYO
Kitchen Facilities: n/a
Tables & Chairs: provided
Linens, Silver, etc.: provided
Restrooms: wheelchair accessible
Dance Floor: provided
Bride's & Groom's Dressing Area: yes
Meeting Equipment: full range CBA
Other: event planning, ice sculpture

Parking: adjacent garages, valet CBA
Accommodations: 591 guestrooms
Telephone: guest or pay phones
Outdoor Night Lighting: n/a
Outdoor Cooking Facilities: no
Cleanup: provided
View: SF Bay, city skyline, Bay and Golden Gate Bridges

RESTRICTIONS:
Alcohol: provided, no BYO
Smoking: outdoors only
Music: amplified OK indoors

Wheelchair Access: yes, elevator
Insurance: not required

First Unitarian Universalist Church of San Francisco

Historic Church

1187 Franklin Street, San Francisco
415/776-4580 x202
www.uusf.org
jroller@uusf.org

●	Rehearsal Dinners	●	Corp. Events/Mtgs.
●	Ceremonies	●	Private Parties
●	Wedding Receptions		Accommodations

As you drive past the bustling corner of Geary and Franklin Streets, you'll notice a beautiful old building that contrasts sharply with its modern neighbors. Built of sandstone in the Gothic Revival-Romanesque style, the First Unitarian Universalist Church of San Francisco looks as if it has existed for over a hundred years—and it has.

Although this is the church's third location in the city, it has occupied this corner since 1889. The First Unitarian Universalist Church marries all loving couples, and does not discriminate based upon gender or spiritual belief.

In the sanctuary, Gothic and modern design elements create an atmosphere that is open and airy, yet visually stimulating. White plaster walls, set with exquisite stained-glass rose windows, soar up to meet the tracery of the carved beam ceiling hung with wrought-iron and gilt chandeliers. On the chancel, the imposing carved Gothic chairs, pulpit and lectern are lightened by a delicate abstract metal candelabra hung on the wall behind them. A custom-built 3,100-pipe organ—said to be one of the best on the West Coast—sits regally in the choir loft. For an extra touch of magic, six-foot-tall candelabras can be fitted into brackets at the ends of the pews, giving an ethereal glow to your ceremony.

The 70-seat Chapel is ideal for smaller weddings. Octagonal in shape, its tall concrete walls are inset with narrow, stained-glass windows in shades of blue and gold, and hung with Oriental rugs and wall hangings. What makes the Chapel truly unique, however, is its fabulous acoustics. Not only do they enhance every type of music from harp to string quartet, they give the Chapel a feeling of real intimacy, and ensure that your guests will hear even your softest-spoken words.

The 35-seat Fireside Room, with fireplace, beamed ceilings and wood paneling is a cozy spot for intimate weddings, receptions or business functions. A favorite place for wedding photos and outdoor celebrations is the Allyne Courtyard, a sunny space whose focal point is a free-form bronze fountain, surrounded by flowering trees and plants.

For indoor events, the Church has two large function areas. The Thomas Starr King Room is named after the Church's beloved minister from 1860 to 1864. This spacious room has a parquet floor, impressive pyramidal beamed skylight hung with wood-and-opaque-glass light fixtures, and a recessed stage area that is perfect for a bride's table or DJ setup. The artwork on the walls is changed monthly. The adjacent Martin Luther King Room, named after the civil rights leader, is a smaller version of the Starr King Room, and sliding doors allow you to combine the two if desired.

Perhaps the most impressive thing about the First Unitarian Universalist Church is its acceptance of diverse faiths, cultures and lifestyles. You are invited to work with their clergy to create a ceremony that celebrates your values and the unique commitment you are making. So, whether you want a traditional wedding with organ music accompanying your procession, or a less conventional ceremony, you're sure to find a warm welcome at the First Unitarian Universalist Church.

CEREMONY CAPACITY: The Sanctuary can accommodate up to 350 seated guests.

EVENT/RECEPTION & MEETING CAPACITY: The church's two reception rooms combined hold up to 270 seated or 300 standing guests indoors.

FEES & DEPOSITS: 50% of the rental fee is required to reserve your date; the balance is due 30 days prior to the event. A $550–1,950 ceremony fee includes an hour for rehearsal, 2 hours for setup, an hour for photos after the ceremony, the organist, and an event coordinator. Rental fees for receptions and business functions range $700–1,500 depending on guest count and space rented. Events running past 10pm incur additional fees.

AVAILABILITY: Year-round, daily, 8am–10pm.

SERVICES/AMENITIES:

Catering: BYO
Kitchen Facilities: prep only
Tables & Chairs: provided
Linens, Silver, etc.: BYO
Restrooms: wheelchair accessible
Dance Floor: yes
Bride's & Groom's Dressing Area: provided
Meeting Equipment: TV/VCR, microphones, sound system, CD/DVD capability

Parking: nearby garages
Accommodations: no guestrooms
Telephone: emergency use only
Outdoor Night Lighting: n/a
Outdoor Cooking Facilities: n/a
Cleanup: through caterer
View: inner courtyard
Other: event coordination

RESTRICTIONS:

Alcohol: BYO
Smoking: outdoors only
Music: amplified OK

Wheelchair Access: yes
Insurance: not required

Foreign Cinema

Restaurant

2534 Mission Street, San Francisco
415/648-7600 x24

www.foreigncinema.com
janine@foreigncinema.com

- Rehearsal Dinners
- Ceremonies
- Wedding Receptions
- Corp. Events/Mtgs.
- Private Parties
- Accommodations

Dinner and a movie…it's the quintessential first date that's probably launched more relationships than any other activity. So what could be more perfect than celebrating the most important day of your relationship by playing out your own romantic wedding scene at Foreign Cinema in San Francisco?

This dynamic and thoroughly original venue in the Mission District has become a magnet for foodies, cinephiles, and loyal locals by artfully editing together critically acclaimed cuisine with several unique dining environments—including a glorious courtyard where films are projected on an exterior wall. If you buy out the restaurant, all of these spaces become yours for the Big Night.

A small marquee-style awning marks the entrance to the restaurant, where two stainless steel doors usher you down a seductively lit hallway, flickering with votive candles. If you're having your ceremony here, your guests will be invited outside to the canopied center Courtyard, which provides a nice long aisle for a dramatic bridal entrance. After the service, friends and family can enjoy a sumptuous cocktail reception in the Modernism West Gallery, a loft-like space with a two-story ceiling. Lining the crisp white walls is an impressive display of visually exciting artwork, which gives the setting a cultural edge and provides a great backdrop for photos. There's a chic bar at one end, and along the other are floor-to-ceiling windows inset with glass doors that lead to a cozy Zen-like Upper Patio. Some couples opt to host their entire event in the gallery.

For larger groups, the festivities continue across the Courtyard with dinner in the rustically elegant Dining Room, whose wood-framed windows open to the outdoors, creating a nice connection between the two spaces. Burgundy banquettes, a stainless steel bar, fireplace, the rich patina of the wood floor and very cool chandeliers made of hanging light bulbs with their cords tied together give the room a warm, yet trendy feel.

Overlooking it all is the Mezzanine, which can serve as a VIP lounge, an intimate rehearsal dinner spot, or a retreat for the bride and groom…all with great views of the action below. And part of that action is the open kitchen, because Foreign Cinema, being chef-owned, is very focused on maintaining the high level of its popular California-Mediterranean dishes, which use only fresh, organic ingredients in inventive ways.

Finally, top off a wonderful evening with dancing in the Gallery and nightcaps in the Courtyard, as your favorite movie or a slideshow of your own love story is projected on the wall.

CEREMONY CAPACITY: The facility holds 100 seated guests indoors or outdoors.

EVENT/RECEPTION CAPACITY: The venue can accommodate up to 175 seated or 400 standing guests.

MEETING CAPACITY: Meeting rooms hold 70 seated guests.

FEES & DEPOSITS: A deposit of varying amounts is required to reserve your date, and the balance is due at the conclusion of the event. Food and beverage minimums range $1,500–35,000 depending on the space reserved and the day of the week of the event. Menus range $55–95/person. Tax, alcohol and a 20% service charge are additional. A facility fee may apply.

AVAILABILITY: Year-round, daily. Call or email for specifics on times available.

SERVICES/AMENITIES:

Catering: provided
Kitchen Facilities: n/a
Tables & Chairs: provided
Linens, Silver, etc.: provided
Restrooms: wheelchair accessible
Dance Floor: provided
Bride's Dressing Area: no
Meeting Equipment: CBA

Parking: on street, valet, garage nearby
Accommodations: no guestrooms
Telephone: house phone
Outdoor Night Lighting: provided
Outdoor Cooking Facilities: none
Cleanup: provided
View: garden courtyard
Other: on-site florals, event coordination, film projection available

RESTRICTIONS:

Alcohol: provided
Smoking: not allowed
Music: amplified OK with restrictions

Wheelchair Access: yes
Insurance: not required

This is important! Tell locations you're reading HERE COMES THE GUIDE and ask if our information is still current.

77

Fort Mason Center

Historic Event Center

Landmark Building A, Fort Mason Center, San Francisco
415/345-7550
www.fortmason.org
weddings@fortmason.org

Rehearsal Dinners	● Corp. Events/Mtgs.
● Ceremonies	● Private Parties
● Wedding Receptions	Accommodations

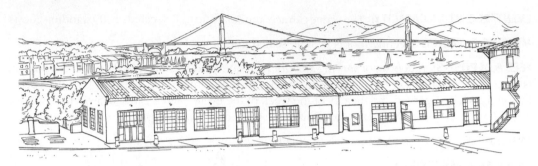

Fort Mason Center embodies what most people love about San Francisco—a nearness to nature (especially the bay) coupled with novel architecture and a dose of the past. Located on some of the most prime real estate in the city, Fort Mason Center's historic buildings sit adjacent to the Marina Green, right on the water, with postcard-worthy vistas of the Golden Gate Bridge, Alcatraz, and Marin. Its well-preserved structures and piers recall a time when troops embarked from this point to the Pacific Theater of Operations during WWII, and military offices occupied the red-roofed warehouses. In the 1970s, the site was re-purposed as an urban national park and Fort Mason Center was established; it's since become a hub for nonprofit arts organizations as well as a desirable spot for weddings and special events.

Alongside the galleries, bookstores, and restaurants that attract the public in droves to Fort Mason, the Center has more than 17 venues that host events of all types and sizes. Two of the most popular for weddings are the Firehouse and the Conference Center. The former, a lovely freestanding hall tucked away in the far northeast corner of the complex, is considered a hidden gem thanks to its divine views and near complete privacy. It edges right up to the bay on one side and a pine-covered hill on the other, and since it's so close to the water, couples often choose to marry outdoors on its intimate patio. From here you can see Marin's rolling hills in the distance and hear the bay lapping gently along the shore. A tent and heat lamps may be added for evening get-togethers, like a cocktail and hors d'oeuvres reception or an informal barbecue. Inside, the high-ceilinged rooms dress up nicely for seated dinners, buffets and dancing.

For larger festivities, the Conference Center—comprised of three adjoining rooms—offers spectacular seascape vistas. In the Golden Gate Room, an entire wall of windows faces the marina. During the day, glittering blue water contrasts with white sailboats and the signature orange-red of the Golden Gate Bridge. At night, the view becomes a galaxy of twinkling lights from the city, yachts and bridge. Guests dine and dance beneath vaulted ceilings, while a band plays on the elevated stage. Two adjacent smaller rooms function well for the buffet line or cocktails during the meet-and-greet hour.

At both the Firehouse and the Conference Center, you can design an event tailored to your taste and budget. The managers of the property are very flexible when it comes to rules, and they embrace people who want a do-it-yourself potluck as much as those planning an elaborate catered affair. And because of the undeniably beautiful location, these venues don't require much in the way of fancy décor—the dramatic panoramas capture everyone's attention, so adding linens and flowers is enough to make them shine.

Though Fort Mason Center certainly serves the needs of those tying the knot, it also has a strong mission to serve the larger community of San Francisco. Booking an event here helps ensure that this landmark—and its affiliated arts organizations—remains for future generations to enjoy. In fact, a portion of facility fees go directly to improving the buildings. This is a win-win arrangement for everyone, and its appeal is not lost on socially conscious couples who realize they can have it all: It's possible to get married in high style, with world-class views, and support a nonprofit in the process.

CEREMONY CAPACITY: The Golden Gate Room can accommodate up to 300 seated guests, the Firehouse 125 seated.

EVENT/RECEPTION CAPACITY: The Conference Center holds 180 seated or 225 standing guests and the Firehouse holds 25 seated or 90 standing.

MEETING CAPACITY: The Center holds 300 guests indoors, seated theater-style.

FEES & DEPOSITS: 50% of the rental fee is required to reserve your date. The balance is due 45 days prior to the event. Rental fees range $1,000–3,600 depending on the time of the event and the space rented.

AVAILABILITY: Year-round, daily, 8am–midnight.

SERVICES/AMENITIES:

Catering: BYO
Kitchen Facilities: limited
Tables & Chairs: provided
Linens, Silver, etc.: some provided
Restrooms: wheelchair accessible
Dance Floor: portable provided
Bride's Dressing Area: CBA
Meeting Equipment: some provided
Other: picnic area, AV equipment, event coordination

Parking: large lot, on street, valet CBA
Accommodations: no guestrooms
Telephone: pay phone
Outdoor Night Lighting: access only
Outdoor Cooking Facilities: BBQ CBA
Cleanup: renter
View: panorama of San Francisco Bay, Alcatraz Island, cityscape and coastline

RESTRICTIONS:

Alcohol: BYO
Smoking: not permitted
Music: amplified OK indoors

Wheelchair Access: yes
Insurance: liability required

Galleria at the San Francisco Design Center

Event Facility

101 Henry Adams Street, San Francisco
415/490-5861
www.sfvenues.com
jschnaps@sfdesigncenter.com

● Rehearsal Dinners	● Corp. Events/Mtgs.
● Ceremonies	● Private Parties
● Wedding Receptions	☐ Accommodations

The exterior of the Galleria building at the San Francisco Design Center gives you no clue as to what's inside—all you see is sky and trees, reflected in a gleaming, four-story façade of more than 700 individual glass panes. Walk through the front doors, however, and you see the world as it would be if top designers were in charge.

The main event space is directly ahead of you, and it becomes immediately clear that the building's architects have made excellent use of the four stories they had to play with. They've created a soaring atrium with a retractable skylight that literally brings the outdoors inside: On nice days, real air and sunshine flood in. The whole space radiates warmth and contemporary sophistication with its open, airy feel, Italian tile floor and exposed brick walls.

Just about any kind of event would feel at home here. The polished light maple hardwood floor in the center can be used for dining or dancing; the elevated stage is right for presentations, a performance or a band, and there's a built-in beverage bar as well. Rising on all sides are three levels of balconies, where *tête-à-tête* tables provide an excellent vantage for people-watching.

On weekdays the Galleria showcases designer furniture, but on weeknights and weekends it comes into its own as a party venue. With its state-of-the-art sound and light system, its stage and dance floor, and its versatile seating options, it's especially suitable for corporate galas, creative receptions and cocktail parties. Not surprisingly, the Galleria has been discovered by high tech, multimedia companies and the media, who love the possibilities it offers. They frequently bring in incredible props and produce large-scale audiovisual presentations to launch a new website or product. Other "transformations" have included a Casablanca Night and a White Christmas party complete with "snow."

There are so many pluses to this unique space, you can do almost anything with it! Entertain an intimate gathering of 100, or throw a bash for 1,600. Take advantage of the full-scale sound system, which allows a band or DJ to hook right in, or experiment with the theatrical lighting to make a dramatic statement on the dance floor and stage. For some truly festive sparkle, set the Tivoli lights on "chasing." Guests can mingle with the crowd on the main floor, or steal away to an upper tier for a quiet conversation, and still feel part of the event.

While this facility is terrific for high-end corporate and private parties, don't overlook the inventive possibilities for a wedding ceremony or reception. Picture the atrium awash in rose petals… or maybe palm trees and toucans for that tropical island ambiance…or a snow motif for winter nuptials. So go ahead and fantasize—truth is, for any event where you want a quality production with endless possibilities, the Galleria has the resources, the space and, above all, the style.

CEREMONY CAPACITY: The Galleria holds 400 seated guests.

EVENT/RECEPTION & MEETING CAPACITY: The Galleria can accommodate up to 750 seated or 1,600 standing guests; the first floor holds 400 seated or 1,000 standing, and three additional floors hold 150 more seated guests per floor.

FEES & DEPOSITS: 50% of the rental fee is required as a deposit to secure your date; the balance is payable 30–90 days prior to the event. The rental fee starts at $6,000 and varies depending on guest count and space rented. Sound and light technicians (at $50/hour per technician) are available. A facility manager and security guards are required; call for specific rates.

AVAILABILITY: Year-round, weekday evenings 5pm–2am, and weekends 8am–2am.

SERVICES/AMENITIES:

Catering: select from list or BYO with approval
Kitchen Facilities: no
Tables & Chairs: provided for up to 300 guests
Linens, Silver, etc.: through caterer
Restrooms: wheelchair accessible
Dance Floor: yes
Bride's Dressing Area: yes
Meeting Equipment: podium, mic, sound system

Parking: on street, pay lots
Accommodations: no guestrooms
Telephone: no
Outdoor Night Lighting: access only
Outdoor Cooking Facilities: CBA
Cleanup: included in rental fee
View: no

RESTRICTIONS:

Alcohol: provided, no BYO
Smoking: outside only
Music: amplified OK

Wheelchair Access: yes
Insurance: liability insurance required

Grand Café at the Hotel Monaco

Hotel & Restaurant

501 Geary Street, San Francisco
415/292-0100 X234

www.grandcafe-sf.com
david.walovich@grandcafe-sf.com

- Rehearsal Dinners
- Ceremonies
- Wedding Receptions
- Corp. Events/Mtgs.
- Private Parties
- Accommodations

Like the diminutive country it was named for, the Hotel Monaco combines French sophistication and Mediterranean charm, and it offers the added attraction of American efficiency and modern conveniences. Its eclectic décor harmonizes with almost any wedding style, whether you're wearing yards of tulle and seed pearls, or sporting a linen suit and a single calla lily. And this versatile hotel also welcomes business or social gatherings of all types.

Situated in San Francisco's bustling theater district two blocks from Union Square, the Hotel Monaco was built in 1910, but has recently undergone a complete renovation. The new owners kept many of the hotel's original Beaux-Arts features, such as tall arched windows, stately columns, and black marble and bronze filigree staircases perfect for a bride to float down. Fanciful *trompe l'oeil* ceiling domes, hand-painted geometrical friezes, and a tasteful selection of modern art keep the look contemporary.

The Paris Ballroom is the hotel's largest reception space. Red velvet screens, black marble buffet tables topped with miniature topiaries, and wrought-iron chandeliers provide warm elegance. Smaller groups can choose either the Vienna or Athens Rooms, both similar in style to the Paris Ballroom. All three rooms can be divided if desired.

For intimate celebrations, the Foyer is ideal. A striking white inglenook fireplace, graceful potted palms, and *trompe l'oeil* ceiling domes depicting fluffy clouds and hot-air balloons give the room a soaring, airy quality. The Sydney Lounge, on the lower lobby level of the hotel, manages to extend the open feeling of the Foyer through the clever use of mirrors, more potted palms and graceful Empire love seats. It even has its own scaled-down marble staircase, so necessary for that grand entrance.

If money is no object, rent the Grand Café Restaurant next door. Decorated in a lively Art Deco/ Nouveau style in earthy shades of gold, brown and maroon, its cozy ambiance and cheerful *fin de siècle* posters are guaranteed to take the chill out of the gloomiest San Francisco day. We don't know if Prince Rainier has ever graced the Hotel Monaco with his presence, but we're sure he'd feel quite comfortable here, and so will you.

CEREMONY CAPACITY: The Sydney Lounge holds 75 standing guests; the north section of the Paris Ballroom 175 seated or 250 standing guests.

EVENT/RECEPTION CAPACITY: The hotel's various spaces hold up to 170 seated or 300 standing guests indoors.

MEETING CAPACITY: There are several spaces available that accommodate 80–200 seated guests.

FEES & DEPOSITS: The room rental fee ranges $250–1,000 depending on the number of guests and rooms rented; the fee may be waived if the event total exceeds a certain amount; call for details. To reserve your date, 25% of the estimated total is required as a refundable deposit; the balance is payable within 72 hours of the event date. Catering is provided through the Grand Café. Seated luncheons start at $30/person, dinners at $42/person. There is a $100 bartender fee; a $2/person fee will apply if you bring in your own wedding cake. Tax and a 20% service charge are additional. For business meetings, the room rental fee starts at $200/half-day block; catering costs, tax and service charges are additional.

AVAILABILITY: Year-round, daily until midnight. Early morning hours by arrangement.

SERVICES/AMENITIES:

Catering: provided, no BYO
Kitchen Facilities: n/a
Tables & Chairs: provided
Linens, Silver, etc.: provided
Restrooms: wheelchair accessible
Dance Floor: CBA, extra charge
Bride's & Groom's Dressing Area: yes
Meeting Equipment: CBA

Parking: nearby garages or valet, extra fee
Accommodations: 201 guestrooms
Telephone: pay phones; analog and DSL CBA
Outdoor Night Lighting: no
Outdoor Cooking Facilities: no
Cleanup: provided
View: no
Other: event coordination

RESTRICTIONS:

Alcohol: provided, or WC corkage $15/bottle
Smoking: designated areas
Music: amplified OK within limits

Wheelchair Access: yes
Insurance: not required
Other: no rice, glitter, birdseed or confetti

Overwhelmed? Use the search criteria on www.HereComesTheGuide.com to narrow down your choices.

83

Great American Music Hall

Historic Music Hall

859 O'Farrell Street, San Francisco
415/202-9812
www.gamh.com
kim@gamh.com

● Rehearsal Dinners	● Corp. Events/Mtgs.
● Ceremonies	● Private Parties
● Wedding Receptions	Accommodations

Standing beneath marble columns, ornately gilded balconies and an elaborate frescoed ceiling, it's easy to imagine this building's allure when it first came on the scene as a flashy French restaurant and San Francisco's grandest nightclub. Opening in 1907 on the heels of the great earthquake, the 5,000-square-foot concert hall symbolized the city's renewed optimism. The popular club flourished for a quarter century in this incarnation, then became the Music Box, where Sally Rand performed her famous fan dances, and later served as a Moose Lodge and yet another French restaurant.

In 1972 it was reborn as the Great American Music Hall, and in 1994 a complete facelift restored the club to its original rococo grandeur. For more than 25 years the hall has showcased the talents of music and comedy greats such as Ray Charles, the Grateful Dead, Bonnie Raitt, Jay Leno, Whoopi Goldberg and Robin Williams. Its intimate setting and wonderful acoustics continue to make it a favorite among locals, as well as with their devoted following throughout the Bay Area.

In addition to countless concerts, the Hall has hosted corporate bashes, fundraisers, holiday parties, product launches and weddings. Its flexible layout—one large room with balconies, a stage, huge oak dance floor and two full bars—makes it party-friendly, and there's not a bad seat in the house. The Music Hall also comes equipped with a state-of-the-art lighting and sound system and all the necessary staff.

Couples getting married here use the stage for the ceremony, with their "audience" seated in chairs on the dance floor and up in the balconies. Once the knot has been tied, the rows of chairs are removed and the Hall is ready for the next phase of the celebration. Tables have been set up for dining all around, and even on the balconies if you like. With a band or a DJ making music on the stage and your guests dancing in the center of the room, the festivities can carry on into the night.

The Great American Music Hall offers a couple of very cool options that take the fun factor up a notch: They'll put the name of your company, your group, your families, or a special message on their marquee (who wouldn't get a kick out of seeing your name in lights?). Considering a theme event? The Hall is the perfect setting for a glitzy casino night, a Barbary Coast bash, or a Phantom of the Opera Night. Swing or '60s dance parties work well here, too.

Close to Union Square and only 10 blocks from Moscone Center, the Music Hall is conveniently situated for post-convention events. The space adapts comfortably to the size of your group, whether you have 100 or 600 guests, and the in-house coordinator will help you book just the right band or DJ.

While you can enhance the mood here with candles or uplighting the columns, the Great American Music Hall is really quite scintillating all by itself. The only building of its kind in The City, it provides a unique window into San Francisco's colorful, exuberant past.

CEREMONY & EVENT/RECEPTION CAPACITY: The Hall can accommodate 50–250 seated and up to 500 standing guests for a reception. Ceremonies can take place on the stage.

MEETING CAPACITY: Up to 250 seated guests.

FEES & DEPOSITS: Half the anticipated total is due when reservations are confirmed; the balance plus a $500 refundable security deposit are payable the business day prior to the event. Facility rental rates are as follows: Sunday–Wednesday $6,500. There is an additional, but refundable, food and beverage minimum of $3,000. The rental rate for Thursday–Saturday is $8,000, with additional $5,000 food and beverage minimum. Food and beverage minimums are subject to a nonrefundable 20% service charge and sales tax. Holiday rates are 20% higher.

There are additional fees for miscellaneous services, as well as a 20% service charge for an open or hosted bar. Evening rates include house manager, bar and janitorial staff, and sound and lighting technicians. If you use the in-house caterer, hors d'oeuvres start at $15/person, luncheons and dinners at $20/person; alcohol, tax and a 20% service charge are additional.

AVAILABILITY: Year-round, daily, 6am–4pm or 4pm–2am. Other blocks of time can be arranged.

SERVICES/AMENITIES:

Catering: provided or BYO
Kitchen Facilities: fully equipped
Tables & Chairs: cocktail tables and chairs are provided or BYO
Linens, Silver, etc.: provided or BYO
Restrooms: wheelchair accessible
Dance Floor: yes
Bride's Dressing Area: 3 dressing rooms
Meeting Equipment: microphones, stage

Parking: valet, garage, nearby lots, on street
Accommodations: no guestrooms
Telephone: house phone
Outdoor Night Lighting: access only
Outdoor Cooking Facilities: no
Cleanup: provided
View: no
Other: event coordination, state-of-the-art sound and lighting systems, entertainment bookings

RESTRICTIONS:

Alcohol: provided
Smoking: no
Music: amplified OK

Wheelchair Access: yes
Insurance: required
Other: no birdseed, rice or confetti; no stick-on name tags

Greens

Waterfront Restaurant

Fort Mason Center, Building A, San Francisco
415/771-7955 x114
www.greensrestaurant.com
events@greensrestaurant.com

- Rehearsal Dinners
- Ceremonies
- Wedding Receptions
- Corp. Events/Mtgs.
- Private Parties
- Accommodations

Greens is a special restaurant, not just because of its waterfront location at Fort Mason, or because it's owned by a Zen Buddhist organization, or because it serves gourmet vegetarian fare with flair. This place is special because the space makes you feel so good.

Greens has enormous multipaned windows extending the entire length of the restaurant. These windows have superb views of the Golden Gate Bridge and of the boat harbor just beyond the building. At sunset, the waning light reflected off the bridge and boats is a stunning sight to see. And for smaller events, Greens can serve you in their private room which features the same wonderful views. The interior of Greens is exceptional, with excellent original artwork, unusual carved wood seating and tables, and a high vaulted ceiling. The overall impression is light, airy and comfortable.

And just in case you think Greens serves bean sprouts and tofu, think again. Their menus are diverse, with wide-ranging entrées that appeal to vegetarians and nonvegetarians alike. Mouth-watering hors d'oeuvres, savory vegetable tarts, hearty pasta and filo dishes and an extensive wine list help make Greens one of the most popular places in San Francisco. We have a feeling that long after the party's over, your wedding guests will return to sample Greens' other culinary delights on their own.

CEREMONY CAPACITY: The Main Dining Room holds 200 standing.

EVENT/RECEPTION CAPACITY: The entire restaurant is available as a buyout for up to 140 guests for a seated meal and up to 200 for a standing reception; the Private Dining Room holds up to 50 guests for a seated meal and up to 65 for a standing reception.

FEES & DEPOSITS: A $1,500 deposit and signed contract with credit card is required to reserve a date. A buyout starts at $8,000 and the Private Dining Room rental fee starts at $175. Prices vary depending on the date rented. Full meal service is provided. Three-course meals start at $35/person for lunch and $50/person for dinner in the private room. All events include linens, printed menus, small flowers and votive candles. Alcohol, tax and an 18% service charge are additional.

AVAILABILITY: Year-round, daily, anytime. Call for details.

SERVICES/AMENITIES:

Catering: provided, no BYO
Kitchen Facilities: n/a
Tables & Chairs: provided
Linens, Silver, etc.: provided
Restrooms: wheelchair accessible
Dance Floor: CBA, extra cost
Bride's Dressing Area: CBA
Meeting Equipment: CBA

Parking: large lot
Accommodations: no guestrooms
Telephone: pay phone
Outdoor Night Lighting: access only
Outdoor Cooking Facilities: no
Cleanup: provided
View: Golden Gate Bridge, Marin Headlands, San Francisco Bay and Marina

RESTRICTIONS:

Alcohol: provided, WBC only
Smoking: outside only
Music: amplified OK

Wheelchair Access: yes, ramp
Insurance: not required

Haas-Lilienthal House

2007 Franklin Street at Washington, San Francisco

415/441-3011

www.sfheritage.org
broldan@sfheritage.org

Historic Home

● Rehearsal Dinners	● Corp. Events/Mtgs.
● Ceremonies	● Private Parties
● Wedding Receptions	Accommodations

The Haas-Lilienthal House is a stately gray Victorian located in Pacific Heights, and it's one of the few houses in the City that remains largely as it was when it was first occupied by the Haas and Lilienthal families in 1886 (they lived in the home until 1972).

Wednesday, Saturday and Sunday afternoons, there are tours through this grand home, showing what it was like to live in San Francisco at the turn of the century, and if you like, you can schedule a docent to give you a tour of the house during your event.

The house provides an unusual and intimate environment for weddings. The main floor has thirteen-foot ceilings, two large parlors, a formal dining room and a foyer and hall. Downstairs, there's a ballroom for larger parties. The interior is very attractive, with subtle colors, Oriental carpets, rich woodwork and many of the original furnishings from the early 1900s. This architectural treasure is very comfortable and warm inside, and would be a most interesting place for your celebration.

CEREMONY CAPACITY: The front and middle parlors, combined, hold 60 seated or up to 100 seated and standing.

EVENT/RECEPTION CAPACITY: The house accommodates 90 seated guests, or 150 standing.

MEETING CAPACITY: The house holds up to 90 seated guests.

FEES & DEPOSITS: A $500 refundable security deposit is required and is returned 30 days after the event. The rental fee runs $2,350–3,400 and includes use of the entire house, tables and chairs, and dressing rooms. At Christmas time, the house is completely decorated for the holidays. For wedding rehearsals, there is an extra $250 fee.

Rates for business functions and meetings vary depending on services selected; call Haas-Lilienthal for specifics.

AVAILABILITY: Year-round, daily. Sunday–Thursday until 10pm; Friday and Saturday until 11pm.

SERVICES/AMENITIES:

Catering: BYO with approval

Kitchen Facilities: moderately equipped

Tables & Chairs: some provided

Linens, Silver, etc.: through caterer or BYO

Restrooms: not wheelchair accessible

Dance Floor: yes

Bride's Dressing Area: provided

Meeting Equipment: fax, copier

Parking: on street, valet CBA

Accommodations: no guestrooms

Telephone: emergency only

Outdoor Night Lighting: access only

Outdoor Cooking Facilities: with approval

Cleanup: caterer

View: no

RESTRICTIONS:

Alcohol: BYO

Smoking: outside only

Music: amplified OK with restrictions

Wheelchair Access: limited

Insurance: not required

The professionals in the back of this book are the best in the business. How do we know? Read page 701.

Hamlin Mansion

2120 Broadway, San Francisco
415/389-8069
www.parties-sf.com
moira@parties-sf.com

Historic Pacific Heights Mansion

● Rehearsal Dinners	● Corp. Events/Mtgs.
● Ceremonies	● Private Parties
● Wedding Receptions	Accommodations

Now and then you may come across a school that occupies a mansion, but only the Hamlin School has a Pacific Heights address with a spectacular panoramic view of the Golden Gate and San Francisco Bay.

The mansion in this case is Stanwood Hall, one of three buildings that make up the school. Designed by Julius Kraft, the 24-room house was constructed in 1901 for James Leary Flood, son of the Nevada silver king, and was part of the last wave of mansion building in The City. Its Italian Baroque exterior is distinguished by Ionic columns, pilasters and pedimented windows arranged in formal symmetry, characteristic of the early 1900s Revival style that succeeded the late Victorians.

Granite steps, flanked by two gray marble lions (nicknamed Leo and Leona by Hamlin students), lead to a mosaic and marble vestibule and a pair of oak-and-plate glass doors. Beyond the vestibule is the two-story Great Hall, a space with columns and wall-to-wall oak paneling that's practically custom-made for ceremonies. The bride makes her entrance by walking down a magnificent staircase, illuminated by a large art glass window with four chipped glass "jewels" embedded in it. Guests are seated throughout the hall, and there's room on the balcony above for an additional group of onlookers.

Cocktails are usually served after the ceremony, giving guests an opportunity to explore the entire house, upstairs and down. Directly beyond the Great Hall is the Library, a warm room with a dark mahogany-paneled interior, striking black marble and gold fireplace and great bay views. Note the carved wood garland over the doorway as you enter. In contrast to the Library is the adjacent Solarium. This mosaic-and-glass space, filled with light and capped by three small Tiffany glass cupolas, also overlooks the bay and Marin County. Upstairs, there is a mezzanine which overlooks the Great Hall.

Receptions are held on the level below the main floor in the new Dining Area, whose East and West Dining Rooms can be reserved individually or combined for large parties. The décor is simple, yet elegant, with ivory walls and maple floors. Large windows provide bay views and natural light during the day, while wall sconces cast soft light at night. If you'd like a more romantic ambiance, candles are permitted.

For over a century, the Hamlin Mansion has impressed all who enter its doors with its classic lines and rich appointments. You'll find that these qualities also make it a wonderful place for an upscale wedding, party or corporate event.

CEREMONY CAPACITY: The Great Hall holds 100 seated, with space around the balcony for an additional 80 standing guests.

EVENT/RECEPTION CAPACITY: The Mansion holds up to 200 seated guests.

FEES & DEPOSITS: A refundable $1,000 security/cleaning deposit is required when the contract is signed. For weddings, a $6,000 rental fee covers use of the facility for 5 hours and is payable 2 months prior to the event. Food services are provided: an hors d'oeuvres buffet starts at $60/person, buffet dinners at $60/person and seated dinners at $65/person. Prices do not include equipment. Tax, staff and alcohol are additional. Brunch and luncheon menus, and full event-planning services are also available. Valet service runs $450–1,500 and a security guard $360/8 hours; both prices depend on guest count.

For corporate events, the rental fee runs $6,000 for groups under 100 guests or $6,500 for groups over 100 guests.

AVAILABILITY: Year-round, weekdays after 6:30pm, weekends and school holidays all day.

SERVICES/AMENITIES:

Catering: provided, no BYO
Kitchen Facilities: n/a
Tables & Chairs: some provided
Linens, Silver, etc.: provided, extra charge
Restrooms: wheelchair accessible
Dance Floor: yes
Bride's Dressing Area: yes
Meeting Equipment: n/a

Parking: valet required, extra charge
Accommodations: no guestrooms
Telephone: CBA
Outdoor Night Lighting: access only
Outdoor Cooking Facilities: no
Cleanup: caterer
View: panorama of SF Bay
Other: baby grand piano, coordination, lawn area

RESTRICTIONS:

Alcohol: BYO or CBA
Smoking: outdoors only
Music: amplified OK; music curfew 10pm Sunday–Thursday, 11:30pm Friday–Saturday; bands have 5-piece instrument maximum

Wheelchair Access: elevator
Insurance: recommended
Other: no rice, rose petals or bubbles

Hornblower Cruises & Events

Yachts

San Francisco and Berkeley
415/438-8300
www.hornblowerweddings.com
sfsales@hornblower.com

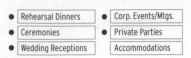

● Rehearsal Dinners	● Corp. Events/Mtgs.
● Ceremonies	● Private Parties
● Wedding Receptions	Accommodations

Offering some of the most spectacular views in the world, the San Francisco Bay is a wedding destination in itself. When you're out on its vibrant blue waters, there are picture-perfect panoramas wherever you look: landmarks like the Bay and Golden Gate Bridges and sun-washed Alcatraz Island; the forested Marin headlands; and San Francisco's famous skyline. One of the best ways to merge these scenic glories with a top-notch celebration is with Hornblower Cruises & Events. From glamorous yachts to a replica of a turn-of-the-century coastal steamer, Hornblower's wide range of vessels combine the facilities of a fine hotel with the excitement of a bay cruise. Whether you're planning a fabulous formal affair or a blowout blast for 2,200 of your closest friends, one of Hornblower's San Francisco Bay-based fleet will provide a spectacular setting.

The *Captain Hornblower* and the *Admiral Hornblower* are similar 60-foot smooth cruising catamarans; each has two decks, a bar and a dance floor, and an outdoor sun deck. The *Commodore Hornblower,* a 90-foot custom-built wood yacht, comes with two decks and two bars. The *Empress Hornblower,* docked in Sacramento, is a 100-foot vessel reminiscent of river ferryboats. Outfitted with the rich woods and shining brass typical of the Hornblower fleet, she features indoor decks, an expansive, awning-covered outdoor deck, two dance floors and two bars. The *Sunset Hornblower* is a 100-foot charter ship that was recently refurbished. She has two decks appointed with mahogany and brass, as well as two bars.

The 183-foot *California Hornblower* is patterned after early 19th-century steamships and is the flagship of the Hornblower fleet. Boasting three decks, dining salons and mahogany bars, spacious promenade decks and multiple dance floors, she can handle even the largest gathering with style. For a dockside event, the *Ferryboat Santa Rosa* combines the charm of being on the water with the convenience of being able to come and go as you please.

One of the most impressive vessels is the 292-foot *San Francisco Belle.* Originally a casino riverboat, she's been remodeled to accommodate sizable groups for special events. She's designed with three large interior decks and an expansive sundeck.

For the ultimate green wedding, reserve the *Hornblower Hybrid,* an eco-showpiece powered by solar panels, wind turbines and fuel-efficient engines. At 64 feet, this re-engineered former dive boat is a fun choice for parties of 100 or fewer. The newest member of the Hornblower fleet is the sleek and modern *San Francisco Spirit.* Live large on this 400-person craft, with marble dance floors and elegant appointments creating a luxurious atmosphere.

All Hornblower events include white linens, china and silver. Their staff can handle as many of your wedding details as you desire, from personalized menus and invitations to photography and custom floral displays. If you get married on board, note that all of Hornblower's captains are licensed ministers. With over 50,000 special events and private parties to their credit, Hornblower Cruises & Events knows how to make the most of an unforgettable setting, and provide all the finery to make your celebration truly memorable.

CEREMONY, EVENT/RECEPTION & MEETING CAPACITY: Depending on the vessel selected, Hornblower's fleet can accommodate 32–1,600 seated or 50–2,200 standing guests. The largest seated meeting capacity on one deck is 560 people.

FEES & DEPOSITS: A $1,500–10,000 deposit is required to book a vessel; the amount varies depending on the vessel selected. Wedding packages start at $89/person and include a 2 to 4½-hour cruise, meal, bar program, champagne and wedding cake. Tax and a 19% service charge are additional. Customized weddings can be arranged; the total cost will include an hourly rate for vessel charter and per-person charges for individualized menus. A confirmed guest count is due 7 working days prior to the event; the final balance 5 working days prior. The captain performs ceremonies at no extra charge. Hornblower's Charter Coordinators offer a multitude of special services, including entertainment.

AVAILABILITY: Year-round, daily, anytime.

SERVICES/AMENITIES FOR ALL VESSELS:
Catering: provided
Kitchen Facilities: n/a
Tables & Chairs: provided
Linens, Silver, etc.: provided
Restrooms: wheelchair accessibility varies per vessel
Dance Floor: available
Bride's Dressing Area: CBA
Meeting Equipment: full range CBA

Parking: various locations
Accommodations: no guestrooms
Telephone: varies per vessel
Outdoor Night Lighting: varies
Outdoor Cooking Facilities: no
Cleanup: provided
View: the entire San Francisco Bay and skyline, Alcatraz and all bridges
Other: full event planning

RESTRICTIONS:
Alcohol: provided with packages, or corkage $15/bottle
Smoking: allowed on outside decks
Music: provided or BYO; amplified OK

Wheelchair Access: varies per vessel
Insurance: not required
Other: no rice or fire on boats

Hotel Kabuki

Hotel

1625 Post Street, San Francisco
415/922-3200 Catering Department
www.hotelkabuki.com or www.jdvhotels.com
rbacon@jdvhotels.com

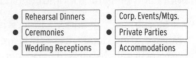

● Rehearsal Dinners	● Corp. Events/Mtgs.
● Ceremonies	● Private Parties
● Wedding Receptions	● Accommodations

Elegantly balancing both Western and Eastern influences, the Hotel Kabuki is a serene retreat in the heart of historic Japantown. This Joie de Vivre property has a modern, sophisticated interior, filled with elements that also reflect the refined beauty of the past.

A distinctively Japanese tone is set by the Summer Garden, a calm enclave featuring a koi pond and waterfall surrounded by a perfectly manicured landscape. This is a lovely spot for a small ceremony and wedding photos.

On every floor you'll discover displays of priceless art, some of it dating back to the 1700s. Downstairs on the Garden Level, the impressive Imperial Ballroom features hand-painted Japanese murals, custom-made chandeliers and sconces, and a parquet dance floor. Through a large picture window you have a view of the Spring Garden, an artful arrangement of white rocks and lush ferns. Prefunction cocktails are often served in the Imperial Ballroom Foyer, whose walls are lined with exquisite, one-of-a-kind Japanese artworks.

Back up on the Lobby level is the hotel's junior ballroom, the Sakura Room. This space is notable for its shoji-coffered ceiling and view of the Summer Garden through a floor-to-ceiling window. Natural light flows into the room during the day, and at night adjustable lighting allows you to create whatever ambiance you like. The Garden, softly lit in the evening, is a tranquil addition to the mood you've created. Additional rooms, some with garden vistas, are available for smaller functions.

If you stay overnight here, you'll enjoy services unique to this premier hotel. Bathing, for example, is taken to a luxurious new level: In guestrooms, deep-soaking tubs are ergonomically designed to let you immerse your entire body up to the neck in hot water enhanced by whatever soothing bath product you've chosen from the inspired bath menu. Just a block and a half away from the hotel is Kabuki Springs and Spa—and hotel guests receive a complimentary pass to the Spa's communal baths, the only facility of its kind in the city. So here's a fun idea: Why not incorporate this Japanese ritual into your bachelorette party festivities? Follow it up with one or two exotic body treatments (think green tea wrap and Javanese Frangipani oil massage) and even an acupuncture session, and you and your gals will look and feel cool, calm and collected for your trip down the aisle.

The Hotel Kabuki is pet-friendly, and its central location puts you within walking distance to shopping, dining, a new Sundance film theater complex, and a variety of music venues. Union Square, the Golden Gate Bridge, Golden Gate Park, Chinatown and the famed cable cars, as well as university and medical center businesses are also nearby.

Whether you're planning an intimate rehearsal dinner, a gala reception or a post-wedding brunch, Hotel Kabuki's variety of options, multilingual staff and emphasis on personalized service will make it a success.

CEREMONY CAPACITY: Several ceremony spaces can accommodate 100–400 seated guests indoors.

EVENT/RECEPTION CAPACITY: The hotel holds 15–400 seated or 30–1,200 standing guest indoors.

MEETING CAPACITY: Meeting spaces can accommodate 12–400 seated guests.

FEES & DEPOSITS: A deposit is required to reserve your date and is applied to the balance. Per-person food costs, not including wine, start at $40 for lunch or $50 for dinner. Alcohol, tax and a 20% service charge are additional.

AVAILABILITY: Year-round, daily, anytime.

SERVICES/AMENITIES:

Catering: provided; Indian, kosher and other cuisine also available
Kitchen Facilities: n/a
Tables & Chairs: provided
Linens, Silver, etc.: provided
Restrooms: wheelchair accessible
Dance Floor: yes
Bride's & Groom's Dressing Area: yes
Meeting Equipment: full-service AV and business center

Parking: Japan Center garage or valet, extra charge
Accommodations: 218 guestrooms
Telephone: guest phones
Outdoor Night Lighting: access only
Outdoor Cooking Facilities: n/a
Cleanup: provided
View: Japanese tea gardens
Other: full-service event coordination, piano, stage

RESTRICTIONS:

Alcohol: provided, corkage negotiable
Smoking: outside only
Music: amplified OK

Wheelchair Access: yes
Insurance: not required

Want to know WHAT TO ASK a potential location or vendor? Check out our Questions to Ask on page 17.

Hotel Nikko San Francisco

Hotel

222 Mason Street, San Francisco
415/394-1111
www.hotelnikkosf.com
sales@hotelnikkosf.com

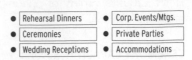

- Rehearsal Dinners
- Ceremonies
- Wedding Receptions
- Corp. Events/Mtgs.
- Private Parties
- Accommodations

Hotel guests stroll across the vast, high-ceilinged, sculpture-filled lobby. Visitors from all over the world lounge in its velvet chairs. Through enormous windows hotel guests can watch the city bustle by, as the soothing sound of a cascading fountain provides a calming contrast to the whirl of activity outside.

High-rise hospitality and a reputation for service and style have long been the hallmarks of the popular Hotel Nikko, an upscale downtown hostelry that can quite literally look down on its neighbors. A favorite spot for grand gatherings, its 25 floors of public and private spaces offer opportunities for entertaining that most smaller establishments can't match. In addition to the 510 tastefully appointed guestrooms and 22 suites, there are good-sized, subdividable meeting rooms on the first, second and third floors, great for social and corporate functions.

But the Nikko Grand Ballroom on the third floor is a real show-stopper; at over 6,600 square feet, it's immense. Its Asian contemporary décor, featuring burnished wall coverings, dark carpeting with a subtle overlay of cherry blossoms, and amber ceiling and wall fixtures, lends it a warmth that is generally lacking in rooms large enough to accommodate a Viennese waltz at full tilt. Subdividable, like so many of the hotel's other meeting and banquet rooms, it breaks down into three smaller chambers, each of which is still suitable for a fairly large function and offers a sense of grandeur in a somewhat cozier setting.

For high-profile parties with a clubbier feel, ascend to Hotel Nikko's 25th floor where an elegant aerie of glass showcases panoramic bay views in an atmosphere of style and restraint. From the floor-to-ceiling windows of the Golden Gate Room one can see Marin County and the Golden Gate Bridge. Bay View Room vistas include the hotel's Financial District and Union Square neighbors, the wooded East Bay hills, and the silvery Oakland Bay Bridge. The Peninsula Room looks south, past AT&T Park, all the way to San Bruno Mountain. Night or day, this spectacular pageant of round-the-clock bayscapes is a hard-to-beat backdrop for glamorous wining and dining. Rooms can be combined to accommodate varying numbers of guests, and there are three boardrooms, as well, on this level. Each of these provides an equally stunning western perspective of the surrounding city, plus fax capability, high-speed internet access and other high-tech amenities.

But the strongest suit of this excellent downtown hotel is service. Legendary Asian hospitality has always been a big part of its legacy, and decades of experience show in the way the expert staff custom caters and creates events with the kind of flair and focus that has earned lofty accolades. From sophisticated menu design and the careful arrangement of flowers to the care and feeding of its distinguished clientele, the attention to detail is exacting. It's no wonder Hotel Nikko partygoers and guests often book a return engagement.

CEREMONY CAPACITY: The Nikko Ballroom holds 600 seated guests and the Golden Gate Room holds 120 seated guests. Various other spaces are available with capacities ranging 10–200 seated guests.

EVENT/RECEPTION CAPACITY: The hotel can accommodate 70–600 seated or 100–1,000 standing guests indoors.

MEETING CAPACITY: 16 different spaces (20,000+ sq. ft.) hold up to 600 seated guests.

FEES & DEPOSITS: 10% of the estimated event total is required to reserve your date. 50% of the estimated event total is due 3 months prior to the event, the balance is due the week of the event. Several wedding packages are offered, and include hors d'oeuvres, meal, wedding cake, champagne toast, and complimentary suite for bride and groom. Also included are floor-length linens, silver service, mirror and votive candles on tables. Packages start at $90/person. Tax, alcohol and service charge are additional.

AVAILABILITY: Year-round, daily, 6am–2am.

SERVICES/AMENITIES:

Catering: provided, no BYO
Kitchen Facilities: n/a
Tables & Chairs: provided
Linens, Silver, etc.: provided
Restrooms: wheelchair accessible
Dance Floor: yes
Bride's & Groom's Dressing Area: yes
Meeting Equipment: full range

Parking: valet CBA or several garages nearby
Accommodations: 532 guestrooms
Telephone: pay phones
Outdoor Night Lighting: no
Outdoor Cooking Facilities: no
Cleanup: provided
View: panoramic cityscape and SF Bay
Other: event coordination

RESTRICTIONS:

Alcohol: provided or BYO, corkage fees apply
Smoking: not allowed
Music: amplified OK

Wheelchair Access: yes
Insurance: not required

Hotel Vitale

Hotel

8 Mission Street, San Francisco
415/278-3711
www.hotelvitale.com
syassin@jdvhotels.com

● Rehearsal Dinners	● Corp. Events/Mtgs.
● Ceremonies	● Private Parties
● Wedding Receptions	● Accommodations

At the Hotel Vitale, the luxury is subtle. A member of the Joie de Vivre family, this boutique hotel along the revitalized Embarcadero strikes the hard-to-find balance between contemporary and warm—think reclaimed wood and river stones mixed with sleek minimal design and you get the idea. The hallmark Joie de Vivre finesse is everywhere, from the swanky circular bar downstairs to the terraces on the upper floors, making this a chic setting for a wedding, reception or post-wedding brunch.

The overall feeling of serenity and vibe of cool permeates every space in the hotel. On the first floor, just off the street-level lobby, the Amalfi Coast Room offers an ultrastylish backdrop for seated dinners and lounging. Almost sheer, platinum-colored curtains filter in daylight (or the city lights at night) but keep the room private, and thanks to its neutral palette the Amalfi Coast dresses up beautifully. Formal dinners here shine, with brocade linens, Chiavari chairs, and candlelight; it also makes an excellent lounge with a bar in the corner, overstuffed white couches and large potted palms.

The hotel's signature restaurant, Americano, provides several options for parties. A circular room at one end works well for private cocktail receptions or brunches; warmth comes from wood floors and dark brown club chairs, which are arranged so that guests can look out the abundant windows to the palm-lined Embarcadero beyond. In the intimate private dining room at the opposite end of the restaurant, a curtain separates rehearsal dinners from the main dining area. An expansive patio right outside is a harmonious counterpart to the adjacent Embarcadero: Tall bamboo and wooden furniture—plus the requisite heat lamps—create a relaxed, yet civilized, ambiance.

Take the elevator to the hotel's peaceful upper levels, and you'll find the terraces and spa that make this place truly special. The fifth-floor terrace overlooks the Ferry Building and bay, and is an excellent spot for a cozy ceremony, cocktail party or small seated dinner. The two-tiered terrace on the seventh and eighth floors is also a stellar location to tie the knot or host a standing reception. With its slightly higher vantage point maximizing the view of the Ferry Building, Embarcadero and the Bay Bridge, this outdoor aerie transforms into a gorgeous above-city party scene.

On the hotel's penthouse level, the Vitale Spa pampers bridal parties in style before—and after—the wedding. Who can say no to an herb-infused soaking tub set amid a rooftop bamboo garden, where all you have to do is "look up at the sky and imagine where your skin ends and the water begins?" Couples can enjoy a side-by-side massage (with a view of the Bay Bridge), not to mention daily private yoga classes.

In the Hotel Vitale, every element is designed with a commitment to subtle visual pleasure and pure comfort. Soft and sultry lighting, fresh lavender scattered throughout, and warm wood accents soothe the senses and make this San Francisco getaway an unlikely urban oasis.

CEREMONY & EVENT/RECEPTION CAPACITY: Indoor spaces can accommodate 100 seated or 150 standing guests. Outdoors, five terraces each hold up to 60 seated or 100 standing.

MEETING CAPACITY: Several spaces accommodate 2–100 guests.

FEES & DEPOSITS: Half of the estimated event total is required to reserve your date. The balance is due 30 days prior to the event. Rental fees range $500–6,000 depending on the space, day and time rented and guest count. Meals range $35–100/person. Tax, alcohol and a 21% service charge are additional.

AVAILABILITY: Year-round, daily. Please call for details on event spaces and availability.

SERVICES/AMENITIES:

Catering: provided
Kitchen Facilities: n/a
Tables & Chairs: provided
Linens, Silver, etc.: provided
Restrooms: wheelchair accessible
Dance Floor: CBA
Bride's Dressing Area: CBA
Meeting Equipment: CBA, extra charge

Parking: valet required
Accommodations: 199 guestrooms
Telephone: house phones
Outdoor Night Lighting: CBA
Outdoor Cooking Facilities: no
Cleanup: provided
View: SF Bay and cityscape
Other: event coordination, spa services, AV equipment

RESTRICTIONS:

Alcohol: provided
Smoking: outdoors only
Music: amplified OK indoors with restrictions

Wheelchair Access: yes
Insurance: liability required

Hotel Whitcomb

Hotel

1231 Market Street, San Francisco
415/487-4439, 415/487-4478
www.hotelwhitcomb.com
weddings@hotelwhitcomb.com

● Rehearsal Dinners	● Corp. Events/Mtgs.
● Ceremonies	● Private Parties
● Wedding Receptions	● Accommodations

Walking through the doors of the Hotel Whitcomb, you leave behind bustling Market Street and enter the relaxed and sophisticated atmosphere of this unique turn-of-the century boutique hotel.

As soon as you step into the lobby you're surrounded by historic grandeur, from the polished marble foyer and the Austrian crystal chandeliers adorning the reception area to the hand-carved wood paneling gracing the high, beamed ceiling. Completed just after the 1906 earthquake, the Whitcomb was chosen by city leaders to serve as a temporary City Hall from 1912 to 1915, a shining stand-in for the building that was destroyed. The words "City Hall" were faintly etched above the hotel's entrance for years, and some of the original jail cells are still intact in the basement.

While the hotel's historic elements captivate visitors, contemporary amenities also abound: a Starbucks coffee shop in the lobby, free high-speed WiFi internet in guestrooms, an internet café and a fitness room. The hotel also features over 17,000 square feet of event space, with free internet access in each meeting room.

Just off the main lobby are the Whitcomb Ballroom and the Ghirardelli Room, the hotel's two main function spaces. With its magnificent crystal chandeliers, a grand staircase for a dazzling bridal entrance, and the largest parquet dance floor in the city, the ballroom is a dream setting for a ceremony and reception. There's even a mezzanine level from which to snap those signature photos of your celebration. The smaller, more intimate Ghirardelli Room, which is popular for rehearsal dinners, features warm, wood paneling and gold leaf accents throughout.

These rooms, however, are not just for weddings. If you're hosting a business function, the ballroom is ideal for large keynote speeches, while the Ghirardelli Room works well for board meetings. Six smaller meeting rooms are also available.

Regardless of the type of event you hold, your guests will appreciate the hotel's experienced catering staff, comfortable, updated guestrooms, and proximity to everything San Francisco is known for: Union Square, Ghirardelli Square, Fisherman's Wharf, the Embarcadero, Chinatown, and Civic Center, which is just steps away from the hotel's main entrance. The Hotel Whitcomb really does offer the perfect mix of vintage charm, modern amenities and world-class hospitality.

CEREMONY CAPACITY: The Whitcomb Ballroom holds 400 seated, and the Ghirardelli Room 100 seated guests. Some standing guests can also be accommodated.

EVENT/RECEPTION CAPACITY: The Whitcomb Ballroom holds 400 seated or 600 standing guests, and the Ghirardelli Room up to 100 seated or standing guests.

MEETING CAPACITY: There are 6 rooms that accommodate 8–400 seated guests.

FEES & DEPOSITS: For weddings, a deposit is required to reserve your date. The event balance is payable 14 business days prior to the event along with a guest count guarantee. Wedding packages start at $35/person; some packages include champagne toast. Menus can be customized.

For other special events and business functions, a deposit is required and varies depending on the services and menu selected. Room rental/setup fees may apply. Call for more specific information.

AVAILABILITY: Year-round, daily, anytime including holidays.

SERVICES/AMENITIES:

Catering: provided, no BYO

Kitchen Facilities: n/a

Tables & Chairs: provided

Linens, Silver, etc.: provided

Restrooms: wheelchair accessible

Dance Floor: provided

Bride's & Groom's Dressing Area: suite provided with package

Meeting Equipment: full range, extra charge

Parking: garage or adjacent parking

Accommodations: 447 guestrooms, 12 suites

Telephone: pay or guest phones

Outdoor Night Lighting: n/a

Outdoor Cooking Facilities: n/a

Cleanup: provided

View: no

RESTRICTIONS:

Alcohol: provided

Smoking: outside only

Music: amplified OK, midnight curfew

Wheelchair Access: yes

Insurance: may be required

Want to find more locations and services? Check out our informative website, www.HereComesTheGuide.com.

101

InterContinental Mark Hopkins

Hotel

Number One Nob Hill, San Francisco
415/616-6959 Catering Dept.

www.intercontinentalmarkhopkins.com
sfoha.sales@ihg.com

- Rehearsal Dinners
- Ceremonies
- Wedding Receptions
- Corp. Events/Mtgs.
- Private Parties
- Accommodations

Since it opened in 1926, the Mark Hopkins has been one of San Francisco's premier hotels. Poised at the crest of Nob Hill, it rises nineteen stories and is as much a San Francisco icon as the cable cars that clang past its grand entrance. So it's no surprise that it evokes lots of romance and history. During WWII, the Top of the Mark was the site of many farewell rendezvous where couples met for a last drink before the men shipped out. Wives and girlfriends stayed behind to watch from the top-story windows as their sweethearts' ships slipped through the Golden Gate.

The Mark Hopkins is still a perfect place for a romantic rendezvous—happily without a tearful farewell. Hold your wedding in the Room of the Dons, notable for its 26-foot ceiling and nine vibrant murals (by Maynard Dixon and Frank Van Sloun) depicting scenes from early California. Painted in a rich medley of reds, blues and browns against gold leaf, they were completed in 1926 for the hotel's grand opening. The seven-foot-high murals, set off by the subtle cream-and-taupe walls and ceiling, create a colorful banner around the room's perimeter. While you're admiring their artistry, say your vows in front of a towering arched window, which is gracefully draped in silk brocade.

Receptions are often held in the Peacock Court, a light, palatial ballroom befitting a grand hotel. Complete with its own stage, its classical details include gold and ivory walls framed by delicately carved plaster moldings, arched windows draped in layers of amber and bronze silk brocade, and a ceiling with intricate plasterwork.

The Mark Hopkins has many smaller event rooms as well, which reflect the hotel's grace and elegance and provide flexible event-planning options. Or for a world-class treat, reserve the Top of the Mark, a glass-walled sky lounge on the 19th floor with a breathtaking 360-degree panorama of San Francisco and much of the Bay Area. The Art Deco theme features dark woods and wrought-iron balustrades, while a 20-foot vaulted ceiling and split-level floor offer unobstructed views from virtually every seat. Let the staff transform the upper terrace for your wedding ceremony with a floor-to-ceiling mirrored backdrop that adds extra glitz. You can choose to have your guests seated so that they overlook either the bay and Golden Gate Bridge or the glittering downtown skyline. Literally one of The City's high points, the sky lounge is also an exceptional spot for impressive receptions and rehearsal dinners—or even a bridal shower brunch. (Famous for its 100 Martini menu, the room hosts great bachelorette parties, too.)

Whatever type of event you have, the Mark Hopkins will leave you and your guests walking on air.

CEREMONY CAPACITY: Six rooms hold 45–600 seated or 30–800 standing guests.

EVENT/RECEPTION CAPACITY: The hotel can accommodate 90–450 seated or 150–800 standing guests indoors.

MEETING CAPACITY: The hotel has 20 rooms with over 19,000 square feet of meeting space and can accommodate 10–450 seated guests.

FEES & DEPOSITS: A 30% deposit is payable when the contract is submitted; the event balance along with a guest count guarantee are due 3 business days prior to the event. Rental fees may apply to corporate meetings and wedding ceremonies, depending on room(s) selected, catering fees, guest count and season. Any menu can be customized. Luncheons start at $52/person, buffets range $43–95/person, and dinners start at $64/person; alcohol, tax and a 21% service charge are additional. Several wedding packages are available that include hors d'oeuvres, open bar, 3-course seated meal, wine with dinner, wedding cake, champagne toast, and suite for the bride and groom. Prices start at $135/person. Tax and service charges are additional. Seasonal discounts may be available for group accommodations.

AVAILABILITY: Year-round, daily, anytime. Weddings take place in 5-hour blocks, with additional time negotiable.

SERVICES/AMENITIES:

Catering: provided
Kitchen Facilities: n/a
Tables & Chairs: provided
Linens, Silver, etc.: provided
Restrooms: wheelchair accessible
Dance Floor: provided
Bride's & Groom's Dressing Area: yes
Meeting Equipment: full range

Parking: limited hotel garage, nearby garages
Accommodations: 382 guestrooms, 33 suites
Telephone: pay and guest phones
Outdoor Night Lighting: n/a
Outdoor Cooking Facilities: no
Cleanup: provided
View: Nob Hill, San Francisco and Bay
Other: baby grand, ice sculptures, event coordination

RESTRICTIONS:

Alcohol: provided, no BYO
Smoking: outdoors in designated areas
Music: amplified OK with volume restrictions

Wheelchair Access: yes, elevator
Insurance: not required
Other: decorations restricted

InterContinental Hotel San Francisco

Hotel

888 Howard Street, San Francisco
415/616-6628

www.intercontinentalsanfrancisco.com
matteo.chiari@ihg.com

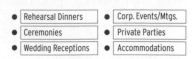

● Rehearsal Dinners	● Corp. Events/Mtgs.
● Ceremonies	● Private Parties
● Wedding Receptions	● Accommodations

The chic InterContinental Hotel San Francisco has pulled off the nearly impossible: It charms like a boutique hotel, while providing all of the amenities and luxuries you expect from an internationally renowned brand. Towering over the burgeoning South of Market district, this 32-story newcomer with its gleaming blue-glass façade makes a streamlined, very modern statement. However, the interior spaces have an unexpected warmth, featuring details that evoke a sense of place...an essence of San Francisco. With all of its assets, this InterContinental is a superb choice for local couples looking to get married in The City, as well as those planning a sophisticated destination wedding.

The hotel offers an array of event spaces on the 3rd, 4th and 5th floors that can accommodate nearly any size or type of wedding imaginable. The Grand Ballroom on floor 3 works best for very large parties: Guests dine at elegantly dressed rounds encircling a generous dance floor, while the bride and groom often sit at a long table in front of floor-to-ceiling windows at one end of the room. The city views beyond add to the expansive feeling, as do the 20-foot-high ceilings. Florists regularly fashion tall, dramatic centerpieces to play up the verticality of the Ballroom, which opens onto a foyer that's perfect for cocktails.

More intimate events are held on all three floors. Floor number 4 boasts the Pacific Terrace, where fair-weather ceremonies and small parties take place outside against a backdrop of the city's angular and colorful skyline. The Terrace can be tented, and it has its own sunny foyer. Up on 5, the InterContinental Ballroom is a smaller version of the Grand Ballroom. Like its counterpart, a wall of windows supplies abundant light and a San Francisco vista. Here, too, the neutral décor allows receptions to shine when set up with copious florals and crisp linens. Breakout rooms on all three floors are excellent for smaller celebrations of any kind; natural light and city views make them distinctive.

The InterContinental has been designed throughout with guests' comfort in mind. Abstract fine art on the walls, soothing color schemes and modern furniture create an atmosphere of calm and ease. Each floor is limited to 22 guestrooms and one natural light-filled hallway instead of the usual maze of corridors you find in a large hotel. The rooms themselves are outfitted with extra outlets, an iPod docking station, flat screen TVs and WiFi, plus spectacular vistas. And then there's the skylit indoor lap pool, and the personalized pampering at the Spa.... Who wouldn't be happy staying here?

Opened in 2008, the InterContinental is the proverbial new kid on the block in San Francisco, and it's actually the newest high-rise hotel downtown. But it joins the ranks of InterContinental hotels sprinkled across the globe in Paris, Tokyo, Nairobi, and Tahiti and, like them, expertly melds world-class service, impeccable facilities, and gourmet cuisine.

CEREMONY CAPACITY: The hotel holds 450 seated indoors and 350 seated outdoors.

EVENT/RECEPTION CAPACITY: The hotel can accommodate 450 seated or 1,000 standing guests indoors and 300 seated or 773 standing outdoors.

MEETING CAPACITY: The hotel holds 870 seated guests.

FEES & DEPOSITS: 30% of the estimated event total is required to reserve your date. The balance is due 7 days prior. Rental fees range $1,000–5,000 depending on the space rented. Meals range $75–175/person. Tax, alcohol and a 22% service charge are additional.

AVAILABILITY: Year-round, daily, anytime. Call for details.

SERVICES/AMENITIES:

Catering: provided
Kitchen Facilities: n/a
Tables & Chairs: provided
Linens, Silver, etc.: provided
Restrooms: wheelchair accessible
Dance Floor: portable provided
Bride's & Groom's Dressing Area: CBA
Meeting Equipment: provided

Parking: valet required
Accommodations: 550 guestrooms
Telephone: house phone
Outdoor Night Lighting: CBA
Outdoor Cooking Facilities: no
Cleanup: provided
View: cityscape
Other: grand piano, on-site wedding cake, on-site florals, spa services, AV equipment, event coordination

RESTRICTIONS:

Alcohol: provided
Smoking: not allowed
Music: amplified OK indoors

Wheelchair Access: yes
Insurance: liability required

The professionals in the back of this book are the best in the business. How do we know? Read page 701.

105

James Leary Flood Mansion

Historic Mansion

2222 Broadway, San Francisco
415/292-3142
www.floodmansion.org
sargeant@sacredsf.org

- Rehearsal Dinners
- Ceremonies
- Wedding Receptions
- Corp. Events/Mtgs.
- Private Parties
- Accommodations

The Flood Mansion is a symphony of classical styles—Italian Renaissance, Rococo, Tudor and Georgian. This elegant building, constructed in 1915, has remained well-preserved since Mrs. Flood donated her home to the Religious of the Sacred Heart in 1939. Although the building is now used as a private school, it's available for special events after school hours and on weekends.

The Mansion is impressive: Its Grand Hall is 140 feet long with marble floors and great views of the bay; the Adam Room, near the entry, has a high, ornate ceiling, specially designed wood tables and chairs, and a marble fireplace; the architecturally complex Reception Room boasts a magnificent coffered ceiling, painted murals in golds, blues and greens, and a parquet floor. And, weather permitting, a pretty enclosed courtyard off of the Grand Hall is available for outdoor gatherings. The Flood Mansion is definitely the place for a stately and elegant party.

CEREMONY CAPACITY: The courtyard holds 175 seated and the Grand Hall 200 seated.

EVENT/RECEPTION CAPACITY: The entire main floor can hold 200 seated or 350 standing guests for cocktail receptions. The courtyard holds 200 standing guests.

MEETING CAPACITY: The main floor can accommodate 200 seated.

FEES & DEPOSITS: The $8,500 rental fee includes security and custodial fees. A $4,250 nonrefundable deposit is required to secure your date; the rental balance and a certificate of insurance are due 1 month prior to the event date.

AVAILABILITY: Year-round, weekdays after 3:30pm, Saturday and Sunday all day. Guests and catering staff must vacate the premises by 11pm Sunday–Thursday, or midnight Friday and Saturday.

SERVICES/AMENITIES:

Catering: select from preferred list
Kitchen Facilities: ample
Tables & Chairs: BYO
Linens, Silver, etc.: BYO
Restrooms: wheelchair accessible
Dance Floor: yes
Bride's Dressing Area: CBA
Meeting Equipment: BYO
Other: grand piano

Parking: valet parking required
Accommodations: no guestrooms
Telephone: pay phone
Outdoor Night Lighting: access only
Outdoor Cooking Facilities: no
Cleanup: caterer
View: SF Bay, Golden Gate Bridge and Alcatraz

RESTRICTIONS:

Alcohol: BYO, must use licensed server
Smoking: courtyard only
Music: amplified OK Sunday–Thursday until 9:30pm; Friday–Saturday until 10:30pm

Wheelchair Access: yes
Insurance: extra liability required

Jewish Community Center of San Francisco

Community Center

3200 California Street, San Francisco
415/292-1269
www.jccsf.org/privateevents
privateevents@jccsf.org

- Rehearsal Dinners
- Ceremonies
- Wedding Receptions
- Corp. Events/Mtgs.
- Private Parties
- Accommodations

If you remember the old Spanish-style red brick Jewish Community Center of San Francisco, you'll be impressed by the new center, which opened in 2004. Though it's three times the size of its predecessor (and has lots more to offer), this new building of sand-colored brick and tawny Jerusalem limestone still manages to fit gracefully into the neighborhood.

The heart of the building is the light-filled three-story Atrium. An airy mobile, appropriately named *Ruach-Bridge of Breath* sails overhead. Its slender steel arches are fitted with panels of dichroic glass that shine different colors depending on how the light strikes them. There are various interpretations of the sculpture, but many like to think it symbolizes the bridge joining the bride and groom and connecting their two families. The floor is paved with more Jerusalem limestone in tones ranging from light almond to amber. If you would like to be married on site, you can descend the glass-walled staircase from the second floor and have your ceremony in front of the two curved walls where life-affirming values are written in Hebrew and English. Or, if you're tying the knot elsewhere, use this space as a prefunction area for cocktails. There is a platform for musicians, and you can set up a bar here as well.

Both of the center's reception rooms open to the Atrium. Kanbar Hall, the larger of the two, has a dramatically high ceiling, walls of rich paprika-red fabric, tall soundproof windows and a full-sized stage. It's also outfitted with state-of-the-art lighting and sound systems (a technician can be arranged, too). The theater seating normally used for performances or lectures is fully retractable and disappears during events. Place your head table on the stage, or have the band here paired with a dance floor set right below.

Smaller receptions are held in the Fisher Family Hall, brightened by white and papyrus-colored walls and light filtering in from the Atrium through one wall of frosted glass. Like Kanbar Hall, it has a complete audiovisual system, and its blond parquet sprung-wood floor is perfect for dancing.

Note that other conference rooms are available on the second floor if you're planning a Ketubah signing, Bedecken or Tisch. Also, there are three separate kitchens, one of which will suit your event: a kosher meat kitchen (under strict rabbinical supervision; kosher meat tableware is available), a dairy/vegetarian kitchen and a non-kosher kitchen.

The JCCSF has some perks you will love: First and foremost in this parking-challenged town is that the center has its own parking garage. Second, the performer's Green Room makes a terrific dressing room. With plenty of mirrors and a sitting room (even a mini-fridge), you and your bridesmaids have ample space for prep and touch-ups.

The JCCSF, organized in 1877, is the oldest Jewish center on the West Coast, and while its mission is specifically to foster a Jewish community, it is open to all. So come and build a little community of your own.

CEREMONY CAPACITY: The Atrium holds up to 250 seated guests.

EVENT/RECEPTION CAPACITY: The Center holds up to 330 seated or 474 standing guests.

MEETING CAPACITY: The Center can accommodate 470 seated guests.

FEES & DEPOSITS: 50% of the rental fee is required to reserve your date, the balance is due 30 days prior to the event. Rental fees range $200–4,200 depending on space rented and day and time rented. A refundable security deposit is required in addition to the rental fee.

AVAILABILITY: Year-round, daily, 8am–midnight.

SERVICES/AMENITIES:

Catering: select from list
Kitchen Facilities: 3, including supervised kosher meat kitchen and tableware
Tables & Chairs: provided
Linens, Silver, etc.: BYO or through caterer
Restrooms: wheelchair accessible
Dance Floor: CBA
Bride's Dressing Area: yes
Meeting Equipment: CBA

Parking: parking garage
Accommodations: no guestrooms
Telephone: pay phone
Outdoor Night Lighting: access only
Outdoor Cooking Facilities: no
Cleanup: caterer or renter
View: no
Other: full sound and lighting

RESTRICTIONS:

Alcohol: BYO, must use licensed server
Smoking: outside only
Music: amplified OK

Wheelchair Access: yes
Insurance: not required

Want to know WHAT TO ASK a potential location or vendor? Check out our Questions to Ask on page 17.

Julia Morgan Ballroom
at the Merchants Exchange

465 California Street, San Francisco

415/421-7730

www.juliamorganballroom.com
info@juliamorganballroom.com

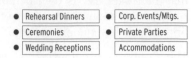

● Rehearsal Dinners	● Corp. Events/Mtgs.
● Ceremonies	● Private Parties
● Wedding Receptions	Accommodations

The Julia Morgan Ballroom at the Merchants Exchange is located in San Francisco's Financial District, but an event held in this historic gem is never business as usual. Designed by Willis Polk and Julia Morgan, its classic Beaux-Arts style echoes that of Hearst Castle, Morgan's most famous architectural creation.

The moment you pass through the street-level doors, you know you've arrived somewhere special. The barrel-vaulted lobby sparkles with marble, gold leaf and bronze, beneath a cross-hatch glass ceiling. Although events are held on the fifteenth floor, this area can be used in conjunction with the ballroom.

The venue has recently been refurbished with a sense of privacy: There are no busy hotel corridors to contend with, no intrusions from the outside world. The space is so expansive and fluid that it's easy to imagine any event being held here, from an elegant formal wedding or holiday party to an annual corporate sales event or training seminar.

The lounge has its own classic coat-check room and foyer. Both rooms are richly appointed with gilded ceilings, and used together they form a comfortable hall with large matching fireplaces of carved stone at either end. The lounge has a 27-foot curved bar that sweeps you toward the ballroom, a venue that is nothing short of grand with over 4,300 square feet of elegance. Light flows in through a wall of soaring floor-to-ceiling arched windows that afford a view of the heart of San Francisco's skyline; mirrors on the opposite wall reflect the light. The view overhead is also impressive—the ceiling is a honeycomb of mahogany octagonals. Like the other rooms, the ballroom is paneled, but here the walls showcase classic columns worked into the wood. At the far end, a 20-foot fireplace creates the final touch of majesty.

The lounge and bar area (over 1,600 square feet) can be rented exclusively, but when you reserve the ballroom, you can use the entire floor. This gives you access to several smaller rooms, perfect for bridal dressing areas or meetings. One bride hired a clown and used one of the small rooms for entertaining the children on her guest list.

If you're looking for a special place to hold an event in the grand tradition, the Julia Morgan Ballroom is not to be missed. Like Hearst Castle it has grace and opulence, but unlike Hearst Castle, it can be yours for a day or night.

CEREMONY & EVENT/RECEPTION CAPACITY: Ceremonies and receptions can be held in the Lobby, Ballroom or Lounge. The Julia Morgan Ballroom holds up to 350 seated or 800 standing. The lounge area holds 60 seated or 350 standing.

MEETING CAPACITY: For large meetings, the Ballroom holds approximately 450 theater-style or 350 conference-style. There are 2 smaller seminar rooms that can accommodate 12–20 seated conference-style.

FEES & DEPOSITS: The rental fee for use of the entire 15th floor starts at $9,500. The rental fee for only the lounge area is $4,500, and for smaller meeting rooms, the fee starts at $600. To secure your date, half the rental fee is required. There is special pricing for Friday and Sunday celebrations, call for details. Meals start at $75/person. Tax, alcohol and service charge are additional.

AVAILABILITY: Year-round, daily. Hours are by arrangement.

SERVICES/AMENITIES:

Catering: provided by in-house chef; choose from preferred list; or BYO licensed, insured and bonded

Kitchen Facilities: fully equipped

Tables & Chairs: provided, mahogany Chiavari chairs and barstools available

Linens, Silver, etc.: BYO or CBA

Restrooms: wheelchair accessible

Dance Floor: provided (mahogany)

Bride's & Groom's Dressing Area: yes

Meeting Equipment: available

Parking: street parking, nearby garages or valet

Accommodations: no guestrooms

Telephone: pay phones

Outdoor Night Lighting: access only

Outdoor Cooking Facilities: no

Cleanup: provided

View: downtown San Francisco cityscape

Other: full-service event production, WiFi, event lighting, stage, setup and breakdown

RESTRICTIONS:

Alcohol: provided

Smoking: outdoors only

Music: amplified OK

Wheelchair Access: yes

Insurance: certificate required

Other: no rice, birdseed, glitter or sparklers

Legion of Honor Museum

Landmark Museum

100 34th Avenue, Lincoln Park, San Francisco
415/750-3698
www.famsf.org
legionevents@famsf.org

●	Rehearsal Dinners	●	Corp. Events/Mtgs.
●	Ceremonies	●	Private Parties
●	Wedding Receptions		Accommodations

Whether you're seeing the Legion of Honor for the first time or the tenth, you can't help but be a little awestruck. The majestic neoclassical building, standing on the highest point of Lincoln Park, represents San Francisco at its absolute best: great architecture, fine art, romance, and stunning coastal views.

Weddings often begin with a ceremony on the Balustrade Lawn, a promontory where couples exchange vows against a breathtaking panorama of the Golden Gate Bridge, the Marin Headlands, and the Pacific Ocean. Or, if palatial is your preference, get married in the regal Court of Honor. Sunrise to sunset, the light is forever changing in this expansive piazza with its soaring wraparound colonnade. August Rodin's famous sculpture, *The Thinker,* sits alone at the entrance, animating the space with its dynamic form.

The Legion of Honor is home to more than 70 Rodin sculptures, and it's the only place on earth where you and your guests may dine and dance sumptuously among the sculptor's masterpieces. They reside in three adjacent galleries with vaulted ceilings—a series of event spaces of princely proportions. Celebrating in any one of these chambers will give your gathering a luxurious feel. But combine all three for unprecedented grandeur: Have cocktails in one gallery, dining in another and dancing in the third. However, you'll probably want to have that first dance, center stage, under the museum's magnificent rotunda, whose gorgeous marble floor is available for just that purpose. You might also opt to include a favorite musical selection played by the museum's designated organist on the Legion's very own walnut, ivory and ebony Skinner pipe organ—one of the finest in the world and a working work of art. Its 4,500 pipes have been seamlessly integrated into the very structure of the museum.

Downstairs on the Terrace Level other interesting choices await. How about a cocktail reception amid the treasures in the dramatic Hall of Antiquities? Guests can meet and mingle surrounded by pottery, sculpture, glass vessels and metalwork created by early artists from Greece, Rome, Egypt and the Ancient Near East. There's room for a large bar, and waiters can serve up champagne and passed hors d'oeuvres here before celebrants step into the adjoining Legion Café to dine.

The Legion Café, with its abundant windows and glass doors, and art-accented walls is an inviting environment for any affair. You can use the whole room or just a section of it for a more intimate atmosphere. Doors open onto the herb-scented Sculpture Garden. Attractive brickwork grounds the airy space, an elegant stone balustrade frames it, and silvery olive trees create a natural canopy.

It feels so removed from the stresses and pressures of everyday life, you might well imagine that you've been spirited away to Paris's Luxembourg Gardens or some other leafy paradise.

The Legion of Honor houses some of the most beautiful art in the world, which elevates every event that's held here. No matter what your occasion—wedding, corporate gala or private party—it will unfold brilliantly in this exquisite Beaux-Arts setting.

CEREMONY CAPACITY: The Balustrade Area, to the right of the museum entrance, and the Court of Honor, each hold up to 275 seated guests. The indoor Rodin Gallery can accommodate 120 seated, and the Florence Gould Theater seats 300.

EVENT/RECEPTION CAPACITY: The Café holds 220 seated or 300 standing guests. An additional 140 guests may be added to that capacity by tenting the sculpture garden at an additional charge. There are three Rodin Galleries, together they hold 225 seated or 250 standing. 130 guests may be seated in the central Rodin Gallery.

MEETING CAPACITY: The museum's Florence Gould Theater holds 316 seated theater-style, plus 3 wheelchair spaces and 2 companion seats.

FEES & DEPOSITS: 50% of the facility fee and a signed agreement are due at the time of booking. Rental fees start at $5,000 and vary depending on the rental package selected. The balance and final guest count are due at least 60 days prior to the event.

AVAILABILITY: Year-round, daily, starting at 6:30pm. Additional hours are available for an extra fee. Closed on major holidays.

SERVICES/AMENITIES:
Catering: select from preferred list
Kitchen Facilities: setup or prep only
Tables & Chairs: some provided
Linens, Silver, etc.: BYO
Restrooms: wheelchair accessible
Dance Floor: provided
Bride's Dressing Area: CBA, extra fee
Meeting Equipment: CBA, extra fee

Parking: large lot
Accommodations: no guestrooms
Telephone: pay phones
Outdoor Night Lighting: yes
Outdoor Cooking Facilities: n/a
Cleanup: provided
View: Lincoln Park, Pacific Ocean, Golden Gate Bridge and Marin Headlands

RESTRICTIONS:
Alcohol: BYO
Smoking: not allowed
Music: amplified OK with volume restrictions

Wheelchair Access: yes
Insurance: certificate required

Mandarin Oriental, San Francisco

Hotel

222 Sansome Street, San Francisco
415/276-9619
www.mandarinoriental.com
tgarcia@mohg.com, mosfo-reservations@mohg.com

- Rehearsal Dinners
- Ceremonies
- Wedding Receptions
- Corp. Events/Mtgs.
- Private Parties
- Accommodations

Mandarin Oriental, San Francisco creates a soothing and sophisticated environment where guests lack for nothing. Borrowing elements from other celebrated Mandarin Oriental hotels in Hong Kong, Thailand and London, this one manages to be both modern and luxurious.

A feeling of calm envelopes guests as they pass through the polished black-and-white marble lobby and up the stairs to the main event spaces. Unlike most hotel banquet rooms, each of them has its own distinctive ambiance—no boring, windowless boxes here.

For a spectacular ceremony, get married on the outdoor Sky Deck on the 40th floor of the hotel. At this height you're presented with a postcard panorama normally only enjoyed by birds: unobstructed views of the Golden Gate Bridge, Coit Tower and Alcatraz Island. You may also tie the knot in the Library, where brass-trimmed bookshelves, a salmon-colored ceiling with gold leaf insets, and crystal chandeliers add warmth and sparkle. Afterwards, you can serve cocktails in the tailored black-and-cream Foyer outside the Library, or go directly into the Embassy Room for your reception. The room's décor reflects a decidedly French influence: Large hand-painted panels are inset in three fabric-covered walls and framed by beveled glass borders; faux-candle chandeliers and wall sconces provide soft lighting. Windows along the second wall let in natural light. Nearby, the triangle-shaped Boardroom can be used for private dining as well. A pale yellow color scheme, recessed lighting and a wall of floor-to-ceiling windows keep the space pleasantly light and airy.

Silks, Mandarin's award-winning restaurant, can also be all yours or, if your event (perhaps a rehearsal dinner or post-wedding brunch) is more intimate, hold it in The Gallery, Silks' private dining room. Both spaces have been recently updated: the main dining room in a sumptuous blend of rich fabrics and warm colors like saffron, plum, pomegranate and cream; The Gallery in more buttery hues.

Although we don't usually devote much space to guestroom descriptions, Mandarin Oriental's are so captivating that if we were going to have an event here, we'd want to include an overnight stay or two. The guestrooms occupy the top eleven floors of this 48-story building (the third tallest in San Francisco), and offer expansive vistas of the bay, both bridges, Alcatraz Island, Marin, the East Bay and the city itself. In fact, two of the suites have terraces large enough to accommodate a small event on their own. You'll appreciate the elegant appointments and windows that actually open to let in fresh air, but it's the bathrooms that give these rooms extra cachet. Each one is done in gorgeous marble, and 22 of them feature a huge picture window next to the bathtub so that you can savor the panorama while you soak. Sample their menu of bath treatments for a sublime tub experience: Before walking down the aisle, relax in a tranquil, Zen tea bath; after the wedding, celebrate with champagne and strawberries in a soap rose-petal bath.

Although it has plenty of international glamour, Mandarin Oriental, San Francisco offers the personality and attentive service of a boutique hotel. We think it's a wonderful choice, not only for a special event, but for a romantic getaway any time of the year. After luxuriating in one of their guestrooms for a couple of nights, you might just want to move in permanently!

CEREMONY & EVENT/RECEPTION CAPACITY: The Embassy Room holds 120 seated or 130 standing guests and the Library 60 seated or 70 standing guests. The Boardroom holds 40 seated or 50 standing.

MEETING CAPACITY: Several spaces accommodate 15–120 seated guests.

FEES & DEPOSITS: 50% of the food and beverage minimum plus applicable room rental is required to reserve your date. The balance is due 10 days prior to the event. Rental fees range $500–1,500 depending on space, day and time rented. Meals range $70–150/person; tax, alcohol and a 20% service charge are additional. A cleanup/setup fee may apply. A complimentary guestroom is available depending on event minimums.

AVAILABILITY: Year-round, daily, anytime.

SERVICES/AMENITIES:

Catering: provided, no BYO
Kitchen Facilities: n/a
Tables & Chairs: provided
Linens, Silver, etc.: provided
Restrooms: wheelchair accessible
Dance Floor: yes
Bride's Dressing Area: CBA
Meeting Equipment: full range, extra fee

Parking: valet or nearby garages
Accommodations: 158 view guestrooms
Telephone: pay and guest phones
Outdoor Night Lighting: access only
Outdoor Cooking Facilities: no
Cleanup: provided
View: San Francisco
Other: event coordination

RESTRICTIONS:

Alcohol: provided
Smoking: not allowed
Music: amplified OK

Wheelchair Access: yes, elevator
Insurance: not required
Other: decorations require approval

Want to find more locations and services? Check out our informative website, www.HereComesTheGuide.com.

115

Marines' Memorial Club & Hotel

Historic Club and Hotel

609 Sutter Street, San Francisco
415/441-8562

www.marineclub.com
sales@marineclub.com

- Rehearsal Dinners
- Ceremonies
- Wedding Receptions
- Corp. Events/Mtgs.
- Private Parties
- Accommodations

The Marines' Memorial Club is a hidden jewel in the heart of San Francisco's Union Square. This Beaux-Arts beauty was built in 1926, and in 1946 was dedicated as a memorial to the Marines who lost their lives during World War II. Today, the landmark is a nonprofit club for veterans and their families—and also a fine hotel and special event facility.

The club's rich architectural heritage, first-class food and service, and nostalgically elegant décor bring extra dimensions to any celebration. The entire 10th and 11th floors of the building are fitted out with wonderful banquet spaces. Weddings on the 11th floor might begin with a ceremony in the exquisite, take-your-breath-away Crystal Ballroom. A vaulted hand-painted ceiling holds three massive crystal chandeliers. Their ornate prisms shimmer over the gleaming candelabra, and the ballroom's oval shape lends a soft intimacy to the magnificent space. For ceremonies, the staff sets up a raised dais flanked by a pair of ficus trees festooned with twinkle lights. After the service, guests retire to the Crystal Lounge, connected to the ballroom by a foyer. Everyone toasts the happy couple, while taking in the sweeping city view from the Lounge's wall of vaulted windows. (Tear your eyes away from the luminous cityscape for a moment, and admire the Lounge's gold-leafed and frescoed ceiling.) When it is time to dine, guests return to the Crystal Ballroom, which has been transformed with white linens and silver candelabra centerpieces. The ballroom also has a built-in dance floor that runs the length of the room, so everyone has plenty of space to kick up their heels.

An equally impressive option awaits on the 10th floor. There's a stately majesty about the Commandant's Ballroom, thanks to a 22-foot-high intricately painted and coffered ceiling, wood detailing, and striking iron chandeliers with matching sconces. Enhancing this ballroom's splendor are vaulted east-facing windows that capture a sparkling city vista. Just as with the Crystal Ballroom, the Commandant's serves as the setting for both ceremonies and lavish receptions. During the cocktail hour, the nearby Heritage and Regimental Rooms, which are connected by an adjoining foyer, are set for cocktail service. Guests can get their drinks from bars set up in either room, then relax at cocktail tables holding flickering votive candles. The Regimental Room looks out toward Nob Hill, and is clad in mahogany paneling. A built-in bar comes in handy during a cocktail hour or rehearsal dinner, and a working fireplace adds to the clubby atmosphere. The Heritage Room enjoys views of Nob Hill and downtown, and Art Deco chandeliers convey a bit of whimsy. Returning to the Commandant's Ballroom for the reception and dancing completes the evening's revelry.

Events at the Club are catered in-house, and feature gourmet contemporary American cuisine. Renovated guestrooms and suites provide a comfortable overnight stay. Newlyweds love Suite #403's oversized tub-for-two; its spacious living room and wall of mirrors are great for pre-wedding primping. The Leatherneck Steakhouse on the 12th floor showcases a stunning panorama with glimpses of the bay over towering skyscrapers—what a dynamic spot for a rehearsal dinner! Though shopping and nightlife is right outside the Club's door, the Marines' Memorial is marvelously self-contained: it also has a health club, an indoor pool, a library, a museum, and its own theater! Whether you are a veteran or civilian, you're sure to find a warm welcome at this timeless club.

CEREMONY & EVENT/RECEPTION CAPACITY: The club can accommodate 25–280 seated guests indoors.

MEETING CAPACITY: Several spaces hold 30–300 seated guests.

FEES & DEPOSITS: For weddings, a nonrefundable deposit is required to reserve the banquet room. There's no rental fee if you meet a food and beverage minimum; however, house catering is required. A guest count along with the estimated event balance is required 7 business days prior to the event. Wedding packages, which include open bar, hors d'oeuvres, champagne and wine service, salad and entrée service and cake cutting range $69–135/person. Seated luncheons start at $29/person and dinners at $40/person. Hors d'oeuvres start at $20/person and buffets (min. 50 people) at $54/person. Tax and a service charge are additional.

For meetings and business functions, rental fees for meeting rooms vary depending on room(s) and/or services selected. Call for additional information regarding food and beverage charges.

AVAILABILITY: Year-round, daily, 7am–11pm. There are overtime charges for events running more than 5 hours.

SERVICES/AMENITIES:

Catering: provided, no BYO
Kitchen Facilities: n/a
Tables & Chairs: provided
Linens, Silver, etc.: provided
Restrooms: wheelchair accessible
Dance Floor: yes
Bride's Dressing Area: CBA
Meeting Equipment: CBA

Parking: nearby garage
Accommodations: 138 guestrooms
Telephone: pay and guest phones
Outdoor Night Lighting: access only
Outdoor Cooking Facilities: no
Cleanup: provided
View: Nob Hill, SF cityscape and Union Square
Other: full event coordination, ethnic cuisine available upon request

RESTRICTIONS:

Alcohol: provided
Smoking: not allowed
Music: amplified OK

Wheelchair Access: yes, elevator
Insurance: required for DJs and entertainers

McCormick & Kuleto's

Restaurant

900 North Point, Suite H301 (at Beach & Larkin), San Francisco
415/929-8374

www.mccormickandkuletos.com
slucas@mccormickandkuletos.com
susanr@mccormickandkuletos.com

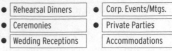

- Rehearsal Dinners
- Ceremonies
- Wedding Receptions
- Corp. Events/Mtgs.
- Private Parties
- Accommodations

If it's true that good food tastes even better when it's served up with a great view, then eating at McCormick & Kuleto's is bound to be a delectable experience. This three-tiered restaurant in Ghirardelli Square specializes in impeccably fresh seafood from all over the world. It overlooks the bay—which just happens to be right across the street—and almost every diner has an unobstructed view of Alcatraz, Marin and a variety of historical ships that are docked at Hyde Street Pier.

The interior scenery is also captivating. In the Main Dining Room, fantastic tortoise shell "boat" chandeliers drop from the vaulted ceiling. Wood-and-copper railings flow from tier to tier, defining each level. The Captain's Room derives its warmth from sumptuous burled redwood paneling throughout and elegant hand-crafted glass lighting fixtures. For larger receptions, this space may be reserved with the Bay View Room, which has its own bar and can be used either for cocktails or additional banquet seating. The Dolphin Room, with its modern décor, adjoining patio and views of the bay, is a nice spot for intimate rehearsal dinners and receptions. Recently remodeled, it features Italian mosaic tiles on the center columns and archways. For smaller receptions or bridal showers, the Alcatraz Room is a more informal space with redwood paneling and pictures of historic ships decorating the walls.

Suffused with sunlight or enhanced by the nighttime glitter of boats docked below, McCormick & Kuleto's provides a generous helping of visual as well as gastronomic appeal.

CEREMONY CAPACITY: Ceremonies for up to 80 guests can be arranged.

EVENT/RECEPTION CAPACITY: The restaurant holds 20–220 seated or 80–220 standing guests in various rooms.

MEETING CAPACITY: Event spaces can accommodate 20–220 seated guests. Buyouts are available for larger groups.

FEES & DEPOSITS: A $500–1,000 deposit is due when reservations are made. For weddings, 80% of the estimated event total is due 3 days prior to the event and the balance is payable the day of the event. Any menu can be customized. Catering costs run $25–40/person for luncheons and $60–80/person for dinners. Tax and a 20% service charge are additional.

Rates for business functions vary; call for more specifics.

AVAILABILITY: Year-round, daily, 11:30am–midnight.

SERVICES/AMENITIES:

Catering: provided, no BYO
Kitchen Facilities: n/a
Tables & Chairs: provided
Linens, Silver, etc.: provided
Restrooms: wheelchair accessible
Dance Floor: CBA, extra charge
Bride's Dressing Area: no
Meeting Equipment: CBA, extra charge

Parking: garage, on street
Accommodations: hotels nearby
Telephone: emergency use only
Outdoor Night Lighting: in Ghirardelli Square
Outdoor Cooking Facilities: no
Cleanup: provided
View: SF Bay, Maritime Museum, historic ships, Angel Island and Alcatraz
Other: event coordination

RESTRICTIONS:

Alcohol: provided
Smoking: outdoors only
Music: amplified OK until 11pm, with volume restrictions

Wheelchair Access: yes
Insurance: not required

New Delhi Restaurant

Landmark Restaurant

160 Ellis Street, San Francisco
415/816-4068

www.newdelhirestaurant.com
ranjan@newdelhirestaurant.com

- Rehearsal Dinners
- Ceremonies
- Wedding Receptions
- Corp. Events/Mtgs.
- Private Parties
- Accommodations

Don't you just love the royal treatment? Then why not set your event in this landmark property in San Francisco's fashionable city center. Named "The Finest Indian Restaurant" by *The New York Times,* New Delhi Restaurant and Bar has service, style and cuisine fit for a maharajah. It's no wonder this colorful venue, situated near Union Square within walking distance of some of the city's finest hotels, has drawn a celebrity crowd for decades. Silicon valley moguls, U.S. Presidents, Indian film stars and spiritual gurus have all basked in the welcoming ambiance. Walter Cronkite sang with Turk Murphy's Jazz Band at their historic reunion here. Bill Clinton, Deepak Chopra and Indian artist Ashwarya Rai are also among past visitors.

Upon entering the restaurant your guests will have fun catching up or getting acquainted in the establishment's long bar over cocktails—a mango or lychee martini, perhaps—and butler-passed hors d'oeuvres. From here they proceed to the dining room where massive hand-carved columns with golden Corinthian-style capitals rise to support the intricately carved coffered ceiling high overhead. The antique brick walls, lustrous mahogany wood accents and handsomely dressed tables add to an atmosphere that is both rich and warm.

Owner and celebrity chef Ranjan Dey, who starred in the PBS series, *My India,* has received numerous awards and gold medals for his culinary expertise and unique line of spice blends. When selecting dishes for your event, you can choose from a menu that revolves around Punjabi, Bengali, Goanese, South Indian, Gujrati, Mughlai, and Kashmiri style regional cuisines.

An expert in Indian food, culture and ceremony who caters events all over the state, Dey draws from a wealth of experience to create spectacular events that feature fresh ingredients excitingly prepared and perfectly presented in the manner prescribed by custom, be it Hindu, Muslim, Buddhist, Jain, Anglo-Indian Christian, Sikh, Parsi, Indian-Chinese, or an eclectic and exotic mix of traditions. "Diversity," explains Dey, "is a part of India." At New Delhi Restaurant and Bar—whether it's a ceremony, reception, social event or corporate affair—diversity is famously celebrated.

Once seated at their tables, everyone can relax as a regional dance troupe glides onto the beautiful, antique Florentine-tile dance floor. This is also a lovely spot for the pre-marriage mehndi or sangeet ceremony; or the day-of var mala, parchan and saptapadi rituals beneath a traditional mandap (wedding tent). Or, depending on the nature of your celebration, you just might want to let your guests get wild and Bollywood as the Indian music swirls around the room and henna artists work their magic on willing hands and arms.

Whether your celebration is one day or many (as Indian weddings often are), everything will be orchestrated to perfection by one of the city's most experienced restaurateurs. Your guests will be gloriously entertained and treated to one exotic dish after another as the courteous and discreet Kashmiri-costumed staff (costumes are by special request) attends to your every need. "We are creating memories that you can treasure for the rest of your life," Dey promises with a smile.

So "Bon appétit!" or, as they say in Hindi, "Shu bhojon!"

CEREMONY CAPACITY: The restaurant accommodates 200 seated indoors.

EVENT/RECEPTION CAPACITY: The restaurant holds 140 seated or 225 standing guests indoors.

MEETING CAPACITY: Meeting spaces accommodate 150 seated guests.

FEES & DEPOSITS: A $500 deposit is required to reserve your date. 50% of the estimated event total is due 4 weeks prior to the event, and the balance is due 2 weeks prior. Rental fees range $1,000–2,500 depending on the day of the week. Meals range $30–70/person. Tax, alcohol and an 18% service charge are additional.

AVAILABILITY: Year-round, daily, 9am–midnight.

SERVICES/AMENITIES:

Catering: provided, no BYO
Kitchen Facilities: n/a
Tables & Chairs: provided
Linens, Silver, etc.: provided
Restrooms: wheelchair accessible
Dance Floor: provided
Bride's Dressing Area: CBA
Meeting Equipment: some provided

Parking: on street, garage nearby
Accommodations: no guestrooms
Telephone: house phone
Outdoor Night Lighting: CBA
Outdoor Cooking Facilities: no
Cleanup: provided
View: Union Square
Other: on-site florals, complimentary event coordination

RESTRICTIONS:

Alcohol: provided
Smoking: not allowed
Music: amplified OK indoors

Wheelchair Access: yes
Insurance: liability required

This is important! Tell locations you're reading HERE COMES THE GUIDE and ask if our information is still current.

121

The Omni San Francisco Hotel

Historic Luxury Hotel

500 California at Montgomery, San Francisco
415/677-9494
www.omnisanfrancisco.com
wjcoale@omnihotels.com

● Rehearsal Dinners	● Corp. Events/Mtgs.
● Ceremonies	● Private Parties
● Wedding Receptions	● Accommodations

The clang of a cable car bell adds just the right touch of romance to the ambiance at the Omni San Francisco Hotel, located in San Francisco at the foot of ever-fashionable Nob Hill. Movie-set perfect, this opulent venue is the result of a painstaking restoration of the old Financial Center Building, one of the city's architectural icons. Completed in 2002 at a cost of $100 million, this 362-room luxury hotel recaptures the bygone grace and Florentine Renaissance style of its illustrious 1926 predecessor.

The elegance of old money still wreaths the interior where the two-story atrium lobby combines the well-upholstered intimacy of a private club and the glamour of a grand salon. Bronzed washed torchères, dark cherrywood and mahogany accents, deep brown Italian marble, dreamy jazz and the scent of exotic blooms ease guests into a world of refined sophistication.

From the lobby, a dramatic grand staircase winds up to a broad wrought-iron-balconied mezzanine just made for receptions. From this airy perch, guests can look out through twenty-foot windows curtained by the cascade of Czechoslovakian crystal that twinkles in the lobby's chandeliers. On the same floor, the Union Square Room offers hush-hush views of the corner of California and Montgomery through its seven arched, draped and betasseled windows. The portrait-friendly lighting and intimate dimensions of this setting make it ideal for everything from rehearsal dinners to brunches to well-arranged seminars. The North Beach Room next door, with its floor-to-ceiling windows and Italian pastoral feel, is another fine choice for smaller functions.

For large parties, guests ascend to the third floor. Here the plushly carpeted and appointed foyer hints at the glamour of the vast Grand Ballroom, outfitted in the rich patterns and tasteful gold tones of the Florentine Renaissance. Lit with chandeliers and wall sconces and paneled in silk, its 2,800 square feet can easily accommodate the most extravagant affair. With acoustics and a sound system that woos divas and DJs alike, it's got what it takes to keep any function from flagging. On the same floor, a terrace (cut into the heart of the building and shielded by the fortress-like walls of the hotel) allows guests to mingle outdoors, free from the wind and fog that bedevil most outdoor events in the city.

When the band has played its last tune, out-of-town and local visitors alike may find it hard to abandon all of this sophistication and style. Not a problem. They can book into guestrooms that feature damask wall coverings, polished brass, Italian marble, Chinese granite, plush terry robes, down duvets and other upscale amenities. And should they want to step out, Chinatown, North Beach, Union Square and the Embarcadero are among the many San Francisco treats to be found mere minutes away.

CEREMONY CAPACITY: The Ballroom holds 200 seated guests, 170 with a dance floor.

EVENT/RECEPTION CAPACITY: The hotel holds 100–200 seated or 125–300 standing guest indoors.

MEETING CAPACITY: 9 meeting rooms are available that can accommodate up to 160 seated guests.

FEES & DEPOSITS: Rental fees range $0–5,000. Lunches range $45–90/person; dinners $65–195/person. Tax, alcohol and a 21% service charge are additional.

AVAILABILITY: Year-round, daily, 6am–midnight.

SERVICES/AMENITIES:

Catering: provided, no BYO
Kitchen Facilities: n/a
Tables & Chairs: provided
Linens, Silver, etc.: provided
Restrooms: wheelchair accessible
Dance Floor: provided
Bride's & Groom's Dressing Area: yes
Meeting Equipment: CBA, extra charge

Parking: valet or nearby garages
Accommodations: 347 guestrooms, 15 suites
Telephone: pay phones
Outdoor Night Lighting: access only
Outdoor Cooking Facilities: no
Cleanup: caterer or renter
View: no
Other: event coordination

RESTRICTIONS:

Alcohol: provided
Smoking: outdoors only
Music: amplified OK

Wheelchair Access: yes
Insurance: not required
Other: decorations require prior approval

The Palace Hotel

Historic Hotel

2 New Montgomery Street, San Francisco
415/546-5060
www.sfpalace.com
palaceweddings@luxurycollection.com

- Rehearsal Dinners
- Ceremonies
- Wedding Receptions
- Corp. Events/Mtgs.
- Private Parties
- Accommodations

The Palace, San Francisco's premier historic hotel, was originally inspired by the most luxurious European hotels of the Gilded Age. It first opened its doors in 1875, and its opulence has since been enjoyed by many generations of society's elite, including President Woodrow Wilson. Today, this beautiful grand dame continues to enchant its visitors, particularly those who envision an elegant wedding in a royal setting.

The Palace's wedding specialists serve as "discovery ambassadors," helping couples explore the variety of event options available at this magnificent location, as well as navigating the many details involved in planning the festivities—such as selecting cuisine, arranging accommodations and organizing the timetable. Every celebration is customized according to each couple's vision, whether it's a classic gala or a contemporary soirée.

Many choose to host a spectacular reception in the world-renowned Garden Court, one of the most exquisite rooms we've ever seen. The magnificent domed ceiling of pale yellow leaded glass floods the restaurant with warm natural light, and the original crystal chandeliers add Old World sparkle. The Ralston Room, which served as The Men's Grille at the turn of the century, is versatile enough to accommodate either a ceremony or reception. Reminiscent of a Gothic cathedral, this room soothes with its cream, gold and jewel tones.

For large wedding receptions, the Grand Ballroom lives up to its name. English classical in style, its charm comes from unique lace plasterwork and shimmering chandeliers decorated with carved crystal pears and apples. The Gold Ballroom is the most popular reception site. Once the hotel's music room, it has the feel of a ballroom in a manor house. Tall draped windows highlight the intricate lattice plasterwork and gold leaf detailing throughout. An antique orchestra balcony, stately fireplace, and rich blue-and-gold carpet complete the lovely décor. For more intimate ceremonies or receptions, the French Parlor features stained-glass skylights, crystal chandeliers, marble fireplaces and a bird's-eye view of the Garden Court ceiling that is guaranteed to take your breath away. And for a more modern ambiance, the Sunset Court accommodates gatherings and ceremonies beneath an arched glass dome.

Overnight guests—and the newlyweds!—enjoy the Palace's health club with its indoor skylit swimming pool. They also appreciate the plush guestrooms and suites, which have mahogany furnishings and a nostalgic flair that blend seamlessly with the latest modern conveniences.

Grand and gorgeous, the Palace Hotel is a place worth visiting even if you're not planning a wedding. Come and see for yourself why it's been a San Francisco landmark for over 125 years.

CEREMONY CAPACITY: The hotel seats 60–500 guests indoors.

EVENT/RECEPTION CAPACITY: The hotel holds 120–600 seated or 150–1,000 standing guests indoors.

MEETING CAPACITY: The Palace has over 20 rooms that can accommodate meetings, seminars, conferences and lectures for 12–1,120 guests.

FEES & DEPOSITS: A nonrefundable deposit in the amount of 50% of the estimated event cost and a signed contract are required to secure your date. Ceremony fees and room rental rates range $1,000–8,000 based on the space selected. Sample wedding packages include butler-passed hors d'oeurvres, 3-course plated dinner, champagne toast and wedding cake. Prices range $135–240/ person. Tax and service charge are additional.

AVAILABILITY: Year-round, daily, 6am–midnight for most venues. Garden Court available late evenings only.

SERVICES/AMENITIES:

Catering: provided
Kitchen Facilities: n/a
Tables & Chairs: provided
Linens, Silver, etc.: provided
Restrooms: wheelchair accessible
Dance Floor: yes
Bride's Dressing Area: yes
Meeting Equipment: full range CBA

Parking: valet CBA at a charge, or lot
Accommodations: 550 guestrooms
Telephone: pay phones
Outdoor Night Lighting: access only
Outdoor Cooking Facilities: no
Cleanup: provided
View: no
Other: coordination

RESTRICTIONS:

Alcohol: provided, or corkage $25/bottle
Smoking: not allowed
Music: amplified OK

Wheelchair Access: yes
Insurance: provided by hotel

Parc 55 Wyndham Hotel

Hotel

55 Cyril Magnin Street, Market at Fifth, San Francisco
415/403-6651
www.parc55hotel.com
sales@parc55.com

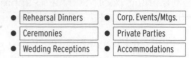

- Rehearsal Dinners
- Ceremonies
- Wedding Receptions
- Corp. Events/Mtgs.
- Private Parties
- Accommodations

It's right off Union Square and unquestionably one of the best and most exciting hotels downtown. Located on a chic little street named after famed businessman and arbiter of style, Cyril Magnin, Parc 55 Wyndham is definitely in the heart of The City's premier shopping, restaurant, gallery and theater district. It's also elegant, modern and one hundred percent San Francisco.

Personal service, a hallmark of this hotel, is apparent in the doorman's greeting as you enter the first-floor gallery. Take the Grand Staircase to the lobby level, and on your way up notice the venue's sleek, contemporary style. Stop at the landing to admire the sculpted art wall (a great backdrop for photos), then proceed up to the lobby where a two-story atrium with floor-to-ceiling windows welcomes you. This floor also houses Parc 55's restaurant, cityhouse, with private space for cocktails, dinner and pre- or post-event brunches.

Escalators and elevators take you to the third floor, where the handsomely appointed Market Street Room, along with several other rooms, can be used for ceremonies, receptions, parties, and conferences. A subtle fascination with geometry is evident in floors and ceilings: rectangular forms etched into the pale slate carpets mirror the sculptural elements in stunning contemporary fixtures and evoke movement and energy without overwhelming.

An ascent to the fourth floor brings you and your guests to the spacious Ballroom Foyer, an expansive prefunction area whose fourteen-foot windows frame views of Market Street and Cyril Magnin Street. Three sets of double doors open to the magnificent 5,600-square-foot Cyril Magnin Ballroom, which can accommodate galas and corporate extravaganzas catered to perfection in an atmosphere of sophistication. It can be sectioned into three smaller chambers with doors leading onto a windowed lounge area. An additional seven meeting salons further multiply options by converting into breakout rooms of various configurations and dimensions. Almost all event spaces feature windows that provide abundant light and great views of the cityscape.

Up on the 31st Floor, the Executive Club Lounge overlooking The City is a marvelous choice for a private rehearsal dinner or cocktail reception. Stainless steel and art glass are combined with dark wood, leather and suede in natural tones to create a visually intriguing setting. The 180-degree views are just the thing to make spirits soar.

Whatever your event at Parc 55 Wyndham, you won't want your sublime experience to end when the party is over, so why retire to less spectacular digs? Book a suite with two bedrooms, a parlor, dining room and Jacuzzi bath or one of the Club Rooms on the top six floors. Plus, any bride and groom can come back on their anniversary and stay for free! Forever! Call for details.

Needless to say there is no shortage of support staff, service and amenities in this strikingly renovated 32-floor property. The 1,010 deluxe rooms offer every comfort, and the hotel retains an intimate feel. Suggest overnighting to all of your guests—that way, they can sit back after the celebration and relax in the lap of luxury.

CEREMONY CAPACITY: The hotel seats 400 guests indoors.

EVENT/RECEPTION CAPACITY: The hotel holds 400 seated or 900 standing guests indoors.

MEETING CAPACITY: The hotel can accommodate 400 seated guests.

FEES & DEPOSITS: 50% of the estimated event total is required to reserve your date. The balance is due 2 weeks prior to the event. Rental fees range $500–7,500 depending on the day and time of the event and the size of the event space and setup needed. Meals range $25–150/person. Tax, alcohol and a 21% service charge are additional.

AVAILABILITY: Year-round, daily, anytime. Call for details.

SERVICES/AMENITIES:

Catering: provided
Kitchen Facilities: n/a
Tables & Chairs: provided
Linens, Silver, etc.: provided
Restrooms: wheelchair accessible
Dance Floor: provided
Bride's Dressing Area: yes
Meeting Equipment: provided
Other: event coordination

Parking: on street, valet required, garage nearby
Accommodations: 1,010 guestrooms
Telephone: pay, house and guest phones
Outdoor Night Lighting: access only
Outdoor Cooking Facilities: no
Cleanup: provided
View: cityscape

RESTRICTIONS:

Alcohol: provided, or BYO with corkage fee
Smoking: not allowed
Music: amplified OK indoors

Wheelchair Access: yes
Insurance: liability required

Overwhelmed? Use the search criteria on www.HereComesTheGuide.com to narrow down your choices.

Presidio Chapel

Historic Chapel

130 Fisher Loop, San Francisco Presidio
415/561-3930
www.sanfranciscoweddings.org
weddings@interfaith-presidio.org

● Rehearsal Dinners	● Corp. Events/Mtgs.
● Ceremonies	● Private Parties
● Wedding Receptions	Accommodations

On a forested hillside overlooking the bay, this elegant Spanish Mission-style chapel is an inspirational place for a wedding. But appealing architecture and panoramic views are only part of what makes the Presidio Chapel so popular. Couples also value the venue's convenient location, secluded setting and affordability. And unlike many houses of worship, here you're welcome to use your own officiant, musicians and cultural style.

In fair weather, gather for pre-ceremony socializing in the memorial garden, a flower-lined tiled patio that faces the Presidio grounds and the bay. This is a wonderful spot for photos, thanks to a stunning backdrop of Angel and Alcatraz Islands framed by sweeping branches of pine and eucalyptus. Here guests await the peal of the church bell summoning them to the sanctuary for the ceremony. Inside the chapel, a soaring redwood-beamed ceiling hung with wrought-iron chandeliers, twelve arched stained-glass windows, and heavy oak doors all contribute to a strong Old World flavor. The Chaplain's office serves as a comfortable private dressing area, and there's even a pipe organ for that traditional rendition of "Here Comes The Bride." The chapel also provides a grand piano, a CD player and iPod docker, as well as the ability to webcast your wedding in real time to far-off family and friends.

Adjacent to the sanctuary, the Mural Room feels like a long, glass-enclosed sun porch. It looks out onto the garden and hillside, but its most notable feature is the mural from which it derives its name. Painted by the same artist who created the famed Coit Tower murals, it depicts St. Francis at its center—a fitting picture considering the variety of wildlife that lives around the chapel and the fact that St. Francis is the patron saint of San Francisco and animals. The room makes a tranquil spot for an intimate reception or post-wedding mingling, while the bride and groom have their photos taken in the picturesque memorial garden.

The chapel is now in the care of the Interfaith Center at the Presidio, a nonprofit organization dedicated to inter-religious dialogue, friendship, education and service. The passing of the chapel into public hands as part of the Golden Gate National Recreation Area is celebrated not only by the Bay Area's diverse religious community, but by everyone who appreciates the sanctity and beauty of this historic spot.

CEREMONY CAPACITY: The chapel holds 150–185 seated guests. Note that you can use your own officiant or one referred by the venue.

EVENT/RECEPTION CAPACITY: The Mural Room can be used for small standing receptions of 40 people; the lower level can accommodate 50 guests, with larger standing receptions held outside.

FEES & DEPOSITS: To reserve your date, a $100 nonrefundable deposit is required. Half the rental balance is due 30 days after submitting your first deposit; the remainder is payable 60 days prior to the event. When you rent the Presidio Interfaith Chapel you have use of the entire facility. On weekends, the rental fee is $1,250 for a 2½-hour block of time; on weekdays, it is $875. Small weddings are $375–500 depending on the guest count and the day of the event. Rehearsals are $150/hour. The fee includes insurance, a Chapel Host and use of the musical instruments. There is a $125 surcharge for events with food and/or beverages.

AVAILABILITY: Year-round, daily, 7am–11pm.

SERVICES/AMENITIES:

Catering: BYO

Kitchen Facilities: no

Tables & Chairs: 10 tables, 60 chairs

Linens, Silver, etc.: BYO

Restroom: limited wheelchair accessible

Dance Floor: no

Bride's & Groom's Dressing Area: yes

Meeting Equipment: n/a

Parking: ample, large complimentary lot

Accommodations: no guestrooms

Telephone: emergency use only

Outdoor Night Lighting: access only

Outdoor Cooking Facilities: no

Cleanup: caterer or renter

View: panorama of San Francisco and bay

RESTRICTIONS:

Alcohol: BYO wine and champagne only, server required, license not required

Smoking: outside only

Music: amplified OK

Wheelchair Access: yes

Insurance: required for aisle runner only

Other: no glitter, confetti, birdseed, rice or balloon releases; some decoration restrictions

Presidio Chapel of Our Lady

Historic Chapel

45 Moraga Avenue, SF Presidio, San Francisco
415/561-5444
www.presidio.gov
events@presidiotrust.gov

Rehearsal Dinners	Corp. Events/Mtgs.
● Ceremonies	Private Parties
● Wedding Receptions	Accommodations

For soldiers stationed at the Presidio during its early years as a military garrison, this little white church was known as the "Ivy-covered Chapel" for the abundance of vines on its walls. The simple wooden building, with its gabled roof and steeple, was built in 1864 to serve as a place of worship for a small group of military officers and their families. These days, both the ivy and the soldiers are gone, but the Chapel of Our Lady has endured and is now a nondenominational church for ceremonies of all religions.

Although the Presidio is only minutes from downtown San Francisco, it's completely removed from the "urban-ness" of The City, and it encompasses some of the most beautiful real estate in Northern California. In fact, this former military base is now part of the Golden Gate National Recreation Area.

To get to the church, we followed Presidio Boulevard from the Marina, but it doesn't matter which road you take through the Presidio—it's a lovely drive from every direction. Our route curved through woods and past old officers' houses and military buildings, all neatly maintained and painted off-white with red roofs. The Chapel of Our Lady is set back from the sidewalk, surrounded by a grove of eucalyptus trees and shrubs. Standing on the front steps, you can see snippets of San Francisco Bay and the Golden Gate Bridge through the trees.

From the outside, the little chapel is still reminiscent of an old country church, but renovations have widened its original footprint and added decidedly modern elements. The chapel has been expanded with side aisles, a baptistery, a dressing room, a choir room, and a sanctuary.

Standing in the chapel on a sunny day, you notice right away how warm and bright it is. The main room is filled with light, flowing in through the two side walls, constructed entirely of clear and multicolored glass block panels. The altar stands in front of a huge floor-to-ceiling window, which lets in even more light. Contemporary-styled wooden pews flank the center aisle, and wooden beams support the vaulted ceiling. Small iron chandeliers and wall sconces provide ambient lighting for ceremonies in the evening or on a misty day.

When the weather is glorious, consider extending the celebration onto the chapel grounds. Guests can gather in the front courtyard to congratulate the happy couple as they emerge from the chapel, then walk over to the side lawn for champagne and light hors d'oeuvres. For a festive touch, add a few umbrella-shaded tables, clad with linens and flowers.

Many couples who get married in the Chapel of Our Lady make life easy on themselves by having their reception at the Presidio Officers' Club, a one-minute stroll down the sidewalk. Once the social epicenter of this retired military establishment, the historic Mission-style building is a popular location for all types of celebrations.

CEREMONY CAPACITY: The Chapel holds 200 seated guests for ceremonies or 100 seated guests in the Courtyard.

RECEPTION CAPACITY: The Chapel Courtyard holds 100 standing for a cocktail reception.

MEETING CAPACITY: The Chapel can accommodate 200 seated.

FEES & DEPOSITS: A $340 reservation fee is required to secure your date. A $250 insurance fee and a refundable $500 security deposit are required. The Chapel rental fee for ceremonies is $1,000.

For ceremonies with Courtyard receptions, there is an additional $100 charge. A 1-hour rehearsal runs $150.

AVAILABILITY: Year-round, daily, 10am–2pm or 3pm–7pm for ceremonies. Not available on national holidays, Christmas Eve or Day, or New Year's Eve or Day.

SERVICES/AMENITIES:

Catering: BYO, licensed and insured
Kitchen Facilities: no
Tables & Chairs: BYO or through caterer
Linens, Silver, etc.: BYO or through caterer
Restrooms: not wheelchair accessible
Dance Floor: no
Bride's Dressing Area: yes
Meeting Equipment: BYO

Parking: large lot nearby
Accommodations: limited, call for details
Telephone: no phone
Outdoor Night Lighting: access only
Outdoor Cooking Facilities: no
Cleanup: caterer or renter
View: courtyard and landscaped grounds

RESTRICTIONS:

Alcohol: BYO, licensed and insured server
Smoking: outside only
Music: amplified OK until 7pm with volume restrictions

Wheelchair Access: no
Insurance: extra liability required ($250)
Other: decorations require prior approval

Presidio Golden Gate Club

Historic Club and Event Facility

135 Fisher Loop, Presidio, San Francisco
415/561-5444
www.presidio.gov
events@presidiotrust.gov

- Rehearsal Dinners
- Ceremonies
- Wedding Receptions
- Corp. Events/Mtgs.
- Private Parties
- Accommodations

Something magical must have come over the army architects who designed the many fine structures that dot San Francisco's Presidio. Instead of fashioning plain barracks or no-frills buildings for the enlisted men and officers, they constructed some of the most exciting examples of Mission-style architecture on California's northern coast.

The Presidio's Golden Gate Club—which once functioned as the Non-Commissioned Officers club—is no exception. With its red-tiled roof, white stucco walls and arcaded courtyard, it's the very picture of rich, Spanish-inspired design. In this well-preserved 1940s-era club, weddings and special events now take place—and the sense of history and period details add real pizzazz to each celebration.

Nestled amongst the towering cypress typical of the Presidio, the club's white-and-red exterior pops in sharp contrast to the deep greens that surround it. As you approach, the wide-open courtyard of the U-shaped building reveals numerous palm trees and a fancy, tropical tile-and-grass patio. This area can accommodate stand-up cocktail receptions beautifully: Box hedges adorned with twinkle lights divide up the space and make it private, while cocktail tables covered in bright linens lend a formal touch.

When the mingling and champagne sipping have concluded, guests then drift past large white columns and through double-glass doors into the stately Ventana Room, undoubtedly the property's most dazzling asset. A two-story wall of windows overlooks a grove of trees, and the bay shimmers in the distance. When you dress up this space for dinner and dancing, that incredible view remains the focal point. Here, you'll also find a cathedral ceiling, a sizable wood dance floor, and a huge fireplace at one end of the long ballroom. As you look around and realize that you're inside an elegant ballroom and intensely close to nature, you feel an overwhelming sense of serenity.

If you want to split up the party or you need more room, two other ballrooms—the Hawthorn and Cypress rooms—offer quiet, versatile areas for children to play, older guests to relax, or for dessert and espresso bars. Up on the second floor, there are three breakout rooms for additional space and a small mezzanine that overlooks the Ventana Room.

It's worth mentioning that there are two charming chapels within walking distance of the Golden Gate Club. Saying "I do" at either one of them and then proceeding with all your guests over to the Club is fun and exhilarating—plus you can take advantage of photo opportunities along the way.

Although it may be hard to imagine soldiers once partying in such an elegant place, it's quite easy to picture your own festivities here. Whether you're planning a wedding, an anniversary bash or another special event, consider yourself lucky that the Golden Gate Club has passed out of army hands and into the public domain, where you can take advantage of its tranquil, sophisticated setting.

CEREMONY CAPACITY: The Club holds up to 200 seated guests depending on room selection and layout.

EVENT/RECEPTION & MEETING CAPACITY: With a buyout, the Club can accommodate up to 450 seated or 850 standing guests. Many configurations are available to accommodate groups of varying sizes; call for details.

FEES & DEPOSITS: A $1,000 reservation fee is required to secure your date. A $250 insurance fee and a $1,500 security deposit are required. Rental fees range $4,500–6,000, depending on the day of the week.

AVAILABILITY: Year-round, daily, 8am–midnight. Not available on national holidays or Christmas and New Year's Days and Eves.

SERVICES/AMENITIES:

Catering: BYO, licensed and insured
Kitchen Facilities: limited, prep only
Tables & Chairs: BYO or limited CBA
Linens, Silver, etc.: BYO or through caterer
Restrooms: wheelchair accessible
Dance Floor: yes, Ventana Room
Bride's Dressing Area: CBA
Meeting Equipment: BYO or limited CBA

Parking: 40 spaces and large lot nearby, restrictions may apply
Accommodations: limited, call for details
Telephone: emergency use only
Outdoor Night Lighting: access only
Outdoor Cooking Facilities: no
Cleanup: caterer or renter
View: SF Bay, Golden Gate bridge, cypress trees

RESTRICTIONS:

Alcohol: BYO, licensed and insured server
Smoking: outside only
Music: amplified OK indoors with volume restrictions until 11:30pm, outdoors until 6pm

Wheelchair Access: yes
Insurance: extra liability required ($250)
Other: decorations require prior approval

The professionals in the back of this book are the best in the business. How do we know? Read page 701.

Presidio Golf Course and Clubhouse

Golfcourse & Clubhouse

300 Finley Road at Arguello Gate, San Francisco Presidio
415/561-4661 x207

www.presidiogolf.com
presidiobanquets@palmergolf.com

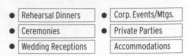

● Rehearsal Dinners	● Corp. Events/Mtgs.
● Ceremonies	● Private Parties
● Wedding Receptions	Accommodations

Since 1776, the year Lieutenant Colonel Juan Bautista de Anza was dispatched to establish a garrison to protect the harbor of St. Francis, the Presidio has guarded the narrow mouth of San Francisco Bay, first for Spain, then Mexico, and finally for the United States. Then, as now, the Presidio was one big beautiful piece of California real estate. Today, its 1,500 acres of eucalyptus, cypress, pine forest, coastal wild flowers, and ocean and bay views belong not to the army, but to the National Park Service, and the 7,000-square-foot clubhouse just inside the old Arguello Gate is a fine place to host a wide spectrum of events.

Set on a rise at the end of a stately drive, the clubhouse has a casually refined look that makes you want to step inside. The interior, a blend of Mission-style architecture and Maybeck-inspired, landscape-friendly details, features cathedral ceilings, exposed fir beams, cherrywood trim and paneling, and a large limestone fireplace. Five French doors extend its largest dining area, the Presidio Cafe, onto a spacious wood-trellised patio with an excellent view of the final green of the Presidio's historic 18-hole golf course. President Theodore Roosevelt reviewed the command on the Presidio Golf Links in 1903, and many a golfer of note—including TR himself, Dwight Eisenhower, Bing Crosby and Arnold Palmer—has played through on its fairways. The patio, with its verdigris tables and chairs, is perfect for any style of function from barbecue to black-tie.

Of course, the close proximity of Bentgrass greens and well-maintained parklands is a powerful lure. Party plans could easily include a bit of golf practice or a short, ranger-led walk. But more likely, guests will simply want to sit back and enjoy the fresh air and the vista—lush green lawns, pine and eucalyptus groves, the blue-roofed towers of distant USF, and the comely neighborhood mansions, all looking very low-rise from this vantage point on a gentle crest.

If those wide open vistas are a tad too distracting, the Palmer Room (named for Arnold Palmer, of course!), provides cozier quarters just right for smaller meetings, breakfasts, luncheons or dinners, and the Palmer Terrace and lawn with its garden setting and pine-curtained bay views allows celebrants once again to take the dining and good times outdoors.

CEREMONY CAPACITY: The Outdoor Terrace holds up to 150, the South Lawn accommodates 220 and the Palmer Lawn holds 60 seated guests.

EVENT/RECEPTION CAPACITY: The Cafe holds 80 seated or 125 standing guests, the Palmer Room 40 seated or 60 standing guests, and the entire Clubhouse 120 seated or 200 standing guests. The Clubhouse and a tented outdoor terrace combined holds 220 seated.

MEETING CAPACITY: The Palmer Room accommodates up to 50 guests seated theater-style or 40 guests seated conference-style. The entire facility holds 120 seated.

FEES & DEPOSITS: For events, 50% of the estimated event total is required to reserve your date; the balance is due 10 days prior to the event. Room rental fees range $250–5,000 depending on space(s) rented. Lunches range $20–40/person. Dinners range $40–125/person. Tax, alcohol and a 21% service charge are additional, as is a $2/person cake-cutting fee.

AVAILABILITY: Year-round, daily, dawn until midnight.

SERVICES/AMENITIES:

Catering: provided, no BYO

Kitchen Facilities: n/a

Tables & Chairs: provided

Linens, Silver, etc.: provided

Restroom: wheelchair accessible

Dance Floor: CBA, extra charge

Bride's Dressing Area: yes

Meeting Equipment: CBA, extra charge

Parking: large lot, complimentary

Accommodations: no guestrooms

Telephone: pay phones

Outdoor Night Lighting: yes

Outdoor Cooking Facilities: no

Cleanup: provided

View: fairways, park

Other: event coordination

RESTRICTIONS:

Alcohol: provided or corkage $15/bottle

Smoking: outside only

Music: amplified OK indoors

Wheelchair Access: yes

Insurance: not required

Presidio Log Cabin and Log Cabin Lawn

Historic Log Cabin & Lawn

1299 Storey Avenue, The Presidio, San Francisco
415/561-5444
www.presidiotrust.gov
events@presidiotrust.gov

● Rehearsal Dinners	● Corp. Events/Mtgs.
● Ceremonies	● Private Parties
● Wedding Receptions	● Accommodations

The name might suggest a humble little structure, but the Presidio Log Cabin is anything but. Although it *is* made of logs, it's more like a grand hunting lodge, with its solid fieldstone foundation and spacious interior.

Hanging across the front of the building, the words "Log Cabin" announce you've arrived—a marker left over from its days as a party hall for soldiers of the Presidio. Since it was built in 1937, the facility has seen its share of festivities, but its sturdy timbers have been beautifully maintained. Ceiling beams and columns are made of actual tree trunks, and there are giant wagon wheel chandeliers overhead. The Old West flavor feels authentic here, and adds a fun element to parties without being over the top. Casual events like company picnics often play up the country-western theme by including cowboy costumes, country music and square dancing. However, for wedding receptions and formal dinner parties, all it takes is candles and flowers to make the place glow with a rustic elegance. In fact, when the huge fireplace is lit and the room is warmed by guests dancing and celebrating, the ambiance is downright cozy.

During warm weather, the Log Cabin is great for an indoor/outdoor event. Get married on the expansive front lawn, either under a tent or in the open sunshine surrounded by nature. From here you have a view of the woods and snippets of San Francisco Bay. Afterwards, host a cocktail reception on the lawn, followed by music and dancing inside the Log Cabin. The large covered patio at the entrance is often set up with small tables and chairs, and used as a cocktail area between the wedding and reception.

You don't come across many log cabins in the sophisticated city of San Francisco, and this may be the only one where you can have a smashing party. It's also probably the only place where you can wear a tux or a cowboy hat and feel equally at home.

CEREMONY & EVENT/RECEPTION CAPACITY: The Log Cabin holds 150 seated or 200 standing, and the Log Cabin Lawn up to 150 seated or 200 standing.

MEETING CAPACITY: The Log Cabin holds 100 seated theater-style.

FEES & DEPOSITS: A $1,000 reservation fee is required to secure your date. A $250 insurance fee and a $1,000 refundable security deposit are required. Rental fees range $2,500–3,500 depending on the day of the event.

AVAILABILITY: Year-round, daily, 8am–midnight. Not available on national holidays or Christmas and New Year's Days and Eves.

SERVICES/AMENITIES:

Catering: BYO, must be licensed and insured

Kitchen Facilities: limited, prep only

Tables & Chairs: BYO, CBA or through caterer

Linens, Silver, etc.: BYO or through caterer

Restrooms: wheelchair accessible

Dance Floor: hardwood floor

Bride's Dressing Area: yes

Meeting Equipment: BYO or limited CBA

Parking: 40 spaces on site, restrictions may apply

Accommodations: limited, call for details

Telephone: no

Outdoor Night Lighting: access lighting only

Outdoor Cooking Facilities: BBQ pit

Cleanup: caterer or renter

View: SF Bay and parts of the San Francisco skyline

RESTRICTIONS:

Alcohol: BYO, licensed and insured server

Smoking: outdoors only

Music: amplified OK with volume restrictions; indoors until 11:30pm, outdoors until 6pm

Wheelchair Access: yes

Insurance: extra liability required ($250)

Other: decorations and any tent or equipment staking on lawn require prior approval

The Regency Center

Landmark Building

1290 Sutter Street, San Francisco
415/673-5716

www.regencycentersf.com
dcronis@aeglive.com

● Rehearsal Dinners		● Corp. Events/Mtgs.	
● Ceremonies		● Private Parties	
● Wedding Receptions		Accommodations	

As you stroll down Van Ness Avenue, you're sure to notice a stately Classical Revival building that looks like it should be on Nob Hill. Completed in 1909 as a Scottish Rite Temple, The Regency also housed a movie theater for many years, and now has a new lease on life as a fabulous event site.

And "fabulous" is not an overstatement. Wait until you see what this three-level architectural gem has in store for you. The Regency's *pièce de résistance* is the Lodge, a showstopper of a room on the building's third floor. If the word "lodge" makes you think of log cabins and pot-bellied stoves, you'll be delightfully surprised by this room's absolute splendor. The 35-foot-high ceilings are traversed by arched dark wood beams, and the carved wainscoting and stained-glass windows give the room the grandeur of a Gothic cathedral. Crimson velvet walls and carpeting add sumptuous warmth. Antique acorn-shaped chandeliers and coach-lantern wall sconces augment the soft amber glow cast by the stained-glass windows lining one wall. Among the Lodge's other amenities are a 1909 Austin pipe organ and a splendid elevated stage with 30 exquisite hand-painted backdrops made in a Hollywood studio during the 1920s.

On this floor you'll also find two other rooms that are ideal for entertaining on a slightly smaller scale. The Regency Room features details that delight the eye wherever you look: moldings and ceiling beams carved with grapevines and other nature motifs; light fixtures constructed of rows of small crystals; and breathtaking silk tapestries, embroidered by hand using gold and copper thread. On the more practical side, this room also has a working fireplace, white oak-paneled walls and solid pocket doors that can be closed for privacy. The elegant Candidate Room is bright and open, with blue carpeting, mirrored walls, gold candle chandeliers and sconces, plus large windows that frame views of San Francisco.

A marble staircase takes you to the center's second level and the Grand Ballroom. From its polished hardwood floor to its 35-foot ceiling, the ballroom is a shining example of turn-of-the-century craftsmanship. The walls, ceiling, moldings and wainscoting are all covered in incredibly detailed neoclassical plasterwork, and painted in shades of silver and gold; 22 teardrop chandeliers hang from the carved beamed ceiling. The Grand Ballroom also has a built-in stage, as well as a horseshoe-shaped balcony, making it a great place for lectures, business seminars and awards banquets. And don't forget that beautiful floor—it simply cries out for dancing! Just outside the Grand Ballroom is the Rotunda, an enchanting foyer with a mosaic floor, crystal chandelier and carved neoclassical ceiling. Though it's too small for functions, it's a lovely place for guests to mingle before an event or take a break from the festivities.

On the center's lower level, the Sutter Room and Sutter Annex introduce you to sophistication on a large scale. Here, creamy white walls, a unique beamed ceiling and blond hardwood floors gleam in the light cast from a series of round frosted glass-and-brass fixtures. The Sutter Room's stage with curtains and the Annex's wet bar make this space versatile enough for any type of function. Sliding pocket doors give you the option of using one or both of these rooms.

It's always a pleasure to see beautiful old landmarks brought back to life, especially when the building is as spectacular as this one. We think that The Regency's gorgeous décor and turn-of-the-century ambiance are the perfect antidote to today's streamlined pragmatic world, and so will you.

CEREMONY/MEETING CAPACITY: The Lodge level seats 300 theater-style, the Grand Ballroom 750, and the Sutter Room 600.

EVENT/RECEPTION CAPACITY: The site can accommodate 240–1,420 seated or 300–2,323 standing guests indoors.

FEES & DEPOSITS: A nonrefundable deposit (50% of the rental fee) is required to reserve your date. The balance is due 30 days prior to the event. The $3,500–25,000 rental fee depends on number of levels rented, day of week and season.

AVAILABILITY: Year-round, daily, until 4am.

SERVICES/AMENITIES:

Catering: select from preferred list
Kitchen Facilities: prep only
Tables & Chairs: tables provided on every level, chairs provided on Lodge and Sutter levels only
Linens, Silver, etc.: through caterer
Restrooms: wheelchair accessible
Dance Floor: provided
Bride's & Groom's Dressing Area: on all levels
Meeting Equipment: BYO

Parking: ample nearby garages, on street or valet
Accommodations: hotels nearby
Telephone: no
Outdoor Night Lighting: access only
Outdoor Cooking Facilities: n/a
Cleanup: caterer
View: no
Other: bar service, built-in bar, one stage per floor, 1909 pipe organ, 31 hand-painted backdrops

RESTRICTIONS:

Alcohol: provided by *Best Beverage Catering*
Smoking: outside only
Music: amplified OK

Wheelchair Access: yes
Insurance: liability required

Want to know WHAT TO ASK a potential location or vendor? Check out our Questions to Ask on page 17.

Rincon Atrium & Yank Sing Restaurant

Banquet, Event Facility & Restaurant

101 Spear Street, San Francisco
415/781-7888
www.yanksing.com
sales@yanksing.com

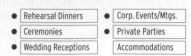

● Rehearsal Dinners	● Corp. Events/Mtgs.
● Ceremonies	● Private Parties
● Wedding Receptions	Accommodations

If you're passionate about Chinese food, and your guest list doesn't exceed 1,000, the Rincon Atrium and Yank Sing Restaurant are a unique combination of event spaces in the Financial District. Both are part of the Rincon Center, an impressive historic building that houses everything from businesses to federal offices to apartments.

The Atrium is at the heart of the center, and Yank Sing is one of the marquee establishments around its perimeter. Anyone who reads restaurant reviews knows about Yank Sing's scrumptious food. And for those foodies out there, Yank Sing is the recipient of the highly coveted James Beard Award. What's rarely mentioned, however, is that the restaurant also has access to the Atrium for special events.

In contrast to its serious Financial District setting, the Atrium is a vibrant indoor courtyard that soars five stories and is topped with a glass ceiling. Built of polished granite with rich wood touches, its contemporary design is softened by an abundance of greenery: potted palms all around, and lush plants cascading off the balconies above. The focal point is a remarkable "rain column" fountain, whose five-story free fall begins at the ceiling and ends in a simple pool, set flush with the floor. And while this is a public use area, a sense of privacy is created by having the storefronts (all done in polished cherrywood) tucked unobtrusively around the outer circumference of the space. Four separate eating areas off the main walk-through also provide intimate gathering places. Events here have included everything from corporate holiday parties and elegant civic functions to weddings staged in front of the dramatic backdrop of the fountain.

Yank Sing is just steps from the Atrium. At the entrance, a picture of Alice Chan, the restaurant's gracious founder, reminds you that this is a family business and welcomes you inside. The large open dining room is designed so that everyone can see each other, and the courtyard is visible through a wall of glass. Diners are surrounded by pale peach silk walls hung with Chinese brush paintings. A black granite bar flecked with copper picks up the warmth from the pastel walls, and gleams in the soft light cast by alabaster chandeliers. The room can be configured any way you want, with movable partitions made of wood and etched glass. In one corner, a glass-enclosed section of the room is often used for a traditional wedding tea ceremony. Hidden shades can be pulled down for complete privacy, so this area can be used as a bridal dressing area or for gifts.

Yank Sing and the Atrium are available separately or together. Some couples have used the Atrium's unconfined space to advantage by having a troupe of lion dancers perform for their guests.

Whether you're planning to serve just dim sum or a complete Chinese banquet, the menu will be customized to your tastes. Yank Sing uses only the freshest ingredients in its award-winning food, and offers hundreds of options, from delicate translucent dumplings and tender noodle dishes to time-honored favorites like Peking Duck and Sharksfin Soup. Chinese couples often schedule their wedding by picking a lucky day from the lunar calendar. In our opinion, any day you choose to celebrate at Yank Sing and the Rincon Atrium is a lucky day.

CEREMONY CAPACITY: The Atrium can accommodate up to 350 seated.

EVENT/RECEPTION & MEETING CAPACITY: The Atrium holds 750 seated or 1,000 standing. Yank Sing Restaurant accommodates 220 seated or 300 standing guests.

FEES & DEPOSITS: A $5,000 nonrefundable deposit is required when the date is reserved and the event is booked. The balance is payable 2 weeks prior to the event. The Atrium rental fee ranges $1,000–4,000 plus a $500 cleaning fee; there's no rental fee for Yank Sing Restaurant. Meals start at $35/person; alcohol, tax and service charges are additional.

AVAILABILITY: Yank Sing and the Atrium, year-round.

SERVICES/AMENITIES:

Catering: provided by *Yank Sing Catering*
Kitchen Facilities: n/a
Tables & Chairs: provided up to 400 guests
Linens, Silver, etc.: provided
Restrooms: wheelchair accessible
Dance Floor: CBA
Bride's Dressing Area: yes
Meeting Equipment: CBA

Parking: free parking in underground garage
Accommodations: no guestrooms
Telephone: emergency use only
Outdoor Night Lighting: access only
Outdoor Cooking Facilities: n/a
Cleanup: provided
View: indoor waterfall
Other: event coordination, entertainment CBA

RESTRICTIONS:

Alcohol: provided, or wine corkage $15/bottle
Smoking: not allowed
Music: amplified OK with volume limits

Wheelchair Access: yes
Insurance: additional may be required
Other: no glitter or confetti

The Ritz-Carlton

600 Stockton at California Street, San Francisco
415/296-7465 x1150
www.ritzcarlton.com
johanna.philipps@ritzcarlton.com

- Rehearsal Dinners
- Ceremonies
- Wedding Receptions
- Corp. Events/Mtgs.
- Private Parties
- Accommodations

Set atop prestigious Nob Hill, The Ritz-Carlton is housed in one of San Francisco's finest examples of neoclassical architecture. Originally built in 1909, the block-long structure has an impressive and stately façade. As you step inside, you're surrounded by The Ritz-Carlton's signature style—handsome, classically designed spaces graced by 18th- and 19th-century museum-quality art and antiques. Gold-framed seascapes and landscapes, Persian carpets, crystal chandeliers, silk wall coverings and enormous fresh floral arrangements lend a sophisticated, yet understated, quality to the hotel's public spaces.

Large parties take place in the Ballroom, which is often used in tandem with adjacent galleries. The galleries themselves are perfect for cocktails and hors d'oeuvres—spacious, with high vaulted ceilings, ornate woodwork, large oil paintings and silk-covered walls in gold tones. Seated receptions follow in the Ballroom, a sizable and regal space that can be partitioned into smaller segments. The room is warm: Light glows from crystal chandeliers suspended from a recessed oval ceiling, and walls are softened by panels of patterned, muted gold silk brocade.

The hotel has more event spaces on the second and third levels, each of which can be used for a private rehearsal dinner or small reception. All are nicely designed with floral arrangements, light wood molding and wainscoting. For outdoor parties, there's a beautiful red-brick courtyard, which has a lovely cityscape and is enclosed by an impeccably manicured garden of roses, lavender, ivy and flowers. Glass-topped tables with umbrellas and wrought-iron chairs dot the courtyard, and the central portion can be tented if the weather doesn't cooperate. After the celebration there's no need to rush off—the bride and groom can unwind in one of the hotel's two Presidential Suites, and be whisked off to the airport the next day by a hotel-arranged limousine service.

CEREMONY CAPACITY: The hotel can accommodate 10–750 seated or 50–1,100 standing guests indoors.

EVENT/RECEPTION CAPACITY: The site holds 16–700 seated or 26–1,100 standing guests indoors.

MEETING CAPACITY: There are 13 spaces that accommodate 26–826 guests seated theater-style, 12–122 conference-style or 16–475 classroom-style.

FEES & DEPOSITS: For weddings, a deposit of 25% of the estimated event charges is due when your contract is submitted. The ceremony setup charge is approximately $4,000. For receptions, buffet luncheons run $63–73/person, seated luncheons $65–70/person and seated dinners $90–100/person. Tax and service charges are additional. The estimated food and beverage total is payable 10 days prior to the event.

For business functions or meetings, fees vary depending on rooms and services selected. Call for specifics.

AVAILABILITY: Year-round, daily, 8am–2am, including holidays.

SERVICES/AMENITIES:

Catering: provided
Kitchen Facilities: n/a
Tables & Chairs: provided
Linens, Silver, etc.: provided
Restrooms: wheelchair accessible
Dance Floor: provided
Bride's Dressing Area: yes
Meeting Equipment: full range CBA

Parking: valet at $35/car for event parking
Accommodations: 336 guestrooms, 59 suites
Telephone: guest phones
Outdoor Night Lighting: CBA
Outdoor Cooking Facilities: CBA
Cleanup: provided
View: SF Bay and skyline from upper floors
Other: event coordination

RESTRICTIONS:

Alcohol: provided
Smoking: designated areas only
Music: amplified OK

Wheelchair Access: yes
Insurance: not required
Other: no rice indoors

St. John's Presbyterian Church

Historic Church

25 Lake Street, San Francisco
415/751-1626
www.sfchurchweddings.com
events@stjohnssf.org

Rehearsal Dinners	Corp. Events/Mtgs.
● Ceremonies	Private Parties
● Wedding Receptions	Accommodations

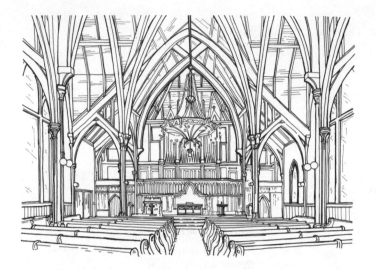

Lovely homes and the bustling Richmond and Presidio Heights neighborhoods have replaced the sand dunes that once surrounded St. John's Presbyterian Church, but things inside the church haven't changed. A welcoming spirit of fellowship and friendship still fills the gracefully turreted 1906 structure, and permeates all of its activities.

The cordiality begins at the bright and airy entrance, where you and your guests can gather for greetings and farewells. From here, turn left into the Narthex, the burgundy-carpeted gallery that opens onto the Sanctuary. In this intimate space, two beautiful stained-glass windows let in filtered daylight, making it an ideal location for a gift table or guest book. During the ceremony, the room can also serve as a retreat for parents with fussy children: They can mind the kids and still watch the wedding through a long row of interior windows.

Step from the Narthex into the Sanctuary, a "wow"-inspiring hall with soaring arches, gothic detailing and rows of burgundy-upholstered pews. Ten stained-glass windows and a large chandelier illuminate the darkly wooded interior, lending it a feeling of grandeur that is equal parts solemnity and warmth. Behind the pulpit and ample stage, an elegant choir loft and magnificent, newly restored Johnson organ (purchased by the church in 1870), suggest the significant role that music has always played in this institution's ministry. A Steinway grand piano is also on hand, and the recently restored original hardwood floors further add to the room's superior acoustics.

Around the corner from the Sanctuary, the white and cheerful Fireside Room offers a contrast to ecclesiastical grandeur. Outfitted with a mini grand piano, burgundy wing-back chairs and conversation-style seating arranged in front of a fireplace, this spacious, light-drenched chamber has been used for tea ceremonies, small receptions and as a haven for the bride, the groom and their families. The adjacent Library, a small room with closet and full-length mirror, offers yet another level of privacy.

If needed, additional reception space is available downstairs in two large community rooms. The Fellowship Hall and the Auditorium can accommodate anything from a dinner dance to a luncheon buffet. In these two rooms, as in all the others under the church's roof, an atmosphere of amiability and versatility governs. It's an attitude mirrored by the staff, who imbue every event here with the same gracious care and attention that has endeared St. John's to its community for nearly a century.

CEREMONY CAPACITY: The Sanctuary holds 300 seated, the Chapel 50 seated guests.

EVENT/RECEPTION CAPACITY: The reception room can accommodate 150 seated or 200 standing guests indoors.

FEES & DEPOSITS: For weddings, a partially refundable $450 security deposit is required to confirm your date. For ceremonies, the $1,400 rental fee is payable 2 weeks prior to the event, and includes an hour for the rehearsal, 2½ hours for the ceremony, plus some coordination. For receptions, room rental fees run $200/hour plus a $250 refundable security deposit. Minister and musician services are extra, as is coordination for receptions.

AVAILABILITY: Year-round, daily. Weddings take place Sundays after 6pm, Saturdays 11am–10pm or weekdays, 9am–10pm; other special events, 11am–midnight. The church is available most holidays, depending on the social schedule, with an additional charge.

SERVICES/AMENITIES:

Catering: BYO
Kitchen Facilities: prep only
Tables & Chairs: some provided, remainder BYO
Linens, Silver, etc.: BYO or caterer
Restrooms: wheelchair accessible
Dance Floor: Fellowship Hall
Bride's & Groom's Dressing Area: CBA
Meeting Equipment: limited, BYO

Parking: nearby garage or on street
Accommodations: no guestrooms
Telephone: emergency use only
Outdoor Night Lighting: no
Outdoor Cooking Facilities: no
Cleanup: renter or caterer
View: no
Other: event coordination, minister, mini grand piano, pipe organ

RESTRICTIONS:

Alcohol: wine and nonalcoholic beverages only
Smoking: not allowed
Music: amplified OK with volume limits

Wheelchair Access: yes, ramp
Insurance: not required
Other: no rice, birdseed or petals

Want to find more locations and services? Check out our informative website, www.HereComesTheGuide.com.

145

The St. Regis San Francisco

Hotel

125 Third Street, San Francisco
415/284-4006
www.stregissanfrancisco.com
barry.peterson@stregis.com

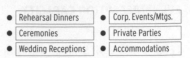

- Rehearsal Dinners
- Ceremonies
- Wedding Receptions
- Corp. Events/Mtgs.
- Private Parties
- Accommodations

Entering The St. Regis San Francisco for the first time feels a little like waltzing into the Manhattan townhouse of a good friend with impeccable taste, an unlimited budget, and a penchant for art and design. In this posh new high-rise hotel, every single surface and element fits together seamlessly so that one is flooded with a sense of comfort and a little awe at the beauty of it all. Here, sumptuous Italian furniture meets hand-blown light fixtures and a world-class art collection—and that's just the beginning.

Located at Third and Mission Streets, The St. Regis has joined the ranks of the San Francisco Museum of Modern Art and the Yerba Buena Center for the Arts in making this area an undisputed hotbed of culture and style. Starting with the lobby, you encounter large vibrant murals, textured leather walls, sleek couches, and lighting and music that evoke an upscale lounge. Plus, the décor throughout the hotel shares an overarching color scheme that soothes: neutral tones of ecru and brown with subtle purple accents sprinkled in.

The first twenty floors of this structure contain the restaurant, event venues, spa, and guestrooms, while the upper floors provide residence for the lucky few. For those looking to throw an epic celebration, three floors dedicated to events offer options galore.

On level two is a pair of the most impressive event spaces we've encountered. Far from being big empty rooms, they feature seventeen-foot ceilings with custom-made glass light fixtures that resemble intricate clusters of vines embedded with glittering purple flowers. Floor-to-ceiling windows look out onto Yerba Buena Gardens, and gray-purple carpet and walls make a cool backdrop for your festivities. Receptions are accommodated here with ease, as are dancing and cake cutting. Right outside the two rooms (which can be combined for large parties), guests flow into a glass atrium with a continuing view of thriving Third Street below.

Up on level four, the Yerba Buena Terrace provides an enormous decadent spot for ceremonies and receptions. Gold Jerusalem marble, and modular teak furniture set the stage for an outdoor fête that overlooks treetops and the urban scene beyond. Brides often choose to tent the space as a hedge against unpredictable weather, and clear sides give guests the best of an outdoor/indoor experience.

Adjacent to the Terrace are three smaller event rooms called the Modernist, Impressionist and Conservatory Suites. Featuring linen-covered walls and aubergine carpets, they further reflect the integration of art and design that distinguishes The St. Regis.

The St. Regis was designed by people who have mastered the art of lavish comfort and impeccable service. The positively serene Remède Spa pampers brides and grooms, and if that's not enough, the hotel's butler service assures that your stay approaches perfection. Wedding menus are also exceptional: They focus on inventive customized cuisine made predominantly from organic local foods. For a wedding that's inspired on every level, The St. Regis San Francisco doesn't disappoint. Here, you can have a celebration that truly reflects your taste for the finer things in life.

CEREMONY CAPACITY: The hotel accommodates 225 seated indoors and 275 outdoors.

EVENT/RECEPTION & MEETING CAPACITY: Indoors, The St. Regis holds 275 seated and 500 standing; outdoors, 300 seated and 600 standing.

FEES & DEPOSITS: 50% of the estimated event total is required to reserve your date. The balance is due 10 working days prior to the event. Rental fees range $1,500–5,000 depending on the event space rented. Meals range $185–350/person. Tax, alcohol and a 21% service charge are additional.

AVAILABILITY: Year-round, daily; outside terraces available until 10pm, ballroom available until 1:30am.

SERVICES/AMENITIES:

Catering: provided
Kitchen Facilities: n/a
Tables & Chairs: provided
Linens, Silver, etc.: provided
Restrooms: wheelchair accessible
Dance Floor: provided
Bride's & Groom's Dressing Area: yes
Meeting Equipment: provided
Other: event coordination; grand piano; on-site wedding cake; spa services; AV equipment

Parking: valet required at hotel; self-parking nearby
Accommodations: 260 guestrooms including 46 suites
Telephone: house phone
Outdoor Night Lighting: CBA
Outdoor Cooking Facilities: BBQ CBA
Cleanup: provided
View: SF cityscape, garden, park

RESTRICTIONS:

Alcohol: provided
Smoking: outside only
Music: amplified OK indoors with restrictions

Wheelchair Access: yes
Insurance: not required

San Francisco Film Centre

Film Center

39 Mesa Street, Suite 107, The Presidio, San Francisco
415/561-3456
www.sffilmcentre.com
propmgr@sffilmcentre.com

● Rehearsal Dinners	● Corp. Events/Mtgs.	
● Ceremonies	● Private Parties	
● Wedding Receptions	☐ Accommodations	

It's always interesting to learn how something built for one purpose ends up being used in a completely different and unforeseen way. The San Francisco Film Centre is a perfect case in point: It occupies one of two attractive Mission-style structures originally designed to house enlisted men and officers stationed at the Presidio. Although the Centre's building never fulfilled its function as a military residence, it has found another calling. In 1999, the Film Centre undertook a historic renovation of the elegantly appointed edifice, and today it's a multi-use facility, providing a variety of resources to the film community.

You don't have to be affiliated with the film industry, however, to have your event in the Palm Room, the Centre's amazingly versatile event space. Fresh white walls and columns and honey-colored hardwood floors, polished to a mirror finish, give the room a natural sophistication. During the day sunlight streams in through attractively shaded multipaned windows, illuminating the room and making the floors gleam (subtle track lighting at night makes them shimmer). East and west windows provide views of the parade ground, the Golden Gate Bridge and the Presidio's meticulously landscaped sylvan setting. On the eastern side, floor-to-ceiling French doors open onto a beautiful Mexican-tile veranda, distinguished by 13 graceful arches and wrought-iron railings. When the weather is warm (or with heaters), you can serve cocktails or dine outdoors.

We think the Palm Room is quite inviting, even if you do nothing at all to it. But with a little imagination, you can transform it in innovative ways. Wrap the columns with green garlands studded with flowers, or make a "hanging" photo album by putting favorite pictures around the room. Many partygivers take full advantage of the state-of-the-art lighting. One bride used copper and yellow uplights on walls and columns to pick up the colors in her floral centerpieces. For a corporate soirée, brown leather banquettes, round red carpets and red tablecloths were brought in to create a rich, clubby feeling. Red uplighting throughout gave the atmosphere just the right touch of sultriness.

The room's excellent acoustics are great for DJs, bands and—as has been demonstrated by previous events—for anything from film screenings to interactive art installations. Twenty-four electrical outlets and internet connections at both ends of the room allow the Palm Room to go high tech.

Also part of the large property and available for rental are the pale yellow Conference Room and Spanish-style Boardroom. They offer breakout arrangements during business functions, or private quarters for bride, groom and attendants. Downstairs, a professionally equipped catering kitchen adds to the marvelous versatility of this venue. The intimate Screening Room, located downstairs as well, seats 24 in a combination of plush leather and comfy theater seating. You can imagine the creative party possibilities: a place to view dailies, enjoy a pre-dinner film or screen that award-winning montage of the bride and groom from childhood to matrimony. Capture your memorable Palm Room celebration on tape, and it might just provide you with the perfect excuse to book a return engagement.

CEREMONY CAPACITY: The Veranda holds up to 100 seated guests.

EVENT/RECEPTION CAPACITY: The Palm Room accommodates up to 180 seated, 150 with dancing or 250 standing guests; the Veranda holds up to 96 seated or 150 standing.

MEETING CAPACITY: The Palm Room seats up to 250 guests theater-style or 100 classroom-style.

FEES & DEPOSITS: 50% of the facility rental fee is required to reserve your date, the balance is due 30 days prior to the event. The rental fee ranges $700–5,000. Rental rates are for an 8-hour time frame, extra time is $250/hour.

AVAILABILITY: Year-round, daily, 7am–midnight.

SERVICES/AMENITIES:

Catering: select from preferred list
Kitchen Facilities: fully equipped
Tables & Chairs: BYO or through caterer
Linens, Silver, etc.: BYO or through caterer
Restrooms: wheelchair accessible
Dance Floor: hardwood floor
Bride's Dressing Area: yes
Meeting Equipment: CBA, extra charge

Parking: large lot
Accommodations: no guestrooms
Telephone: emergency use only
Outdoor Night Lighting: yes, Veranda
Outdoor Cooking Facilities: CBA
Cleanup: caterer
View: Main Post and Golden Gate Bridge, Presidio Officers' homes

RESTRICTIONS:

Alcohol: provided
Smoking: outside only
Music: amplified OK indoors only

Wheelchair Access: yes
Insurance: liability required

Sir Francis Drake Hotel

Hotel

450 Powell Street, San Francisco
415/395-8509

www.sirfrancisdrake.com
catering@sirfrancisdrake.com

- Rehearsal Dinners
- Ceremonies
- Wedding Receptions
- Corp. Events/Mtgs.
- Private Parties
- Accommodations

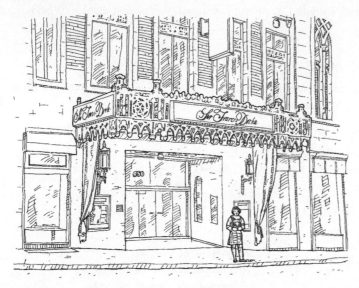

The Sir Francis Drake Hotel's 21-story, Gothic-style tower just off Union Square and its Beefeater-attired doormen have been beloved San Francisco attractions since 1928.

Stepping into the Drake's opulent Italian Renaissance lobby is just like stepping back into the 1920s: Marble staircases, walls and pillars convey a stately air; crystal chandeliers shine and the lofty, ornately detailed ceiling sparkles with gold leaf. The main event spaces, the Empire Ballroom and the Franciscan Room, have a high-society, Age of Innocence ambiance. In the gold-and-ivory Empire Room, beautiful hand-painted murals turn the walls into works of art. Overhead, three crystal chandeliers suspended from a vaulted ceiling painted with ribbons of gold leaf give the room a delicate amber glow. The adjoining wood-paneled Walnut Room, with its club-like, Edwardian atmosphere and built-in bar, makes a great prefunction space.

Located just off the mezzanine, the spacious and grand Franciscan Room is an excellent choice for a formal wedding. It's a regal setting, featuring a 21-foot ceiling with intricate gold embossing, chandeliers, windows draped with blue silk curtains, and columns with carved gold capitals. Guests can enjoy cocktails and hors d'oeuvres on the adjacent mezzanine, which offers a cozy fireplace and a bird's-eye view of the vibrant hotel lobby below.

And for those who have a yen for a panoramic 180-degree view of San Francisco, try Harry Denton's Starlight Room on the 21st floor. It not only has a built-in dance floor and shiny baby grand piano, it features floor-to-ceiling windows that wrap around the room, making it seem like you're floating in the clouds.

Steeped in 80 years of history, the Drake is a true classic. Brides may fall in love with its enchanting vintage architectural details, but they'll also appreciate the modern amenities and personal service this landmark hotel has to offer.

CEREMONY & EVENT/RECEPTION CAPACITY: The hotel can accommodate 100–250 seated or 200–350 standing guests indoors.

MEETING CAPACITY: The Hotel has 13,000 square feet of meeting and conference space with 14 different rooms accommodating groups from 10 to 350 people.

FEES & DEPOSITS: For weddings, a nonrefundable deposit is required to confirm your date. Half the total food and beverage payment is payable 4 months prior to the event; the balance and guest count guarantee are due 3 days prior. Wedding packages range $115–135/person and include open bar, passed hors d'oeuvres, champagne, wine, wedding cake and a 3-course dinner. Tax, and a 21% service charge are additional. Per-person prices for seated meals are as follows: luncheons start at $35, dinners at $47, luncheon buffets at $40, and dinner buffets at $66. Alcohol, tax and a 21% service charge are additional. Bride and groom receive a complimentary suite, and group discounts for overnight guests can be arranged.

Fees for meetings and business functions vary depending on rooms and services selected; call for specifics.

AVAILABILITY: For special events and business functions, year-round, daily, 6am–midnight. Weddings usually take place on Saturdays 11am–5pm or 6pm–midnight; other days have more flexible time frames. The Starlight Room is available Saturday 3pm–8pm, and Sunday 6pm–midnight.

SERVICES/AMENITIES:

Catering: provided, no BYO
Kitchen Facilities: n/a
Tables & Chairs: provided
Linens, Silver, etc.: provided
Restrooms: wheelchair accessible
Dance Floor: provided
Bride's & Groom's Dressing Area: no
Meeting Equipment: AV
Other: event coordination, baby grand piano

Parking: nearby garages or valet, extra fee
Accommodations: 417 guestrooms
Telephone: guest and pay phones
Outdoor Night Lighting: n/a
Outdoor Cooking Facilities: n/a
Cleanup: provided
View: Starlight Room has 180° view of San Francisco skyline

RESTRICTIONS:

Alcohol: provided, no BYO
Smoking: designated areas
Music: amplified OK

Wheelchair Access: yes, elevator
Insurance: not required
Other: no rice or open flames

The Stanford Court Renaissance
San Francisco Hotel

905 California Street, atop Nob Hill, San Francisco
415/989-3500, Catering Department
www.stanfordcourt.com
sfosc.leads@renaissancehotels.com

Hotel

- Rehearsal Dinners
- Ceremonies
- Wedding Receptions
- Corp. Events/Mtgs.
- Private Parties
- Accommodations

Few San Francisco venues can boast as prestigious a provenance as this imaginatively re-envisioned top-of-Nob Hill hotel. Built on the lofty site selected by 19th-century railroad baron and California governor Leland Stanford as the setting for his palatial multimillion-dollar mansion, The Stanford Court Renaissance San Francisco Hotel commands the cityscape.

The original edifice was destroyed in the fire that followed the 1906 earthquake, but part of the 30-foot basalt and granite wall that surrounded the spectacular two-acre estate was carefully restored and can be seen on the eastern side of the building. Privacy is still very much a part of this property's charm. The keyhole street entrance opens onto a beautiful courtyard beneath a Tiffany-style dome of sunlit stained glass.

That sophisticated blend of the elegant and the urbane continues inside under another sparkling rotunda where Aurea, the hotel's extraordinary new dining and lounge environment, offers numerous ways to relax and revitalize. Your guests can greet one another over drinks in attractive, semiprivate cocktail "cubbies," chat or nosh in intimate dining nooks, or gather pre- or post-event at one of the expansive communal tables.

From the lobby a white marble staircase descends to the ballroom level. The staircase, with its two-story waterfall of light at the top, is a stunning frame for bridal portraits. But don't linger too long in front of the camera; other alluring settings await. The dreamy ballroom foyer has cream-colored walls set off by a glorious gold carpet that vibrates with exuberant, sun-splashed colors and shapes. Arrange cocktail tables here or use the area for champagne and passed hors d'oeuvres. White double doors open onto the California Ballroom, a great space for smaller sit-down receptions and ceremonies. The mood in this room is joyous, upbeat and uplifting: Champagne-colored walls effervesce with a soft, bubble pattern, while the balloon shapes in the carpet design create movement. Elegant white crown moldings and trim add grace and a touch of serenity.

Four more white double doors lead from the foyer to the similarly caparisoned Stanford Ballroom, where unforgettable features like twin Baccarat crystal chandeliers—that once graced the Grand Hotel in Paris—establish an exciting ambiance. Gala affairs are easily accommodated here, and the ballroom can be partitioned for more intimate gatherings. For real extravaganzas, book the entire ballroom level and let the party flow seamlessly from one enchanting room to the next.

Remarkably, the luxury doesn't end here. Fournou's Ovens has a selection of gorgeous ultraprivate dining rooms and is a great place to extend the fun, as is the Nob Hill Room with its views from atop Nob Hill. And don't forget the additional meeting rooms, fitness center and 393 handsome guestrooms and suites. You can definitely have your entire event here, from the rehearsal dinner to the post-wedding brunch. But if you'd like to get married in a church, there are several nearby, including the famous Grace Cathedral, just two blocks from the hotel.

The Stanford Court Renaissance is also a wonderful getaway for a "Bride's" or "Groom's" weekend before or after the wedding. There's so much to do in San Francisco and the hotel's stellar location makes it easy: Guests can simply hop on a cable car right outside the front door and go explore the city.

CEREMONY CAPACITY: The Stanford Ballroom accommodates up to 450 seated guests. The California Ballroom holds up to 140 seated and the Nob Hill up to 45 seated guests.

EVENT/RECEPTION CAPACITY: The Stanford Ballroom holds up to 320 seated with a dance floor.

MEETING CAPACITY: Event spaces accommodate 12–520 seated guests.

FEES & DEPOSITS: 25% of the estimated food and beverage total is required to reserve your date. The balance is due 72 hours prior to the event. Rental fees range $750–4,000 depending on your guest count and the day of the event. Wedding packages range $145–190/person. Tax, alcohol and a 22% service charge are additional.

AVAILABILITY: Year-round, daily, anytime.

SERVICES/AMENITIES:
Catering: provided, no BYO
Kitchen Facilities: n/a
Tables & Chairs: provided
Linens, Silver, etc.: provided
Restrooms: wheelchair accessible
Dance Floor: provided
Bride's & Groom's Dressing Area: CBA
Other: event coordination, on-site wedding cake and florals, AV equipment

Parking: valet or public garage
Accommodations: 393 guestrooms
Telephone: house and guest phones
Outdoor Night Lighting: CBA
Outdoor Cooking Facilities: no
Cleanup: provided
View: cityscape and bay views
Meeting Equipment: full range

RESTRICTIONS:
Alcohol: provided, no BYO
Smoking: outside only
Music: amplified OK indoors

Wheelchair Access: yes
Insurance: liability required

Terra

Art Gallery

511 Harrison Street, San Francisco
415/896-1234
www.terrasf.com
info@terrasf.com

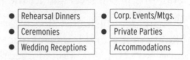

● Rehearsal Dinners	● Corp. Events/Mtgs.
● Ceremonies	● Private Parties
● Wedding Receptions	☐ Accommodations

The collective creativity of entrepreneurs, artists and tech whizzes has made SOMA the hippest neighborhood in The City, vibrating with a diversity of businesses, restaurants, clubs and galleries.

One of the most intriguing of these is Terra, a collection of newly renovated galleries and event spaces that epitomizes the synergy of art and technology. At this urban-chic venue, just blocks from the Bay Bridge, you're encouraged to turn your celebration into a work of art—literally. The whole place is like a big blank canvas on which you can paint whatever vision you have in mind. Terra's two diverse levels have separate entrances, so you can reserve a floor individually or take over all the galleries and offer your guests multiple environments.

The upper floor has a spacious, open feeling: 5,000 square feet of Brazilian cherry hardwood floors, white brick walls and support columns rising 20 feet to the ceiling, and at the end of the room 40 feet of floor-to-ceiling windows that showcase the downtown skyline. Light pours in during the day, and at night city lights turn the wall of glass into a vast glittering tableau—a dreamy backdrop for a wedding ceremony. A carpeted area with leather furniture and a baby grand piano lets guests relax and enjoy the view.

Equally impressive is Mer, a lounge-style space on the lower floor that gives off the ultra-hip vibe of a private club. Serpentine bars inlaid with glass tiles let the staff serve up signature cocktails with style and ease. A built-in oak stage at one end holds your entertainment, while guests dance on the gleaming hardwood floor. Mer adjoins a 3,000-square-foot landscaped patio, which can be left open to the stars or elegantly tented. Bamboo, lush foliage and abundant water features evoke a garden atmosphere for cocktails or an outdoor ceremony.

Terra's staff will work with you to develop a theme, and ensure that your wedding is seamlessly choreographed. You're welcome to incorporate the current exhibit's paintings and sculptures into your event, or turn Terra into your own personal gallery by exhibiting blown-up photos of the bride and groom on the walls, or projecting a slide show set to music. If you'd like something more, the artistic folks at Terra will do almost anything to satisfy your decorative fantasies. Terra's state-of-the art Bose sound system, gallery lighting and multimedia capabilities allow for the ultimate in customization. And if you're having a destination wedding here, they're able to provide a live feed to guests who can't attend.

You're free to bring your own licensed caterer, and there's plenty of nearby parking with valet service available upon request. To make it easy for out-of-town guests who want to take advantage of nearby museums, entertainment and sightseeing, Terra has partnered with local hotels for special group rates.

Terra's versatility makes it an inspired choice for just about any type of event. And if you're short on imagination, don't worry: They offer full production services, adapted to your personality and budget. Whether you desire a quiet and refined affair or a totally theatrical experience, Terra has all the elements.

CEREMONY CAPACITY: The Gallery can accommodate up to 300 seated guests on one floor, or 500 using both.

EVENT/RECEPTION CAPACITY: This facility holds 300 seated or 725 standing guests per floor.

MEETING CAPACITY: The Gallery holds 300–500 seated guests, or 1,400 seated theater-style.

FEES & DEPOSITS: A $2,000 deposit is required to reserve your date. The balance is due 30 days prior to the event. Rental fees range $2,000–11,000 depending on date of event, guest count, facility usage and type of organization.

AVAILABILITY: Year-round, daily. Weekdays 10am–4am, weekends 10am–6am.

SERVICES/AMENITIES:
Catering: BYO or CBA
Kitchen Facilities: 2 prep kitchens
Tables & Chairs: BYO or CBA
Linens, Silver, etc.: BYO or CBA
Restrooms: wheelchair accessible
Dance Floor: provided at no charge
Bride's & Groom's Dressing Area: yes
Meeting Equipment: CBA, extra fee

Parking: garages nearby or valet CBA
Accommodations: hotels nearby
Telephone: house phone
Outdoor Night Lighting: provided
Outdoor Cooking Facilities: yes
Cleanup: provided
View: cityscape, landscaped grounds
Other: full event coordination and production; up to 108mbps of dedicated bandwidth

RESTRICTIONS:
Alcohol: provided
Smoking: outside only
Music: amplified and live music OK

Wheelchair Access: yes
Insurance: required, CBA

ThirstyBear Brewing Company

661 Howard Street, San Francisco
415/974-0905 x208
www.thirstybear.com
events@thirstybear.com

Restaurant & Brewery

- Rehearsal Dinners
- Ceremonies
- Wedding Receptions
- Corp. Events/Mtgs.
- Private Parties
- Accommodations

The marriage of hand-crafted, organic San Francisco beers and Spanish tapas is celebrated with panache and gourmet flair at ThirstyBear Brewing Co. An unlikely match? Perhaps. But within this upscale brewpub in the city's South of Market district, it's a perfect combination for rehearsal dinners. Here, the traditional (and often stuffy) seated meal with in-laws before the big day has been replaced by a comfortable and relaxed dining experience. In fact, you and your closest family and friends may find yourselves sipping a Brown Bear Ale (brewed on the premises) while noshing on tuna crostini, empanadas and shrimp skewers—*and* having a lot of fun.

Walking into ThirstyBear, you pass a classic long bar, banquettes and exposed brick on your way to the private and semiprivate event spaces upstairs. As you ascend the modern, industrial staircase, the brewing tanks for the house-made beers come into view, letting you know this is in fact a working brewery. On the second floor, the friendly, yet sophisticated, atmosphere continues in the semiprivate Billar Room. Vividly colored contemporary art and a private bar highlight this open area, while a pool table and dartboards lend a casual touch. It's ideally suited for a cocktail hour, beer tasting, or a buffet of tapas.

The adjacent Sillón Room provides total privacy and a lounge-like ambiance. Here you can host a lively sit-down meal animated by vibrant artwork and a colored-glass wall that adds pizzazz day or night. Family-style repasts complete with customized platters of tapas or large pans of paella (a menu specialty) work well in this open, airy spot. ThirstyBear's knowledge of all things Spanish also extends to music: They're happy to bring in a Spanish guitarist to play exclusively at your party in either the Sillón or Billar Room.

If your guest list tops 200 or more, why not reserve the whole place? Then you can take advantage of the entire downstairs restaurant/bar in addition to the rooms upstairs. One couple who did a buyout booked a guitarist and flamenco troupe to perform *and* teach partygoers some dance moves. It was a true Spanish extravaganza.

What ThirstyBear brings to all celebrations, whether they're large or small, elaborate or low-key, is a lack of pretense and a true dedication to hassle-free entertaining. Amazing to note, too, is that ThirstyBear can often be booked for a party with as little as two months' notice, something nearly unheard of at most Bay Area venues, much less at one so desirable. Add to that the delectable array of Spanish food, fresh sangria, full bar and handcrafted organic beers, and you have a recipe for *una buena fiesta*.

CEREMONY CAPACITY: Ceremonies do not take place at this location.

EVENT/RECEPTION CAPACITY: This facility holds 175 seated or 500 standing guests.

MEETING CAPACITY: Smaller rooms hold 40 seated guests.

FEES & DEPOSITS: A small deposit may be required to reserve your date, call for details. The event total is due at the conclusion of the event. Rental fees range $100–500 depending on your guest count. If you have 25 or more guests, the room rental fee is waived. Meals range $22–55/person. Tax, alcohol and a 20% service charge are additional.

AVAILABILITY: Year-round, Monday–Saturday, 9am–midnight. Sundays 5pm–10pm, but may be flexible depending on the event.

SERVICES/AMENITIES:

Catering: provided
Kitchen Facilities: n/a
Tables & Chairs: provided
Linens, Silver, etc.: provided
Restrooms: wheelchair accessible
Dance Floor: CBA
Bride's Dressing Area: CBA
Meeting Equipment: CBA

Parking: on street, garage nearby
Accommodations: no guestrooms
Telephone: emergency use only
Outdoor Night Lighting: CBA
Outdoor Cooking Facilities: no
Cleanup: provided
View: no
Other: brewery tours and tasting, flamenco dancing and lessons, event coordination

RESTRICTIONS:

Alcohol: provided
Smoking: not allowed
Music: amplified OK indoors with restrictions

Wheelchair Access: yes
Insurance: not required

Overwhelmed? Use the search criteria on www.HereComesTheGuide.com to narrow down your choices.

University Club of San Francisco

Historic Social Club

800 Powell Street, San Francisco
415/781-0900 x149
www.univclub.com
barbaral@univclub.com

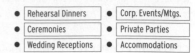

● Rehearsal Dinners	● Corp. Events/Mtgs.
● Ceremonies	● Private Parties
● Wedding Receptions	● Accommodations

San Francisco's past and present meet downtown at the city's most prestigious location: Nob Hill. Here, at the intersection of California and Powell, cable cars roll by as they have for more than 100 years, past century-old buildings erected by our Barbary Coast forebears.

One structure that's stood the test of time on this very corner is the venerable University Club, a glorious brick facility that has occupied this spot since 1909. The Club's first organizers purchased the property from city founder Leland Stanford, relocating their social club here because the original UC clubhouse on Sutter Street had been destroyed in the 1906 earthquake.

Today, the University Club still echoes those long-ago beginnings. However, while it continues as a private membership-based social and athletic club, it also rents out a plethora of fancy, history-rich event spaces on its third and fourth floors to nonmembers. The fourth-floor lounge is downright stunning, with one long wall of windows that open out onto the intricate geometric pattern of San Francisco's Financial District skyline. Couples who get married in this room not only benefit from the city as a backdrop, they're surrounded by opulent wood and gilt trim, brocade wallpaper, and glittering chandeliers.

Right down the hall, past original artwork, is the more subdued library room. Warm and cozy, it has green leather couches, red carpets, a working fireplace and a multitude of shelves containing over 3,000 leather-bound books. It also boasts windows overlooking downtown to the east, and serves as a convenient getaway for brides and grooms who want to find some alone time, commune with the wedding party, or simply relax during the festivities.

Partygoers can also take advantage of two additional spaces on this floor: the wood-paneled game room with a pool table for a little diversion, and the circular Old World bar next to it. Both provide overflow areas for the ceremony, and encourage guests to linger over cocktails while taking in details like the red carpets and wood accents.

Down on the third floor, the attractive dining room allows brides to truly personalize their event. Bright linens and flowers embellish this wide-open banquet room, which features exposed wood beams overhead. Add to this the Club's award-winning cuisine and your reception will shine.

After dinner, cake and aperitifs can be served in the adjacent Black Cat Bar, a congenial choice for winding down your celebration.

The University Club has eleven traditional guestrooms and five suites, enabling the wedding party to make the entire club "home" for the weekend. Host a "morning after" brunch before guests depart for the airport, with box lunches that contain a special note from the newlyweds!

At the University Club, events aren't just *in* the city, they're *of* the city in a very elemental way. The action happens right downtown, in a setting where every visual motif harks back to another era. Like former members John Muir and Herbert Hoover, who once sipped cocktails here themselves, you'll appreciate this elegant yet comfortable destination that has a special place in San Francisco history.

CEREMONY CAPACITY: The Fourth Floor Lounge holds up to 150 seated guests.

EVENT/RECEPTION & MEETING CAPACITY: The Dining Room accommodates 200 seated or 300 standing guests.

FEES & DEPOSITS: A 50% deposit is required to reserve your date. The balance is due 2 weeks prior to the event. Wedding packages start at $75/person, wedding cake included. Tax, alcohol and a 20% service charge are additional, as is a $5/person cake-cutting fee for cakes brought in from the outside. Site fees are $2,500 for Saturday night, $1,500 for Sunday and $500 for Friday. Please inquire for special rates for corporate meetings and events.

AVAILABILITY: Year-round, daily.

SERVICES/AMENITIES:

Catering: provided, no BYO
Kitchen Facilities: n/a
Tables & Chairs: provided
Linens, Silver, etc.: provided
Restrooms: wheelchair accessible
Dance Floor: provided
Bride's Dressing Area: yes
Meeting Equipment: some provided, more CBA

Parking: valet parking available upon request
Accommodations: 16 guestrooms
Telephone: pay phone
Outdoor Night Lighting: access only
Outdoor Cooking Facilities: no
Cleanup: provided
View: panorama of SF cityscape and SF Bay
Other: event coordination, grand piano; complimentary guestroom for bride and groom on the event date (subject to availability)

RESTRICTIONS:

Alcohol: provided, no BYO
Smoking: outside on balconies or street only
Music: amplified OK

Wheelchair Access: limited
Insurance: not required

Westin St. Francis on Union Square

Historic Hotel

335 Powell Street, Union Square, San Francisco
415/774-0126
www.westinstfrancis.com
bill.hedgepeth@westin.com

- Rehearsal Dinners
- Ceremonies
- Wedding Receptions
- Corp. Events/Mtgs.
- Private Parties
- Accommodations

Commonly referred to as the Grand Dame of Union Square, The Westin St. Francis has so many rooms in which to hold an elegant wedding ceremony, a grand reception, or business bash of any kind, that they can't all be fully described on these two little pages. They can, however, be divided into two categories: Historic Elegance and Modern Luxury.

In the first category are the numerous ballrooms of the original turn-of-the-century building, stunning spaces with marble floors, gilt pillars, intricately carved ceilings, and a hundred years' worth of history. They include: the Borgia Room, a jewel-box chamber with oak-paneled walls, a six-foot-tall marble fireplace, and a vaulted, delicately painted ceiling (originally the hotel's chapel, it's perfect for a wedding ceremony); the St. Francis Suite (just right for a smaller ceremony and reception); and the Colonial Room, appointed with Italian murals, elaborate candelabras, and gold-leafed columns separating regal opera balconies. Large events are held in the Grand Ballroom, which is easily transformed by your choice of décor and can accommodate up to 800 guests. Receptions often start with cocktails in the Colonial Room, then flow into the adjacent Grand Ballroom for the main affair.

The two rooms in the second category, Modern Luxury, are 32 stories up on the Imperial Floor. Five glass elevators overlook spectacular downtown panoramas as they whisk guests to Victor's and Alexandra's, a pair of sophisticated settings with breathtaking views. Glowing chandeliers combined with hundreds of sparkling pin-spots provide adjustable illumination, while wraparound San Francisco vistas—from the Bay Bridge to the Golden Gate—are framed in fourteen-foot-high bay windows draped with floor-to-ceiling silk curtains. Gold Chiavari chairs, custom Wedgwood china and your own Imperial Floor concierge make having a celebration up here a sublime experience.

The range and quality of options at the Westin St. Francis is astonishing, and your choice will not be easy. Are you looking for Old San Francisco glamour or a more contemporary ambiance? If you can't decide, why not combine both eras with a ceremony in the Borgia Room followed by dinner and dancing in Alexandra's. Whatever spaces you select, your event will most certainly be magical.

CEREMONY CAPACITY: The hotel can accommodate 20–1,000 seated guests.

EVENT/RECEPTION CAPACITY: The St. Francis has 31 banquet rooms with 54,000 square feet of event space; some of the larger rooms hold 80–800 seated or up to 1,200 standing guests indoors.

MEETING CAPACITY: The facility has 31 rooms and over 54,000 square feet of meeting space that hold 20–1,500 seated theater-style, 15–800 classroom-style or 10–50 conference-style.

FEES & DEPOSITS: For social events, a nonrefundable deposit based on the estimated event total is required when the contract is signed; the remaining balance and a final guest count are due 72 business hours prior to the event. Wedding packages start at $165/person, and include hors d'oeuvres, 4-hour bar, 2-course meal, wedding cake, champagne toast, wine with meal, and a luxury suite for the bride and groom. Tax and a 22% service charge are additional. A ceremony setup fee may be required. Customized wedding and bar mitzvah packages can be arranged; kosher catering under strict rabbinical supervision is available. Persian, Indian and Chinese catering is also available.

AVAILABILITY: Year-round, daily, anytime, including holidays.

SERVICES/AMENITIES:

Catering: provided
Kitchen Facilities: n/a
Tables & Chairs: provided
Linens, Silver, etc.: provided
Restrooms: wheelchair accessible
Dance Floor: provided
Bride's & Groom's Dressing Area: suite provided
Meeting Equipment: full range; AV extra charge
Other: kosher and Indian catering, wedding cakes

Parking: limited in-house; many nearby garages
Accommodations: 1,195 guestrooms
Telephone: pay phones
Outdoor Night Lighting: n/a
Outdoor Cooking Facilities: n/a
Cleanup: provided
View: sweeping cityscape from upper floors

RESTRICTIONS:

Alcohol: provided
Smoking: outside only
Music: amplified OK

Wheelchair Access: yes
Insurance: not required

North Bay

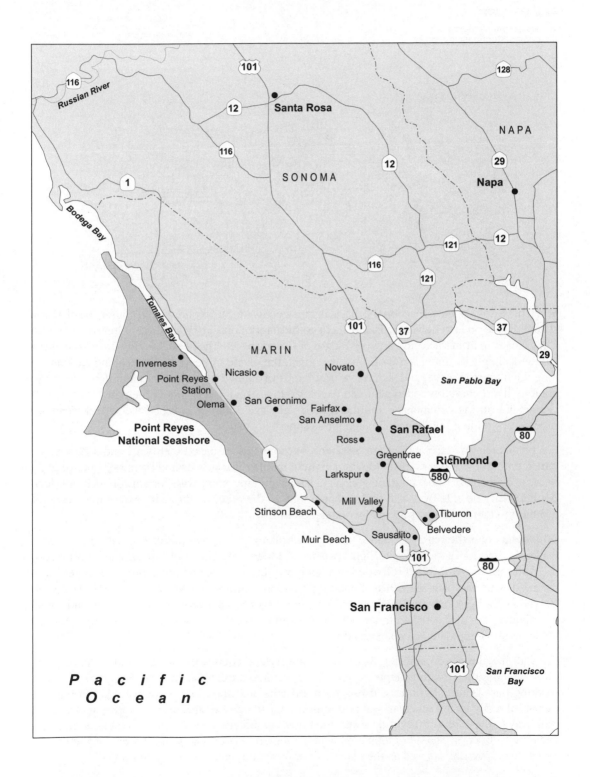

St. Stephen's Episcopal Church

Church

3 Bay View Avenue, Belvedere
415/435-4501
www.ststephenschurch.org
kitchen@ststephenschurch.org

Rehearsal Dinners	● Corp. Events/Mtgs.
● Ceremonies	● Private Parties
● Wedding Receptions	Accommodations

You'll have an "Ah, yes!" reaction the moment you step inside St. Stephen's. The church, nestled in a shady hillside on lush Belvedere Island, has a gothic interior of soaring concrete columns and walls. They create an immediate and powerful sense of sacred space—the perfect setting if you're seeking eloquent simplicity and a sense of connection with the divine. A heavenly blue ceiling crowns the long, high, narrow nave, and slender vertical bands of stained glass filter sunlight down onto the church's hand-carved wooden altar and baptismal font. Small torches flank the pews, casting soft candlelight during ceremonies, and the church's massive organ of polished wood and gleaming pipes is played in a building long noted for its superb acoustics.

For post-ceremony celebrations, St. Stephen's beckons with a paved courtyard and a handsome parish hall. The courtyard, planted with Japanese maples, flowerbeds and bamboo, smells lightly of rich, damp earth and fragrant greenery. It's an inviting spot, with an almost secluded feel, bounded on one side by a wall of the church and on the other by the hall's exterior, a façade of ground-to-ceiling windows and tall wooden columns.

When you enter the hall, you realize you're in a brilliantly designed place. The hall's main space is like the interior of an exquisite, light-splashed wooden box. The floors are simple blond wood, the walls are rough-finished softwood of slightly varying shades, and the gently curved ceiling is trimmed with eye-pleasing lattice. Gentle light passing through the courtyard-facing glass wall, as well as the windows that look out to Belvedere Lagoon, Tiburon's tiered mansions and Angel Island, gives the airy room an inner glow. The artfulness of the hall's design shows through in its ability to accommodate any color palette.

The hall has direct access to a full-size restaurant-style kitchen with tons of counter space. Most local caterers (the church is happy to recommend some) are familiar with St. Stephen's and love working here. There's a bridal dressing room upstairs, and the groom's room leads through the sacristy directly to the sanctuary—a perfect setup for the groom and his men to discreetly make their way to the altar as everybody awaits the bride's grand entrance. (An important note: Remember to ask about St. Stephen's requirements for premarital counseling and the use of the church by baptized persons, as well as the playing of appropriate music at the ceremony.)

This is a place of lovely spaces, each of them wonderfully suited to its purpose. From the pageantry and solemnity of the wedding ceremony to the hours of celebratory laughter and joy that follow, everyone who moves through and around St. Stephen's will remember the experience with pleasure.

CEREMONY CAPACITY: The church holds 200 seated guests indoors.

EVENT/RECEPTION CAPACITY: The Parish Hall accommodates 120 guests seated banquet-style or 275 standing indoors and 60 seated or 100 standing outdoors.

MEETING CAPACITY: Meeting spaces hold 125 seated guests.

FEES & DEPOSITS: 25% of the rental fee (plus a $250 refundable damage deposit) is required to reserve your date. The balance is due 10 days before the event. Rental fees range $1,500–5,000 depending on the space rented and the number of hours used.

AVAILABILITY: Year-round, daily, except the week before Easter and the week before Christmas. The church is available 11am–10pm except Thursdays (11–6pm) and Sundays (3pm–9pm).

SERVICES/AMENITIES:

Catering: BYO
Kitchen Facilities: fully equipped
Tables & Chairs: some provided or through caterer
Linens, Silver, etc.: through caterer
Restrooms: wheelchair accessible
Dance Floor: provided
Bride's & Groom's Dressing Area: yes
Meeting Equipment: some provided

Parking: large lot, on street, limited
Accommodations: no guestrooms
Telephone: emergency use only
Outdoor Night Lighting: some provided
Outdoor Cooking Facilities: BBQ CBA
Cleanup: renter
View: garden patio, hills, lagoon, fountain
Other: grand piano, clergy on staff, pipe organ, event coordination

RESTRICTIONS:

Alcohol: BYO WBC
Smoking: not allowed
Music: amplified OK with restrictions

Wheelchair Access: yes
Insurance: liability required

The professionals in the back of this book are the best in the business. How do we know? Read page 701.

The Tavern at Lark Creek

Restaurant & Garden

234 Magnolia Avenue, Larkspur
415/924-1602

www.larkcreek.com
tavernevents@larkcreek.com

● Rehearsal Dinners	● Corp. Events/Mtgs.
● Ceremonies	● Private Parties
● Wedding Receptions	Accommodations

The Tavern at Lark Creek, one of the most popular restaurants in the Bay Area, is a delightful place for a wedding or reception. Built in 1888, this former Victorian country home is nestled in a grove of redwoods, next to a flowing creek. Sunlight filters through trees and windows, warming the tables in the Main Dining Room. Overhead, an enormous skylight creates an open, airy ambiance. Muted colors, rich wood paneling and rotating exhibits of original art complete the tasteful interior. Outdoors, the Creekside Patio is perfect for a romantic outdoor ceremony, and the formal front garden with fountain provides a lovely backdrop for photographs.

The Tavern at Lark Creek has received national acclaim as well as local restaurant awards, and we have found the food here to be some of the best we've ever tasted. Note that the special events manager is available to coordinate all aspects of your party, including rehearsal, ceremony and reception. Add to that the outstanding atmosphere and you'll understand why your wedding celebration here will receive rave reviews.

CEREMONY CAPACITY: The Creekside Patio holds 150 seated or 200 standing guests. Indoors, the Inn holds up to 50 seated guests.

EVENT/RECEPTION & MEETING CAPACITY: Private rooms hold 24–40 seated or 40–60 standing guests indoors. The patio holds 60 seated or 100 standing outdoors. The entire restaurant, including the patio, can accommodate 180 seated or 300 standing guests.

FEES & DEPOSITS: A nonrefundable deposit of 25% of the food and beverage minimum is required to book your date. Additional deposits may be required with the remaining balance due on the day of the function. Room rental fees are $150 for the Private Dining Room, $225 for the Sunroom, $500 for the Creekside Patio or $750 for the entire restaurant. Food and beverage minimums for the entire restaurant start at $6,000 and vary depending on the day of the week, time of the event and the time of year. Tax, ceremony fees and service fees are additional.

AVAILABILITY: Year-round, daily. Dinners nightly 5:30pm–11pm, Sunday brunch 10:30am–3:30pm and Saturday lunch 11am–4pm, but you must reserve the entire restaurant. Closed Christmas, New Year's Day and July 4th.

SERVICES/AMENITIES:

Catering: provided, no BYO
Kitchen Facilities: n/a
Tables & Chairs: provided
Linens, Silver, etc.: provided
Restrooms: wheelchair accessible
Dance Floor: yes
Bride's Dressing Area: yes
Meeting Equipment: CBA, extra fee

Parking: large lot, valet CBA
Accommodations: no guestrooms
Telephone: emergency use only
Outdoor Night Lighting: yes
Outdoor Cooking Facilities: n/a
Cleanup: provided
View: garden, redwoods and creek
Other: in-house pastry chef

RESTRICTIONS:

Alcohol: provided, no BYO
Smoking: designated area only
Music: amplified OK indoors and outdoors
with restrictions

Wheelchair Access: yes
Insurance: not required

Acqua Hotel

Hotel

555 Redwood Highway, Mill Valley
415/380-0400
www.marinhotels.com/acqua.html
jgilmore@jdvhotels.com

- Rehearsal Dinners
- Ceremonies
- Wedding Receptions
- Corp. Events/Mtgs.
- Private Parties
- Accommodations

Experienced travelers will tell you that in Mediterranean countries, the long, often blank public walls of houses and buildings hide marvels within—fountains and gardens that create soul-nourishing private islands of repose.

Acqua Hotel in Mill Valley is like that. Travelers along the freeway behind it see a three-story building with an inconspicuous façade of warm stucco and some windows. But step into the hotel and walk through to its other side—the one that unfolds along an arm of Richardson Bay—and suddenly the world opens up. There, across a sweep of water, loom the wooded ridges of Mill Valley and the southern flank of Mt. Tamalpais. Many of the hotel's rooms, designed by a canny architect, have balconies and front on this side, facing the mountain.

The ultramodern Acqua, opened in August 1999, has quickly acquired a local reputation as a hip, stylish location. Its spare visual details rely on an expert meeting of horizontal and vertical planes made from stark and simple materials. Even the concrete floors, unadorned but buffed to a high shine, lend an industrial elegance to the hotel. Variations in paint tones, such as brilliant flat whites juxtaposed with light earth tones, make the eyes race from one pleasing volume and shape to another. The waterfall that flanks the fireplace in the airy lobby has a deliberately sculptural feel to it.

The hotel's bayside area, accessed through the lobby's great glass doors, is a natural wedding site. A spacious lawn runs from one end of the property to the other, bordered on one side by a pedestrian promenade that runs along the water and on the other by a large patio area that has quickly become a favorite gathering place for knowledgeable locals seeking a drink or meal with a beautiful view. A wide brick walkway bisects the lawn and connects the promenade to the patio. With its backdrop of bay and hills, the walkway can double perfectly as a bridal aisle.

The main architectural element of this hidden-from-the-freeway side of the hotel is a dramatic outdoor spiral staircase that leads from the patio to a second-floor terrace. The terrace is sheltered under a large arching steel canopy, itself a beautiful architectural statement. Couples often marry on the terrace, then glide down the staircase in a stately procession to a reception on the patio.

Indoors, the Richardson Room features floor-to-ceiling windows, with easy access to the bayside patio. This event space can be divided into three smaller rooms.

Catering for weddings and meetings is provided by *Piazza D'Angelo,* a Mill Valley restaurant that consistently ranks among local residents' favorites in the *Pacific Sun's* annual "Best of Marin" contest. The hotel provides a liaison who works with the caterer and client.

The Acqua Hotel is part of a welcome trend among suburban Bay Area hotels: small, stylish suburban properties that meld city sophistication with the great natural beauty surrounding them. When you come to visit, take a few moments to relax in the lobby with one of Acqua Hotel's exotic collection of Oriental hot teas (a refreshing little amenity provided for guests). From your comfy couch you can appreciate the hotel's serene interior and the equally calming view. Listen to the fountain and watch the clouds float by...you have all the time in the world.

CEREMONY CAPACITY: The Bayside Lawn holds up to 120 seated guests.

EVENT/RECEPTION CAPACITY: The Richardson Room accommodates up to 120 seated guests.

MEETING CAPACITY: Event spaces accommodate 18–120 seated guests.

FEES & DEPOSITS: The rental fee is the deposit, and is required to reserve your date; the event balance is payable at the event's conclusion. Rental fees range $1,800–4,000 depending on space(s) rented. Rental of the lawn for a standing ceremony is an addtional $2,000. Meals range $36–150/ person; tax, beverages and labor charges are additional. The gratuity is optional. The in-house caterer, *Piazza D'Angelo,* may be reached directly at 415/388-2000 or catering@piazzadangelo.com.

AVAILABILITY: Year-round, daily, 7am–10pm.

SERVICES/AMENITIES:

Catering: provided by *Piazza D'Angelo*
Kitchen Facilities: n/a
Tables & Chairs: provided
Linens, Silver, etc.: provided
Restrooms: wheelchair accessible
Dance Floor: yes
Bride's Dressing Area: CBA
Meeting Equipment: some provided, more CBA, extra fee

Parking: large lot
Accommodations: 50 guestrooms
Telephone: pay phones
Outdoor Night Lighting: no
Outdoor Cooking Facilities: n/a
Cleanup: provided
View: Richardson Bay
Other: event coordination

RESTRICTIONS:

Alcohol: provided, no BYO
Smoking: outdoors only
Music: amplified OK indoors until 10pm

Wheelchair Access: yes
Insurance: not required

Mill Valley Community Center

Community Center

180 Camino Alto, Mill Valley
415/383-1370

www.millvalleycenter.org
sallingham@cityofmillvalley.org

● Rehearsal Dinners	● Corp. Events/Mtgs.
● Ceremonies	● Private Parties
● Wedding Receptions	Accommodations

How blessed is Mill Valley? Let us count the ways: dramatic location at the foot of Mt. Tamalpais; redwood groves; proximity to the bay and San Francisco; sophisticated citizenry and small-town feel.

And, since April 2001, add the Mill Valley Community Center to that list—it's become the town's pride and joy. Every day, from early morning to late evening, people flock here to swim, dance, work out or attend meetings.

The two-building complex, connected by arcades and enclosed walkways, is clad in olive-green wood siding that calls to mind the leaves of the oak trees on nearby hills. While it has the inviting silhouette of an Adirondack-style resort from 100 years ago, this structure deftly combines wood, concrete, painted steel, copper and glass to create a facility with all the light-admitting spaciousness and crispness of good modern architecture.

The Center's main event space is the Cascade Room, and to reach it visitors first pass through a dramatic entrance atrium. Their eyes are immediately drawn up to a vaulted ceiling supported by four slender concrete pillars. The atrium's distinctive reddish-gray slate floor is made of stone quarried in China. (The floor generates steady inquiries from landscapers whose clients have fallen in love with the slate and want to know where they can get some for themselves.)

The generous use of glass in the Cascade Room is particularly effective at night, when light pours out through the windows. Motorists on the nearby main road often slow down to look in longingly on its festive scenes, and imagine themselves dancing the night away in this warm, bright place. By day, the two-story space is lit by sunlight falling through the tall windows that run the length of its side walls. The cathedral-style ceiling is supported by laminated wood trusses, an airy architectural element that makes the room soar. Perhaps the nicest touch is the wood floor, left uncarpeted to allow the richness of its eucalyptus floorboards to dazzle the eye. They range along a spectrum of earthy reds, from reddish-browns and near maroons to lighter-colored planks. An adjoining professional kitchen can accommodate any catering operation.

The large patio on the east side of the Cascade Room has no walls or fences, so people don't feel hemmed in. It runs right up to a three-acre lawn (part of a community playing field), so that in one step you can move from stone to grass. This is a well-thought-out design that provides a sense of space, and invites parties to spill happily beyond the patio. The level lawn is a fine place to pitch a tent or two if you want to host an outdoor event.

Smaller rooms are available for wedding-related activities, including the Terrace Room, which can handle a cocktail party or small dinner. Wedding parties can also rent the whole facility if they'd like, including the 25-yard swimming pool, Jacuzzi, giant water slide and adjoining patio.

Mill Valley has always had a nice hum, and this well-maintained new facility only adds to it. People instinctively sense it's a great place to hold a celebration.

CEREMONY CAPACITY: The Cascade Room holds 400, and the lawn area 200 seated.

EVENT/RECEPTION CAPACITY: The center can accommodate 12–285 seated or 30–400 standing guests indoors.

MEETING CAPACITY: The facility has 6 rooms which can accommodate 2–400 theater-style, or up to 200 classroom-style.

FEES & DEPOSITS: For special events, a $100–500 refundable deposit is required when the contract is signed. Room rental fees for the Cascade Room range $120–195/hour on weekdays and $2,400–2,900 on weekends (for an 8-hour block). The Terrace Lounge is $45–81/hour on weekdays, and $75–101/hour on weekends. Other rooms range $26–101/hour. An attendant fee runs $15/hour, for weeknights and weekends.

AVAILABILITY: Year-round, daily, 8am–1am.

SERVICES/AMENITIES:

Catering: BYO
Kitchen Facilities: commercial kitchen
Tables & Chairs: provided to 250 guests
Linens, Silver, etc.: BYO or caterer
Restrooms: wheelchair accessible
Dance Floor: hardwood floor in Cascade Room
Bride's Dressing Area: CBA
Meeting Equipment: lectern, TV/VCR, screen, dry erase boards, microphone and sound system, portable stage

Parking: large lot, complimentary
Accommodations: no guestrooms
Telephone: pay phones
Outdoor Night Lighting: CBA
Outdoor Cooking Facilities: no
Cleanup: provided
View: Mt. Tamalpais
Other: baby grand piano

RESTRICTIONS:

Alcohol: BYO
Smoking: outside only
Music: amplified OK indoors, OK outdoors with curfew and volume restrictions

Wheelchair Access: yes
Insurance: certificate required
Other: decorations require approval

Want to know WHAT TO ASK a potential location or vendor? Check out our Questions to Ask on page 17.

Mountain Home Inn

Retreat

810 Panoramic Highway, Mill Valley
415/381-9000
www.mtnhomeinn.com
mountainweddingevents@gmail.com

● Rehearsal Dinners	● Corp. Events/Mtgs.
● Ceremonies	● Private Parties
● Wedding Receptions	● Accommodations

Perched on a forested ridge between the lofty peaks of Mt. Tamalpais and Mill Valley 1,000 feet below, the Mountain Home Inn has been enticing guests with stunning views and rustic charm for almost a century.

This bed and breakfast was built in 1912 as a mountain getaway for San Franciscans seeking an escape to nature, and has since served the entire Bay Area as a welcome stop for hiking enthusiasts, writers, lovers and even celebrities (Jack London and the Grateful Dead have stayed here). An abundance of wood, both inside and out, lends warmth to all the rooms, as do numerous fireplaces and homey details like the vintage photos of the inn framed on guestroom doors.

Everyone who comes here is mesmerized by the breathtaking panorama from the Upper Deck: A vast redwood forest flows down and away to the distant foothills of Mt. Tam, and on a clear day you can see past Tiburon and Angel Island to the East Bay. Although the inn is only 25 minutes from The City, it feels like it's at the edge of the wilderness. No wonder so many couples decide to get married here.

When you book your wedding at Mountain Home Inn, you can have exclusive use of the venue, which includes indoor and outdoor event spaces on three levels plus ten guestrooms. You're free to choreograph your day any way you like, but it has to be said that the Upper Deck, with its spectacular vista and endless sky overhead, is the premier spot for any warm-weather ceremony or reception. If the temperature drops, couples get married in front of the fireplace in the cozy Mountain View Room, where large picture windows frame all three peaks of Mt. Tamalpais. Other ceremony options include the nearby woods and beach (permits are required for these sites). The terraced gardens just below the deck are filled with purple Mexican sage, rosemary and salvia, making them a lovely setting for photos.

Cocktails and hors d'oeuvres are generally served either outside right in front of the inn or downstairs in the Bayview Room, which has French doors that open to a view-filled terrace. While your guests are mingling, tables for the reception are set up on the deck or in the Mountain View

Room. Simple decorations such as candles, leaves and tree branches are easy to come by and complement the natural surroundings.

All of the guestrooms face east, so your family and friends will wake up to the sunrise. Some of the rooms also have Jacuzzi tubs, fireplaces and terraces. Mountain Home Inn's sister property, the English Country-style Pelican Inn, is only ten minutes away and offers a convenient place for a rehearsal dinner or post-wedding brunch. A shuttle can be arranged to transport your guests between the inn and any other local lodging.

Mountain Home Inn offers a number of wedding packages, and their on-site wedding coordinator is happy to customize a package for you. She can also assist in organizing activities for your guests, such as hiking on Mt. Tam, cycling, picnicking or going to the beach. Designated a Bay Area Green Business, the inn keeps its grounds pesticide-free, uses eco-friendly cleaning products and supports local farmers and artisans.

CEREMONY CAPACITY: The Inn holds 50 seated guests indoors and 110 seated outdoors.

EVENT/RECEPTION CAPACITY: The facility accommodates 110 seated or standing, indoors and outdoors.

MEETING CAPACITY: Meetings do not take place at this facility.

FEES & DEPOSITS: 33% of the total event cost is required to reserve your date and the balance is due on the day of the event. Rental fees range $1,000–2,200 depending on the season. Meals range $42–62/person. Tax, alcohol and a 20% service charge are additional.

AVAILABILITY: Year-round, daily.

SERVICES/AMENITIES:

Catering: provided
Kitchen Facilities: n/a
Tables & Chairs: provided
Linens, Silver, etc.: provided
Restrooms: wheelchair accessible
Dance Floor: portable provided
Bride's Dressing Area: yes
Meeting Equipment: BYO
Other: on-site florals, AV equipment, event coordination

Parking: large lot, on street
Accommodations: 10 guestrooms
Telephone: house, office and guest phones
Outdoor Night Lighting: yes
Outdoor Cooking Facilities: no
Cleanup: provided
View: panorama of ocean, mountains, hills, forest, valley and cityscape

RESTRICTIONS:

Alcohol: provided
Smoking: not allowed
Music: amplified OK

Wheelchair Access: yes
Insurance: not required

The Outdoor Art Club

Historic Landmark

1 West Blithedale Avenue, Mill Valley
415/383-2582
www.theoutdoorartclub.org
rental@theoutdoorartclub.org

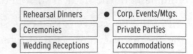

Rehearsal Dinners	● Corp. Events/Mtgs.
● Ceremonies	● Private Parties
● Wedding Receptions	Accommodations

The Outdoor Art Club, located in the heart of downtown Mill Valley, is one of Marin's favorite (and most sought-after) event spots. You enter through a quaint, arched gate into a restful garden patio area that immediately removes you from the hustle and bustle of everyday life. A sprawling native oak tree provides a leafy canopy to the lovely, large garden patio. Guests can mingle informally under the oak with cocktails and hors d'oeuvres, or they can be seated on the patio for a ceremony. Annuals, perennials and an abundance of shrubbery around two sides of the patio area add to the feeling of serenity.

The clubhouse, which borders two sides of the patio, is a charmer with a capital "C". Designed in 1904 by Bernard Maybeck, this classic Arts and Crafts structure has a rustic brown-shingled exterior, multipaned windows and multiple sets of French doors that bring the outside in when they're all opened. The interior is spacious, with a beamed vaulted ceiling, hardwood floor and raised stage along one end, perfect for a head table or band setup. The Sun Porch, which is suitable for the cake table or buffets, is a smaller space with two sets of French doors opening out onto a wide deck behind the clubhouse. The deck runs almost the full length of the building, connected with the kitchen area at one end, and at the other end with wide, shallow steps leading down to the shaded wedding patio area.

This sheltered patio is the optimal spot for a wedding ceremony. Guests can be seated in rows here, while the bride and groom say their vows in front of a backdrop of dense trees and shrubbery. It's no mystery why the Outdoor Art Club is so popular—it has an Old World appeal that's hard to resist.

CEREMONY CAPACITY: The wedding patio holds 120 seated guests and the front patio area 125 seated guests.

EVENT/RECEPTION CAPACITY: The facility seats a maximum of 160 guests inside for dining.

MEETING CAPACITY: The Main Room can accommodate approximately 200 seated in rows; the Sun Porch and Library seat approximately 60 guests each.

FEES & DEPOSITS: The Club's rental fee is $3,500. Half of the rental fee is required as a deposit to reserve a date, and is due 10 days after receipt of the written contract. The balance of the rental fee, along with an insurance fee and $1,500 security deposit, is due 60 days before your event. Renters are required to use and pay for the Club's one-day rental insurance fee, which is based on the number of guests. A custodian is provided for 2 hours for table and chair setup. The security deposit is refunded after the site has been checked and the Clubhouse key has been returned.

AVAILABILITY: Weekends only. Saturdays 8am–1am; Sundays 8am–10pm. Note that the City of Mill Valley's noise ordinance is strictly observed.

SERVICES/AMENITIES:

Catering: BYO

Kitchen Facilities: fully equipped

Tables & Chairs: provided for 160

Linens, Silver, etc.: BYO, or through caterer

Restrooms: wheelchair accessible

Dance Floor: yes

Bride's Dressing Area: yes

Meeting Equipment: state-of-the-art AV system

Parking: on-street only

Accommodations: no guestrooms

Telephone: pay phone

Outdoor Night Lighting: yes

Outdoor Cooking Facilities: no

Cleanup: caterer

View: garden

RESTRICTIONS:

Alcohol: BYO

Smoking: not allowed

Music: moderately amplified OK inside until midnight; volume limits

Wheelchair Access: yes

Insurance: required, extra charge

Other: decorations require prior approval; no candles allowed

The Pleasure is Mine at Harbor Point

Waterfront Club & Restaurant

475 East Strawberry Drive, Mill Valley
415/381-6400, The Pleasure Is Mine Catering

www.thepleasureismine.com
thepleasureismine@harbor-point.com
potnpanchick@aol.com

- Rehearsal Dinners
- Ceremonies
- Wedding Receptions
- Corp. Events/Mtgs.
- Private Parties
- Accommodations

If you're a tennis buff, and the word "love" tugs at more than your heart strings, the Harbor Point Tennis and Swim Club may be the perfect place to celebrate your love match. And even if you're not a tennis aficionado, you can still score a winning shot by holding an event here.

Tucked at the base of Mill Valley's rolling hills, the clubhouse is unpretentious, and with its peaked, shake-shingled roof, looks almost like a private residence—albeit one surrounded by tennis courts and a large lap pool. The glass-and-wood clubhouse sits right at the edge of a lagoon in a quiet unhurried corner of the bay, where sea birds from a nearby preserve loll offshore and there are few reminders of city life.

The newly remodeled main room is intimate and relaxed, yet feels spacious, thanks to an open-beamed ceiling and floor-to-ceiling windows. There's an expansive bayview panorama, and if you prefer to do your viewing outside, slip out onto one of the wide decks surrounding the building. For those evenings when it can get chilly on the bay, there are two large fireplaces—one in the main room and the other in a smaller adjoining room, an ideal spot in which to set up a buffet.

While the clubhouse is certainly a favorite locale for wedding receptions, the congenial setting has witnessed all sorts of special occasions—anniversary parties, bar and bat mitzvahs, memorial services and fundraisers, to name a few. You can also hold an intimate wedding ceremony in one section of the main room, and still have space to wine and dine your guests in the other.

Whatever type of event you celebrate at Harbor Point, you probably won't have to exhaust your life savings to pay for it. Site manager Bob Kaliski says, "When you come to us, we make a real effort to work within your budget. Our goal is not just to give you a good time, but to give you the best event we can at the best price."

Note: The Pleasure is Mine also caters events at other locations, some of which can accommodate larger functions.

CEREMONY CAPACITY: The site accommodates up to 150 seated guests.

EVENT/RECEPTION CAPACITY: The main room and enclosed patio, combined, hold 150 seated with a dance floor, or up to 200 for a cocktail reception. Additional tenting may be used for larger events.

MEETING CAPACITY: The main room accommodates 175 seated guests, theater-style or conference-style; the smaller room seats 10–35.

FEES & DEPOSITS: A $500 refundable security deposit fee is required to reserve your date. The rental balance is due 90 days prior to the event. Rental fees are: $750 for up to 60 guests; $850 for 61–100 guests; $950 for over 100 guests.

In-house catering is provided: Hors d'oeuvres start at $12/person, lunches at $15/person and buffets or seated dinners range $25–150/person; alcohol, tax and service charge are additional. A $1,000 fee applies if an outside caterer is used; the caterer must be insured and preapproved by the club. A signed credit card receipt is required prior to the event to guarantee final payment.

AVAILABILITY: Year-round, daily, 6pm–11pm. Additional hours and time blocks may be rented.

SERVICES/AMENITIES:

Catering: provided
Kitchen Facilities: fully equipped
Tables & Chairs: provided
Linens, Silver, etc.: provided
Restrooms: some wheelchair accessible
Dance Floor: provided
Bride's & Groom's Dressing Area: yes
Meeting Equipment: PA, lectern, easels, large screen, TV, VCR

Parking: large lot or on street, valet
Accommodations: no guestrooms
Telephone: pay phone
Outdoor Night Lighting: yes
Outdoor Cooking Facilities: BBQs
Cleanup: provided
View: Strawberry Point Lagoon
Other: on-site event planner, florist, DJ, photographer, and tape player available

RESTRICTIONS:

Alcohol: full bar provided, or wine corkage $10/bottle, $15/magnum
Smoking: not allowed
Music: amplified OK until 11pm; after 11pm, volume restrictions are required

Wheelchair Access: yes
Insurance: not required

Want to find more locations and services? Check out our informative website, www.HereComesTheGuide.com.

177

Rancho Nicasio

1 Old Rancheria Road, Nicasio
415/662-2219

www.ranchonicasio.com
maxbrown@ranchonicasio.com

Historic Restaurant & Grounds

- Rehearsal Dinners
- Ceremonies
- Wedding Receptions
- Corp. Events/Mtgs.
- Private Parties
- Accommodations

In the Broadway play *Brigadoon*, an enchanted village appears on the Scottish moors for a single day each century, then disappears for another 100 years. In the geographic center of Marin County, the little town of Nicasio must look like a Brigadoon to the frazzled city dwellers who often happen upon it during rambling weekend drives. Fortunately, Nicasio, set in a secluded valley and surrounded by grassy hills, woods and placidly grazing ranch animals, never fades from view (except, perhaps, on the rare foggy day). Although travelers who discover it leave reluctantly, they're consoled by the thought that this little country retreat is only half an hour away from the clamor of Highway 101.

Often they come back to get married, heading straight for Rancho Nicasio, the town's heart and soul. You can't miss it: Set at the north side of Nicasio's New England-style town square, Rancho Nicasio is the busiest and most important building in town. That's because it's the area's all-in-one post office, general store, bar, restaurant and social center. Even without the hubbub surrounding it, Rancho Nicasio's Spanish-style white stucco façade, red trim, sloping tile roof and long porch (where locals invariably gather to schmooze) set it apart from its Victorian neighbors.

Two settings create Rancho Nicasio's appeal for weddings. Indoors, the Rancho Room, with its beautiful wooden ceiling trusses, brass-trimmed fixtures and permanent oak dance floor, has a built-in stage equipped with professional lighting and sound (Rancho Nicasio is West Marin's main live music venue). Curtains on the north wall open to a view of a deep green lawn, a vine-festooned gazebo, a shady grove of pines, and distant pastures, farm buildings and soft-shouldered knolls. There's a touch of whimsy, too: The moose head above the fireplace wears different hats throughout the year.

Just outside the Rancho Room, an open-air deck looks out over Rancho Nicasio's grand lawn, which has been the memorable venue for many a wedding. Remember, Marin has one of the best climates in the world, and Nicasio sits at its sunny center. Couples love exchanging vows outdoors—usually in front of the gazebo—while musicians play across the way on a small stage. Afterwards, guests socialize by the full-service al fresco bar on the lawn's east side, or enjoy the aroma of food cooking on the two big grills next to it. A professional chef provides on-site catering.

Besides the lawn and the Rancho Room, Rancho Nicasio also boasts Marin's quintessential western barroom. There are lots of animal heads on the walls, wagon wheel chandeliers, a long oak bar with glass mirrors, a brick fireplace, dark wood trusses and knotty pine paneling. The bar adjoins a meeting room that has its own private, oak-sheltered deck—a splendid rehearsal dinner location. (There's even a cottage tucked away at the far end of the green that's ideal for the bridal party. It has a tub and shower, full-length mirror, living room and bedroom.)

Locals brag that Rancho Nicasio "is 25 minutes from everywhere." The couples who come here from "everywhere" leave with lifelong memories. They look back on having pledged their love under a canopy of warm country light, enveloped by happy friends and great music. It's just the kind of experience you'd expect to have at Marin's own Brigadoon.

CEREMONY CAPACITY: The lawn holds up to 300 seated guests. Indoors, the Rancho Room holds up to 200 seated guests.

EVENT/RECEPTION CAPACITY: Outdoors, Rancho Nicasio holds 300+ guests; indoors, 200 seated guests.

MEETING CAPACITY: Event spaces hold 30–200 guests for meetings.

FEES & DEPOSITS: A 25% nonrefundable deposit is required to reserve your date and the balance is due on the day of the event. Rental fees start at $500. The rental fees and packages vary depending on the guest count, space rented, the day of the week, time of the event and the time of year. All-inclusive wedding packages range $16,000–20,000 for up to 150 guests. Tax and gratuity are additional.

AVAILABILITY: Year-round, except Christmas and New Year's Days.

SERVICES/AMENITIES:

Catering: provided, no BYO
Kitchen Facilities: n/a
Tables & Chairs: provided
Linens, Silver, etc.: provided
Restrooms: wheelchair accessible
Dance Floor: yes
Bride's Dressing Area: yes
Meeting Equipment: CBA, extra charge
Other: on-site event coordinator, professional sound and lighting technician on staff, on-site music coordinator for assistance with musical entertainment and bands

Parking: on site
Accommodations: no guestrooms
Telephone: pay phones
Outdoor Night Lighting: CBA
Outdoor Cooking Facilities: chefs can prepare buffet on outdoor brick barbecue
Cleanup: provided
View: 5-acre site, panorama of hills and valley, landscaped grounds

RESTRICTIONS:

Alcohol: provided or wine corkage $15/bottle
Smoking: designated outdoor areas only
Music: amplified OK indoors, outdoors CBA, stages available both inside and outside

Wheelchair Access: yes
Insurance: typically not required

Stonetree Golf Club

Golf Club

9 Stonetree Lane, Novato
415/209-6296
www.stonetreegolf.com
ebugg@stonetreegolf.com

● Rehearsal Dinners	● Corp. Events/Mtgs.
● Ceremonies	● Private Parties
● Wedding Receptions	Accommodations

For years, the tree-studded site at Novato's Black Oak Point was where the Bay Area's Renaissance Faire revelers gathered each September to recreate Elizabethan England. These days the area's beautiful oak woods sweep down to the great clubhouse at StoneTree Golf Club. With its stone columns, picture windows, rafter beams and handsome dark furniture, the clubhouse evokes the grand lines of a mountain lodge.

This is a place carefully designed to host weddings and events, indoors or out. The attractive entrance hall sets an elegant tone with its large window at the far end that drinks in the light, and a floor-to-ceiling stone fireplace. Throughout the building, the walls are a warm yellow accented by dark-stained wood. From the hall, guests can head off to the Black Point Bar & Grill or to the Black Oak and Waterfall Salon, the clubhouse's main reception room, or outside to the Sunset Terrace. Some couples use the Black Point Bar & Grill for their ceremony, reciting their vows in front of the picture window. This area is especially popular for winter weddings when the warmth of the fireplace adds to the intimate setting.

The Black Oak and Waterfall Salon is named after a spring-fed waterfall just outside it that tumbles down from the woods to one of three ponds near the base of the clubhouse. Every view from this spacious room is pleasant, ranging from nearby ponds and Black Point's oaks to the intricate stonework alongside the club's main road. The Salon, which can be split into smaller sections, has an adjacent arcaded balcony that's visible through tall windows and accessible through French doors. The balcony's sheltering colonnade, formed by tapering wood pillars set on stone bases, reinforces the feeling of being in a grand lodge.

The Sunset Terrace is a generous patio marked by trellises and exquisitely crafted stone walls. Its view takes in the golf course below, and a panorama that extends from Mt. Tamalpais and the San Rafael hills to the south, all the way north to Novato's wooded ridges and Black Point's oak woods. The golf course undulates over terrain that's an artful mix of sharply manicured greens and natural vegetation. Wedding parties often begin with a ceremony and/or cocktail hour on the Sunset Terrace, then move to the Black Oak and Waterfall Salon for dinner. The Sunset Terrace is also perfect for a casual rehearsal lunch or dinner.

With architecture that inspires but never overwhelms, StoneTree Golf Club makes people feel that they're part of a grand occasion. That sensibility, combined with beautiful views and masterful catering, makes this facility a prime prospect among North Bay wedding venues.

CEREMONY CAPACITY: The Terrace holds 250 seated or 300 standing guests.

EVENT/RECEPTION CAPACITY: The Black Oak Salon seats 70 guests; the Waterfall Salon seats 130. Combined they accommodate 200 guests with space for a dance floor.

MEETING CAPACITY: The Black Oak and Waterfall Salon holds up to 220 seated guests.

FEES & DEPOSITS: 20% of the estimated total is required when the contract is signed. The balance is due 14 days prior to the event. Wedding packages start at $75/person. Tax, alcohol and service fee are additional. There are no fees for room rental, cake cutting or dance floor.

AVAILABILITY: Year-round, daily 6am–midnight, except Christmas Day.

SERVICES/AMENITIES:

Catering: provided
Kitchen Facilities: n/a
Tables & Chairs: provided
Linens, Silver, etc.: provided
Restrooms: wheelchair accessible
Dance Floor: portable provided
Bride's & Groom's Dressing Area: yes
Meeting Equipment: CBA, extra fee

Parking: 2 large complimentary lots
Accommodations: no guestrooms
Telephone: pay phones
Outdoor Night Lighting: yes
Outdoor Cooking Facilities: CBA
Cleanup: provided
View: coastal range, Mt. Tamalpias, Mt. Burdell, Big Rock Ridge, golf course
Other: coordination CBA

RESTRICTIONS:

Alcohol: provided, or BYO with corkage fee
Smoking: outdoor designated areas
Music: amplified OK indoors, OK outdoors until 10pm

Wheelchair Access: yes
Insurance: not required
Other: no rice, confetti, birdseed or sparklers; limited real flower petals are permitted

Unity Center

Chapel and Banquet/Events Facility

600 Palm Drive, Hamilton Center, Novato
415/475-5000
www.unityinmarin.com
events@unityinmarin.com

● Rehearsal Dinners	● Corp. Events/Mtgs.
● Ceremonies	● Private Parties
● Wedding Receptions	Accommodations

Step back in time to the sun-kissed days when California belonged to Spain and town centers displayed flowing fountains, colonnades, bell towers, gardens and charming baroque façades. The Unity Center invites you to do just that. Nestled in the rolling hills of southern Novato, this Marin County wedding venue includes a chapel; the spacious Unity Hall for receptions; a commercial kitchen; and a lawn and courtyard with fountain, garden and shaded colonnade.

The chapel, which blends pleasingly with the Spanish Colonial-style buildings in the adjacent town center, is surrounded by roses, wisteria, palms and a broad lawn. Its charming interior welcomes ceremonies and/or receptions, with light-colored walls and cushioned chairs for flexible seating. Windows line the top of each side wall, bringing in views of the ever-changing sky. Pendant chandeliers, suspended from a spectacular exposed-wood-beam ceiling, cast up and down lighting. The room's ambiance is further enhanced by an ethereal half-dome ceiling over the maple-floored chancel/stage area.

The balcony is backlit by a colorful stained-glass window with an arch of clear glass beneath it. Old pews from the original Hamilton Chapel have been restored for additional seating. To the side, a state-of-the-art media booth controls a world-class sound system, theater lights and a rear-lit projection screen. The 8' x 10' screen, designed to be a discreet architectural element over the chancel area, appears as an opaque window when not in use. With this sophisticated AV system, you can project favorite photos, engagement pictures, videos or background images prior to or during the ceremony or reception.

In the vestibule area, there's a soundproof family or "cry" room. This carpeted area has a picture window that allows families with babies or crying children a comfortable place from which to view the ceremony. Adjoining the chapel is a bride's room with its own bathroom and full-length mirror, perfect for treasured moments of privacy and as a place to change before and after the wedding.

Unity Hall is ideal for receptions and banquets, and can also be partitioned into four smaller meeting rooms. Floor-to-ceiling windows and multiple doors offer views of the courtyard, while other windows look out to the back hillside. The countertops and granite serving counter work well for buffets, and the adjacent full-size commercial kitchen—with all new appliances—can accommodate any caterer.

Outdoor weddings are easily arranged here because Unity, in a masterstroke, added a grassy courtyard with a fountain as its centerpiece, then built a covered walkway to enclose it. With unobtrusive built-in lighting and sound, the courtyard can be used any time of day.

The campus' newest addition is the Meditation Garden, a beautiful backdrop for photos. A wisteria-covered trellis beckons you down a winding path through naturally landscaped gardens. Wooden benches along the way encourage you to relax and enjoy the surrounding native trees, flowers and greenery.

Unity Center is both romantic and spiritually uplifting. When you come by for a visit, take a moment to sit on a bench near the fountain and appreciate how deftly this venue has melded past and present together. We think its combination of carefully rendered classical Mission architecture and cutting-edge facilities is hard to beat.

CEREMONY CAPACITY: Several spaces accommodate 50–300 seated guests.

EVENT/RECEPTION CAPACITY: Unity Center can accommodate 80–210 seated or 150–275 standing guests indoors, and 80–300 seated or 400 standing outdoors.

MEETING CAPACITY: The chapel holds up to 300 seated theater-style, 200 for a sit-down banquet or up to 80 seated classroom-style. Unity Hall holds up to 145 seated theater-style, 120 for a sit-down banquet or 50 seated conference-style.

FEES & DEPOSITS: 50% of the rental fee is required to reserve your date. The rental balance and a $150–900 refundable security deposit are due 30 days prior to the event. Rental fees range $1,200–3,900 depending on spaces selected, date of the event and guest count. Catering packages with preferred vendors start at $120/person and include: full use of Unity Center; several menu options to fit your taste and budget; beverage and coffee service; linens; table service; wedding cake; DJ; professionally attired waitstaff and banquet coordination.

AVAILABILITY: Year-round, daily, 7am–10pm; extended hours can be negotiated.

SERVICES/AMENITIES:
Catering: provided, or BYO licensed and full-service
Kitchen Facilities: commercial, fully equipped
Tables & Chairs: CBA
Linens, Silver, etc.: BYO or caterer
Restrooms: wheelchair accessible
Dance Floor: CBA
Bride's Dressing Area: yes
Meeting Equipment: WiFi internet access, state-of-the-art AV, lighting and sound available, extra fee

Parking: ample, complimentary
Accommodations: no guestrooms, hotels nearby
Telephone: office phone
Outdoor Night Lighting: yes
Outdoor Cooking Facilities: no
Cleanup: renter or caterer
View: courtyard and Novato hills
Other: ministers available

RESTRICTIONS:
Alcohol: BYO or through caterer
Smoking: designated areas only
Music: amplified OK indoors, outdoors with limits

Wheelchair Access: yes
Insurance: liability required

This is important! Tell locations you're reading HERE COMES THE GUIDE and ask if our information is still current.

183

Point Reyes Seashore Lodge
and Restaurant

10021 Coastal Highway One, Olema
415/663-9000

www.pointreyesseashore.com
lodgekeeper@pointreyesseashore.com

Lodge, Restaurant & Retreat

- Rehearsal Dinners
- Ceremonies
- Wedding Receptions
- Corp. Events/Mtgs.
- Private Parties
- Accommodations

With a setting you're likely to see in one of those gorgeous photographic coffee table books, the lodge has long maintained a reputation as a terrific romantic hideaway. It's on one of the prettiest sections of the Northern California coast, flanked by giant redwoods and Point Reyes National Seashore Park. Many of its guestrooms feature fireplaces and whirlpool tubs with pastoral views of the lodge's landscaped grounds and the park's meadows and mountains beyond (yes, you can see the view from the tub!). Given its natural appeal, the lodge increases its romantic possibilities by not only hosting weddings and receptions, but by offering your family, friends and guests the opportunity to have an exclusive retreat for a long weekend celebration.

With the lodge as a backdrop and the expansive, sloping lawn and blooming English garden of the hotel grounds before you, outdoor weddings here are a special treat. You can tie the knot under the branches of a blossoming magnolia tree, or beneath any one of the mature olive, oak and shady alder trees that border the grounds.

For smaller weddings consider the lodge's Casa Olema Retreat, which includes a cottage and lawn. Walk down a flagstone path behind the lodge and under a redwood arch, and you'll be in a separate grass-covered area, surrounded by a formal herb and flower garden and apple, fig, pear and magnolia trees. On one side of the lawn is an arbor containing a built-in table and benches. Crafted from the lodge's trademark golden fir and thickly draped with ivy, it's a charming setting. For larger gatherings, you can set up tables and chairs on the lawn itself.

For small weddings held midweek, the delightful Creekside Cottage, located right on Olema Creek, is ideal for up to 10 people.

Adjoining the lodge is the 1865 Historic Farm House Restaurant, Bar and Deli. In addition to being available for rehearsal dinners and post-wedding brunches, it's an option for intimate indoor weddings. When the weather's warm you can also get married outside on the restaurant's Clemente Garden Patio, which is bordered by a lawn and the Olema Creek.

Included with the rental of the main lodge, the Casa Olema cottage provides both a small kitchen for caterers and a bride's dressing room. Plush furnishings, a fir-manteled fireplace and wainscoting create a room as quaint and personable as any one of the lodge's guestrooms. The cottage's eight-person outdoor hot tub, set within an enclosed brick patio, is a relaxing treat for bride and groom or members of the wedding party. You'll have the exclusive use of its cozy breakfast room, where you can warm yourself in front of a massive stone fireplace, and the downstairs game room, outfitted with an antique billiard table. If you're inviting out-of-town guests, there are also 21 quiet and restful rooms, all with private baths. The Point Reyes Seashore Lodge makes it possible to combine getting married and getting away in one of the state's most scenic and secluded areas.

CEREMONY CAPACITY: The main lawn behind the Lodge holds 150 seated or standing guests.

EVENT/RECEPTION CAPACITY: The Casa Olema Retreat lawn accommodates 150 seated or standing for a variety of events. Tents may be advisable depending on weather conditions. The Farm House can accommodate up to 100 guests.

MEETING CAPACITY: The Casa Olema Retreat holds 20 seated conference-style or 25 theater-style; the Creekside Cottage holds 10 for meetings. The Farm House Restaurant's Park Room holds 40 guests conference-style and 50 theater-style.

FEES & DEPOSITS: For weddings or special events, 50% of the rental fee is the nonrefundable deposit required to secure your date. The rental fee (which ensures exclusive use of the entire Lodge and grounds for your event) ranges $3,500–5,000 and includes tables and chairs and 2 nights' lodging at the Casa Olema Cottage. A $500 cleaning/damage deposit and a certificate of insurance are due 8 weeks prior to the event. There is some flexibility in fees for midweek ceremonies and receptions. There is a fee if you bring in your own caterer.

For business functions, fees are based upon date reserved, number of rooms booked and services requested. Please call for rates.

AVAILABILITY: Mid-May through mid-October, weather permitting. A 6-hour block (1pm–7pm) is allowed for ceremonies and receptions.

SERVICES/AMENITIES:

Catering: provided by *Farm House Restaurant* or select from preferred list
Kitchen Facilities: prep only
Tables & Chairs: provided
Linens, Silver, etc.: BYO
Restrooms: not wheelchair accessible
Dance Floor: provided, extra charge
Bride's Dressing Area: yes
Meeting Equipment: VCR, TV, projector and screen, flip charts; secretarial services CBA

Parking: ample
Accommodations: 21 guestrooms, 2 cottages
Telephone: in guestrooms; pay phone nearby
Outdoor Night Lighting: access only
Outdoor Cooking Facilities: BBQ
Cleanup: caterer or renter
View: coastal mountains, creek, meadows

RESTRICTIONS:

Alcohol: provided by *Farm House Restaurant*
Smoking: outdoors only
Music: acoustic only

Wheelchair Access: limited
Insurance: certificate required
Other: no confetti, rice or birdseed

Marin Art & Garden Center

Art Center & Garden

30 Sir Francis Drake Boulevard, Ross
415/454-1301
www.magc.org
rental@magc.org

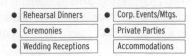

● Rehearsal Dinners	● Corp. Events/Mtgs.
● Ceremonies	● Private Parties
● Wedding Receptions	Accommodations

The Marin Art & Garden Center, an eleven-acre historic estate in the exclusive town of Ross, is a dream come true for anyone seeking exquisitely landscaped gardens and a serene, private atmosphere. Within these lush, tree-shaded grounds are various indoor and outdoor sites available for weddings, parties, meetings, workshops and other special events.

The Livermore Pavilion is a wonderful venue for large events. Spacious and airy, it offers an uninterrupted view of the gardens through a wall of windows. Rustic stone gas-jet fireplaces add warmth both inside the room and on the adjoining deck, which is shaded by an attractive awning. The Pavilion is air-conditioned and can be divided into two smaller spaces, making it ideal for corporate meetings. Two AV screens are available on request.

The inviting Garden Room opens to an expansive garden area. When the weather is warm, you won't be able to resist having your event outside. The garden is enclosed by ivy-covered walls, live oaks, redwoods and Japanese maples. Below these trees huge mossy boulders, heavenly bamboo and flourishing shrubs heighten the woodsy atmosphere. A lava rock fountain whispers to itself in one corner; a Japanese stone lantern sits serenely in another. Tables with white umbrellas provide seating in the sun-dappled center of the space. Buffet service or a string quartet can be set up on a slightly raised area, shaded by redwoods. Evening events are made magical by discreet lighting and the bubbling fountain.

The room itself is elegant, yet relaxed. French doors and generous skylights bring in plenty of light, and connect you visually to the garden. Faux-finished walls, painted in a montage of Impressionist-style colors, extend the garden feeling. Other tasteful features include a fireplace and glass wall sconces twined with metal grapevines. The room opens to a diminutive brick-walled flower garden containing a patio, rose and camellia bushes, and a seashell fountain. Though most couples exchange vows elsewhere on the Center grounds, intimate weddings can be accommodated here, too.

For couples getting married at the Center, the woodsy grounds offer a host of attractive ceremony sites. The Fountain area is perfect for an outdoor ceremony, reception or party. Here, a large fountain pool sends its glittering spray into the air. A floral rainbow of daylilies, blue catnip, verbena, Santa Barbara daisies and iris blooms around the fountain, all enclosed by an aggregate-concrete path. On one side, a forest of mature elms, Lombardy poplars, deodar cedars and honey locusts forms a backdrop behind a curving wooden bench beneath a pergola. To the left, couples tie the knot in the Memory Garden, a shady glade decorated with garden ornaments. Other spots for ceremonies include the Magnolia Tree Lawn and the Gazebo Lawn, a large swath of velvety grass graced by a rare dawn redwood, elm and horse chestnut trees.

Though its fabulous gardens and tranquil atmosphere make the Marin Art & Garden Center seem a world away, it's centrally located near Highway 101, and only 20 minutes from San Francisco. When you have your event here, you not only have a chance to "get away from it all," you also experience a little piece of Paradise close to home.

If you want to contact Marin Art and Garden Center by mail, the address is P.O. Box 437, Ross, CA 94957.

CEREMONY CAPACITY: Indoor and outdoor spaces can seat 300+ guests.

EVENT/RECEPTION CAPACITY: The center can accommodate 200 seated or 300 standing guests indoors.

MEETING CAPACITY: The Livermore Pavilion holds 200+ guests seated classroom-style or 225 guests theater-style and the Garden Room seats 80 guests theater-style.

FEES & DEPOSITS: Half of the total rental fee is required to secure your date; the rental balance and a $500 refundable cleaning/security deposit are due 1 month prior to the function. Rental fees range $1,000–7,000 depending on space selected and date of event. Use of additional areas runs an extra $500. Rates for weekday meetings start at $150.

AVAILABILITY: Year-round, weekends, 8am–11pm at the Livermore Pavilion and in the Garden Room.

SERVICES/AMENITIES:

Catering: BYO licensed and certified
Kitchen Facilities: ample, fully equipped
Tables & Chairs: provided
Linens, Silver, etc.: BYO or through caterer
Restrooms: wheelchair accessible
Dance Floor: yes
Bride's Dressing Area: yes
Meeting Equipment: sound systems, AV screens, mics, wireless internet

Parking: large lot
Accommodations: no guestrooms
Telephone: pay phone
Outdoor Night Lighting: access only
Outdoor Cooking Facilities: no
Cleanup: through caterer or renter
View: gardens, pond, hills, Mt. Tamalpias
Other: security guard CBA

RESTRICTIONS:

Alcohol: BYO
Smoking: outdoors only
Music: amplified OK with restrictions

Wheelchair Access: yes
Insurance: liability required
Other: no rice or birdseed; decorations restricted

San Francisco Theological Seminary

105 Seminary Drive, San Anselmo
800/447-8820 x836

www.sfts.edu/rentals
hliencres@sfts.edu

- Rehearsal Dinners
- Ceremonies
- Wedding Receptions
- Corp. Events/Mtgs.
- Private Parties
- Accommodations

When they first see a photograph of this place, many people remark that it looks like a castle on a wooded Scottish brae or a medieval village in central Europe. It's easy to understand why this seminary on a hill evokes such romantic associations. First there's Montgomery Memorial Chapel, a graceful stone church near the seminary's main entrance that is one of its two most popular wedding sites. Then, up the hill, there's Stewart Memorial Chapel at Geneva Hall, a splendid white church with an arcade, a soaring campanile, a terrace that overlooks a breathtaking view, and stained-glass windows whose intense colors rival those of Europe's cathedrals.

In between the two ceremony venues is a tree-shaded campus with grand lawns, weathered moss-covered stone walls, classrooms, Victorian homes for faculty members and rock-faced administration buildings that evoke the allure of historic citadels. The most popular reception site is the Geneva Hall terrace, a curving sweep of stone that provides one of the most stunning panoramas in Marin: the north flank of Mt. Tamalpais; Ross Township's redwood-covered ridges; Red Hill; the seminary's signature stone academic buildings; and views down the Ross Valley.

There's a more prosaic form of beauty here, too: Because the seminary is a religious nonprofit entity, it can offer its beautiful grounds and facilities at prices that are considered quite competitive by Marin County standards.

The seminary has another deal sweetener—a Victorian home available for small prenuptial parties or a pre-wedding stay. You can rest overnight at the seminary, then awaken fresh the next morning, knowing you don't have to travel anywhere for the big day. The seminary also has a 28-room dorm-style retreat center, which allows close friends and family to lodge together. Keeping so many of your loved ones nearby makes it easy to turn your wedding into a destination weekend.

Besides a choice of romantic chapels and the campus' overall enticing feel, couples also like the unlimited parking and almost universal accessibility for their disabled guests. This site is like a good day that just keeps getting better. First, the drive here takes you through some of Marin's loveliest, leafiest neighborhoods, and then the campus itself charms you with its meandering lanes, compelling architecture and one-of-a-kind vistas in a county famous for its views. Once it wins you over, any other venue just won't feel as right.

CEREMONY, EVENT/RECEPTION & MEETING CAPACITY: This location holds up to 110 seated or standing guests indoors and up to 170 seated or standing guests outdoors.

FEES & DEPOSITS: A nonrefundable deposit of 50% of the estimated event total is required to reserve your date. The balance is due 2 months prior to the event. Rental fees range $800–2,900 depending on the space rented.

AVAILABILITY: Year-round. Call for details.

SERVICES/AMENITIES:

Catering: BYO
Kitchen Facilities: none
Tables & Chairs: provided
Linens, Silver, etc.: through caterer
Restrooms: wheelchair accessible
Dance Floor: through caterer
Bride's & Groom's Dressing Area: yes
Meeting Equipment: some provided

Parking: large lot or on-street
Accommodations: 33 guestrooms
Telephone: no
Outdoor Night Lighting: access only
Outdoor Cooking Facilities: no
Cleanup: caterer or renter
View: mountains, meadow, garden, forest
Other: pianos, picnic area, AV equipment

RESTRICTIONS:

Alcohol: through caterer
Smoking: not allowed
Music: amplified OK indoors and outdoors with restrictions

Wheelchair Access: yes
Insurance: liability required

Overwhelmed? Use the search criteria on www.HereComesTheGuide.com to narrow down your choices.

Falkirk Mansion

1408 Mission Avenue, San Rafael
415/485-3328
www.falkirkculturalcenter.org
beth.goldberg@ci.san-rafael.ca.us

Historic Mansion

- Rehearsal Dinners
- Ceremonies
- Wedding Receptions
- Corp. Events/Mtgs.
- Private Parties
- Accommodations

Magnificent oaks and magnolias frame the historic Falkirk Mansion, a lovely Queen Anne Victorian in the heart of Marin. Built in 1888, the house is the creation of Clinton Day, the architect who designed the Stanford University campus chapel. In keeping with the style of the day, it has a complex and intriguing roof line of gables and chimneys, variously shaped bays and plenty of decorative details.

The property was purchased in 1906 by Captain Robert Dollar, a Scotsman who'd made his fortune in timber and shipping. He added many features to the estate, including the brick steps and pond, rolling lawns, the greenhouse and a carriage house. A civic-minded man, he donated generously to both San Rafael and his hometown of Falkirk, Scotland—hence the name of the Mansion.

Today, Falkirk Cultural Center serves as a historic site, contemporary art gallery, cultural and educational center, as well as a popular spot for weddings. You can have your ceremony in the outdoor Wedding Garden, on the sprawling lawns or in the parlor. The Mansion's interior is beautifully rendered in rich redwood paneling, and features ornate mantelpieces, hardwood floors and elegant wall coverings. When you reserve the Mansion, you have use of the entire first floor. The foyer has a huge decorative fireplace and floor-to-ceiling stained-glass windows. Have your reception indoors or, during warmer months, dine and dance on the veranda. This secluded wooden porch is enclosed by camellia bushes and an ancient oak. It doesn't matter how you orchestrate your wedding, Falkirk will imbue it with intimacy and a century's worth of Victorian charm.

CEREMONY CAPACITY: The Parlor holds 50 seated or 75 standing; outdoors the site can accommodate 125 seated guests.

EVENT/RECEPTION CAPACITY: October–April, standing capacity is 100; seated capacity 50–60 guests. April–October, the house and veranda hold up to 125 guests.

MEETING CAPACITY: Indoors, the venue holds 60 seated theater-style or 20 seated conference-style; outdoors it holds 80 seated theater-style.

FEES & DEPOSITS: Half of the rental fee is a nonrefundable deposit required to reserve your date. Weekend rates for a 6-hour minimum block are $1,800 from April 15 to October 14, and $1,200 from October 15 to April 14. Additional charges will apply for overtime hours. A refundable $500 security deposit and any remaining balance are payable 45 days in advance of your event. Weekday rates vary; call for more information. Special rates can be arranged for nonprofits.

AVAILABILITY: Year-round, Saturdays and Sundays 1pm–11pm. Weekdays 9am–11pm by arrangement.

SERVICES/AMENITIES:

Catering: select from approved list or BYO

Kitchen Facilities: minimal

Tables & Chairs: provided

Linens, Silver, etc.: BYO

Restrooms: wheelchair accessible

Dance Floor: no

Bride's Dressing Area: yes

Meeting Equipment: limited

Parking: large public lot

Accommodations: no guestrooms

Telephone: emergency use only

Outdoor Night Lighting: yes

Outdoor Cooking Facilities: no

Cleanup: caterer

View: wooded park and grounds

RESTRICTIONS:

Alcohol: BYO

Smoking: restricted area only

Music: amplified OK to 90 decibels

Wheelchair Access: yes

Insurance: extra liability required

Other: no candles, decorations restricted

Osher Marin Jewish Community Center

Community Center

200 North San Pedro Road, San Rafael
415/444-8084
www.marinjcc.org
pday@marinjcc.org

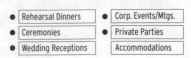

- Rehearsal Dinners
- Ceremonies
- Wedding Receptions
- Corp. Events/Mtgs.
- Private Parties
- Accommodations

When this long-anticipated architectural gem opened in 1991, it was an immediate hit with Marin County residents. It continues to be one of the county's main social hubs, with a constant stream of people attending exercise classes, lectures, dances, theatrical productions and parties. It's also one of Marin's favorite places to hold a wedding, and just one look at this facility's design tells you why.

Set at the base of a high forested ridge, this three-story Craftsman-style building is a masterpiece of exquisite proportions and detailing—including one of the Bay Area's most beautiful interior staircases.

Its façade, screened by maple trees, is faced with brick on the bottom and finished with a smooth, soft beige stucco on the top. Rust-red window sashes and rain gutters complete the building's subdued exterior palette. Inside, past the reception area, are three contiguous spaces that form the nucleus of the JCC's wedding venue: the Hoytt Theater, an enclosed atrium that opens to a garden courtyard and the impressive Main Hall that connects them.

The Theater, with its broad stage, extensive seating area and professional sound and lighting equipment, is a flexible space suitable for ceremonies, receptions and dinners. Its sconces and light fixtures, which resemble white pyramids stacked upside down upon one another, give it an Art Deco look. For event coordinators this place is like catnip: one whiff of its ample size and high-level amenities, and their imaginations start buzzing with ideas. The venue is a classy blank slate that lends itself to almost any theme, and dresses up beautifully for a wedding.

Just outside the Theater, the terracotta-paved Main Hall has a peaked 30-foot ceiling of white tiles, supported by light-colored wood trusses. A row of glass doors along one wall leads into the spacious Kurland Center, which can be used as one large room, or can be closed off with movable walls to create three separate spaces. The central area, filled with natural light, opens onto the intimate garden courtyard.

Then there's the JCC's most compelling interior feature: the Elaine Rosenberg Stairway. This grand staircase has to be one of the Bay Area's loveliest. It curves out in wide welcome at the bottom, then narrows and climbs, first to a spacious mezzanine landing and then up to the facility's lofty top floor. The stairway ascends so steeply (a clever visual trick) that you get the impression it's aspiring to reach Heaven itself. Many brides can't resist descending this remarkable flight of steps during their pre- or post-ceremonial entrances.

Management here is fond of saying, "This isn't your grandmother's JCC," and they're right. Grandma never had access to such an architecturally satisfying, state-of-the-art facility. And her JCC probably didn't have this community center's reputation for hospitality, either. While the Osher Marin JCC is set up to accommodate pre-wedding minyans and other traditional Jewish activities, it is a famously "come one, come all" place. It doesn't matter who you are; when you're here, you *are* somebody.

CEREMONY CAPACITY: The Hoytt Theater holds up to 500 seated guests; outdoors, the courtyard holds up to 150 seated guests.

EVENT/RECEPTION CAPACITY: The Hoytt Theater holds up to 265 seated or 650 standing guests; outdoors, the courtyard holds up to 150 seated or 200 standing guests. The Kurland Center holds up to 185 seated or 200 standing guests.

MEETING CAPACITY: The Hoytt Theater holds up to 500 guests; the Kurland Center accommodates up to 200 guests.

FEES & DEPOSITS: A $750 deposit is required to reserve your date. The balance is due 1 month prior to the event. Rental fees range $450–4,500 depending on space rented.

AVAILABILITY: Year-round, daily, 4pm–midnight on weekends, 6pm–midnight on weekdays.

SERVICES/AMENITIES:

Catering: BYO
Kitchen Facilities: fully equipped, no catering equipment
Tables & Chairs: provided
Linens, Silver, etc.: BYO or through caterer
Restrooms: wheelchair accessible
Dance Floor: yes
Bride's Dressing Area: yes
Meeting Equipment: yes

Parking: large lot
Accommodations: no guestrooms
Telephone: pay phone
Outdoor Night Lighting: yes
Outdoor Cooking Facilities: no
Cleanup: renter or caterer
View: garden patio
Other: internet access

RESTRICTIONS:

Alcohol: BYO
Smoking: not allowed
Music: amplified OK

Wheelchair Access: yes
Insurance: extra liability required

Palm Ballroom at the Seafood Peddler

Waterfront Restaurant

100 Yacht Club Drive, San Rafael
415/460-6669
www.seafoodpeddler.com
lisa@seafoodpeddler.com

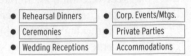

● Rehearsal Dinners	● Corp. Events/Mtgs.
● Ceremonies	● Private Parties
● Wedding Receptions	Accommodations

The Palm Ballroom is located in scenic Marin County on the San Rafael Canal, framed by a sweeping view of the oak-studded hills of San Rafael. The draw of the Palm Ballroom is that it's a plush banquet hall—the kind of space usually only found in a large hotel—directly connected to the Seafood Peddler, a fresh seafood restaurant that has been voted Marin's Best Seafood Restaurant for seven years by the *Pacific Sun's* readers.

"We host weddings, rehearsal dinners, dances, holiday events, monthly groups, seminars and retirement parties," says the Banquet Manager. "Any event that needs a spacious room and superb, made-to-order food." People often comment after a Palm Ballroom event: "I can't remember the last time I've had a hot meal at a banquet that was actually served hot!"

The Palm Ballroom's exceptional service will ensure that your wedding and reception will go off without a hitch. They offer a customizable menu and are happy to help you select a compatible vintage from their extensive wine list. Their all-inclusive wedding package covers virtually every detail. "There aren't too many one-stop facilities like us," the Banquet Manager observes. "We customize everything—colors, linens, bar setups, seating arrangements, and even stationery."

The Palm Ballroom has a separate entrance from the restaurant. As you walk through the double French doors, you notice the unique light fixtures designed by a local artist. Matching wall sconces cast a soft glow on the custom wallpaper, a frieze of stylized light olive palm trees on a desert sand-colored background. The room has several live palm trees that can be moved to change the mood and layout. French doors on the back wall lead out to a small latticework patio, where people can take a break from the festivities. Plush red velvet stage curtains serve as an excellent backdrop for the wedding party. The full-service bar in the corner invites a lively flow of guests through the room.

The Waterfront Patio with its flower-lined arbor is a lovely spot for a wedding ceremony next to the water. Smaller events are held in the Waterfront Room, an informal second-floor space with huge picture windows that's great for dancing, banquets or cocktail parties. The cozy Chart Room is popular for showers, board meetings and small rehearsal dinners.

With its beautifully appointed banquet room and personalized services, the Palm Ballroom has developed a loyal following in the North Bay. They believe in giving clients flawless, memorable events. "We don't have a set formula for doing parties," promises the Banquet Manager. "Everything we do here is customized."

CEREMONY CAPACITY: The Patio holds up to 150 seated guests.

EVENT/RECEPTION & MEETING CAPACITY: The Palm Room holds 220 seated or 350 standing guests, the Waterfront Room 100 seated or 150 standing guests and the Chart Room up to 45 seated or 80 standing guests. For outdoor events, the Waterfront Patio accommodates up to 150 seated or 200 standing guests.

FEES & DEPOSITS: A $600 deposit is required to reserve your date. The event balance is payable 10 days before the event. For events taking place in the Palm Ballroom, a $350 rental fee applies and includes setup, linens, a full-service bar and professional staff, candles and cordless microphones.

AVAILABILITY: Year-round, daily, 11am–2am.

SERVICES/AMENITIES:

Catering: provided
Kitchen Facilities: n/a
Tables & Chairs: provided
Linens, Silver, etc.: provided
Restrooms: wheelchair accessible
Dance Floor: yes
Bride's Dressing Area: yes
Meeting Equipment: podium and projection screen

Parking: ample
Accommodations: no guestrooms
Telephone: emergency use only
Outdoor Night Lighting: yes
Outdoor Cooking Facilities: no
Cleanup: provided
View: bay outlet, harbor and hills
Other: event coordination; elevated stage with theater lighting

RESTRICTIONS:

Alcohol: provided, or wine corkage $12/bottle
Smoking: outdoors only
Music: amplified OK

Wheelchair Access: limited
Insurance: not required
Other: no rice, confetti, birdseed, no open flames

Unitarian Universalist Congregation of Marin

Church

240 Channing Way, San Rafael
415/479-4131
www.uumarin.org
events@uumarin.org

- Rehearsal Dinners
- Ceremonies
- Wedding Receptions
- Corp. Events/Mtgs.
- Private Parties
- Accommodations

Exploring Marin County can be a lifetime passion, especially as you discover the region's wonderful hidden vistas, many of which are seldom publicized in guidebooks and tourist literature. One of those little-known views can be enjoyed at the Unitarian Universalist Congregation of Marin. From its hilltop setting high above Terra Linda, the center offers a grand panorama of the north flank of Mt. Tamalpais that most people will never see.

Superb as the view is, the heart of this venue is a simple, tranquil courtyard, graced by a grove of mulberry trees whose broad leaves spread bountiful shade over a lush lawn. A curving three-level terrace rises toward an arbor-topped knoll along two sides of the space, and an ornamental pool and fountain in the center teems with goldfish and water lilies. Water gurgles over a sandstone ledge and spills into the pool creating a calming, almost musical sound.

Beginning at the courtyard, a gravel path winds up past flowers, herbs and succulents to a flagstone-paved area on top of the knoll. With a tall oak and an arbor as backdrops, this is a compelling spot for photos. From this height you can see a quintessential Marin panorama: Terra Linda and Mt. Tam to the west and southwest; the wooded hills that run south of Santa Venetia from Civic Center to China Camp; and a commanding view of San Pablo Bay.

The center's Fellowship Hall is the most popular site for dining and dancing (or for winter indoor ceremonies). It has a high ceiling of pine beams and rafters, an oak floor and picture windows on three sides, including one that looks out over Terra Linda and that impressive Mt. Tam view. The more modest Fireside Room is warm and intimate, ideal for a small wedding or reception. Its focal point is a tall sandstone-faced fireplace, flanked by picture windows that look out to a dense oak wood. The room has direct access to the courtyard, and in winter a roaring fire makes it especially inviting. Whichever space you use, your guests can party till 11pm.

Caterers will find counter space galore and a professional range in the large kitchen, and UUCM is happy to refer brides to a preferred list of seasoned vendors.

Their first look at the courtyard is usually all it takes to convince many brides to get married here. But if more reasons are needed, the center's great views, affordability, and beautiful setting quickly clinch their decision.

CEREMONY CAPACITY: The Courtyard holds up to 200 seated guests; the Fellowship Hall up to 250.

EVENT/RECEPTION CAPACITY: The Courtyard accommodates up to 200 seated or 250 standing guests; the Fellowship Hall up to 200 seated or 320 standing.

MEETING CAPACITY: The Fellowship Hall holds 12–250 seated guests.

FEES & DEPOSITS: For a wedding, a $900 deposit is required to reserve your date. The package fee is due 4 weeks prior to the event. Packages range $1,750–2,750 depending on the space rented and the day and time of the event. There is a 25% discount for November–March weddings. Hourly rental of the facility is also available, call for pricing. Packages include use of entire facility, attendant, tables and indoor chairs (for up to 150 guests), custodial service (setup, breakdown and cleaning). The Saturday wedding package includes use of the facility for a half day the Friday before to decorate, rehearse, etc. Outdoor chairs are not provided. For rentals and other services, select from their preferred vendor list.

AVAILABILITY: Year-round, Monday–Saturday, 7am–11pm and Sunday, 2pm–11pm.

SERVICES/AMENITIES:

Catering: select from preferred list
Kitchen Facilities: fully equipped
Tables & Chairs: provided indoors
Linens, Silver, etc.: BYO or through caterer
Restrooms: wheelchair accessible
Dance Floor: provided
Bride's Dressing Area: yes
Meeting Equipment: some provided

Parking: large lot and on-street
Accommodations: no guestrooms
Telephone: office phone
Outdoor Night Lighting: limited, BYO, CBA
Outdoor Cooking Facilities: BBQ CBA
Cleanup: provided
View: panorama of bay, woods and mountains
Other: grand piano, clergy on staff, picnic area, AV equipment

RESTRICTIONS:

Alcohol: BYO
Smoking: outside only
Music: amplified OK

Wheelchair Access: yes
Insurance: liability required

The professionals in the back of this book are the best in the business. How do we know? Read page 701.

197

Cavallo Point
The Lodge at the Golden Gate

Historic Landmark

601 Murray Circle, Fort Baker, Sausalito

415/339-4709

www.cavallopoint.com
jessica@cavallopoint.com

- Rehearsal Dinners
- Ceremonies
- Wedding Receptions
- Corp. Events/Mtgs.
- Private Parties
- Accommodations

It's been awarded honor status by the National Trust for Historic Preservation; it has LEED Gold Certification from the U.S. Green Building Council; and it's on *Condé Nast Traveler's* "Hot List" and *Travel+Leisure's* Top 10 New Green American Landmarks. History, ecology and luxury all seem to come seamlessly together at Cavallo Point Lodge, the meticulously restored Colonial Revival complex tucked away like a gorgeous surprise at the northern foot of the Golden Gate Bridge.

The views are breathtaking from anywhere on this property set on 75,000 acres of sunny national parkland, but especially from the Mission Blue Chapel. Named after an endangered California butterfly, this pristine, cream-colored structure stands high on a hillside covered with tufted grasses and California native plants. Its adjoining terrace is ideal for light-hearted gatherings, and affords a vista of San Francisco, the sparkling bay, and the towers of the Golden Gate Bridge rising above the pines and eucalyptus through tiaras of clouds.

There are no pews in the chapel, which has large picture windows, gleaming honey-colored floors, and a low stage that make it an excellent setting for anything from a meeting of the minds to a wedding ceremony or reception. But perhaps you'll want to take your celebration outdoors to the Mission Blue Lawn, where your guests can enjoy an elegant hilltop affair or an exchange of vows framed by the incomparable natural panorama.

At the foot of the hill, the Callippe Terrace—named for the endangered Callippe butterfly—is another prime party venue. This one comes with a welcoming fire pit, comfortable seating and a lovely view of historic Fort Baker. Team it up with the Callippe Ballroom and the Callippe Foyer for an ultra-grand indoor-outdoor fête. The foyer alone is roomy enough for cocktails and dancing. Large, lounge-like alcoves flanking the doors add to the sense of grandeur. If you need a place for additional activities, the handsome Silverspot Room on the opposite side of the ballroom can be used as a minitheater, a children's playroom and more.

Not enough possibilities? The lodge offers an amazing 14,000 square feet of adaptable function rooms and formal meeting space. Traipse upstairs to where the balconied Verbena Room and Foyer, La Mariposa Borracha Room and the Cavallo Point Cooking School kitchen multiply ways to maximize your event experience. Imagine serving cocktails or dinner in a graceful salon with fireplace and thrilling wraparound views, or a group lesson in the art of fine cuisine in the warmth of a spotless, professionally equipped, wine country-style kitchen.

Added to all this are day-of accommodations for the bride, a luxurious Healing Arts Center & Spa, the award-winning Murray Circle restaurant, the Farley Bar and a dreamy veranda designed for sitting back and soaking up the wild beauty of the surrounding terrain. You won't want to leave the grounds and you don't have to. The magnificently renovated two-bedroom family-friendly suites and guestrooms and glamorous contemporary lodgings are a great place for you and your guests to settle in and relax for a weekend...or embark on an extended stay full of fun-filled exploration. Rest assured, any journey that begins here is bound to be a glorious one.

CEREMONY CAPACITY: The facility holds 208 seated guests, indoors or outdoors.

EVENT/RECEPTION CAPACITY: The site can accommodate 180 seated or 250 standing indoors, and 325 seated or standing outdoors.

MEETING CAPACITY: Meeting rooms hold 300 seated guests.

FEES & DEPOSITS: 50% of the total event cost is required to reserve your date and the balance is due 30 days prior to the event. Rental fees range $5,000–8,000 depending on the season and the number of guests. Meals, including wine, beer and wedding cake range $208–365/person. Tax, alcohol and a 21% service charge are additional.

AVAILABILITY: Year-round.

SERVICES/AMENITIES:
Catering: provided
Kitchen Facilities: n/a
Tables & Chairs: provided, CBA
Linens, Silver, etc.: provided, CBA
Restrooms: wheelchair accessible
Dance Floor: portable provided
Bride's Dressing Area: yes
Meeting Equipment: provided, CBA
Other: on-site wedding cake, spa services, picnic area

Parking: large lot
Accommodations: 142 guestrooms
Telephone: house phone
Outdoor Night Lighting: CBA
Outdoor Cooking Facilities: BBQ CBA
Cleanup: provided
View: garden patio, landscaped grounds; panorama of fields, hills, cityscape, coastline, forest, mountains, ocean and park

RESTRICTIONS:
Alcohol: BYO with corkage fee
Smoking: designated areas only
Music: OK with restrictions

Wheelchair Access: yes
Insurance: not required

Spinnaker Restaurant

Waterfront Restaurant

100 Spinnaker Drive, Sausalito
415/332-1500
www.thespinnaker.com
jeff@thespinnaker.com

- • Rehearsal Dinners
- • Ceremonies
- • Wedding Receptions
- • Corp. Events/Mtgs.
- • Private Parties
-   Accommodations

The Spinnaker Restaurant, on Sausalito's waterfront, has recently added a spacious new banquet facility to its list of delicious offerings. The new wing is adjacent to the Sausalito Yacht Harbor, and is completely separate from the main dining room. It even has its own kitchen area that caters solely to the new facility. Like the restaurant, the banquet room is partially built on piers over the water, and has floor-to-ceiling glass throughout, a warm interior in shades of cream and rose and the same distinctive wood-slat ceiling. From any spot in the room you have sweeping views that include Belvedere, Angel Island, the Bay Bridge and San Francisco's skyline. Sliding glass doors open onto an adjoining outdoor deck that offers an additional 1,000 square feet of bayside space. From here you can read the names of the boats as they glide past, their colorful spinnakers fluttering and white sails billowing in the breeze.

The banquet room can be set up any way you like. Audiovisual systems are available for business functions, and there is ample space for a band and portable dance floor for wedding receptions and holiday parties. It's also a great setting for a small private affair, such as a bridal shower luncheon or an anniversary or birthday party. Quiet and tasteful, the Spinnaker is an inviting and welcome addition to waterfront dining.

CEREMONY & EVENT/RECEPTION CAPACITY: The deck holds 60 seated or 80 standing, the banquet room 160 seated or 220 standing guests.

MEETING CAPACITY: The Banquet Room holds 200 seated theater-style or 160 seated conference-style.

FEES & DEPOSITS: To reserve your date, a $1,500 nonrefundable deposit is required (which is applied towards the event balance). The food and beverage balance is payable at the event's completion. The food and beverage minimum is $3,000 Monday–Thursday, $4,500 Friday and Sunday, and $8,000 Saturday. In-house catering is provided. Buffets or seated meals run $40–50/person; alcohol, tax and an 18% service charge are additional. A $1,000 room charge, $175 bartending fee and $225 dance floor fee may apply. For ceremonies, there's a $450 setup charge.

For business luncheons and dinners, or for smaller groups, special rates can be arranged.

AVAILABILITY: Year-round, daily, 7am–midnight, in 4-hour blocks.

SERVICES/AMENITIES:

Catering: provided, no BYO
Kitchen Facilities: n/a
Tables & Chairs: provided
Linens, Silver, etc.: provided
Restrooms: wheelchair accessible
Dance Floor: CBA, extra fee
Bride's Dressing Area: no
Meeting Equipment: PA, microphones

Parking: valet parking
Accommodations: no guestrooms
Telephone: pay phone
Outdoor Night Lighting: on deck
Outdoor Cooking Facilities: no
Cleanup: provided
View: San Francisco Bay and bridges
Other: event coordination, cakes, music CBA

RESTRICTIONS:

Alcohol: provided or corkage $14–16/bottle
Smoking: designated areas
Music: amplified OK

Wheelchair Access: yes
Insurance: not required

Stinson Beach Community Center

Community Center & Chapel

32 Belvedere Avenue, Stinson Beach
415/868-1444
www.stinsonbeachcommunitycenter.org
info@stinsonbeachcommunitycenter.org

- Rehearsal Dinners
- Ceremonies
- Wedding Receptions
- Corp. Events/Mtgs.
- Private Parties
- Accommodations

Stinson Beach is one of the Bay Area's natural treasures. This curving stretch of white sand extends three miles along Marin County's Pacific coastline and has a visual advantage many other beaches lack: To reach it, you drive down a scenic mountain road whose views are often as dramatic as those along the French Riviera. But even better than Stinson Beach's gratifying appearance is the little town that has grown up beside it: a quiet seaside community whose very existence is a restorative balm to almost any visitor's hectic life.

This is a beautiful place for a wedding, and the best place to celebrate is at the Stinson Beach Community Center, a building that's been at the heart of Stinson Beach's civic life for decades. Located just off Shoreline Highway, up from the fire station and next door to Stinson Beach Community Church, the Center looks like a small lodge. The exterior is finished with brown wood siding with white trim. Wood predominates inside, too: Three impressive trusses under a ceiling of pine rafters span the Center's large sunny interior, the walls have four-foot-high wainscoting, and the floors are Canadian maple hardwood. Delightful murals of sunlit clouds are painted on the east and west walls, adding a whimsical touch. Across the room from the entrance, the Center's focal point is a tall light-brick fireplace capped with a huge log mantel. On either side of it are large wood-trimmed windows and French doors.

The French doors open out to a patio enveloped by nature. A flower- and bush-lined fence runs along one side, separating it from a gurgling creek edged with fragrant cedars, mulberry trees and pines. While flowerbeds and potted plants adorn the patio, its most compelling visual attribute is a magnificent maple tree whose trunk has grown out horizontally. The trunk—easily 2.5 feet in diameter—runs parallel to the ground for about 20 feet, finally coming to rest on the pavement, where it hurls three long branches 30 feet up into the air. It's an impressive conversation piece, to say the least.

Some couples marry on nearby Stinson Beach, while others opt for a ceremony in the church next to the Center. The church's bright interior of light fir walls and pews soars to pointed arches, and the altar is backed by floor-to-ceiling glass. A mezzanine accommodates an organ and a choir. The church has an intimate feel inside and a small-town look outside, with its wooden siding and steeply angled roof culminating in a little belfry.

Stinson Beach has a best-of-both-worlds air about it. Although it's only a 45-minute drive from San Francisco, it's just far enough removed to possess an enticing away-from-it-all quality. And, it may be just the place to have a memorable, uncomplicated wedding day.

CEREMONY CAPACITY: The Community Center holds 150–200 seated guests with room for 299 standing. The Chapel holds 115 seated guests and up to 130 including standing guests.

EVENT/RECEPTION & MEETING CAPACITY: The Community Center holds 200 seated or 299 standing. Tenting can be arranged to increase capacity.

FEES & DEPOSITS: For special events, a $500 security deposit is required to secure your date. The rental fee ranges $2,300–2,500. The fee includes the full use of the industrial kitchen and a block of time from 8am–midnight. The Chapel rents for $450/day and includes a rehearsal the day prior to the ceremony.

Please call for affordable meeting rates.

AVAILABILITY: Year-round, daily, 8am–midnight.

SERVICES/AMENITIES:

Catering: BYO or CBA
Tables & Chairs: provided, call for details
Kitchen Facilities: new, fully equipped
Linens, Silver, etc.: BYO
Restrooms: wheelchair accessible
Dance Floor: hardwood floor indoors
Bride's Dressing Area: yes
Meeting Equipment: limited, ask for specifics
Other: grand piano, organ

Parking: Center's parking area and on street
Accommodations: nearby hotels and beach house rentals
Telephone: emergency use only
Outdoor Night Lighting: on porch and patio
Outdoor Cooking Facilities: CBA
Cleanup: caterer, basic cleanup provided
View: Stinson Beach hills, part of Mt. Tamalpais

RESTRICTIONS:

Alcohol: BYO
Smoking: outside only
Music: amplified OK until 11pm, call for details

Wheelchair Access: yes
Insurance: certificate required

Want to know WHAT TO ASK a potential location or vendor? Check out our Questions to Ask on page 17.

Corinthian Yacht Club

Historic Yacht Club

43 Main Street, Tiburon
415/435-4812

www.corinthiancatering.com
leila@cyc.org

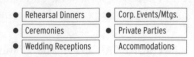

● Rehearsal Dinners	● Corp. Events/Mtgs.	
● Ceremonies	● Private Parties	
● Wedding Receptions	Accommodations	

The setting of the Corinthian Yacht Club is truly spectacular. Even its members, who've been coming here for years, never fail to be awed by its sweeping view. It is easily one of the great panoramas in all of California, taking in Tiburon's rustic downtown, the deep waters of Raccoon Strait, Angel Island's wooded profile, the silvery Bay Bridge, the high hills and towers of San Francisco, Alcatraz's ship-like silhouette, and Belvedere Island's leafy slopes and grand mansions. Only steps away, in the club's harbor, spars and spinnakers bob everywhere, and there's a steady flow of craft setting out to ply the bay or return home from it.

This beloved Marin landmark—a Colonial Revival building with a shimmering white façade and soaring 40-foot namesake columns—could be tempted to let its prime waterfront address do all the work. But the club has never rested on its scenic laurels. "Location, location and location" is matched with a high level of service, thanks to a cadre of employees who have worked exclusively for Corinthian for several years. Their experience shows through in their uncanny ability to anticipate guests' desires, providing little touches that may not be much in the larger scheme of things, but are remembered over the years by grateful clients: glasses that get refilled without prompting; a server conjuring up a bobby pin that saves a bride from a hair disaster.

Corinthian's award-winning kitchen team has worked together for years, and is proud of its menu and flexible pricing. Their attitude reflects the club's client-friendly philosophy: Make the venue highly competitive when it comes to cost and value.

Bridal parties can take over the entire second story, an ensemble of four distinctive spaces that tie wonderfully well together to create a terrific flow. People love to circulate here, knowing that each area they stroll to presents its own visual reward. Start with the Grand Ballroom, a redwood-paneled room with a 22-foot-high ceiling, large stage for musicians, imposing stone fireplace and an oak floor that's ready for dancing no matter how you configure the dining tables. Guests often amble into the adjoining solarium, which runs along one side of the ballroom, and take in Corinthian's dramatic bay view through giant picture windows. (With such an impressive backdrop, the solarium is a favorite site for the cake cutting, too.) It accesses an outdoor deck that not only presents a fine harbor and breakwater view, but can function as a bar or reception area. Both the deck and ballroom have doorways to a separate salon that features a granite-topped bar. The bar's nautical-motif plaques, pendants and photos create an enjoyable clubby feel.

Because it offers access to one of the Bay Area's stellar locales at an affordable rate, Corinthian is a "best of both worlds" proposition. It's nice to know that you don't have to choose between the site and service—your guests will take away fond memories of both.

CEREMONY CAPACITY: The Solarium accommodates 115 seated with additional room for 30 standing guests; the Deck holds 35 seated guests.

EVENT/RECEPTION CAPACITY: The Ballroom holds 250 seated or up to 300 standing guests.

MEETING CAPACITY: The Ballroom seats 300.

FEES & DEPOSITS: A $2,000 deposit is applied towards the total event cost and is required at the time of booking. The facility rental fee ranges $1,500–4,000, depending on your guest count and the date of the event. Fees cover a 5-hour block; extra hours can be negotiated. 80% of the estimated total is due 6 weeks prior to the event, and the balance is due 4 days prior to the event.

Catering is provided; menu prices range $65–85/person, plus a 20% service charge and tax. On average, bar prices range $30–55/person based on consumption, including service and tax.

AVAILABILITY: The Ballroom is available daily 9am–11pm.

SERVICES/AMENITIES:
Catering: provided, no BYO
Kitchen Facilities: n/a
Tables & Chairs: provided
Linens, Silver, etc.: china, silverware, glassware provided; no linens
Restrooms: wheelchair accessible
Dance Floor: yes
Meeting Equipment: limited

Parking: public lot nearby
Accommodations: no guestrooms
Telephone: emergency use only
Outdoor Night Lighting: yes
Outdoor Cooking Facilities: no
Cleanup: provided
View: San Francisco Bay and skyline, Angel Island and Alcatraz

RESTRICTIONS:
Alcohol: provided, or wine and champagne with corkage fee
Smoking: on decks only
Music: amplified OK with volume restrictions

Wheelchair Access: yes, all levels
Insurance: not required
Other: security required

North Coast

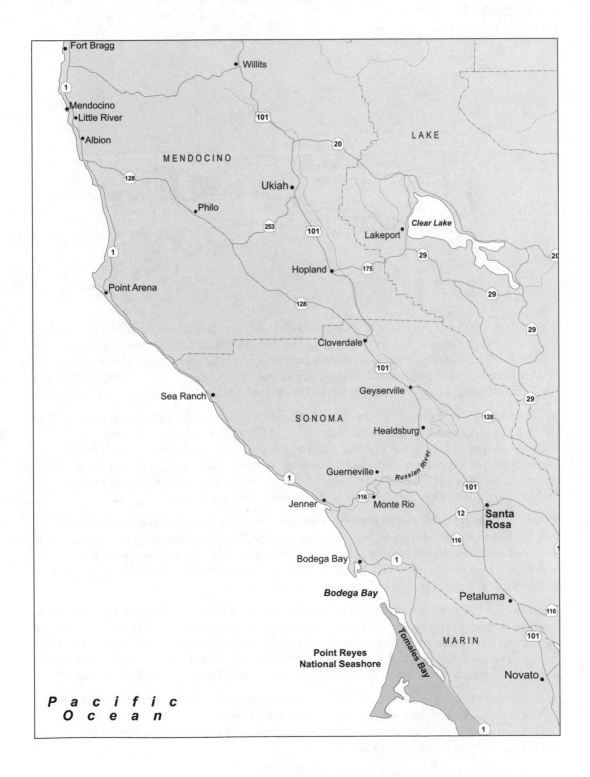

Bodega Harbour Yacht Club

Yacht Club

565 Smith Brothers Road, Bodega Bay
707/875-3519 x40
www.bodegayachtclub.com
avineyard@kempersports.com

● Rehearsal Dinners	Corp. Events/Mtgs.
● Ceremonies	● Private Parties
● Wedding Receptions	Accommodations

West of Petaluma, there's a scenic two-lane road that takes you through rolling hills and past dairy farms and sheep ranches until you reach the coast and Bodega Bay. This is the kind of sheltered estuary small craft owners, fishermen, and weekend sailors all along the Pacific love. It's a beautiful seaside outpost that's been passed by in the "grand scheme of things," which suits the natives just fine—they're quite happy enjoying the relaxed small-town pace of this little port.

In 1970 a historic waterfront structure was refurbished and turned into a charming meeting place dubbed "The Bodega Harbour Yacht Club." Over the years it's become a favorite for wedding parties and special events. The two-story cedar structure, with fieldstone accents, lies beyond a copse of mature cypress trees on a quiet waterside location. The building rests on sturdy pilings directly over the water, so visitors looking out the floor-to-ceiling windows facing the bay often feel as though they're on a vessel slipping out of its berth to go to sea.

These tall windows frame the Yacht Club's centerpiece stone fireplace. Guests can't resist sitting on its wide hearth to chat and enjoy their champagne, as well as admire the fireplace's construction. The bold fieldstone façade extends from floor to ceiling, and the flue is faced with vertical cedar boards that soar like organ pipes. The entire space is strikingly finished in knotty cedar, an effect that continues in the supporting columns and crossbeams.

Couples often host a pre-wedding reception downstairs, followed by a ceremony next to the fireplace in front of the bayfront windows. Afterwards, the party moves upstairs to a wood-lined mezzanine-style room overlooking the first floor's dramatic glass-and-stone façade. The room comfortably seats 120 guests for a buffet-style dinner. Professional catering services, including food prepared with pride by the Club's own chef, are provided exclusively by the Bluewater Bistro.

Although the Yacht Club is a self-contained building that easily handles both weddings and receptions, couples sometimes hold their ceremony at St. Teresa's church in the town of Bodega, a ten-minute drive from the Yacht Club. This small church is an appealing Colonial-style building made famous by photographer Ansel Adams.

The club also offers elegant beach ceremonies for couples who want to combine romance and nature. Another amenity is the availability of rental housing and numerous inns in the Bodega Bay area for relatives and guests.

Few places like the Yacht Club exist on the waterfront between San Francisco and Mendocino. Its architectural beauty, bayside location and scenic harbor views make it a natural for couples seeking a bucolic, yet very civilized, setting.

CEREMONY CAPACITY: The Yacht Club's ground floor holds 125 seated.

EVENT/RECEPTION CAPACITY: The Club holds 120 seated or 200 standing guests.

FEES & DEPOSITS: A deposit of $500 is required at the time of reservation. 90% of the estimated total is due within 7 days of the event and the remaining balance is due on the day of the event. These payments are nonrefundable. For receptions only, the Club rental fee is $2,500 for a 5-hour period. For receptions with ceremonies, the fee is $3,500 (5 hours plus ceremony time). Buffets range $35–60/person; alcohol, hors d'oeuvres, tax and a 20% service charge are additional.

AVAILABILITY: Year-round, daily, 8am–midnight, including holidays.

SERVICES/AMENITIES:

Catering: provided, no BYO
Kitchen Facilities: n/a
Tables & Chairs: provided
Linens, Silver, etc.: provided
Restrooms: wheelchair accessible
Dance Floor: hardwood floor lower level
Bride's Dressing Area: no
Meeting Equipment: n/a

Parking: on-street and lot, complimentary
Accommodations: no guestrooms, hotels nearby
Telephone: no
Outdoor Night Lighting: yes
Outdoor Cooking Facilities: no
Cleanup: provided
View: Bodega Bay and marina
Other: some coordination

RESTRICTIONS:

Alcohol: provided, or WC corkage $20/bottle
Smoking: outside only
Music: amplified OK indoors until 11pm

Wheelchair Access: yes
Insurance: certificate required

Compass Rose Gardens

Private Garden

Corner East Shore & Bay Flat Roads, Bodega Bay

707/875-2343

www.compassrosegardens.com
info@compassrosegardens.com

- Rehearsal Dinners
- Ceremonies
- Wedding Receptions
- Corp. Events/Mtgs.
- Private Parties
- Accommodations

When we passed through the Compass Rose Gardens' humble iron gate, we felt as if we had encountered Narnia—the magical, otherworldly kingdom that C.S. Lewis wrote of in his famed children's books. Entering the gardens, you're immersed in a world of unbridled beauty. In every direction the eye is delighted: here the abundant blooms of rhododendrons, irises and camellias; over there delicate Japanese maples, cherry trees and towering redwoods. A year-round running brook unspools the length of the gardens, pausing now and again to calm itself in one of several lovely ponds. It is truly an idyllic place to hold a celebration.

Donna Cook Freeman is the exuberant owner and green thumb responsible for coaxing such beauty from what was once three acres of tangled briars, willows and blackberries. She began work on the grounds in 1986; the foliage was so thick she had to crawl in on her hands and knees to reach the interior. There she sat for hours in contemplation, dreaming her garden into existence. A ten-year labor of love ensued, during which Donna and her family hauled, excavated, pruned and thinned. They built footbridges and cottages, planted flowers and trees, eventually wrangling a magnificent garden from a tenacious coastal jungle. Then in homage to Bodega Bay's long seafaring history, she christened the gardens "Compass Rose" (a compass rose is the starlike insignia found on mariners' maps and compasses).

A variety of scenic spots are available to tie the knot; however, most couples prefer to marry on an oval lawn overlooking the property's largest pond. Guests are seated on the opposite bank (still within earshot) where they are afforded a perfect view of the bride and groom as they exchange vows underneath a venerable willow. After the ceremony, folks can lose themselves along the gardens' meandering paths before joining the feasting and festivities at the handsome pavilion at the far side of the gardens. The newlyweds may want to slip away to share a quiet moment in the meditation garden. Nestled in a ring of redwoods, it's just the place to collect oneself after all the hubbub. Couples are also welcome to participate in what has now become a Compass Rose tradition—the planting of a "wedding" sapling or placing a personalized birdhouse in a nearby tree, serve as both living memory and future promise for their journey together as husband and wife.

Although the Compass Rose is an ideal spot for outdoor weddings, it is also an excellent gathering place for any number of events—seminars, retreats, bar mitzvahs and anniversaries. For those who desire lodging nearby, there are both luxury hotels and more modest accommodations nearby. And movie buffs will be interested in the gazebo from Hitchcock's famous film *The Birds*. The owners of the Gardens, who were extras in the movie, have decided to share their favorite memento by setting it into a hillside where everyone can enjoy it.

The Compass Rose Gardens used to be Bodega Bay's best kept secret, but given their extraordinary beauty, of course word got out. They were also featured on HGTV and A&E, and in *Town and Country* magazine, radio and other media! So if your heart is set on a garden party, call sooner rather than later—this is one opportunity you won't want to miss!

CEREMONY & EVENT/RECEPTION CAPACITY: The Ceremony Area holds 200 seated and the Pavilion up to 150 seated guests.

MEETING CAPACITY: Meetings spaces accommodate up to 200 guests.

FEES & DEPOSITS: 50% of the rental fee is required to reserve your date, the balance and a $1,000 refundable security deposit are due 1 month prior to the event. Engagement photos and a 1-hour rehearsal are included. The weekend rental fee starts at $4,900; call for midweek rates. Extra hours are available.

AVAILABILITY: Daily, May through October.

SERVICES/AMENITIES:

Catering: select from preferred list or with approval
Kitchen Facilities: yes, limited outdoor
Tables & Chairs: through caterer
Linens, Silver, etc.: through caterer
Restrooms: not wheelchair accessible
Dance Floor: large dance area
Bride's Dressing Area: yes
Meeting Equipment: BYO

Parking: ample on-street and in private lot
Accommodations: no guestrooms, hotels nearby
Telephone: no
Outdoor Night Lighting: yes
Outdoor Cooking Facilities: yes, area available
Cleanup: caterer or renter
View: gardens, pond, creek and redwoods

RESTRICTIONS:

Alcohol: BYO, insurance required, no corkage fees
Smoking: not allowed
Music: amplified OK until 10pm

Wheelchair Access: limited
Insurance: certificate required

Want to find more locations and services? Check out our informative website, www.HereComesTheGuide.com.

211

Little River Inn Resort and Spa

Seaside Inn

7901 Highway One, Little River
888/INN-LOVE, 888/466-5683

www.littleriverinn.com
melissap@littleriverinn.com

- Rehearsal Dinners
- Ceremonies
- Wedding Receptions
- Corp. Events/Mtgs.
- Private Parties
- Accommodations

California boasts some of the most gorgeous coastline in the world, and when early settler Silas Coombs came here in 1863, he scoped out and purchased the absolute best that the state had to offer. He built his Victorian home on 225 wooded oceanside acres just a few miles south of what is now charming Mendocino village, and a century and a half later it's become the historic Little River Inn, the toast of the coast and an ideal setting for your own piece of history.

The North Coast hasn't changed much since Silas's day. It's still wildly beautiful: craggy and pristine with startling bluffs, miles of trails, sheltered coves, and little trafficked yet easily accessible beaches. But his property has blossomed. Today, it's a much-praised establishment with a unique collection of guestrooms, cottages and indoor and outdoor meeting spaces, as well as a full-service salon and day spa, tennis courts, golf course, excellent restaurant/bar and cute little antique shop. The inn sprawls over the hillsides, offering a felicitous mix of privacy, community and spectacular Pacific views.

Your conference, retreat, reunion, wedding—in fact, any kind of celebration—will be expertly handled by dedicated innkeepers whose family has been hosting outstanding events for nearly a hundred years.

They can help you pick the event sites that are right for you—not an easy decision with so many options! Share vows or cocktails in a picturesque multilevel courtyard surrounded by a profusion of colorful flowers. Lilies, lavender, daffodils, nasturtiums, poppies, fuchsias and more peek out from between the ferns and pines, perfuming the air and brightening moods. Just up the steps, the wedding-cake-white Abalone Room with its large deck and ocean views suits any kind of standing or seated function. Scattered with shells, looped with veils, garlanded in flowers or hung with white paper lanterns, it's an inviting blank canvas for your wedding masterpiece. Let the property's meandering grounds inspire you. You might want to plan a rehearsal dinner at the restaurant, a picnic by the golf course, and if absolute privacy and rugged coastal views are your preference, the stand-alone Mallory House a short drive down the coast also provides stunning vistas and still more of the inn's many special event options.

For a destination wedding like no other, extend the festivities. Your happily-ever-after can begin right here in the lovely people-friendly—and in some cases pet-friendly—accommodations. The comfortable rooms feature fireplaces, wet bars, Jacuzzis and individual hot tubs and all have spectacular ocean views. You won't want to leave and neither will your guests.

So stay and enjoy the on-site activities or explore the splendor of the North Coast. Hiking, kayaking, sightseeing and wine tasting adventures may beckon during the day, but afterwards you'll want to rush back to the inn to wind down in style. Start with a delicious dinner, then perhaps a stroll around the grounds, and finally, share a romantic toast with a glass of wine on your private deck in this blissful, ocean-kissed hideaway.

CEREMONY CAPACITY: The inn holds 100 seated guests indoors and 200 seated outdoors.

EVENT/RECEPTION CAPACITY: The inn accommodates 200 seated or standing guests indoors.

MEETING CAPACITY: Meeting rooms hold 80 seated guests.

FEES & DEPOSITS: A 50% nonrefundable deposit is required to reserve your date. The balance is due at the end of your event. Rental fees range $3,000–10,000 depending on guest count. Meals range $30–75/person. Tax, alcohol and a 20% service charge are additional.

AVAILABILITY: Year-round, daily.

SERVICES/AMENITIES:

Catering: provided, no BYO
Kitchen Facilities: n/a
Tables & Chairs: provided
Linens, Silver, etc.: provided
Restrooms: wheelchair accessible
Dance Floor: portable provided
Bride's & Groom's Dressing Area: CBA
Meeting Equipment: CBA

Parking: large lot
Accommodations: 65 guestrooms
Telephone: guest and house phones
Outdoor Night Lighting: CBA
Outdoor Cooking Facilities: BBQ CBA
Cleanup: provided
View: Pacific Ocean, gardens
Other: on-site florals, spa services, picnic area, AV equipment, gift shop, beach access, event coordination

RESTRICTIONS:

Alcohol: provided, no BYO
Smoking: outside only
Music: amplified OK indoors

Wheelchair Access: yes
Insurance: not required

Peninsula

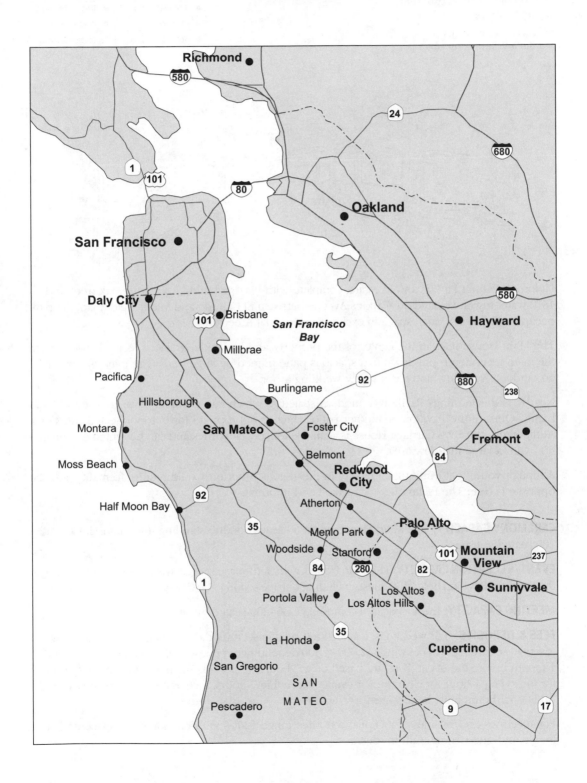

Holbrook Palmer Park

Historic Park

150 Watkins Avenue, Atherton
650/752-0534
www.ci.atherton.ca.us
jcardona@ci.atherton.ca.us

● Rehearsal Dinners	● Corp. Events/Mtgs.
● Ceremonies	● Private Parties
● Wedding Receptions	Accommodations

Holbrook Palmer Park is an old estate, complete with historic buildings, mature oak trees and an 1870 water tower. Located on Watkins Avenue between El Camino and Middlefield Road, the park occupies 22 acres of open space in exclusive residential Atherton.

The Main House rests in the center of the property and has wide, gracious steps that lead from the main reception room down to a spacious patio framed by large trees. The patio is perfect for an outdoor ceremony and has a lovely wedding arbor.

Nearby is the Jennings Pavilion, a modern structure which can accommodate large events and bands. Outside the Pavilion is another patio which is appropriate for outdoor seated functions. Additionally, the 1896 Carriage House is available for special parties and can be rented in conjunction with a large meadow area.

Although you might think that a facility in prestigious Atherton would require formality, just the opposite is true: The feeling here is relaxed and informal.

CEREMONY CAPACITY: The Main House holds 60 seated or 100 standing; the Main House Patio, 200 seated guests.

EVENT/RECEPTION CAPACITY: The Main House, with outdoor seating, can accommodate 100 guests; the Jennings Pavilion holds 200 guests including outside seating; the Carriage House seats 60 guests.

MEETING CAPACITY: Event spaces accommodate 30–200 seated guests.

FEES & DEPOSITS: For weddings, a $1,000 refundable security/damage deposit is required when reservations are made. Fees range $2,000–4,500 depending on guest count. The use fee is required 1 month before the event. Fees are based on a 7-hour use period: 1–2 hours for setup; 4–5 hours for the event; 1 hour for cleanup. For events exceeding 7 hours, a charge of $100/hour will apply. Additional hours must be arranged in advance.

For meetings and business functions, the rates range $200–600 depending on space and time rented and guest count. Call for details.

AVAILABILITY: Saturday weddings or special events, 10am–5pm or 5pm–midnight, including setup and cleanup. Sundays (only one event/day), 10am–9pm; cleanup must be completed by 10pm. Friday weddings and social events, 5pm–midnight, including cleanup.

Business functions, year-round, daily. Half-day events are held 8am–noon or 1pm–5pm; full-day events 8am–5pm; evening events 5pm–10pm. Additional hours can be arranged.

SERVICES/AMENITIES:

Catering: BYO or provided

Kitchen Facilities: yes

Tables & Chairs: provided

Linens, Silver, etc.: BYO

Restrooms: wheelchair access in Pavilion only

Dance Floor: CBA

Bride's & Groom's Dressing Areas: yes

Meeting Equipment: CBA

Parking: several lots

Accommodations: no guestrooms

Telephone: pay phones

Outdoor Night Lighting: yes

Outdoor Cooking Facilities: BYO

Cleanup: caterer

View: 22-acre landscaped park

RESTRICTIONS:

Alcohol: BYO

Smoking: outside only

Music: amplified OK inside only

Wheelchair Access: yes

Insurance: CBA or BYO

Ralston Hall Mansion
at Notre Dame de Namur University

1500 Ralston Avenue, Belmont
650/508-3501
www.ralstonhall.com
ralstonhall@ndnu.edu

- Rehearsal Dinners
- Ceremonies
- Wedding Receptions
- Corp. Events/Mtgs.
- Private Parties
- Accommodations

This registered National Historic Landmark is a stunning Victorian mansion, completed in 1867 by William Chapman Ralston, founder of the Bank of California. Ralston purchased the land in 1864, and modified the original Italian villa with touches of Steamboat Gothic and Victorian details to create a lavish and opulent estate. The delicately etched glass panes of the front doors and the windows dressed in striped awnings give you an indication of what you'll see inside.

The interior reflects the charm of a bygone era, featuring a magnificent ballroom, delightful parlors, and a picturesque opera box gallery. Each room is decorated with beautiful antiques, stunning crystal chandeliers and colorful Oriental rugs. The ballroom is particularly appealing. Its patterned hardwood floor is encircled by mirrored walls, and three impressive chandeliers hang gracefully from the skylight. At the far end of the room is a large bay window, with a curving fabric-covered bench seat and regal matching draperies. Musicians can set up in an alcove without interfering with the grandeur and flow of the ballroom. The spacious dining rooms were decorated with an attention to detail that is unparalleled by today's standards. Because of Ralston Hall's size and layout, you can choose from a variety of setups utilizing the entire first floor or the expansive front lawn. This facility is one of the Peninsula's few mansion locations and makes a terrific venue for a sophisticated and memorable wedding.

CEREMONY CAPACITY: The Ralston lawn holds 200 seated or standing; the Ballroom 200 seated or standing.

EVENT/RECEPTION CAPACITY: The facility accommodates 200 seated guests or 275 standing guests.

MEETING CAPACITY: Several spaces accommodate 13–150 seated guests.

FEES & DEPOSITS: For weddings and special events, a $4,500 booking deposit is required to reserve your date. This amount includes a $500 refundable security deposit. For an 8-hour event, the rental fee runs $7,000–9,500 and is payable 6 months prior to the function. Fees include a facility manager and 2 hours for setup and 1 hour for cleanup. The security deposit is returned if the property is left in good condition.

The fee for meetings and other special events is $400/hour, Monday–Thursday, with a 4-hour minimum.

AVAILABILITY: Year-round, daily, 9am–midnight.

SERVICES/AMENITIES:

Catering: select from exclusive list
Kitchen Facilities: moderate
Tables & Chairs: provided
Linens, Silver, etc.: through caterer
Restrooms: wheelchair accessible
Dance Floor: provided
Bride's Dressing Area: yes
Meeting Equipment: BYO

Parking: ample
Accommodations: no guestrooms
Telephone: local calls only
Outdoor Night Lighting: limited
Outdoor Cooking Facilities: BBQ
Cleanup: caterer
View: lawn with fountain
Other: security available

RESTRICTIONS:

Alcohol: through caterer or BYO
Smoking: not permitted inside
Music: amplified OK

Wheelchair Access: yes
Insurance: certificate required
Other: candles not permitted

This is important! Tell locations you're reading HERE COMES THE GUIDE and ask if our information is still current.

Mission Blue Center

Community Center

475 Mission Blue Drive, Brisbane
415/657-4320

www.ci.brisbane.ca.us
www.ablacktieaffairinc.com
julieweidner@ci.brisbane.ca.us

● Rehearsal Dinners	● Corp. Events/Mtgs.
● Ceremonies	● Private Parties
● Wedding Receptions	Accommodations

Brisbane is like the librarian in romantic comedies whose beauty—until the doofus leading man finally figures out to take off her glasses and undo her hair—remains unseen. It's hidden away in a nook of Mt. San Bruno and isolated by wetlands from the tens of thousands of commuters who pass by it daily on Highway 101.

But those who leave the freeway and do some exploring will find an unspoiled little town that climbs up its hill like an Italian fishing village. Brisbane has its share of wealth, but it has yet to be yuppified or see its main street turned into a stretch of chain stores. You sense right away that this is a tight-knit place that knows it has a good thing going. Part of that good thing is Mission Blue, the community center the town built in 2000. It has everything a building of its type should have, including appealing architecture, a great hillside location with a fine view, and the ability to seamlessly accommodate a wedding and reception. There's a poetic touch, too: Mission Blue is named after a rare butterfly whose preservation inspired the saving of open space on Mt. San Bruno, the imposing palomino-colored ridge that dominates the view from the center's terrace.

Mission Blue's main entrance takes you to a soaring glass-walled foyer that's often used for a post-ceremony champagne reception. It opens into the spacious room at the center's heart, cleverly designed with visual cues that separate it into two distinct areas. The first half of the room, with its hardwood floor and light-colored walls, is perfect for an indoor ceremony or dancing. The second half, carpeted and tiled, and painted a slightly darker color, is ideal for dining. The two areas can be partitioned or used in combination, and are easily accessed from the nearby full-service kitchen.

Glass doors lead from the interior to a beautifully fashioned, stone-finished terrace that runs the length of Mission Blue's west and north sides. It sweeps out from the building toward a well-kept lawn that many couples have used to recite their vows. Standing on the terrace, you can look across a valley to Mt. San Bruno, and south to a view of Brisbane's little houses clambering up the hill. There are fine design touches everywhere, including a wooden pergola at one end of the lawn and a colonnade along the terrace whose eye-catching beams and supports call to mind the sophisticated carpentry of a Chinese temple. Planters and flowerbeds abound, and the simple black railing that stands between the lawn and the hillside is sculptural in form. Even Mission

Blue's exterior colors have a sensual appeal—the olive green, creamy white and light chocolate tones give it an almost luscious appearance.

This site's architects certainly understood how to create a welcoming place: Mission Blue is a harmonious interplay between space and light, colors and materials, indoors and outdoors. But when you have your celebration here, you won't be thinking about how all the elements work so well together—you'll just be having a great time.

CEREMONY CAPACITY: Mission Blue Center holds up to 250 seated indoors and 200 seated outdoors.

EVENT/RECEPTION & MEETING CAPACITY: This location holds 250 seated at tables or 350 guests seated theater-style. The large room can be broken into smaller spaces.

FEES & DEPOSITS: A $500 refundable cleaning deposit is required to reserve your date; the balance is due 21 days prior to the event. The rental fee is $260/hour, discounts are available for Brisbane residents and for partial hall rentals. Meals range $18–26/person. Tax, alcohol and a 15% service charge are additional.

AVAILABILITY: Year-round, daily, 8am–midnight.

SERVICES/AMENITIES:

Catering: preferred caterer is *A Black Tie Affair Catering*
Kitchen Facilities: full kitchen
Tables & Chairs: provided
Linens, Silver, etc.: through caterer
Restrooms: wheelchair accessible
Dance Floor: yes
Bride's Dressing Area: CBA
Meeting Equipment: wall-mounted projection screen, LCD projector, PA system, CD/tape player, DVD/VCR, stage

Parking: 40-space lot and on-street
Accommodations: no guestrooms
Telephone: house phone
Outdoor Night Lighting: access only
Outdoor Cooking Facilities: no
Cleanup: caterer or renter
View: Mt. San Bruno and bay
Other: event coordination, cake, ice carving; chocolate fountain available through caterer

RESTRICTIONS:

Alcohol: provided by caterer
Smoking: outdoors only
Music: amplified OK

Wheelchair Access: yes
Insurance: proof of liability provided by caterer or renter
Other: no wall decorations

Kohl Mansion, "The Oaks"

Historic Mansion & Grounds

2750 Adeline Drive, Burlingame
650/762-1136 or 650/762-1137

www.kohl-mansion.com
ddevin@mercyhsb.com
tbaldocchi@mercyhsb.com

● Rehearsal Dinners	● Corp. Events/Mtgs.
● Ceremonies	● Private Parties
● Wedding Receptions	Accommodations

Commissioned by Frederick Kohl and his wife in 1912, the Kohl Mansion was built on 40 acres of oak woodlands in Burlingame. Kohl, heir to a shipping fortune, loved to entertain and created this grand estate to include a manor house, pool, rose garden, tennis courts, greenhouses, and a large carriage house. Now, decades later, the elegant rosebrick Tudor mansion is again available for parties, and has many inviting rooms for weddings, special events, business functions and picnics.

The wood-paneled Library features a large marble fireplace, bookcases and graceful French doors that open to a center courtyard. The room's Gothic bay window catches the light filtered through the oaks on the lawns just beyond. The sizable Great Hall, a copy of the Arlington Tudor Hall in Essex, England, was built for music and entertaining. Its very high ceiling, oak paneling and walnut floor create a fine acoustical setting for music. A lighter twin of the Library, the spacious and airy Dining Room has delicate, pristine-white plaster relief on the walls and ceiling. This marvelous dining environment shares the Library's view of the oak-studded lawns through its own bay windows.

The Morning Room, with white lattice walls and black-and-white marble floors, adds a touch of formality to the East Wing. It overlooks the English Rose Garden and surrounding manicured grounds, where guests can stroll over the lawns or sample hors d'oeuvres on the large terrace. The Kohl Mansion is, indeed, a fabulous facility for anyone planning a stylish event.

CEREMONY & EVENT/RECEPTION CAPACITY: Various rooms in the mansion hold 50–250 seated and 75–300 standing guests. The patio and lawn areas each accommodate 300 seated or standing.

MEETING CAPACITY: Event spaces accommodate 12–200 seated guests.

FEES & DEPOSITS: Rental fees range $6,500–13,750, for an 8-hour minimum, depending on guest count and date of event. To reserve your date, half the rental fee is due at the time of booking; the remainder is due 90 days prior to the event. The rental fee includes a $500 refundable security deposit and a $500 setup fee.

AVAILABILITY: From mid-August through June, parties and special events are held after 3:30pm on weekdays, and anytime on Saturday and Sunday. June through mid-August, every day, anytime. Meetings can be held year-round, time frames subject to availability.

SERVICES/AMENITIES:

Catering: select from preferred list
Kitchen Facilities: full
Tables & Chairs: provided
Linens, Silver, etc.: BYO
Restrooms: wheelchair accessible
Dance Floor: provided
Bride's Dressing Area: yes
Meeting Equipment: podium, stage

Parking: large lots, valet required for over 200 guests
Accommodations: no guestrooms
Telephone: phone CBA
Outdoor Night Lighting: no
Outdoor Cooking Facilities: BYO
Cleanup: caterer
View: San Francisco Bay and coastal hills
Other: baby grand piano; swimming pool; tennis, basketball and volleyball courts; children's room, coatcheck room

RESTRICTIONS:

Alcohol: BYO, licensed bartender required
Smoking: outside only
Music: amplified OK indoors, acoustic only outdoors; time restrictions vary depending on the day of the week; sound check required hourly

Wheelchair Access: yes
Insurance: certificate required or CBA for a small fee

Wedgewood Wedding & Banquet Center
at Crystal Springs Golf Course

Event Facility

6650 Golf Course Drive, Burlingame
866/966-3009
www.wedgewoodbanquet.com
sales@wedgewoodbanquet.com

- Rehearsal Dinners
- Ceremonies
- Wedding Receptions
- Corp. Events/Mtgs.
- Private Parties
- Accommodations

One of the most picturesque wedding sites in the Bay Area has something very few people ever have the privilege of seeing: a bird's-eye view of the protected land around Crystal Springs Reservoir. San Francisco stores its precious drinking water in this jewel of a lake, and the city jealously guards access to the reservoir—only rangers, scientists and certain officials can visit the heavily wooded semi-wilderness surrounding it.

But if you wed outdoors at Crystal Springs Golf Course, you are among the rare outsiders who get to enjoy this vista, and with it comes much more than simple bragging rights. The ceremony site, a city-owned meadow at the southern end of the golf club, has a gazebo that stands on a grassy knoll overlooking the reservoir. The view from here is sensational, with glistening reservoir waters below and tree-covered ridges behind it. In the distance, high hills slope toward the bay. There are no houses in sight, and deer often graze nearby. The backdrop is so spectacular that the gazebo needs little adornment—put some flowers in front or over the entry, and voilà, all eyes are upon it. There's plenty of room for a limo to drop off the bride, and if she wants to add a little more pizzazz to the moment, she can arrive in a horse-drawn carriage. A well-tamped earthen aisle cuts through a beautifully tended lawn to the gazebo, where the couple exchanges vows.

The reception takes place up a tree- and greens-lined road at the Wedgewood Banquet Center. The club's main building, painted creamy white with gray-green trim, is set at the edge of gentle terraces that drop toward the reservoir. To reach its two banquet rooms and deck, you walk along a red-carpeted terrace that has a sweeping view down to the golf course. Best of all is spotting the deer that placidly graze the course.

The Wedgewood's Vista Room is the primary dining-reception area. The entire west wall, which faces the Vista Deck, is glass windows and doors, with airy, white sheers framing the view outside. If you reserve this space, you also get the adjoining Vista Deck, a large glassed-in area shaded by a canopy. The vista looks west toward woods and north toward neighboring hills and the golf course's gorgeous landscape.

Wedgewood's all-inclusive packages offer the best values in the Bay Area, saving time and money, and make planning your event here a breeze. Services range from a basic ceremony at the gazebo with seating (and of course the view!), to such amenities as invitations, DJ, food, cake, beverages, florals and the honeymoon suite.

The elements for a fine, fine day are here in splendid array: the gazebo in its unforgettable setting; a personable, attentive staff; good food; fresh, sea-kissed air (the ocean is only a few ridges away); and nature's intense blues and greens. Lastly, nearby Highway 280 makes the course easily accessible from San Francisco, the Peninsula and the South Bay. Now, that's a list that should satisfy anyone.

CEREMONY CAPACITY: This location accommodates up to 275 guests indoors or 400 outdoors.

EVENT/RECEPTION CAPACITY: Indoors, the Wedgewood Banquet Room holds 275 seated or 375 standing guests.

MEETING CAPACITY: Event spaces accommodate 50–200 seated guests.

FEES & DEPOSITS: 25% of the estimated event total is required to reserve your date. The next 25% is due 90 days prior to the event; the balance is due 10 days prior. Wedding area fees range $1,000–2,000 depending on services needed. There is no room charge for the reception area. Meals range $25–40/person. Tax, alcohol and a 20% service charge are additional. There are several wedding packages available.

AVAILABILITY: Year-round, anytime.

SERVICES/AMENITIES:

Catering: provided
Kitchen Facilities: n/a
Tables & Chairs: provided
Linens, Silver, etc.: provided
Restrooms: wheelchair accessible
Dance Floor: yes
Brides Dressing Area: yes
Meeting Equipment: CBA, extra charge

Parking: large lot
Accommodations: no guestrooms
Telephone: emergency use only
Outdoor Night Lighting: yes
Outdoor Cooking Facilities: no
Cleanup: provided
View: fairways, lake, meadows, mountains
Other: event coordination

RESTRICTIONS:

Alcohol: provided
Smoking: outside only
Music: amplified OK with some restrictions

Wheelchair Access: yes
Insurance: not required
Other: no rice, confetti or glitter; no open flames

Overwhelmed? Use the search criteria on www.HereComesTheGuide.com to narrow down your choices.

225

Crowne Plaza Foster City-San Mateo

Hotel

1221 Chess Drive, Foster City
650/295-6129
www.eventscp.com
irene@cpfcc.com

● Rehearsal Dinners	● Corp. Events/Mtgs.
● Ceremonies	● Private Parties
● Wedding Receptions	● Accommodations

"Location, location, location!" may be the byword of people who deal in real estate, but hoteliers are pretty hip to the idea, too. That's certainly the case at the Crowne Plaza Foster City-San Mateo, a bustling 351-room hotel conveniently situated at a major Bay Area crossroads. Right off the western end of the San Mateo Bridge, and just minutes south of San Francisco International Airport, it's easily accessible from The City, South Bay, East Bay and the Peninsula. Free parking and a complimentary airport shuttle to SFO are provided, and nearby restaurants, shopping and parks add even more to the hotel's appeal.

But a great location is only part of what makes the Crowne Plaza a thriving site for weddings. The five-story garden atrium certainly has brides talking. Its most impressive feature has to be the room-length waterfall along the east side: Four streams of water cascade among flower-strewn rocks, creating a soothing and arresting backdrop. For obvious reasons, many couples love having their ceremony in here. The two-level space (split between a bar and café) can be closed off with lattice, and decorated with flowers and an arch. Brides often descend dramatically from above in one of the hotel's glass elevators, then walk to a wooden bridge at the center of the atrium to exchange vows. Palms, ficus and other plants give this glassed-in area a tropical feel.

Receptions usually start in the Magellan Foyer where cocktails are set up, and then move into the adjoining ballroom, which can be divided into four sections depending on the size of your event. Rehearsal dinners and post-wedding brunches are often held on site, too. The Marco Polo Room, directly off the atrium, is especially well suited for smaller gatherings where family and close friends want to mingle and catch up with each other. An abundance of rich wood creates a lot of warmth, and the glass wall facing the atrium can be curtained for privacy or left open for people watching.

Bridal suites, which are a standard part of the hotel's wedding package, are located in the Executive Tower, a twin building reached via a covered driveway. The Crowne Club there has a cocktail and hors d'oeuvre serving area that you can reserve for an intimate reception. The adjacent Bay View Ballroom, which hosts dinners and dancing and is sometimes used for ceremonies, is a favorite with smaller wedding parties. For musical entertainment, bring your own band or DJ or, if your event is on a Friday or Saturday night, you have another option: Accompany your guests over to the Clubhouse Bistro just off the atrium, where the house DJ rocks the crowd three nights a week.

The final component of this hotel's appeal is its experienced wedding staff. They're not only flexible about letting you decorate early so you'll have plenty of time to spare, they also go out of their way to accommodate the needs of almost any ethnic group. For example, when there's a traditional Chinese wedding, which involves a pre-ceremony tea ritual, the staff here always sets aside a proper space for it.

The wedding manager says the first thing she asks any prospective client is, "What is it that you want to do?" When she gets the answer to that question, she and her team quickly go about the business of making each reception reflect the couple's wishes.

CEREMONY CAPACITY: The Atrium holds 150 seated guests.

EVENT/RECEPTION CAPACITY: Various rooms hold up to 650 seated or 800 standing guests. Smaller events can be accommodated; call for detailed configuration options.

MEETING CAPACITY: Event spaces accommodate 25–600 seated guests.

FEES & DEPOSITS: A $2,500 deposit is required to reserve your date and a second deposit, which is equal to 50% of your estimated event total, is due 4 months after the original booking date; the final balance is due 10 days prior to the event. There are no separate room rental fees. Meals range $36–90/person. Packages are available ranging $68–105/person. A 20% service charge and tax are additional. A $4/chair ceremony setup fee and a $3/person cake-cutting fee may also apply. Group room rates are available, as is a complimentary bridal suite for the wedding couple. Call for details about honeymoon packages.

AVAILABILITY: Year-round, daily, 6am–1am.

SERVICES/AMENITIES:

Catering: provided
Kitchen Facilities: n/a
Tables & Chairs: provided
Linens, Silver, etc.: provided
Restrooms: wheelchair accessible
Dance Floor: yes
Bride's & Groom's Dressing Areas: yes
Meeting Equipment: full range

Parking: complimentary self-parking
Accommodations: 351 guestrooms
Telephone: pay phones
Outdoor Night Lighting: CBA
Outdoor Cooking Facilities: no
Cleanup: provided
View: bay views in some spaces
Other: event coordination

RESTRICTIONS:

Alcohol: provided
Smoking: outside only
Music: amplified OK indoors

Wheelchair Access: yes
Insurance: not required

Half Moon Bay Golf Links

Golf Resort

Two Miramontes Point Road, Half Moon Bay
650/773-8895
www.hmbgolflinks.com
AMcNeil@hmbgolflinks.com

● Rehearsal Dinners		● Corp. Events/Mtgs.
● Ceremonies		● Private Parties
● Wedding Receptions		Accommodations

With a rich history and honors from top publications like *Travel + Leisure*, the Half Moon Bay Golf Links is one of the most prestigious championship golf resorts in California—and it's also one of the most beautiful. Comprised of 300 acres of parkland, lakes, breathtaking oceanside bluffs and beach access, the Links are understandably a favorite with couples in search of an incomparable setting for their celebration.

For a phenomenal ceremony, choose from several view-filled locales right on the golf course. The Oceanview Practice Green embraces an astonishing coastal panorama, while in the opposite direction, a landscaped pond with a weathered brick canal looks like an artist's watercolor. Another stunning choice is the Old Course 18th Tee. Couples pledge their vows on a gentle rise at the edge of a dramatic cliff dotted with native wildflowers, as the surf crashes against the shore below. These vistas are so cinematic that they've been featured in major motion pictures.

Marrying at the Links has its privileges, and one of the most enticing is a custom "photographic tour" of their exclusive and oh-so-picturesque grounds. During the cocktail hour, the newlyweds are chauffeured to a variety of positively awe-inspiring backdrops, including a golden sand beach for those romantic "frolicking in the sand and surf" portraits. Just imagine how magnificent your wedding album will be!

Meanwhile, friends and family mingle on a manicured lawn that sweeps from the banks of the pond. Amethyst salvia, rose bushes and lithe reeds line the shore as duck families paddle by, putting the finishing touch on this the fairy-tale tableau.

The inviting Mullins Bar & Grill accommodates your reception in several adjoining areas. The bar is a great spot for the band and dance floor, while guests look on from the cozy Fireplace Lounge with leather club chairs clustered around a hearth. Curtains separate (or open up to) the Dining Room, a comfortable yet refined space where everyone can relax and enjoy the party. Large westward-facing windows frame the Pacific, the perfect accompaniment to gourmet cuisine. The banquet team knows how to dress a table, too, using Chiavari chairs and luxurious linens to set a stylish tone. Doors open from the Dining Room to a brand new Oceanview Deck for scenic outdoor gatherings. On weekends, the poignant notes of a bagpiper at the neighboring Ritz-Carlton usher in the sunset. (Another benefit of having the Ritz next door—luxurious accommodations and a spa are within easy walking distance.)

The event pros at the Links can take you beyond the traditional with innovative rehearsal dinners or farewell brunches. How about a "drive-in movie night," with guests relaxing in convertible golf carts beneath customized keepsake blankets, as "carhop" waiters on roller-skates ply them with cotton candy and buttered popcorn? Fancy a game of nighttime "glow-in-the-dark" golf? Or a private round of play on one of their award-winning courses? Ask and ye shall receive at Half Moon Bay Golf Links.

In fact, with only one wedding at a time, the staff strives to exceed your expectations. From complimentary valet service to an optional rose petal send-off for the newlyweds, they go out of their way to make you feel pampered and appreciated. And that's almost as impressive as the views!

CEREMONY, EVENT/RECEPTION CAPACITY: The resort holds 150 seated or 200 standing guests indoors, and 200 seated or standing outdoors

MEETING CAPACITY: The resort can accommodate 150 seated guests, conference-style.

FEES & DEPOSITS: A $2,000 deposit and signed contract are required to reserve your date. The balance is paid according to a customized plan based on your event. Ceremony packages start at $2,450 including the right to take photographs on the exclusive oceanside bluffs as well as on the beach. Room fees start at $300 for the Palmer Private Dining Room (capacity 35), and $850 for the Main Dining Room (capacity 150) plus food and beverage minimums (inquire for more information). Receptions include use of upgraded Chiavari chairs, basic tables with linens, and classic tableware. Lunch receptions start at $50/person and dinners at $65/person plus beverages, tax and service charge. Valet is complimentary.

AVAILABILITY: Year-round, daily, 6am–midnight.

SERVICES/AMENITIES:

Catering: provided
Kitchen Facilities: n/a
Tables & Chairs: provided
Linens, Silver, etc.: provided
Restrooms: wheelchair accessible
Dance Floor: CBA
Bride's & Groom's Dressing Area: yes
Meeting Equipment: provided
Other: beach access, AV equipment

Parking: large lot, valet required, limited
Accommodations: hotel and resort next door
Telephone: house phone
Outdoor Night Lighting: CBA
Outdoor Cooking Facilities: BBQ CBA
Cleanup: provided
View: park, garden, lagoons, fairways, landscaped grounds; panorama of Pacific Ocean, harbor, coastline and oceanside bluffs

RESTRICTIONS:

Alcohol: provided or BYO with corkage $20/bottle
Smoking: outside only
Music: amplified OK

Wheelchair Access: yes
Insurance: not required

Liquid Sky Oceanfront Estate

Waterfront Private Estate

By Appointment Only, Scenic Highway 1, Half Moon Bay
650/726-4090 x112

www.liquidskyestate.com
events@cetrella.com

Rehearsal Dinners	Corp. Events/Mtgs.
● Ceremonies	● Private Parties
Wedding Receptions	Accommodations

The beauty of the California coast is legendary, and the scenic stretch of Highway 1 between Half Moon Bay and Santa Cruz is particularly entrancing. Largely undeveloped, there's nothing to distract from the drama of the crashing surf or the transcendent vision of jagged shoreline and cool blue ocean panorama. This is the stuff wedding dreams are made of, and if you long for a pretty piece of this earthly paradise for your ceremony, just reserve Liquid Sky Oceanfront Estate.

Sequestered behind iron gates, Liquid Sky is perched on a secluded coastal bluff. The imaginative two-story home, built in the shape of a cylinder, curves toward the expanse of sea and sky like a minicoastal citadel of old. The rolling waves are a stirring roar in the background, punctuated by the occasional cry of a gull or the lilting notes of a songbird. Sea-grass and ice plants form green patches along the sandy cliffs that cascade down to the shore. It's easy to get lost in the surroundings, but more delights beckon further on.

A short path between the home and a sheltered hillside culminates at a sweep of manicured lawn overlooking the vast seascape. Imagine the scene, set with white chairs, flowers and aisle runner; perhaps you've chosen to accent your ceremony with a pair of Grecian columns, or a garlanded arch or *chuppah*. Or maybe you prefer to have the wild ocean backdrop be your sole embellishment as you pledge your vows…. In addition to the captivating setting, Liquid Sky offers couples complete privacy; with nothing except meadows and ocean around you, the stunning natural elements accentuate the sense of occasion, as well as the shared passion and deep commitment between you.

After the first kiss, serve a champagne toast right in the garden. Then invite guests to enjoy cocktails and hors d'oeuvres up on the rooftop deck, which may be enhanced with twinkle lights or paper lanterns for added romantic flair. While some guests mingle, others are taken with a sense of exultation as they pause to survey the scenery. This view-filled aerie is the perfect vantage point for appreciating the estate's evocative name—"Liquid Sky," which refers to the fluid, ever-changing horizon on display. One minute daylight glimmers through wispy clouds and puffs of sea mist; the next, all is clear, just in time for a glorious sunset to burnish the landscape.

This singular property is owned by Dave Labuda, local restauranteur and burgeoning winemaker. There's a small building on a nearby hill where he retreats to work his oenophilic magic. The Liquid Sky vintage made its debut in 2010, but Dave's fine dining restaurant, Cetrella, is already a well-established Half Moon Bay landmark. Just 10 minutes from the estate, Cetrella is a tasteful (and tasty) venue to hold your reception. What a perfect way to end a spectacular day!

CEREMONY CAPACITY: The estate accommodates 125 seated guests outdoors.

EVENT/RECEPTION CAPACITY: The estate holds 125 standing guests for a 1-hour reception following a ceremony.

MEETING CAPACITY: Receptions and meetings do not take place at this location.

FEES & DEPOSITS: 25% of the estimated event total is due upon signing your contract. The next 50% is due 90 days prior, and the final balance is due 14 days prior to the event. Rental fees range $5,000–6,000 depending on your guest count. The rental fee includes chairs, restrooms, sound system for the ceremony, and shuttle service for your guests to and from the ceremony site. For a cocktail reception, hors d'oeuvres start at $20/person. Tax, alcohol and service charge are additional. Seated receptions usually occur at Cetrella restaurant in downtown Half Moon Bay.

AVAILABILITY: April–October, call for details.

SERVICES/AMENITIES:

Catering: provided or BYO
Kitchen Facilities: ample
Tables & Chairs: some provided
Linens, Silver, etc.: CBA
Restrooms: not wheelchair accessible
Dance Floor: provided
Bride's Dressing Area: yes
Meeting Equipment: CBA
Other: Shuttle service included

Parking: shuttle service required, and included in rental fee
Accommodations: no guestrooms
Telephone: house phone
Outdoor Night Lighting: CBA
Outdoor Cooking Facilities: no
Cleanup: provided
View: landscaped grounds; panorama of ocean, bay and coastline

RESTRICTIONS:

Alcohol: provided through Cetrella
Smoking: not allowed
Music: amplified OK outdoors

Wheelchair Access: limited
Insurance: liability required

The professionals in the back of this book are the best in the business. How do we know? Read page 701.

Oceano Hotel and Spa

280 Capistrano Road, Half Moon Bay
650/726-5400
www.oceanohalfmoonbay.com
nancyn@oceanohalfmoonbay.com

Waterfront Hotel and Spa

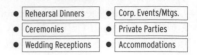

- Rehearsal Dinners
- Ceremonies
- Wedding Receptions
- Corp. Events/Mtgs.
- Private Parties
- Accommodations

A quaint, artsy Main Street... miles of shoreside trails and nature habitats...world-class golf, surfing and fishing.... As if there wasn't enough to love about Half Moon Bay, we've discovered another compelling reason to celebrate in this secluded oasis: Oceano Hotel and Spa. Conceived as a cutting-edge model of environmental sensitivity, Oceano is not only one of the greenest hotels in California, it's also one of the most inviting.

First off, consider the location, just a few minutes north of town center overlooking Pillar Point Harbor. Sailboats bob and sway in the marina, dolphins cavort beyond the breakers, and in the distance the Santa Cruz coastline is etched along a watery-blue panorama. The hotel lobby's creamy marble elegance is equally uplifting, and the Great Room just beyond the foyer has all the charm of a luxurious, sun-washed beach house. Three stories of guestrooms encircle this cozy yet airy space, bathed in a natural light from its vaulted atrium ceiling. The magic of the sea whispers at Oceano: A replica of a schooner sits atop a grand fireplace mantle, and overstuffed sofas surround a whimsical glass coffee table that encases starfish, seashells and coastal mementos in a bed of sand. The entire boutique hotel is peppered with such well-chosen decorative details, all of which maintain the seaside motif.

You and your event guests will also be delighted by your spacious accommodations. High ceilings, fireplaces and plantation-style furniture make you want to move right in. Thoughtful amenities like Aveda bath products, super-soft towels and organic bamboo sheets seduce you with plush comfort. Step out to your oceanview balcony and experience Half Moon Bay's dual personality: On an easy, breezy afternoon, sunlight glistens on the waves and brown pelicans dive for their dinner; then in an instant, curls of mist roll in with the setting sun and the bellow of foghorns adds a romantic mystique.

Speaking of romance, ceremonies are utterly picturesque out on the Wedding Garden, a sweep of landscaped lawn facing the harbor. A stone pathway leads to a white gazebo where you can exchange vows. Afterwards, serve cocktails on the adjoining Cypress Courtyard before retiring to the ballroom for the reception.

This beautiful new banquet space is embellished with ornate crown molding, Art Deco wall sconces and a trio of crystal chandeliers. The soothing neutral palette—soft gold, vanilla and a touch of sea-green—lends an upscale ambiance to your wedding dinner. (Incidentally, Oceano has superb cuisine, and their knowledgeable and experienced Executive Chef will sit down with you to design your menu.) When it's time for dancing, five sets of double doors swing open to the Atrium, a stylish annex aglow in moonlight from a skylit ceiling.

Though Half Moon Bay has plenty of diversions, your guests really don't need to leave Oceano at all. There's an on-site spa offering indulgent treatments, and the hotel's shopping promenade, Harbor Village, features select boutiques, cafés and galleries—all with colorful façades reminiscent of a Nantucket village. The enclosed promenade, which is flooded with natural light thanks to a greenhouse roof, is a great place for a stroll year-round and it's also available for events.

Perhaps the most endearing aspect of this sea-inspired sanctuary is its warm and enthusiastic service: The staff is genuinely eager to help you realize your own personal wedding vision. In short, Oceano is a real class act.

CEREMONY CAPACITY: The hotel holds 200 seated indoors and 400 seated outdoors.

EVENT/RECEPTION CAPACITY: The hotel accommodates 350 seated or 450 standing guests indoors and 400 seated or 800 standing outdoors.

MEETING CAPACITY: The hotel holds 350 seated guests.

FEES & DEPOSITS: 30% of the total event cost is required to reserve your date. A portion is due 90 days prior to the event and the balance is due 2 weeks prior. Rental fees range $1,000–5,000 depending on the space rented. Meals range $50–100/person. Tax, alcohol and a 20% service charge are additional.

AVAILABILITY: Year-round, daily, 6am–midnight.

SERVICES/AMENITIES:

Catering: provided
Kitchen Facilities: n/a
Tables & Chairs: provided
Linens, Silver, etc.: provided
Restrooms: wheelchair accessible
Dance Floor: provided
Bride's Dressing Area: yes
Meeting Equipment: provided
Other: spa services, picnic area, AV equipment, shopping promenade, event coordination

Parking: large lot
Accommodations: 95 guestrooms
Telephone: house, office and guest phones
Outdoor Night Lighting: CBA
Outdoor Cooking Facilities: BBQ CBA
Cleanup: provided
View: landscaped grounds, garden, courtyard; panorama of mountains, ocean/bay and fields

RESTRICTIONS:

Alcohol: provided or BYO with corkage fees
Smoking: not allowed
Music: amplified OK with restrictions

Wheelchair Access: yes
Insurance: not required
Other: no birdseed, rice, glitter or confetti

Sam's Chowder House

Waterfront Restaurant

4210 North Cabrillo Highway, Half Moon Bay
650/712-0245
www.samschowderhouse.com
events@samschowderhouse.com

- Rehearsal Dinners
- Ceremonies
- Wedding Receptions
- Corp. Events/Mtgs.
- Private Parties
- Accommodations

Oh, Sam's Chowder House in glorious Half Moon Bay, how do brides love thee? Let us count the ways! They love thee for your warm, welcoming atmosphere and waterfront setting; they love thee for your fresh, delicious cuisine; they love thee for your savvy, unpretentious service and versatile, ocean-view event spaces. *(Pssst... if you haven't met Sam's yet, be prepared to be swept off your feet!)*

Perched on a beachside bluff, this sublime restaurant, with its Cape Cod-style façade and hearty menu that's more surf than turf, was inspired by the traditional seafood houses of New England. Yet Sam's also evokes a California-casual sensibility that makes even refined celebrations feel relaxed and cheerful. The interior is decked out with wood and windows that frame scenic snapshots in all directions: *seabirds soaring over the blue Pacific...sailboats moored at the neighboring harbor...sweethearts strolling hand in hand along the shore*. A ramble of banquet rooms and refreshing sea-scented terraces (all with windbreaks and heaters) provide an array of mix-and-match event options.

The private Harbor View Room boasts a dark hardwood floor and a fireplace, especially cozy during the cooler seasons. It opens onto its own terrace, lined with Adirondack chairs and fire pits, offering a comfortable vantage for sipping cocktails and admiring sunsets. These spaces are often used together with the Terrace Room, a clear-covered patio that retains an open-air feel. The South Beach Bar is a private, two-level patio with an informal, beach-shack vibe and built-in bar. Sporting café tables with colorful umbrellas, it's also dog-friendly in case you want your pup for your ring-bearer. Planning a large bash? Then consider buying out the entire restaurant, including the Main Dining Room with its marble-topped oyster bar and row of picture windows.

Yet another reason brides love Sam's is for its private Beachfront Lawn, a sand-skimming meadow outfitted with umbrellas, strings of lights, and appropriate event accouterments. The staff will set up your wedding arch for picturesque "I do's" right on the beach, with the gentle whoosh of the waves enhancing the naturally romantic ambiance. Guests then dine at long tables, arranged family-style, on the lawn.

Sam's super-scrumptious menu focuses on sustainable and locally sourced ingredients. With so many culinary temptations to choose from, we have a hot tip: Treat your guests to Sam's famous three-course Lobster Clambake, prepared right in front of your guests. Whole Maine lobsters, clams, mussels and fresh ears of corn layered with seaweed are steamed in authentic New England-style wooden boxes, and served along with clam chowder and other tasty accompaniments. Add a raw seafood bar and margaritas to your cocktail hour, and let the flavorful aroma of the cooking feast create mouth-watering anticipation. *Mmmmm…*

Amazingly, all of this food and fun is value priced—there are no rental fees, just food and beverage minimums. Sam's Director of Private Dining will help you sort it all out to match your wedding vision. By the way, wedding couples aren't the only ones that have fallen for Sam's. Since its opening in 2006, the award-winning restaurant has garnered an impressive string of accolades. Which just goes to prove our point that to know Sam's is to love Sam's, for oh so many reasons.

CEREMONY, EVENT/RECEPTION & MEETING CAPACITY: Indoors, the restaurant holds 175 seated or 350 standing guests; outdoors, the Beachfront Lawn area holds 100 seated or 150 standing and Sam's South Beach Bar holds 60 seated or 80 standing.

FEES & DEPOSITS: An event date can be held for 4 days without a deposit. 50% of the estimated event total, a signed contract and credit card authorization are required to reserve your date. The balance is due on the day of the event. There is no room rental fee, but food and beverage minimums apply and vary depending on space rented. Lunch and dinner range $35–75/person. Tax, alcohol and a 20% service charge are additional.

Cancellation charges will be applied if notice is given 30 days or less before the confirmed event date.

AVAILABILITY: Year-round daily, 11am–10pm, except major holidays.

SERVICES/AMENITIES:

Catering: provided
Kitchen Facilities: n/a
Tables & Chairs: provided
Linens, Silver, etc.: provided
Restrooms: wheelchair accessible
Dance Floor: CBA
Bride's Dressing Area: yes
Meeting Equipment: CBA, extra charge

Parking: large lot, valet CBA
Accommodations: no guestrooms
Telephone: emergency use only
Outdoor Night Lighting: provided
Outdoor Cooking Facilities: yes
Cleanup: provided
View: harbor and Pacific Ocean
Other: cakes, flowers, music CBA, event coordination

RESTRICTIONS:

Alcohol: provided, full bar, no BYO
Smoking: not allowed
Music: amplified OK

Wheelchair Access: yes
Insurance: not required

Hillsborough Racquet Club

Historic Club

252 El Cerrito, Hillsborough
650/343-2062
www.hillsboroughracquetclub.org
info@hillsboroughracquetclub.org

● Rehearsal Dinners	● Corp. Events/Mtgs.
● Ceremonies	● Private Parties
● Wedding Receptions	Accommodations

The venerable Hillsborough Racquet Club has a lot in common with Katherine Hepburn. Like the actress, this venue has a great profile—polished looks and a dignified demeanor. But also like Hepburn, it doesn't have an ounce of stiffness or stuffiness. HRC's members love their place and enjoy all of its amenities, from its ballroom, patio and bar to the indoor badminton games they've played here for years. They have a lot to appreciate and they're happy to share it with brides and grooms.

Located in a lovely residential neighborhood, the Club is surrounded by elms, cypresses and laurel hedges. The entrance faces away from the street, and it's not until you walk around to it that you see just how beautiful the Club's architectural elements are. The building's design is based on the classical Greek Doric order with clean, elegant lines. A handsome portico sweeps along the front in a shallow curve, opening to a patio with flowerbeds and the main entrance. Visitors enter a domed, parquet-floored foyer with hallways that lead off to a bridal changing room, a servers' entrance, dining and music rooms, and the ballroom.

The ballroom is the heart of the Club and it's easy to see why. It's a large and airy, but not over-whelming space—ideal for dinner and dancing. The walls are finished in off-whites and orna-mentation is simple and subdued. The room's main visual focuses are a large working fireplace capped with a Tudor arch on one side, and a wall of windows and French doors on the opposite side that open to the patio (which is a wonderful place for cocktails and outside dining). Interior designers enjoy the room's good "bones," and since HRC never hosts more than one function per weekend, there's plenty of time for decorating.

Adjoining the ballroom is a bar and a "domino room." The bar, its white walls adorned with badminton racquets, is backed by a mirror that reflects light pouring in from the windows. The domino room next door has a very clubby feel with its green plaid-covered cane furniture. It's a fine place to sit and relax, and many wedding parties use it as a "quiet room" for guests who want to take a break from the festivities.

The dining room has a fireplace, brass chandelier and "hounds and hunters" prints on the walls. French doors off the adjacent music room lead to the patio, a sunny space between the portico and main entrance that's sheltered by a shade tree and lined with flowers and small hedges. The music room has a grand piano that stands against a light-loving wall of windows that's often used as a backdrop for small ceremonies. (Couples can also wed in the ballroom or on the patio, and HRC is close to several neighborhood churches.) Caterers love the very manageable staging kitchen off of the dining room. The changing room/ladies' lounge next to the foyer is spacious enough so that a bride and her attendants would never feel cramped.

Built in 1913 as a polo club, HRC predates the incorporation of Hillsborough. Now, almost a century old, it's an honored local institution. The bride who gets to have her function here knows she's getting a special place. She has exclusive use of the facility during her event, and an experienced live-in manager is available to provide discreet and efficient assistance. From the moment you step through the entrance to your first glimpse of the ballroom, this is a place that grows on you by leaps and bounds. Indeed, like Kate Hepburn, it's a class act that's hard to resist.

CEREMONY & EVENT/RECEPTION CAPACITY: Indoors, the Club holds 225 seated or 322 standing guests; the patio holds up to 50 seated or 60–70 standing guests.

MEETING CAPACITY: The Ballroom holds 225 guests seated theater-style.

FEES & DEPOSITS: A $500 deposit is required. 50% of the rental fee is due 6 months prior to the event, the balance is due 3 months prior. Rental fees range $3,500–4,000 (depending on guest count) for a 5-hour block of time. An extra hour is allowed for a wedding ceremony ($300 ceremony fee).

AVAILABILITY: Year-round, daily (except Thursdays) until 11pm.

SERVICES/AMENITIES:

Catering: BYO
Kitchen Facilities: warming kitchen
Tables & Chairs: provided
Linens, Silver, etc.: through caterer
Restrooms: wheelchair accessible
Dance Floor: yes
Bride's Dressing Area: yes
Meeting Equipment: BYO

Parking: ample on site
Accommodations: no guestrooms
Telephone: no
Outdoor Night Lighting: CBA
Outdoor Cooking Facilities: through caterer
Cleanup: caterer and resident manager
View: landscaped terrace
Other: exclusive use of facility during event

RESTRICTIONS:

Alcohol: BYO
Smoking: outdoors only
Music: amplified OK indoors with restrictions

Wheelchair Access: yes
Insurance: liability required

Want to know WHAT TO ASK a potential location or vendor? Check out our Questions to Ask on page 17.

Chateau La Joye

Private Estate

Address withheld to assure privacy, La Honda
650/747-0163

www.chateaulajoye.com
joanne@chateaulajoye.com

Rehearsal Dinners	Corp. Events/Mtgs.
● Ceremonies	● Private Parties
● Wedding Receptions	Accommodations

There are two routes to Joye, at least as far as the wedding venue is concerned: You can travel fifteen miles south of Half Moon Bay on Highway 1 and savor magnificent coastal vistas. Or take a leisurely drive inland from Woodside that curves past creek-watered meadows, nature preserves and picturesque countryside. Either route is magical, but they're just a prelude to the beauty of Chateau la Joye, a private home on sixteen acres where every detail radiates relaxed hospitality.

Upon arrival, your guests pull into a treelined drive and park in a large field, bordered by horses grazing in green pastures with low hills etched along the horizon. Passing beneath a rose-covered arbor into a courtyard, they're greeted by a triple-tiered fountain burbling a soothing welcome. The chateau's cheery façade includes multipaned windows trimmed in dark green and a balcony overflowing with a froth of climbing pink and white roses. Together with a quaint rooftop weathervane, distressed wooden shutters and a rustic barn in the distance, the scene recalls a charming Provençal village.

A covered breezeway—spacious enough for a gift table and a vintage wine barrel that holds the guestbook—connects the front and rear grounds. Friends and family are served cool drinks and snacks before taking their seats on the ceremony lawn. This sweep of grass faces a grand rectangular white gazebo next to a magnificent rose garden that perfumes the air. Meanwhile, you and your bridal party survey the crowd from an adorable hilltop bridal cottage, set amidst a terraced lavender garden. When you hear your musical cue, you descend a flight of wooden steps to the back of the lawn and then down the final stretch of wedding aisle—at Chateau la Joye, this spotlight moment isn't rushed!

After exchanging vows, you and your husband take advantage of the photogenic scenery, while your loved ones meander back to the front courtyard for drinks and hors d'oeuvres. (By the way, you save a bundle here by bringing in your own wine and liquor. The chateau provides the bartender—with no corkage fee!) Meals are served beneath a long wisteria-clad pergola that borders the ceremony lawn, which has been reset with tables, chairs and market umbrellas. At one end of the pergola, another fountain and built-in benches make an inviting conversation nook. At the opposite end, the chateau's award-winning caterer cooks up freshly prepared entrées and tasty accompaniments in an outdoor kitchen.

Following a hearty meal, you and your new husband kick off the dancing on a large patio strung with jazzy café lights on the far side of the lawn. Nearby, chairs clustered around a fire pit are a comfortable spot from which to survey the festivities.

Celebrating at the chateau is not only lovely, it's also easy. Owner Joanne Joye-Francesconi is a natural hostess and a trained wedding coordinator, and day-of coordination is included with your site rental (a significant savings to you!) so you can fully experience your big day rather than worrying about the details. What could be more joyful than that?

CEREMONY & EVENT/RECEPTION CAPACITY: The site holds 250 seated or 500 standing guests outdoors. Tenting is available.

MEETING CAPACITY: Meetings do not take place at this facility.

FEES & DEPOSITS: A $1,000 deposit is required to reserve your date and the balance is due 2 weeks prior to the event. Rental fees are $33/person. Meals start at $59/person. Tax, alcohol and service charge are additional.

AVAILABILITY: Seasonal from May to October, Friday, Saturday or Sunday, 10am–10pm. By appointment only.

SERVICES/AMENITIES:

Catering: provided
Kitchen Facilities: n/a
Tables & Chairs: provided
Linens, Silver, etc.: through caterer
Restrooms: not wheelchair accessible
Dance Floor: provided
Bride's Dressing Area: yes
Meeting Equipment: n/a

Parking: large lot
Accommodations: no guestrooms
Telephone: guest phones
Outdoor Night Lighting: provided
Outdoor Cooking Facilities: BBQ on site
Cleanup: provided
View: fountain, garden, hills, fields, valley, landscaped grounds
Other: event coordination

RESTRICTIONS:

Alcohol: BYO
Smoking: outdoors only
Music: amplified OK outdoors with restrictions

Wheelchair Access: yes
Insurance: liability required

Los Altos History Museum

51 South San Antonio Road, Los Altos
650/948-9427 X12
www.losaltoshistory.org
mperry@losaltoshistory.org

History Museum & Special Event Facility

● Rehearsal Dinners	● Corp. Events/Mtgs.
● Ceremonies	● Private Parties
● Wedding Receptions	Accommodations

Not so very long ago, apricot orchards, vineyards, and walnut groves cloaked the fertile plains of the Peninsula, and dairy farms and greenhouses dotted the hillsides. The transition from pristine agricultural paradise to Silicon Valley hub is skillfully realized at the Los Altos History Museum, where the past comes alive right before your very eyes. We thought this place was so interesting and so lovely that we would come here even if we weren't planning a special event. But make no mistake—there's plenty here to entice party-givers of all types.

In a model of team spirit, a group of Los Altos go-getters banded together to create this local museum, a captivating window in time set among acres of delightful parks and gardens. Open since Spring 2001, the History Museum resides in a folksy, wood-plank building. The vaulted entryway and the indoor balcony, which encircles the three-story space, generate an open, welcoming look and feel. Most of the main floor is taken up by the changing exhibits gallery, which features visiting collections, some on loan from notable institutions like the Smithsonian. Up a winding staircase to the permanent exhibit you'll find engaging interactive displays of Los Altos area history. There's more history just across the landscaped courtyard in the landmark J. Gilbert Smith History House. This adorable Craftsman-style shingled farmhouse from 1905 sets a nostalgic tone for your outdoor wedding or special event.

Surrounding both buildings, the pretty museum gardens offer several spots to enjoy the inspiring beauty of flowers in bloom, treetops swaying in the breeze, and squirrels scampering about their natural habitat. Why not exchange marriage vows under the dappled shade of oak trees? The front yard of the History House is a darling scene for memorable photos, the newlyweds framed by an archway wrapped in wild roses, or the wedding party posed on the broad porch steps in an old-fashioned tableau. In fair weather, you may want to hold your reception outdoors too, skillfully arranged by the museum's expert event coordinator.

A more formal outdoor ceremony and reception site is the spacious red-brick courtyard between the main Museum and the quaint façade of the History House. Your walk down the aisle is accented by antique-style verdigris lamps, potted blooms and delicate saplings, and a redwood pergola lets you say your vows while facing the lush garden. Afterwards, you can dine outdoors and even have your first dance under the stars.

Then the party moves through sliding glass doors into the Changing Exhibits Gallery, where polished blonde wood floors and works of art lend an air of distinction to your celebration. Here, the cake is served and guests can dance the night away. Those who prefer quieter pursuits might meander upstairs to enjoy the interactive displays, artifacts and vintage clothing, or step outside for a stroll along the moonlit garden lanes. This is the way museums should be—hands-on, fun, and fascinating. To further enhance your event, arrange a guided tour of the History House. The quaintly furnished rooms replicate in amazing detail the lifestyle of a 1930s farm family. You'll feel like you stepped through a time tunnel into the simple, wholesome world of a bygone era.

The Los Altos History Museum is more than just a peek into the past; it's also a vision of the future, a future that embraces family, community, and traditional values, while honoring a connection to the land. When you hold your special celebration here, you'll become part of this ideal tomorrow, because most of the proceeds from your event go towards supporting the museum and its grounds for generations to come.

CEREMONY CAPACITY: The Garden accommodates 200 seated, and the Changing Exhibits Gallery 100 seated guests.

EVENT/RECEPTION CAPACITY: The Garden holds 200 seated or standing, and the Changing Exhibits Gallery 100 seated or 150 standing guests.

MEETING CAPACITY: The Gallery holds 100 seated theater-style or 60 seated classroom-style.

FEES & DEPOSITS: The entire rental fee, along with a $1,000 security deposit and a $500 application fee, are required to reserve your date. Rental fees range $2,000–4,500. Liability insurance is required. There is also an alcohol permit fee required.

AVAILABILITY: Tuesday–Sunday, 4pm–11pm, mid-April through mid-October. Setup access at 3pm.

SERVICES/AMENITIES:

Catering: select from preferred list
Kitchen Facilities: fully equipped, caterer's kitchen
Tables & Chairs: provided; extra fee
Linens, Silver, etc.: BYO or through caterer
Restrooms: wheelchair accessible
Dance Floor: hardwood floor or brick patio
Bride's & Groom's Dressing Area: yes
Meeting Equipment: full range, extra fee
Other: coordination, docent-led tours

Parking: large lot, complimentary
Accommodations: no guestrooms
Telephone: pay phone at library
Outdoor Night Lighting: yes
Outdoor Cooking Facilities: through caterer
Cleanup: through caterer
View: garden courtyard, Peninsula coastal hills and landscaped grounds

RESTRICTIONS:

Alcohol: BYO, licensed and insured server
Smoking: not allowed
Music: amplified OK indoors and outdoors until 8pm with volume restrictions

Wheelchair Access: yes
Insurance: extra liability required
Other: no rice, birdseed, confetti or glitter

Allied Arts Guild

Historic Landmark & Garden

75 Arbor Road at Cambridge, Menlo Park
650/322-2405
www.alliedartsguild.org
events@alliedartsguild.org

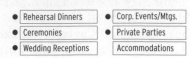

● Rehearsal Dinners	● Corp. Events/Mtgs.
● Ceremonies	● Private Parties
● Wedding Receptions	Accommodations

The Allied Arts Guild is an extraordinary place. It hits you instantly as you walk through the entry and gaze at the fountains, the wrought-iron details, colorful frescos and intricate tilework. The beautiful and tranquil gardens draw you further into the central courtyard, where you say to yourself, "I can't believe I'm in Menlo Park."

No wonder. This serene oasis is a historic landmark located amidst three and a half acres that were once part of an original Spanish land grant. Allied Arts is so hidden, you'd never know that it's located here, tucked away in a quiet, residential neighborhood not far from the Stanford University campus. The founders' original dream of a European-style crafts guild was realized in 1929 by California artist Pedro deLemos and architect Gardner Dailey. Both were responsible for creating the gardens, buildings and shops of the complex, and adhering to a romantic palette with a strong Spanish emphasis.

After more than 70 years, the site holds a major place in California history. Luckily for all of us, this jewel-of-a-venue has been recently and completely restored back to its original splendor. The complex is designed in the Spanish Colonial style, with meandering courtyards and terraces, burbling fountains, and handsome buildings with white plaster walls topped by terracotta tiles. The lush gardens were inspired by gardens in Granada, Spain, with an emphasis on color, fragrance and seasonal flowers. During the summer months, a floral profusion of intense color makes a great background for wedding photos. Just imagine getting married outdoors in a spot called "Garden of Delight," encircled by blue Nile lilies, aster, salvia and hydrangeas or "The Court of Abundance," with splashing fountain surrounded by gold and yellow marigolds, wallflowers and nasturtiums!

If the weather is uncooperative, you can have your ceremony or reception indoors in the Restaurant or Sunset Room. Both have rustic, high-beamed ceilings and wrought-iron chandeliers. The cement floors are worthy of note: They were painstakingly handcarved by Pedro deLemos to look like stone. The homey Spanish fireplaces are made of adobe, and when a fire is burning, they give the rooms a warm glow.

You can rent one part of the complex, or go for broke and celebrate by renting the entire facility. You'd be hard pressed to find a more relaxed and striking setting on the Peninsula with both indoor and outdoor event spaces. And there's an added benefit: Because Allied Arts is a nonprofit organization, all proceeds are donated to the Lucile Packard Children's Hospital at Stanford—which means a significant portion of your rental fees are tax deductible!

CEREMONY & EVENT/RECEPTION CAPACITY: The site accommodates 140 seated or standing indoors and 140 seated or standing outdoors.

MEETING CAPACITY: The site holds 120 seated guests, or up to 44 seated conference-style.

FEES & DEPOSITS: Ceremonies start at $2,000; for receptions the use fee ranges $3,000–6,500. Weekday events range $400–1,500.

AVAILABILITY: Year-round, Monday–Saturday 8:30am–9pm.

SERVICES/AMENITIES:

Catering: select from preferred list
Kitchen Facilities: prep only
Tables & Chairs: some provided
Linens, Silver, etc.: through caterer
Restrooms: wheelchair accessible
Dance Floor: CBA
Meeting Equipment: provided
Bride's Dressing Area: yes

Parking: on-site lot for 100 cars, and on-street
Accommodations: no guestrooms
Telephone: house phone
Outside Night Lighting: yes
Outdoor Cooking Facilities: CBA
Cleanup: provided
View: garden, landscaped grounds
Other: AV equipment

RESTRICTIONS:

Alcohol: provided
Smoking: designated area only
Music: amplified OK indoors, acoustic only outdoors

Wheelchair Access: yes
Insurance: certificate required
Other: no birdseed or rice; no swimming

Want to find more locations and services? Check out our informative website, www.HereComesTheGuide.com.

243

Stanford Park Hotel

Hotel

100 El Camino Real, Menlo Park
650/330-2776
www.stanfordparkhotel.com
weddings@stanfordparkhotel.com

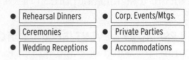

- Rehearsal Dinners
- Ceremonies
- Wedding Receptions
- Corp. Events/Mtgs.
- Private Parties
- Accommodations

Renowned for its sophisticated décor and gracious service, the Stanford Park Hotel is an outstanding choice for your celebration.

You feel the welcoming atmosphere as soon as you walk through the brass entry doors and into the softly lit lobby with its immense brick fireplace and cascading oak staircase.

Just past the lobby is a beautiful bi-level courtyard that exudes an Old World ambiance. The two levels, separated by a vine-covered brick wall and original garden sculptures, are expertly landscaped with multicolored flowers, trees and handsome stone benches. Together they create a tranquil garden setting that's custom-made for outdoor ceremonies and receptions.

Couples exchange vows on the upper level, where the bridal processional walks down a lovely pathway bordered by seasonal flowers. Every ceremony here has an unexpected guest—a full bronze statue of Benjamin Franklin, permanently seated on his own bench. Receptions take place in the lower courtyard, with tables arranged around a small fountain. On sunny days, freestanding market umbrellas are available to shade guests.

Inside the hotel, the Stanford and Menlo Rooms are popular for receptions and rehearsal dinners. Featuring high vaulted ceilings, and furnished with pieces designed specifically for the Stanford Park, these pleasant spaces convey a classic style with a contemporary touch. For larger events reserve the Woodside Room, which has a cathedral ceiling, expansive bay windows and an adjacent foyer.

The Stanford Park is a convenient destination for out-of-town guests who want to explore the Bay Area, and the hotel's very special room rates make it easy for them to extend their stay. After a long day of sightseeing they'll look forward to dining in the award-winning restaurant, relaxing over a glass of wine (or decadent dessert) in the Lounge, or just calling it a night in their elegantly appointed guestrooms.

CEREMONY & EVENT/RECEPTION & MEETING CAPACITY: The hotel can accommodate up to 120 seated or 200 standing guests indoors and 250 seated or 300 standing outdoors

FEES & DEPOSITS: Rental fees range $600–2,000. For weddings, a nonrefundable deposit of 25% of the estimated total is required to reserve your date. For any time over 5 hours there is an additional rental fee. All catering is provided by the hotel. Wedding packages range $79–129/person. Alcohol, tax and a 20% service charge are additional.

For weekday business meetings and corporate events, call the catering department for additional information.

AVAILABILITY: Year-round, daily, 7am–midnight. The Courtyard, when weather permits, 9am–10pm.

SERVICES/AMENITIES:

Catering: provided
Kitchen Facilities: n/a
Tables & Chairs: provided
Linens, Silver, etc.: provided
Restrooms: wheelchair accessible
Dance Floor: yes
Bride's Dressing Area: CBA
Meeting Equipment: CBA, extra fee

Parking: large lot
Accommodations: 163 guestrooms
Telephone: house phone
Outdoor Night Lighting: yes
Outdoor Cooking Facilities: no
Cleanup: provided
View: courtyard
Other: event coordination

RESTRICTIONS:

Alcohol: provided
Smoking: designated area
Music: amplified OK with volume limits; indoors until midnight, outdoors until 9:30pm

Wheelchair Access: yes
Insurance: not required
Other: no birdseed or rice

Westin San Francisco Airport

Hotel

One Old Bayshore Highway, Millbrae
650/872-8118
www.westin.com
vicki.idzal@westin.com

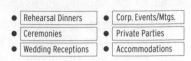

- Rehearsal Dinners
- Ceremonies
- Wedding Receptions
- Corp. Events/Mtgs.
- Private Parties
- Accommodations

The name Westin San Francisco Airport Hotel is a bit of a misnomer, because even though it's close to the airport this venue is really more like an elegant resort. With its refined décor, warm ambiance and long list of amenities, it's one of the Peninsula's most popular places for weddings, receptions and parties.

Set on the cusp of a palm-lined drive near the edge of the bay, and just two minutes from the airport, the Westin is surprisingly quiet and peaceful. Even the lobby has a calming influence, designed in warm natural shades and outfitted with modern, comfortable furnishings and lush floral arrangements.

From here it's a short walk to the banquet rooms, and by the time you reach them, you're expecting something sophisticated and tasteful. You won't be disappointed. The Westin Ballroom, where most weddings, large meetings and special events take place, is very lovely. Brides are usually overjoyed with the décor and have been known to exclaim, "Oh, this will match my dress perfectly!" That's because the walls are papered in a neutral champagne-and-taupe print that gives off a subtle gold sheen, and the coffered ceiling is white. One of the most striking features of this ballroom is the lighting. Instead of traditional chandeliers, there are fixtures fashioned from white globes seemingly "scattered" behind a veil of pearl strands. When the lights are dimmed, you feel like you're gazing at clusters of stars, shining through golden clouds. Additional romantic lighting comes from alabaster-and-brass wall sconces. Although the ballroom can be divided into four sections, only one event at a time is scheduled so you can tailor the size of the space to fit your needs.

The expansive foyer area in front of the ballroom is not only refreshing to the eye, it's large enough to be set up with fountains, plants and an hors d'oeuvre buffet and still have plenty of room left over for a crowd to mingle comfortably. And if you have kids at your event, you'll be ever-grateful to the Westin—they make a room with childcare available just off the foyer.

Smaller weddings and meetings are held in the Bayshore Ballroom, an intimate space with crystal chandeliers, alabaster wall sconces, and floor-to-ceiling windows overlooking the pool atrium. The atrium itself is ideal for cocktail parties and more informal receptions. Huge potted ferns and rubber trees, as well as colorful flowers set around the pool soak up the sunlight from the vaulted skylit "ceiling" and create a tropical ambiance.

Two dozen other rooms are available for functions, and award-winning chefs will create custom, culturally diverse menus. Guests staying overnight sleep well, thanks to the Westin's supercomfy Heavenly Bed and triple-paned windows that create a virtually soundproof environment. There's one more amenity just for weddings: a customized web page for each couple to facilitate reserving guestrooms and providing information to attendees.

The combination of beautiful facilities, excellent food and personal service generates lots of repeat business for the hotel. Their "Letters To The Hotel" binder includes pages of laudatory comments such as, "The Westin is the only place to hold an event in San Mateo County! Period!" and "My daughter's dream of a perfect wedding day came true!" Read them all and you come away with a sense that guests feel quite welcomed here and very well taken care of. It's absolutely clear why they return to the Westin time after time—for many of them it's like coming home.

CEREMONY CAPACITY: The Bayshore Ballroom holds 200, the Westin Ballroom 600, and the Aspen Room 150 seated guests.

EVENT/RECEPTION CAPACITY: The hotel can accommodate from 48–410 seated or 125–600 standing guests indoors.

MEETING CAPACITY: The Westin has over 22,000 square feet of function space, including 31 flexible rooms, from ballrooms and salons to suites and boardrooms. Spaces can accommodate 4–700 guests for business events.

FEES & DEPOSITS: For weddings, a nonrefundable $5,000 deposit is required to secure your date; the event balance is due 3 weeks prior to the event. There are 3 wedding packages, ranging $75–125/person, that include centerpieces, champagne reception and toast, 3-course meal, hors d'oeuvres, wine with meal, overnight accommodations and breakfast for the bride and groom. If you don't want a package, all menus can be customized; luncheons range $34–55/person, dinners $45–65/person. Tax and a 22% service charge are additional. There is a $500 ceremony setup charge.

For other social events or business functions, prices will vary depending on the menu and services selected; call for specific rates. Meeting packages are also available.

AVAILABILITY: Year-round, daily including holidays, until 1am. For Saturday weddings, time frames are 11am–5pm or 6pm–1am.

SERVICES/AMENITIES:
Catering: provided, no BYO
Kitchen Facilities: n/a
Tables & Chairs: provided
Linens, Silver, etc.: provided
Restrooms: wheelchair accessible
Dance Floor: provided
Bride's & Groom's Dressing Area: guestroom CBA
Meeting Equipment: full range and business center, in-room data port lines

Parking: ample, gated and secure lots
Accommodations: 400 guestrooms
Telephone: guest phones
Outdoor Night Lighting: access only
Outdoor Cooking Facilities: no
Cleanup: provided
View: no
Other: event coordination, baby grand piano, ice sculpture, wedding cakes, limo service, customized web page

RESTRICTIONS:
Alcohol: provided, or WC corkage negotiable
Smoking: outside only
Music: amplified OK

Wheelchair Access: yes
Insurance: not required
Other: no rice, birdseed, glitter or confetti

La Costanera—Contemporary Peruvian Cuisine

Waterfront Restaurant

8150 Cabrillo Highway, Montara
650/728-1600

www.lacostanerarestaurant.com
info@lacostanerarestaurant.com

● Rehearsal Dinners	● Corp. Events/Mtgs.
● Ceremonies	Private Parties
● Wedding Receptions	Accommodations

La Costanera, a new culinary destination just north of Half Moon Bay, is an upscale all-in-one event venue with gourmet panache. Perched on a bluff above Montara Beach, this gorgeous restaurant is nothing short of a masterpiece. The three-level 10,000-square-foot building is shaped like half of a modern Mesoamerican pyramid, with slanting windows and skylights that embrace a breathtaking ocean view. Its overall design reflects a contemporary global aesthetic, artfully blending rustic, natural elements—rich woods, sea shells, distressed metal—into the décor of the geometrically shaped rooms. Cleverly styled furnishings and accents, such as old-fashioned maps inlaid into some of the tabletops and nautically inspired mobiles, convey an antique seafaring flair. The effect is beautifully original.

La Costanera's layout offers supreme event versatility, and whether you buy out the entire restaurant for your event or reserve individual sections, there are no rental fees as long as you meet the food and beverage minimums. The main floor houses the restaurant and a semiprivate dining area called the Greenhouse, with its own fireplace and atrium. Glass doors open to an oceanview patio, complete with fire pit, for outdoor dining or an intimate ceremony. Back inside, a staircase leads to a skylit balcony that overlooks the action on the main floor. This private enclave can host rehearsal dinners, showers or small gatherings.

The lower level holds the bar and lounge, a very cool space for receptions, social hours and after-parties—La Costanera can stay open until 2am. A long bar serves up the drinks (we recommend the house-made sangria or their pisco sour, a Peruvian cocktail that's one of our all-time favorites). Gleaming tile floors and Oriental carpets enhance the space's exotic luxe; a sunken lounge area, normally outfitted with velour couches and club chairs, can be cleared ahead of time for dancing. Glass doors open onto a beachfront patio, whose glorious panorama of sea and sky makes it quite the romantic spot for ceremonies. A footpath leads directly to the sand, so while your guests are sipping sangria, you and your bridal party can pose for photos alongside the waves.

The food and drink is as impressive as the setting. Chef-owner Carlos Altamirano already has two critically acclaimed restaurants to his credit, Mochica and Piqueos, and this latest venture is sure to add to his culinary fandom. Altamirano's fusion dishes reflect his country's Asian and Mediterranean influences, and introduce some fascinating indigenous components like yucca fries, sweet plantains and blue potatoes. Seafood is the star here, but entrées like lamb chops in mint chimichurri sauce will keep carnivores contented, too. La Costanera brilliantly showcases

Peru's national dish, *cebiche,* in a dozen or so provocative interpretations, and they even have a cute cart to serve it up to your guests. Round out the appetizers with an assortment of tapas and anitcuchos (South American-style skewers), and you have a cocktail hour that's pure foodie fun. Just don't forget the pisco! La Costanera has an entire menu of pisco variations, ensuring your signature cocktail will be unique (mojitos are so 2008…).

The expert staff will help you navigate the novel food and drink options, and can assist with event extras—entertainment, late-night service, valet parking, flowers, favors and more. With its hip vibe, cutting-edge cuisine and stunning atmosphere, La Costanera is definitely a venue to put on your short-list.

CEREMONY CAPACITY: The restaurant holds 50 seated guests indoors and 30 seated outdoors.

EVENT/RECEPTION CAPACITY: The facility can accommodate 250 seated or 300 standing indoors and 50 seated or standing outdoors.

MEETING CAPACITY: Meeting rooms hold 200 seated guests.

FEES & DEPOSITS: 20% of the total event cost is required to reserve your date. Rental fees range $0–1,000 depending on the space rented. Meals range $50–100/person. Tax, alcohol and a 20% service charge are additional.

AVAILABILITY: Year-round, Tuesday–Sunday, 5pm–midnight.

SERVICES/AMENITIES:

Catering: provided or BYO
Kitchen Facilities: fully equipped
Tables & Chairs: provided
Linens, Silver, etc.: provided
Restrooms: wheelchair accessible
Dance Floor: provided
Bride's Dressing Area: CBA
Meeting Equipment: BYO

Parking: large lot
Accommodations: no guestrooms
Telephone: house phone
Outdoor Night Lighting: provided
Outdoor Cooking Facilities: none
Cleanup: renter or caterer
View: coastline, mountains, ocean/bay
Other: event coordination

RESTRICTIONS:

Alcohol: provided or BYO with corkage fee
Smoking: outdoors only
Music: amplified OK with restrictions

Wheelchair Access: yes
Insurance: liability required

This is important! Tell locations you're reading HERE COMES THE GUIDE and ask if our information is still current.

249

Cypress Meadows

343 Cypress Avenue, Moss Beach
650/728-8045
www.cypressmeadows.net
info@cypressmeadows.net

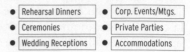

Private Banquet Facility

- Rehearsal Dinners
- Ceremonies
- Wedding Receptions
- Corp. Events/Mtgs.
- Private Parties
- Accommodations

Tucked inside a quaint residential neighborhood just north of Half Moon Bay Airport, Cypress Meadows is a welcome addition to the San Mateo coastal scene. This private banquet facility is hidden behind a pretty flower farm, and offers a secluded milieu for your wedding celebration. On these nine pleasant acres, adjacent to the Fitzgerald Marine Reserve, the air is sweet, tinged with a hint of salt from the nearby sea, and the atmosphere mellow and relaxed.

Your congenial proprietors are Randy and Sharon Dardenelle, who designed Cypress Meadows specifically to host social events. They've outfitted meeting areas and guestrooms with the latest modern technology; yet, they've managed to instill the place with a timeless simplicity, beginning with the cedar board-and-batten building. Trimmed with river rock pillars and copper handrails, the structure conveys a comfortable, rustic vibe. Yet it's a fairly new venue, so everything is neat and fresh inside. Guests enter through the foyer, where a trio of skylights, a travertine tile floor, and a gas fireplace in one corner make an inviting first impression. Brides often place their gift table and guest book here.

Indoor gatherings congregate in the Cypress Room, a warm and friendly space bookended by two gas fireplaces glowing beneath tall, stacked-stone hearths. Depending on your preferred setup, the room can accommodate up to 75 guests, with overflow seating on an adjacent terrace (which can be tented in case the weather doesn't cooperate).

The terrace is also a sublime spot for your cocktail hour, with a low trickling waterfall pond and potted plants setting the scene. The most striking feature, however, is the bird's-eye view of a lovely hillside garden, with a sprawling meadow down below. From the terrace, follow a loose gravel path that cascades downward through native plantings—flowering herbs, blooming succulents and fragrant lavender—that spill over low walls. Several stone seating areas built into the landscape entice you to pose for photos, framed by purple salvia and wispy ornamental grasses. Or steal a few moments with your sweetie, snuggling together on the old-fashioned driftwood swing.

At the bottom of the path, a vast green meadow, kissed with bursts of yellow wildflowers, spreads before you. On one side, a copse of lofty cypress trees feathers the sky; on another, a bank of lithe willows bends in the breeze. Opposite, Montara Mountain forms a jagged silhouette against the mercurial skyline. Wedding ceremonies on the meadow take on an informal, country charm coupled with a sense of wild majesty. Little decoration is needed to improve upon what Nature provides, which includes peek-a-boo ocean views.

Unlike at some locations, you're free to hire any caterer you wish to take advantage of the commercial kitchen with separate, easy access. Another bonus at this property: two guestrooms on opposite sides of the building, each with its own private entrance. The nicely styled suites—one for the bride, one for the groom—open to a balcony overlooking the meadow. What an inspired spot for tossing your bridal bouquet, as you savor the culmination of your memorable celebration at Cypress Meadows.

CEREMONY CAPACITY: The facility holds 80 seated guests indoors, and 150 seated outdoors.

EVENT/RECEPTION CAPACITY: Cypress Meadows can accommodate 65 seated or 80 standing guests indoors and 100 seated or 150 standing outdoors.

MEETING CAPACITY: The facility holds 60 seated guests.

FEES & DEPOSITS: A $1,000 deposit is required to reserve your date. The balance is due 30 days prior to the event. Rental fees range $1,500–5,000 depending on the day of the week and the type of event.

AVAILABILITY: Year-round, daily, 8am–10pm.

SERVICES/AMENITIES:

Catering: BYO
Kitchen Facilities: fully equipped
Tables & Chairs: some provided
Linens, Silver, etc.: CBA
Restrooms: wheelchair accessible
Dance Floor: provided
Bride's & Groom's Dressing Area: yes
Meeting Equipment: provided
Other: on-site florals, AV equipment

Parking: large lot
Accommodations: 2 guestrooms
Telephone: office phone
Outdoor Night Lighting: provided
Outdoor Cooking Facilities: BBQ CBA
Cleanup: caterer & facility
View: forest, fountain, garden, courtyard, meadow, mountains, ocean

RESTRICTIONS:

Alcohol: BYO
Smoking: not allowed
Music: amplified OK with restrictions

Wheelchair Access: yes
Insurance: liability required

Ristorante Portofino
at the Best Western Lighthouse Hotel

105 Rockaway Beach Avenue, Pacifica
650/359-0302, 650/355-6300

www.ristorante-portofino.com, www.bestwesternlighthouse.com
ristoranteportofino@yahoo.com

Waterfront Restaurant & Hotel

- Rehearsal Dinners
- Ceremonies
- Wedding Receptions
- Corp. Events/Mtgs.
- Private Parties
- Accommodations

You're walking down the aisle, breathing in the fresh sea air. Just ahead, your betrothed watches you approach, smiling proudly. A hundred yards behind him, ocean waves crash in white peaks against a rocky bluff, then play out in gentle ripples along a secluded sandy beach. The western sky is turning an orange-purple as the sun sets. You hear a guest whisper to someone beside him, "What a view!" Without a doubt, you know you've picked the right spot for your seaside wedding: Ristorante Portofino in Pacifica.

The restaurant is located on the San Marlo Esplanade in Pacifica's Rockaway Beach area. Butting up against the Pacific Ocean, this paved boardwalk gives you all the benefits of a beach wedding, minus the sand in your shoes. And while it's close to the surf, it's not so close that it drowns out the "I do's." The staff does a great job of staging your ceremony—they'll even pull out special charts to help you synchronize your ceremonial kiss with the setting sun. Best of all, since Ristorante Portofino is in a sunbelt, the coastal fog rarely makes an appearance, leaving the view unspoiled.

Reception options abound here. You not only have the choice of renting out part or all of the restaurant, but you also have access to the event spaces in the adjoining Best Western Lighthouse Hotel. Built behind the restaurant, the hotel was designed to preserve Portofino's charm, while ensuring that almost all of its guestrooms have an ocean view.

Within the restaurant the fireplace glows, antique red lanterns and nautical artifacts add romance, and guests have an unobstructed view of the ocean from every seat. For a small reception, reserve the semiprivate area around the fireplace in the main dining room. The Boardroom, a private sunlit dining room, cries out "rehearsal dinner." The Cove, Portofino's most popular room, is right off the esplanade. Formerly a nightclub, it has a large built-in bar and a wooden dance floor. And there's that vista again! If your guest list is too long for the restaurant, have your party in the Bounty Room on the hotel's second floor. When used in conjunction with the adjacent Sea Witch Room (great for the buffet or bar), it can accommodate over 200 guests! Naturally the view plays a significant role here: Tall draped windows across the entire oceanfront wall frame the crescent-shaped beach and vast sea beyond.

Another beautiful sight besides the ocean is the food at Portofino's. The restaurant's world-renowned chef, Giovanni Galati, has been in the business over 24 years. His creations include 45 kinds of homemade pasta and his signature dish, a unique seafood cioppino combining crab legs, mussels, clams and shrimp in his own "Red Bone Sauce."

After the last dance, you don't have to get in your car and drive home. Included in some of Ristorante Portofino's special event packages is a room in the hotel for your wedding night. Why not splurge a little and upgrade to a Beachfront Junior Suite or the luxurious Presidential Suite with a Jacuzzi tub! San Francisco is just minutes away, making this restaurant/hotel a convenient choice if you're inviting out-of-town guests. Plus the staff make it so easy to plan a wedding here, one couple flew in from Florida to tie the knot.

Everyone likes to relive a wonderful experience, and at Ristorante Portofino you can do just that. Simply return every year on your anniversary: When you share a candlelight dinner and take a walk on the beach, those sweet wedding memories will come flooding back to you.

CEREMONY & MEETING CAPACITY: The restaurant holds up to 150 seated guests, indoors or outdoors.

EVENT/RECEPTION CAPACITY: The restaurant accommodates up to 180 seated or 200 standing guests.

FEES & DEPOSITS: A nonrefundable room deposit is required to reserve your date. The balance is due 2 weeks prior to the event. Rental fees range $325–1,400 depending on space rented. Meals start at $48+/person. Tax, alcohol and a 20% service charge are additional.

AVAILABILITY: Year-round, daily, 7:30am–midnight.

SERVICES/AMENITIES:

Catering: provided
Kitchen Facilities: fully equipped
Tables & Chairs: provided
Linens, Silver, etc.: provided
Dance Floor: provided (built-in)
Restrooms: wheelchair accessible
Bride's Dressing Area: CBA
Meeting Equipment: CBA

Parking: complimentary
Accommodations: 97 guestrooms
Telephone: in sleeping rooms
Outdoor Night Lighting: yes
Outdoor Cooking Facilities: no
Cleanup: provided
View: panorama of ocean

RESTRICTIONS:

Alcohol: provided
Smoking: outside only
Music: amplified OK with restrictions

Wheelchair Access: yes
Insurance: not required

Crowne Plaza Cabaña Palo Alto

Hotel

4290 El Camino Real, Palo Alto
650/857-0787
www.cppaloalto.crowneplaza.com
sales.catering@cabanapaloalto.com

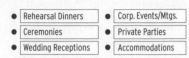

- Rehearsal Dinners
- Ceremonies
- Wedding Receptions
- Corp. Events/Mtgs.
- Private Parties
- Accommodations

What do the Beatles, Frank Sinatra, and President Clinton's security dogs have in common? They've all been guests at the Crowne Plaza Cabaña! Originally owned by movie star Doris Day, the Cabaña Hotel opened its doors in 1962 and immediately became a magnet for Hollywood luminaries. Described by *Life Magazine* as "one of the best hotels on the West Coast," it's now "the Cabaña reinvented," thanks to a 21st-century makeover that completely updated the décor, event spaces and guestrooms. However, the venue still retains the breezy, relaxed elegance and innovative design elements that made it a California classic.

With the largest event capacity on the Peninsula, the Crowne Plaza Cabaña offers numerous choices for functions, especially weddings and other fabulous fêtes. In the expansive Grand Mediterranean Ballroom, two-toned gold walls painted in a subtle swirling pattern complement the carpet. Overhead, eye-catching half-dome light fixtures made from tortoise shell and opaque glass panels are set into the high, coffered ceiling. Just outside, a spacious and sunny courtyard is perfect for a smaller ceremony or reception. It can be used alone, or as a prefunction area in conjunction with the ballroom. Other first-floor facilities include the intimate Bacchus Room, with a fireplace, new fixtures and plantation-shuttered windows.

On the second floor, you'll find the sophisticated Cyprus Room, the hotel's most sought-after venue. With its unique oval shape, wraparound floor-to-ceiling windows, and elegant touches (like the sky-blue wallpaper and fabric valances), this room's charms are hard to resist. During the day, natural light streams in through the windows, which provide ample views of the trees, courtyard and sparkling swimming pool below. At night, lights may be dimmed for a soft, romantic ambiance. If you prefer a more theatrical or dynamic look, specialty lighting can be added for an extra fee.

The Cyprus Room opens to the Sun Deck, which accommodates overflow reception seating and also works well for a wedding ceremony or social hour. Six Cabaña Suites next to the deck provide even more options: For example, you might reserve one for the bride's changing room and another for a hospitality room. One of the suites connects to both the Cyprus Room and the Sun Deck, creating a wonderful indoor-outdoor flow.

A host of smaller rooms are available, too, so you should be able to find a space that perfectly suits your occasion. In addition, the staff is extremely flexible and will work with you to deliver the event you envision. The Crowne Plaza Cabaña has always impressed its guests, and it continues to do so with inspired service, modern amenities and comfortable accommodations.

CEREMONY CAPACITY: The hotel accommodates up to 800 seated guests indoors and 400 seated outdoors.

EVENT/RECEPTION CAPACITY: The facility holds 640 seated and 800 standing indoors; 350 seated and 750 standing outdoors.

MEETING CAPACITY: Event spaces accommodate 800 seated guests.

FEES & DEPOSITS: 50% of the estimated event total is due at contract signing. The balance is payable 30 days prior to the event. Ceremony fees start at $1,000. Event and wedding packages start at $39/person and may include appetizers, meals, wine, champagne, linens, chair covers with colored sash, dance floor, staging and bridal suite, depending on the package selected. Tax, alcohol and a 20% service charge are additional. Room rental fees may apply if certain minimums are not met.

For business meetings, room rental fees range $150–15,000 depending on space rented and day of the event. Meals range $14–80/person. Tax, alcohol and a 20% service charge are additional.

AVAILABILITY: Year round, daily, 6am–midnight.

SERVICES/AMENITIES:

Catering: provided or BYO approved ethnic caterer
Kitchen Facilities: n/a
Tables & Chairs: provided
Linens, Silver, etc.: provided
Restrooms: wheelchair accessible
Dance Floor: yes
Bride's & Groom's Dressing Areas: yes
Meeting Equipment: provided

Parking: large lot
Accommodations: 184 guestrooms and 10 suites
Telephone: house phones
Outdoor Night Lighting: yes
Outdoor Cooking Facilities: no
Cleanup: provided
View: mountains
Other: event coordination, complimentary bridal suite with minimum number of rooms booked

RESTRICTIONS:

Alcohol: provided
Smoking: outside only
Music: amplified OK indoors

Wheelchair Access: yes
Insurance: not required

Overwhelmed? Use the search criteria on www.HereComesTheGuide.com to narrow down your choices.

255

Elizabeth F. Gamble Garden

Historic Home & Garden

1431 Waverley Street, Palo Alto
650/329-1356 x201

www.gamblegarden.org
admin@gamblegarden.org

●	Rehearsal Dinners	●	Corp. Events/Mtgs.
●	Ceremonies	●	Private Parties
●	Wedding Receptions		Accommodations

The Elizabeth F. Gamble Garden is one of the most perfect garden ceremony/reception sites we've seen. Miss Gamble, granddaughter of the co-founder of the Procter and Gamble Company, willed the home and its grounds to the City of Palo Alto. The estate is now run by the Elizabeth F. Gamble Horticultural Foundation.

The main house is a 1902 Colonial/Georgian Revival-style structure built in a lovely, older residential area of Palo Alto. Inside, a dining room, drawing room and library are available for receptions. Each room has been carefully restored using colorful, turn-of-the-century reproduction wallpapers. Dark natural wood wainscoting has been returned to its original splendor and there are graceful, molded ceilings and nicely finished oak floors throughout. Each room has its own fireplace. A set of French doors in the Library opens onto a brick porch that leads down to the first of many beautifully landscaped spaces.

Our favorite spots are the formal and informal gardens—the collective work of a full-time horticulturist and 300 volunteers. Each separately landscaped area feels like a private secret garden: The Rose Garden (with its 100 species of roses), the Wisteria Garden, and the Victorian Grotto—separately or combined—provide elegant settings for small wedding ceremonies and receptions.

After the ceremony, guests are invited to gather at the Tea House, where hors d'oeuvres and beverages are served. The bride and groom often slip away from the festivities at this time for a quiet moment together in the Gazebo, an Edwardian-inspired garden house.

The reception is usually held at the Carriage House. While the buffet is set up inside, guests are seated on the adjoining brick terrace. Five sets of French doors make it easy for people to move indoors and out, giving them the feeling of being in a garden pavilion.

Miss Gamble succeeded in creating a place of serenity and beauty. We recommend it highly.

CEREMONY CAPACITY: The Wisteria Garden, Rose Garden, Tea House Patio and Carriage House each hold 50 seated or standing guests; the Drawing Room holds 30 seated or standing guests.

EVENT/RECEPTION CAPACITY: The facility hosts events for up to 50 guests.

MEETING CAPACITY: The Carriage House Main Room holds 30 seated conference-style, the Dining Room 12 seated boardroom-style, and the Drawing Room 30 seated conference-style.

FEES & DEPOSITS: For events, a deposit of half of the total rental fee is required when reservations are confirmed. The rental fee on Saturdays is $1,200 for an 8-hour block; Monday–Friday daytime, $100/hour; weekday evenings, $600 minimum with a 50-guest maximum. The rental balance and an $800 cleaning/damage deposit are due prior to the date reserved. The damage/cleaning deposit is generally refunded within 3 weeks following your event.

For meetings and business functions, fees vary based on rooms rented and rental time frames; call for more details.

AVAILABILITY: For weddings, Saturdays and Sundays noon–10pm, Monday–Friday 4pm–10pm. For business functions, year-round, Monday–Thursday, 9am–5pm.

SERVICES/AMENITIES:
Catering: BYO
Kitchen Facilities: fully equipped
Tables & Chairs: BYO
Linens, Silver, etc.: BYO
Restrooms: wheelchair accessible
Dance Floor: yes
Bride's Dressing Area: yes
Meeting Equipment: screen, wireless

Parking: lot
Accommodations: no guestrooms
Telephone: house phone
Outdoor Night Lighting: yes
Outdoor Cooking Facilities: no
Cleanup: renter or caterer
View: Edwardian gardens
Other: piano available, event coordination

RESTRICTIONS:
Alcohol: BYO wine, beer or champagne; no beer kegs in main house
Smoking: not allowed
Music: acoustic only; no amplified or recorded music

Wheelchair Access: yes
Insurance: required
Other: rose petals only (no rice, birdseed, etc.)

Garden Court Hotel

520 Cowper Street, Palo Alto
800/824-9028, 650/323-1912

www.gardencourt.com
hotel@gardencourt.com

● Rehearsal Dinners	● Corp. Events/Mtgs.
● Ceremonies	● Private Parties
● Wedding Receptions	● Accommodations

The Garden Court Hotel is one of the few venues on the Peninsula where you can host your wedding ceremony and reception and your guests can stay. Newly remodeled in 2010, this hotel provides a warm, relaxed atmosphere combined with modern sensibilities and five-star personalized service.

Designed around a beautiful open-air European-style courtyard, the hotel is visually impressive. The large central fountain and tiers of flower-laden balconies create the feeling of an old Mediterranean town square. Arches abound, planters and urns are filled with colorful flowers and evergreen foliage, and trees are lit with twinkle lights. Celebrations often begin with champagne and hors d'oeuvres around the fountain in the courtyard, before guests are invited into the spacious Courtyard Ballroom for the main event.

The Grove Ballroom on the second floor is another favorite reception space. Floor-to-ceiling arched windows wrap around the room and overlook a lushly landscaped balcony. Here, guests may enjoy an al fresco cocktail hour out on the balcony followed by dinner and dancing inside. Both ballrooms are popular for their indoor/outdoor flow and inviting ambiance.

There are many benefits that contribute to the complete guest experience at the Garden Court. A few of them are exclusively available to wedding couples with a guaranteed guest list of 75 or more: preferred room rates for guests staying at the hotel; a complimentary guestroom with fireplace or Jacuzzi for the wedding couple on the night of the event; and a complimentary seven-night "Honeymoon in Spain" option at a sister hotel. What more could you ask for?

CEREMONY CAPACITY: The Grove Ballroom accommodates 225 seated or 300 standing. The Courtyard Ballroom holds 120 seated or 200 standing.

EVENT/RECEPTION & MEETING CAPACITY: Various rooms can accommodate 8–230 seated or 8–300 standing for a reception. For a meeting, the hotel seats 8–60 conference-style or 8–200 theater-style. Removable dividing walls can vary the room size.

FEES & DEPOSITS: For weddings, a $1,000–3,000 nonrefundable deposit is due at the time of booking, an additional $3,000 nonrefundable deposit is due 6 months prior to your event date, and the final estimated total is due 10 days prior to the event. All deposits are applied to the total cost of the event. Facility fees start at $1,000 and vary depending on the day of the week and space reserved. Menu and beverage packages range $65–95/person. Tax and a 20% service charge are additional. All pricing is guaranteed 90 days prior to the event date, with some specialty items subject to market change.

Facility fees for meetings and corporate events vary based on group size, room(s) selected and catering requirements. Please call for more details. Customized estimate and an event packet will be emailed or mailed directly.

AVAILABILITY: Year-round, daily, 8am–midnight. Please call for specific time frames for events.

SERVICES/AMENITIES:

Catering: provided
Kitchen Facilities: n/a
Tables & Chairs: provided
Linens, Silver, etc.: provided
Restrooms: wheelchair accessible
Dance Floor: provided
Bride's Dressing Area: CBA, extra fee
Meeting Equipment: full range CBA, extra fee

Parking: complimentary valet, large lot
Accommodations: 62 guestrooms and suites
Telephone: pay phones
Outdoor Night Lighting: yes
Outdoor Cooking Facilities: no
Cleanup: provided
View: Mediterranean courtyard and downtown Palo Alto

RESTRICTIONS:

Alcohol: provided or WC corkage $17.50/bottle
Smoking: outside only
Music: amplified OK indoors only, outdoors acoustic music only

Wheelchair Access: yes
Insurance: not required
Other: no birdseed or rice

Lucie Stern Community Center

Community Center

1305 Middlefield Road, Palo Alto
650/463-4900
www.cityofpaloalto.org
mary.constantino@cityofpaloalto.org

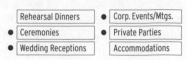

Rehearsal Dinners	● Corp. Events/Mtgs.
● Ceremonies	● Private Parties
● Wedding Receptions	Accommodations

With its white-stucco archways, red tile roof and vibrant courtyard, the Lucie Stern Center is a gracious example of Spanish-Mediterranean architecture. Designed by Birge Clark and donated by Lucie Stern, an heir of Levi Strauss, it was originally built in 1931 as a community theater. But since then, the center has matured into a welcoming hacienda that offers a variety of options for weddings.

You can rent individual areas or the whole center. For instance, if your wedding is small and informal, consider having it in the mid-sized Community Room, whose windows overlook a Mission-style promenade. The adjacent patio, which is enclosed by the U-shaped building and a vine-covered brick wall, has a two-tiered lawn bordered by an array of colorful flowers. The upper level is an ideal spot for your ceremony or live entertainment. Another choice for an intimate event is the Fireside Room. It features a large fireplace constructed of brick and stucco, and also adjoins the patio.

If you rent the entire center, you have carte blanche to utilize its event spaces any way you like. One of the most popular areas for gathering during a celebration is the Municipal Courtyard, a brick-paved retreat surrounded by flowers of every conceivable color. Enhancing this picturesque setting is the majestic stucco theater, standing tall in the background—it's evocative of a centuries-old Spanish church.

From the courtyard, guests walk through double glass doors into the Lucie Stern Center Ballroom, a large space complete with beautiful hardwood floors, dark wood wainscoting and two tiled fireplaces. Done in a rustic, early-California style, the room has a cathedral ceiling with exposed wooden beams and six cylindrical chandeliers crafted of black wrought iron. A row of windows overlooks the lush lawn in front of the facility.

From the blooming white roses at the courtyard entry to the open-air promenade and Mission-style rooms, the Lucie Stern Center is a classic Old World setting. And it's this abundance of old-fashioned elements that makes the Center such a charming spot for weddings.

CEREMONY CAPACITY: The Center holds 300 seated guests indoors or up to 250 seated guest outdoors.

EVENT/RECEPTION & MEETING CAPACITY: The Center holds 200 seated or 300 standing guests indoors or up to 150 seated or 200 standing guest outdoors.

MEETING CAPACITY: The Center holds up to 300 guests seated theater-style.

FEES & DEPOSITS: A reservation deposit in the amount of $300–1,000 (depending if alcohol is being served) is due within 10 days of obtaining an approved permit. The balance is due in 2 payments; the final payment is payable 4 weeks prior to the event. If a cancellation occurs, 33% of the total fees and charges is nonrefundable. Cancellations within 2 weeks of an event receive no refund. The 5-hour minimum exclusive use fee ranges $1,000–1,250 for Palo Alto residents, $1,500–2,000 for nonresidents. If you don't rent the entire facility, individual rooms can be rented on an hourly basis; call for rates. A $25–30/hour fee is charged for a city employee to be on premises during the event.

AVAILABILITY: Year-round, daily, 6am–1am.

SERVICES/AMENITIES:

Catering: BYO

Kitchen Facilities: fully equipped

Tables & Chairs: most provided or through caterer

Linens, Silver, etc.: BYO or through caterer

Restrooms: wheelchair accessible

Dance Floor: ballroom

Bride's Dressing Area: no

Meeting Equipment: BYO or CBA

Parking: ample on-site

Accommodations: no guestrooms

Telephone: emergency use only

Outdoor Night Lighting: yes

Outdoor Cooking Facilities: through caterer

Cleanup: caterer or renter

View: garden patio

RESTRICTIONS:

Alcohol: BYO WBC

Smoking: outside only

Music: amplified OK with restrictions

Wheelchair Access: yes

Insurance: extra liability required

The professionals in the back of this book are the best in the business. How do we know? Read page 701.

Palo Alto Hills Golf & Country Club

Country Club

3000 Alexis Drive, Palo Alto
650/917-5101
www.pahgcc.com
ltbeaton@pahgcc.net

● Rehearsal Dinners		● Corp. Events/Mtgs.
● Ceremonies		● Private Parties
● Wedding Receptions		Accommodations

Set high in the rolling hills above Silicon Valley and nestled next to the Arastradero Open Space Preserve, the Palo Alto Hills Golf & Country Club boasts spectacular Bay Area vistas. And although this is one of the most prestigious private clubs in the United States, you don't have to be a member to host a special event here.

The country club is known for its welcoming atmosphere, and its Grand Ballroom could not be more inviting. Considered one of the loveliest spaces on the Peninsula, it's an ideal setting for any celebration. Windows on three sides showcase the golf course, signature 18th-hole green and cascading waterfall (a fabulous backdrop for a wedding ceremony and photos). The venue is also spacious enough to accommodate a seated reception for 275 with a dance floor.

The ballroom opens onto a landscaped terrace that's popular for wedding ceremonies, rehearsal dinners or post-ceremony cocktail receptions. Your guests will appreciate both the fresh air and the irresistible view: verdant fairways bordered by majestic redwoods, pine and oak trees. The park-like setting not only brings nature into your event, it offers endless photo opportunities.

For smaller gatherings, reserve the sophisticated Members Dining Room, whose warm cherrywood walls are crisscrossed with a distinctive pattern of brass inlay. In the evening, add a romantic glow with candles on the tables, or simply enjoy the captivating panorama of city lights sparkling against the night sky. Two meeting rooms, which can be used individually or combined, are available for rehearsal dinners.

Award-winning Executive Chef Orlin Marcus, formerly the Chef de Cuisine at the renowned Beach and Tennis Club in Pebble Beach, has made Palo Alto Hills Golf & Country Club his "home away from home" since 2000. He takes pride in using the freshest ingredients and supporting many local and organic farms and vendors. Chef Orlin and his staff have created three distinct wedding packages, but if you have something else in mind they're happy to customize a menu for your occasion.

Impeccable service is the top priority at the Palo Alto Hills Golf & Country Club. Whether you're planning an elegant black-tie affair, a casual poolside party or something in between, you'll be impressed with their entire staff, from the valet parking attendants to the professional event coordinator who will help you personalize your festivities.

CEREMONY, EVENT/RECEPTION & MEETING CAPACITY: The clubhouse holds up to 275 seated or 400 standing guests, both indoors and outdoors.

FEES & DEPOSITS: Rental fees range $500–3,000 depending on the day of the week. Meals range $85–130/person. All wedding packages include a 1-hour hors d'oeuvres reception, salad course, entrée, champagne toast and cake-cutting fee. Tax, alcohol and a 20% service charge are additional.

AVAILABILITY: Year-round.

SERVICES/AMENITIES:

Catering: provided
Kitchen Facilities: n/a
Tables & Chairs: provided
Linens, Silver, etc.: provided
Restrooms: wheelchair accessible
Dance Floor: provided
Bride's Dressing Area: yes
Meeting Equipment: provided, extra fee

Parking: self-parking or valet, extra fee
Accommodations: no guestrooms
Telephone: emergency use only
Outdoor Night Lighting: yes
Outdoor Cooking Facilities: n/a
Cleanup: provided
View: bay, fairways, grounds, hills, pool, waterfall
Other: event coordination

RESTRICTIONS:

Alcohol: provided or BYO wine with corkage fee
Smoking: outdoors only
Music: amplified OK

Wheelchair Access: yes
Insurance: not required

Sheraton Palo Alto

Hotel

625 El Camino Real, Palo Alto
650/328-2800
www.sheraton.com/paloalto
kbowne@pahotel.com

- Rehearsal Dinners
- Ceremonies
- Wedding Receptions
- Corp. Events/Mtgs.
- Private Parties
- Accommodations

Picture a clear, rocky stream running beneath footbridges, past bushy ferns and flower gardens. Sounds more like a combination of the mountains and a tropical island than Palo Alto, but that's exactly where it is. At the Sheraton Palo Alto, you have a variety of event spaces, each with its own unique look, from the Spanish-tiled, glass-enclosed courtyard to the ballroom decorated with authentic Chinese antiques. The hotel is located on a commercial boulevard within walking distance of downtown Palo Alto, but because it's set back off the road and imaginatively landscaped, the Sheraton maintains an air of exclusivity.

A walk through the mostly glass lobby, suffused with light from windows and skylights, takes you to the large rectangular swimming pool area. It's the perfect spot for a splashy cocktail hour: A brick-paved patio is bordered by trees and gardenias, and at night the pool is illuminated by underwater lights and the trees glow with twinkle lights.

The Reception Room is set in its own wing, and the adjoining lawn is equally suited for ceremonies or stargazing. A semicircular wall encloses the lawn, so only your group can access it. The room itself features two large crystal chandeliers, a dance floor and vaulted ceiling, and fold-out glass doors that open onto the lawn.

Justine's Ballroom is highlighted by a beautiful glass-enclosed interior courtyard between spacious banquet rooms. It has Spanish tile, white stucco archways, arched mirrors and a glass ceiling. The setting makes a picturesque backdrop for your ceremony, photographs and even the cake cutting. Use the banquet room that opens out onto a streamside patio for cocktails, then spread out into both dining rooms for dinner. Beneath Justine's Ballroom is the Cypress Ballroom, an imperial room that features deep burgundy custom carpeting and royal white columns inset in the wall. Works of art from China are displayed in softly lit shadow boxes.

With its variety of event spaces, the Sheraton Palo Alto gives you plenty of options, and their creative and experienced staff guarantee to work wonders on your special day.

CEREMONY CAPACITY: The hotel can accommodate 150–300 seated or 200–350 standing guests indoors, and up to 110 seated or 200 standing outdoors.

EVENT/RECEPTION CAPACITY: The site holds 150–350 seated or up to 500 standing guests indoors.

MEETING CAPACITY: Small meeting rooms and parlors are available in addition to 3 larger spaces that seat 30–300 guests.

FEES & DEPOSITS: For weddings and special events, 25% of the estimated event total is required to secure your date. Lunches start at $45/person and wedding packages start at $68/person. Alcohol, a 20% service charge and tax are extra. The anticipated food and beverage total is due 10 days prior to the event. Bride and groom receive a complimentary room with champagne toast for the reception, and group rates can be arranged for overnight wedding guests. For meetings, room rental fees start at $400.

AVAILABILITY: Year-round, daily, anytime. Weddings take place on Saturdays and Sundays, 11am–4pm or 6pm–midnight.

SERVICES/AMENITIES:

Catering: provided; some ethnic caterers permitted
Kitchen Facilities: n/a
Tables & Chairs: provided
Linens, Silver, etc.: provided
Restrooms: wheelchair accessible
Dance Floor: portable indoors or Piazza Courtyard
Bride's & Groom's Dressing Area: CBA
Meeting Equipment: full range CBA

Parking: large lot, valet available
Accommodations: 350 guestrooms and suites
Telephone: pay phones
Outdoor Night Lighting: yes
Outdoor Cooking Facilities: n/a
Cleanup: provided
View: flower gardens, fountain, koi ponds
Other: event coordination

RESTRICTIONS:

Alcohol: provided or corkage $15/bottle, $25/magnum
Smoking: outdoors only
Music: amplified OK

Wheelchair Access: yes
Insurance: not required
Other: no birdseed or rice; no fog machines

Westin Palo Alto Hotel

Hotel

675 El Camino Real, Palo Alto
650/321-4422
www.westin.com/paloalto
kbowne@pahotel.com

- Rehearsal Dinners
- Ceremonies
- Wedding Receptions
- Corp. Events/Mtgs.
- Private Parties
- Accommodations

It may look like simply another nice hotel from the outside, but as soon as you step into the marble-clad lobby of the Westin Palo Alto you experience its extraordinary appeal. This boutique-style venue combines clean, harmonious Feng Shui with a cosmopolitan sophistication that is warmed by understated Mediterranean architecture. Facing the entrance, a sleek marble staircase is flanked by a tableau of up-lit Oriental ferns in creamy ceramic vases. Above you, a ceiling inset with a serene shade of sky-blue introduces the hotel's design motif: *celestial*.

The expansive feeling of connection to heavenly elements is most artfully realized in the hotel's peaceful garden courtyards. Each is defined by two five-storied façades, whose guestroom windows are embellished with wrought-iron balconies and pastel-hued shutters that recall Old World town squares. The Court of the Moon & Stars is favored by many brides for ceremonies because of its striking water feature: Along one ivy-decked wall, a row of fountain urns the color of cobalt blue overflows with water into a rectangular pool. At night, white globes glow like full moons in the background. Opposite this wall are French doors opening to a luxurious fireplace suite, often reserved by the bridal couple for the perfect grand entrance. Your attendants and overnight guests might stay in the other rooms overlooking the courtyard, turning it into your own private party haven.

But feel free to spread your event out into other delightful enclaves. The Court of the Sun features a bronze sundial at its center, cheerful yellow umbrellas, and a trellis climbing with golden honeysuckle. A large celadon fountain urn gurgles at the center of the Court of the Wind, while reeds and grasses arch along one wall as if bending to a gentle breeze. Either of these are pleasant spots for a social hour or an al fresco reception; or serve cocktails in the Court of Water around the swimming pool!

Indoor receptions are equally charming in the sumptuous Siena-Carrara Ballroom, commodious enough to accommodate your exclusive fête while still keeping things cozy. Leave the doors open, and guests can meander into the tastefully appointed Foyer, furnished with club chairs and sofas for relaxed conversation.

The Westin Palo Alto caters to intimate celebrations, that convivial kind of gathering where you're actually well acquainted with each guest. Since yours is the one and only event on site, the Westin staff is dedicated to making it quite special indeed.

You would expect a venue with such style and personal service to be very costly; however, Westin offers reasonably priced wedding packages that include champagne and butler-passed hors d'oeuvres for the social hour; plated gourmet dinner with wine; elegant centerpieces; and a complimentary suite for the newlyweds. Speaking of wedding nights: Most of the hotel suites include romantic touches like a fireplace and whirlpool tub, and all rooms have Westin's signature Heavenly Bed, which boasts "10 layers of comfort"...so if you and your new spouse decide to leave the "do not disturb" sign on your door indefinitely, everyone will understand.

CEREMONY CAPACITY: The Courtyard holds 50 seated guests; the Siena-Carrara Ballroom 100.

EVENT/RECEPTION CAPACITY: The Siena-Carrara Ballroom holds up to 60 seated or 100 standing guests; the Courtyard up to 50 seated or 60 standing guests.

MEETING CAPACITY: Event spaces accommodate 12–80 seated guests.

FEES & DEPOSITS: 25% of the estimated event total is required to reserve your date. The balance is due 10 days prior to the event. Rental fees range $300–800 depending on the food and beverage minimum. Lunches start at $45/person, wedding packages start at $70/person. Tax, alcohol and a 20% service charge are additional.

AVAILABILITY: Year-round, daily, anytime. Weddings take place on Saturdays and Sundays, 11am–4pm or 6pm–midnight.

SERVICES/AMENITIES:

Catering: provided
Kitchen Facilities: n/a
Tables & Chairs: provided
Linens, Silver, etc.: provided
Restrooms: wheelchair accessible
Dance Floor: provided
Bride's & Groom's Dressing Areas: CBA
Meeting Equipment: CBA

Parking: large lot, valet available
Accommodations: 184 guestrooms
Telephone: pay phone
Outdoor Night Lighting: yes
Outdoor Cooking Facilities: no
Cleanup: provided
View: pool, courtyard, fountain, grounds
Other: event coordination

RESTRICTIONS:

Alcohol: provided, or corkage $15/bottle
Smoking: outside only
Music: amplified OK with restrictions

Wheelchair Access: yes
Insurance: not required

Want to know WHAT TO ASK a potential location or vendor? Check out our Questions to Ask on page 17.

Woman's Club of Palo Alto

Historic Woman's Club

475 Homer Avenue, Palo Alto
650/321-5821

womansclubofpaloalto.org
rentals@womansclubofpaloalto.org

- Rehearsal Dinners
- Ceremonies
- Wedding Receptions
- Corp. Events/Mtgs.
- Private Parties
- Accommodations

On June 20, 1894, 24 women gathered together to formally organize the Woman's Club of Palo Alto. Their goals were friendship, self-improvement, and community involvement, and they didn't waste any time fulfilling them. Within the first four years of the club's existence, they'd founded the city's first reading room and library, as well as its first elementary school and high school.

Their dream of having their own clubhouse, however, was not realized until 1916. After twelve years of continuous fundraising, they'd managed to raise $5,300, and their Tudor-Craftsman-style "home" was built. At the time, they worried that it was too far removed from the center of town, but its location in a quiet residential neighborhood has proved a felicitous one.

Weddings are held in the Ballroom, a simply designed space with grand proportions. On two sides, tall windows flood the room with light, which reflects off polished maple floors. Eight brass-and-glass fixtures suspended from the high ceiling, and dark wood wainscoting and trim throughout add period character. Have your ceremony on the stage, which is framed by a red velvet curtain and illuminated by footlights. There's even a pair of baby grand pianos for musical accompaniment. Buffets are usually set up in the adjacent Fireside Room, aptly named for its tiled fireplace, and joined to the Ballroom by folding French doors.

The founders of the Woman's Club of Palo Alto may not have envisioned their clubhouse being used for matrimonial celebrations, but today its spacious airy interior and ample kitchen facilities make it a popular spot for weddings. And besides, it's one of the few places we know of that has twice as many restrooms for women as for men. Good planning, ladies.

CEREMONY, EVENT/RECEPTION & MEETING CAPACITY: The Ballroom and Fireside Room hold 150 seated guests.

FEES & DEPOSITS: For weekend special events or weddings, the full-day rental fee is $2,000 plus a $500 security deposit and a $100 janitorial fee. Half the rental fee and the security deposit are due with your signed contract; the balance is payable 2 weeks prior to the event.

For weekday meetings and multi-day bookings, the rental fee varies depending on usage. The base rate is $150/hour with a minimum of 6 hours.

AVAILABILITY: Year-round, daily, anytime.

SERVICES/AMENITIES:

Catering: BYO
Kitchen Facilities: fully equipped
Tables & Chairs: some provided
Linens, Silver, etc.: BYO
Restrooms: wheelchair accessible
Dance Floor: on stage, in Ballroom
Bride's Dressing Area: yes
Meeting Equipment: WiFi

Parking: on-street and nearby lots
Accommodations: no guestrooms
Telephone: no phone
Outdoor Night Lighting: access only
Outdoor Cooking Facilities: BYO BBQ
Cleanup: caterer or renter
View: residential neighborhood

RESTRICTIONS:

Alcohol: BYO, CBW only
Smoking: outdoors only
Music: amplified OK indoors only until 10pm

Wheelchair Access: yes
Insurance: liability required

Costanoa Resort

Resort

2001 Rossi Road at Highway 1, Pescadero
650/879-7306
www.costanoa.com
sales@costanoa.com

- Rehearsal Dinners
- Ceremonies
- Wedding Receptions
- Corp. Events/Mtgs.
- Private Parties
- Accommodations

The drive along Highway 1 between Half Moon Bay and Santa Cruz is more than just the distance between two (wonderful) points: It's a destination all its own. In the morning, foghorns sound from Pigeon Point Lighthouse, but the afternoon sunshine usually pierces through mist, letting you admire everything you pass: white sand dunes dotted with yellow bottlebrush and lavender sea daisies; parasails floating like colored balloons above the foamy surf; and handmade farmstand billboards announcing "seaside pumpkins," "u-pick berries" and "jam tasting." In this piece of paradise, it's all about slow food, savoring the scenery, and having a great time doing it.

The same is true of Costanoa, an eco-adventure resort that's ideally situated where the forest meets the sea. Poised at the foot of the Santa Cruz Mountains, Costanoa is connected to four state parks, a wilderness preserve and 30,000 miles of hiking and biking trails. The recreational activities are boundless—whether you're kayaking or horseback riding, exploring tide pools or enjoying a couple's massage at the on-site spa, Costanoa inspires you to tune in to the rhythm of Nature.

The rhythm of romance is also alive at this sublime sanctuary, and Costanoa is THE place for eco-chic weddings. The resort has two main hubs of action: the stunning mountain-style Lodge on the east side of the main road, and the General Store and its neighboring Cascade Restaurant to the west. From the restaurant, a path winds through cypress trees to a hidden enclave for oceanview wedding ceremonies—the Coastal Bluff, a rustic meadow with a breathtaking vista of sea and sky. After the vows, it's just a short stroll back to the Cascade Lawn, which can be elegantly tented for a reception or left open to the great outdoors.

Larger weddings are celebrated at the Lodge, whose lovely "back yard" consists of two tiers of landscaped lawns. Ceremonies are held on the lower tier, the Lodge Lawn, which embraces a magnificent canyon and mountain panorama. Then receptions spread out on the Lodge Terrace. You can have a tent here too, but if the weather is fine—and it often is—why not stage your festivities in the open air? That way, you might spy some of the resident wildlife…a squirrel, a rabbit, a hawk…and hear the tranquil harmonies of Costanoa's 371 species of birds. As sunset gives way to night, you and your sweetheart can make a wish on any one of a multitude of stars.

Costanoa is Bay Area Green Certified, providing farm-to-table cuisine that's as fresh, local, organic and sustainable as possible. The genuinely caring staff helps you organize your destination weekend, whether you want a rehearsal dinner barbecue complete with s'mores or need assistance arranging group activities.

The resort offers a variety of accommodations to suit all tastes and budgets. A honeymoon suite at the Lodge is the most luxurious, but even campers—or "Glampers," as they're called here—can relax in a tent bungalow outfitted with a four-poster bed and maid service. However, none of the rooms have televisions, as its Costanoa's objective that its guests "discover the pace of nature," a pace that you'll want to return to again and again.

CEREMONY CAPACITY: The resort holds 80 seated guests indoors and 250 seated outdoors.

EVENT/RECEPTION CAPACITY: The facility can accommodate 64 seated or 80 standing indoors and 250 seated or standing outdoors.

MEETING CAPACITY: Meeting rooms hold 80 seated guests.

FEES & DEPOSITS: A deposit equal to the first night's lodging is required to reserve your date and the balance is due 14 days prior to the event. Rental fees range $1,500–4,500 depending on the day of the event and the number of guests. Meals range $65–100/person. Tax, alcohol and a 20% service charge are additional.

AVAILABILITY: Year-round, daily. Outdoor events must end by 10pm. On-site restaurant and bar available for after hours parties 10pm–1am.

SERVICES/AMENITIES:

Catering: provided
Kitchen Facilities: n/a
Tables & Chairs: provided
Linens, Silver, etc.: provided
Restrooms: wheelchair accessible
Dance Floor: CBA
Bride's Dressing Area: CBA
Meeting Equipment: some provided
Other: on-site wedding cake and florals, spa services, picnic area, event coordination, free WiFi available

Parking: large lot
Accommodations: 130 guestrooms
Telephone: house phone
Outdoor Night Lighting: CBA
Outdoor Cooking Facilities: BBQ on site
Cleanup: provided
View: landscaped grounds, canyon, garden; panorama of mountains, ocean/bay and fields

RESTRICTIONS:

Alcohol: provided or BYO with corkage fees
Smoking: designated areas only
Music: amplified OK with restrictions

Wheelchair Access: yes
Insurance: not required
Other: no birdseed, rice, glitter or confetti

Valley Presbyterian Church

Church

945 Portola Road, Portola Valley
650/851-2848
www.valleypreschurch.org
wedding@valleypreschurch.org

Rehearsal Dinners	Corp. Events/Mtgs.
● Ceremonies	Private Parties
Wedding Receptions	Accommodations

From its breathtaking sanctuary to its wooded grounds, Valley Presbyterian Church draws on the purity of the natural world to enhance your spiritual experience. "There's a sense of peace here," explains one congregant. "You feel like a part of Nature, and thus closer to God."

The heart of Valley Presbyterian Church is the awe-inspiring sanctuary. The sanctuary's simplicity and unpretentious beauty evoke serenity and wonder. Guests enter through four heavy wooden doors, richly carved with images of New Testament figures. Flanking each side of the church are stone planters filled with lush greenery. Oak pews are upholstered in green fabric, and the A-frame pine ceiling is accented by dark beams. Polished riverbed stones in the washed aggregate floor echo the sanctuary's earthy aesthetic.

However, it's the soaring sanctuary windows behind the communion table that take your breath away: They frame a grove of majestic redwood trees reaching heavenward, while a filigree of sunbeams streams into the church. Guests face this magnificent forest scene, while from the steps below the communion table the bridal party enjoys its own striking tableau: the six-foot-tall stained-glass panel above the front doors that depicts a simple golden cross in a blue-toned mosaic. When the sun shines through it, the amber cross is reflected across the church onto the view of the redwoods, and seems to float mysteriously in the air—a sparkling vision that heightens the mood of peaceful reverence.

The church comes with the services of a minister, coordinator, organist, wedding hostess and hostess assistant. Every couple that marries at Valley Presbyterian attends a one-day Marriage Preparation Workshop, as well as a separate private meeting with their assigned officiant. All are welcome here, and though a Valley Presbyterian minister will be the main officiant of the wedding, you may invite a guest minister to assist with the ceremony. Also included, but optional, are candelabras and candles, unity candle, silk floral arrangement, pew decorations and aisle runner.

Valley Presbyterian Church believes in giving back to the community, and is known for its outreach and children's programs. This is a church that actively promotes family, community, and spiritual values—a promising environment for starting a new life together.

CEREMONY CAPACITY: The Sanctuary holds 225+ guests. Call for details.

FEES & DEPOSITS: A $1,000 nonrefundable deposit is required to reserve your date. The fee through 2012 is $1,850 for a 2½-hour time frame. Fees subject to change without notice. Couples need not be members of Valley Presbyterian Church; however, it is necessary that the ceremony be a Christian service.

AVAILABILITY: Year-round. Ceremonies on Saturday begin at 10am, noon, 2:30pm and 5pm, and on Sunday at 2:30pm and 5pm. Rehearsals take place on the Friday before the wedding.

SERVICES/AMENITIES:

Catering: n/a
Kitchen Facilities: n/a
Tables & Chairs: n/a
Linens, Silver, etc.: n/a
Restrooms: wheelchair accessible
Dance Floor: n/a
Bride's & Groom's Dressing Area: yes
Meeting Equipment: n/a

Parking: lot for 175 guests
Accommodations: no guestrooms
Telephone: house phone
Outdoor Night Lighting: yes
Outdoor Cooking Facilities: n/a
Cleanup: provided
View: redwood forest

RESTRICTIONS:

Alcohol: not permitted
Smoking: not allowed
Music: acoustic only

Wheelchair Access: yes
Insurance: not required
Other: no birdseed or rice

Want to find more locations and services? Check out our informative website, www.HereComesTheGuide.com.

Pacific Athletic Club at Redwood Shores

Athletic Club

200 Redwood Shores Parkway, Redwood City
650/593-1112
www.pacclub.com

● Rehearsal Dinners	● Corp. Events/Mtgs.
● Ceremonies	● Private Parties
● Wedding Receptions	☐ Accommodations

You know you're almost there once you see the distinctive, green copper pyramid-shaped roofs of this seven-acre complex of event spaces, restaurant, pools and athletic courts. Enter the foyer and step onto the tan mosaic flagstone floor. The space soars to 35 feet, with huge Douglas fir poles supporting an enormous skylight.

Wedding guests are led to the lounge and reception area, the latter an octagon-shaped room with an unusual two-tone floor of Brazilian walnut and cherry hardwoods. There are several mirrored arches, one of which cleverly pushes back to provide a place for a band. Hors d'oeuvres and cocktails are served here before an event, and after a seated meal elsewhere, guests often return to dance. The adjacent Main Dining Room is large and light-filled, with a sizable skylight and two walls of floor-to-ceiling glass. The other two walls feature pastel-colored landscapes. Four large Douglas fir poles that match those in the foyer support a very high vaulted ceiling. Attached to these poles are multitiered pinpoint fixtures, making evening functions sparkle. Tables are dressed with crisp cream-colored linens.

Beyond the glass walls and doors is the garden courtyard, lushly planted and landscaped to accommodate outdoor ceremonies and cocktail receptions.

This is a must-see location for receptions. Be prepared to be impressed—we think that the Pacific Athletic Club is one of the better event sites on the Peninsula.

CEREMONY CAPACITY: Indoors the club can seat up to 250 guests, outdoors the garden courtyard holds up to 130 seated.

EVENT/RECEPTION CAPACITY: The club holds 240 seated or 300 standing guests indoors, and 60–300 seated or 150–300 standing outdoors.

MEETING CAPACITY: The Cypress and Sequoia Rooms each hold 12 guests conference-style. Combined they accommodate 36 classroom-style, 25 in a U-shape, 20 boardroom-style and 50 theater-style. The Dining Room holds 240 seated theater-style or 110 conference-style.

FEES & DEPOSITS: For special events, a $2,000 nonrefundable deposit, which is applied to your event rental, is required to secure your date. The room rental fee is $1,000–2,000 depending on the day of the week reserved, and covers a 4½-hour block of time. Half the anticipated food and beverage cost is payable 180 days in advance; the balance, along with a confirmed guest count, is due 5 working days prior to the function. Seated meals start at $30/person, not including hors d'oeuvres or beverages. Alcohol, tax and a 20% service charge are additional.

For meetings, room rentals are as follows: Cypress and Sequoia Rooms $150 each, or $300 combined.

AVAILABILITY: Year-round. Saturday and Sunday weddings or special events take place noon–4:30pm or 6pm–10:30pm. Overtime is $500 for the first hour and $1,000 for each additional hour. Monday–Friday corporate or special events begin after 3pm in the Dining Room. Meetings take place in the Cypress and Sequoia Rooms, and can be scheduled 7 days a week, anytime.

SERVICES/AMENITIES:

Catering: provided
Kitchen Facilities: n/a
Tables & Chairs: provided
Linens, Silver, etc.: provided
Restrooms: wheelchair accessible
Dance Floor: yes
Bride's Dressing Area: CBA
Meeting Equipment: CBA, extra fee

Parking: valet available, large lot
Accommodations: no guestrooms
Telephone: pay phones
Outdoor Night Lighting: yes
Outdoor Cooking Facilities: yes
Cleanup: provided
View: (from dining room) garden courtyard
Other: event coordination

RESTRICTIONS:

Alcohol: provided, corkage available
Smoking: designated areas
Music: amplified OK

Wheelchair Access: yes
Insurance: not required
Other: no birdseed, rice or helium balloons

San Mateo County History Museum

Museum

2200 Broadway, Redwood City
650/299-0104 X225
www.historysmc.org
sue@historysmc.org

● Rehearsal Dinners	● Corp. Events/Mtgs.
● Ceremonies	● Private Parties
● Wedding Receptions	☐ Accommodations

Domes are wondrous things, and there's no end to our fascination with them. Fortunately, you don't have to go to Rome (St. Peter's), Washington, DC (the Capitol) or Istanbul (the Hagia Sophia) to get a great dome fix—or even to get married beneath one. Just take the much shorter trip to Redwood City, where the San Mateo County History Museum has preserved one of the Bay Area's most remarkable domes.

The museum inhabits the venerable 1910 county courthouse, a sandstone structure that retains all of the dignity of that era, with its tile floors, Corinthian columns and tall wooden doors opening to stately courtrooms. But it's the dome that's easily the magnificent and overwhelming centerpiece of this venue. A towering concoction of skylit glass panes colored brilliant red, green, amber and opaque white, it rises above sculpted eagles and ornamental arches to a constellation of gold stars on a deep blue background. The dome is a full-tilt, rock-your-head-back-on-your-shoulders-and-stare-at-it-in-wonder kind of thing. Get married under it and you'll be talking about it for years to come.

Many couples also use the rotunda for their post-ceremony receptions or dinners. If your party is a large one, take advantage of the balcony-like second floor, where you can put additional tables. Here guests not only have a better vantage of the gorgeous glass overhead, they can stroll over to the railing and enjoy a bird's-eye view of the festivities below.

A second favorite location for wedding ceremonies is Courtroom A on the second floor. You reach it via a grand staircase distinguished by marble-topped risers, brass railings and mahogany banisters. Couples love its elegance and often pose for wedding photos on it. Courtroom A, recently restored to its former splendor, has rich oak moldings and furnishings, including the traditional long railing that separates the jury and bar members from the public. The ceiling features an oblong skylight of green, red and gray-blue glass arranged in abstract floral patterns. Stylized plaster wreathes of fruits and grains border the skylight, and four heavy Federal-style chandeliers with scalloped sconces hang low from the ceiling. Large oak-framed windows along two walls come down almost to the floor, and a Roman-style broken pediment spans the main entrance. The thick English carpet, red with gold highlights, feels absolutely wonderful underfoot. The original clerk, bailiff and judge's benches are still there, as are the jury chairs. This immensely refined room bestows an extra element of grace on any wedding.

The rotunda is so phenomenal that it needs little decoration, and the same goes for Courtroom A. For an added diversion (and fee), arrange to have the museum's exhibits open to your guests. This is a place for couples who love history or simply want something delightfully unconventional. If you're interested in making a different kind of beautiful memories, it would be hard to beat this domed museum.

CEREMONY CAPACITY: Courtroom A holds 120 seated guests and the Rotunda holds 150 seated guests.

EVENT/RECEPTION CAPACITY: The entire courthouse holds 400 standing guests. The Lower Rotunda holds 120 seated guests and the Upper Rotunda up to 170 seated guests.

MEETING CAPACITY: The Museum holds up to 120 guests for meetings.

FEES & DEPOSITS: A $750 deposit is required to reserve your date. The balance is due 30 days prior to event. Rental fees range $2,895–4,900 depending on space, services selected and staffing needed for the event.

AVAILABILITY: Year-round, daily: Monday all day; Tuesday–Sunday 4pm–midnight.

SERVICES/AMENITIES:

Catering: BYO
Kitchen Facilities: full catering kitchen
Tables & Chairs: tables provided, extra fee
Linens, Silver, etc.: CBA
Restrooms: wheelchair accessible
Dance Floor: yes
Bride's Dressing Area: yes
Meeting Equipment: full range CBA,
including teleconferencing and internet access

Parking: on-street
Accommodations: no guestrooms
Telephone: no
Outdoor Night Lighting: yes
Outdoor Cooking Facilities: no
Cleanup: caterer and staff janitorial
View: park, hills, fountain, grounds
Other: access to exhibits, extra fee

RESTRICTIONS:

Alcohol: BYO
Smoking: outdoors only
Music: amplified OK indoors

Wheelchair Access: yes
Insurance: required

Sofitel San Francisco Bay

Hotel

223 Twin Dolphin Drive, Redwood City
650/598-9000
www.sofitel-sanfrancisco-bay.com
sofitel.sanfranciscobay@accor.com

- Rehearsal Dinners
- Ceremonies
- Wedding Receptions
- Corp. Events/Mtgs.
- Private Parties
- Accommodations

Poised on the banks of a serene lagoon, Sofitel San Francisco Bay conveys a contemporary elegance. Sofitel's European heritage and French-inspired cuisine are complemented by a California-style friendliness and an experienced staff that make guests feel right at home.

The marble-clad lobby boasts a striking abstract blown-glass chandelier in shades of sapphire blue, reminiscent of the sun-splashed waters of the bay. Throughout the public spaces, the same vibrant blues play against the interior's muted hues as eye-catching accents—throw pillows on a dove-gray sofa in *bay bar*; painted library alcoves; and restaurant *bay 223's* modern dining banquettes. In fact, the hotel décor is stunning, applied with sleek, fresh brushstrokes befitting its uniquely presented luxury.

Wedding ceremonies sparkle out on the dock, which overlooks a tranquil waterway where egrets and blue herons feed alongside flocks of ducks and geese. Follow up with a cocktail hour on the landscaped patio surrounding the swimming pool, with the glistening lagoon as a picturesque backdrop.

There are plenty of event options indoors as well—fifteen rooms in all, including Sofitel's 6,200-square-foot Grand Ballroom. Serve cocktails and hors d'oeuvres in the Foyer, adorned with illuminated swags of blue crystals. Inside, the recently renovated Grand Ballroom is done in a refined color scheme of gold, sand and cream with accents of blue. Avant-garde lighting fixtures incorporate wavy sheets of striped glass that are in harmony with shimmery drapes in the same honey and copper earthy hues. One wall of floor-to-ceiling windows looks out to a porte-cochère, where water flows from a Mediterranean fountain. The Grand Ballroom can be used in its entirety or divided in half, depending on the size of your party.

Wedding showers and rehearsal dinners take on an air of exclusive intimacy in the Grand Salon or Blue Room. Small receptions are held in the Veranda, a room enclosed entirely by glass walls. Marble detailing and floors inlaid with dark wood add extra flair.

Cuisine is not an afterthought at Sofitel—the kitchen has a reputation for superbly prepared gourmet fare, best described as Bay Area French. Creative menus employ fresh local ingredients and the expertise of a French culinary staff for a marvelous dining experience.

To help you relax after the big event, Sofitel offers a complimentary suite for the bride and groom, with champagne and strawberries upon arrival, and special group rates for out-of-town guests.

All the rooms feature Sofitel's signature SoBed, a plush featherbed oasis of comfort. There will be plenty of takers for any overnight accommodations you arrange, as guests will want to extend their visit to this fashionable establishment as long as possible!

CEREMONY CAPACITY: Dockside (next to the lagoon) accommodates up to 175 seated; the Ballroom holds 450 seated guests.

EVENT/RECEPTION CAPACITY: The hotel holds 80–450 seated or 100–700 standing guests indoors.

MEETING CAPACITY: 15 rooms are available, including the Ballroom, the Executive Board Room, and a variety of salons. The facility holds 10–400 classroom-style, 12–30 conference-style, 14–50 in a U-shape and 10–700 seated theater-style.

FEES & DEPOSITS: For events, 10% of the estimated total is required as a nonrefundable deposit when you book your date; 50% of the estimated total is due 6 months prior, and another 25% is due 1 month prior to the event. The remaining balance is required 1 week prior to the event, and a guaranteed guest count is due 3 business days prior. Any remaining charges are payable at the conclusion of your event. Wedding packages range $100–150/person; sales tax and a 20% service charge are additional. The Sofitel offers a discount for Friday and Sunday receptions. For meetings, room rental fees start at $400/day.

AVAILABILITY: Year-round, daily, 11am–1am. Call for details on specific spaces.

SERVICES/AMENITIES:

Catering: provided
Kitchen Facilities: n/a
Tables & Chairs: provided
Linens, Silver, etc.: provided
Restrooms: wheelchair accessible
Dance Floor: provided
Bride's Dressing Area: yes
Meeting Equipment: CBA, extra fee

Parking: ample parking, valet available
Accommodations: 421 guestrooms
Telephone: private lines CBA
Outdoor Night Lighting: no
Outdoor Cooking Facilities: no
Cleanup: provided
View: lagoon, hills, fountain
Other: complete event coordination and wireless internet available

RESTRICTIONS:

Alcohol: provided
Smoking: designated areas
Music: amplified OK

Wheelchair Access: yes
Insurance: may be required
Other: no rice, birdseed or confetti

This is important! Tell locations you're reading HERE COMES THE GUIDE and ask if our information is still current.

San Mateo Marriott

Hotel

1770 South Amphlett Boulevard, San Mateo
650/653-6093

www.sanmateomarriott.com
info@marriott-sanmateo.com

- Rehearsal Dinners
- Ceremonies
- Wedding Receptions
- Corp. Events/Mtgs.
- Private Parties
- Accommodations

The intersection of 101 and 92 is the true crossroads of the San Francisco Bay Area, linking east to west, north to south, and bay to coast. At that exact nexus, just minutes from San Francisco International Airport, sits the San Mateo Marriott.

Remodeled in 2007, the hotel's exterior is topped with Spanish-style red tile roofs, and the interior is decidedly contemporary. The circular marble-clad lobby and many of the lounges sport whimsical wrought-iron chandeliers and sconces with brightly colored, hand-blown glass shades. French doors everywhere open to patios, terraces and courtyards, and there are more windows than usual for such a large hotel, giving the venue a light and airy feel.

Stage your ceremony in the courtyard beneath the white-pillared gazebo with its decorative wrought-iron dome. Afterwards your guests can enjoy cocktails and hors d'oeuvres in the nearby lobby lounge with its full bar and fireplace, while you take advantage of the beautiful courtyard for photographs. From here, make your grand entrance into the spacious Engage Ballroom for the reception. Wood molding, silky gold drapes and a fireplace framed in green stone tiles give this space an almost European flavor. During the day the room is flooded with light, flowing in through French doors.

More event options are available on the second floor. Have cocktails in the Synergy Lobby and your banquet in the Inspire Ballroom, which can be employed as one large space or partitioned for smaller celebrations. Off the grand foyer is the circular Synergy, with unusual, brick-lined walls and massive glass doors. Set the buffet and bar in the boardroom, and let your guests mingle in the foyer, or wander out onto the adjacent terrace for some fresh air.

Windows on both sides of the capacious Convene Ballroom are framed in pale gold drapes, and the room is lit with impressive alabaster and verdigris chandeliers. Invite your guests to sip champagne in the sconce-lit Convene Lobby to the sound of soft music played on the grand piano, before they move into the ballroom for the reception.

If there are many children on your guest list, consider offering them their own kid-friendly banquet in the adjacent Synergy 1, with a child-size (and child-safe) buffet of pizza, chicken tenders and other readily accepted kid fare.

San Mateo Marriott specializes in California cuisine, but the hotel will cater to any preference, be it pork and poi or roast beef and potatoes. They'll handle all the details, from flowers to fire-eaters (really!), or you can plan your whole event yourself.

If your guests are coming from far and wide, San Mateo Marriott is in the single most convenient location possible. It can be reached easily from anywhere in the greater Bay Area, and there are enough luxury rooms and suites (476 to be precise) to accommodate the largest of weddings. There are even brand new bridal suites with lofted bedrooms, Jacuzzi tubs and full-length mirrors. Making everyone happy is a difficult goal to achieve, but San Mateo Marriott does it with ease.

CCEREMONY CAPACITY: The hotel seats 600 indoors and 300 outdoors.

EVENT/RECEPTION CAPACITY: The Marriott accommodates 350 seated or 700 standing indoors, and 170 seated, 200 standing outdoors.

MEETING CAPACITY: The hotel holds 600 seated guests.

FEES & DEPOSITS: A $1,000 deposit is required to reserve your date. The balance is due 7 days prior to the event. Rental fees range $1,800–4,500 depending on the space rented. Meals range $70–120/person. Tax, alcohol and a 22% service charge are additional.

AVAILABILITY: Year-round, daily, anytime.

SERVICES/AMENITIES:
Catering: provided or BYO
Kitchen Facilities: minimal
Tables & Chairs: provided
Linens, Silver, etc.: provided
Restrooms: wheelchair accessible
Dance Floor: patio, deck or portable
Bride's Dressing Area: yes
Meeting Equipment: provided

Parking: large lot, valet available
Accommodations: 476 guestrooms
Telephone: house phone
Outdoor Night Lighting: yes
Outdoor Cooking Facilities: BBQ on site
Cleanup: provided
View: hills, pool area, landscaped grounds
Other: AV equipment

RESTRICTIONS:
Alcohol: provided
Smoking: outside only
Music: amplified OK

Wheelchair Access: yes
Insurance: may be required

The Mountain Terrace

Special Event Facility

17285 Skyline Boulevard, Woodside
650/851-1606

www.themountainterrace.com
info@themountainterrace.com

- Rehearsal Dinners
- Ceremonies
- Wedding Receptions
- Corp. Events/Mtgs.
- Private Parties
- Accommodations

Whether you're driving down from San Francisco or up from San Jose, the final six miles to The Mountain Terrace are sensational. They ascend a mountainside on state route 84, one of California's most magnificent sections of highway. The winding road is flanked by sturdy old oaks, dense fragrant redwood groves and huge chateau-like mansions. There are spectacular bay and ridge views at several spots along the way and, in a couple of places, imposing trees thrust their branches out across the road to form living archways.

If the last leg of the trip is a revelation, a second surprise awaits at the top. Where Highway 84 meets up with redwood-edged Skyline Blvd., there's a small crossroads settlement. The Mountain Terrace is an unassuming wooden building at the far end of this little village. However, as they say, appearances can be deceiving: The Mountain Terrace's prosaic exterior conceals glories inside. Once you cross the parking lot and pass through a redwood arbor, what you see takes your breath away: a brilliant green acre of lawn, shimmering in the sunlight, rimmed by oaks and dozens of soaring redwoods. At its far boundary, where the mountain begins to slope to the lowlands, it draws your eyes to a sweeping view of the southern part of San Francisco Bay all the way down to the Fremont hills.

By itself, the lawn makes a perfect spot for an outdoor wedding and reception. But there's more—once you've taken in the lawn, you turn to see a large two-level redwood deck. Right away you know it would make a superb setting for a stand-up reception, sit-down dinner or any kind of function in between. On its upper level, a vine-covered trellis shelters half the deck. The lower deck, only a couple of steps down from the upper, has a deftly crafted octagonal-shaped extension that's built around a mature oak tree. Just beyond the deck there are more oaks (one with a tree swing) shading chairs beneath them. The little grove makes a perfect nook partygoers can use to take a break from the main festivities while not losing touch.

There's still more: Glass doors connect the deck to a substantial indoor space, divided into a dining room and a bar/dance area by a large stone fireplace. The antique bar, made of solid oak, has hefty Doric columns carved into it and is backed by a massive three-part mirror. The room's hardwood floor invites carefree dancing (there's an area where a band or DJ can set up). The dining area looks out through picture windows onto the deck and lawn. In winter, with a roaring fire inside and mist-shrouded redwoods outside, it makes a cozy wedding and reception site by itself.

As a facility, The Mountain Terrace is a "three-fer": stunning lawn and view, inviting interior and grand redwood deck. Then there's the drive up, which will put your guests in such a good mood, by the time they arrive they'll be ready to fully enjoy the charms of this very special place.

CEREMONY CAPACITY: The meadow accommodates up to 400 seated guests.

EVENT/RECEPTION & MEETING CAPACITY: Indoors, the site holds 130 seated guests. The patio holds up to 200 seated guests. If combined, the indoor and outdoor spaces accommodate a maximum of 330 seated guests.

FEES & DEPOSITS: A $500 refundable security deposit plus half the rental fee is required to reserve your date. The remainder, along with any estimated bar charges, is due 15 days prior to the event, and the balance is payable on the day of the event. Rental fees range $750–4,000 depending on the date and time rented. Meals start at $26/person. Tax, alcohol and service charge are additional.

AVAILABILITY: Year-round, daily.

SERVICES/AMENITIES:

Catering: provided or approved caterer
Kitchen Facilities: fully equipped
Tables & Chairs: provided for up to 150 guests
Linens, Silver, etc.: BYO or through caterer
Restrooms: wheelchair accessible
Dance Floor: indoor area
Bride's Dressing Area: yes
Meeting Equipment: CBA

Parking: on-site lot or shuttle
Accommodations: no guestrooms
Telephone: house phone
Outdoor Night Lighting: yes
Outdoor Cooking Facilities: CBA, extra fee
Cleanup: caterer
View: redwoods, partial bay view

RESTRICTIONS:

Alcohol: provided
Smoking: designated areas
Music: amplified OK indoors only, outdoors acoustic only

Wheelchair Access: yes
Insurance: not required

Thomas Fogarty Winery and Vineyards

Hilltop Winery

19501 Skyline Boulevard, Woodside
650/851-6772
www.fogartywinery.com
events@fogartywinery.com

● Rehearsal Dinners	● Corp. Events/Mtgs.
● Ceremonies	● Private Parties
● Wedding Receptions	Accommodations

If we were to rate facilities on a scale from 1 to 10, the Fogarty Winery would be a 10! Located off Skyline Boulevard, this has to be one of the best places we've seen, not only for weddings, but for private parties and corporate functions, too.

Commanding an extraordinary panorama of the bay and Peninsula, the Winery sits high on a ridge in a quiet vineyard setting. As you drive in, vineyards and a lovely pond come into view. At the top of the ridge is a large lawn, beautifully landscaped around the perimeter—a perfect spot for an outdoor ceremony.

Receptions and special events are held in the Hill House and/or the outdoor Pavilion. True to its name, the former steps down the hill, and is designed with incredible attention to detail, featuring a stone fireplace, fine woodwork, skylights, a wine bar and professional kitchen. From comfortable seating indoors, as well as from the semiglass-enclosed terrace, you can see for miles—past the neighboring vineyard all the way to the distant bay.

Adjacent to the Hill House is the Pavilion, a covered redwood deck suspended over the hillside. Calling it a "covered deck" may be something of an understatement: This 4,000-square-foot architectural treat is constructed of teal-painted columns and beams which support a peaked cedar roof inset with skylights. You have a 270-degree view of the surrounding oak-dotted hills and the Chardonnay vineyards below. The Pavilion is truly the perfect spot for cocktails and hors d'oeuvres or an open-air seated reception—no matter how hot the day is, there's always a breeze blowing here. You can reserve the House or Pavilion individually or use them in combination—they're connected by a deck, so there's a wonderful flow between them.

For small private dinners, the Redwood Room is light and airy, arranged with custom-built "barrel" tables, handcrafted leather chairs, a wood burning stove and full kitchen. Even the restroom is unique, with a blue-green slate and stone bathtub! And if you'd like to have a meeting in this glorious setting, hold it in the Board Room or the Hill House. A recent landscaping project has covered the hillside with ferns, manzanita and native plantings, not to mention tons of river rock.

The improvements only add to the sense you get that the Winery has been designed with taste and sophistication to blend in with its surroundings. We can't recommend this facility highly enough.

CEREMONY CAPACITY: The Garden holds 200 seated or 216 standing.

EVENT/RECEPTION CAPACITY: The Hill House accommodates 216 seated guests without space for dancing, or 180 with dancing. The Pavilion holds up to 216 seated guests.

MEETING CAPACITY: Event spaces accommodate 20–150 seated guests.

FEES & DEPOSITS: For weddings, 50% of the rental fee is required as a nonrefundable deposit, due when reservations are confirmed; the balance is payable 6 months prior to your function. The rental fee includes use of the lawn area, Hill House and the Pavilion for 8 hours. The wedding rental fee for the entire facility is $7,000 Monday–Friday, year-round. The weekend rental fee ranges $4,500–10,000 year-round.

For other special events and business functions, fees vary depending on spaces selected, event duration, day of week and season. Call for rates.

AVAILABILITY: Year-round, daily. For weddings and receptions, weekends 8am–11pm. For corporate events, any day 7am–11pm. Closed Thanksgiving, Christmas and New Year's Days and Eves.

SERVICES/AMENITIES:

Catering: select from preferred list
Kitchen Facilities: fully equipped
Tables & Chairs: some provided
Linens, Silver, etc.: BYO
Restrooms: wheelchair accessible
Dance Floor: inside Hill House
Bride's Dressing Area: yes
Meeting Equipment: full range
Other: site manager, wine tasting

Parking: for weddings, valet included in fee
Accommodations: no guestrooms
Telephone: pay phone
Outdoor Night Lighting: yes
Outdoor Cooking Facilities: CBA
Cleanup: caterer
View: panorama of SF Bay, including all major mountain peaks

RESTRICTIONS:

Alcohol: WC provided, no BYO
Smoking: outside only
Music: must select band or DJ from preferred list; acoustic only in lawn area

Wheelchair Access: yes
Insurance: certificate required

Overwhelmed? Use the search criteria on www.HereComesTheGuide.com to narrow down your choices.

South Bay

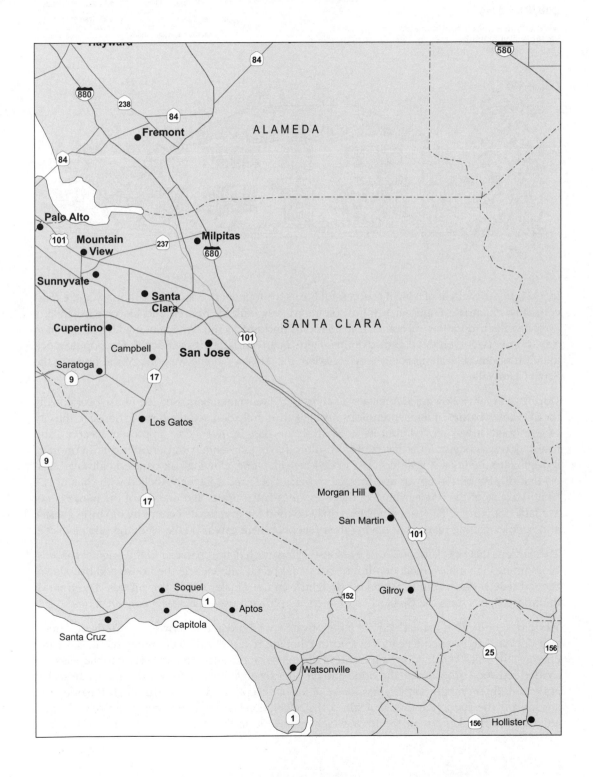

Ainsley House and Gardens

Historic House & Gardens

300 Grant Avenue, Campbell
408/866-2119

www.cityofcampbell.com/museum
kerryp@cityofcampbell.com

● Rehearsal Dinners		● Corp. Events/Mtgs.	
● Ceremonies		● Private Parties	
● Wedding Receptions		Accommodations	

In 1925, in the twilight of a highly successful life as the founder of a local fruit cannery and export company, expatriate Englishman John Colpitts Ainsley built for himself and his wife, Alcinda, a lovely English Tudor Revival home. With 15 rooms (including a modern kitchen with a refrigerator, a six-burner two-oven stove, and adjoining maid's quarters), large bay windows, a swooping mock thatch roof, and blooming English-style garden, the Ainsley's home was one of the finest in the Santa Clara Valley.

During the years following JC Ainsley's death in 1937, family members used the house occasionally for Christmas parties and other reunions. In 1989, the family donated the historic house to the city of Campbell. It was moved from its original site on Bascom Avenue to its present location, and restoration was begun immediately. The result is a living museum with period furniture (most of it original to the house), walls covered in delicate silk fabric, glowing oak-paneled hallways, closets that display period gowns and tiny flapper-era shoes, and a kitchen stocked with cans of JC's fruit! Because of the fragile nature of these antiques and artifacts, the interior of the house is not available for parties. The parlor, however, may be used for an intimate ceremony (up to 15 guests), and couples getting married or having their reception here can also take wedding photos inside.

The gardens that now surround Ainsley House retain much of the character of the original gardens. Blossoming crabapples, rhododendrons, irises, and bridal veil encircle the house and back lawn. Several rose bushes were transplanted straight from the Ainsley's 1925 flowerbeds. The front of the house opens onto the Orchard City Green, a lush lawn used for a local concert series.

Weddings are held in the backyard, a large private lawn bordered by flowers and redwood trees, and enclosed by latticed fencing covered in climbing roses. For the ceremony, the bridal party emerges through French doors at the rear of the house, and walks across the lawn to the wisteria-shaded redwood arbor where the bride and groom exchange vows. Afterwards, guests are seated at beautifully set tables on the grass for an al fresco reception. With colorful English gardens all around and the Tudor house as a backdrop, the celebration is infused with considerable Old World charm. Dancing takes place in the arbor, which is romantically lit at night by hanging period lanterns.

Ainsley House provides elegance, beauty and a taste of a time when life was more relaxed. If JC Ainsley could come back for a visit, he would be pleased to see that his home is still one of the finest in the region.

CEREMONY CAPACITY: The garden holds 200 seated guests.

EVENT/RECEPTION & MEETING CAPACITY: The garden holds 200 seated or 250 standing for a cocktail reception.

FEES & DEPOSITS: For special events, a $500 refundable security deposit and half the entire rental fee are required to secure your date. For ceremonies and rehearsals, the rental fee starts at $925 for a 3-hour minimum. For a reception, the fee is $1,425 for a 6-hour minimum and for a ceremony and reception, the fee starts at $1,925 for an 8-hour minimum. For each additional hour, there's a $200/hour charge.

AVAILABILITY: May–October. Call for more information.

SERVICES/AMENITIES:

Catering: BYO

Kitchen Facilities: no

Tables & Chairs: BYO

Linens, China, etc.: BYO

Restrooms: wheelchair accessible

Dance Floor: cement area

Bride's Dressing Area: yes

Meeting Equipment: BYO

Parking: ample, complimentary

Accommodations: no guestrooms

Telephone: emergency use only

Outdoor Night Lighting: yes

Outdoor Cooking Facilities: no

Cleanup: renter or caterer

View: English cottage garden

RESTRICTIONS:

Alcohol: BYO, champagne, wine and beer only

Smoking: restricted

Music: amplified OK, volume limits until 10pm

Wheelchair Access: yes

Insurance: not required

Other: no rice, birdseed, petals or confetti

The PruneYard Plaza Hotel

Hotel

1995 South Bascom Avenue, Campbell
800/559-4344

www.pruneyardplazahotel.com
sales@pruneyardplazahotel.com

● Rehearsal Dinners	● Corp. Events/Mtgs.
● Ceremonies	● Private Parties
● Wedding Receptions	● Accommodations

Not long ago, Campbell was home to miles of rustic prune orchards. The city has since become a busy South Bay mecca, highlighted by cosmopolitan restaurants, shops and nightlife. In the midst of this sophisticated urban environment you'll find a bit of Tuscany, courtesy of the PruneYard Plaza Hotel.

As you approach the hotel, you're greeted by a graceful, tri-level stone fountain in the center of the circular driveway out front. The soothing sound of cascading water quickly begins to wash away the stress of your day, and the promise of calm beckons you into this golden-hued getaway. Inside the spacious lobby, enormous earth-toned terracotta tiles cover the expansive floor, while moss green-gray walls play up dramatic area rugs featuring a pattern of fall colors. Large cushy chairs clustered around a fireplace invite conversation.

Through the lobby and past the small, tastefully appointed dining room (where your out-of-town guests will find plenty of healthful options for a morning-after brunch), a storybook-perfect terrace awaits, enclosed by a picturesque fence. This spot would be lovely for a day or evening ceremony, and it works equally well for a reception. From spring through fall, scarlet hibiscus flowers cover the latticed arbors that bookend the space. Huge clay pots filled with lavender peonies are placed around the used-brick terrace, instantly bringing to mind a neighborhood square in northern Italy.

Intimate indoor receptions are held in the Orchard Room on the third floor. Its vaulted fifteen-foot ceiling lends an airy feel to the room. During the day, tall windows bathe the muted pastel-green walls in light; to create a more subdued ambiance, just close the wooden shutters. Wall-to-wall carpeting in burgundy and gold echoes the pattern of the rugs in the lobby, and a Mediterranean breakfront and smaller side tables complete the "rustic elegance" theme.

For a larger celebration, reserve the Harvest Room on the mezzanine level. It's similar in décor to the Orchard Room and has a light oak dance floor. One of the best things about having an event here is that you have access to the mezzanine itself. It's a wonderful prefunction space where guests can mingle, or simply stand at the black wrought-iron-and-brass railing with cocktail in hand and watch the activity in the Lobby below.

Naturally, the PruneYard Plaza Hotel can accommodate the newlyweds, the wedding party and visiting guests in style. The parents of the bride and groom often stay in Executive Suites, while the couple reserves one of the two penthouse honeymoon suites. Both feature a fireplace, decorator-quality Euro-country furnishings and a roomy spa tub, as well as a private balcony that faces the pool and outdoor hot tub. All rooms include high-end amenities; some have kitchenettes for those booking an extended stay. Perhaps most convenient, the property adjoins the PruneYard Plaza, a full-service shopping area where the bride and her attendants can be coiffed and made up (and gowned, if need be), while the groomsmen can rent tuxedos or have theirs pressed. Plan your wedding at this boutique hotel, and you'll enjoy Old World charm combined with the best of modern-day hospitality.

CEREMONY, EVENT/RECEPTION & MEETING CAPACITY: Indoors, the hotel holds up to 80 seated guests; outdoors, up to 100 guests.

FEES & DEPOSITS: 50% of the estimated event total is required to reserve your date. The balance is due 2 weeks prior to the event. Rental fees start at $500, and depend on space rented, guest count and catering costs. Packages start at $35/person. Tax, alcohol and a 20% service charge are additional.

AVAILABILITY: Year-round, daily, 7am–11pm.

SERVICES/AMENITIES:

Catering: provided
Kitchen Facilities: n/a
Tables & Chairs: provided
Linens, China, etc.: provided
Restrooms: wheelchair accessible
Dance Floor: CBA
Bride's & Groom's Dressing Area: suite CBA
Meeting Equipment: CBA, extra charge

Parking: ample, complimentary
Accommodations: 171 guestrooms
Telephone: emergency use only
Outdoor Night Lighting: yes
Outdoor Cooking Facilities: CBA
Cleanup: provided
View: garden and landscaped grounds
Other: event coordination

RESTRICTIONS:

Alcohol: provided
Smoking: designated areas only
Music: amplified OK with restrictions

Wheelchair Access: yes
Insurance: not required
Other: no rice, birdseed, or confetti

Villa Ragusa

Special Events Facility

35 South Second Street, Campbell
408/364-1900
www.delvillas.com
info@delvillas.com

Rehearsal Dinners	● Corp. Events/Mtgs.
● Ceremonies	● Private Parties
● Wedding Receptions	Accommodations

Some couples opt for a small wedding, with just their nearest and dearest in attendance. Then there are those exuberant souls who want to share their once-in-a-lifetime experience with everyone, from next of kin and good friends to third cousins twice removed. If you fall into the latter category, we've got a great suggestion for you: Check out Villa Ragusa, located in the historic downtown section of Campbell.

Built in traditional Mediterranean style, with a stucco façade and red-tile roof, Villa Ragusa blends in so seamlessly with its vintage neighbors it's hard to believe it's only been here since 2001. Inside, the simple European-style décor gives the Villa an Old World ambiance, yet everything is freshly painted and polished to a high gloss.

When you enter the facility, a grand staircase leads to the Foyer, whose flawless limestone-and-granite floor glistens like a frozen pond. Four wooden double doors lead from the Foyer to the immense room that is the heart of Villa Ragusa. Here, the visual details are spare but carefully chosen. The thick carpeting, patterned in shades of maroon, green, gold and cream, looks as if no one has ever walked on it, and the dark wood bar that occupies one side of the space is immaculate and gleaming. Round frosted-glass-and-brass chandeliers are suspended from the coffered white ceiling, and arched windows let natural light stream in. The walls, painted in soft neutral shades of gray-green and cream, are enlivened by architectural elements such as pilasters, molding and wooden wainscoting. French doors lead to a covered deck that wraps around two sides of the building, making a great place for guests to mingle and enjoy Campbell's salubrious climate.

Although Villa Ragusa can accommodate 600 people, it can be divided into smaller galleries holding from 100 to 400 seated guests. Naturally, they provide portable bars and dance floors, and some of the galleries are available for wedding ceremonies. Villa Ragusa is also more than happy to book other types of events. They've hosted everything from Little League dinners to giant corporate parties, and the City of Campbell is one of their frequent clients. Last, but not least, there's plenty of parking in the 350-space garage just down the street. So go ahead and send a wedding invitation to that cousin from back east that you haven't seen since you were five years old, and anyone else you can think of. There's room for everyone up at Villa Ragusa.

CEREMONY CAPACITY: The Campbell Gallery holds 300, and the West Gallery holds 250 seated guests.

EVENT/RECEPTION & MEETING CAPACITY: Event spaces accommodate 100–600 seated guests.

FEES & DEPOSITS: For events, half of the room rental fee is a nonrefundable deposit required to hold your date. For Saturday events, the fee ranges $2,500–6,000. For other days of week, the fee ranges $500–4,000. 25% of the catering total is payable 3 months prior to the event. The catering and rental balance are due 1 week prior to the event, along with the beverage package balance and any other fees. Beverage packages range $6–28/person, and include beverages and bar service. The ceremony fee is $700, including chairs, setup and use of the facility.

AVAILABILITY: Year-round, daily, 8:30am–midnight, except all major holidays.

SERVICES/AMENITIES:

Catering: provided
Kitchen Facilities: fully equipped commercial
Tables & Chairs: provided
Linens, Silver, etc.: provided
Restrooms: wheelchair accessible
Dance Floor: hardwood and 2 portable available
Bride's Dressing Area: yes
Meeting Equipment: AV available, extra fee

Parking: public, free parking nearby
Accommodations: no guestrooms
Telephone: emergency use only
Outdoor Night Lighting: access only
Outdoor Cooking Facilities: no
Cleanup: caterer
View: downtown Campbell
Other: some event coordination

RESTRICTIONS:

Alcohol: provided, or corkage $10/bottle
Smoking: outside only
Music: amplified OK until midnight

Wheelchair Access: yes
Insurance: not required
Other: no confetti or glitter; decorations require approval

The professionals in the back of this book are the best in the business. How do we know? Read page 701.

Wedgewood Wedding & Banquet Center
at Eagle Ridge Golf Club

Golf Club

2951 Club Drive, Gilroy
866/966-3009

www.wedgewoodbanquet.com
sales@wedgewoodbanquet.com

- Rehearsal Dinners
- Ceremonies
- Wedding Receptions
- Corp. Events/Mtgs.
- Private Parties
- Accommodations

Mention the town of Gilroy and most people immediately think of farm stands, orchards, and of course—garlic! But ever since the high-tech boom of the 1980s and '90s, Gilroy has quietly been undergoing a transformation from a sleepy farm town to a thriving bedroom community, with fine homes, shopping centers and other amenities. The only thing missing was a sophisticated special event facility, and now, Wedgewood Wedding and Banquet Center at Eagle Ridge Golf Club has filled that niche.

As befits its name, this lovely golf club perches high on the hills above Gilroy, affording a 360-degree view of the surrounding countryside. Closer in, the greens and fairways of the golf course are draped over the golden hills like a cape of emerald velvet. Warm breezes are redolent with the scent of roses, thanks to the dozens of flourishing bushes planted in front of the clubhouse. This graceful, two-story structure was built in the "Monterey Colonial" style, combining elements from both New England and Spanish Colonial architecture. With its white clapboard siding, green shutters, and wisteria-twined veranda, it looks as refreshing as a cold glass of lemonade in the summer, and quite cheerful in the midst of winter. But no matter what the time of year, the clubhouse blends in with its surroundings as effortlessly as the hundred-year-old oaks that shade the golf course and adjacent countryside.

Inside, the club is every bit as appealing as it is outside. In the Lounge, you'll find a freestanding double fireplace of brick and wood, an impressive marble-and-wood bar, and circular wrought-iron chandeliers hanging from a soaring, vaulted, open-beamed ceiling. Guests can relax in overstuffed leather chairs as they sip cocktails before moving into the dining room for dinner. This space has creamy walls with white trim, carpeting in shades of rust and green, and plenty of windows to showcase the sweeping golf course vista.

Upstairs, the Terrace is ideal for more intimate events, including small ceremonies. For parties or receptions, they can set up a dance floor and portable bar. And since the Terrace is enclosed on three sides and covered, your guests can revel in the fabulous outdoors (and fabulous views) while keeping their cool on hot days; a built-in fireplace adds warmth when the sun goes down.

Just outside the clubhouse, a great swath of lawn serves as the main ceremony site. Exchange vows in a white gazebo, with the golf course as a beautiful backdrop.

Though Eagle Ridge is visually stunning, one of its most valuable assets is the professionalism and service provided by the Banquet Center's expert planning staff. Wedgewood offers the same trademark on-site coordination that has distinguished the company for decades. Five lavish wedding packages include invitations, flowers, cake, and music, as well as the DJ, minister and menu—all of which are carefully sampled, screened and priced to ensure top quality, affordability and maximum satisfaction. Menu options are varied and generous, with room for customization.

CEREMONY CAPACITY: The Lawn Area holds up to 275 seated guests.

EVENT/RECEPTION & MEETING CAPACITY: The Banquet Room accommodates 275 seated and 375 standing.

FEES & DEPOSITS: 25% of the estimated event total is required to reserve your date. The next 25% is due 90 days prior to the event, and the balance is due 10 days before the event, along with the final guest count. Wedding packages start at $39/person and include rental fee, bartenders, outside ceremony setup and cleanup. Tax, alcohol and a service charge are additional. Customized packages are also available.

AVAILABILITY: Year-round, daily, 6am–11pm.

SERVICES/AMENITIES:

Catering: provided, no BYO

Kitchen Facilities: n/a

Tables & Chairs: provided

Linens, Silver, etc.: provided

Restrooms: wheelchair accessible

Dance Floor: yes, extra charge

Bride's Dressing Area: yes

Meeting Equipment: full range CBA, extra charge

Parking: large lot

Accommodations: no guestrooms

Telephone: emergency use only

Outdoor Night Lighting: yes

Outdoor Cooking Facilities: no

Cleanup: provided

View: fairways, foothills

Other: event coordination

RESTRICTIONS:

Alcohol: provided

Smoking: outdoors only

Music: amplified OK with volume restrictions

Wheelchair Access: yes

Insurance: not required

Other: no rice, confetti or glitter; no open flames

San Juan Oaks Golf Club

Golf Club

3825 Union Road, Hollister
831/636-6125
www.sanjuanoaks.com
dvarner@sanjuanoaks.com

● Rehearsal Dinners	● Corp. Events/Mtgs.
● Ceremonies	● Private Parties
● Wedding Receptions	Accommodations

Old World charm meets modern day amenities at San Juan Oaks Golf Club, a peaceful California-style hacienda and 18-hole championship golf course, set amongst the creeks and foothills near historic San Juan Bautista.

The drive to San Juan Oaks is a relaxing one, meandering through the valley floor, past a green and golden landscape dotted with colorful seasonal flowers. And when you pull into the club's circular brick entranceway with its softly flowing fountain, you realize that this place is as serene as its surroundings. "It's such a beautiful site—people arrive and find themselves in good spirits," says David Varner, Director of Food & Beverage services.

Architecturally, the club takes a nod from the town's 200-year-old Mission, with a tile roof, wide hallways, broad windows and arched entryways. A gorgeous, wraparound terrace spills onto the lush golf course, and offers an unobstructed view of the shimmering lake just beyond. Inside, the club's foyer features tiled floors and comfortable oversized chairs. High ceilings throughout the 19,000-square-foot facility are punctuated by dramatic exposed wooden trusses and sleek, hanging light fixtures.

All three of San Juan Oaks' event spaces open out onto the terrace through a series of French doors, so no matter where you celebrate, you have a clear view of the fairways, lake and distant foothills. Guests can kick off an event with a drink or appetizer at the gorgeous cherrywood bar in the Lounge, then stroll into the adjacent Oaks Room for the main reception. This versatile space accommodates large weddings, showers, rehearsal dinners or corporate functions, and can be divided into two smaller rooms for more intimate events. When the weather's balmy, guests like to dine on the terrace and take in the sunset, and if the evening turns cool, they're quickly warmed by the wood-burning stone fireplace. If you're planning a small conference or meeting, the Fred Couples Room next door is a private space with its own bar and fireplace, and an interesting display of Couples' trophies, photos and memorabilia.

The cuisine at San Juan Oaks is overseen by their talented chef, who incorporates the freshest ingredients into his culinary creations. He and his team specialize in regional California dishes with artistic presentations. Customized menus are available, and may feature wine pairings from the club's wine list, which includes a selection of favorite local wines.

Although you don't have to be a golfer to host your event at San Juan Oaks, lovers of the game will be in heaven here. In a recent ranking of 5,000 North American public and resort courses by *Golf Digest Magazine,* San Juan Oaks received four out of five stars for customer service, value and golf course quality. Designed by PGA great Fred Couples, the Front Nine winds through five lakes and interconnecting creeks on the valley floor; the Back Nine climbs 200 feet into the foothills, and includes elevated tees and fairways with spectacular views. The Pro Shop is experienced in organizing a wide range of golf-related events, including "Shotgun" tournaments, charity events, and golf clinics. Lodging options in neighboring San Juan Bautista, or in the Monterey Bay area (just 35 minutes away), can be arranged.

A great deal of care has gone into making San Juan Oaks blend seamlessly into its natural environment, and an equal amount of effort has been put into providing topnotch facilities and service. Much to the delight of golfers and non-golfers alike, they've succeeded on both counts.

CEREMONY CAPACITY: The Patio holds 300 seated.

EVENT/RECEPTION CAPACITY: The Fred Couples Room holds 50 seated guests, the Adobe Room 80 seated or 100 standing, the Oaks Room 160 seated or 200 standing and the Oaks and Adobe Rooms together hold 300 seated or 350 standing guests indoors.

MEETING CAPACITY: The Fred Couples Room holds 30 guests seated conference-style. The Oaks Room seats 200 theater-style.

FEES & DEPOSITS: A $1,000 nonrefundable deposit is required to reserve your date and is applied towards the event total. A $2,000 nonrefundable payment is due 90 days prior, and the estimated event balance is payable 5 days prior to the event. Events range $60–100/person depending on the day of the week and guest count; tax, alcohol and an 18% service charge are additional. Facility fees range $250–2,000 depending on the room selected. A $750 ceremony fee is additional.

AVAILABILITY: Year-round, daily, 7am–midnight.

SERVICES/AMENITIES:

Catering: provided, no BYO
Kitchen Facilities: n/a
Tables & Chairs: provided
Linens, Silver, etc.: provided
Restrooms: wheelchair accessible
Dance Floor: yes
Bride's Dressing Area: yes
Meeting Equipment: screen, podium, wireless microphones

Parking: large lot
Accommodations: no guestrooms
Telephone: emergency use only
Outdoor Night Lighting: access only
Outdoor Cooking Facilities: BBQ CBA
Cleanup: provided
View: fairways, rolling hills, lake
Other: event coordination

RESTRICTIONS:

Alcohol: provided
Smoking: patio only
Music: amplified OK

Wheelchair Access: yes
Insurance: not required
Other: no rice or birdseed, no open flames

Creekside of Los Gatos

Private Estate

Address withheld to ensure privacy. Los Gatos
408/559-7733, Panetta's Catering
www.creeksidelosgatos.com
lbeesley@msn.com

● Rehearsal Dinners	● Corp. Events/Mtgs.
● Ceremonies	● Private Parties
● Wedding Receptions	Accommodations

Creekside of Los Gatos was born of the romantic vision of two people in love. Pat and Augusto purchased this view-filled spread with the idea of designing an awe-inspiring wedding location; it was bound to turn out fantastically, since the couple also planned on using it for their own summer wedding.

Though conveniently located near a main highway, Creekside is totally secluded. A private treelined drive takes visitors onto the grounds, a gently sloping hillside surrounded by coastal oaks. Tucked between unspoiled hills and a forested stream, this exclusive haven feels oh-so-close to nature.

The first part of the couple's dream project involved renovating the 100-year-old genuine log cabin, which is poised atop a narrow plateau. Quaint and welcoming beneath a canopy of leafy boughs, the cabin's burnished redwood façade seems as fresh as if its planks had just been hewn. At the same time, embellishments like river-rock steps and trim contribute a nostalgic charm. With a pretty lawn and garden, and several small areas paved with textured rose-colored concrete, the cabin's immaculate front yard is a delightful milieu for preparty mingling or cocktail gatherings. Inside the cabin, Pat and Augusto have outfitted the rooms for bridal party preparations, with separate quarters for guys and gals. The Great Room has a picture window that lets a bride preview the unfolding scene before making her grand entrance.

While the cabin's ambiance is warm and down to earth, the event areas are breathtaking and dramatic. Broad steps lead from the cabin to two descending terraces fashioned of river rock. With teak benches, upscale café tables and umbrellas, and an outdoor stone fireplace, terrace receptions take on a mood of Tuscan-style conviviality. On the other side of the stairs, flagstone and rocks have been artfully arranged into a magnificent tropical waterfall. As the watery cascade glistens in the waning rays of the sun, guests succumb to the hypnotic sound of the water's flow.

Another captivating element at Creekside is the view. From the terraces, a vast carpet of manicured lawn makes a gradual descent towards the forest's edge. Through billowy trees, glimpses of a meandering creek seem like a beguiling mirage. The placid vision of sparkling Lexington Reservoir is a sweep of blue in the distance. There are a total of four possible ceremony spots that take advantage of this picturesque tableau, including a lush cathedral of redwood trees and a timbered pergola.

Pat and Augusto had intended to say their vows beneath the pergola, but a funny thing happened on the day of their wedding. The guest chairs were arranged on the grass and everything was in place for the arrival of friends and family. Then Pat was suddenly struck by an adventurous impulse: Why not get married on one of the waterfall's flagstone landings amid the mist and ornamental ferns? Being the bride, her whim was gratified, seating was quickly rearranged, and Pat officially inaugurated the waterfall as a resplendent ceremony option!

Creekside of Los Gatos is available exclusively through *Panetta's Catering,* event pros whose attractively priced, full-service packages expertly pull all the elements together. *Panetta's* joins Pat and Augusto in extending a gracious invitation to bask in this estate's many charms.

CEREMONY, EVENT/RECEPTION & MEETING CAPACITY: The site holds a maximum of 150 seated or 200 standing guests outdoors.

FEES & DEPOSITS: A $1,000 deposit is required to reserve your date. The balance is due 30–90 days prior to the event. Rental fees range $3,000–5,000 depending on the date rented. Meals start at $60/person. Tax, alcohol and an 18% service charge are additional.

AVAILABILITY: Available from late April–early October. Just one event takes place on the property per day. Hours are flexible, and amplified music must be over by 10pm.

SERVICES/AMENITIES:

Catering: provided by *Panetta's Catering*
Kitchen Facilities: n/a
Tables & Chairs: some provided
Linens, Silver, etc.: through caterer
Restrooms: wheelchair accessible
Dance Floor: provided
Bride's & Groom's Dressing Areas: yes
Meeting Equipment: CBA

Parking: limited
Accommodations: no guestrooms
Telephone: office phone
Outdoor Night Lighting: yes
Outdoor Cooking Facilities: no
Cleanup: renter or caterer
View: meadow, lake, garden, waterfall, hills
Other: event coordination

RESTRICTIONS:

Alcohol: BYO
Smoking: outside only
Music: amplified OK outdoors with restrictions

Wheelchair Access: limited
Insurance: required

Want to know **WHAT TO ASK** a potential location or vendor? Check out our Questions to Ask on page 17.

Hazlwood

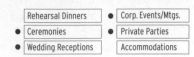

Private Estate

Address withheld to ensure privacy. Los Gatos

408/429-4381

www.hazlwood.com
barbarahzwd@yahoo.com
jknipe@yahoo.com

○ Rehearsal Dinners		● Corp. Events/Mtgs.	
● Ceremonies		● Private Parties	
● Wedding Receptions		○ Accommodations	

Just like every bride is uniquely beautiful, so, too, is each private estate charming in its own way. Hazlwood boasts charm aplenty, beginning with a bucolic and secluded location in the foothills of Los Gatos. It's only a few minutes off the highway, but Hazlwood's congenial, storybook personality makes you feel as if you were dropped into the middle of an enchanted forest.

A driveway lined with birdhouses leads to a parking area bordered by redwoods; a flower-covered archway marks a footpath onto Hazlwood's bi-level grounds, and from here you get an overview of the lush property. On a rise to the left sits a comely wood-frame home, whose broad wraparound deck invites your guests to sit back and enjoy the view. Just beyond this home is a spacious brick patio flanked by a quaint summer house. Abundant fruit trees frame garden lawns that cascade down towards a magnificent site: a waterfall and water garden ringed with river rocks, reedy bamboo and wild grasses. The trickling of water and a breeze whispering through the treetops harmonizes with birdsong, while bullfrogs and fish dart among the water lilies. Below the water garden is the ceremony area, a rambling emerald-green lawn edged with coastal redwoods. A brick-lined aisle makes a gentle descent to a simple white-columned pergola, set against a dense grove of redwood trees, nature's chapel for your wedding vows.

During the social hour, guests mingle around the water garden or have a friendly game of bocce on the two courts near the entrance. Drinks are served on the broad porch of the summer house, while cedar and apple trees provide shade for hors d'oeuvres stations. Dining tables are spread out over the patio and on the lawns; nearby, a petite greenhouse, decorated with café lights and flowers, holds the buffet.

After dinner, guests can enjoy dancing on the patio under the stars or relaxing in the two-room summer house. A vaulted ceiling and tall, multipaned windows create a bright and airy atmosphere. The pretty first room has a polished wood floor, and while it's reserved for the bride's preparations before the ceremony, it's open to guests afterwards. Up a step, an adjoining salon features a fireplace and Italian-tile floor, making it a great choice for after-dinner dancing, as well as cake cutting and coffee service. Both rooms have French doors that are left open to the patio, so guests can easily roam inside and out.

Hazlwood has one more arrow in its quiver of delights: James and Brenda Knipe, who cater many of the events here and are devoted to making your celebration special. We have it on good authority that they cook up a storm; and since James is the brother of owner Robert Knipe, festivities at Hazlwood take on the convivial spirit of a real family affair. Together, they extend a genteel welcome to you and your loved ones.

CEREMONY CAPACITY: The Ceremony Lawn holds 300 seated guests.

EVENT/RECEPTION CAPACITY: The brick and lawn areas accommodate up to 300 guests. The Summer House holds up to 75 seated or 150 standing guests.

FEES & DEPOSITS: 50% of the rental fee is required to secure your date. The balance is due 30 days prior to the event. Rental fees range $3,000–9,000 depending on guest count. There is a 10% discount for Friday events and 15% for Monday–Thursday. Meals start at $34.50/person. Tax, alcohol and service charge are additional.

AVAILABILITY: May–October, daily, 10am–10pm.

SERVICES/AMENITIES:

Catering: provided, or BYO approved
Kitchen Facilities: n/a
Tables & Chairs: through *Prestigious Provisions*
Linens, Silver, etc.: through *Prestigious Provisions*
Restrooms: wheelchair accessible
Dance Floor: provided
Bride's Dressing Area: yes
Meeting Equipment: n/a

Parking: limited, valet CBA
Accommodations: no guestrooms
Telephone: emergency use only
Outdoor Night Lighting: yes
Outdoor Cooking Facilities: through caterer
Cleanup: caterer
View: garden, water garden, forest
Other: coordination available, extra charge

RESTRICTIONS:

Alcohol: BYO
Smoking: designated areas only
Music: amplified OK with restrictions

Wheelchair Access: limited
Insurance: liability required

Laurel Mill Lodge

Lodge

Address withheld to ensure privacy. Los Gatos
408/353-5851

www.laurelmilllodge.com
proprietors@laurelmilllodge.com

- Rehearsal Dinners
- Ceremonies
- Wedding Receptions
- Corp. Events/Mtgs.
- Private Parties
- Accommodations

Whether you're seeking a place with unspoiled natural beauty for your wedding, a quiet atmosphere for a writer's retreat, or just a place to get in touch with your "inner child," Laurel Mill Lodge has a variety of packages to suit your needs. Nestled in the tall trees of the Santa Cruz Mountains, this delightfully rustic establishment is not only a special event facility, but a virtual summer camp for grown-ups (and their kids, too.) The stresses and strains of the everyday world will float away like so much dandelion fluff, as you experience the extraordinary effect of the Laurel Mill Lodge.

This 27-acre facility occupies the site of a lumber mill that operated over a century ago, and part of the Lodge dates back to when it was the mess hall for the lumberjacks. Today, the property is equipped to handle any kind of event, from an elegant wedding to a laid-back family reunion. In the Lodge itself, you'll find a spacious room that works well for meetings, sit-down dinners or just relaxing. Paneled entirely in very old redwood, with windows along one wall framing views of the surrounding trees, the room features a large fireplace, a baby grand piano and a big screen TV with VCR/DVD player. The adjacent sunny deck, with its umbrella-shaded tables, overlooks a pavilion that can be used as a stage, a dance floor, or for an outdoor luncheon or dinner. The convenient arrangement of event spaces allows you to have your celebration indoors, outdoors or both. And from the commercially equipped and caterer-friendly kitchen, you'll be able to serve gourmet meals to a crowd.

One of Laurel Mill Lodge's most attractive features is a vast verdant meadow, surrounded by magnificent redwoods and bordered by Soquel Creek. This sun-splashed space, carpeted in lush "barefoot grass," can seat a sizeable group for a wedding ceremony, concert or theater production. An octagonal redwood stage with detachable handrails and arch can be placed anywhere on the meadow, which is also an ideal setting for camping, picnics, barbecues and outdoor games. After dining and dancing, guests often soak in the twenty-person hot tub, bake in the sauna or gather around a campfire with guitars and marshmallows.

Laurel Mill Lodge specializes in long, leisurely celebrations. In times past, when the mountain residents traveled by horseback, they didn't just get together for an afternoon or an evening—they partied for days! This charming custom is still observed here, thanks to a variety of overnight options. Across the footbridge over Soquel Creek and up a short winding path through redwoods, ferns and forget-me-nots, you will find simple but cozy cabins, each with a king-size sleeping loft and a deck overlooking the creek. Another footbridge leads to six A-frame bunkhouses, each of which sleeps four. Camping is permitted on the meadow. Just think—you could extend your rehearsal, wedding and reception over several days, so that your close friends and family have time to really get to know each other. Guests can stay even longer if they wish. Best of all, when you hold your wedding at Laurel Mill Lodge, you get the entire property to yourself. The same could be said for reunions, parties, bar/bat mitzvahs and retreats.

We could go on and on about the beauty and versatility of Laurel Mill Lodge, but only a visit will convince you how special this facility really is. To protect the privacy of each event in progress, site visits are arranged by appointment only.

CEREMONY, EVENT/RECEPTION & MEETING CAPACITY: The site holds up to 150 guests indoors or outdoors. Spaces are available for smaller events.

FEES & DEPOSITS: For weddings, 50% of the estimated event total is required to reserve your date; the balance is due 21 days before the event. Rental fees range $2,650–6,800 for 6-hour to 48-hour wedding packages. When you rent the site for a wedding, you have access to the entire facility. Some overnight accommodations are additional. If your event includes more than 5 children, childcare will be provided by the facility at an additional charge.

For business meetings or seminars, rental fees for the conference room range $10–25/person depending on length of time rented. For family reunions, $30–45/person/day includes camping and many other amenities.

AVAILABILITY: Year-round, daily.

SERVICES/AMENITIES:

Catering: BYO
Kitchen Facilities: commercially equipped
Tables & Chairs: provided
Linens, Silver, etc.: CBA, extra charge
Restrooms: narrow wheelchairs OK
Dance Floor: on deck
Bride's & Groom's Dressing Area: yes
Meeting Equipment: TV with VCR/DVD, whiteboards, projection screen, podium; other CBA, extra charge

Parking: 60 spaces available
Accommodations: 8 cabins, 6 bunkhouses and tent camping
Telephone: available upon request
Outdoor Night Lighting: yes
Outdoor Cooking Facilities: yes
Cleanup: provided
View: redwood trees, creek, meadow, starry night sky
Other: piano, large hot tub, sauna, outdoor fire pit, stage lighting

RESTRICTIONS:

Alcohol: BYO, licensed server
Smoking: outdoors only
Music: amplified OK until 10pm

Wheelchair Access: limited
Insurance: liability required
Other: no fireworks, torches, lighter fluids or pets

Los Gatos History Club

123 Los Gatos Boulevard, Los Gatos
408/559-7733
www.losgatoshistoryclub.com
lbeesley@msn.com

Historic Club

● Rehearsal Dinners		● Corp. Events/Mtgs.	
● Ceremonies		● Private Parties	
● Wedding Receptions		Accommodations	

Would you like to have your wedding at a lovely, full-service facility while supporting a worthwhile cause? You can easily accomplish both aims at the Los Gatos History Club. This unique organization has been a Los Gatos fixture since 1897, when six women met in the Los Gatos library and decided to form a club to study the history of other countries. By 1907, the group had grown too big to meet in private homes, so the women decided to build their own clubhouse. Determined to pay for it themselves, they borrowed the money, and one year later the "History Club of Los Gatos" held its grand opening. From its beginning, this unusual club has concerned itself with the needs and interests of the women in the community, and in its early years joined with other women's groups to influence policy-making on a state and national level. Today, the club continues to promote friendship among women, aids local educational and charitable institutions, and encourages community awareness and involvement. And though the Los Gatos History Club may not be the most well-known fundraising organization in the South Bay, it's garnered national recognition, as evidenced by the framed letters from such luminaries as former president Bill Clinton, congressman Tom Lantos, and former governor Pete Wilson.

Located in a woodsy residential neighborhood, the Los Gatos History Club occupies a modest, yet charming, ranch-style building whose simple lines and neutral taupe exterior give it the kind of unobtrusive elegance often found in Japanese architecture. Inside, the History Club's gleaming hardwood floors, fresh white walls and unusual peaked, buttressed ceiling provide the perfect backdrop for any type of decorating scheme you desire. At one end of the room is a raised stage with a grand piano; at the other, a floor-to-ceiling window frames a fenced garden lush with lacy Japanese maples and flourishing tree ferns. This greenery is echoed by potted ficus trees placed strategically throughout the room. Dimmable main lights and a variety of stage lighting options help to create that special mood. Along one wall, large windows and French doors look out onto a fenced patio where ceremonies are held. Chock-full of colorful roses and sheltered by mature trees, it's as cozy and private as any couple could wish. A wooden arbor, covered with climbing roses and wisteria vines, is the preferred spot for exchanging vows. The building's deep eaves shade part of the patio, outfitted with ceiling fans and heat lamps to make it comfortable no matter what the weather.

Perhaps the club's elegant simplicity and historical relevance have piqued your interest, but you're wondering about the other elements so necessary for a smashing event: food, drink and service.

Well, let us put your mind at ease right now—this facility specializes in weddings. In fact, the staff has probably handled more weddings than a Las Vegas justice of the peace! They also pride themselves on making your event stress-free, by taking care of as many details as possible. And they'll put together a wedding package that fits your tastes and budget as beautifully as your wedding gown fits you. Speaking of wedding gowns, the Los Gatos History Club also has a spacious ladies room, equipped with a large mirror, makeup table and a generous closet for use by you and your bridal party. Needless to say, the club's expertise in coordinating weddings can be applied to other special events as well. Whatever you're planning, the Los Gatos History Club will make sure your event comes off without a hitch. You may not get a letter of commendation from the president, but you'll get heaps of praise from your happy guests.

CEREMONY CAPACITY: The garden holds 150 seated guests.

EVENT/RECEPTION CAPACITY: Indoors, the site holds 150 seated or 200 standing for a cocktail reception.

MEETING CAPACITY: Indoors, the site holds 150 seated classroom-style or 200 seated theater-style.

FEES & DEPOSITS: For special events, a $300 refundable security deposit is required to secure your date. Site rental fees are paid through *Panetta's Catering* and may be paid in installments. Site fees range $600–1,200 depending on the day of the event. *Panetta's Catering* offers a special wedding package which includes the bridal buffet, beverage package, wedding cake, DJ for 5 hours, all service labor, china, flatware and linen napkins starting at $4,995, based on the first 100 guests. For each guest over 100, the cost is $39/person. Individual consultations and tastings are offered at no extra charge.

AVAILABILITY: Year-round, daily, 11am–10pm, including holidays.

SERVICES/AMENITIES:

Catering: provided by *Panetta's Catering*

Kitchen Facilities: yes

Tables & Chairs: provided

Linens, China, etc.: provided

Restrooms: wheelchair accessible

Dance Floor: provided, in front of stage

Bride's Dressing Area: yes

Meeting Equipment: CBA, extra fee

Parking: limited on-site, ample off-site

Accommodations: no guestrooms, hotels nearby

Telephone: emergency use only

Outdoor Night Lighting: access lighting only

Outdoor Cooking Facilities: CBA

Cleanup: caterer

View: rose garden patio

Other: event coordination

RESTRICTIONS:

Alcohol: BYO

Smoking: designated areas

Music: amplified OK indoors only

Wheelchair Access: yes

Insurance: not required

Want to find more locations and services? Check out our informative website, www.HereComesTheGuide.com.

305

Los Gatos Lodge

Hotel and Garden

50 Los Gatos-Saratoga Road, Los Gatos
408/354-3300

www.losgatoslodge.com
sales@losgatoslodge.com

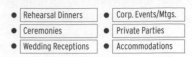

- ● Rehearsal Dinners
- ● Ceremonies
- ● Wedding Receptions
- ● Corp. Events/Mtgs.
- ● Private Parties
- ● Accommodations

Los Gatos Lodge is an oasis of serenity, just minutes away from the center of picturesque downtown Los Gatos. Nestled in the Santa Cruz Mountains on ten beautifully landscaped acres, it's an attractive garden setting with a warm, unpretentious atmosphere. Its accessible location—close to three major airports—makes it very convenient for out-of-town wedding guests and business travelers alike.

The two-story lodge offers 128 newly renovated guestrooms, including thirteen suites with fireplaces, and over 5,000 square feet of banquet facilities, featuring five meeting rooms (equipped with screens and whiteboards) for seminars, retreats, conferences, weddings, and receptions. Among the outdoor event spaces are the Wedding Garden (designed exclusively for ceremonies), a large pool and patio with ample space for a band or DJ, and emerald-green lawns (great for wedding photos, cocktail receptions, or just a quiet stroll).

The Wedding Garden is a private covered arbor set slightly outside of the circle formed by the lodge's main buildings. It's available for rental whether you're holding your reception at the Lodge or elsewhere, and it nicely combines both natural and decorative elements. Guests are seated on white garden chairs, while the wedding party makes its entrance through a frame of trees and flowers. They walk along an aisle runner, taking their places under a lattice arch decorated with silk ivy. The bride can make a dramatic entrance from a nearby room that has been provided as a changing area.

After the ceremony, the tree-shaded covered patio provides a pleasant reception option. You can dance poolside until 10pm (when outside music must end), then move your party to the indoor lounge, with its massive fireplace and full bar. If you decide to hold your entire affair indoors, the large El Gato Room is a good choice. With its plush carpet and soft lighting, the space has a sophisticated feel. It can be outfitted with a dance floor, and there will still be plenty of room left for tables.

The guestrooms and additional facilities at Los Gatos Lodge offer many advantages. If you're planning a large wedding with a lot of out-of-town guests, you can reserve a block of rooms. Both wedding and business guests will appreciate the putting green, regulation bocce ball court, and the in-house food and beverage services. Here, your dining experience is enhanced by views of the lush garden through large picture windows. You might consider organizing a morning-after-the-wedding brunch in one of the smaller banquet rooms, easily arranged by the Lodge's experienced wedding consultants. However you decide to utilize this flexible facility, you'll find the management extremely knowledgeable, friendly and accommodating.

CEREMONY CAPACITY: The Wedding Garden holds 150 seated or 250 standing guests.

EVENT/RECEPTION CAPACITY: The El Gato Room holds 120 seated guests, and the Gardenside Patio and pool area hold 250 seated guests. For other events, the Vasona Room holds 30, the DeAnza Room 80, the Saratoga Room 40, and the Garden Room 75 seated guests.

MEETING CAPACITY: Event spaces accommodate 15–250 seated guests.

FEES & DEPOSITS: For social events, deposits range $250–1,000 depending on the space reserved, due within 7 days of making reservations. The event balance is due 5 days prior to the event. Room rental fees run $300–1,500. Wedding packages range $59–90/person, and à la carte meals $30–50/person; tax, alcohol and a 20% service charge are additional. A $1.50/person cake-cutting fee applies.

For business functions, a deposit may be required. The event balance is due 5 days prior to the function. Meeting rooms run $200–500 and meals run $15–35/person; tax, alcohol and a 20% service charge are additional.

AVAILABILITY: Indoor spaces and the Wedding Garden are available year-round, daily, including holidays, 7am–midnight. Gardenside Patio and Grass are available April 1–October 31, until 10pm.

SERVICES/AMENITIES:
Catering: provided
Kitchen Facilities: prep only
Table & Chairs: provided
Linens, Silver, etc.: provided
Restrooms: wheelchair accessible
Dance Floor: CBA, $200 extra charge
Bride's Dressing Area: yes
Meeting Equipment: CBA, extra charge, WiFi access, business center

Parking: free, ample and on-site
Accommodations: 128 guestrooms, including 13 suites with fireplaces
Telephone: emergency use only
Outdoor Night Lighting: yes
Outdoor Cooking Facilities: no
Cleanup: provided
View: garden courtyard
Other: event coordination

RESTRICTIONS:
Alcohol: provided or BYO with corkage fee for wine
Smoking: outside only
Music: amplified OK outdoors until 10pm, indoors until midnight

Wheelchair Access: yes
Insurance: required for outside catering
Other: decorations must have prior approval

Nestldown

Private Estate

Address withheld to ensure privacy. Los Gatos Mountains
408/353-5311

www.nestldown.com
info@nestldown.com

●	Rehearsal Dinners	●	Corp. Events/Mtgs.
●	Ceremonies	●	Private Parties
●	Wedding Receptions	●	Accommodations

A bride at Nestldown descends a broad stairway through redwoods to a lakeside bower where she will say her vows. About halfway down, she experiences a sublime moment when, for a few seconds, it's possible for her to look up to the tops of the soaring trees and down to their bases far below, as though she's suspended in the air among them, a bird waiting to glide to earth.

This is not the only ethereal moment she or her groom and guests will enjoy here. Nestldown, an enchanted hideaway in a mountain forest, evokes magic over and over.

Years ago it was a fruit farm in the Santa Cruz Mountains that grew apples, peaches and kiwis. Its current owners have spent the past decade creating a wonderland of gardens, whimsical sculptures, topiary figures, and fanciful structures on 35 acres at the property's heart. The result is a place where so many things delight and amaze: redwoods standing gray under morning clouds that suddenly blaze cinnamon in sunlight; flowers splashed along every path; barely-there trails and unexpected stairways that lead the curious to bentwood benches and chairs set smack in the middle of the forest. But all of these sensory treats are just preludes to the beauty of Nestldown's outdoor chapel and the breathtaking architecture of its signature building, The Barn.

You reach the chapel on an earth-and-wood staircase that meanders down a forested hillside. Its destination is a flagstone-paved amphitheater, sheltered by trees and ferns, that faces a wisteria-covered pergola. The pergola, set at the edge of a small, forest-fringed lake, is built from redwood saplings with their bark left on. It's so natural in appearance that it looks as though it sprang by itself from the ground. Just beyond it is another grace note, a wooden bridge, Japanese in its simplicity, that arches over a rivulet at the foot of a small waterfall.

Post-ceremony celebrations take place in The Barn and on its adjoining grand lawn. The Barn is one of the most beautiful wooden structures built in Northern California in recent years. Almost everybody who enters it for the first time gasps at the interior of this soaring glass-and-fir structure. The interior rises to a steep-pitched ceiling, supported by slender wooden columns. The timbers, stained a glowing reddish-amber, still have the wonderful smell of fresh-cut wood lingering about them. Gardens and trees hug two sides of The Barn. Flowers bloom year-round—petunias, red hot salvias, alyssum, candytufts, begonias, violas, irises and calla lilies—and there are fanciful critters everywhere: a brass bear peers out from one garden and in another a topiary serpent undulates through a sea of long, slender-bladed fescue. A large koi pond in front of The Barn is lined with willows and birch, and embellished by a brass stork. Just off The Barn's terrace, a grand meadow sweeps out to a copse of redwoods where a hand-carved wooden bench reveals the image of three cavorting bears.

Nestldown is sheer exhilaration. You feel a giddy sense of expectation and joy, as you discover nature's best so skillfully combined with the fruit of human imagination.

CEREMONY CAPACITY: The outdoor chapel holds 225 seated guests, the Foxglove Meadow 300 seated guests, The Barn holds 150 seated, and the Main Lawn 300 seated guests.

EVENT/RECEPTION & MEETING CAPACITY: There is one indoor and several outdoor spaces available that hold up to 300 seated guests. Smaller events can also be accommodated.

FEES & DEPOSITS: 50% of the rental fee is required to reserve your date; the balance is due 60 days prior to the event. The rental fees range $3,500–15,000 depending on guest count, space rented and time of year.

AVAILABILITY: Year-round, daily, 8am–11pm. Limited capacities apply December–March.

SERVICES/AMENITIES:

Catering: select from list
Kitchen Facilities: prep only
Tables & Chairs: provided up to 200 guests
Linens, Silver, etc.: through caterer
Restrooms: wheelchair accessible
Dance Floor: yes
Bride's Dressing Area: yes
Meeting Equipment: CBA, extra charge
full A/V on site

Parking: on-site for up to 125 cars, shuttle CBA
Accommodations: guest house holds 8 guests
Telephone: emergency only
Outdoor Night Lighting: some areas
Outdoor Cooking Facilities: CBA
Cleanup: provided
View: pond, meadow, redwoods, garden

RESTRICTIONS:

Alcohol: BYO, licensed server
Smoking: designated area only
Music: amplified OK

Wheelchair Access: limited
Insurance: certificate required
Other: no rice or birdseed; some types of balloons are restricted

Opera House

Landmark Building

140 West Main Street, Los Gatos
408/354-1218

www.operahouselosgatos.com
events@operahouselosgatos.com

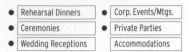

● Rehearsal Dinners	● Corp. Events/Mtgs.
● Ceremonies	● Private Parties
● Wedding Receptions	Accommodations

For large weddings, the Opera House is still the only game in town. Occupying a 1904 landmark brick building with crisp white trim, its 8,000 square feet can seat up to 350 guests!

Enter the downstairs foyer and wind your way up the formal sweeping staircase to the main event floor. Award-winning Bradbury & Bradbury wallpaper in blues, creams and golds adorns the stairwell. Walls and ceilings are covered with original pressed tin in 15 different Victorian motifs, and antique light fixtures abound. The Grand Ballroom has a 24-foot ceiling, with a rectangular skylight in the center that brings in natural light. From the Balcony up above, you can toss your bouquet or watch the dancing below. The lower portion of the room, called the Mezzanine, has a wall of windows facing north. Soft pastels, cream and taupe predominate, and a large mural on an upper wall facing the Ballroom depicts the Opera House's original theater curtain.

Because of the way this facility is configured, groups of 100 or fewer won't feel dwarfed in this space. Additional enhancements are a movable dance floor and a beautiful turn-of-the-century-style mahogany bar. And if you haven't been able to whittle down your invitation list, we think the Opera House is a must-see.

CEREMONY CAPACITY: The Mezzanine holds 100 seated; the Main Room up to 300 seated.

EVENT/RECEPTION CAPACITY: The site holds 50–300 seated or 110–350 standing guests indoors.

MEETING CAPACITY: The facility holds 39–300 seated conference-style or theater-style.

FEES & DEPOSITS: A nonrefundable $1,000 deposit is required within 1 week of confirming reservations. A second deposit, the amount dependent on size and type of event, is due 180 days prior to the event. The balance for the entire event, including a $500 refundable security deposit, is due 1 week prior to your function. Customized wedding receptions are available. Meals start at $50/person, including tax and service charge. Alcohol is additional.

For weekday functions, the rental fee starts at $1,000. Food and beverage service is provided; rates will vary depending on services requested.

AVAILABILITY: Year-round: Sunday–Thursday until midnight; Friday and Saturday until 1am.

SERVICES/AMENITIES:

Catering: provided or BYO with approval

Kitchen Facilities: prep only

Tables & Chairs: provided for 350 guests

Linens, Silver, etc.: through caterer

Restrooms: wheelchair accessible

Dance Floor: yes

Bride's Dressing Area: yes

Meeting Equipment: CBA

Parking: valet or self-parking

Accommodations: no guestrooms, hotels nearby

Telephone: no

Outdoor Night Lighting: access only

Outdoor Cooking Facilities: no

Cleanup: provided

View: Santa Cruz Mtns., Old Town Los Gatos

Other: event coordination

RESTRICTIONS:

Alcohol: provided, no BYO

Smoking: not allowed

Music: amplified OK

Wheelchair Access: yes, elevator

Insurance: not required

Other: decorations restricted

This is important! Tell locations you're reading HERE COMES THE GUIDE and ask if our information is still current.

Testarossa Winery

300-A College Avenue, Los Gatos
408/354-6150

www.testarossa.com
events@testarossa.com

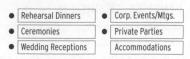

Historic Winery

● Rehearsal Dinners	● Corp. Events/Mtgs.
● Ceremonies	● Private Parties
● Wedding Receptions	Accommodations

Located in the scenic foothills just above downtown Los Gatos, Testarossa Winery is one lovely spot. The road leading up to this site winds through a pleasant residential neighborhood, but once you enter the historic winery's stone and wrought-iron gates, you leave the modern world behind.

It was on top of this knoll that Jesuits began missionary work in California in the late 1860s. The first seminary was built here in 1888, giving way to a more permanent winery building in 1893. Known as the Novitiate Winery in honor of the seminary students (called "novices"), it's a fine example of a 19th-century, three-story, gravity-flow winery, and amazingly, it's still in operation today. The Jesuits stopped making Novitiate wines in 1985 and leased the winery to Testarossa in 2003. The original building still stands, forming the core of the present-day venue.

A variety of options are available for weddings, special events and business functions. Outside, the sunny, flower-lined courtyard patio is a sweet spot to hold an open-air reception in the summer. Trees border one side, and on the other there's a bank of ivy containing a recessed, two-stepped wooden deck that's perfect for ceremonies and musicians.

Indoors, Testarossa has a unique group of spaces. As you pass through the front door, you find yourself in a cool stone tunnel that's one of the most interesting ceremony sites you'll ever see. It feels exactly like a cave, with its century-old limestone walls and vaulted ceiling. A photographic history of the Novitiate is displayed on one wall, and artwork graces the other. Antique chandeliers softly light the way, as the bride walks down the center aisle, flanked on both sides by her seated guests.

The Castello Room, which normally serves as Testarossa's tasting room, is a wonderful place for sampling wine and appetizers. The larger Palazzio Room is spacious enough for dinner and dancing when used in conjunction with the neighboring Castello Room. Rehearsal dinners are cozy and elegant in the Niclaire Room, whose stone walls rise to a wood-beamed ceiling and enclose a grand table that extends the length of the room. Add beautiful linens, crystal and candles to make dining here a romantic affair.

Inside and out, Testarossa Winery conveys warmth and a sense of a rich past. You couldn't ask for a more tranquil and beautiful environment for any kind of event.

CEREMONY CAPACITY: The cave holds 80 seated guest and the patio holds 150 guests.

EVENT/RECEPTION CAPACITY: Various indoor spaces hold 15–150 seated or 35–150 standing guests. Combined, the Castello and Palazzio Rooms hold up to 200 guests. These 2 rooms combined with the patio hold a maximum of 300. The patio alone accommodates 100 seated or 200 standing guests outdoors.

MEETING CAPACITY: Event spaces accommodate up to 60 guests seated theater-style.

FEES & DEPOSITS: Half of the total purchase is required to reserve your date; the balance is due 2 weeks prior to the event.

Testarossa Winery offers two choices when planning your wedding. One option is to rent the facility and work directly with a preferred caterer to create a menu specialized to your needs. All-inclusive wedding packages range $100–150/person and include the rental fee and a selection of gourmet menus from which to choose. The rental fees for a wedding range $4,000–6,500 depending on the size and day of the event. Weddings may be held on any day of the week.

Corporate meals range $90–175/person, including food, wine and service. Tax is additional.

AVAILABILITY: Year-round, daily, 6:30pm–11pm. Please call for date availability.

SERVICES/AMENITIES:
Catering: provided or select from approved list
Kitchen Facilities: prep only
Tables & Chairs: provided up to 150 guests
Linens, Silver, etc.: basic linens provided
Restrooms: wheelchair accessible
Dance Floor: yes
Bride's Dressing Area: yes
Meeting Equipment: wireless broadband internet; more CBA, extra charge

Parking: 2 lots
Accommodations: no guestrooms
Telephone: conference phone available
Outdoor Night Lighting: yes
Outdoor Cooking Facilities: no
Cleanup: caterer
View: Los Gatos hills
Other: event coordination

RESTRICTIONS:
Alcohol: wine, beer and champagne by Testarossa; no BYO
Smoking: outside only
Music: amplified OK indoors only

Wheelchair Access: yes
Insurance: certificate required
Other: no rice, birdseed or confetti

The Toll House Hotel

Boutique Hotel

140 South Santa Cruz Avenue, Los Gatos
408/884-1044

www.tollhousehotel.com
bkessler@larkspurhotels.com

● Rehearsal Dinners	● Corp. Events/Mtgs.
● Ceremonies	● Private Parties
● Wedding Receptions	● Accommodations

Nestled at the base of the Santa Cruz Mountains, the Toll House Hotel in Los Gatos offers a friendly, unpretentious atmosphere and quaint charm. Its shingled walls, cheerful balconies and mansard-roofed clock tower give it an old-fashioned feel. Those planning a special event appreciate its convenient location—it's within easy walking distance of downtown shops and restaurants, 30 minutes from Santa Cruz, and 60 minutes from Monterey Bay via Highway 17.

The hotel has both indoor and outdoor event areas. Inside, the aptly named Capitola Room is tailor-made for corporate functions. The Larkspur Ballroom is used for weddings and receptions and has plenty of space for dancing. Prefunction events are held in the adjacent Lobby, whose overstuffed green damask chairs and loveseats tempt you to relax and contemplate the classical paintings hung on the walls. There's also Three Degrees, a private dining room off the Toll House Restaurant.

In the center of the Toll House Hotel, the sunny courtyard is a favorite place for weddings and receptions. A splashing fountain adds refreshing coolness. On the second floor, a small deck overlooks the courtyard. This is also a nice spot for weddings and related events, and rehearsal dinners are frequently held here. The five adjoining rooms that open onto this deck are often rented by the wedding party or close friends. No need for a designated driver when the party is right outside your room!

The Toll House's relaxed atmosphere makes it popular for bar and bat mitzvahs as well. It's the kind of place that's posh enough to make adults feel really pampered, but casual enough to make children feel at home, too.

CEREMONY CAPACITY: The Courtyard holds 200 seated; the Ballroom 140 seated.

EVENT/RECEPTION CAPACITY: The Courtyard accommodates 170 seated with dance floor and the Ballroom 120 seated with dance floor, or up to 150 without.

MEETING CAPACITY: Event spaces accommodate 14–180 seated guests.

FEES & DEPOSITS: A nonrefundable deposit equal to 25% of the event total is required to reserve your date; the balance is payable 1 month prior to the event. Room rental fees range $225–1,900 depending on guest count, catering costs and selected room(s).

Meal prices run $36–58/person, and alcohol $10–12/person; tax and a 20% service charge are additional. A $150/bartender charge for each 4-hour block may apply.

AVAILABILITY: Year-round, daily, 7am–11pm.

SERVICES/AMENITIES:

Catering: provided, no BYO
Kitchen Facilities: n/a
Tables & Chairs: provided
Linens, Silver, etc.: provided
Restrooms: wheelchair accessible
Dance Floor: in Courtyard and Ballroom
Bride's Dressing Area: no
Meeting Equipment: CBA

Parking: garage, complimentary
Accommodations: 115 guestrooms
Telephone: pay phones
Outdoor Night Lighting: yes
Outdoor Cooking Facilities: no
Cleanup: provided
View: Santa Cruz Mtns., Old Town Los Gatos
Other: event and wedding coordination

RESTRICTIONS:

Alcohol: provided, no BYO
Smoking: designated areas
Music: amplified OK with volume limits

Wheelchair Access: yes
Insurance: not required
Other: no confetti, birdseed, rice or glitter

Summitpointe Golf Club

Golf Club

1500 Country Club Drive, Milpitas
408/262-2500

www.countryclubreceptions.com
catering@summitpointegc.com

● Rehearsal Dinners	● Corp. Events/Mtgs.
● Ceremonies	● Private Parties
● Wedding Receptions	Accommodations

Clearly, the designers of Summitpointe Golf Course understood the meaning of the expression "photo op." Nestled in a canyon between rolling East Bay foothills, this Milpitas golf course offers sweeping views in every direction, not to mention an absolutely world-class ceremony site.

Encompassing the far end of the driving range (which is closed whenever events are held) and the huge expanse of lawn beyond, the site adjoins the largest of the course's three natural lakes. Place an arch at the water's edge, and the weeping willows that dip towards the lake provide all the decoration necessary. Brides typically make their entrance via limousine, but for more drama, consider making the journey in a horse-drawn carriage. Golf carts are also available to transport any elderly or physically challenged guests.

In spring and summer months, your entire wedding day can be staged outdoors. Following the ceremony, guests amble over to the broad area in the driving range for an al fresco reception. Have rounds set up in the shade of umbrellas, or long banquet tables arranged beneath a large canopy. Either way, your guests will appreciate the fresh air and beautiful scenery.

If you prefer an indoor celebration (or just indoor dancing), Summitpointe's Lakeview Room will comfortably accommodate most groups. Large windows on two walls reveal views of the hills and lakes. On chilly evenings, a generous mirrored fireplace at one end creates a warmly romantic atmosphere. And guests who need to take a break will enjoy stepping outside onto the roomy brick patio where they can order up their favorite drink from the full-service indoor bar nearby. The patio is also an event site in its own right: It's covered year-round with a canvas tent, whose clear walls can be rolled up for maximum access to balmy afternoon breezes, or rolled down to provide protection from the elements.

Next to its photogenic setting, this golf club's most appealing feature may be its affordability. If you long for a wedding at a country club but don't belong to one, Summitpointe is a wonderful alternative. Their friendly, helpful staff will gladly streamline your to-do list by making arrangements for everything from a champagne fountain to deluxe chair coverings. And with their flexible menu options, you're sure to find a combination of dishes that perfectly suits you and your budget.

CEREMONY CAPACITY: The Lakeview Room holds 130 seated; the Lawn holds 300 seated.

EVENT/RECEPTION CAPACITY: The Lakeview Room accommodates 130 seated or 200 standing guests; the Lawn area holds 250 seated with tent option and the Lakeview Patio holds 200 seated guests.

MEETING CAPACITY: Event spaces accommodate up to 90 seated guests.

FEES & DEPOSITS: A nonrefundable deposit, which is applied to your food and beverage total, is required to reserve your date. The amount of the deposit is equal to 25% of the estimated event total. 50% is due 6 months prior, and 100% of the final estimated balance is due 10 days prior to the event date. Rental fees range $500–1,500 depending on space, day and time rented. Meals range $18–76/person. Tax, alcohol and a 20% service charge are additional.

AVAILABILITY: Year-round, daily, 6am–midnight.

SERVICES/AMENITIES:

Catering: provided, no BYO
Kitchen Facilities: n/a
Tables & Chairs: provided
Linens, Silver, etc.: provided
Restrooms: wheelchair accessible
Dance Floor: CBA, extra charge
Bride's Dressing Area: no
Meeting Equipment: CBA, extra charge

Parking: ample on-site
Accommodations: no guestrooms
Telephone: pay phone
Outdoor Night Lighting: yes
Outdoor Cooking Facilities: BBQ CBA
Cleanup: provided
View: panorama of fairways, hills, valley, lakes
Other: event coordination

RESTRICTIONS:

Alcohol: provided, no BYO
Smoking: designated areas
Music: amplified OK indoors

Wheelchair Access: yes
Insurance: not required
Other: no confetti, birdseed or rice

Overwhelmed? Use the search criteria on www.HereComesTheGuide.com to narrow down your choices.

Guglielmo Winery

Winery

1480 East Main Avenue, Morgan Hill
408/779-2145
www.guglielmowinery.com
eventcenter@guglielmowinery.com

● Rehearsal Dinners	● Corp. Events/Mtgs.
● Ceremonies	● Private Parties
● Wedding Receptions	○ Accommodations

There is practically no event that this versatile venue can't handle. Corporate dinners, private parties and seminars keep this family winery hopping all year long. They even host a Harvest Festival complete with a grape stomping competition, and a Holiday Gift Faire in December. But from the first weekend in May through the second weekend in October, the winery's charming Villa Emile Event Center is most popular for rehearsal dinners and weddings.

Emilio Guglielmo, whose family passed down a winemaking craft for generations in Italy, came to the Santa Clara Valley in 1908 and by 1925 had established his winery in Morgan Hill. Today, Emilio's grandsons run the winery, and their custom-designed event space, Villa Emile, is a pleasing complement to their award-winning winery. Creativity is encouraged here, and the staff will help you custom-design your event, too, including personalized labels for small bottles of wine you can use as favors.

Villa Emile is immediately adjacent to the winery itself. Pass through the iron gates, topped by a stained-glass window with the family name "Guglielmo" encircled by grapevines, and you'll find yourself in the courtyard. This area consists of a cobblestone patio bordered by beds of assorted flowers, an appropriate setting for small parties or pre-dinner drinks and hors d'oeuvres. Nearby is a large granite bar where wine, champagne and beer are served under an arbor covered by a luxuriant 80-year-old grapevine.

A redwood pergola and concrete walkway separate the courtyard from the larger event space, a vast green lawn where tables and chairs can be set up—with umbrellas, if the weather is hot. At one end of the lawn is an enormous covered stage supported by rugged sandstone pillars (perfect for live music or a DJ). In front of the stage, a large dance floor invites you to get out there and boogie. At the other end of the lawn is a charming red-tile-roofed arbor, where couples often exchange wedding vows. To the right, a new building contains a spacious, beautifully appointed dressing room for the bride and her attendants. A small balcony off this room overlooks the vineyard and rolling hills, and is a favorite spot for wedding photos.

The structures here—all built out of terracotta stucco—seem to have sprung from the earth as naturally as the grapevines themselves, and their red tile roofs are reminiscent of Tuscany. Geraniums, lilies-of-the-Nile, and petunias are colorful accents in front of the stage and along the paths. In this lovely setting, with its relaxed, Old World ambiance, you and your guests will feel that time spent at Guglielmo Winery is time well spent indeed.

CEREMONY, EVENT/RECEPTION & MEETING CAPACITY: Indoors, Guglielmo holds up to 72 seated guests, outdoors up to 450 seated guests.

FEES & DEPOSITS: The rental fee starts at $600 for indoor events, and at $3,500 for outdoor events, and varies depending on space rented, day and time of event and guest count.

AVAILABILITY: Indoors, year-round. Outdoors, May–October.

SERVICES/AMENITIES:

Catering: select from list
Kitchen Facilities: fully equipped
Tables & Chairs: provided
Linens: provided, variety of colors
Restrooms: wheelchair accessible
Dance Floor: cement floor near stage
Bride's & Groom's Dressing Area: yes
Meeting Equipment: BYO

Parking: ample, lot nearby
Accommodations: no guestrooms
Telephone: no
Outdoor Night Lighting: yes
Outdoor Cooking Facilities: no
Cleanup: caterer or renter
View: vineyards and surrounding hills
Other: event coordination, private wine tasting and tours CBA

RESTRICTIONS:

Alcohol: provided, no BYO
Smoking: designated areas
Music: amplified OK

Wheelchair Access: yes
Insurance: certificate required

Bella Montagna

Hilltop Private Estate

Address withheld to ensure privacy. San Jose
408/267-0773, Marcia Coleman-Joyner, CWC

www.eventswithaview.net
www.bellamontagna.net
info@bellamontagna.net

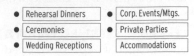

- Rehearsal Dinners
- Ceremonies
- Wedding Receptions
- Corp. Events/Mtgs.
- Private Parties
- Accommodations

The short drive into the San Jose foothills and the winding, olive-lined driveway will not prepare you for the sweep and grandeur of the view from Bella Montagna. Standing at the site where bride and groom exchange vows is like standing on top of the world, with vistas of the peaks of the Santa Cruz Mountains to the west, and on a clear day, the spires of San Francisco and the glittering waters of the bay to the north. No wonder couples can't wait to get married here.

Once guests arrive outside this classic California-adobe villa and their cars are whisked away by valets, they enter through a wide porte-cochère into a grassy arena ringed by trees. But the sparkling vista of the Santa Clara Valley remains Bella Montagna's centerpiece—until the bride appears to steal the show.

The grounds are impeccably landscaped with Italian cypress and olive trees, a vineyard and Old World stone, giving the property a very distinct taste of Tuscany. Add to this the warm glow of the home's natural adobe brick walls and the golden rolling hills, and you'll have a hard time believing you're only minutes away from a city.

A handsome curving deck under the canopy of a grand old tree allows guests to admire the view prior to the event, and provides more than ample space for musicians during the ceremony. The grassy seating area is dappled with shade from the trees for much of the day.

Bella Montagna is the home of Victor and Stacie Klee, who decided to make their rustic villa available for outdoor weddings after one of their friends had a spectacularly successful wedding on the property. They built a special bride's dressing room/salon where the bride and her attendants can take advantage of Stacie's professional services as a beautician. The Klees' attentions will make you feel as though you're spending the day with family friends.

Bella Montagna is indeed a welcome retreat from the everyday world below. The panorama is majestic, and the sound of rustling leaves and the warmth of the setting make it an intimate and peaceful place. A wedding at this private estate is like having your celebration with all the comforts of home—if your home was perched on a hillside with a breathtaking 45-mile view.

CEREMONY CAPACITY: The site holds up to 200 seated guests.

EVENT/RECEPTION CAPACITY: The site holds up to 200 seated guests outdoors. Private and corporate parties of up to 200 seated guests may be accommodated; please call for details.

MEETING CAPACITY: Meetings do not take place at this locaton.

FEES & DEPOSITS: 50% of rental fee deposit is required to reserve your date. The balance is due 60 days prior to the event. Rental fees range from $2,500 for a ceremony only, to 6,500 depending on the date, time and type of event.

AVAILABILITY: Open May–October. Weddings take place Friday–Sunday. Corporate events may take place 7 days a week, anytime.

SERVICES/AMENITIES:

Catering: select from preferred list, or BYO
Kitchen Facilities: fully equipped
Tables & Chairs: provided for up to 125
Linens, Silver, etc.: through caterer
Restrooms: wheelchair accessible
Dance Floor: yes
Bride's Dressing Area: yes
Meeting Equipment: n/a

Parking: valet required, extra charge
Accommodations: no guestrooms
Telephone: emergency only
Outdoor Night Lighting: yes
Outdoor Cooking Facilities: yes
Cleanup: caterer
View: mountains, cityscape, valley, hills
Other: professional beautician on site

RESTRICTIONS:

Alcohol: BYO, licensed server
Smoking: allowed
Music: amplified OK outdoors

Wheelchair Access: yes
Insurance: liability required
Other: no rice, glitter, birdseed or confetti; children require supervision

The Corinthian Event Center

Historic Private Club

196 North Third Street, San Jose
408/938-2332

www.corinthiangrandballroom.com
rmendoza@corinthiangrandballroom.com

● Rehearsal Dinners	● Corp. Events/Mtgs.
● Ceremonies	● Private Parties
● Wedding Receptions	Accommodations

Located in the heart of historic downtown San Jose, this 1924 landmark is no ordinary venue. As you walk up the broad granite steps, past the enormous urns and soaring columns, you can't help but be impressed by the stately elegance of its neoclassic design.

That impression carries through to the interior spaces as well. The Corinthian Room is the Event Center's main ballroom, and it has all the elements of a true ballroom. You enter through a foyer, regally outfitted with a crystal chandelier and a hand-painted wood-beam ceiling. Once inside the Corinthian Room, you're struck by its grand proportions and majestic features. The 60-foot ceiling has massive wood beams, and is inset with alternating panes of blue glass and intricately detailed panels of gold leaf grillwork. Six extraordinary wrought-iron-and-glass lanterns hang from the ceiling like giant luminous earrings, while five 30-foot palm trees embedded with twinkle lights add sparkle. At one end of the room is a stage with a carved stone proscenium arch framing red velvet curtains; at the other end is a carved granite balcony, where just-married couples often dance their first dance. Banquettes along the sides of the room make cozy seating areas, and there's a raised section that's ideal for the head table. The hardwood dance floor is permanently ensconced in front of the stage.

Smaller functions take place in the Gold, Silver and Bronze Rooms. All have crystal chandeliers, cream walls, red carpeting and ceilings baffled for sound. You can reserve these rooms individually, or combine them to make one long room—the perfect space for a wedding ceremony. And all three rooms have access to the Columns Lounge, a more casual space with faux-candle chandeliers and a mix of antiques and contemporary furnishings. The Olympia Room, a large private room with white walls and pastel detailing, is available for small meetings and as a bride's dressing area.

Whether you're getting married or planning a company meeting or party, the Center's staff will help you orchestrate it. And if you're inviting out-of-town guests, they'll appreciate being close to many of San Jose's best hotels and cultural activities.

CEREMONY CAPACITY: The Gold, Silver and Bronze Rooms, combined, hold up to 150 seated guests; the Olympia and Decathlon Rooms hold 60 seated guests each, and the Corinthian Room 300 seated guests.

EVENT/RECEPTION CAPACITY: The facility holds 5–300 seated or up to 500 standing guests indoors. The ballroom can accommodate 300 seated or 500 standing.

MEETING CAPACITY: Event spaces accommodate 5–350 seated guests.

FEES & DEPOSITS: For special events and weddings, a $2,000 nonrefundable deposit secures your date and is required when reservations are made. Full payment is due 5 days prior to your event. For 5 hours' use, the rental fee ranges $500–2,000 depending on the space selected. There is a ceremony setup charge. In-house catering is provided: Meals start at $35/person; alcohol, tax and a 20% service charge are additional. Note that there's a $10,000 minimum for functions held on Saturday evenings. All wedding events have private use of the Event Center when the food and beverage minimum is met. Off-site catering is also available.

For business functions, weekday morning and afternoon rental rates run $150–500 depending on the room(s) selected. Food prices will vary depending on the type of function, guest count and event duration.

AVAILABILITY: Year-round, daily, 7am–1am. Weddings are in 5-hour blocks; extra hours may be available for an additional $300/hour.

SERVICES/AMENITIES:
Catering: provided
Kitchen Facilities: n/a
Tables & Chairs: provided
Linens, Silver, etc.: provided
Restrooms: wheelchair accessible
Dance Floor: yes
Bride's Dressing Area: CBA
Meeting Equipment: AV, other CBA, extra fee
Other: event coordination, poolside parties

Parking: on-street or nearby garage, free on weekends and weekdays after 6pm
Accommodations: no guestrooms
Telephone: emergency use only
Outdoor Night Lighting: yes
Outdoor Cooking Facilities: no
Cleanup: provided
View: no

RESTRICTIONS:
Alcohol: provided
Smoking: outside only
Music: amplified OK indoors

Wheelchair Access: yes
Insurance: not required
Other: no helium balloons in Corinthian Room; no confetti, birdseed or rice indoors

The professionals in the back of this book are the best in the business. How do we know? Read page 701.

323

Dolce Hayes Mansion

200 Edenvale Avenue, San Jose
408/226-3200

www.dolcehayesmansion.com
info_hayesmansion@dolce.com

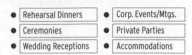

Historic Mansion & Grounds

● Rehearsal Dinners	● Corp. Events/Mtgs.	
● Ceremonies	● Private Parties	
● Wedding Receptions	● Accommodations	

There must be 1,001 places for romantic photographs in the award-winning Dolce Hayes Mansion. The front of the impressive Belle Epoque mansion is an obvious choice, but there are picturesque inglenooks, gorgeous doorways with beveled glass insets and shining wood trim, graceful archways, mysterious stairways lit with Art Deco fixtures, and lawns and flowers aplenty. And that's just in the daytime—by night it's a completely different and dramatic experience.

Built in 1905 for Mary Hayes Chynoweth and designed by architect George Page, it's a marriage of Queen Anne, Mission and Mediterranean styles. Oddly enough, these diverse architectures meld together well, resulting in a beautifully preserved jewel of a building. The mansion is lovingly managed by Dolce Hotels & Resorts, specialists in event, resort and conference destinations around the world.

Hold your ceremony on the front lawn and let the entire mansion, with its grand entryway and four-story central tower, create the backdrop. Or get married at one of the entrances to the East or West Lawns, each with a carved archway and sweeping steps flanked by flowers. If an intimate indoor wedding is your preference, exchange vows in the Willow Glen Room, standing in front of a marble fireplace beneath a gleaming wooden arch. These are just a tiny sampling of your many ceremony options.

Reception possibilities range from several smaller rooms like the Parlors, all the way up to the Grand Hayes Ballroom, which enjoys its own separate building. Serve cocktails and hors d'oeuvres in the vast foyer of the ballroom, whose French doors open to a vista of the lawn and mansion. Then dine elegantly in the ballroom, with its 20-foot ceilings, chandeliers, stage, drop-down screens, projectors, sound system, dance floor—the works.

Dolce Hayes Mansion offers several banquet packages with an amazing array of delicacies. Some of the featured dishes are: mini beef Wellingtons with mushroom duxelles; foie gras and truffle reduction; dungeness crab-crusted Pacific salmon; and pepper crusted filet mignon with lobster tail. The selection of vegetarian dishes is equally enticing.

Wedding packages include a luxury suite in the mansion for the bride and groom. Relaxing in your plush surroundings, you could easily imagine you're the privileged guest of Mary Hayes Chynoweth, enjoying the good life at the turn of the 20th century (well, you could if it weren't for the refrigerator, Jacuzzi tub and other modern amenities). There are also 214 spacious rooms for your guests, many with views of the Santa Cruz Mountains. For a delightful twist on bridesmaid gifts, surprise your female entourage with a day at Being Spa, the mansion's Asian-inspired spa. All the stresses of planning a wedding will slip away as you luxuriate with a soothing massage, manicure and pedicure, or indulge in a multitude of other beautifying treatments.

One of the charms of Dolce Hayes Mansion is its lack of restrictions. The facility once hosted a wedding with a live elephant, so it's unlikely you can come up with anything that they can't accommodate (though the management says you're welcome to try). The range of event spaces runs the gamut from grand and impressive to intimate and homelike, and from enormous swaths of lawn and scenery to small, sun-dappled patios. The only problem you'll have is trying to choose between so many seductive possibilities.

CEREMONY CAPACITY: The San Jose Room, Westwood Patio and Guadalupe Room each seat up to 140 guests; the Edenvale Room holds 200 seated and the East Lawn up to 1,200 seated or 1,500 standing.

EVENT/RECEPTION CAPACITY: Various rooms hold 10–450 seated or 50–1,000 standing; the entire mansion can accommodate 2,000 for a standing reception. Patio areas seat 10–100, and the East Lawn holds 800 seated or 1,200 standing.

MEETING CAPACITY: There are 24 rooms, some that hold up to 720 guests seated theater-style.

FEES & DEPOSITS: For weddings, 50% of the estimated event total is the deposit required to book any portion of the facility, an additional 30% is due 60 days prior to the event; the balance is due 10 days prior. Customized wedding packages range $99–150/person, and include hors d'oeuvres, salad, 2 entrées, wedding cake and overnight accommodations for the bride and groom. For a 1-hour ceremony, the wedding package includes 200 chairs, rehearsal and setup.

For other special events and business functions, 50% of the estimated total is required to confirm reservations; 30% is due 60 days prior to the event; and the estimated event balance is payable 10 days prior to the event. Rental fees range $595–5,000 depending on guest count and space(s) selected. Meals start at $50/person. Alcohol, tax and a 22% service charge are additional.

AVAILABILITY: Year-round, daily, anytime. Weddings take place on Saturdays and Sundays; other days and time frames may be negotiated.

SERVICES/AMENITIES:

Catering: provided, no BYO
Kitchen Facilities: n/a
Tables & Chairs: provided
Linens, Silver, etc.: provided
Restrooms: wheelchair accessible
Dance Floor: provided
Bride's & Groom's Dressing Area: provided, extra fee
Meeting Equipment: computer networking capabilities, video conferencing equipment, wireless, high-speed internet service, lighting packages, LCD packages, microphones

Parking: complimentary valet; large lots
Accommodations: 214 guestrooms and suites
Telephone: house phone
Outdoor Night Lighting: yes
Outdoor Cooking Facilities: BBQ
Cleanup: provided
View: Santa Cruz Mountains
Other: outdoor pool, tennis, volleyball, full-service spa, fitness center

RESTRICTIONS:

Alcohol: packages provided
Smoking: designated areas
Music: amplified OK, outdoors until 9pm

Wheelchair Access: yes
Insurance: not required
Other: no birdseed, rice or confetti

Fairmont Hotel San Jose

Hotel

170 South Market Street, San Jose
408/998-1900 x3520

www.fairmont.com
george.patten@fairmont.com

● Rehearsal Dinners		● Corp. Events/Mtgs.	
● Ceremonies		● Private Parties	
● Wedding Receptions		● Accommodations	

For almost one hundred years, the words "Fairmont Hotel" have represented the *ne plus ultra* in grand hotels, and the Fairmont San Jose lives up to this reputation admirably. Winner of the *AAA Four Diamond Award*, the Fairmont San Jose offers not only the elegant décor, luxurious accommodations and exemplary service that has made the chain famous around the world, but an entire floor of ballrooms and meeting spaces tailor-made for sophisticated celebrations and business functions.

Planning a sit-down dinner for 1,000 guests, or a banquet for 800? Then you'll want to check out the 13,000-square-foot Imperial Ballroom and the 8,000-square-foot Regency Ballroom. Both of these majestic spaces feature 20-foot molded ceilings with crystal chandeliers, and the Imperial Ballroom has a Foyer that's lovely enough for a wedding ceremony or prefunction cocktail party. It's full of natural light, thanks to an enormous arched window overlooking César Chavez Plaza. For ceremonies, a stage is set up beneath the fanciful wrought-iron-and-crystal chandelier that hangs from the Foyer's vaulted ceiling, and guests are seated in a "theater in the round" configuration. A host of smaller rooms are available for more intimate gatherings, whether festive or business oriented. All are similar in décor to the Imperial and Regency Ballrooms, but with more modest twelve-foot ceilings. Many of them have large windows with views of the Plaza or the trees lining First Street, giving the rooms an open, airy feel.

One of the most delightful spaces at the Fairmont is the Club Regent. Formerly a dinner theater, its octagonal shape, terracotta walls and curtained stage give this room plenty of personality, while split-level seating makes it surprisingly intimate and versatile. It's ideal for sit-down receptions of up to 240, since the room's unique layout allows guests to be seated around a central head table, making everyone feel close to the "action." But it's also a favorite spot for bar and bat mitzvahs, since the kids can cut loose on the main floor, while adults observe the festivities from the relatively sedate upper level (the Club Regent would also be great for a graduation party, or any event where different generations might each like their own "space").

As you would expect from an award-winning hotel, the Fairmont provides much more than just beautifully appointed ballrooms and meeting spaces. They're one of the only hotels in the South Bay to offer kosher catering, and they specialize in Asian, Indian and Persian weddings. Perks for brides and grooms include a complimentary bridal suite and a spotlit, tulle-draped stage to showcase the wedding cake. The hotel's layout keeps large and small events separate, and solid padded walls mean that your string quartet won't be drowned out by the DJ next door. And the Fairmont's fabulous lobby, with its marble columns, statuary, chandeliers and floral displays makes an opulent backdrop for your wedding photos.

With all the amenities we've listed above, plus a great central location in the heart of Silicon Valley, it's easy to see why the Fairmont has been awarded such high accolades. Don't be afraid to expect perfection at this first-rate establishment—you won't be disappointed. After all, this is the Fairmont!

CEREMONY CAPACITY: There are 22 rooms which can accommodate 10–1,000 seated guests.

EVENT/RECEPTION CAPACITY: The hotel has 22 banquet rooms that hold 30–1,000 seated or 50–3,200 standing guests. In addition, the Club Regent holds 240 seated or 300 standing guests.

MEETING CAPACITY: The hotel has 65,000 square feet of meeting space, with 22 rooms that hold 28–1,400 seated guests.

FEES & DEPOSITS: For weddings, a nonrefundable $2,500 minimum deposit is required to secure your date. A month before the event, 50% of the anticipated total is due, and 5 business days prior, the balance is payable. Rental charges vary depending on room size and the event time frame. There are 4 wedding packages ranging $95–120/person, which usually include hors d'oeuvres, a 2-course dinner, ice carving, wedding cake, champagne toast, and bridal suite. Tax and service charges are extra.

For business functions, all services are customized; call for more information and rates. The hotel has an on-site full-service business center.

AVAILABILITY: Year-round, daily, including holidays until 2am.

SERVICES/AMENITIES:
Catering: provided; outside caterers allowed only for Indian cuisine, and must be approved
Kitchen Facilities: n/a
Tables & Chairs: provided
Linens, Silver, etc.: provided
Restrooms: wheelchair accessible
Dance Floor: provided
Bride's & Groom's Dressing Area: CBA
Meeting Equipment: full range AV

Parking: valet or nearby parking lots
Accommodations: 805 guestrooms
Telephone: pay phones
Outdoor Night Lighting: CBA
Outdoor Cooking Facilities: CBA
Cleanup: provided
View: César Chavez Park, Circle of Palms
Other: baby grand pianos, ice sculpture, event coordination, wedding cakes

RESTRICTIONS:
Alcohol: provided, no BYO
Smoking: allowed outdoors
Music: amplified OK until 1am

Wheelchair Access: yes
Insurance: not required
Other: no fog machines

First Unitarian Church of San Jose

160 North Third Street, San Jose
408/841-7542

sanjoseuu.org/AboutUs/Rentals/index.html
rentals@sanjoseuu.org

Reception Facility and Church

- Rehearsal Dinners
- Ceremonies
- Wedding Receptions
- Corp. Events/Mtgs.
- Private Parties
- Accommodations

For many brides and grooms, the dream starts with a big church wedding, preferably a place with lots of charm, a sense of history and a warm, inviting atmosphere. Well, dreams can come true, because the First Unitarian Church of San Jose offers all that and more. Built in 1891 and recently restored to its former glory, the venue's Romanesque Revival architecture incorporates graceful domes, arched entryways, a sun-kissed stucco façade and some of the most beautiful stained-glass windows you're likely to find. Perhaps equally important, the church, with its long tradition of community outreach and social equality, welcomes all couples—regardless of religious affiliation or sexual persuasion—to celebrate their union in its unique circular sanctuary.

Arriving guests enter through three sets of double doors at the top of the terracotta steps (there's a side ramp and elevators, too). Once inside the two-story, domed space, you're struck by the lack of hard edges as one design motif flows into another, reinforcing a sense of continuity. Rows of old wooden seats, their antique patina glowing in the light from dozens of floral stained-glass windows, are arranged in a semicircle on both the main floor and the mezzanine. They face an inspiring stained-glass panel that flanks the graceful, triple-arched altar. Etched right into the carpet below is a large labyrinth, adding a note of contemplation to the spirituality of the surroundings. And speaking of notes, the acoustics in a room without angles are superb for savoring the sound of either the Steinway baby grand or the Galanti organ during your service.

If you have your reception here, you may want to start with cocktails and hors d'oeuvres in the parlor-style Fireside Room, which features an upright piano, wainscoted walls and a barrel ceiling. Dominating one wall is the Arts and Crafts wooden fireplace, while throughout the room there are notable antique touches like an intricately carved buffet. When it's time for dinner, just swing open the French doors and invite your guests into the adjacent Hattie Porter Hall. This spacious, high-ceilinged dinner and dancing area, set off by moss green walls and dark wood floors, is filled with light from more stained-glass windows and twinkling chandeliers. For a quiet moment away from the crowd, retreat to the casual upstairs lounge (which also serves as your bridal room) and enjoy a bird's-eye view of the festivities from windows that look down on the action in the hall below.

Just remember before you leave to take advantage of photo opportunities at the historic St. James Park across the street. Among its illustrious designers was Frederick Olmstead, one of this country's pre-eminent landscape architects and the mastermind behind outdoor treasures such as New York's Central Park.

CEREMONY CAPACITY: The sanctuary holds 237 seated guests.

EVENT/RECEPTION CAPACITY: Indoors the facility holds 150 seated or 200 standing guests.

MEETING CAPACITY: Meeting rooms accommodate 150 seated guests.

FEES & DEPOSITS: A $1,000 refundable deposit is required to reserve your date. The balance is due 3 months prior to the event. Rental fees range $1,200–2,500 depending on the space rented.

AVAILABILITY: Year-round, daily, 9am–midnight.

SERVICES/AMENITIES:

Catering: BYO
Kitchen Facilities: prep only
Tables & Chairs: provided
Linens, Silver, etc.: BYO
Restrooms: wheelchair accessible
Dance Floor: provided
Bride's & Groom's Dressing Area: yes
Meeting Equipment: some provided

Parking: garage nearby
Accommodations: no guestrooms
Telephone: emergency use only
Outdoor Night Lighting: access only
Outdoor Cooking Facilities: none
Cleanup: provided
View: cityscape
Other: grand piano, AV equipment, complimentary event coordination

RESTRICTIONS:

Alcohol: BYO
Smoking: allowed outdoors only
Music: amplified OK indoors

Wheelchair Access: yes
Insurance: not required

Want to know WHAT TO ASK a potential location or vendor? Check out our Questions to Ask on page 17.

Hilton San Jose

Hotel

300 Almaden Boulevard, San Jose
408/947-4450 Sales, 408/287-2100 Main
www.sanjose.hilton.com
sales@sanjosehilton.com

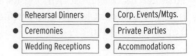

● Rehearsal Dinners	● Corp. Events/Mtgs.
● Ceremonies	● Private Parties
● Wedding Receptions	● Accommodations

Given its prominence in downtown San Jose (which is, after all, the heart of Silicon Valley) it's only natural that the Hilton San Jose would embrace the culture of innovation and constant improvement. Their forward-thinking approach is evident in the venue's recent $11.5 million, top-to-bottom transformation that seamlessly integrates leading-edge technology, eye-catching design and an expansion of its public space… all without losing the kind of hands-on, personal touch that makes you and your event feel special.

Drop off your car with the valet and enter the new classic modern lobby where soft, recessed lighting and wall panels in rich earth colors create a soothing atmosphere. Nearby, a dramatic interior fountain features stainless steel sculptures rising from a pool of water in front of the Affinity Lounge, the hotel's casually chic restaurant for meeting, greeting and dining on the chef's inventive European-inspired cuisine.

Just a few steps from the restaurant is the Affinity Patio, an open-air, urban oasis and a great place to start your celebration. Located on the McEnery Convention Center Plaza, this charming spot is shielded from view by an artistically sculpted metal screen. There's a cascading water wall and movable fire pits set amongst the dark rattan sofas and chairs—a perfect locale for your cocktail reception. While many brides opt to have their ceremony at one of the nearby houses of worship, like St. Joseph's Cathedral, you can also exchange vows on the Patio (they even have an officiant on staff!).

Afterwards, invite your guests back inside the hotel to the beautifully proportioned Market Room. Ambient light from skylights gracing the three-story vaulted ceiling along with a series of picture windows that look out towards the Patio give you a sense of the outdoors. White glass chandeliers and billowing swags hung from the high, steel beams add a romantic note.

For a completely different ambiance, or if you have a larger group, begin with cocktails at the Winchester Room on the other side of the lobby. You can get more of a city vibe here with hip, lounge-type, retro-cool furnishings and floor-to-ceiling windows that provide a view of the energetic street scene outside. When you're ready for dinner and dancing, the spacious Almaden

Ballroom is just across the lobby. High ceilings, hanging chandeliers and an optional hardwood dance floor make this an elegant setting for your main reception.

One of the most mesmerizing aspects of the Hilton is the panoramic view you get from the top floors, and there's no better way to appreciate it than from your exquisite bridal suite. Many hotels offer complimentary honeymoon suites, but this one is extraordinary. This VIP space, with full living room and luxurious bedroom, has curving, wraparound walls of windows that offer 90-degree vistas of downtown's twinkling lights and recognizable landmarks...a truly fabulous retreat to cap off a memorable night.

CEREMONY CAPACITY & EVENT/RECEPTION CAPACITY: The Almaden Ballroom holds 240 seated or 400 standing guests. Various other rooms hold 25–150 seated or 30–250 standing. Outdoors, the Affinity Patio holds 100 seated or standing guests.

MEETING CAPACITY: There are 14 meeting rooms which can accommodate 10–190 seated guests, classroom-style.

FEES & DEPOSITS: For weddings, a $1,000 nonrefundable deposit is required when the contract is signed. Half of the anticipated event total is due 3 months in advance, the balance is payable 7 days prior.

There are multiple wedding packages, ranging $76–97/person, which include linen décor package, 1-hour hors d' oeuvres reception, dinner with wine service on the tables, wedding cake, champagne toast and complimentary bridal suite for one night, breakfast in bed the following morning and shuttle service to the airport. Group discounts are available for out-of-town guests. Also included is a complimentary overnight stay on your 1-year anniversary.

AVAILABILITY: Year-round, daily.

SERVICES/AMENITIES:

Catering: provided

Kitchen Facilities: n/a

Tables & Chairs: provided

Linens, Silver, etc.: provided

Restrooms: wheelchair accessible

Dance Floor: portable provided

Bride's Dressing Area: yes

Meeting Equipment: CBA

Parking: valet required, garage nearby

Accommodations: 353 guestrooms

Telephone: house, office and guest phones

Outdoor Night Lighting: CBA

Outdoor Cooking Facilities: BBQ CBA

Cleanup: provided

View: no

Other: on-site wedding cake and florals, clergy on staff, AV equipment, event coordination

RESTRICTIONS:

Alcohol: provided, or BYO with corkage fee

Smoking: outdoors only

Music: amplified OK indoors, outdoors with limits

Wheelchair Access: yes

Insurance: not required

Other: decorations require approval

Il Fornaio at the Sainte Claire, a Larkspur Hotel

Historic Hotel

302 South Market Street, San Jose
408/271-3350
www.ilfornaio.com
catering@ilfo.com

● Rehearsal Dinners	● Corp. Events/Mtgs.
● Ceremonies	● Private Parties
● Wedding Receptions	● Accommodations

In 1992, when the stately Sainte Claire was undergoing a major refurbishing, workmen broke through a false wall and stumbled onto something that had been completely forgotten for years: an exquisite little Mediterranean courtyard with graceful arches, hanging terracotta planters and intricate, jewel-like geometric tile work that an Italian noblewoman would envy. The crowning achievement of the multi-million-dollar project was enclosing the courtyard with a vaulted atrium ceiling. The restoration of this beautiful 1926 hotel returned the registered National Historic Landmark to its former glory.

Today, the hotel is called the Sainte Claire, a Larkspur Hotel, and the dining and event rooms are operated by Il Fornaio. Together, they have resurrected the nostalgic glamour of the historic rooms. The most spacious is the luxurious Grande Ballroom, which features wrought-iron chandeliers and candelabras that complement the hotel's Jazz-era sophistication. French doors topped with arched cutaways open to the Courtyard, the pinnacle of the hotel's vintage majesty. Leafy saplings thrive in the dappled sunlight, while narrow arched leaded-glass windows add Deco flair. A curved marble-topped bar is shared with the adjacent Palm Room, named for the potted palms spread throughout the lounge-like space. Decked out in dark wood, gold-leafed moldings and velvet furnishings, the Palm Room is reminiscent of the high-society clubs from the Roaring Twenties. With wrought-iron chandeliers hanging from a hand-painted leather beamed ceiling and a fire blazing in the hearth, the Palm Room makes a gracious setting for a cocktail hour. The Sala Del Vino, named for its rows of wine racks, is a stylish private dining room framed in glass. In the Sala Del Fornaio, the chef's personal dining room, culinary accouterments are on display, and a wall of windows looks out to the boulevard.

Such appealing and diverse spaces present a variety of wedding scenarios. One possibility: Imagine saying your vows in the sunlit Courtyard. An opaque skylight casts a diffused glow, subtly highlighting the room's rich granite floor. Follow the ceremony with a champagne toast, then serve cocktails and tasty appetizers in the Palm Room. Perhaps hire a pianist to entertain guests with old-time tunes on the Palm Room's black baby grand. Continue the festivities with dinner and dancing in the Grande Ballroom. Finally, gather once more in the pretty Courtyard for that favorite wedding ritual—cutting the cake. If you're staging an entire wedding weekend, why not have the rehearsal dinner and post-wedding brunch in the Sala Del Vino or Sala del Fornaio?

Flexibility and understated elegance are also in evidence when Il Fornaio hosts business events in any of their well-appointed, state-of-the-art conference rooms on the second floor.

Il Fornaio is a full-service restaurant/caterer, offering packages at price levels for every kind of event, business or pleasure. And eating the authentic Old World dishes brought to you by Il Fornaio is a pleasure all its own. Their culinary creations blend the fresh bounty of seasonal foods with Italian flavors, accompanied by their award-winning, fresh-baked bread and olive oil. The Sainte Claire can also accommodate all your out-of-town guests, while you and your new spouse lounge in the Jacuzzi tub in your own junior suite. If you're looking for an all-in-one facility that can handle everything with a touch of class, Il Fornaio at the Sainte Claire could be the place for you.

CEREMONY CAPACITY: The Courtyard holds up to 160 seated guests; other indoor arrangements can be made to accommodate up to 300 seated guests.

EVENT/RECEPTION CAPACITY: Various rooms hold 120–350 seated without a dance floor or 80–300 with one. The courtyard seats 80 outdoors.

MEETING CAPACITY: There are 8 rooms which hold 35–350 seated theater-style or 24–165 seated classroom-style.

FEES & DEPOSITS: For weddings, a $1,500 nonrefundable deposit is required 2 weeks after making reservations. The estimated event balance is payable 3 working days prior to the event; the balance is due at the event's conclusion. The Courtyard rental fee is $750. Three all-inclusive wedding packages include hors d'oeuvres, champagne toast, wine with served meals, cake cutting, tax and service charges. Wedding packages start at $85/person. Menus can be customized. Luncheons start at $20/person and dinners start at $30/person. Tax, alcohol and a 20% service charge are additional.

For other special events, deposits range $250–1,500 depending on the room and services selected. Meals and cocktail/hors d'oeuvres parties vary in price. Meeting packages include a continental breakfast, lunch and 2 mid-meeting breaks and room rental; call for more details.

AVAILABILITY: Year-round, daily, anytime until 1am. Saturday weddings in the Grande Ballroom usually take place 10am–4:30pm or 6pm–1am.

SERVICES/AMENITIES:
Catering: provided by *Il Fornaio*, no BYO
Kitchen Facilities: n/a
Tables & Chairs: provided
Linens, Silver, etc.: provided
Restrooms: wheelchair accessible
Dance Floor: provided
Bride's & Groom's Dressing Area: CBA
Meeting Equipment: full range including AV

Parking: nearby lots or valet
Accommodations: 170 guestrooms
Telephone: emergency use only
Outdoor Night Lighting: no
Outdoor Cooking Facilities: n/a
Cleanup: provided
View: no
Other: full event coordination

RESTRICTIONS:
Alcohol: provided, or wine and champagne corkage CBA
Smoking: outdoors only
Music: amplified OK indoors only

Wheelchair Access: yes
Insurance: not required
Other: decorations must be approved

Paolo's Restaurant

Restaurant

333 West San Carlos Street, San Jose
408-294-2558
www.paolos.com
carolyn@paolos.com

- Rehearsal Dinners
- Ceremonies
- Wedding Receptions
- Corp. Events/Mtgs.
- Private Parties

  Accommodations

Like a chameleon, Paolo's Restaurant transforms itself into just the right setting for your wedding reception or any special event. Its location in a sleek, granite office tower overlooking the beautiful Guadalupe River Park is surprisingly versatile—add a little creative magic with flowers, linens, and lighting and—voila! You've got a candlelit gala on a terrace overlooking a wooded creek. Or an elegant soirée in the building's gleaming main lobby. Or a cozy get-together in the Wine Room upstairs. Or…you get the idea; Paolo's shapes itself to your personal vision.

There's an understated richness about Paolo's décor. The walls are a soft, burnished gold reminiscent of an old Tuscan village sleeping in the afternoon sun. Quiet lighting and artfully gathered jewel-tone drapes showcase the original, modern paintings and sculptures that grace every room and passageway.

All three dining rooms look out on a sweeping terrace, which also features a stairstep waterfall cascading down to a lower level—another possible spot for a ceremony or reception. The trees along the creek form a pastoral foreground that softens the view of the city's towers, and the bridge across the creek to the Center for the Performing Arts is an irresistibly dramatic entrance point for the bridal party. If you have a large group, consider reserving the entire restaurant. When weather permits, special arrangements can be made to dine outdoors, too.

Paolo's specializes in authentic regional Italian cuisine that emphasizes fresh, seasonal foods and skillful combinations of flavors. When we dined here we had broad maltagliate noodles accompanied by rabbit braised with fresh vegetables until the meat melted off the bone and the vegetables gently disappeared into a luscious sauce. The rabbit, tender and flavorful, was perfectly complemented by the al dente noodles. We also tried a house-made gnocchi, which we declared the best we've ever tasted: soft potato pillows that melted on the tongue, made even more *squisito* by baby wild mushrooms and black truffle butter.

In addition to providing a choice of wedding packages, Paolo's special event coordinator can work with you to custom-design a menu. And if Cucina Italiana isn't what you have in mind, Chef Carolyn Allen-Samavarchian—daughter of Jack Allen, who founded the restaurant a half a century ago—will exert her considerable culinary talents to accommodate your preferred cuisine. Sommelier/Maitre d' and husband-of-the-chef Jalil Samavarchian has compiled a handpicked, 34-page wine list with selections from Italy, France, and California. For their efforts, Paolo's has been a consistent *Wine Spectator* "Best of Excellence" and *Distinguished Restaurants of Northern America* award winner.

Conveniently located right downtown, Paolo's is close to the many churches and upscale hotels of central San Jose. In fact, it's within walking distance of at least three of the best hotels the city has to offer, something your overnight guests will appreciate—especially if they've fully partaken of Paolo's exquisite cuisine and fine wines. Another plus is the validated on-site parking.

A successful and memorable wedding is often about pleasing the greatest number of people possible, which means convenience and flexibility become nearly as important as ambiance, great food and service. This restaurant impresses in all of these areas and possesses one more quality that's often harder to come by: *il cuore,* or "heart." Paolo's puts love into everything they do.

CEREMONY CAPACITY: The restaurant holds 90 seated guests indoors and 250 seated outdoors.

EVENT/RECEPTION CAPACITY: The restaurant can accommodate 180 seated or 300 standing indoors and 250 seated or 350 standing outdoors.

MEETING CAPACITY: Meeting spaces hold 110 seated.

FEES & DEPOSITS: For weddings, 25% of the total anticipated event cost or $2,000 (whichever is greater) is required to reserve your date. Call for nonrefundable policy terms and conditions. The balance is due 5 business days prior to the event. Rental fees range $0–2,000 depending on the day and time of the event, guest count and the space rented. Wedding packages range $52–95/person. Tax, alcohol and a 20% service charge are additional.

For private, corporate or special events, a $250–2,500 deposit is required. Contact the Special Events Department for pricing details.

AVAILABILITY: Year-round, Monday–Saturday, 9am–midnight. The restaurant is closed most Sundays and major holidays except by prior arrangement. Call for availability and details.

SERVICES/AMENITIES:

Catering: provided
Kitchen Facilities: n/a
Tables & Chairs: provided
Linens, Silver, etc.: provided
Restrooms: wheelchair accessible
Dance Floor: CBA
Bride's & Groom's Dressing Area: yes
Meeting Equipment: some provided, CBA
Other: grand piano, event coordination

Parking: validated parking in covered garage on site
Accommodations: no guestrooms
Telephone: emergency use only
Outdoor Night Lighting: CBA
Outdoor Cooking Facilities: BBQ CBA
Cleanup: provided
View: cityscape, river, park, fountain, landscaped grounds, garden patio

RESTRICTIONS:

Alcohol: provided, or BYO with corkage fee
Smoking: outdoors only
Music: amplified OK with restrictions

Wheelchair Access: yes
Insurance: not required

Want to find more locations and services? Check out our informative website, www.HereComesTheGuide.com.

335

The Pavilion Event Center at Boulder Ridge

Event Center

1000 Old Quarry Road, San Jose
408/323-9900 x125
www.boulderridgegolf.com
events@boulderridgegolfclub.com

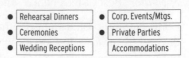

- Rehearsal Dinners
- Ceremonies
- Wedding Receptions
- Corp. Events/Mtgs.
- Private Parties
- Accommodations

At the top of a picturesque road that starts at Almaden Lake and heads up into the Santa Theresa Hills, there's a new wedding venue that's sure to seduce you with its spectacular, unobstructed views in virtually all directions.

Perched high on a plateau overlooking Boulder Ridge golf course, The Pavilion Event Center was named for the dramatic sandstone rock formations that dot the hillside fairways. These striking boulders, which were part of land that was once home to the Ohlone Indians, now contribute to this location's unique landscape.

The Pavilion's rough-hewn stone and earth-colored exterior blends organically with the natural tones of the Santa Cruz Mountains in the distance. Spreading out in front of the building is a verdant lawn, adorned with several Craftsman-style arbors, each framing a different vista. The Welcome Arbor, with its nearby fountain, faces north, presenting arriving guests with a bird's-eye view of downtown San Jose's skyline. The Bridal Arbor, which you can decorate with your choice of flowers, garlands, crystals, etc., becomes the focal point when everyone takes their seats and turns to watch the bride begin her walk down the aisle. Vows are exchanged at the Gazebo, facing west towards the Almaden Valley, allowing the setting sun to form the perfect, glowing backdrop for the ceremony.

After the "I do's," invite everyone to enjoy cocktails and hors d'oeuvres on the adjoining Terrace, where a large granite-topped bar is a great place to get the party started. Since there's something interesting to catch your eye no matter where you look, it may be hard to tear your friends and family away from the scenery, but even after they sit down to dinner in the Pavilion they're never far from the natural beauty and twinkling lights outside.

Wraparound windows framed in hand-stained sustainable wood cover three sides of the dining room and a floor-to-ceiling fireplace with stone hearth dominates the fourth. Chandeliers with mottled glass shades and California *plein air* paintings reinforce the indoor/outdoor motif of the open, airy space.

An on-site coordinator will help you choreograph your event from start to finish, but she's also happy to work with your own wedding planner. And when it comes to food, the chef can customize your menu, including ethnic specialties.

Before your shuttle or limo whisks you away to your new life, take a quiet stroll under the stars with your beloved—a truly romantic end to a memorable celebration.

CEREMONY CAPACITY: The facility holds 300 seated guests indoors or outdoors.

EVENT/RECEPTION CAPACITY: The site can accommodate 299 seated or 300 standing guests indoors and 225 seated or 299 standing outdoors.

MEETING CAPACITY: Meeting spaces hold 200 seated guests.

FEES & DEPOSITS: A $2,000 deposit is required to reserve your date and the balance is due 30 days prior to the event. Rental fees range $500–10,000 depending on the type of event, the season, and day of the week. Meals range $25–150/person. Tax, alcohol and a 20% service charge are additional.

AVAILABILITY: Year-round, daily, 7am–midnight.

SERVICES/AMENITIES:

Catering: provided
Kitchen Facilities: n/a
Tables & Chairs: provided
Linens, Silver, etc.: provided
Restrooms: wheelchair accessible
Dance Floor: CBA
Bride's Dressing Area: yes
Meeting Equipment: CBA
Other: spa services, AV equipment, parking shuttle, event coordination

Parking: large lot
Accommodations: no guestrooms
Telephone: emergency use only
Outdoor Night Lighting: provided
Outdoor Cooking Facilities: none
Cleanup: provided
View: fairways, landscaped grounds, panorama of mountains, hills and valley

RESTRICTIONS:

Alcohol: provided, or BYO with corkage fee
Smoking: outdoors only
Music: amplified OK with restrictions

Wheelchair Access: yes
Insurance: not required

San Jose Country Club

Country Club

15571 Alum Rock Avenue, San Jose
408/258-4901 x16

www.sanjosecountryclub.org
troberts@sanjosecountryclub.org

- Rehearsal Dinners
- Ceremonies
- Wedding Receptions
- Corp. Events/Mtgs.
- Private Parties
- Accommodations

107 years ago, the San Jose Country Club really was out in the country, nestled against the Diablo Range foothills and surrounded by ranchland. Today, even though the city has encroached upon it and the 680 freeway is just minutes away, the club retains its peaceful sense of being far from the hurly-burly of civilization.

San Jose Country Club is private, but you need not be a member to have your wedding here. One of its great advantages is flexibility—you can stage an intimate little gathering, a medium-sized celebration, or pull out all the stops for a wedding with 250 guests.

For ceremonies, the club provides the quintessential California setting: Exchange vows in the dappled shade of a centuries-old California live oak at the 6th hole of the golf course—the old tree is so huge and spreading that it forms a natural cathedral on the velvety greens. Or choose a sunny spot between a nearby oak and a willow, with a view of the foothills on one side and a distant vista of downtown San Jose on the other.

If your reception is large, you can have the entire, newly remodeled main floor of the club to yourself. The main dining room is spacious and airy, with windows spanning two sides overlooking the fairway. Crystal chandeliers provide sparkle for nighttime events. There's a built-in hardwood dance floor, and ample room for a live band or a DJ booth.

Next to the main dining room is the bar, with a semicircular dining area facing the greens and the ancient oak tree. Dark wood trim, a parquet tile floor and wrought-iron sconces create a clean, contemporary look. A smaller dining area just off the main lobby looks out over the Olympic-size pool below.

Take advantage of the shiny black concert grand piano in the lobby by serving cocktails and hors d'oeuvres accompanied by a jazz trio or soft classical music prior to the banquet. Your guests can sip and nibble in front of the tall fieldstone fireplace, or enjoy the view of the fairway and the distant city beyond through every window. The décor throughout the main floor is updated yet classic, with touches of gleaming brass and mahogany wood trim.

Using only the freshest and finest ingredients, San Jose Country Club specializes in Contemporary American cuisine. Menu options are varied, and designed to offer something for every occasion.

If you're fond of golf, or just enjoy the outdoorsy ambiance of a golf course, the San Jose Country Club may suit you to a tee. The club's close-to-the-city convenience combined with its pretty surroundings may make it a match for you.

CEREMONY CAPACITY: The club accommodates up to 240 seated guests indoors or outdoors.

EVENT/RECEPTION CAPACITY: The club holds up to 240 seated indoors.

MEETING CAPACITY: Event spaces accommodate 20–350 seated guests.

FEES & DEPOSITS: 50% of the event total is required to reserve your date. A further deposit will be required prior to the event with full payment due upon final invoicing. Event fees range $3,200–4,500 depending on the space, day and time rented. Meals start at $30/person, plated or buffet-style.

AVAILABILITY: Year-round, daily, anytime.

SERVICES/AMENITIES:

Catering: provided
Kitchen Facilities: n/a
Tables & Chairs: provided
Linens, Silver, etc.: provided, choice of color
Restrooms: wheelchair accessible
Dance Floor: provided
Bride's Dressing Area: yes
Meeting Equipment: some provided

Parking: large lot or on-street
Accommodations: no guestrooms
Telephone: emergency use only
Outdoor Night Lighting: yes
Outdoor Cooking Facilities: no
Cleanup: provided
View: fairways, hills, cityscape, pool, grounds
Other: event coordination, grand piano, AV equipment

RESTRICTIONS:

Alcohol: provided
Smoking: outside only
Music: amplified OK

Wheelchair Access: yes
Insurance: not required

San Jose Woman's Club

Historic Woman's Club

75 South Eleventh Street, San Jose
408/772-6667

sjwomansclub.org
rentals@sjwomansclub.org

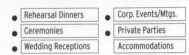

- Rehearsal Dinners
- Ceremonies
- Wedding Receptions
- Corp. Events/Mtgs.
- Private Parties
- Accommodations

With its façade of tall arched windows and imposing entryway, the San Jose Woman's Club building makes a graceful impression. Completed in 1929, the Spanish-style structure has hosted a wide variety of events over the years, and many couples continue to be married here.

The foyer, with its fireplace niche and tiled stairway, is often used for small ceremonies; the stairs serve as both an entrance for the bride and a convenient spot for photos. It's also a relaxed space for sipping champagne and mingling.

The Ballroom, however, is the building's *pièce de résistance*. A high, slightly vaulted ceiling spans the enormous room, and light from a wall of tall arched windows brings out the shine on the maple floor. The floor itself is unusual in that it has a special "spring" construction to enhance dancing. Up above, the beams crisscrossing the ceiling are all hand-stenciled, and the ornate parchment-and-wrought-iron chandeliers glow amber when lit. You can exchange vows on the curtained stage, while your favorite tune is played on the Steinway baby grand piano.

The Ballroom has plenty of space for a large reception, but if you need additional seating, the adjacent Tea Room comes in very handy. Separated from the Ballroom by two sliding glass pocket doors, it has easy access to the kitchen via a pass-through counter at one end. Like the Ballroom, its pastel unadorned walls make a neutral backdrop for potted plants and flowers. The Club offers a great deal of flexibility, not only for weddings, but for private parties, seminars, concerts or lectures—and its fees are very affordable.

CEREMONY CAPACITY: The Club holds 400 seated theater-style.

EVENT/RECEPTION CAPACITY: The Ballroom holds 300 seated and the Tea Room holds 72 seated guests, banquet-style.

MEETING CAPACITY: The Ballroom holds 400 seated theater-style and the Tea Room holds 90 seated theater-style. The Fireside Room holds 25 seated conference-style.

FEES & DEPOSITS: A refundable security deposit is required to hold your date, and is returned 20 days after the event if the site is left in good condition and all the rules are followed. For weekday events, Monday–Thursday, the rental is $1,500; Friday or Sunday $2,000; and Saturday $2,750. The rental fee is payable 60 days prior to the event. These prices cover a 5-hour event, each additional hour runs $250. Smaller rooms may be available, call for pricing. Security personnel are required at $46.50/officer: 1 off-duty police officer for up to 150 guests, 2 for over 150 guests.

For weekday business functions or meetings, the rental rate varies depending on guest count and event duration. Call for specifics.

AVAILABILITY: Year-round, daily, 9am–11pm.

SERVICES/AMENITIES:

Catering: select from preferred list or BYO, extra fee
Kitchen Facilities: prep only
Tables & Chairs: provided
Linens, Silver, etc.: BYO
Restrooms: wheelchair accessible
Dance Floor: in Ballroom
Bride's Dressing Area: yes
Meeting Equipment: lighted podium, stage with lights, projector. projection screen, stands. DVD/video player & sound system

Parking: adjacent lot, on-street
Accommodations: no guestrooms
Telephone: no
Outdoor Night Lighting: yes
Outdoor Cooking Facilities: BYO
Cleanup: renter
View: no

RESTRICTIONS:

Alcohol: provided or BYO, licensed server
Smoking: outside only
Music: amplified OK with restrictions; amplification not required in many cases, acoustics are superb

Wheelchair Access: yes
Insurance: certificate required; special event insurance available
Other: no rice, birdseed or confetti; no tacks or tape on walls

---

This is important! Tell locations you're reading HERE COMES THE GUIDE and ask if our information is still current.

Silicon Valley Capital Club

Private Club

50 West San Fernando, 17th Floor, San Jose
408/971-9300
www.sanjoseclub.com
jenna.torres@ourclub.com

- Rehearsal Dinners
- Ceremonies
- Wedding Receptions
- Corp. Events/Mtgs.
- Private Parties
- Accommodations

Located on the penthouse floor of the Knight Ridder Building in the heart of downtown San Jose, this private club offers a genteel ambiance, fine dining and sensational views. The elaborate furnishings, coffered ceiling, marble floors and picture windows of the Capital Club's lobby seem just right for a post-ceremony reception area. Its ivory, gold and navy blue color scheme is carried throughout the club, along with an abundance of ash-colored oak paneling and millwork. A grand piano and the adjacent Buena Vista Bar also make the lobby a pleasant place for cocktails before moving on to one of the club's dining rooms for a seated reception.

The formal main dining room features walls of windows, hardwood tables and ivory upholstered chairs. On the south side of the room, doors open onto a wide terrace, where the Penthouse's sweeping views of downtown San Jose and the Silicon Valley are breathtaking. If you're hosting an intimate affair, you might want to celebrate in one of the Capital Club's six private dining rooms; each comes with panoramic vistas, and some have private balconies.

If you're planning a soirée, we can't think of a more fitting location. At night, when the sun goes down and the sunset begins to fade, you'll feel like you're on top of the world. A glittering carpet of twinkling lights spreads beneath you, creating a dramatic ambiance for a ceremony, wedding reception or any type of special event.

CEREMONY CAPACITY: The North Terrace holds 150 seated or standing, and the indoor Lounge 160 seated or standing.

EVENT/RECEPTION CAPACITY: The club accommodates 200 seated guests indoors, 300 with indoor and outdoor seating.

MEETING CAPACITY: Meeting rooms accommodate 2–200 seated guests.

FEES & DEPOSITS: A $2,000 nonrefundable deposit is required to book the club. Food and beverage service is provided; meals run $25–60/person. Half of the estimated catering total is due 90 days prior to event and the balance 96 hours prior. Alcohol, tax and a 22% service charge are additional, as are ceremony setup fees.

AVAILABILITY: Year-round, daily. Closed most major holidays.

SERVICES/AMENITIES:

Catering: provided, no BYO
Kitchen Facilities: n/a
Tables & Chairs: provided
Linens, Silver, etc.: provided
Restrooms: wheelchair accessible
Dance Floor: portable, extra fee
Bride's & Groom's Dressing Area: yes
Meeting Equipment: AV equipment

Parking: garage with validation
Accommodations: no guestrooms
Telephone: house phones
Outdoor Night Lighting: yes
Outdoor Cooking Facilities: n/a
Cleanup: provided
View: panorama of Silicon Valley
Other: coordination, piano

RESTRICTIONS:

Alcohol: provided, no BYO
Smoking: outside only
Music: amplified OK

Wheelchair Access: yes, elevator
Insurance: not required
Other: no rice, birdseed or confetti

Silver Creek Valley Country Club

Country Club

5460 Country Club Parkway, San Jose
408/239-5888

www.scvcc.com
catering@scvcc.com

● Rehearsal Dinners	● Corp. Events/Mtgs.
● Ceremonies	● Private Parties
● Wedding Receptions	Accommodations

Whoever invented the phrase "storybook wedding" must have attended one at Silver Creek Valley Country Club (SCVCC). Every last detail at this upscale facility has been carefully thought out to ensure the most memorable experience possible for all guests.

Driving into the Club, you pass through a master-planned gated community. Here, swaying palms keep watch over sprawling houses that echo the earth tones of nearby Mount Hamilton and the adjoining foothills. At the end of a long, curving driveway stands the main clubhouse, a golden-hued edifice reminiscent of an Italian villa. Inside, every visitor experiences stunning grandeur and personalized service.

As you make your way through the expansive foyer, you immediately take note of the marble flooring and large columns. However, what really commands your attention is the imposing and ornate rotunda. Encircled by gold-tipped wrought iron and capped by a vast domed skylight, it soars over dual curving staircases that descend to the floor below. (Note that photographers love to pose the wedding party on the landing halfway down the stairs. Flooded with light, it's a prime spot for photos.)

French doors off the foyer lead to the Yerba Buena Ballroom, Silver Creek's main event space. Like the rest of the building's valley-facing side, this unusual crescent-shaped room features a back wall made entirely of glass. Every guest enjoys spectacular views of the championship golf course and the evergreen valley beyond, and at night thousands of twinkling lights from the surrounding homes yield a panorama that's even more dramatic.

The Ballroom's décor creates a seamless visual connection with the outdoor scenery: Pale green carpets and drapes and beige walls reflect the palette of the surrounding hills and foliage. Over-head, three Mediterranean-modern chandeliers cast a warm glow, while a cream-colored marble floor in the center invites everyone to dance.

If you have a smaller-sized gathering, or you'd like to serve cocktails and hors d'oeuvres while pictures are being taken, consider the adjoining Chaboya Lounge. This L-shaped space boasts a wood-paneled, granite-topped bar, cozy fireplace, and a terracotta patio that shares the Club's sweeping vistas.

Have you always dreamed of saying your vows in an exotic South Sea setting? Silver Creek Valley Country Club can save you the plane fare. It's just a short pleasant walk from the clubhouse to a majestic waterfall, where couples exchange vows on a raised flagstone Ceremony Landing at the base of this triple-level water feature. Or get married in front of the Cypress Dome with your guests seated on a rolling expanse of lawn. The site itself is certainly photogenic, but photographers also like to snap pictures of the bride and bridesmaids arriving via golf cart (the SCVCC mode of transport), as well as the just-marrieds departing for the reception in the same fashion.

From the custom-designed china to the tasteful furnishings and friendly, accommodating staff, Silver Creek Valley Country Club offers still more amenities that will make planning your wedding easy and enjoyable. Put yourself in the hands of the Club's on-site event coordinators, and prepare for a "storybook wedding" that has the happiest of endings.

CEREMONY CAPACITY: The outdoor ceremony area holds up to 300 seated guests.

EVENT/RECEPTION CAPACITY: The Club accommodates 300 seated or 500 standing guests indoors.

MEETING CAPACITY: Meeting rooms accommodate up to 250 seated guests.

FEES & DEPOSITS: Rental fees for weddings and events range $5,000–10,000 depending on event date. Rental fees for meetings start at $250. Meals range $34–128/person. Tax, alcohol and a 20% service charge are additional. Valet parking service is available upon request.

AVAILABILITY: Year-round, daily, 8am–midnight.

SERVICES/AMENITIES:

Catering: provided; outside ethnic cuisine caterers upon approval
Kitchen Facilities: n/a
Tables & Chairs: provided
Linens, Silver, etc.: provided
Restrooms: wheelchair accessible
Dance Floor: provided
Bride's & Groom's Dressing Area: yes
Meeting Equipment: CBA, extra charge

Parking: self-parking or valet, extra charge
Accommodations: no guestrooms
Telephone: house phones
Outdoor Night Lighting: yes
Outdoor Cooking Facilities: n/a
Cleanup: provided
View: panorama of valley and hills
Other: event coordination

RESTRICTIONS:

Alcohol: provided, no BYO
Smoking: outdoors only
Music: amplified OK indoors and outdoors

Wheelchair Access: yes
Insurance: required for outside ethnic cuisine caterer
Other: no rice, birdseed or glitter

The Tech Museum of Innovation

Museum

201 South Market Street, San Jose
408/795-6221
www.thetech.org
maureenl@thetech.org

● Rehearsal Dinners	● Corp. Events/Mtgs.
Ceremonies	● Private Parties
● Wedding Receptions	Accommodations

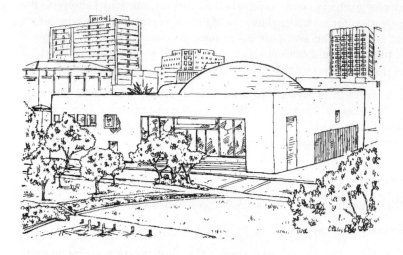

All you people who yawn at the prospect of going to a museum listen up: The Tech is not just a museum, it's an adventure. In fact, The Tech may be the most exciting thing to happen to the South Bay in years.

Located in downtown San Jose, facing Plaza de César Chavez and just across from the Fairmont Hotel, this bright mango building houses 300 high-tech interactive exhibits that will energize the most jaded visitor. And wonder of wonders!—if you host an event here, the exhibits are available for your guests' enjoyment.

Events are held in the museum lobby, the four major exhibit galleries, and the Hackworth IMAX Dome Theater. You can reserve any combination of spaces or rent the entire museum. The lobby is a fantastic place for a large party. It's a three-level atrium with a 45-foot cylindrical tower rising up through it and, when used in conjunction with the adjacent New Venture Hall, it can accommodate 500 for a sit-down dinner.

The galleries lend themselves to standing receptions. They're thoroughly modern, displaying a mix of steel, glass and plastic, with walls and ceilings painted in jewel shades of purple, yellow and blue. Each gallery has a different theme. *Innovation: Silicon Valley and Beyond* focuses on the story of Silicon Valley, and the people and inventions that made it famous. Have you ever wanted to know how they make silicon chips? In here you can take an air shower, put on a bunnysuit and watch grains of sand become polished silicon wafers. *Life Tech: The Human Machine* shows us how technologies save lives and enhance human performance. Take a tour of a virtual hospital operating room or ultrasound yourself and watch an image of your bones wiggling on a monitor. *Exploration: New Frontiers* gives you the opportunity to go places you've only been able to imagine. Here you can shake in an earthquake, explore under the sea and fly over the surface of Mars. And in *NetPl@net,* you'll be inspired to use the internet in different ways. Try your strength in a virtual Arm Wrestle against museum visitors in New York or Alaska. Create your own character and chat online in a 3D world or tour the globe with worldwide webcams.

In addition to these extraordinary galleries, The Tech has one more cutting-edge gem that will dazzle you and your guests: the Hackworth IMAX Dome Theater. The only one of its kind in Northern California, it features a giant hemispherical screen whose image dwarfs that of a conventional theater and puts the audience in the center of the action. Outfitted with state-of-the-art audiovisual equipment, the theater can be reserved exclusively for a performance or presentation, but we recommend you also use it for viewing an IMAX film. Experience rafting down the world's deadliest river, traveling to the Red Planet, a spellbinding climb up sheer vertical walls to the summit of Everest or the adventure, drama and emotion of some of your favorite Hollywood movies.

The Tech aims to inspire the innovator in everyone; yet, even if you don't come away wanting to be a scientist when you grow up, you'll have to admit that this place makes traditional meeting rooms and party themes feel obsolete. Part of the next generation of museums, The Tech triumphs at making science, math and technology not only accessible, but positively fun.

CEREMONY CAPACITY: Ceremonies don't take place at this venue.

EVENT/RECEPTION CAPACITY: The Tech can accommodate 500 seated guests or 2,500 standing.

MEETING CAPACITY: The Large Group Meeting Room holds up to 65 seated guests, and the New Venture Hall, 400 seated guests. The Noyce Center for Learning holds a maximum of 125 seated guests and can be divided into three separate meeting rooms.

FEES & DEPOSITS: 50% of the rental fee is the deposit required to secure your date, along with a $1,000–2,500 security/cleaning deposit. The rental fee ranges $500–12,500 depending on the space(s) used. Exclusive use of the Hackworth IMAX Dome Theater can be arranged at an additional cost. Fees are based on a 4-hour time period. An additional 30% per hour will be charged after the first 4 hours. Meals start at $20/person. Tax, alcohol and service charge are additional.

AVAILABILITY: Year-round, daily, 6pm–midnight. Closed Thanksgiving Day, Christmas Eve and Day and New Year's Eve.

SERVICES/AMENITIES:
Catering: provided, or select from list
Kitchen Facilities: prep only
Tables & Chairs: BYO or through caterer
Linens, Silver, etc.: through caterer
Restrooms: wheelchair accessible
Dance Floor: CBA
Meeting Equipment: CBA, extra charge
Other: on-site coordinator

Parking: Convention Center garage, nearby lots
Accommodations: no guestrooms
Telephone: pay phone
Outdoor Night Lighting: no
Outdoor Cooking Facilities: no
Cleanup: through caterer
View: no

RESTRICTIONS:
Alcohol: provided
Smoking: outdoors only
Music: amplified OK

Wheelchair Access: yes
Insurance: certificate required

Overwhelmed? Use the search criteria on www.HereComesTheGuide.com to narrow down your choices.

The Villages Golf and Country Club

Golf & Country Club

5000 Cribari Lane, San Jose
408/223-4687

www.thevillagesgcc.com
theclubhouse@the-villages.com

- Rehearsal Dinners
- Ceremonies
- Wedding Receptions
- Corp. Events/Mtgs.
- Private Parties
- Accommodations

We've heard the sad tale before: You'd love to have a country club wedding, but there's one tiny little problem—you don't belong to a country club. Lucky for you, membership isn't required at the Villages Golf and Country Club. Perched in the hills above southeastern San Jose, this facility has everything you're looking for: a handsome Spanish Mission-style clubhouse; lovely banquet rooms; well-tended gardens, and a verdant, meticulously groomed golf course. You get all this, plus a variety of wedding packages, at a price that won't make you dip into your honeymoon fund.

In the clubhouse, you'll find three special event rooms that can be used separately or in combination. Though all three have a versatile cream-and-tan color scheme and frosted-glass-and-brass chandeliers, each one has its own distinct design elements: The Oak Room features a gleaming hardwood oak dance floor; the Sunset Room has a large window that takes advantage of the view of the Santa Clara Valley; and the elegant Fairway Room boasts panoramic golf course views. Adjacent to this trio of rooms is a foyer area with a grand piano. The Oak and Fairway Rooms are particularly lovely when used together, but no matter what configuration of these areas you choose, they're all brimming with sophisticated country club ambiance.

So, now that we've introduced you to the Villages Golf and Country Club, you won't have to give up your dream of a country club wedding. And if there's no wedding in your future, but you'd still like to book your event here, go right ahead—the flexible, competent staff can help you with whatever type of gathering you've got in mind. The price is right, the setting is fabulous and they'll be happy to see you even if you don't have a membership card.

CEREMONY CAPACITY: Limited indoor ceremony space available. Contact facility for more information.

EVENT/RECEPTION & MEETING CAPACITY: The Clubhouse holds up to 250 seated or 600 standing guests. This space can be divided into smaller reception areas.

FEES & DEPOSITS: A $2,100 room rental deposit is required to reserve your date. The estimated event total is due 7 working days prior to the event. Meals range $34–68/person. Tax, alcohol and an 18% service charge are additional. One or more security officers are required (depending on guest count) at the rate of $100/officer.

AVAILABILITY: Year-round, Tuesday–Sunday, 6am–11pm.

SERVICES/AMENITIES:

Catering: provided, no BYO

Kitchen Facilities: n/a

Tables & Chairs: provided

Linens, Silver, etc.: provided

Restrooms: wheelchair accessible

Dance Floor: hardwood floor

Meeting Equipment: projection screen

Other: on-site coordinator, PA system

Parking: large lot

Accommodations: no guestrooms

Telephone: pay phone

Outdoor Night Lighting: yes

Outdoor Cooking Facilities: no

Cleanup: provided

View: golf course, Santa Clara Valley, city lights

RESTRICTIONS:

Alcohol: provided, or wine corkage $10/bottle

Smoking: outdoors only

Music: amplified OK indoors only

Wheelchair Access: yes

Insurance: not required

Other: no rice or open flames

Clos LaChance

One Hummingbird Lane, San Martin
408/686-1050 x106

www.clos.com
kristin@clos.com

Winery

● Rehearsal Dinners	● Corp. Events/Mtgs.
● Ceremonies	● Private Parties
● Wedding Receptions	Accommodations

If you've seen the movie classic, *The Wizard of Oz,* you'll recall the scene where Dorothy arrives in Oz, looks around, and says to her little dog, "I don't think we're in Kansas anymore, Toto."

Well, you won't think you're in *California* anymore when you see Clos LaChance Winery. This majestic facility, with its white stucco and fieldstone walls, red-tile roof and exquisitely landscaped gardens, will have you wondering if you've been magically transported to the hills of Provence. But the only magic involved here was the unique vision of owners Bill and Brenda Murphy, brought to reality by talented designers and architects.

Located adjacent to the sixth hole of the exclusive CordeValle Golf Course, and overlooking acres of vineyards and open land, Clos LaChance surrounds you with beauty and elegance the minute you enter the grounds. A petite courtyard, graced by a bubbling fountain and abloom with fragrant herbs and flowers, welcomes you to the winery. A small ceremony or champagne reception is enchanting in this sunlit space.

After pausing here to savor its delights, continue on into the winery itself and the aptly named Grand Salon. This expansive room has tiled floors, pale taupe walls and ceiling with dark wood moldings, and French doors framed in deep red-and-brown brocade drapes. The room's focal point is an imposing stone fireplace; above it, a gilded mirror reflects the light cast by the wrought-iron chandelier, embellished with gilt leaves and flowers. A gorgeous tapestry, depicting a Roman scene, adorns one wall. Incidentally, throughout the winery, all of the furnishings and art are genuine antiques—even the books in the bookcase in the Salon's foyer!

Just off the Grand Salon is the Tasting Library, a cheerful room featuring an unusual zinc-topped tasting bar, a massive wooden back-bar, and little cocktail tables that came from an English pub. For something really unusual, entertain your guests in the Cellar Room. Built entirely of dry-stacked sandstone, and lit by a wrought-iron candle chandelier, this cozy underground space can host intimate dinners, bridal toasts or photos around the antique refectory table.

Outside the Salon and Tasting Library is the Grand Terrace, paved with flagstones and bordered by white rose bushes. Seated dining takes place here, before moving into the Grand Salon for music and dancing. Below the Grand Terrace, a velvety semicircle of grass called the Tapestry Lawn is enclosed by a stone wall and framed by a silhouette of the rolling hills. A wooden arbor laced with climbing roses is the preferred place for couples to tie the knot. Another option is the Mulberry Grove, a pretty spot for sun-dappled ceremonies and social hours.

The outdoor areas are all lavished with horticultural treasures, such as lush chestnut trees and oleanders; colorful Santa Barbara daisies and salvias; aromatic lavender and roses. Even the briefest visit to Clos LaChance reveals a meticulous attention to detail, a quality shared by the topnotch event planning and wedding coordination services offered here. Clos LaChance was named after co-owner Brenda LaChance Murphy, but "chance" is also the French word for "luck," and we're sure that you'll feel extremely fortunate when you discover this outstanding facility.

CEREMONY CAPACITY: The winery accommodates 125 seated indoors or 200 outdoors.

EVENT/RECEPTION CAPACITY: The facility holds 100 seated and 130 standing indoors; 200 seated or standing outdoors.

MEETING CAPACITY: Event spaces accommodate 200 seated guests.

FEES & DEPOSITS: Half the anticipated event total is required as a nonrefundable deposit to reserve your date. The event balance is due 3 months prior to the event, any remaining balance for extra services is due 14 days prior to the event. Rental fees range $600–10,000 depending on space rented and guest count.

AVAILABILITY: Year-round, daily, 8am–11pm, except Thanksgiving, Christmas and New Year's Days.

SERVICES/AMENITIES:

Catering: select from approved list
Kitchen Facilities: n/a
Tables & Chairs: some provided
Linens, Silver, etc.: CBA
Restrooms: wheelchair accessible
Dance Floor: yes
Bride's & Groom's Dressing Areas: yes
Meeting Equipment: some provided

Parking: limited, valet required
Accommodations: no guestrooms
Telephone: house phone
Outdoor Night Lighting: yes
Outdoor Cooking Facilities: BBQ CBA
Cleanup: provided
View: vineyards, hills, fairways, gardens
Other: event coordination, picnic area

RESTRICTIONS:

Alcohol: provided
Smoking: outside only
Music: amplified OK indoors and outdoors with restrictions

Wheelchair Access: yes
Insurance: required

CordeValle, A Rosewood Resort

Resort

One CordeValle Club Drive, San Martin
408/695-4585
www.cordevalle.com
kristi.hogue@rosewoodhotels.com

● Rehearsal Dinners	● Corp. Events/Mtgs.
● Ceremonies	● Private Parties
● Wedding Receptions	● Accommodations

Nestled in the foothills of the Santa Cruz Mountains, CordeValle, a Rosewood Resort, may very well be Northern California's answer to Shangri-la. Rising gently above a rural valley midway between Monterey and San Jose, this destination location, which strikes the perfect balance between understated elegance and natural beauty, instantly casts its spell over you.

Driving past a series of ponds, waterfalls and picturesque vines from the winery on property, you're waved through the guard gate and arrive at the sprawling lodge-style clubhouse. Framed by mountains in the distance, the vaulted, cross-beamed entryway with its outdoor seating and fireplace beckons you and your guests with a warm welcome.

The lobby, a subtle mix of honeyed woods, stone pillars and earth tones, conveys luxury without a hint of pretension. Just to the left is the Library. Decorated with vibrant modern art and a rich kilim rug, it makes a cozy setting for an intimate wedding or reception. Larger ceremonies are held in the glorious outdoors on a nicely manicured practice facility, which affords wide-angle views of the 1,700-acre property. Continue your celebration with cocktails in the Rose Garden, a lovely spot abloom with fragrant and colorful flowers planted around a center patio. Several modern sculptures—a couple holding hands and a mother swinging her child—seem to convey sheer joy. There's even a nearby stand of old oaks where a family of owls has nested.

When dinner is served, there's no need to leave the vistas behind, because each of the four banquet event rooms looks out onto the verdant Robert Trent Jones Jr.-designed golf course. Most notable is the 2,300-square-foot Main Ballroom, whose high, coffered ceiling and stained-glass chandeliers enhance the rich décor. Here, wood-framed, wraparound windows reveal the panoramic landscape outside.

Inevitably you'll find that just as the visitors to the fictional Shangri-la didn't want to leave their heavenly valley, you and your nearest and dearest will want to linger at CordeValle. Their beautifully appointed bungalows and villas let you kick back in first-class homes away from home that feature top-of-the-line linens, organic toiletries, large living rooms and private, landscaped patios—some with outdoor spas and wisteria trees. If you'd like some extra relaxation, their lush

Sense™ Spa, will pamper you into a state of bliss. Throw in world-class golf, hiking trails up to Lion's Peak, a vineyard tour and gourmet dining and you'll find much to tempt you into extending your stay in paradise.

CEREMONY CAPACITY: The resort holds 60 seated guests indoors and 200 seated outdoors.

EVENT/RECEPTION CAPACITY: The resort can accommodate 180 seated or 200 standing indoors and 100 seated or 200 standing outdoors.

MEETING CAPACITY: Meeting rooms hold 120 seated guests.

FEES & DEPOSITS: A deposit equal to the rental fee is required to reserve your date and the balance is due 14 days prior to the event. Rental fees range $700–7,500 depending on the day of the week, the season and the space rented. Meals range $60–110/person. Tax, alcohol and a 22% service charge are additional.

AVAILABILITY: Year-round.

SERVICES/AMENITIES:

Catering: provided
Kitchen Facilities: n/a
Tables & Chairs: provided
Linens, Silver, etc.: provided
Restrooms: wheelchair accessible
Dance Floor: yes
Bride's Dressing Area: CBA
Meeting Equipment: provided
Other: spa services, AV equipment, golf course printed menus and place cards, event coordination

Parking: large lot
Accommodations: 44 guestrooms
Telephone: office phone
Outdoor Night Lighting: provided
Outdoor Cooking Facilities: BBQ CBA
Cleanup: provided
View: creek, fairways, landscaped grounds, garden patio; panorama of hills, mountains and valley

RESTRICTIONS:

Alcohol: provided
Smoking: outdoors only
Music: amplified OK with restrictions

Wheelchair Access: yes
Insurance: not required

The professionals in the back of this book are the best in the business. How do we know? Read page 701.

Adobe Lodge

University Club

Santa Clara University, Santa Clara
408/554-4059
www.scu.edu/adobelodge
adobelodgecatering@scu.edu

- Rehearsal Dinners
- Corp. Events/Mtgs.
- Ceremonies
- Private Parties
- Wedding Receptions
- Accommodations

Set in the lovely Mission Gardens just steps from the historic Mission Santa Clara Church, the Adobe Lodge is the oldest structure on the Santa Clara University Campus and one of the area's most beloved event venues. Originally built in 1822, the building has been completely updated with modern amenities, but it still retains the flavor and charm of its Mission-era architecture.

The garden itself is an enviable spot for an al fresco or tented reception. Its focal point is an amazing wisteria-laden pergola, entwined with vines dating back 150 years. In spring, the pergola becomes an enchanting pathway (and an irresistible backdrop for photos), covered in a breathtaking cloud of lavender blossoms. The surrounding landscaping is delightful as well, from the palms dotting the lawns to the beds of multihued roses and seasonal flowers.

At the end of the pergola is the Adobe Lodge, whose Spanish-tiled fountain and wraparound vine-covered porch evoke the gracious quality of a bygone time. Several indoor and outdoor spaces can be used individually or in combination, and all look equally fabulous when decorated casually or dressed to the nines.

If the weather is fine, consider serving cocktails or having your reception on the patio, an intimate tiled courtyard bordered by Chinese elms, greenery and flowers. Prefer an indoor affair? The main dining room and its adjoining porch connect to each other through tall windows and doors, and there's a nice flow between them. The porch is custom-made for a rehearsal dinner, buffet setup, or drinks and hors d'oeuvres, while the light and airy dining room is ideal for a seated reception. It also works well for dancing, as it's outfitted with a permanent raised dais that holds your band or DJ.

Couples who want to get married here, too, can exchange vows in the Mission Santa Clara Church. The exquisite interior—featuring walls lined with graceful arches, hand-painted designs on every surface, and stunning chandeliers suspended from the 25-foot-high ceiling—will imbue your ceremony with beauty and awe.

An on-site event planner is happy to help with ideas and recommend vendors, and if you don't have your own wedding coordinator she'll provide day-of coordination. At the Adobe Lodge, you're encouraged to be creative, and use any or all of the event areas in the way that suits you best. Whether you host a picnic with gingham tablecloths or a black-tie gala with elegant linens and crystal, you'll feel that you've chosen exactly the right place.

CEREMONY CAPACITY: Ceremonies do not take place at this venue. Mission Santa Clara is nearby and hosts ceremonies. Call for details.

EVENT/RECEPTION CAPACITY: The Main Dining Room holds 100–125 seated guests or 200 standing; the adjacent Porch seats 24; the Patio holds 40 seated or 90 standing. The Mission's Gardens can accommodate 150–600 seated guests during warmer months. Tented events can be arranged.

MEETING CAPACITY: The Main Dining Room accommodates 80 seated theater-style; two Private Dining Rooms seat up to 12 guests each.

FEES & DEPOSITS: For wedding receptions, a nonrefundable $1,800 rental fee, which includes use of the facility for 4 hours, is required at the time of booking. A final guest count is due 10 days prior to the wedding. Food services are provided. Special wedding menus for served or buffet-style meals, including passed hors d'oeuvres, range $68–89/person. Customized menus are also available. Alcohol, tax and an 18% service charge are additional. The food and beverage balance is payable 10 days prior to the event. Extra hours may be arranged at $450/hour.

For other special events and business functions, the rental fee ranges $50–500 depending on room(s) selected. Fees are based on a 3-hour rental period; additional time can be arranged for an extra fee. Prices for breakfast meetings and luncheons vary depending on services requested.

AVAILABILITY: Year-round, daily, 7:30am–midnight.

SERVICES/AMENITIES:

Catering: provided, no BYO
Kitchen Facilities: n/a
Tables & Chairs: provided
Linens, Silver, etc.: provided
Restrooms: wheelchair accessible
Dance Floor: yes
Bride's Dressing Area: no
Meeting Equipment: full range CBA, extra fee

Parking: large lot
Accommodations: no guestrooms
Telephone: emergency use only
Outdoor Night Lighting: CBA
Outdoor Cooking Facilities: CBA
Cleanup: provided
View: Mission Gardens, Mission Santa Clara

RESTRICTIONS:

Alcohol: provided, or corkage $10/bottle
Smoking: outside only
Music: amplified OK indoors, outdoors with volume limits

Wheelchair Access: yes
Insurance: certificate required
Other: no rice or birdseed; decorations require approval

David's Restaurant & Banquet Facility

Restaurant and Event Facility

5151 Stars & Stripes Drive, Santa Clara
408/986-1666 x21

www.davidsbanquetfacility.com
jean@davids-restaurant.com

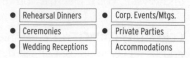

- Rehearsal Dinners
- Ceremonies
- Wedding Receptions
- Corp. Events/Mtgs.
- Private Parties
- Accommodations

For many couples, nothing says romance like a golf course, and for them there's David's Restaurant and Banquet Facilities, two neighboring venues on the Santa Clara Golf Course that share the same beautiful panorama of velvety green fairways.

With its sharply steepled roof, wood-beamed ceiling and huge windows overlooking the greens, the restaurant feels like a cathedral—especially at night by candlelight. During cold weather, the natural stone fireplace makes a beautiful backdrop for an indoor ceremony, but on a sunny day you might prefer to get married outside on the adjacent patio.

Just steps away is David's Banquet Facility, which has five rooms facing the fairways. Clean and modern, with baffled wood ceilings, stylish chandeliers, wood trim, and large picture windows, the rooms can be opened up into one grand space with a fireplace at either end, or partitioned into smaller spaces for a more intimate event. Stage your ceremony on the grassy landscaped area next to the fairway, or in front of one of the granite-faced fireplaces. A long foyer with a high ceiling provides plenty of room for pre-banquet cocktails.

David's can arrange any type of affair, from an informal barbecue to an elegant sit-down dinner, with equal ease. They specialize in Continental cuisine, offering a choice of 44 hors d'oeuvres, from petit beef Wellington suxelles to sushi. Feast on entrées as elaborate as chicken Voldostano with proscuitto and gruyère cheese, or as simple and delicious as broiled salmon filet. For vegetarians, there is an array of choices, like stuffed red bell pepper and charbroiled polenta with fresh seasonal squash.

Other options include international custom menus and a variety of buffets, from Mexican or Italian-style to the Grand Buffet with a wide selection of hors d'oeuvres, salads, pastas and entrées. Buffet desserts, such as chocolate-dipped strawberries, double lemon cake and mini éclairs, are an irresistible finale to a great meal.

Its golf course location lends David's an open, breezy, out-in-the-country feeling; yet it's right in the heart of Silicon Valley, within walking distance to major hotels. David's has over 35 years of restaurant and banquet experience and can handle every detail of your event. If you want to make planning your celebration easier, put yourself in their capable hands.

CEREMONY, EVENT/RECEPTION & MEETING CAPACITY: The location holds up to 500 seated or 600 standing guests, indoors or outdoors.

FEES & DEPOSITS: A $1,000 deposit is required to reserve your date. The balance is due 7 days prior to the event. Rental fees range $0–1,000 depending on the space, day and time rented. Meals range $30–45/person. Tax, alcohol and a 19% service charge are additional.

AVAILABILITY: Year-round, daily, 7am–midnight or later.

SERVICES/AMENITIES:

Catering: provided
Kitchen Facilities: n/a
Tables & Chairs: provided
Linens, Silver, etc.: provided
Restrooms: not wheelchair accessible
Dance Floor: provided
Bride's & Groom's Dressing Areas: yes
Meeting Equipment: provided

Parking: large lot
Accommodations: no guestrooms
Telephone: pay and house phones
Outdoor Night Lighting: yes
Outdoor Cooking Facilities: BBQ
Cleanup: provided
View: park, garden, landscaped grounds
Other: event coordination, on-site florals, chair covers

RESTRICTIONS:

Alcohol: provided
Smoking: outside only
Music: amplified OK

Wheelchair Access: yes
Insurance: not required

Decathlon Club

3250 Central Expressway, Santa Clara
408/736-3237
www.decathlon-club.com
catering@decathlon-club.com

Private Club

● Rehearsal Dinners	● Corp. Events/Mtgs.
● Ceremonies	● Private Parties
● Wedding Receptions	☐ Accommodations

One of Silicon Valley's finest resort/health clubs, the Decathlon Club is ingeniously designed to accommodate private events, corporate functions and wedding receptions. As you enter, there is a shaded atrium setting with a bubbling stream that flows through the building, beautifully separating the social-function spaces from the club's spa and athletic areas. Ficus trees glow with white twinkle lights at night, and abundant greenery creates a lush indoor garden.

For special events, guests are invited into their private area without having to mingle with Club members. The large skylit dining area is filled with natural light during the day, and on a clear night you can see stars sparkling overhead. There is a lot more sparkle inside, however, and it comes from the chairs. *Chiavari* chairs to be more precise. Ornate and gilded, these special seats add elegance and a bit of glamour to your dining experience. After enjoying your meal, take a turn on the raised hardwood dance floor.

A nine-acre complex, the Decathlon Club is extremely well suited for corporate functions. For team building, company picnics, grad nights and other group activities, many of the Club's sports facilities are available for rental. Corporate challenges or interoffice games can be played here, all supported by a helpful and experienced staff.

In fact, no matter what kind of event you have at the Club, the staff is committed to making it a total success. The executive chef and professional event planners will coordinate everything for you, including entertainment, flowers, photography and overnight accommodations—that's great news for brides who feel overwhelmed. "They can relax when they come through our door," says the Catering Director. "We will handle all the details, and help them plan the wedding of their dreams."

CEREMONY CAPACITY: The Garden Terrace holds 90 seated guests and the Main Dining Room holds 400 seated theater-style.

EVENT/RECEPTION CAPACITY: Indoors, the Club accommodates 650 guests seated or standing.

MEETING CAPACITY: The Monterey Room holds 10 seated conference-style and the Peninsula Room 20 seated conference-style. Meeting rooms come with screen and white board. The newly renovated Vista Room holds up to 120 guests seated banquet-style and has many audiovisual amenities as well as wireless internet access.

FEES & DEPOSITS: Rental fees are $3,500 for Saturday evenings and $2,000 for Fridays and Sundays. The rental fee covers a 5-hour period; overtime is available. A nonrefundable $2,500 deposit is due when your reservation is confirmed; 50% of the estimated food and beverage total is due 6 months prior to the event and the balance is due 72 hours prior. Per-person rates are: dinners $31–45, buffets $40–48; hors d'oeuvres range $325–450 per 100 pieces. Beverage packages start at $12/person. Tax and a 19.75% service charge are additional. A $1,000 wedding ceremony fee includes setup, cleanup, coordinator and rehearsal. Food and beverage minimums are required for functions taking place during prime dates and times.

For other events or corporate functions, rates vary depending on rooms and services selected. Conference rooms start at $400/event.

AVAILABILITY: Special events and business functions, year-round, daily until 1am. Wedding receptions take place in a 5-hour block on Saturdays, 11am–4pm or 6pm–11pm, or on Fridays and Sundays, anytime.

SERVICES/AMENITIES:

Catering: provided, BYO with approval
Kitchen Facilities: fully equipped
Tables & Chairs: provided
Linens, Silver, etc.: provided
Restrooms: wheelchair accessible
Dance Floor: yes
Bride's Dressing Area: yes
Meeting Equipment: full range

Parking: large lots, complimentary
Accommodations: no guestrooms
Telephone: pay phone
Outdoor Night Lighting: yes
Outdoor Cooking Facilities: no
Cleanup: provided
View: indoor garden, outdoor coastal hills
Other: event coordination

RESTRICTIONS:

Alcohol: provided, or WC corkage $17/bottle
Smoking: outside only
Music: amplified OK indoors

Wheelchair Access: yes
Insurance: not required
Other: no birdseed, rice, freefloating balloons or bubbles inside the Club

---

Want to know WHAT TO ASK a potential location or vendor? Check out our Questions to Ask on page 17.

Freedom Hall and Gardens

Gardens and Event Facility

Address withheld to ensure privacy. Santa Clara
408/379-FREE (3733)
www.freedomhall.com
info@freedomhall.com

Rehearsal Dinners	Corp. Events/Mtgs.
● Ceremonies	Private Parties
● Wedding Receptions	Accommodations

You would never in a million years guess that it was there. It's woodsy and flowery, with splashing fountains—perfect for taking the most idyllic of wedding photos. Yet the recently remodeled Freedom Hall and Gardens is right in the middle of Silicon Valley's high-tech empire in Santa Clara. What could be more convenient?

On weekends, this little oasis is as private and quiet as a desert island. Tucked away amid the silent office buildings, it's practically invisible to anyone passing by. But oh what this place has to offer: a fountain-pond surrounded by carpets of colorful flowers; natural stone formations; towering redwoods and weeping willows; and butterflies flitting across the pond by the rocky waterfall.

Ceremonies here are lovely. Picture your guests seated on the lawn at one end of the pond. You glide across the bridge spanning the water in front of them, and down the grassy aisle to stand in front of the fountain with your husband-to-be. Your music plays (via the professional outdoor sound system) as clouds drift through the blue sky overhead.

After exchanging vows, you and the wedding party walk the few yards to Freedom Hall, whose floor-to-ceiling windows command a panorama of the gardens. While the guests assemble, you wait in the Bride's Room, decorated with glass cases displaying a collection of wedding favors commemorating every wedding at Freedom Hall since the first one in 1995. You make your grand entrance through the bridal arch into the hall.

Dinner is served in the completely transformed Hall, which now features a gleaming hardwood floor, a granite bar, and Tuscan-inspired wrought-iron chandeliers. But the facility's most beautiful "decoration" is its view of the gardens. Guests are free to stroll outside, champagne glasses in hand, and meander along the winding brick paths through the redwoods.

Although the setting is quite appealing, what you don't see is the well-coordinated operation behind the event. Freedom Hall and Gardens hosts 170 weddings a year, and they know their stuff. The venue is Diamond-certified, which means that brides and grooms who were married here have been interviewed by an independent organization to determine the rate of customer satisfaction. Freedom Hall has consistently achieved a near-perfect score. It's not surprising that Freedom Hall and Gardens was voted "Best Wedding Reception Facility" by *The Knot* magazine from 2007 through 2010.

The cuisine features classic American dishes such as a chef's carving station with New York roast steak, chicken Madeira, rice pilaf, pasta marinara, steamed vegetables and fresh-baked breads. There's a selection of passed hors d'oeuvres such as jumbo prawns, stuffed mushrooms and blue cheese pastries. As for dessert, any menu you choose includes complimentary chocolate-dipped strawberries as a sweet surprise before the wedding cake.

If you yearn for a ceremony in the redwoods, but your practical side requires a central location, Freedom Hall and Gardens offers both. You and your guests get the charm of a forest sanctuary, while being within walking distance of the Santa Clara Marriott and Great America. This place has everything you need.

CEREMONY & EVENT/RECEPTION CAPACITY: The site holds up to 250 guests indoors or outdoors, maximum.

MEETING CAPACITY: Meetings do not take place at this location.

FEES & DEPOSITS: A $1,500 deposit is required. The balance is due 10 days prior to the event. There are no separate rental fees. Price per person, including the meal and alcohol starts at $77.50. There is a 100 person minimum charge. Tax and an 18% service charge are additional.

AVAILABILITY: Year-round, Friday 6:30pm–midnight, Saturday and Sunday 10am–midnight. Weekdays by special arrangment.

SERVICES/AMENITIES:

Catering: provided
Kitchen Facilities: n/a
Tables & Chairs: provided
Linens, Silver, etc.: provided
Restrooms: wheelchair accessible
Dance Floor: provided
Bride's Dressing Area: yes
Meeting Equipment: n/a

Parking: large lot
Accommodations: no guestrooms
Telephone: office phone
Outdoor Night Lighting: yes
Outdoor Cooking Facilities: no
Cleanup: provided
View: garden, pond, fountain, grounds
Other: event coordination, on-site wedding cake, professional DJ

RESTRICTIONS:

Alcohol: provided with package
Smoking: designated areas only
Music: amplified OK

Wheelchair Access: yes
Insurance: not required

Hilton Santa Clara

Hotel

4949 Great America Parkway, Santa Clara
408/562-6704

www.hiltonsantaclara.com
Lia.Dulay@hilton.com

- Rehearsal Dinners
- Ceremonies
- Wedding Receptions
- Corp. Events/Mtgs.
- Private Parties
- Accommodations

The Silicon Valley isn't the first place most people think of when planning a wedding or social gathering, and that's a shame. It means they're missing out on one of the nicest hotels in the area—the Hilton Santa Clara. Given its location, it's been a popular place for high-tech industry meetings, but it also has a number of features that make it an excellent choice for festive occasions.

The Hilton Santa Clara's exterior has the sleek, modern good looks you'd expect a large upscale hotel to have, but when you enter the lobby, you'd swear you were in an exclusive boutique hotel. Utilizing Classical, Art Nouveau and modern design elements, the lobby has an enticing air of relaxed, understated luxury. The neutral color scheme is anything but bland, while marble floors, wall panels and blond wood molding add natural luster to the room. Wall sconces, standard lamps and light fixtures, all made of sinuously curving wrought iron and frosted glass, make a stunning visual statement. Wherever you look, there is something to captivate your eye: two life-sized sculptures that could have been done by Rodin or Degas, richly colored and textured upholstery, framed prints and paintings.

All of the function areas in the Hilton Santa Clara reflect the imaginative style and attention to detail displayed in the lobby. There are two large ballrooms available for weddings and events: the 2,800-square-foot Sierra and the 1,500-square-foot Coastal. Each ballroom can be divided into three smaller rooms if desired. Another option for smaller, more casual get-togethers is the Lounge. Just off the lobby, it has an intimate feel, thanks to gold-and-ocher brocade armchairs and deep green walls. Softly lit by unusual disc-shaped fixtures hanging from the coffered ceiling, and enlivened by modern paintings, it's made-to-order for cocktail parties, receptions and "welcome" parties. By special arrangement, and depending on availability, you can rent the Concierge Room, a sort of super-deluxe "den" where guests watch TV, play games or just sit and chat over drinks. It's the perfect place for family and friends to relax after the reception.

In our opinion, the Hilton Santa Clara needs no more to recommend it than what we've already described, but we can't help mentioning just a few more benefits. They have a superb staff that can assist you in everything from menu selections to room rentals for your guests. The bridal package includes a complimentary suite for the bride and groom with chocolate-covered strawberries and a bottle of champagne. And the Hilton Santa Clara's location can't be beat—the Great America theme park is literally steps away, and the streetcar stops right outside the hotel, giving you access to all the attractions of downtown San Jose. Should you wish to venture further afield, major freeways leading to the Monterey Peninsula or San Francisco are within easy reach. With all it has to offer, this Hilton qualifies as one of the South Bay's undiscovered treasures.

CEREMONY CAPACITY: The Coastal Ballroom holds 115, and the Sierra Ballroom 250.

EVENT/RECEPTION CAPACITY: The Coastal Ballroom accommodates 60–100 seated or 200 standing, and the Sierra Ballroom 150–200 seated or 250–300 standing guests.

FEES & DEPOSITS: For weddings, a $2,000 nonrefundable deposit is required when the contract is signed. The event balance and a final guest count are due 1 week prior to the event.

There are a variety of packages from which to choose. Prices range $66–80/person. Tax and a 20% service charge are additional. All packages include hors d'oeuvres, butler-passed champagne and sparking cider during the cocktail hour, champagne toast, two bottles of house wine per table, elegant floor-length linens, 2-course dinner and complimentary cake-cutting service. Complimentary wedding-night accommodations are provided for the bride and groom.

AVAILABILITY: Year-round, daily, 6am–midnight, including holidays.

SERVICES/AMENITIES:

Catering: provided
Kitchen Facilities: n/a
Tables & Chairs: provided
Linens, Silver, etc.: provided
Restrooms: wheelchair accessible
Dance Floor: yes
Bride's & Groom's Dressing Area: guestroom
Other: on-site wedding coordinator

Parking: complimentary
Accommodations: 280 guestrooms
Telephone: pay and guest phone, internet
Outdoor Night Lighting: access only
Outdoor Cooking Facilities: no
Cleanup: provided
View: Great America amusement park

RESTRICTIONS:

Alcohol: provided, or wine corkage $15/bottle
Smoking: outside only
Music: amplified OK, volume limits after 11pm

Wheelchair Access: yes
Insurance: not required
Other: no open flames or fog machines; decorations need approval

Hakone Estate and Gardens

Japanese Gardens

21000 Big Basin Way, Saratoga
408/741-4994 x103
www.hakone.us
events@hakone.com

● Rehearsal Dinners	● Corp. Events/Mtgs.
● Ceremonies	● Private Parties
● Wedding Receptions	Accommodations

We all have our own idea of the perfect getaway, a place to escape to when the world is too much for us. For some, it's a little grass hut on a tropical island; for others it's a villa on the Riviera. For Oliver and Isabel Stine, however, it was a Japanese garden.

Inspired by exhibits they saw at the 1915 Panama-Pacific Exposition, the Stines purchased 16 acres near Saratoga on which to build Hakone Gardens, their summer home. In 1932, the property was bought by a financier, who owned it until 1960 when six families bought it. Then the City of Saratoga purchased the Gardens in 1966, and hired a Japanese landscape gardener to restore them to their former splendor. The Gardens are now maintained under the watchful eye of the nonprofit Hakone Foundation.

Because Hakone is open to the public seven days a week until 5pm, outdoor events must be held after 5. If you're an early bird, you can also schedule your event in the morning before the facility opens. During these times you have the entire Garden to yourself. Larger weddings often take place in the gravel area near the Koi Pond (the Garden area) while truly intimate ceremonies of 15 or fewer are held in the Wisteria Pavilion, a charming wooden structure perched on the banks of the pond and entwined with wisteria. Afterwards, guests can walk the short distance to the Madrone Mound, a gravel-topped rise shaded by an arching oak tree and bamboos, which is equally fine for a seated or standing reception.

Those wishing to tie the knot during more conventional hours are welcome to do so—indoors. Hakone features two meticulously detailed and authentic Japanese structures that are available for four-hour or all-day rentals. The Lower House has redwood walls in the reception area, a tea ceremony room (not available to the public unless you're going to have a tea ceremony there) and a shoe-removal rock near the entrance. The Cultural Exchange Center is a replica of a 19th-century Kyoto tea merchant's shop and living quarters. Built in 1991, the building was assembled in Japan using traditional methods and materials, then set up on its present site by Japanese carpenters. Display cases containing various Japanese artifacts line the walls of the reception area, and elsewhere in the building there is a traditional tatamied tea ceremony room. The Cultural Exchange Deck, overlooking the Santa Clara Valley, is perfect for a breathtaking ceremony, formal seated dinner or a more relaxed cocktail reception.

Weddings are popular at Hakone Gardens, and on moonlit summer nights they're nothing short of enchanting. Business functions also benefit from the quiet and peaceful atmosphere. In fact, the way we see it, any type of event—whether indoors or out—will be enhanced by these beautiful surroundings.

CEREMONY CAPACITY: The Garden Area or the Madrone Mound holds 150 seated or standing guests; the Cultural Exchange Center holds 80 seated theater-style; the Lower House 60 seated theater-style.

RECEPTION CAPACITY: The Cultural Exchange Center accommodates 60 seated or standing indoors, with an additional 40 guests seated on the adjacent deck. The Madrone Mound holds 150 seated or standing outdoors. The Lower House holds 40 seated guests.

MEETING CAPACITY: The Cultural Exchange Center accommodates 80 seated theater-style or 35–40 seated conference-style. The Lower House holds 60 guests seated theater-style or 20 seated conference-style.

FEES & DEPOSITS: To secure your date, a $600 refundable deposit plus half the rental fee is required; the balance is due 90 days prior to the event. For weddings and special events taking place between May and October, use fees range $1,050–6,600 depending on space(s) rented. Overtime is $400–600/hour, not to exceed 10pm. Off-season rates available. Part of your fees may be tax-deductible, as Hakone is a nonprofit organization.

For business meetings, use fees range $120–200/hour depending on space(s) rented.

AVAILABILITY: For weddings and receptions, the Garden Area and Madrone Mound are available 8am–11am or 5pm–9pm (or 10pm with overtime fee); Lower House and Cultural Exchange Center 9am–9pm (or 10pm with overtime fee). For business functions, year-round, daily, 8am–5pm, except Christmas Day and New Year's Day.

SERVICES/AMENITIES:

Catering: preferred list
Kitchen Facilities: prep only
Tables & Chairs: provided
Linens, Silver, etc.: through caterer
Restrooms: limited wheelchair accessibility
Dance Floor: yes
Bride's Dressing Area: yes
Meeting Equipment: DVD player, LCD projector/screen, white boards, easels, wireless internet

Parking: large lot, free parking for guests
Accommodations: no guestrooms
Telephone: emergency use only for meetings
Outdoor Night Lighting: yes
Outdoor Cooking Facilities: no
Cleanup: renter or caterer
View: Santa Clara Valley, Japanese gardens, cascading waterfalls and koi pond
Other: gift shop, picnic tables; access to gardens, trails and paths; tea ceremony and guided tours

RESTRICTIONS:

Alcohol: WCB only, through caterer or BYO
Smoking: parking lot only
Music: amplified OK indoors with volume limits

Wheelchair Access: limited
Insurance: not required
Other: no rice, decorations restricted

Want to find more locations and services? Check out our informative website, www.HereComesTheGuide.com.

The Mountain Winery

Mountaintop Winery

14831 Pierce Road, Saratoga
408/913-7125

www.mountainwinery.com
weddings@mountainwinery.com

● Rehearsal Dinners	● Corp. Events/Mtgs.
● Ceremonies	● Private Parties
● Wedding Receptions	☐ Accommodations

Set high up in the Saratoga foothills, this historic winery has wonderful sweeping views of the entire Silicon Valley. Amazingly, it only takes 15 minutes to drive here from the valley, and once you arrive, you'll be delighted with everything you see on the mountaintop.

The two main buildings on the property, the Historic Winery Building and the Chateau, were constructed in 1905 by French winemaker Paul Masson. Both are fashioned of stone masonry, and represent fine examples of French country architecture. Masson lived in the Chateau, where he often entertained guests like John Steinbeck and Charlie Chaplin (who had a fondness for pressing grapes himself). Host your own event here, and you'll understand why Chaplin was such a frequent visitor.

If you're planning a large indoor event, like a fundraising gala, wedding reception or casino night, reserve the ivy-covered Winery Building. Its stone walls and fragrant oak casks give the space a delicious, Old World ambiance. Outdoor ceremonies, champagne receptions and wine tastings are held in the Vista Point area, a tranquil slate patio bordered by trees and lush landscaping.

Expecting a crowd? The perfect spot is the Chateau Deck, an expansive terrace at the edge of the crest. Flanked by gardens and oak trees, it provides a view of the valley that will take your breath away. If you need a theater setting for your event, the Amphitheater is seasonally available. It has a stage with a striking backdrop: the stone portal of a San Jose cathedral that crumbled in the 1906 quake.

This venue is so versatile you're bound to find an area that fits your needs. In addition, corporations looking for team building programs will appreciate the innovative packages available, including gourmet cooking, treasure hunts and California wine tours.

The Mountain Winery has expanded its scope since its early days as a family winery, but still offers the same beauty and serenity that enchanted Paul Masson when he first came here almost a century ago.

CEREMONY & EVENT/RECEPTION CAPACITY: The winery can accommodate 20–200 seated or 25–300 standing indoors, and 20–2,500 seated or 20–5,000+ standing outdoors.

MEETING CAPACITY: There are 3 different indoor meeting rooms that can accommodate 10–300 seated, and multiple outdoor areas that can hold upwards of 2,500 people.

FEES & DEPOSITS: The rental fee, contract and estimated guest count are required when the facility is reserved. The final balance is due 1 week prior to the event. Site fees range $1,500–8,500 depending on guest count. Meals start at $50/person, plus tax and a 20% service charge.

The rental fee includes use of the site, rentals, setup, cleanup and staff. For business functions, it also includes meeting equipment.

AVAILABILITY: Year-round, daily, 8am–midnight.

SERVICES/AMENITIES:

Catering: provided
Kitchen Facilities: n/a
Tables & Chairs: provided
Linens, Silver, etc.: provided
Restrooms: wheelchair accessible
Dance Floor: provided
Bride's Dressing Area: yes
Meeting Equipment: flipcharts, overhead projector, screen, LCD projector

Parking: large lot
Accommodations: no guestrooms
Telephone: house phone
Outdoor Night Lighting: yes
Outdoor Cooking Facilities: CBA
Cleanup: provided
View: panorama of the valley floor and coastal hills

RESTRICTIONS:

Alcohol: provided, or wine corkage fee
Smoking: outside only
Music: amplified OK with volume limits

Wheelchair Access: yes
Insurance: liability required
Other: no rice, confetti

Saratoga Country Club

Country Club

21990 Prospect Road, Saratoga
408/253-0340

www.saratogacc.com
lthibeault@saratogacc.com

● Rehearsal Dinners	● Corp. Events/Mtgs.
● Ceremonies	● Private Parties
● Wedding Receptions	Accommodations

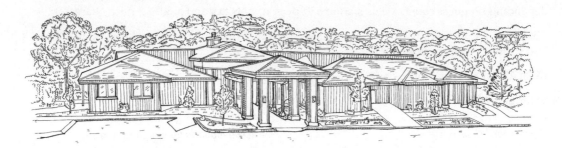

Perched high in the wooded hills above the Santa Clara Valley, the Saratoga Country Club offers everything you need for a superb wedding or festive gathering: beautiful surroundings, a romantic ceremony spot, a casually elegant clubhouse and fabulous food. And best of all, you don't have to be a member to host your event here.

The ceremony site, on top of a gentle hill, is one reason couples gravitate to the club. Drenched in sunlight and surrounded by panoramic hillside views, it's as pretty as a wedding bouquet. The centerpiece is a majestic, one-of-a-kind, fifteen-foot-high white wrought-iron dome gazebo, set on cobblestones. Encircled by a large lawn and enclosed by a decorative fence, it's a private haven for family and friends to witness your exchange of vows. After the ceremony, it's just a short walk to the clubhouse reception by way of a spectacular lighted staircase with white railings, flanked by pines and oleanders.

The contemporary clubhouse is a well-appointed two-story structure painted in soft beige that harmonizes with the encompassing hillsides. An imposing portico and pergola-shaded walkway add drama to the building's entrance, where the exquisitely crafted cherrywood and cut-glass double doors are reminiscent of the work of Frank Lloyd Wright. In the Main Dining Room, the cream-colored walls are awash in sunlight, thanks to plenty of large windows interspersed with stately columns. French doors lead to spacious decks overlooking the verdant golf course below and the Santa Clara Valley in the distance. There's also a dance floor and stage area, and the soft, neutral beige-and-white color scheme of the dining room allows you to dress it up or down to your taste. Needless to say, this facility is not limited to wedding receptions; in fact, when we viewed it, it was set up for a graduation party with bright colored napkins, star-garlanded centerpieces and displays of yearbook photos and other school-related decorations. The dining room is also available on a limited basis during the week for business functions.

Are all these great features beginning to intrigue you? Well, let us sweeten the pot just a little bit more. When you book your event at the Saratoga Country Club, you also get the services of events manager extraordinaire, Linda Thibeault. Her assistance is invaluable, especially for weddings. Every year, she updates a minutely detailed wedding guide outlining everything you need to know to plan your wedding, from a reception schedule to a list of preferred vendors. She's a calming influence for brides and a welcome resource for advice. Linda even provides a detailed map to send out with your invitations, in case some of your guests are directionally impaired (the country club's secluded location is just minutes from highways I-280, SR-85 and I-880). So, schedule a trip to the Saratoga Country Club. Even if you're not a member, you'll be given VIP treatment!

CEREMONY CAPACITY: The Lawn Area holds up to 250 seated guests.

EVENT/RECEPTION & MEETING CAPACITY: The Dining Room accommodates 250 seated guests. Conference rooms are available for smaller groups.

FEES & DEPOSITS: A nonrefundable deposit, based on a percentage of the room rental fee and/or catering costs, is required when the contract is signed. The balance may be paid in installments, depending on the amount of time remaining between the signing of the contract and the date of the event, with the final payment due 10 days prior to the event. Any additional balance accrued is due at the end of the event. Room rental fees range $360–3,600 depending on the space(s) rented. (Be sure to ask about any special offers!) Banquet and buffet meals are available and start at $54/person. Tax, alcohol and a 20% service charge are extra.

AVAILABILITY: Year-round, daily, 7am–1am.

SERVICES/AMENITIES:

Catering: provided, no BYO
Kitchen Facilities: n/a
Tables & Chairs: provided
Linens, Silver, etc.: provided
Restrooms: wheelchair accessible
Dance Floor: yes
Bride's Dressing Area: yes
Meeting Equipment: CBA, extra fee

Parking: ample on-site
Accommodations: no guestrooms
Telephone: house phone
Outdoor Night Lighting: no
Outdoor Cooking Facilities: no
Cleanup: provided
View: golf course and Santa Clara Valley
Other: event coordination

RESTRICTIONS:

Alcohol: provided, no BYO
Smoking: outdoors only
Music: amplified OK with restrictions

Wheelchair Access: yes
Insurance: not required
Other: no rice or birdseed

Saratoga Foothill Club

Historic Women's Club

20399 Park Place, Saratoga
408/867-3428
www.saratogafoothillclub.com
lbeesley@msn.com

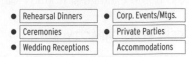

● Rehearsal Dinners	● Corp. Events/Mtgs.
● Ceremonies	● Private Parties
● Wedding Receptions	○ Accommodations

In a spot you'd never expect, on a quiet residential street near the crossroads of Big Basin and Sunnyvale/Saratoga Roads, lies the Foothill Club. This decorative 1915 Arts and Crafts-style building was designed by Julia Morgan as a women's club, and houses the oldest social organization in Saratoga. This structure ranks among the distinguished small redwood buildings of California, and in 1978 the clubhouse received the distinction of being listed in the National Register of Historic Landmarks.

The old-fashioned brown-shingled façade has a wood trellis framing unusually shaped windows. An adjoining paved courtyard is dotted with Japanese maples. It's small but very pretty and private.

The Club's formal redwood entry ushers you into a room that's perfect for a buffet arrangement. It has a 30-foot-high ceiling, a raised platform stage, hardwood floor and an elaborate window that filters in glorious sunlight, setting the room aglow. A buffet table can be situated in front of the window, creating a special and highlighted place for the wedding cake and cutting ceremony. With its overall feeling of Old World comfort and warmth, the Saratoga Foothill Club provides a pleasant and intimate environment for reception celebrations.

CEREMONY CAPACITY: The outdoor patio holds 100 seated, and the Club's interior holds 120 seated.

EVENT/RECEPTION CAPACITY: The site's maximum seated capacity is 150.

MEETING CAPACITY: The Main Room holds 200 seated theater-style.

FEES & DEPOSITS: A $500 refundable security deposit is required when reservations are made. The rental fee ranges $600–1,400. There is only one event per day. Wedding packages (based on 100 guests) start at $4,995 and include buffet, service, china, linens, cake, DJ and beverage package.

AVAILABILITY: Tuesday through Sunday, 9:30am–10pm.

SERVICES/AMENITIES:

Catering: provided by *Panetta's Catering*
Kitchen Facilities: moderate
Tables & Chairs: provided
Linens, Silver, etc.: through caterer
Restrooms: not wheelchair accessible
Dance Floor: yes
Bride's Dressing Area: yes
Meeting Equipment: BYO

Parking: call for details
Accommodations: no guestrooms
Telephone: house phone
Outdoor Night Lighting: yes
Outdoor Cooking Facilities: no
Cleanup: caterer or renter
View: of coastal hills and courtyard
Other: new air conditioning, baby grand piano available

RESTRICTIONS:

Alcohol: BYO wine, champagne and beer in bottles or cans; no kegs
Smoking: on patio only
Music: amplified OK with volume limits

Wheelchair Access: limited
Insurance: certificate required

This is important! Tell locations you're reading HERE COMES THE GUIDE and ask if our information is still current.

Villa Montalvo at Montalvo Arts Center

Historic Mansion & Grounds

15400 Montalvo Road, Saratoga
408/961-5856
www.montalvoarts.org
kkirkpatrick@montalvoarts.org

● Rehearsal Dinners	● Corp. Events/Mtgs.
● Ceremonies	● Private Parties
● Wedding Receptions	Accommodations

Nestled against a wooded slope in the private and secluded Saratoga hills is Montalvo Arts Center, a lovely complex with a variety of venues for concerts, weddings, corporate events and private parties. For weddings, the focal point of this estate is its beautiful Mediterranean-style mansion, Villa Montalvo. Built in 1912 as the private summer residence of Senator James Duval Phelan, this National Register Historic Landmark is now home to an arboretum and a nonprofit center for the arts.

An inviting one-way road leads up to Villa Montalvo. As you round the last turn, you get your first glimpse of the estate's expansive manicured lawns and colorful gardens, as well as the mansion's terracotta-tile roof, light stucco walls and wide veranda. To your left, you'll also see the Love Temple, one of two ceremony sites on the grounds; it's an open-air, white-columned pavilion set at the end of a wide, rose-lined brick path featuring historic marble statues. Couples get married on its steps, with a view of the surrounding Mediterranean garden and the Villa and woods in the background.

Directly behind the Villa, the Oval Garden offers a lush garden setting complete with classical statues and wisteria-covered pergolas. This open-air courtyard is an intimate and delightful place for a ceremony; a brick pathway serves as the center aisle, and a column-supported arcade is the backdrop for taking vows.

The Villa's first floor and outdoor patios are available for receptions. Guests can mingle on the veranda, sipping champagne and sampling hors d'oeuvres while enjoying splendid views of the estate's lawns and gardens. Reserve well in advance. The Montalvo Arts Center is an extraordinary site for an elegant and sophisticated wedding.

CEREMONY CAPACITY: The Oval Garden accommodates 200 seated. The Side Veranda seats 130 in case of inclement weather. The Love Temple capacity is 140.

EVENT/RECEPTION CAPACITY: The Villa's indoor capacity is 190 seated or 200 standing; outdoors, it's 300 seated or 1,000 standing. The Love Temple accommodates 140 seated. Events with over 300 guests may incur an additional cost, and require special arrangements with the Events Manager.

MEETING CAPACITY: Meeting venues accommodate groups of 4–300 people; the Villa's main floor holds up to 100. The Carriage House Theatre can accommodate up to 300 people seated theater-style. The outdoor Garden Theatre accommodates 1,100 guests. The upper Villa has 3 large rooms for staff meetings or dressing rooms. The Cottage accommodates up to 14 guests.

FEES & DEPOSITS: For weddings, the rental fee for 9 hours' use ranges $8,000–15,000. Note that rental fees paid over $3,500 are tax deductible. Half the total fee is required as a nonrefundable deposit when the site is booked; the balance is payable 6 months prior to the event along with a refundable $1,000 damage deposit and a certificate of insurance. For a Love Temple or Oval Garden ceremony only, the rental fee is $3,500. Call for details and for weekday and winter rates. Special rates apply for last-minute events.

For other special events and business functions, the Villa can accommodate groups of 4–2,000. For fees and details, call the Event Manager at 408/961-5856.

AVAILABILITY: Ceremonies are held year-round, and take place 10am–1pm. Ceremony/receptions are held year-round, 2pm–11pm in 9-hour blocks. For other special and business functions, contact the Events Manager.

SERVICES/AMENITIES:

Catering: select from preferred list
Kitchen Facilities: ample
Tables & Chairs: provided
Linens, Silver, etc.: caterer
Restrooms: wheelchair accessible
Dance Floor: yes
Bride's & Groom's Dressing Areas: yes
Meeting Equipment: full range CBA, extra fee

Parking: valet may be required for over 200 guests, carpooling encouraged
Accommodations: no guestrooms, hotel partners
Telephone: pay phone
Outdoor Night Lighting: yes
Outdoor Cooking Facilities: no
Cleanup: caterer
View: manicured lawns, formal gardens, historic sculptures and Santa Clara Valley vista

RESTRICTIONS:

Alcohol: through caterer
Smoking: outdoors only, designated area
Music: amplified OK with restrictions until 10pm

Wheelchair Access: yes
Insurance: certificate required

The Historic Del Monte Building

Banquet & Event Facility

100 South Murphy Avenue, Sunnyvale
408/735-7680
www.delvillas.com
info@delvillas.com

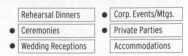

Rehearsal Dinners	● Corp. Events/Mtgs.
● Ceremonies	● Private Parties
● Wedding Receptions	Accommodations

Built in 1904 and originally used for drying and packing the Valley's apricots, peaches and prunes, the three-story Del Monte Building had been long neglected when a local developer decided to save and restore it. The process wasn't easy. First they had to hire three trucks to carefully move the wooden structure from its location beside railroad tracks to a breezy corner across the street. Then they spent a year rebuilding it from the outside in. Their hard work has paid off, and the beautifully refurbished Historic Del Monte Building is now a terrific place for wedding receptions or corporate meetings—right in the heart of Sunnyvale's vibrant downtown.

The main entrance is on a lovely treelined street. Take the wide carpeted staircase (or the elevator at the rear entrance) to the second and third floors where the fully equipped banquet facilities are located. When you step into the Grand Ballroom, everything you see is totally inviting, from the golden Wilshire chandeliers set against a stark white ceiling to the warm mahogany wainscoting. A gleaming hardwood dance floor dominates the room's center. During the day, light filters into the room through white-framed windows and French doors. Set back into another wall is a handcrafted bar fashioned out of mahogany and beveled glass mirrors.

The third floor houses the Del Monte Room, a smaller space with a cathedral ceiling supported by five white fluted columns. At night, a dozen gold-plaited faux candle chandeliers glow overhead, while during the day natural light flows in through windows along two sides. Like the Ballroom, the Del Monte Room has a built-in bar, and it also has a spacious outdoor terrace.

When you gaze up at the Del Monte Building, fronted by tall sycamore trees and illuminated by old-fashioned lamp posts, it's hard to believe that it was the first commercial structure erected in the city, that it led such a rugged prior existence and that it almost disappeared. By breathing new life into it, the developer not only preserved a little bit of Sunnyvale's past, but created a delightful place to celebrate.

CEREMONY CAPACITY: The building can accommodate up to 225 seated guests.

EVENT/RECEPTION CAPACITY: The Del Monte Room holds 170 seated with dancing or 350 standing; the Grand Ballroom, 280 seated with dancing or 500 standing guests.

MEETING CAPACITY: The Grand Ballroom holds 500 seated theater-style or 180 seated classroom-style. The Del Monte Room holds 275 theater-style or 100 seated classroom-style.

FEES & DEPOSITS: For wedding receptions, 50% of the rental fee is required when the site is booked; a second deposit is due 6 months prior to the event, with the remaining balances due 1 week prior to the event. Wedding packages start at $45/person, and can include meals, wedding cake, flowers and DJ. Beverage packages and tax are additional. December pricing may vary; call for specific information. For other months, rental fees range up to $3,550 depending on date, time and space rented. Call for specific details.

AVAILABILITY: Year-round, Monday–Thursday 7am–11pm; Friday and Saturday 7am–midnight or Sundays until 9pm. Ceremonies take place Friday evenings 6:30pm–7:30pm or Sundays noon–4pm.

SERVICES/AMENITIES:

Catering: provided
Kitchen Facilities: n/a
Tables & Chairs: provided
Linens, Silver, etc.: provided
Restrooms: wheelchair accessible
Dance Floor: provided
Bride's Dressing Area: no
Meeting Equipment: full range

Parking: lots and on street
Accommodations: no guestrooms
Telephone: pay phone
Outdoor Night Lighting: deck only
Outdoor Cooking Facilities: no
Cleanup: provided
View: downtown Sunnyvale
Other: full event coordination

RESTRICTIONS:

Alcohol: provided, no BYO
Smoking: deck only
Music: amplified OK indoors

Wheelchair Access: yes
Insurance: not required

Orchard Pavilion
at the Sunnyvale Community Center

550 East Remington Drive, Sunnyvale
408/730-7751
http://weddings.insunnyvale.com
rcotter@ci.sunnyvale.ca.us

Banquet & Community Facility

● Rehearsal Dinners	● Corp. Events/Mtgs.
● Ceremonies	● Private Parties
● Wedding Receptions	Accommodations

Gazing out the towering windows at the lush, rolling grounds, the lake with dancing fountains, and the sun-drenched patio area, you'd swear you'd landed at an exclusive country club. You'd be absolutely wrong. This lovely locale—the Orchard Pavilion at the Sunnyvale Community Center—is one of the most reasonably priced, yet visually appealing, venues in the South Bay.

The Pavilion is actually located in the complex's new Senior Center, which opened its doors in July of 2003. But banish any visions of cramped, gloomy rooms full of endless bingo games. Instead, prepare to experience 32-foot ceilings, bleached parquet floors, and graceful curving architecture that affords sweeping views of the 11-acre gardens and grounds.

Accented by several extraordinary glass and bronze sculptures, the Center's design has already received several awards. Wander past the reception area and down a vast, whitewashed hallway that's open to the second story, and you'll find almost limitless options for events both large and small.

The centerpiece of the facility is undisputedly the Orchard Pavilion. An airy room of nearly 5,000 square feet, it can be used in its entirety or divided into three smaller spaces. Skylit cupolas top each section, allowing a natural brightness to wash over the light-colored floors and walls. All three sections also feature south-facing, floor-to-ceiling windows and doors that open to the 4,000-square-foot patio and uninterrupted views of the lake and fountains just beyond.

Specifically designed with events in mind, the Pavilion comes with a separate service entrance that provides easy access to the industrial-sized kitchen, as well as unobtrusive deliveries to the banquet rooms. Behind a full-length curtain on one wall is a raised stage area that's perfect for either the band or the wedding party.

Couples who prefer to say their vows in the open air often choose the patio for the ceremony. Afterwards, everyone drifts inside for the reception and dancing, or the entire event can be staged al fresco. Low-slung granite seats along the patio's border invite guests to relax and enjoy the meticulously groomed gardens, which are adorned with flowers year-round.

If you have a more intimate event in mind, the Center's Oak Lounge is ideally suited with its dark-oak floors, comfy leather couches and chairs, and scattering of tables that encourage conversation. You might also use this space for a pre-ceremony cocktail party or the receiving line.

The Community Center houses still more alternatives for the cost-conscious. A ballroom in an adjoining building has a dark wood parquet floor and ample space for dining and dancing. With its floor-to-ceiling windows, and a pass-through bar revealing a patio bedecked with clay tubs full of flowers, the room encourages guests to stroll outside and take in the views. Here, a small pond with cubist-style concrete fountains makes the perfect backdrop for a sunlit ceremony.

There's no shortage of smaller rooms that may be used as the bridal party's changing spaces, for gift display, or anything else your wedding requires. One visit and you'll agree: This stunning facility is much more "Ritz" than Rec Center.

CEREMONY, EVENT/RECEPTION & MEETING CAPACITY: The facility holds up to 300 guests, seated or standing.

FEES & DEPOSITS: A deposit ranging $500–1,000 is required to reserve your date. The balance is due 30 days before event. Rental fees range $60–300/hour depending on space rented.

AVAILABILITY: Year-round. Events must conclude no later than midnight (including cleanup time).

SERVICES/AMENITIES:

Catering: BYO, licensed and insured
Kitchen Facilities: fully equipped
Tables & Chairs: provided
Linens, Silver, etc.: through caterer
Restrooms: wheelchair accessible
Dance Floor: yes
Bride's Dressing Area: CBA
Meeting Equipment: provided, may be extra charge

Parking: public lot
Accommodations: no guestrooms
Telephone: pay phone
Outdoor Night Lighting: yes
Outdoor Cooking Facilities: BYO
Cleanup: caterer or renter
View: pond, fountain, landscaped grounds
Other: sound system

RESTRICTIONS:

Alcohol: BYO with licensed server
Smoking: designated areas
Music: amplified OK indoors

Wheelchair Access: yes
Insurance: liability required

Overwhelmed? Use the search criteria on www.HereComesTheGuide.com to narrow down your choices.

Tri-Valley and Livermore Area

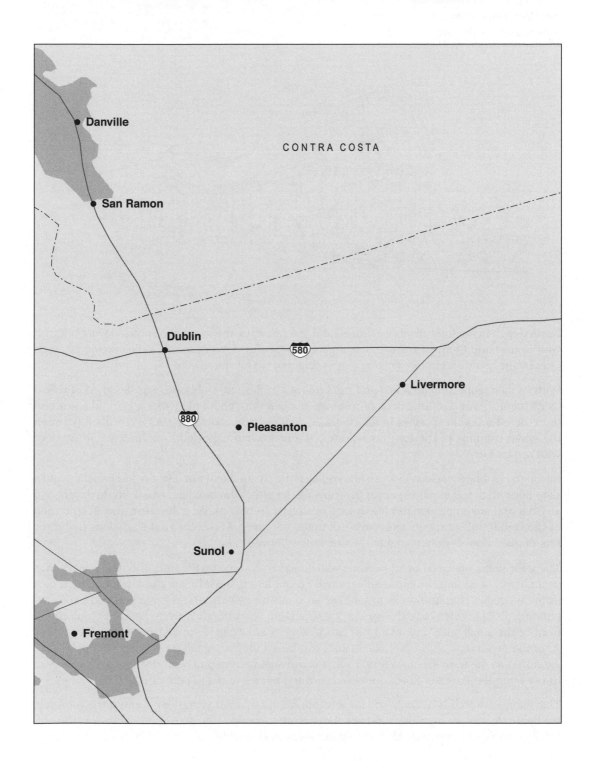

Danville

CONTRA COSTA

San Ramon

Dublin

580

Livermore

880

Pleasanton

Sunol

Fremont

Dublin Ranch Golf Course

5900 Signal Hill Drive, Dublin
925/556-7040 X201
www.dublinranchgolf.com
kmoran@dublinranchgolf.com

Golf Course and Clubhouse

● Rehearsal Dinners	● Corp. Events/Mtgs.
● Ceremonies	● Private Parties
● Wedding Receptions	Accommodations

Nestled high in the foothills above the 680 and 580 freeways, the recently completed Dublin Ranch Golf Course and Clubhouse enjoys uncommonly beautiful views of the Tri-Valley previously seen only by the cattle and horses grazing on the neighboring hillsides.

With its pale taupe shingle siding and gambrel-roof gables, the clubhouse was designed to reflect its 21st-century rural setting. Beds of roses are planted throughout the parking lot, and a graceful three-tiered fountain splashes in the center of a large circular driveway. As we walked between the white columns of the enormous porte-cochère we half expected to be greeted at the door with a mint julep.

Inside the clubhouse, clean modern lines replace the pastoral exterior. Light wood paneling and a slate floor mark the expansive foyer that runs the length of the building. Guests in the bright and airy bar and adjoining Banquet Room look out at the 18-hole public golf course and steep terrain of the Dublin hills through wide panels of tinted windows. At the end of the spacious hall three sets of glass double doors open to the Clubhouse Terrace.

The wide patio, enclosed by a low stone wall edged with crepe myrtle trees and rose bushes, was created with weddings in mind. All eyes will be on the bride as she approaches the garden gate from an outside path and walks toward her groom, waiting beneath the large portico next to the building. Couples also have the option of exchanging vows beside a white lattice arch placed in front of the small gate, and additional lattice screens are available to add privacy to the setting. After the ceremony, umbrella-shaded tables can be set up for a small outdoor reception or as an extension to the festivities held inside. On a warm summer's night you and your guests can even throw open the Banquet Room doors and turn the terrace into an open-air dance floor.

The Banquet Room is a lovely site for a reception at any time of the day. During the morning, sunlight streams through the windows. Later in the evening, the soft dome lamps on the coffered ceiling cast a romantic glow on the guests, seated at tables set with white linens and china.

Dublin Ranch offers a variety of banquet menus, with your choice of plated or buffet service, that are designed to please even the most finicky of palates. Everyone from the Executive Chef and Event Manager to the service staff is eager to work with the bride and groom making them feel right at home. In addition, only one event is scheduled at a time, ensuring that each couple gets the attention they deserve.

CEREMONY CAPACITY: The Terrace holds up to 150 seated guests; the Ceremony Lawn up to several hundred seated guests. Indoors, the Banquet Room up to 180 seated guests.

EVENT/RECEPTION CAPACITY: The Clubhouse Terrace holds up to 120 seated or 180 standing guests; the Banquet Room can accommodate up to 180 seated or 200 standing guests. The venue can hold up to 275 seated guests if you combine both indoor and outdoor spaces.

MEETING CAPACITY: Event spaces hold up to 180 guests seated theater-style.

FEES & DEPOSITS: A $1,000 deposit is required to reserve your date. 50% of the event total is due 6 months prior and the balance is due 14 days prior to the event. Rental fees range $250–1,500 depending on nature of event, day and time. Meals range $25–58/person. Tax, alcohol and a 19% service charge are additional.

AVAILABILITY: Year-round, anytime.

SERVICES/AMENITIES:

Catering: provided
Kitchen Facilities: n/a
Tables & Chairs: provided
Linens, Silver, etc.: provided
Restrooms: wheelchair accessible
Dance Floor: yes
Bride's Dressing Room: yes
Meeting Equipment: CBA, extra charge
Other: event coordination, use of clubhouse grounds for photography

Parking: complimentary large lot, valet available
Accommodations: many hotels nearby
Telephone: emergency use only, excellent cell phone reception
Outdoor Night Lighting: yes
Outdoor Cooking Facilities: BBQ
Cleanup: provided
View: mountains, golf course, cityscape

RESTRICTIONS:

Alcohol: provided, full-service bar
Smoking: outdoors only
Music: amplified OK indoors and outdoors with restrictions, live musicians welcome

Wheelchair Access: yes
Insurance: not required

The Clubhouse at Las Positas

Golf Course and Clubhouse

915 Clubhouse Drive, Livermore
925/455-7070
www.clubhousecatering.com, www.beebsatlaspositas.com
jensolaro@yahoo.com

- Rehearsal Dinners
- Ceremonies
- Wedding Receptions
- Corp. Events/Mtgs.
- Private Parties
- Accommodations

Used to be a town like Livermore was simply a place you passed through on your way to somewhere bigger and better; but not anymore. These days, Livermore is often called "Little Napa" for its growing wine industry, and folks from all over the Bay Area routinely stop here to sample the wines and enjoy the combination of small-town hospitality and rural flavor. They've also discovered another local attraction: the Clubhouse and Golf Course at Las Positas. This popular facility is in demand not just for golf, but for weddings, corporate banquets and other special celebrations. What makes it so appealing? Great service and a versatile setting for a reasonable price.

The Clubhouse includes Beeb's Sports Bar & Grill, a private banquet room, and a patio—all with lovely views of the manicured grounds. The enthusiastic staff are genuinely pleased to serve, so it's no wonder that the two words that come to mind when you visit the clubhouse are "friendly" and "fun."

The "fun" starts at Beeb's Sports Bar & Grill, which has been consistently voted "Best Sports Bar in Alameda County." The restaurant's lively atmosphere and built-in service area are just right for a casual celebration. Boasting an impressive collection of sports memorabilia, games, and television sets, Beeb's has plenty to keep the sports enthusiast engaged. Seated guests can even enjoy a little golf (vicariously, of course) by watching the putting action just beyond the bank of dining room windows.

For something more formal, opt for the Clubhouse's banquet room with its own private entrance and dance floor. A high, pyramid-shaped ceiling meets walls of windows trimmed in wood; a ledge above the windows decked with ivy and twinkle lights adds a festive touch. One of the nicest features of the banquet room is that it opens onto the patio, allowing your event to become instantly al fresco. The ample patio, shaded by a deep, wooden overhang, is delightful for a buffet or barbecue. It's also a great spot for cocktails and appetizers before inviting your guests inside for a buffet reception. And whether you're on the patio or in the banquet room, the pastoral vista is always there, lending a feeling of peaceful contentment.

That view also makes a picturesque backdrop for couples who get married here. Ceremonies usually take place out on the private lawn under an archway. The surrounding hillsides cradle acres of lawn dotted with trees and colorful blooms, while several quaint footbridges arch over a running stream.

As you can see, you don't need to be a sports aficionado to fully appreciate the Clubhouse at Las Positas. However, if you would like to make sports an integral part of your event, it's very easy to do: The banquet room has TV monitors ready and waiting. Show an instructional video to improve your group's golf game, or entertain guests with "athletic" home movies. One group of partying skydivers played tapes of their most spectacular jumps! Brides and grooms have even made use of the AV equipment to show a retrospective of them growing up. And don't forget golf—a tournament can be incorporated into any event—including a wedding!

Wherever inspiration takes you, the Clubhouse staff will follow. As the folks here are fond of saying, "If we don't have it, we will find it and provide it for you." Now, that's the kind of attitude that has made Las Positas not just a local favorite, but a bona fide Bay Area destination.

CEREMONY CAPACITY: The Ceremony Site holds 270 seated guests; the Clubhouse, 130 seated guests.

EVENT/RECEPTION CAPACITY: The Banquet Room can accommodate 130 seated or 150 standing guests; the Patio holds 140 seated or 220 standing guests.

MEETING CAPACITY: Event spaces accommodate 30–150 seated guests.

FEES & DEPOSITS: For weddings and social functions, a $1,000 deposit is required to reserve your date; the balance is due 10 days prior to the event. Room rental fees range $800–1,400. Buffets run $30–36/person. Wedding packages are available starting at $36/person and include appetizers, champagne toast and dinner. Beverage packages start at $15/person. Custom menus are available. Tax, alcohol and a 19% service charge are additional. A $400 ceremony setup fee is extra.

For business functions, a $100–500 deposit is required to reserve your date. The balance is due the day of the event. Room rental fees range $200–500 depending on space rented. Meals run $6–19/person; tax, alcohol and a 19% service charge are additional.

AVAILABILITY: Year-round, daily, 6am–1am. Site tours are by appointment only.

SERVICES/AMENITIES:

Catering: provided
Kitchen Facilities: n/a
Tables & Chairs: provided
Linens, Silver, etc.: provided
Restrooms: wheelchair accessible
Dance Floor: provided
Bride's Dressing Area: yes
Meeting Equipment: some provided, more CBA

Parking: large lot
Accommodations: no guestrooms
Telephone: emergency use only
Outdoor Night Lighting: yes
Outdoor Cooking Facilities: BBQ CBA
Cleanup: provided
View: 22-acre landscaped park
Other: event coordination, big screen TV, projector screen

RESTRICTIONS:

Alcohol: provided or WC with corkage fee
Smoking: outside only
Music: amplified OK

Wheelchair Access: yes
Insurance: not required
Other: no birdseed or rice

Concannon Vineyard

Winery

4590 Tesla Road, Livermore
925/583-1570
www.concannonvineyard.com
jennifer.franklin@concannonvineyard.com

- Rehearsal Dinners
- Ceremonies
- Wedding Receptions
- Corp. Events/Mtgs.
- Private Parties
- Accommodations

Here is a property that began with a personal dream and became a shared one. When James Concannon first settled on his land in 1883 and started making the wines that would one day win awards, he couldn't possibly have known that his vision and success would come to be appreciated by so many. Perhaps it was the luck of the Irish; certainly that ebullient and fortunate spirit is the essence of Concannon Vineyard.

Set on 200 acres in the middle of Livermore Wine Country, Concannon Vineyard is an instant charmer. The red roses and whimsical topiary creatures that dot the vine-bordered drive, the faint fragrance of developing wine, and the beautiful structures and grounds immediately win visitors over. But they're only a prelude to delights in store.

You might want to linger in the historic Tasting Room sampling the vineyard's renowned wines and hospitality, but tear yourself away and move on to the private event spaces for a truly dazzling experience.

Have your ceremony or celebration on the lawn in front of the Ellen Rowe Concannon Victorian. Pretty as a wedding cake, its graceful white balconies, banisters and porch can be easily wrapped or draped in ribbons of color, light, greenery or flowers. Clay-colored walkways crisscross the grass; rose bushes, silvery olive trees and a gorgeous vineyard surround lend a natural elegance. The mansion's handsomely appointed interior is a great place for a private meeting, a tête-à-tête that means business, or a luxurious hideaway for the bride.

Sound exquisite? Well, there's also the Concannon Grape Arbor, nearly 2,500 linear feet of peaceful, grape-shaded space set between new vineyard and maturing vines. Have a sunny luncheon, a starlit dinner or walk down the aisle under the shining leaves and grape clusters. It's also a spectacular spot in which to set up an ultralong king's table for a glittering Wine Country repast.

Of course one of the treats that vintners sometimes offer is access to the dramatic barrel room and Concannon is no exception. You could also dine in the property's Cask and Barrel Room, where French white oak upright barrels lining the entrance soar toward the lofty ceiling. The smaller French roll barrels can be arranged in any configuration and offer a fragrant backdrop for a fête of regal dimensions. The space is both intimate and grand, great for a cocktail reception and passed hors d'oeuvres or a sit-down affair; the polished floor is an eloquent invitation to dance.

The adjacent Trade Development Center provides additional options for entertaining when your group demands an even bigger space. Equipped with portable podiums, a built-in screen and projector, a DVD player, wireless handheld and lavalier microphones and more, it's ideal for corporate retreats, meetings and large banquet-style celebrations. Sliding partitions can divide the venue into two separate rooms, and a spacious patio framed by the estate's cherished vines allows you to take your festivities outdoors. So many possibilities for a glorious gathering…and best of all: You can toast your success with fabulous Concannon wines.

CEREMONY CAPACITY: The facility holds 250 seated guests indoors and 350 seated outdoors.

EVENT/RECEPTION CAPACITY: The vineyard can accommodate 400 seated or 500 standing indoors and 250 seated or 350 standing outdoors.

MEETING CAPACITY: Meeting spaces hold 100 seated guests.

FEES & DEPOSITS: 50% of the total event cost is required to reserve your date and the balance is due 30 days prior to the event. Rental fees range $500–6,500 depending on the day and time of the event and the space rented.

AVAILABILITY: Year-round, 8am–10pm for indoor locations and 8am–8pm for outdoor locations.

SERVICES/AMENITIES:

Catering: select from preferred list
Kitchen Facilities: n/a
Tables & Chairs: some provided
Linens, Silver, etc.: through caterer
Restrooms: wheelchair accessible
Dance Floor: provided
Bride's Dressing Area: CBA
Meeting Equipment: some provided

Parking: large lot
Accommodations: no guestrooms
Telephone: emergency use only
Outdoor Night Lighting: CBA
Outdoor Cooking Facilities: BBQ CBA
Cleanup: provided
View: garden courtyard, landscaped grounds, panorama of vineyards
Other: picnic area, event coordination

RESTRICTIONS:

Alcohol: provided
Smoking: designated areas only
Music: amplified OK with restrictions

Wheelchair Access: yes
Insurance: liability required

The professionals in the back of this book are the best in the business. How do we know? Read page 701.

Garré Vineyard & Winery
and Martinelli Event Center

7986 Tesla Road, Livermore
925/371-8200
www.garrewinery.com
garre@garrewinery.com

Vineyard & Winery

● Rehearsal Dinners	● Corp. Events/Mtgs.
● Ceremonies	● Private Parties
● Wedding Receptions	Accommodations

Garré Vineyard & Winery is a bit like a small village—a charming one surrounded by grapevines. One of the Livermore Valley's original wineries, this gem, with its Italian Wine Country style, has always drawn a crowd. Maybe it's because of the café on the premises, the park-like setting, the Tasting Room or the jazz they serve up with the food and the bocce ball.

That popularity has increased even more with Garré's Martinelli Event Center, a private facility located just a short drive up the hill from the winery. Set on an elevated vineyard, it's a grand Hacienda-style venue with wrought-iron gates, a bell tower, and palm trees at the entrance. The ballroom, which has been designed for both beauty and versatility, features a vaulted beamed ceiling, wood wainscoting and accents, high windows, and contemporary chandeliers. There are three built-in, remote-controlled projection screens (for that slide show of the bride and groom), as well as wireless microphones for the toasts. The building's stone-paved inner courtyard with fireplace and fountain is ideal for a bar setup and appetizers, or for a reception under the stars. A nearby ceremony site is not only surrounded by vines, but also offers views of vineyard-laced rolling hills. The entire facility—including an enormous patio and lawn, an exquisite bridal suite, and a comfortable groom's dressing area—is laid out in a way that allows for seamless transitions from ceremony to hors d'oeuvres to dining and dancing.

Back down the hill on the winery property is the Grand Pavilion and Oak Staging Area, another gorgeous wedding site. Old-fashioned 19th-century streetlamps line the paths and illuminate the area at night. One walkway leads up to a small stage beneath the property's centuries-old oak tree. Bordered by flowerbeds and Italian cypress and backed by rows of Cabernet vines, this is a dignified spot for a ceremony. Across the grass, an elegant white pavilion provides 6,000 square feet of banquet and dance space for large parties. During the summer, the walls of the "big white tent" can come down, revealing the surrounding vineyards and gardens and connecting the ceremony area with the reception site. It's an incredibly festive environment and a marvelous place to sample the masterful pairings of food and wine recommended and prepared by Chef Ty Turner. Try a Garré Vineyard Cabernet Sauvignon with pan-seared fillet mignon wrapped in bacon with wild mushroom demi-glaze and freshly grated horseradish mashed potatoes. Or, indulge in a Cabernet Franc with Dijon-herb encrusted rack of lamb with truffled white bean ragout and Cabernet

Franc reduction. Two full-size bocce ball courts that are lit at night offer a before- and after-dinner diversion, adding to the Old World ambiance.

In 2011 Garré plans to break ground on an additional 15,000-square-foot building that will showcase a larger café and a new event center with environmentally friendly features like solar panels and a recycled cork floor. Executive Chef Turner also intends to offer a "green" wedding package, focusing on locally grown and organic ingredients.

Tours of Garré Winery's event sites are by appointment only. We suggest that to really experience what Garré is like, make a reservation for lunch or dinner, too. That way you'll be able to stroll the grounds, take in the views, and taste their award-winning food and wine.

CEREMONY CAPACITY: The Martinelli Event Center holds up to 250, and the Pavilion up to 300 seated guests.

EVENT/RECEPTION CAPACITY: The Café holds up to 75 seated guests, the Café Courtyard up to 100, the Martinelli Center up to 250, and the Pavilion up to 300.

MEETING CAPACITY: Spaces are available for 12–200 guests. Facilities include conference capabilities.

FEES & DEPOSITS: A $1,200 nonrefundable deposit is required to reserve your date, and the balance is due 2 weeks prior to the event. Rental fees range $400–4,000 depending on the venue, day and guest count. Meals range $35–75/person. Tax, alcohol and a 20% service charge are additional.

AVAILABILITY: Year-round, daily, anytime.

SERVICES/AMENITIES:

Catering: provided
Kitchen Facilities: n/a
Tables & Chairs: provided, Chiaviari chairs at Event Ctr.
Linens, Silver, etc.: provided
Restrooms: wheelchair accessible
Dance Floor: yes
Bride's Dressing Area: yes
Meeting Equipment: video projectors, DVD/VCR, amplifier, electronically operated projection screen, program speakers, wireless microphone, wireless connections

Parking: ample on-site
Accommodations: no guestrooms
Telephone: emergency use only
Outdoor Night Lighting: yes
Outdoor Cooking Facilities: no
Cleanup: provided
View: vineyards, valley, mountains, meadow, fountain, gardens

RESTRICTIONS:

Alcohol: provided, WBC only
Smoking: outdoors only
Music: amplified OK

Wheelchair Access: yes
Insurance: liability required

Murrieta's Well

Wine Estate

3005 Mines Road, Livermore
925/456-2425

www.murrietaswell.com
catering@wentevineyards.com

● Rehearsal Dinners	● Corp. Events/Mtgs.
● Ceremonies	● Private Parties
● Wedding Receptions	Accommodations

An almost operatic love for romance might seize you when you first set eyes upon this lovely little wine estate, tucked away in a pastoral fold of picturesque Livermore Valley. Named for the artesian well where Joaquin Murrieta, the notorious Robin Hood of El Dorado, and his band of desperados purportedly watered their horses, this history-rich property is just the place for an event worth singing about for decades.

Your celebration can begin on the graceful Vineyard Patio. The enchanting 100-year-old winery building with its huge double doors and second-story balcony provides an elegant backdrop to every party played out here. Artistically and fragrantly framed in bright bursts of crimson—red roses, geraniums, wispy bottlebrush and a delicate Japanese maple—and by the 92-acre vineyard that yields the grapes for the property's handcrafted blends of Meritage, Zarzuela and Zinfandel wines, this attractive outdoor space is ideal for a wedding ceremony, a reception, or any other affair set—California style—under a canopy of brilliant blue or starry-night skies.

For show-stopping entrances and tasteful transitions, use the terracotta stairway accented with antique Spanish tiles that winds its way, via a gentle, lushly planted slope, from the patio to the quiet Upper Terrace. A red-carpet-caliber stop for photo ops, it looks out over the small adobe fountain that caps the well of legend and lore. Guests can stroll up this stairway after the ceremony to cocktails, passed hors d'oeuvres and gorgeous views that stretch from the chestnut mares whinnying in a lower pasture to a skyline of oaks and palms.

Dinner and dancing are served up in style in the wonderful old winery building. In its appropriately named Barrel Room, located on the ground floor, heavy wood beams and pillars, high ceilings, rustic stone walls and ancient wine barrels create a dramatic ambiance. The twinkling lights and twining vines that climb the broad wooden columns add a theatrical touch designed to transport your guests to another place and time. Any little additions—white-clad tables, glassware and cutlery, simple arrangements of flowers—look remarkable in this room. It's an interior rich with the flavor of tradition and good living that typifies the wine country experience, one that's sure to enhance the sparkle of your event.

At the back of the Barrel Room a wooden staircase leads upstairs to the broad tasting room foyer, where a trellised breezeway offers guests a private place to take a breather from all the excitement. At the foot of the stairway, an enormous gilt mirror doubles the pleasure of admiring your wedding cake. And throughout your reception, Wente Vineyards' award-winning restaurant and catering staff (set up out of sight on the second floor) whisks upstairs and down with their mouthwatering pairings of fabulous food and fine Murrieta's Well and Wente Vineyards wines.

CEREMONY CAPACITY: Outdoor spaces are available, seating up to 110 guests.

EVENT/RECEPTION & MEETING CAPACITY: Indoor and outdoor spaces are available, holding up to 110 seated or 150 standing guests.

FEES & DEPOSITS: A $500–2,000 deposit is required to reserve your date. An estimated 50% of the final balance is due 6 months prior to the event. The anticipated balance is payable 2 weeks prior to the event; all incurred expenses are due the day of the event. Rental fees range $500–2,000 depending on the day and season of the event. *Wente Catering* provides sit-down dinners and buffets, including a custom-designed wedding cake. These range $45–75/person. Tax, beverages, rentals and a 20% service charge are additional.

AVAILABILITY: Year-round, daily, 6pm–11pm.

SERVICES/AMENITIES:

Catering: provided
Kitchen Facilities: n/a
Tables & Chairs: provided
Linens, Silver, etc.: provided
Restrooms: wheelchair accessible
Dance Floor: CBA
Bride's & Groom's Dressing Areas: no
Meeting Equipment: CBA

Parking: large lot
Accommodations: no guestrooms
Telephone: emergency use only
Outdoor Night Lighting: yes
Outdoor Cooking Facilities: no
Cleanup: provided
View: vineyards, garden, hills
Other: event coordination, custom-designed wedding cake

RESTRICTIONS:

Alcohol: provided
Smoking: outside only
Music: amplified OK

Wheelchair Access: yes
Insurance: not required

Poppy Ridge Golf Course
Rees Jones Scottish Heathland Course

Golf Course and Clubhouse

4280 Greenville Road, Livermore
925/447-6779
www.poppyridgegolf.com
jahlman@poppyridgegolf.com

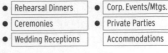

- Rehearsal Dinners
- Ceremonies
- Wedding Receptions
- Corp. Events/Mtgs.
- Private Parties
- Accommodations

You might expect thoroughbreds to canter up to the white fence that lines the drive to Poppy Ridge. The narrow road, divided by young grapevines along the median strip, winds through the biscuit-colored hills to a graceful hacienda-style clubhouse. Set on a hill, the spacious, tile-roofed edifice overlooks the forever-verdant fairways and greens of the Poppy Ridge Golf Course, one of the Northern California Golf Association's two premier golf facilities. First opened for play in 1996, the 27-hole course and clubhouse is the sister facility of top-ranked Poppy Hills Golf Course in Pebble Beach and, like the flower it's named for, it epitomizes the sunny charm of the Golden State.

Friendly double doors open to a siesta-quiet lobby, where a large round table invites guests to sign in. Sunlight cascades through skylights, warming the rich earth tones of the carpet and drenching the pale yellow walls. On the far side of the lobby, the high-ceilinged Poppy Ridge Grill and Bar is a picturesque place for weddings, company celebrations, tournament banquets and more. It has two walls of windows, an expansive wraparound deck and a full walk-up bar. The north window's commanding view of the Chardonnay and Zinfandel courses was voted "Best Restaurant View" by the *Tri-Valley Herald* in 2003, making it a prime spot to situate a banquet table or buffet.

In addition to its enviable vista, the restaurant has also earned high marks from repeat clientele for great food: The menus for hors d'oeuvres, sit-down dinners and buffets are mouthwatering. Start out with smoked salmon crostini with herb cream cheese, vegetable spring rolls with chili-garlic dipping sauce and crispy coconut prawns. Move on to marinated tri-tip of beef with wild mushroom sauce or ginger-sesame glaze, baked Alaskan salmon with fresh pineapple salsa, or applewood-smoked pork loin chops with apricot-cherry sauce. The site fee—an incredible value—includes an event planner and on-site coordinator, bartender, and all the props for the right presentation. And, of course, the staff is expert at personalizing any event.

If you'd rather entertain outdoors, reserve one of the building's wide sun-splashed decks with their unobscured backdrops of sapphire lakes and emerald greens. There's plenty of room for a ceremony on the pleasant east deck, where the accommodating staff will set up a beautiful arbor and chairs for your guests. Crystal and flatware sparkle in the natural light on the partially covered north deck, with its lofty Spanish-style tower and sweeping, flower-lined stairway. Whatever the occasion, this is a glorious setting for making merry. Lean out over the balustrade to admire the scenic surround, retire to a shady spot for an appreciative pause or raise a toast in the archway of the tower, where a delicate lantern hangs and swallows occasionally flit back and forth into the shadows. Then, grab colleagues, family and friends for a photo shoot on the property—with so much lovely scenery around, your photographer will have no trouble creating perfect portraits to add to your album of memories.

CEREMONY CAPACITY: Poppy Ridge holds up to 200 seated guests, indoors or outdoors.

EVENT/RECEPTION CAPACITY: Indoors, Poppy Ridge holds up to 160 seated or 300 standing guests; outdoors, up to 175 seated or 200 standing guests.

MEETING CAPACITY: Spaces are available which hold up to 100 guests.

FEES & DEPOSITS: The rental fee is required to reserve your date. The balance is due 14 days prior to the event. Rental fees range $300–3,000 depending on the type of event. Meals range $39–48/person. Tax, alcohol and service charge are additional.

AVAILABILITY: Year-round, daily, 6am–midnight. Site tours by appointment.

SERVICES/AMENITIES:
Catering: provided, no BYO
Kitchen Facilities: full kitchen
Tables & Chairs: provided
Linens, Silver, etc.: provided
Restrooms: wheelchair accessible
Dance Floor: yes, extra fee
Bride's Dressing Area: yes
Meeting Equipment: CBA, extra charge

Parking: for up to 300 cars
Accommodations: no guestrooms
Telephone: emergency use only
Outdoor Night Lighting: yes
Outdoor Cooking Facilities: yes
Cleanup: caterer or renter
View: vineyards, fairways, hills, pond
Other: event coordination; event security, extra fee

RESTRICTIONS:
Alcohol: provided or BYO WC with corkage fee
Smoking: outdoors only
Music: amplified OK

Wheelchair Access: yes
Insurance: may be required

Want to know WHAT TO ASK a potential location or vendor? Check out our Questions to Ask on page 17.

Shrine Event Center

Banquet Facility

170 Lindbergh Avenue, Livermore
925/373-4880
www.shrineeventcenter.com
sales@shrineeventcenter.com

● Rehearsal Dinners ● Corp. Events/Mtgs.
● Ceremonies ● Private Parties
● Wedding Receptions Accommodations

Towering palms and lithe willow trees flank the Shrine Event Center, whose spacious interior has hosted many a wonderful celebration. The grand ballroom is larger than most event facilities in the area, and it can take on any theme you have in mind.

Events often begin in the Lounge, where two built-in, brass-trimmed bars with mirrored backsplashes make serving cocktails both attractive and easy. Matching nearby counters can hold the appetizer or dessert display. The Lounge is also a fun retreat for after-dinner cordials.

The Lounge leads directly into the Lindbergh Ballroom, the centerpiece of the venue. Open, airy and contemporary, the ballroom features a dramatic vaulted ceiling with polished wooden beams. Rows of fabric swags overhead lend a soft, elegant look. At one end of the ballroom, an east-facing stage is perfect for your band or DJ, while risers are available for elevating the head table just below. The state-of-the-art sound system ensures that everyone will be able to hear everything clearly, whether they're listening to live music, a DJ or an emcee.

One of the best things about the Shrine Event Center is its adaptability. The ballroom magically takes on whatever ambiance you have in mind. For a sophisticated soirée, deck the space out in white linen and crystal. If you're planning something more informal, like a luau-style banquet, the room easily transforms into a Caribbean paradise with vibrant colors and tropical décor. Add tulle, flowers, or twinkle lights as the spirit moves you. Track lighting on dimmers allows you to adjust the mood throughout your party. There's also a retractable screen for showing a photo or video montage, and even a disco ball in case you want to turn it up a notch when the dancing gets going. The on-site coordinator will work with you to design your event, and can recommend vendors to help you bring your ideas to life.

If you like, host both your ceremony and reception in the ballroom. Movable room dividers let you create separate areas if desired. Large conferences or banquets can combine adjacent breakout rooms with the ballroom, and seat up to 1,000 guests theater-style! It's no wonder this venue is so in demand for receptions, proms, quinceañeras, bar/bat mitzvahs, trade shows and other big events.

The Shrine Event Center is easily accessible by freeway and close to local hotels (one within walking distance), restaurants and nightclubs—something you'll appreciate if you're inviting out-of-town guests. Plus, there are plenty of nearby wineries, hiking trails and other attractions to keep your family and friends happily occupied before and after your event.

Noted worldwide for their philanthropy, the Shriners and other charities are making a real difference. It's good to know that when you rent the Shrine Event Center, you're helping these dedicated volunteers continue their good works.

CEREMONY CAPACITY: Ceremonies take place upon request.

EVENT/RECEPTION CAPACITY: The main ballroom accommodates 450 seated guests for dining and dancing.

MEETING CAPACITY: The facility holds up to 1,000 guests seated theater-style.

FEES & DEPOSITS: A nonrefundable deposit is required to hold your event date. The rental fee, which includes a 5-hour event plus 2 hours for setup and 1 hour post-event for cleanup, ranges $800–3,500 depending on the date and number of guests attending the event. Overtime is available at $100/hour. A refundable $500 security deposit is also required.

AVAILABILITY: Year-round, daily.

SERVICES/AMENITIES:

Catering: BYO licensed and pre-approved or select from list
Kitchen Facilities: fully equipped
Tables & Chairs: provided
Linens, Silver, etc.: through caterer or BYO
Restrooms: wheelchair accessible
Dance Floor: yes
Bride's Dressing Area: yes
Meeting Equipment: AV equipment CBA, extra charge

Parking: large lot
Accommodations: hotels nearby
Telephone: emergency use only
Outdoor Night Lighting: yes
Outdoor Cooking Facilities: CBA
Cleanup: provided
View: East Bay foothills

RESTRICTIONS:

Alcohol: through caterer or BYO licensed server
Smoking: outside only
Music: amplified OK

Wheelchair Access: yes
Insurance: certificate required

Wente Vineyards
Event Center, Golf Course & Vineyard Lawn

5050 Arroyo Road, Livermore
925/456-2425
www.wentevineyards.com
catering@wentevineyards.com

Restaurant & Golf Course

● Rehearsal Dinners	● Corp. Events/Mtgs.
● Ceremonies	● Private Parties
● Wedding Receptions	Accommodations

Situated in a picturesque canyon at the southern end of the Livermore Valley, Wente Vineyards Restaurant, Event Center and Golf Course is surrounded by grapevines, sycamore groves and rolling hills. The site, with its beautifully landscaped grounds, is a versatile setting for corporate retreats, special events, and of course, Tri-Valley Wine Country weddings!

Founded 125 years ago, Wente Vineyards is the country's oldest continuously operated family-owned winery. It's no wonder, then, that the architecture reflects a sense of California history. White Spanish-style stucco buildings are accented with tile roofs and floors, and terracotta pots full of flowering plants set a cheery tone. The event center includes the Cresta Blanca Room, where indoor receptions are held, and the adjacent Terrace Lawn, a pretty spot for a garden wedding ceremony. There's space here, too, for an elegantly tented reception. Or use an open-sided tent for dancing, and set up tables and chairs outside to enjoy the view, which includes the changing seasonal colors of the sycamore trees.

Speaking of views: One of the best can be had on the new Vineyard Lawn near a pond at the golf course's 18th hole. Ceremonies and receptions on this green expanse can accommodate up to 1,000 of your nearest and dearest; in the background, lush vineyards and the golden Sandstone Hills cast a romantic spell.

Wente's award-winning restaurant casts a spell of its own. Three private dining rooms and terraces with vineyard views accommodate intimate receptions, rehearsal dinners, bridal showers or any other celebration. Wente, which has been Green Certified by Alameda County, has earned much critical acclaim for its cuisine, wine and sustainability. (They're among the first wineries in the state to be recognized by the recently established Certified California Sustainable Winegrowing Alliance.) Menus focus on simple foods with complex flavors, and incorporate the freshest locally grown and organic ingredients. Experienced staff will assist you with menu choices and wine selection, as well as recommendations for event services such as photography, floral design and overnight accommodations.

Wente also offers private wine tastings in their wine caves (a superb idea for your rehearsal dinner) and customized wine labeling for wedding favors. Sometimes event hosts organize a round of golf on Wente's Greg Norman-designed course, located just a chip shot away from the Conference Center. In keeping with their environmental sensitivity, the course was recently designated a "Certified Audubon Cooperative Sanctuary" by the Audubon International Program.

With its first-rate facilities, acres of vineyards and warm, Mediterranean ambiance, Wente is an extremely popular event site. They book up quickly, so don't wait too long to pay this East Bay oasis a visit.

CEREMONY CAPACITY: The Lawn and Garden can accommodate 350 seated; the Charles Wetmore and Cresta Blanca Rooms each hold 60–100 seated guests.

EVENT/RECEPTION CAPACITY: The site holds 15–150 seated indoors, and 20–500 seated outdoors.

MEETING CAPACITY: Event spaces hold 16–100 seated guests.

FEES & DEPOSITS: For weddings, a $500–4,000 nonrefundable deposit is required to reserve your date. An estimated 50% is due 6 months prior, and the estimated event balance is payable 2 weeks prior to the event; all incurred expenses are due on the day of the event. Facility rental fees range $500–4,000 depending upon day and season. Catering is provided: Buffets, luncheons and dinners, including a custom-designed wedding cake, range $45–75/person. Tax, beverages, rentals and a 20% service charge are additional.

For business functions, social events and meetings, facility rental fees range $150–4,000 depending on the spaces rented. Food is provided; prices will vary depending on menus and services selected. Call the sales department for specific rates.

AVAILABILITY: Year-round, daily, 7am–11pm.

SERVICES/AMENITIES:

Catering: provided
Kitchen Facilities: n/a
Tables & Chairs: provided
Linens, Silver, etc.: provided
Restrooms: wheelchair accessible
Dance Floor: available
Bride's Dressing Area: yes
Meeting Equipment: full range, extra charge

Parking: large lot with parking attendants
Accommodations: no guestrooms
Outdoor Night Lighting: yes
Outdoor Cooking Facilities: no
Telephone: pay phones
Cleanup: provided
View: vineyards surrounded by rolling hills
Other: event coordination

RESTRICTIONS:

Alcohol: beer, champagne, spirits and Wente wine provided
Smoking: outside only
Music: amplified OK

Wheelchair Access: yes
Insurance: not required
Other: no birdseed, rice or petals

Casa Real at Ruby Hill Winery

Winery, Garden & Ballroom

410 Vineyard Avenue, Pleasanton
925/931-0200

www.casarealevents.com
info@casarealevents.com

- Rehearsal Dinners
- Ceremonies
- Wedding Receptions
- Corp. Events/Mtgs.
- Private Parties
- Accommodations

The name, Casa Real, means House of Royalty, and we have no doubt that you and your guests will feel to the manor born when you arrive at this dramatic property set in the heart of the Livermore Wine Country.

Landscaped drives and acres of vineyards frame the 20,000-square-foot villa. The beautiful Mediterranean-style fountain surrounded by roses is a paparazzi-pleasing backdrop for red carpet arrivals and departures. Enormous hand-carved mahogany doors with wrought-iron hinges open into the jaw-dropping Entrance Hall with its 32-foot ceiling, Italian tile floor and white limestone trim. Three huge chandeliers; artisan-crafted limestone niches, rosettes and medallions; and clerestory-style windows set high in the walls lend the space a classical, yet romantic, feel. It's a gallery fit for rows of marble statues or shining suits of antique armor, but you might be perfectly happy with a roomful of celebrants and a beautiful floral arrangement atop the round mahogany table that sits at its center.

From this hall five additional sets of massive mahogany doors lead in other directions. To the east, the similarly trimmed Amber Room with its honey and cocoa accents embraces you in an atmosphere of luxury and intimacy. Large enough for a sizeable indoor ceremony or sit-down gathering, its focal point is a twelve-foot hand-carved limestone fireplace before which vows, performances and spirited toasts are surely in order. The Entrance Hall's north doors lead to the 9,000-square-foot Grand Salon, ideal for magnificent fêtes and feasts, with its soaring ceiling, mahogany bar and expansive windows. Twenty massive half-moon chandeliers, star-like pin lights, and sconces around the room's perimeter vary the mood; the champagne-colored Italian tile floor invites dancing; and handsome mahogany king's tables suggest banqueting in grand style.

No detail goes unattended in this regal oasis. In addition to the spacious, elegantly appointed restrooms, a posh chamber the size of a small condo (with couch, credenza, standing mirror, private bathroom and a granite-topped vanity that seats up to four) serves as a corporate closing room, a lounge for the bride and attendants or a peaceful semiprivate retreat.

For outdoor ceremonies, cocktails and other activities, the Sun Garden's terrace, walkways, limestone fountains and plants provide an idyllic setting. Views of the vineyards and the rolling East Bay hills abound, and a canopy of blue sky caps its protective walls. Within them Valencia orange trees, lavender, white tree roses and other beautiful blooms share space with twelve lovely magnolia trees that border the garden's central lawn. A remembrance niche in one of the walls is the perfect place to honor missing friends or family. And don't forget the historic Ruby Hill Winery right next door; it's a great spot for a rehearsal dinner or optional wine tasting activities.

CEREMONY CAPACITY: The facility holds 400 seated guests indoors and 450 seated outdoors.

EVENT/RECEPTION CAPACITY: The site can accommodate 550 seated or 700 standing guests.

MEETING CAPACITY: The site holds 600 seated guests.

FEES & DEPOSITS: A deposit equal to the rental fee is required to reserve your date. 50% of the estimated event costs is due 4 months before the event. The balance is due the week of the event. Rental fees range $800–5,000 depending on the day of week, the time of year and the space rented. For ceremonies there is a $475 setup fee. Meals range $45–60/person. Tax, alcohol and an 18% service charge are additional.

AVAILABILITY: Year-round, Sunday–Thursday, 9am–10pm; Friday and Saturday (and Sundays before a national holiday), 9am–11pm.

SERVICES/AMENITIES:

Catering: provided
Kitchen Facilities: n/a
Tables & Chairs: provided
Linens, Silver, etc.: provided
Restrooms: wheelchair accessible
Dance Floor: provided
Bride's Dressing Area: yes
Meeting Equipment: CBA, extra charge
Other: event coordination

Parking: valet required for over 250 guests
Accommodations: no guestrooms
Telephone: emergency use only
Outdoor Night Lighting: provided
Outdoor Cooking Facilities: n/a
Cleanup: provided
View: fountains, landscaped grounds, garden, courtyard, hills, valley and vineyards

RESTRICTIONS:

Alcohol: provided
Smoking: outside only
Music: amplified OK with restrictions

Wheelchair Access: yes
Insurance: certificate required

Want to find more locations and services? Check out our informative website, www.HereComesTheGuide.com.

397

Castlewood Country Club

Golf Club

707 Country Club Circle, Pleasanton
925/485-2237
www.castlewoodcc.org
thunt@castlewoodcc.org

● Rehearsal Dinners	● Corp. Events/Mtgs.
● Ceremonies	● Private Parties
● Wedding Receptions	Accommodations

Once the site of the fabulous "La Hacienda Del Pozo de Verona" and the former estate of Phoebe Apperson Hearst, California's beloved hostess and first lady of philanthropy, the Castlewood Country Club still retains the aura of elegance and grace that were the hallmarks of its famous resident. And the drive up Pleasanton Ridge, which overlooks the Amador Valley and is flanked by green fairways and gated estates, continues to generate a feeling of opulence and success. Giant palms line the Clubhouse approach, while the Country Club pool, built by Mrs. Hearst, sparkles like a huge aquamarine amid emerald lawns.

The princely porte-cochère that marks the entrance to the Clubhouse is reminiscent of the palatial 53-room California Mission-style mansion that once crowned the rise. This red carpet-style entrée through a beautiful colonnade is a fitting introduction to the spaces within.

Guests can gather in the handsomely furnished Grand Lobby with its soaring ceiling and majestic fireplace. Gleaming terracotta-colored floors reflect light in a way that adds warmth and splendor. The lobby leads to the Del Pozo Bar, a 2,000-square-foot private prefunction space of castle-like splendor. A magnificent granite and marble bar in the back of the room draws guests in to relax and lounge with a cocktail in hand before stepping into the 6,000-square-foot Del Pozo Ballroom. The room's twelve-foot-high windows let in breathtaking valley and golf course views, and ten massive Spanish-style chandeliers combine with other ambient lighting to halo festivities in just the right light. Event menus are customized by Castlewood's award-winning chef, and served up by a staff experienced in fine dining and topnotch service.

Let a waltz across the polished hardwood floors lead to the Del Pozo Terrace, where 4,000 additional square feet of function space and more stunning valley and woodland vistas expand the party possibilities. Perfect for pre-dinner or après-dinner drinks and tête-à-têtes, it's also an excellent ceremony space. But brides and grooms might want to tie the knot instead on Castlewood's Oak Tree Lawn. The property's ancient oak tree, whose branches spread overhead like a lacy fan, is a spectacular natural backdrop for the wedding couple.

If the bride and her retinue need to freshen up, they can do so in quarters fit for a queen. Entrance is through the Ladies Card Room, where rich carpeting, card tables, wingback chairs and golf course views create an inviting vibe. The bathrooms feature vanities and wraparound counters with upholstered cream- and bronze-colored seating. The groom and his groomsmen also have their own space, but we're betting they'll spend little time there. After all, how often can you party like a Spanish grandee in a 21st-century castle?

CEREMONY CAPACITY: The facility holds 200 seated guests indoors and 250 seated outdoors.

EVENT/RECEPTION CAPACITY: The site can accommodate 400 seated or 500 standing indoors, and 500 standing outdoors.

MEETING CAPACITY: The site holds 400 seated guests.

FEES & DEPOSITS: A $2,500 deposit is required to reserve your date and the balance is due 30 days prior to the event. Rental fees range $500–2,500 depending on the day and time of the event and the space rented. Meals range $20–60/person. Tax, alcohol and a 20% service charge are additional.

AVAILABILITY: Year-round.

SERVICES/AMENITIES:

Catering: provided or BYO
Kitchen Facilities: fully equipped
Tables & Chairs: provided
Linens, Silver, etc.: provided
Restrooms: wheelchair accessible
Dance Floor: provided
Bride's Dressing Area: yes
Meeting Equipment: some provided

Parking: large lot
Accommodations: no guestrooms
Telephone: emergency use only
Outdoor Night Lighting: CBA
Outdoor Cooking Facilities: BBQ CBA
Cleanup: caterer or renter
View: fairways, landscaped grounds, pool area; panorama of hills and valley
Other: AV equipment, event coordination

RESTRICTIONS:

Alcohol: provided
Smoking: designated areas only
Music: amplified OK with restrictions

Wheelchair Access: limited
Insurance: not required

Palm Event Center in the Vineyard

Winery, Garden & Ballroom

1184 Vineyard Avenue, Pleasanton
925/426-8666

www.palmeventcenter.com
info@palmeventcenter.com

- Rehearsal Dinners
- Ceremonies
- Wedding Receptions
- Corp. Events/Mtgs.
- Private Parties
- Accommodations

The ambiance here is purely palatial or maybe "palazzo," since the feeling you'll get is that you've stepped into the Italian countryside. Set on a 110-acre California winery estate and fashioned in a size, scale and simplicity that emphasize the beauty and character of its vineyard setting, the Palm Event Center is certainly a magnificent place for a party.

The facilities are surrounded by vineyards and enjoy views of Mt. Hamilton and Ruby Hill. Guests arrive via a graceful palm-lined approach to find themselves in front of an imposing winery with its roots in the past. The atmosphere is one of privacy and refinement. The adjacent Palm Event Center, which is where your event will take place, has been built using antique brick recycled from an old historic winery. Carefully designed in a manner that combines Early California and Italian Romanesque styles, it is a majestic edifice that bespeaks both taste and means.

The enchantment continues when you step into the Ballroom through the Palm's massive redwood doors. They're made from wine barrels that were aged over 50 years, and constructed by a master carpenter. Inside, a twenty-foot-high ceiling and stone-colored Italian-tile floor define the grand scale of this spacious room. High Roman windows connect you with the outdoors: Look through them and you can see the tops of the palms. Weddings, fancy fundraisers, high-end dinner dances and corporate celebrations will all look impossibly posh in this sumptuous interior. Bigger-than-life appointments include French oak barrels and two 800-pound king's tables ideal for presenting cakes, registration, buffets or banquets in royal style. Handsome portable screens can partition off any area, including the sleek tan-and-black granite bar. And the magnificent catering kitchen enables an all-star staff to turn out delicious contemporary cuisine, guaranteed to dazzle your palate. The sky is the limit on lighting, but even better than the stars, this heaven of dual pin spots is on adjustable dimmers. Even the seating is exquisite: Italian designer chairs are ultracomfy and welcoming after a mad whirl (or two or three) around the ballroom.

On the eastern wall, huge floor-to-ceiling windows and glass doors open onto a sizeable, two-tiered patio, which can also be accessed from a trellis- and trumpet-vine-bordered walkway on the side of the building. Floored in tasteful gray stone and attractively lit, it's perfect for cocktails and hors d'oeuvres or for after-dinner drinks under the stars. The well-manicured lawn is another lovely gathering place, perhaps for a ceremony beneath the eastern-influenced arch, or for a convivial chat.

The cavernous Estate Room, lined with wine barrels and glittering tealights, provides more space and is a beautiful setting for an indoor ceremony. The room can also host extra activities and sideshow attractions like an auction, dance hall or disco. Clean, crisp and cool, it's full of wine-cave romance and the fragrance of ripening vintages.

CEREMONY CAPACITY: The site holds 350 seated guests outdoors and 400 seated indoors.

EVENT/RECEPTION CAPACITY: The Palm accommodates 450 seated or 650 standing guests.

MEETING CAPACITY: The site seats 600 guests.

FEES & DEPOSITS: A deposit equal to the rental fee is required to reserve your date. 50% of the estimated event total is due 4 months prior to the event. The balance is due a week before the event. Rental fees range $800–5,000 depending on day and time of the event. Meals range $40–55/person. Tax, alcohol and an 18% service charge are additional. A $475 ceremony setup fee is additional.

AVAILABILITY: Year-round, daily, 8am–11pm.

SERVICES/AMENITIES:

Catering: provided
Kitchen Facilities: n/a
Tables & Chairs: provided
Linens, Silver, etc.: provided
Restrooms: wheelchair accessible
Dance Floor: yes
Bride's Dressing Area: yes
Meeting Equipment: CBA, extra charge

Parking: valet required for over 275 guests
Accommodations: no guestrooms
Telephone: emergency use only
Outdoor Night Lighting: yes
Outdoor Cooking Facilities: n/a
Cleanup: provided
View: vineyards, garden, hills, landscaped grounds, fountain
Other: event coordination

RESTRICTIONS:

Alcohol: provided
Smoking: outside only
Music: amplified OK with restrictions

Wheelchair Access: yes
Insurance: certificate required

Palm Pavilion

Event Center

4501 Pleasanton Avenue, Pleasanton
925/426-7600

www.alamedacountyfair.com
fcater@alamedacountyfair.com

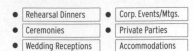

- Rehearsal Dinners
- Ceremonies
- Wedding Receptions
- Corp. Events/Mtgs.
- Private Parties
- Accommodations

Set on 267 beautifully landscaped acres in the heart of downtown Pleasanton, the Palm Pavilion is home to many events year-round, including weddings, private parties and corporate affairs.

Surrounded by its namesake trees, the versatile facility enables you to celebrate indoors and out. Inside, the golden oak bar, pale terracotta tiles and cream walls lend the space an inviting warmth, while a variety of lighting options make this large (5,000-square-foot) space feel surprisingly intimate. Generous windows on three sides showcase views of the golf course and main lawn area. Three adjoining patios—two open and one covered—let you and your guests revel in the balmy Pleasanton weather. In addition, the building is fully air-conditioned, and boasts up-to-date audiovisual technology for those with more business-oriented functions in mind.

Just a few steps away is the Wine Garden where ceremonies are held. Couples exchange vows on a raised platform near a burbling fountain, against a lush backdrop of flowers, ferns and other greenery. The stucco wall enclosing the garden ensures privacy.

If you're a bride on a budget, you won't find a better venue than the Palm Pavilion. The experienced staff will give you as much (or as little) assistance as you want, and they can handle everything from an upscale wedding to a quinceañera to a company barbecue. Plus, they provide services and amenities you won't find at smaller facilities, such as an on-site plant nursery, acres of nearby parking, security, and plenty of privacy.

And because the Pavilion is part of the nonprofit Alameda County Fairgrounds, the revenue they generate goes back into maintaining and improving the property, ensuring that the grounds and buildings are always in tip-top shape.

With so much to offer, the Palm Pavilion could be the surprise perfect place for your special event!

CEREMONY CAPACITY: Various outdoor locations hold in excess of 2,000 guests; the Palm Pavilion up to 275 seated guests.

EVENT/RECEPTION CAPACITY: Indoor spaces accommodate 225 seated or 275 standing guests. The Garden holds up to 200 seated or 250 standing guests.

MEETING CAPACITY: Spaces are available which hold up to 3,000 guests.

FEES & DEPOSITS: 50% of the estimated event total is required to reserve your date. The balance is due 30 days prior to the event. The rental fee is $700 Sunday–Thursday and $1,400 Friday and Saturday. Meals start at $27/person. A 22% service charge and sales tax are additional.

AVAILABILITY: Year-round, daily, 8am–midnight.

SERVICES/AMENITIES:

Catering: provided, no BYO
Kitchen Facilities: n/a
Tables & Chairs: provided
Linens, Silver, etc.: provided
Restrooms: wheelchair accessible
Dance Floor: yes, permanent
Bride's Dressing Area: CBA
Meeting Equipment: some provided, more CBA

Parking: large lots
Accommodations: partner hotels nearby
Telephone: emergency use only
Outdoor Night Lighting: yes
Outdoor Cooking Facilities: BBQ
Cleanup: provided
View: golf course, garden, park, grounds
Other: coordination available for fee; on-site florals, picnic area, AV equipment

RESTRICTIONS:

Alcohol: provided
Smoking: outside only
Music: amplified OK with restrictions

Wheelchair Access: yes
Insurance: not required

This is important! Tell locations you're reading HERE COMES THE GUIDE and ask if our information is still current.

Ruby Hill Golf Club

Private Golf Club

3400 West Ruby Hill Drive, Pleasanton
925/461-3504
www.rubyhill.com
bfitzsimmons@rubyhill.com

● Rehearsal Dinners	● Corp. Events/Mtgs.
● Ceremonies	● Private Parties
● Wedding Receptions	Accommodations

Judging by its beautiful entrance, with a Tuscan-style gatehouse, trellised driveway and meticulous landscaping, Ruby Hill is no ordinary golf club. In fact, what lies beyond the impressive gates is not just a golf course, but an exclusive private community surrounded by vineyards and spread over acres of open land. It's so exclusive that in order to take a peek at this lovely facility you have to make an appointment.

The clubhouse and fairways are a short drive up the hill, and as you make your way to the top, you pass dozens of spectacular homes whose graceful architecture defines the development. Most of these houses are reminiscent of Italian villas, and when you finally reach the clubhouse, you're hardly surprised to find that it's the largest and most striking "villa" of them all.

Step through the arched front door into the Fireside Room and you're more than a little awestruck by the grand scale and inviting ambiance. The vast marble floor gleams softly, bathed in natural light from a stunning domed skylight overhead. Elegant conversational seating is arranged beneath the skylight and in front of a large stone fireplace. You can't help but notice rich details, like the crown molding, wall sconces and window trim, all seemingly fashioned from stone, and the eclectic antiques and art, which add a personal touch.

From the Fireside Room, walk down the regal staircase into the Main Dining Room, where indoor receptions and special events are held. The sheer grandeur of the space makes you want to sit down to fully appreciate the soaring 40-foot ceiling, giant potted palms and abundant light streaming in through a multitude of high windows and glass doors. Walls are painted a warm Tuscan wheat accented with creamy white trim, and the Florentine motif in the custom carpet swirls beneath your feet in muted earth tones.

To one side of the Main Dining Room is a similarly appointed small private dining room for rehearsal dinners or meetings. On the other side is the Lounge, a clubby space with dark maple woodwork, a marble fireplace and granite-topped bar that's well suited for cocktails. All three rooms open out onto an expansive arcaded patio that overlooks a formal garden and emerald lawn, as well as views of the golf course, the Livermore hills and Mt. Diablo.

The patio also overlooks a stunning oval terrace that's custom-made for al fresco ceremonies and receptions. Paved with smooth Napa Valley stone and enclosed by two wisteria-covered trellises, the terrace feels intimate despite the fact that it's completely open to the sky, the breeze and panoramic vistas.

The effort that has gone into making Ruby Hill Golf Club a showplace is evident in unexpected places, too. The women's lounge (and carpeted "locker room") is practically palatial, not only in size but in amenities such as elaborately tiled bathrooms with gorgeous granite counters, plush seating and mirrors everywhere. Even the telephone booths are refined private nooks with their own doors, granite counters and art on the wall!

This is a glorious spot for any upscale affair or holiday party. And if you're interested in a corporate golf tournament, Ruby Hill Golf Club has the first Jack Nicklaus-designed golf course in Northern California. The clubhouse was built to exacting standards so you'd feel right at home. We're quite sure you will.

CEREMONY CAPACITY: The Fireside Room holds 200 seated, and the Terrace 250 seated.

EVENT/RECEPTION CAPACITY: The Main Dining Room accommodates 220 seated guests or 300 standing. The Terrace holds 250 seated or 300 standing guests.

MEETING CAPACITY: Several spaces accommodate 8–45 seated guests.

FEES & DEPOSITS: A $3,000 nonrefundable deposit is required to reserve your date. The estimated food and beverage total is due 1 month prior to the event. Meals range $36–49/person; tax, alcohol and a 20% service charge are additional. Customized menus available.

AVAILABILITY: For weddings, Ruby Hill Golf Club is available January–November. The facility is available year-round for other events, daily 10am–11pm.

SERVICES/AMENITIES:
Catering: provided, no BYO
Kitchen Facilities: n/a
Tables & Chairs: provided
Linens, Silver, etc.: provided
Restrooms: wheelchair accessible
Dance Floor: yes
Bride's & Groom's Dressing Rooms: yes
Meeting Equipment: CBA, extra charge

Parking: large lot and valet
Accommodations: no guestrooms
Telephone: emergency use only
Outdoor Night Lighting: yes
Outdoor Cooking Facilities: yes
Cleanup: provided
View: vineyards, Jack Nicklaus Golf Course
Other: full event and day-of coordination

RESTRICTIONS:
Alcohol: provided or corkage $15/bottle
Smoking: outside only
Music: amplified OK with restrictions

Wheelchair Access: yes
Insurance: not required
Other: no rice, birdseed or glitter

Elliston Vineyards

Winery

463 Kilkare Road, Sunol
925/862-2377
www.elliston.com
info@elliston.com

Rehearsal Dinners	● Corp. Events/Mtgs.
● Ceremonies	● Private Parties
● Wedding Receptions	Accommodations

When gold rush pioneer Henry Ellis carved out an estate for himself in 1890, he picked a prime setting: a sheltered canyon tucked between two tree-covered ridges. Here he set up house in a three-story mansion constructed of thick sandstone from nearby Niles Canyon, and went about enjoying life in the country. Today his lovely homestead, now surrounded by vineyards, has become a prime setting for hosting weddings, receptions and private parties.

Garden-style ceremonies are held outdoors alongside the historic mansion, in a garden brimming with native flora and including an expansive lawn and arbor. Stage your photos here, and you'll have some striking options for a backdrop—the century-old stone house, vibrant displays of azaleas and camellias and sprawling vineyards. But if you'd like to search for more photographic possibilities, go right ahead—there are plenty of photo opportunities at Elliston.

A short walkway takes you from the garden to the newly remodeled Terrace Room, a secluded 2,000-square-foot banquet room set into the hillside. Its vaulted ceiling and glass walls add to the feeling of spaciousness, while the surrounding deck gives guests a chance to dine al fresco at umbrella-shaded tables. A Victorian gazebo next to the deck is large enough for a bridal table or a quartet of musicians to serenade partygoers. The entire site is sheltered by oak, eucalyptus and olive trees, creating an ideal venue for you and your guests to celebrate.

Whether you're a bride planning your wedding or a wine aficionado, Elliston Vineyards is a destination worth seeking. Centrally located, with access from several East Bay freeways, you're close to civilization but you'd never know it—the quiet country atmosphere will give you the delicious feeling of being a million miles away.

CEREMONY CAPACITY: Outdoors, the South Lawn holds 225 seated; indoors the Terrace Room can accommodate 125 seated guests.

EVENT/RECEPTION CAPACITY: The Terrace Room and adjoining deck seat 225 guests, with 125 guests seated indoors and 100 guests seated outdoors.

MEETING CAPACITY: The facility accommodates up to 150 seated guests.

FEES & DEPOSITS: A nonrefundable $2,000 deposit is required when reservations are confirmed. 50% of the estimated event total is due 6 months prior to your function, with additional 25% payment due 2 months prior to the event. The remaining balance, with a confirmed guest count, is due 2 weeks prior to the event. Event minimums may apply. Minimums include meals, beverages, facility fees, service charge and tax. The actual cost will depend on the menu and beverage package selected, and guest count. Three-course luncheon and dinner menus, including hors d'oeuvres, start at $42/person; buffets start at $39/person and require a 50-person minimum.

For meetings and conferences, a nonrefundable $500 deposit is required when reservations are confirmed. Room fees range $500–750. minumums may apply. Continental breakfast, full lunch and afternoon snack run $44/person.

AVAILABILITY: Year-round, daily.

SERVICES/AMENITIES:

Catering: provided
Kitchen Facilities: n/a
Tables & Chairs: provided
Linens, Silver, etc.: provided
Restrooms: wheelchair accessible
Dance Floor: yes
Bride's Dressing Area: yes
Meeting Equipment: AV, overhead projector, screen, flip charts, podium, DVD/VCR and monitor, extra charge

Parking: large lot, parking attendants
Accommodations: no guestrooms
Telephone: office phone
Outdoor Night Lighting: yes
Outdoor Cooking Facilities: no
Cleanup: provided
View: vineyards and hills
Other: event planning and day-of coordination

RESTRICTIONS:

Alcohol: WCB provided, no BYO
Smoking: outside only
Music: amplified OK inside only

Wheelchair Access: yes
Insurance: not required
Other: no rice, birdseed or confetti

Sunol Valley Golf Club

Golf Club

6900 Mission Road, Sunol
925/862-2408
www.sunolvalley.com
catering@sunolvalley.com

● Rehearsal Dinners	● Corp. Events/Mtgs.
● Ceremonies	● Private Parties
● Wedding Receptions	Accommodations

Two weddings, an awards banquet and a corporate function— they're all in a day's play at the Sunol Valley Golf Club. Situated amid lush fairways, shimmering ponds and tall desert palms in the sun-drenched Sunol Valley, this popular facility has been serving up exceptional events with efficiency and expertise for 40 years. Not many places can comfortably host a thousand guests, but here, in an oasis of leisure and calm, large parties and small are accommodated with ease.

Imagine your guests relaxing and enjoying themselves in the easy elegance of rooms with a country club feel. Outstanding vistas that blend artful golf course landscaping with the area's natural rural charm distinguish the property. It's as private and pristine as an island paradise—only *this* island paradise has topnotch amenities *and* it's perfectly groomed. The attractively appointed Coronado Room, with its built-in bar, corner stage and chandeliers, easily seats around 220 and boasts one of the largest permanent dance floors in the valley. Sunlight streams in through windows that open onto a deck overlooking the surrounding hills. Larger parties spill into the Pavilion Room, with more floor-to-ceiling windows, balconies and a breathtaking view of the velvety greens, ponds and palms of the links. Everyone from business execs to golf pros to visiting out-of-state cousins is certain to be charmed by the setting. If your special event is a wedding, consider this room for your ceremony. A changing room furnished with mirror, dress racks and vanity provides private space for the bride.

Just outside the Pavilion Room, the Mediterranean Room, with its lobby-like length and appeal, is a welcoming prefunction space and a super spot for guests to mingle and meet over drinks, buffet service or passed hors d'oeuvres.

The Mission Room, though smaller and more casual than the Coronado and Pavilion Rooms, has the same clubby feel. Floored in slate and a tasteful taupe-colored carpet, it's dominated by a handsome granite bar and a spectacular outlook onto the course. There's even room for a small dance floor so guests can swing, cha-cha, rock or trance out to the heartbeat of your celebration. The beamed ceiling, illuminated by chandeliers, makes this an elegant environment for nighttime events.

If low-key and lovely is a mood you prefer, the Garden Room downstairs is a cheerful enclave with private patio access, a large dance floor and a built-in bar. And if the golf course beckons, there's no need to resist. Book a tee time or ask the staff to coordinate a photo shoot out where the grass is perpetually greener.

CEREMONY CAPACITY: Indoors, the Club holds up to 500 seated guests. Outdoors, the lawn area holds up to 250 seated guests.

EVENT/RECEPTION CAPACITY: The Club accommodates up to 500 seated or 800 standing guests.

MEETING CAPACITY: The facility accommodates up to 500 seated guests.

FEES & DEPOSITS: A $1,000–3,000 deposit is required to reserve your date, and the balance is due 10 days prior to the event. Rental fees range $500–1,500 depending on space rented. Meals range $26.95–40.95/person. Tax, alcohol and a 20% service charge are additional.

AVAILABILITY: Year-round, daily, 7am–midnight.

SERVICES/AMENITIES:

Catering: provided or BYO
Kitchen Facilities: n/a
Tables & Chairs: provided
Linens, Silver, etc.: provided
Restrooms: wheelchair accessible
Dance Floor: yes
Bride's Dressing Area: yes
Meeting Equipment: CBA, extra charge

Parking: large lot
Accommodations: no guestrooms
Telephone: house phone
Outdoor Night Lighting: access only
Outdoor Cooking Facilities: no
Cleanup: provided
View: garden, fairways and hills
Other: event coordination

RESTRICTIONS:

Alcohol: provided
Smoking: outside only
Music: amplified OK

Wheelchair Access: yes
Insurance: not required
Other: no rice, birdseed or confetti

Overwhelmed? Use the search criteria on www.HereComesTheGuide.com to narrow down your choices.

East Bay

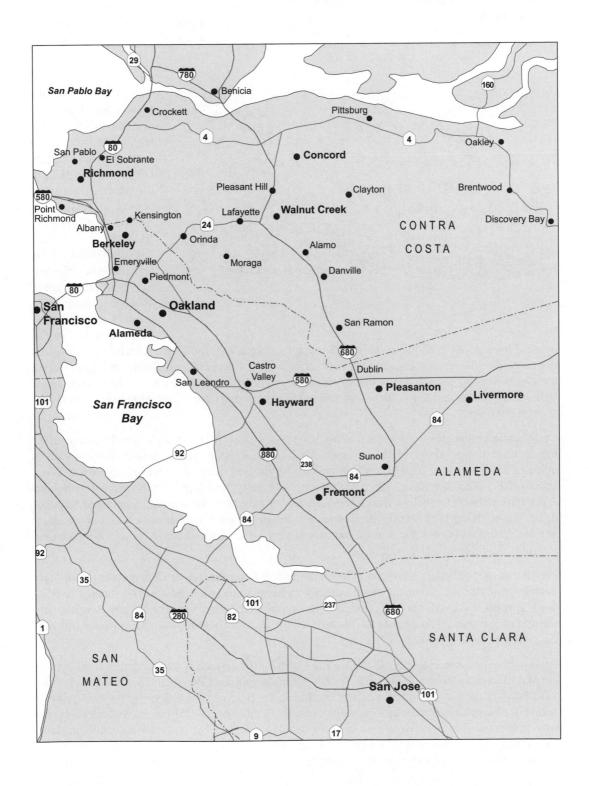

Albert H. DeWitt O'Club

Historic Officer's Club

641 West Red Line, Alameda
510/747-7529
www.ci.alameda.ca.us/arpd
arpd@ci.alameda.ca.us

● Rehearsal Dinners	● Corp. Events/Mtgs.
● Ceremonies	● Private Parties
● Wedding Receptions	Accommodations

The "O" in "O'Club" stands for "Officers," and the officers who frequented this club certainly lived like gentlemen. It was built at the Alameda Naval Air Station in 1941, when America was entering World War II, and Uncle Sam didn't stint on the luxuries. Even the entrance is imposing: A 40-foot-long canopy shelters the walkway from the street to the massive front doors. Walking under it makes you feel like a VIP, and it's no stretch of the imagination to picture the glamorous arrival of famous military, political and entertainment figures during the Club's heyday. John F. Kennedy, for example, attended a gala in his honor here, and Lucille Ball, Henry Fonda and Van Johnson were fêted at a wrap party for *Yours, Mine and Ours,* a film shot on the base.

Once inside, you get the impression that nothing was too good for the Navy's elite. There are tables handcrafted from solid oak, chairs covered with the highest grade calfskin leather, and chandeliers made of leaded crystal; the O'Club was built and furnished in an era when people really cared about quality. And then there's the palpable sense of history, which practically oozes from behind every dark redwood panel. In the cozy Squadron Room, where Naval aviators gathered for a last drink before flying off to battle, their squadron insignia stare down in mute testimony to their heroics. You couldn't ask for a more intimate setting for a small wedding, or a better changing room for the bride at a large one.

Events that shaped history were conceived in the Trident Room next door. Officers planned military strategy from the comfort of the same leather wingback chairs you see here. The stately fireplace, plush carpets, dark oak paneling and antique crystal chandeliers give the Trident Room a rich, warm, comfortable feel—acoustically as well as visually. It's the ideal room for drinks and hors d'oeuvres before the wedding ceremony.

You might even be tempted to use the Trident Room for the ceremony itself—that is, until you see the Main Ballroom, which echoes the Trident Room's sumptuous décor, and has some innovative touches of its own. Along one wall, separated from the parquet dance floor by a gleaming brass railing, is a two-foot elevated platform with overstuffed leather booths. Above each booth is a crystal sconce that matches the chandeliers in every detail. It's the perfect place for the wedding party, family and guests of honor. To the right of the platform is a stage for the band, with a superb sound system and a large pull-down movie screen, in case you want to show slides, movies or videos.

If you're planning a smaller wedding and don't need the space of the Main Ballroom or the Trident Room, the Terrace Room, with its hand-painted floral motifs and green lattice work, provides a serene atmosphere. Or on sunny days, you can move outdoors into the lovely Terrace Garden for a ceremony al fresco.

The O'Club was built to provide rest and relaxation for America's fighting men and women. But now that times have changed, it's proving to be a much better place for love than it ever was for war.

CEREMONY CAPACITY: Outdoors, the Main Patio holds 300 or the Terrace Garden 200 seated; indoors, the Trident Room holds 225 seated.

EVENT/RECEPTION & MEETING CAPACITY: Individual spaces at the center can accommodate 30–250 seated or 50–450 standing indoors, and up to 200 seated or 400 standing outdoors. The entire facility holds 500 seated or 1,100 standing guests.

FEES & DEPOSITS: A $500 refundable cleaning and security deposit is required when reservations are made. For an outdoor ceremony, the setup fee is $150. Rental fees range $30–175/hour depending on the day of the week and room selected. The rental balance is payable 14 days prior to the event.

AVAILABILITY: Year-round, daily, except major holidays, 9am–midnight.

SERVICES/AMENITIES:

Catering: BYO caterer; contract and insurance required
Kitchen Facilities: n/a
Tables & Chairs: provided
Linens, Silver, etc.: BYO or caterer
Restrooms: wheelchair accessible
Dance Floor: parquet floor, portable and patio
Bride's & Groom's Dressing Area: yes
Meeting Equipment: CBA, extra charge

Parking: large lots; complimentary parking
Accommodations: no guestrooms, CBA
Telephone: emergency use only
Outdoor Night Lighting: yes
Outdoor Cooking Facilities: no
Cleanup: renter or caterer
View: landscaped garden

RESTRICTIONS:

Alcohol: BYO; insurance required
Smoking: outside only
Music: amplified OK with volume limits; curfew 11pm weekdays, midnight Fri and Sat

Wheelchair Access: yes
Insurance: extra liability may be required
Other: no rice or confetti; decorations require approval

CommodoreEvents.com

Yachts

Docked at Mariner Square, Alameda (boarding at 15 other ports)
510/337-9000

www.commodoreevents.com
events@commodoreevents.com

● Rehearsal Dinners	● Corp. Events/Mtgs.
● Ceremonies	● Private Parties
● Wedding Receptions	Accommodations

If you are a lover of ocean liners, cruise ships, yachts, and all the grandeur and pampering they imply, why not charter one of CommodoreEvents.com's six luxury yachts for your special day? Their fleet serves fifteen ports around San Francisco Bay, including San Francisco, Alameda, and Sausalito, and its founders have been maintaining the fine tradition of elegant entertaining at sea for over 30 years. The white glove treatment is no empty promise on these yachts: Their expert staff—from the uniformed U.S. Merchant Marine Officer captains to the waiters—really do wear them! And the service, whether the event is a wedding, black-tie gala, themed ball, corporate mixer or any other kind of celebration, is impeccable.

The glamorous $6 million *Cabernet Sauvignon Commodore* is the flagship. It boasts five enormous decks: a luxurious lounge deck outfitted with ultra leather couches and tables; a dining deck for grand sit-down dinners or buffets; a large dance floor deck equipped with an excellent sound system; and an open-air sky deck that will make you feel like you're on top of the world. Carpeting is plush with an understated nautical theme, and four handsome staterooms on a deck of their own provide a private space for brides and bridesmaids. There's even an elevator to take guests from one level to the next.

Their fleet also features a trio of finely appointed Mega Yachts: the *Pinot Noir, Merlot,* and *Chardonnay.* The *Pinot Noir,* with its long white bar and mirrored ceilings, looks like the chic set for a James Bond movie. Its sister yacht, the *Chardonnay Commodore,* is equally stunning. Couples who desire an intimate outdoor ceremony framed by sunlight-spangled waters and blue skies might want to consider the *Merlot Commodore.* Popular because it serves large groups and small, it has a roomy dance floor on the second deck that spills out onto the open-air deck. The *Zinfandel Commodore,* a true trimaran, boasts fabulous views from a dining deck with floor-to-ceiling glass. Then there's the magnificent *Fumé Blanc Commodore,* a three-deck replica of a New York State Hudson River steamboat. It has a 30-foot dance floor, roomy viewing platforms on the bow, and accommodates up to 468 guests and crew.

All vessels offer well-appointed settings for dining, relaxing and entertaining; decks outdoors on bow, stern and topside; gorgeous wraparound views of the bay; and multiple options for a wide variety of social and corporate functions. CommodoreEvents.com has all-inclusive packages for every budget and makes it easy to put together the wedding of your dreams. Before booking any other venue, make reservations for one of their open houses where you may "Meet the Fleet." *Bon Voyage!*

CEREMONY, EVENT/RECEPTION & MEETING CAPACITY: Maximum capacity is 450 guests aboard *Fumé Blanc* and 400 aboard *Cabernet Sauvignon*. Many events are hosted with 20–150 guests aboard smaller yachts.

FEES & DEPOSITS: 25% of the estimated event total is a nonrefundable deposit required to reserve your date. Another 25% is due 120 days prior to the event. The balance is due 14 days prior to the event. Fees, including meals, a full bar and 4 hours aboard, range $62–200/person. The yachts are also available à la carte.

AVAILABILITY: Year-round, anytime.

SERVICES/AMENITIES:

Catering: provided or BYO
Kitchen Facilities: fully equipped
Tables & Chairs: provided
Linens, Silver, etc.: provided
Restrooms: some wheelchair accessible
Dance Floor: yes
Bride's Dressing Area: CBA
Meeting Equipment: CBA

Parking: large lot
Accommodations: guestrooms nearby
Telephone: onboard radio and cellular phones
Outdoor Night Lighting: yes
Outdoor Cooking Facilities: n/a
Cleanup: provided
View: entire San Francisco Bay
Other: wedding cakes, florals, referrals

RESTRICTIONS:

Alcohol: provided, or BYO with corkage fee
Smoking: restricted to back deck
Music: sound system provided

Wheelchair Access: yes
Insurance: not required

Grandview Pavilion

300 Island Drive, Alameda
510/865-5322

www.grandviewpavilion.com
info@grandviewpavilion.com

Banquet & Special Event Center

- Rehearsal Dinners
- Ceremonies
- Wedding Receptions
- Corp. Events/Mtgs.
- Private Parties
- Accommodations

Fairy tales begin in places like this. Set in the tranquil community of Harbor Bay on historic Bay Farm Island in Alameda, the perfectly picturesque Grandview Pavilion does seem almost too good to be true. The lovely ivy-covered Mediterranean-style building sits just at the edge of the championship 36-hole Chuck Corica Golf Course, far enough away from the main complex to maintain an aura of seclusion without sacrificing the lush tree-dotted green and fairway views.

There is a soft sheen to the handsome Spanish-style doors that open onto the elegantly tiled foyer and spacious Ballroom. Full-size French windows cover the facing wall, creating a backdrop of eucalyptus, pine trees and meticulously manicured lawns. The Edenic surroundings find their way inside in the luxuriant garden feel of the carpet's pale floral tones and the sunlit brilliance of the cream-colored walls and white crown moldings and trim. Coppered chandeliers hang from the airy coffered ceilings, and the built-in granite, copper and mahogany bar and service area has back-to-back access from either room.

It's a magnificent stage for any high-end social or corporate event, but weddings are truly exceptional here. In the Ballroom, enormous mirrors overlook the polished, hand-laid cherrywood dance floor, amplifying the area and the energy. There's even a professional DJ booth seamlessly tucked away behind one retractable mirror for clutter-free entertaining. If dancing isn't on the agenda, the dance floor is an ideal place to set up a dramatic serpentine table showcasing an exquisite food presentation.

Did we mention that all the food for this venue is provided by one of the Bay Area's top caterers? *Grand Catering* has been wowing clients with excellent service and delectable dining experiences for decades. Their offerings look and taste like works of art. Whether your plans are simple (French bistro, BBQ, California cuisine) or extravagant (Asian fusion, luau with full roast pig, mashed potato bar with martini glass service), the eats will be outstanding—a true feast for the eyes and palate.

As if this weren't enough, the facility has recently added a spectacular tri-peaked tent pavilion. When the weather's warm, its clear "walls" are opened to let in balmy breezes. During cooler months or for evening events, the pavilion can be enclosed and heated for guests' comfort. But no matter what the season, this venue provides a garden experience with views of the surrounding flowers, plants and golf course. If you have your ceremony in the Garden Tent Pavilion, a white trellis at one end serves as an arch. Two indoor fountains create their own soothing music, while chandeliers and twinkle lights add an enchanting sparkle.

There's even a beautiful room for the bride and her attendants with pink champagne walls, soft moss-colored carpeting and private restrooms with peach marble accents, but our guess is the ladies will spend little time there.

CEREMONY CAPACITY: The Garden Tent Pavilion holds up to 200 seated guests.

EVENT/RECEPTION & MEETING CAPACITY: The Ballroom holds up to 275 seated guests with a dance floor or 450 standing. The total seated capacity for a reception is 420. The Garden Tent Pavilion can accommodate up to 120 seated guests.

FEES & DEPOSITS: For weddings, the rental fee is required to reserve your date; the estimated event total is due 30 days prior to the event. Room rental fees range $1,600–3,800. Wedding reception food and beverage minumum is $50/person. Tax and an 18% service charge are additional.

For corporate meetings, room rental fees start at $200. Breakfast starts at $10/person, lunch at $18/person.

AVAILABILITY: Year-round, daily.

SERVICES/AMENITIES:

Catering: provided, no BYO
Kitchen Facilities: n/a
Tables & Chairs: provided
Linens, Silver, etc.: provided
Restrooms: wheelchair accessible
Dance Floor: yes
Bride's Dressing Area: provided
Meeting Equipment: full sound system, wireless mics, 2 LCD projectors, 2 built-in projection screens

Parking: large lot
Accommodations: no guestrooms
Telephone: emergency use only
Outdoor Night Lighting: yes
Outdoor Cooking Facilities: CBA
Cleanup: provided
View: golf course
Other: event coordination

RESTRICTIONS:

Alcohol: provided
Smoking: outdoors only
Music: amplified music indoors only, acoustic music outdoors OK

Wheelchair Access: yes
Insurance: not required

The professionals in the back of this book are the best in the business. How do we know? Read page 701.

Oakland Yacht Club

Yacht Club

1101 Pacific Marina, Alameda
510/522-6868

www.oaklandyachtclub.com
emendes@oaklandyachtclub.com

● Rehearsal Dinners	● Corp. Events/Mtgs.
● Ceremonies	● Private Parties
● Wedding Receptions	Accommodations

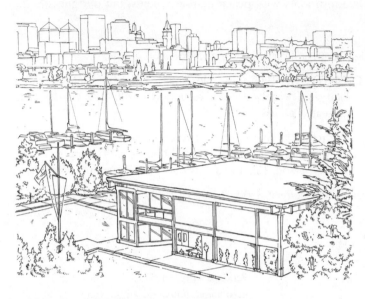

Jack London would not recognize the place! The famous author-adventurer was a member of the Oakland Yacht Club in 1913, when access was by dinghy only and members tied up at wood pilings driven into the mud. Today, many decades and moves later, the organization's airy, well-appointed clubhouse occupies a quiet, park-like setting in a treelined Alameda neighborhood with a private 220-slip marina and views of the Oakland skyline and the Oakland/Alameda Estuary. There's no stress here. The atmosphere is relaxed, and the friendly staff will bend over backwards to make certain every aspect of your affair is shipshape.

Your guests will have plenty of parking and easy access to the two-story facility. Event spaces include the Regatta Room downstairs, with a built-in wet bar, big windows, a sheltered patio and excellent views of the marina and estuary where kayaks and sailboats drift by at eye level. It's perfect for small meetings and gatherings, or as a roomy hideaway for the groom and his groomsmen or the bride and her attendants. Adjacent restrooms have showers, dressing areas and patio access.

For the main event, the Commodore's Hall upstairs is a gorgeous room with a view. Its pale blue hue mirrors the water and sky and fills the space with a pleasant sense of peace and possibility. Brightly colored burgees—the flags from yacht clubs with reciprocating privileges—festoon the walls near the entrance, where an ample vestibule houses a cloakroom that can double as gift storage.

Like the waters it rests beside, the room has a natural flow and a nautical feel. The floor-to-ceiling windows on its north side open onto a series of individual balconies, set with tables and chairs, that look down on the boats berthed in the marina below and out toward the East Bay hills and the dramatic Oakland skyline. On the far end of the hall, a built-in oak dance floor can serve as an indoor ceremony space, a stage, or a place to move to the music. A circular oak bar occupies the opposite end of the room. Sizable celebrations of every kind can be easily accommodated in the area in between and serviced from the club kitchen where a well-trained staff expertly prepares fine party fare. Add a podium for speakers and a pull-down screen and you have a room fit for any occasion. There's even a windowed alcove with city and sea vistas just right for framing the couple's first bite of cake.

The peaceful city park, situated between a tranquil lagoon and the picturesque marina, is an outdoor option for exchanging your wedding vows. OYC staff adds guest seating, flowers, an arch, chairs for your harpist or string quartet—whatever you want to personalize your special ritual. Nature provides the rest: live oaks, willow, birdsong and, of course, the spectacular estuary view.

Next door to the clubhouse, an attractive hotel makes visiting attendees' accommodation easy and offers additional venues for rehearsal dinners, brunches and other pre- and post-function mixers. Those with a boat may want to make use of the club's guest dock—it might be just the spot to park that getaway launch and set sail for the future.

CEREMONY CAPACITY: The facility holds 200 seated guests outdoors.

EVENT/RECEPTION CAPACITY: Indoors, the club can accommodate 200 seated or 225 standing guests.

MEETING CAPACITY: The club holds 200 seated.

FEES & DEPOSITS: The rental fee is required to reserve your date. 90% of the estimated event total is due 10 days prior to the event, the balance is due on the day of the event. Rental fees range $150–500 depending on the space and time rented. Meals range $7.50–40/person. Tax, alcohol and a 20% service charge are additional.

AVAILABILITY: Year-round, Tuesday–Sunday, 9am–midnight. Times vary depending on already scheduled member events.

SERVICES/AMENITIES:

Catering: provided
Kitchen Facilities: n/a
Tables & Chairs: provided
Linens, Silver, etc.: provided
Restrooms: wheelchair accessible
Dance Floor: provided
Bride's Dressing Area: yes
Meeting Equipment: some provided

Parking: large lot
Accommodations: no guestrooms
Telephone: emergency use only
Outdoor Night Lighting: CBA
Outdoor Cooking Facilities: no
Cleanup: provided
View: panorama of ocean/bay and coastline
Other: grand piano, picnic area, AV equipment, event coordination

RESTRICTIONS:

Alcohol: provided, or BYO with corkage fee
Smoking: not allowed
Music: amplified OK with restrictions

Wheelchair Access: yes
Insurance: liability required

Round Hill Country Club

3169 Round Hill Road, Alamo
925/934-8211
www.rhcountryclub.com
debbies@roundhillcc.org, laurens@roundhillcc.org

● Rehearsal Dinners	● Corp. Events/Mtgs.
● Ceremonies	● Private Parties
● Wedding Receptions	○ Accommodations

Set atop a gentle rise, the clubhouse at Round Hill Country Club presides over a sun-dappled golf course amidst the rolling hills and upscale homes of the exclusive community of Alamo. It's so quiet and secluded here you feel like you're in your own little world, yet the venue is only a mile from Highway 680 and minutes from lodging and shopping in nearby Walnut Creek and San Ramon. Fortunately for you, this private club makes its beautiful event facilities available to nonmembers.

Round Hill has been a favorite site for social and corporate events for decades. With four distinctly different interior event areas and an expansive patio, it offers many options for choreographing your celebration. Another plus are their in-house Catering Directors, who will help you organize all the details so you don't need to hire a coordinator. Flexibility is key at the club, and they rarely say "no" to requests. Planning a Persian, Indian, Chinese, Korean or other ethnic wedding? Not a problem. The staff will customize your cuisine and your ceremony setup to your particular needs.

Formal affairs are often held in the Vista Ballroom, whose refined décor features a Romanesque fresco at each end, textured beige walls trimmed in polished oak, and mirrors that enhance the feeling of spaciousness. Icicle lights seem to float from the ceiling, highlighting the dance floor. A series of arched windows look out onto the Breezeway, a light-filled prefunction space that extends the entire length of the ballroom. As friends and family mingle over cocktails here, they have a view of the outdoor pool area. The most intimate spot is the adjoining Living Room, where guests can take a break from the festivities by relaxing on comfortable sofas in a homey atmosphere. These three areas work extremely well together, and create a wonderful flow to an event.

For something less formal, but equally appealing, consider the casual elegance of the Fairway Grill & Lounge. Dining is hosted in the Grill, designed with an exceptionally high, open-beamed ceiling. On one side of the room, a fire blazing in the cast stone fireplace lends a cozy warmth, while on the other side floor-to-ceiling windows overlook manicured golf greens and the Fairway Patio. The Lounge, with its built-in bar, is also where the dance floor is set up. During fair weather, guests enjoy easy access from the Grill & Lounge to the patio, which serves as a lovely spot for dining overflow or al fresco cocktails.

The President's Room is ideal for small events and is often used in combination with the Ballroom and/or the Grill & Lounge. It's popular for rehearsal dinners and anniversary parties—some groups have even used it for a casino games evening! When the weather turns cool, it also doubles as an indoor ceremony site.

Outdoors, exchange vows on the Upper Patio Terrace against a postcard-perfect backdrop: the 18th green and the picturesque Alamo hills.

Hosting your event at Round Hill is like inviting guests to enjoy your own private villa. For the day at least, they can indulge in the privileges and amenities of this prestigious country club.

CEREMONY CAPACITY: The President's Room holds 200 seated guests. The outdoor wedding site accommodates 200 guests

EVENT/RECEPTION CAPACITY: The Vista Ballroom accommodates 300 seated or 400 standing guests, and the Fairway Grill 160 seated or 200 standing. The President's Room holds up to 100 seated or 120 standing guests, and can be divided into 2 smaller spaces that each hold 50 seated or 60 standing guests.

MEETING CAPACITY: The Vista Ballroom holds 400 guests seated theater-style or 150 classroom-style; the President's Room 200 guests seated theater-style or 64 classroom-style.

FEES & DEPOSITS: A $2,000 deposit is required to reserve your date; the balance is due 14 days prior to the event. Room rental fees range $200–2,000 depending on space rented. Luncheons range $15–25/person, dinners $35–50/person. Tax, alcohol and a 20% service charge are additional. A $600–1,000 ceremony setup fee is extra.

AVAILABILITY: Year-round, daily, 6am–1am.

SERVICES/AMENITIES:

Catering: provided, no BYO
Kitchen Facilities: n/a
Tables & Chairs: provided
Linens, Silver, etc.: provided
Restrooms: wheelchair accessible
Dance Floor: parquet floor
Bride's & Groom's Dressing Area: CBA
Meeting Equipment: CBA, extra charge

Parking: valet required, extra charge
Accommodations: no guestrooms
Telephone: emergency use only
Outdoor Night Lighting: yes
Outdoor Cooking Facilities: CBA
Cleanup: provided
View: pool, rolling hills, trees, golf course
Other: event coordination

RESTRICTIONS:

Alcohol: provided or WC corkage $15/bottle
Smoking: outside only
Music: amplified OK indoors

Wheelchair Access: yes
Insurance: not required
Other: no rice, confetti, birdseed, or rose petals

Albany Community Center

1249 Marin Avenue, Albany
510/524-9283
www.albanyca.org
jcosby@albanyca.org

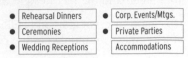

Community Center

● Rehearsal Dinners	● Corp. Events/Mtgs.
● Ceremonies	● Private Parties
● Wedding Receptions	Accommodations

"A small town in a big city" could best describe Albany, tucked as it is between Richmond, El Cerrito and Berkeley. Although it has all the conveniences of a modern metropolis, it's still a throwback to a more sociable time: Brightly painted wood frame storefronts on Solano Avenue are right out of an old-fashioned "Main Street," and delightful shops and sidewalk cafés inspire a leisurely pace. Many of Albany's homes have broad front porches that are garlanded with climbing rose bushes and shaded by oak trees, inviting you to extend your stroll through pretty neighborhoods. And while you're at it, stop in at the Albany Community Center, an appealing gathering place that embodies the same congenial spirit as the rest of the town.

You'll recognize the snappy Community Center by its Observation Tower, rising above the contemporary complex and surrounding trees. Hedgerows and leafy saplings form a fringe of greenery along the front of the Center, whose entrance leads into a spacious foyer called the Terrazzo. The Center was designed to house the town library on one side and the recreation center on the other, and the cheerful Terrazzo links the two. Bathed in natural light from a lofty skylight, it provides a warm welcome for you and your guests. The Terrazzo also doubles as an art gallery, and a few comfortable chairs make it possible to sit down, relax and admire the paintings and photographic exhibits featuring prominent Northern California artists.

When you're ready to attend your special event, turn into a smaller lobby that adjoins the Terrazzo and the Community Room. It serves as your prefunction area, where friends and family mingle and sign the guest book before moving on into the Community Room.

This versatile banquet area can set the stage for almost any kind of celebration. Sunshine or moonlight filters through a vaulted pyramid of glass that crowns the room, contributing to an open, expansive quality. Features like highly polished oak floors, wood trim and demi-panels of matching oak lend the simple space distinction, while providing a neutral palette for your own decorating scheme. A long row of French doors along one side of the room leads outdoors to the patio.

Out here guests can enjoy their cocktails and hors d'oeuvres, while watching the sparrows flit among the trees and shrubbery. Enhance the festive atmosphere by hanging twinkle lights or other decorations from a narrow Asian-style pergola that defines the outer edge of the patio.

You can bring your own caterer, and there's a full modern kitchen to help them serve up an impressive feast. The facility is not only audiovisually complete, but also has a friendly staff that's on duty during your event. Albany Community Center is very reasonably priced, making it very much in demand. So don't wait too long to book here, or you may miss out on this popular venue.

CEREMONY CAPACITY: The Community Room holds 240 guests, and several meeting rooms hold 25–45 seated.

EVENT/RECEPTION CAPACITY: The Community Room holds 160 seated at tables or 260 standing; meeting rooms hold 35–45 seated or 40–50 standing guests.

MEETING CAPACITY: Several meeting rooms accommodate 20–45 classroom-style or 35–45 theater-style. The Community Room holds 80 classroom-style or 200 theater-style.

FEES & DEPOSITS: A $33 application fee and a $350 refundable security deposit are required when reservations are made. Rental fees range $61–125/hour, depending on the day of the week and type of event. The rental fee balance is payable 60 days prior to the event. Insurance is required and can be purchased through the City of Albany; there are processing charges. Stage setup and sound system fees are additional.

AVAILABILITY: Year-round, daily: Sunday–Thursday 7:30am–10pm, Friday 1pm–midnight, and Saturday 7:30am–midnight.

SERVICES/AMENITIES:
Catering: BYO
Kitchen Facilities: commercial kitchen
Tables & Chairs: provided up to 160 guests
Linens, Silver, etc.: BYO or caterer
Restrooms: wheelchair accessible
Dance Floor: hardwood floor
Bride's & Groom's Dressing Area: CBA
Meeting Equipment: full range, extra charge

Parking: on street or parking lot
Accommodations: no guestrooms
Telephone: pay phones
Outdoor Night Lighting: access only
Outdoor Cooking Facilities: no
Cleanup: renter or caterer
View: no

RESTRICTIONS:
Alcohol: BYO
Smoking: outside only
Music: amplified OK indoors with volume limits

Wheelchair Access: yes
Insurance: required through City of Albany
Other: no rice, confetti or birdseed; no open flames, decorations need approval

Want to know WHAT TO ASK a potential location or vendor? Check out our Questions to Ask on page 17.

ASUC Student Union

Bancroft & Telegraph, Berkeley
510/642-1141
eventservices.berkeley.edu
reservations@berkeley.edu

Student Union

● Rehearsal Dinners	● Corp. Events/Mtgs.
● Ceremonies	● Private Parties
● Wedding Receptions	Accommodations

Whether you're a Cal alumnus who dreams in blue and gold, or a bride (or groom!) looking for a room-with-a-view that won't cost a bundle, consider the ASUC Martin Luther King, Jr. Student Union. Overlooking Sproul Plaza at the heart of the UC Berkeley Campus, the five-story building offers a variety of flexible event facilities.

The Main Lobby is a modern, open space with a dramatic focal point: a wide marble staircase that brides decorate with garlands or greenery entwined in the banisters. Photographers usually pose the wedding party on these stairs, which also lead guests up to the Ballroom and Lounge for a reception or cocktail hour.

For wedding ceremonies, ride the elevators to the newly renovated Tilden Room at the top of the building. Here, the simple décor showcases a magnificent wall-size mosaic of boldly colored stained glass done in deep scarlet, glittering white and shades of blue. The splendid work of art—a glorious backdrop for exchanging vows—is especially evocative of a Renaissance masterpiece when backlit by the sun's rays.

After the ceremony, open the doors wide on both sides of the room so that guests can flow out to the East and West Patios for more visual treats. The West Patio takes in a spectacular Bay Area skyline, with the Golden Gate Bridge poised above the blue-green waters of the bay; in the evening, sunset gives way to the twinkling lights of San Francisco in the distance. A promenade leads to the East Patio, which faces the verdant Berkeley Hills. Stately Sproul Hall lies below, and the venerable Campanile seems almost within reach. Wooden planters brimming with flowering greenery of the season edge these outdoor spaces, and you can add Tivoli lights or paper lanterns for greater effect. Even if you hold your ceremony at one of the local houses of worship, you can still use the Tilden Room for your cocktail hour; leave the room's doors open, and up to 250 of your friends and family can mingle in this refreshing milieu.

For a cocktail hour with a relaxed formality, reserve Kerr Lounge, located at the top of the Lobby staircase. This open area, defined by blue carpeting, wood paneling and tall windows, conveniently adjoins the foyer of Pauley Ballroom.

Seated receptions for up to 600 can be staged in this spacious ballroom, where oak paneling, a high ceiling, modern light fixtures, and a gleaming hardwood floor create a timeless blend of the traditional and contemporary. The star here, however, is the row of floor-to-ceiling windows that let guests peer over leafy treetops to far-reaching vistas of rolling hillsides, historic buildings and star-filled skies. Not only does the view make the room feel even more expansive, but it also connects your celebration to the surrounding community. There's also a service kitchen, and you're free to use the caterer of your choice—even your Aunt Millie!

Event Services at the Student Union will assist in all aspects of your event, from preferred vendors, linens and equipment rentals to recommendations for local activities, lodging and dining options. With its accommodating staff and very attractive pricing, the Student Union is catching on as a prime venue for any important occasion.

CEREMONY & MEETING CAPACITY: The Ballroom holds up to 900 guests, seated theater-style.

EVENT/RECEPTION CAPACITY: Various indoor spaces hold up to 600 seated at round tables or 999 standing guests.

FEES & DEPOSITS: 50% of the rental fee is required to reserve your date. The balance is due 30 days prior to event. Rental fees range $1,000–3,000 depending on space rented.

AVAILABILITY: Year-round, subject to University activities and availability.

SERVICES/AMENITIES:
Catering: BYO
Kitchen Facilities: fully equipped
Tables & Chairs: CBA
Linens, Silver, etc.: BYO
Restrooms: wheelchair accessible
Dance Floor: yes
Bride's Dressing Area: yes
Meeting Equipment: CBA, extra fee

Parking: on-street or on-site and nearby garages
Accommodations: no guestrooms
Telephone: emergency use only
Outdoor Night Lighting: access only
Outdoor Cooking Facilities: no
Cleanup: caterer and facility
View: cityscape and rolling hills

RESTRICTIONS:
Alcohol: BYO
Smoking: outdoors only
Music: amplified OK indoors

Wheelchair Access: yes
Insurance: liability required

Bancroft Hotel

Boutique Hotel

2680 Bancroft Way, Berkeley
510/549-0113

www.bancrofthotel.com
kelly@bancrofthotel.com

- Rehearsal Dinners
- Ceremonies
- Wedding Receptions
- Corp. Events/Mtgs.
- Private Parties
- Accommodations

Housed in a historic landmark building across the street from the University of California and next door to the Berkeley Art Museum, the Bancroft Hotel has become one of the premier hotels in the East Bay. Originally built in 1928 as the home of the College Women's Club, it was designed by Walter T. Steilberg, an associate of architect Julia Morgan (of Hearst Castle fame).

After a complete renovation of the property, the Bancroft Hotel had its much-acclaimed grand opening in 1994. Guests admired the handsome public spaces, graced with antiques, vintage-style furniture and period reproductions; furnishings in the Bancroft's 22 beautifully appointed guestrooms were reproduced from Walter Steilberg's original drawings, and many of the rooms are enhanced with balconies and views of the bay. There's an ambiance of timeless elegance, and whether you're dreaming of a celebration with an air of romantic nostalgia or quiet refinement, the Bancroft Hotel is an absolute must-see.

Most receptions unfold in the Great Hall, a glamorous event space inspired by the turn-of-the-century Arts and Crafts movement. This one-of-a-kind 4,000-square-foot room is lavished with floor-to-ceiling woodwork, period fixtures and stained-glass transoms. Gleaming hardwood floors and lofty ceilings add to the sense of tradition and grandeur, and two giant fireplaces provide warmth and atmosphere. The Hall actually has three distinct sections, which can be used for different aspects of your event. The raised hardwood stage at one end can hold musicians, a dance floor or the head table, while the recessed middle section can be transformed into an intimate dining space. Use the other end for additional reception seating, or for a buffet and bar setup. The Great Hall is not only spacious, but also extremely flexible—you could arrange your party in a variety of ways and still have it work fabulously.

The light and bright Steilberg Conference Room is distinguished by pale, gently curving walls and a magnificent fireplace trimmed in tile and rich mahogany. Windows at one end frame a pleasing view of the city and a slice of the San Francisco Bay in the distance. Another way to savor the vista is to sneak away to the Rooftop Terrace and share a champagne toast with your sweetie.

The Bancroft Hotel does have comfortable and attractive accommodations for your out-of-town relatives and friends—but why not reserve the entire boutique hotel exclusively for you and your guests for a destination weekend? A complete buyout gets you all the event spaces, guestrooms—even the parking lot! In fact, *Bancroft Catering* can customize all your meals to your liking throughout your stay, so you never really have to leave the hotel at all—unless it's to visit their sister location, Adagia Restaurant, just two doors away, a wonderful option for your rehearsal dinner.

If you plan on "going green" for your wedding, then you'll appreciate the Bancroft's environmentally safe cleaning products, luxurious bamboo towels, organic linens and other "green" amenities. Eco-weddings are a specialty, and the in-house culinary team offers earth-friendly tableware alternatives and organic menus.

Whether you're hosting a large bash or a cozy gathering, the Bancroft Hotel is a distinctive indoor wedding site with a conveniently located, yet very serene environment.

CEREMONY CAPACITY: Indoors, up to 250 seated guests. Three tiered sections in the Great Hall available for smaller groups to have more intimate gatherings.

EVENT/RECEPTION CAPACITY: The facility holds 175–250 seated guests (depending on whether or not a dance floor is required), or 300 for a standing reception.

MEETING CAPACITY: The Hotel accommodates 250 seated theater-style.

FEES & DEPOSITS: To secure your date, the entire rental fee is required as a deposit when you sign your contract. The rental fee runs $800–2,000 and varies depending on the season and day of week. The entire hotel is available for a buyout. Luncheons start at $18.95/person, dinners at $35.95/person. Tax, alcohol and service charge are additional.

AVAILABILITY: Year-round, daily, anytime.

SERVICES/AMENITIES:

Catering: provided
Kitchen Facilities: n/a
Tables & Chairs: provided
Linens, Silver, etc.: CBA, extra charge
Restrooms: wheelchair accessible
Dance Floor: provided
Bride's Dressing Area: CBA
Meeting Equipment: banquet tables, flip charts, extra fee for TV/VCR and overhead projector

Parking: adjacent lot or valet CBA
Accommodations: 22 guestrooms
Telephone: emergency use only
Outdoor Night Lighting: CBA
Outdoor Cooking Facilities: no
Cleanup: provided
View: SF Bay and Berkeley hills
Other: event coordination available

RESTRICTIONS:

Alcohol: CBA
Smoking: not allowed
Music: amplified OK until 10:30pm unless all guestrooms are booked by client

Wheelchair Access: conference room only
Insurance: not required

Berkeley City Club

Historic Hotel and Social Club

2315 Durant Avenue, Berkeley
510/280-1532

www.berkeleycityclub.com
events@berkeleycityclub.com

- Rehearsal Dinners
- Ceremonies
- Wedding Receptions
- Corp. Events/Mtgs.
- Private Parties
- Accommodations

The Berkeley City Club, located just one block from the UC Berkeley campus, is a sensational landmark building and a proud member of Historic Hotels of America®. Although it's long been a private member social club, its hotel and event facilities welcome the public.

Designed in 1929 by famed architect Julia Morgan, the popular venue is like a miniature Hearst Castle. The Venetian Mediterranean-style building features landscaped inner courtyards and fountains, plus a wealth of graceful arches, domed ceilings, pillars, leaded-glass windows and doors, and art. Together they create a gorgeous backdrop for your wedding—and your photos!

The detailing and craftsmanship are impressive throughout. The Drawing Room and Members' Lounge are large and gracious, with beamed ceilings, pianos, fireplaces, wall tapestries, tiled floors, Oriental carpets and sizable leaded-glass windows. The Ballroom, which has a stage, parquet floor, concert grand piano, and its own leaded-glass windows overlooking the courtyard, also has plenty of room for dancing along with your reception. For an outdoor affair, the sheltered, ivy-covered Terrace is a wonderful spot on a warm day or evening. And because many of these event spaces are connected to one another, they can be used individually or in combination.

The Camelia Courtyard is perfect for an intimate ceremony or cocktail reception. Filled with greenery and framed by the building's arches, it's evocative of a Mediterranean garden. A smaller, lushly planted fountain courtyard on the opposite side of the club lends itself to a cozy luncheon or rehearsal dinner. Even if you don't host an event in one of these courtyards, you'll definitely want to take advantage of their photogenic qualities for your wedding album.

Many couples like to host both their ceremony and reception here: The club's soaring architecture and private, contemplative areas provide a spiritual atmosphere for exchanging vows; at the same time, the versatile reception facilities and experienced staff ensure a flawless event.

Speaking of flawless, the club's hair salon and aesthetic services make it easy for you and your bridesmaids to look and feel your best for the wedding. Whether you arrive the day before or the day of, you'll be able to relax while the on-site professionals take you from stressed to beautiful.

The Berkeley City Club is a tranquil oasis in this bustling college town. Family and friends who stay overnight will appreciate the newly renovated guestrooms, all of which offer outstanding views of the San Francisco Bay or Berkeley hills. And as hotel guests, they'll be able to take a dip in the magnificent swimming pool, enjoy the Dining Room's outstanding cuisine, and sample premier wines in the Venetian Room. From this conveniently located getaway, exploring Berkeley couldn't be easier: Famed Telegraph Avenue, museums, restaurants, the theater district and public transit are all close by.

CEREMONY, EVENT/RECEPTION CAPACITY: Event spaces hold 14–200 seated guests. The Venetian Ballrooom holds up to 300 standing guests.

MEETING CAPACITY: The Berkeley City Club has 5 meeting rooms that accommodate up to 280 seated theater-style or 125 seated classroom-style.

FEES & DEPOSITS: A $775 nonrefundable rental deposit is required when the reservation is confirmed; the balance and a final guest count are due prior to the function. Rental fees range $300–1,300 depending on space or day selected. For a separate bar setup, a bartender fee will apply. On weekdays, luncheons begin at $22.50/person, and dinners at $35/person. Dinners on weekends begin at $46/person. Menus and event details can be arranged with the event coordinator. If your group would like to stay overnight, bed and breakfast rates will apply. Call for more information.

AVAILABILITY: Year-round, Tuesday–Friday, 8am–11pm; Saturday–Sunday, 2pm–11pm. Closed Thanksgiving, Christmas and New Years Days.

SERVICES/AMENITIES:

Catering: provided, no BYO
Kitchen Facilities: n/a
Tables & Chairs: provided
Linens, Silver, etc.: provided
Restrooms: wheelchair accessible
Dance Floor: yes
Bride's Dressing Area: yes
Meeting Equipment: full range CBA

Parking: small lot, valet or prepaid CBA
Accommodations: 36 guestrooms
Telephone: pay and guest phones
Outdoor Night Lighting: yes
Outdoor Cooking Facilities: BBQ CBA
Cleanup: provided
View: indoor courtyards
Other: event coordinator, candelabras, fireplaces, pianos; complimentary amenities for overnight guests include dining room buffet, hot made-to-order breakfast, and a pass to the UC Berkeley Recreational Sports Facility

RESTRICTIONS:

Alcohol: provided, no BYO
Smoking: not allowed
Music: amplified OK

Wheelchair Access: yes
Insurance: sometimes required
Other: security sometimes required

Want to find more locations and services? Check out our informative website, www.HereComesTheGuide.com.

Brazilian Room

Tilden Park, Berkeley (operated by East Bay Regional Parks)
510/544-3164
www.brazilianroom.org
brazil@ebparks.org

Historic Banquet Facility

- Rehearsal Dinners
- Ceremonies
- Wedding Receptions
- Corp. Events/Mtgs.
- Private Parties
- Accommodations

High in the hills of North Berkeley lies Tilden Park, popularly considered "the Jewel of the East Bay." Hiking trails with names like Seaview or Skyline wind past creeks, mineral springs, and sylvan meadows, up to the sweeping panorama offered at Inspiration Point. Yet just about every vista in Tilden Park is inspirational. Encompassing the Tilden Nature Area, most of the park's 2,077 acres serve as tranquil shelters for native plants and wildlife. Rangers here are serious about preserving this magnificent habitat—they even close one of their roads seasonally to protect migrating newts—and the result is a cornucopia of natural beauty. Visitors also enjoy the abundance of recreational activities, including steam trains, a golf course and an antique merry-go-round. For generations of Bay Area residents, outings to Tilden Park have been part of a happy tradition, beginning with a youngster's first pony ride and perhaps culminating in a wedding ceremony at the historic Brazilian Room.

Once part of the 1939 Golden Gate Exposition on Treasure Island, the Brazilian Room was presented as a gift to the East Bay Regional Park District by the country of Brazil. The original interior hardwood paneling was kept intact, while a new exterior of local rock and timber was constructed by the Works Project Administration to permanently house the room.

To reach the Brazilian Room, follow Grizzly Peak Boulevard to Wildcat Canyon Road, and behold a cascading glen dotted with thick stands of fragrant pine, oak and eucalyptus. Add to this scene a building of remarkable architectural achievement with its own beautiful garden, and you have a striking location for any celebration.

Wedding ceremonies are extremely popular on the flagstone patio, with its dramatic panorama of sloping lawn and tree-studded hillsides. After toasting the newlyweds, guests can sip their champagne among the colorful mix of agapanthus, hydrangea and other flowers that make up the small garden adjoining the patio, or sample hors d'oeuvres under the cherry tree, abloom in April with perfumey-pink blossoms.

The setting at the Brazilian Room is just as lovely indoors as out. The building's Old English-style façade is defined by a trio of leaded-glass doors, each with dormer-style threshold. When guests move inside for the reception, they'll find that floor-to-ceiling leaded-glass windows run the length of the other side of the room as well. These rear windows also offer a close-up look at the forest, evoking the romance of a light-filled mountain cabin. Dark wooden beams create a novel pattern on the ceiling, and polished wood flooring and a huge stone fireplace give the space additonal rustic charm.

The serene pastoral surroundings at the Brazilian Room offer an environment free from noise and distraction, where Nature's gifts are honored and preserved and the modern world is in harmony with the building's heritage. It's a place you'll want to make part of your own family tradition.

CEREMONY CAPACITY: The patio holds 180 seated; the main room, up to 150 seated or 225 standing guests.

EVENT/RECEPTION CAPACITY: The main room holds 225 standing guests or 150 seated.

MEETING CAPACITY: The main room accommodates 150 seated conference-style or 225 seated theater-style.

FEES & DEPOSITS: A $300 deposit is required to secure your date. If cancelled more than 120 days prior to the event, $100 of this deposit is refundable. For a 12-hour block, a $600 deposit is required. $200 of that is refundable if cancellation is made more than 120 days prior to the event. Signed contracts are required 2 weeks after the initial deposit, the fee balance and cleaning and-damage deposits are due 120 days prior to the event date. For events reserved fewer than 120 days away, the entire rental balance and all deposits are due when the contract is signed.

Weekend rates for Friday night, Saturday, Sunday and holidays (min. 7 hours) range $1,900–3,800 depending on the day and time frame reserved. Weekday rates range $300–750 depending on day and length of time rented. The seasonal Sunday rate November through March is $1,900 for a 7-hour block, 9am–midnight. Each additional hour is $250. For nonresidents of Alameda and Contra Costa Counties, there is a surcharge that equals 20% of the room rental fee. Optional services are available at an extra charge.

AVAILABILITY: Saturday, Sunday and holidays 9am–4pm or 5pm–midnight; Friday evening 5pm–midnight; Friday day 8am–4pm; Monday, Wednesday, Thursday 8am–midnight; Sunday, November through March 9am–midnight

SERVICES/AMENITIES:
Catering: select from preferred list
Kitchen Facilities: ample
Tables & Chairs: provided
Linens, Silver, etc.: BYO
Restrooms: wheelchair accessible
Dance Floor: yes
Bride's Dressing Area: yes
Meeting Equipment: PA, projector and screen, microphones, extra fee

Parking: in lot, no fees
Accommodations: no guestrooms
Telephone: pay phone
Outdoor Night Lighting: yes
Outdoor Cooking Facilities: yes
Cleanup: caterer
View: great views of Tilden Park with lots of trees and relative privacy
Other: fireplace available, extra fee

RESTRICTIONS:
Alcohol: BYO; WCB only, kegs of beer restricted to patio and kitchen
Smoking: outside only
Music: amplified OK indoors, outdoors with restrictions

Wheelchair Access: yes
Insurance: extra liability is required
Other: decorations restricted

Claremont Hotel Club and Spa

Landmark Hotel

41 Tunnel Road, Berkeley
510/549-8591
www.claremont-hotel.com
catering@claremont-hotel.com

- Rehearsal Dinners
- Ceremonies
- Wedding Receptions
- Corp. Events/Mtgs.
- Private Parties
- Accommodations

The brilliant white, castle-like Claremont Hotel Club & Spa has been a Bay Area landmark since 1915 when it debuted. Spread over 22 acres, the hotel is set high in the Berkeley Hills and commands one of the best views in the Bay Area. Along with its panoramic vista, the hotel's grand design, fragrant rose gardens and luxurious amenities have made it a perennial favorite, drawing admirers from around the globe. A long list of presidents, Hollywood stars and other famous guests have stayed here. Among them was architect Frank Lloyd Wright, who proclaimed the Claremont "one of the few hotels in the world with warmth, character and charm." We tend to agree. After all, could the esteemed Mr. Wright be wrong?

The Claremont's assets have also made it a sought-after locale for weddings. Couples can host their entire event here, from a rehearsal dinner at the Meritage at the Claremont to a sublime honeymoon in a grand suite. A variety of ballrooms—each one with its own distinctive ambiance—accommodate groups of every size, from an intimate gathering to a gala reception. In the Horizon Room, warm tones and vintage crystal chandeliers create a delicate, timeless elegance—and the panoramic view from the wall of west-facing windows encompasses both bridges and the San Francisco skyline. The adjacent Lanai Room is a lovely indoor ceremony space and comes complete with an outdoor balcony for great photo opportunities.

The Claremont also boasts a 20,000-square-foot fitness center, Pilates studio, and lap pool. You'll definitely want to spend some time being pampered at Spa Claremont, which offers wedding packages that include facials, hairstyling, manicures, pedicures and makeup application, ensuring that you'll be picture-perfect on your wedding day.

Planning your event here is stress-free, thanks to a team of wedding experts who will guide you through every decision and take care of all the details. And when you're ready to wind down after the festivities, you'll find an atmosphere of relaxation in the Claremont's guestrooms. All feature plush bathrobes and slippers, cable TV, video-game consoles and high-speed internet access. Many also provide exceptional views of San Francisco Bay.

Conceived as an English estate, this historic hotel and grounds have surrounded guests with elegance, sophistication and charm for nearly a century. So, whether you come here to get married in style or simply enjoy a delectable dinner for two, the Claremont is a peaceful and romantic retreat from the world.

CEREMONY CAPACITY: Indoor spaces hold 20–300 seated; outdoor spaces up to 150 seated guests.

EVENT/RECEPTION CAPACITY: The largest ballroom accommodates 300 seated with dancing, 360 seated without, or 500 standing for a cocktail reception. Capacities for the 20 other rooms range 10–350 seated guests.

MEETING CAPACITY: There are 20 rooms that hold 20–400 seated theater-style, 30–275 classroom-style, or 8–60 conference-style.

FEES, DEPOSITS & AVAILABILITY: For special events and weddings, a $1,500 nonrefundable deposit is required to hold your date. Half of the total estimated bill is due 4 months prior to the event; the balance is due 14 days prior to the event.

Wedding packages are available starting at $59/person, and include dinner, wedding cake, setup, breakdown, linens, tableware, dance floor, room rental fee, tax and service charges. Any menu can be customized. There is a $1,500 charge for an indoor ceremony in a ballroom or an outdoor ceremony. Tax and services charges are additional.

Fees for business functions and meetings vary depending on room(s) and services selected. Corporate day meeting packages are available; call for specific pricing.

AVAILABILITY: Year-round, daily, 6am–midnight.

SERVICES/AMENITIES:
Catering: provided, no BYO
Kitchen Facilities: n/a
Tables & Chairs: provided
Linens, Silver, etc.: provided
Restrooms: wheelchair accessible
Dance Floor: provided
Bride's & Groom's Dressing Area: CBA
Meeting Equipment: full range AV
Other: event coordination, spa, fitness center

Parking: self-parking and valet
Accommodations: 279 guestrooms
Telephone: pay and guest phones
Outdoor Night Lighting: access only
Outdoor Cooking Facilities: BBQ
Cleanup: provided
View: entire East Bay and San Francisco Bay plus San Francisco skyline

RESTRICTIONS:
Alcohol: provided, or corkage $19/bottle
Smoking: outdoors only
Music: amplified OK indoors only

Wheelchair Access: yes
Insurance: required

The Faculty Club

University of California at Berkeley
510/643-0834
www.berkeleyfacultyclub.com
info@berkeleyfacultyclub.com

Historic Campus Club

- Rehearsal Dinners
- Ceremonies
- Wedding Receptions
- Corp. Events/Mtgs.
- Private Parties
- Accommodations

UC Berkeley has many picturesque settings, but the loveliest one may well be that of the Faculty Club. Located in the heart of campus, it's quietly ensconced in a grove of redwoods, oaks and maples next to meandering Strawberry Creek. Built in 1902 by the renowned architect Bernard Maybeck in traditional Arts and Crafts style, it's designed to create a cozy, intimate feeling.

The crowning glory of the Club is the three-story Great Hall. With its vaulted ceiling, massive stone fireplace, and stained-glass windows featuring heraldic crests of the great universities of the world, it's reminiscent of many a European cathedral. Light from the floor-to-ceiling windows warms the redwood paneling and suffuses the Hall in a golden glow.

Two charming smaller spaces are also available for functions. The Heyns and Seaborg rooms (named respectively after a chancellor and a distinguished University Nobel Laureate) both have French doors leading to a private outdoor area with a garden view. The Seaborg Room is especially striking, with its open-beamed A-frame ceiling and wisteria-framed windows overlooking the peaceful Faculty Glade Lawn.

The Faculty Club has long been a favorite site for meetings, bar and bat mitzvahs, anniversary parties, class reunions, retreats and retirement dinners. But it really comes into its own during weddings. Many couples like to have the ceremony right outside on the Faculty Glade Lawn, then move into the Great Hall for the wedding feast. (The Heyns and Seaborg rooms also have private terraces for al fresco ceremonies.) Aside from the building itself, the staff is the Faculty Club's greatest asset. They've been producing events since 1902, and they're experienced at accommodating a wide range of special requests. Do any of your guests have particular dietary needs? The Faculty Club can provide nonfat, vegetarian or vegan dishes. For the ultimate in convenience, your family and friends are welcome to stay overnight in the Club's hotel bedrooms (which are often reserved for visiting scholars). From these comfortable lodgings, it's just a quick walk down the stairs to the ceremony. Also, if the bride needs a room for changing, or for storing flowers or gifts, the Club will provide one.

The Faculty Club's full catering service handles all the food and beverages—including the bar—and they offer menus for every type of event, from a brunch buffet to a formal sit-down dinner. Their catering staff hails from all over the world, and can create authentic cuisine from many countries including India, Mexico, Peru, Greece and Spain. The Faculty Club has been serving its members and guests for over a hundred years, and will do everything possible to make your event successful and enjoyable.

CEREMONY CAPACITY: The Faculty Glade holds 250 seated guests; indoor spaces hold up to 300 seated.

EVENT/RECEPTION CAPACITY: The Great Hall holds 300 seated (260 with a dance floor and buffet) or 400 standing for a cocktail party.

MEETING CAPACITY: The Club can accommodate 300 guests seated theater-style.

FEES & DEPOSITS: The room rental fee is required as a nonrefundable deposit to secure your date; the event balance is due 15 days prior to the event. Catering is provided; meal prices range $15–42/person; beverages, alcohol, tax and an 18% service charge are additional. A $2/person cake-cutting fee is extra, and for ceremonies there's a $2/chair fee for setup on the Glade.

AVAILABILITY: Year-round, daily, anytime (except days on which there is a Cal home football game)

SERVICES/AMENITIES:
Catering: provided
Kitchen Facilities: n/a
Tables & Chairs: provided
Linens, Silver, etc.: provided
Restrooms: wheelchair accessible
Dance Floor: yes
Bride's & Groom's Dressing Area: yes
Meeting Equipment: BYO or CBA, extra charge
Other: event coordination, baby grand and upright pianos, wireless internet connection in hotel and banquet rooms

Parking: on campus, pay parking available evenings and weekends
Accommodations: 23 guestrooms
Telephone: pay and house phones
Outdoor Night Lighting: yes
Outdoor Cooking Facilities: no
Cleanup: provided
View: lawn, creek and garden

RESTRICTIONS:
Alcohol: provided or BYO wine, corkage $15/bottle
Smoking: not allowed
Music: amplified OK until 11pm

Wheelchair Access: except to Seaborg Room
Insurance: not required
Other: no rice or glitter; decorations restricted, no nails, staples or tacks on walls

---

This is important! Tell locations you're reading HERE COMES THE GUIDE and ask if our information is still current.

Hotel Durant

2600 Durant Street, Berkeley
510/845-8981

www.hoteldurant.com
durantsales@jdvhotels.com

● Rehearsal Dinners	● Corp. Events/Mtgs.
● Ceremonies	● Private Parties
● Wedding Receptions	● Accommodations

A Berkeley landmark with strong ties to the UC campus, this historic Spanish Mediterranean-style establishment has charmed visitors from around the world since 1928. Recently, the Joie de Vivre property underwent a multi-million dollar renovation, making it an extremely accommodating setting with many options for a warm celebration.

The hospitality begins in the high-ceilinged lobby with its unique appointments, friendly staff and comfortable seating. A blue-and-gold color scheme echoes the University's colors and gives a respectful nod to the nearby campus.

Just off the lobby are three popular yet completely different options for events. The first two are in the hotel's restaurant, Henry's, where delectable breakfast, luncheon, appetizer and dinner combinations are created for your guests. The Main Dining Room, filled with natural light from grand, double-paned bay windows overlooking Durant Avenue, is ideal for upscale gatherings and every type of private function. More casual get-togethers are held in the dashing and congenial pub. The third option is the Board Room, an intimate space that can be booked on its own or in conjunction with some of the other rooms in the hotel.

Upstairs is the California Room, a favorite of the scholarly crowd. Its four large windows framed in champagne draperies have showered light on plenty of parties over the years, from sedate sit-down dinners to boisterous mixers to high-powered meetings and corporate events. Off Durant Avenue by way of a private entrance, the University Room provides yet another very flexible event space. Its neutral décor is brightened by skylights and double-paned windows that afford more Durant Avenue views.

Having too much fun at the party to leave? You can take the elevator home to one of Hotel Durant's 143 rooms, including upscale suites like those on the Graduate Floor, a club floor named after the famous movie. All rooms feature a 37″ flat-screen TV, high-speed wireless internet access, an honor bar, refrigerator, in-room safe and iPod docking station. And for the business person's convenience, there's a business center in the lobby.

Nearby attractions like the Lawrence Hall of Science, Zellerbach Hall, the UC Art Museum across the street, Julia Morgan Center, the Botanical Gardens and, of course, dynamic Telegraph Avenue undoubtedly add to the appeal of this much-loved Berkeley hotel. Book early; this one sells out.

CEREMONY CAPACITY: The hotel accommodates up to 75 seated guests indoors.

EVENT/RECEPTION & MEETING CAPACITY: Hotel Durant holds up to 60 seated and 90 standing indoors.

FEES & DEPOSITS: A $400 deposit is required to reserve your date. The balance is due 10 days prior to the event. Rental fees range $300–900 depending on space and time rented. Meals range $22–45/person. Tax, alcohol and a 20% service charge are additional.

AVAILABILITY: Year-round, daily, 7am–midnight.

SERVICES/AMENITIES:

Catering: provided
Kitchen Facilities: n/a
Tables & Chairs: provided
Linens, Silver, etc.: provided
Restrooms: wheelchair accessible
Dance Floor: CBA
Bride's & Groom's Dressing Areas: CBA
Meeting Equipment: some provided

Parking: limited on-site, nearby lots
Accommodations: 143 guestrooms
Telephone: house phone
Outdoor Night Lighting: access only
Outdoor Cooking Facilities: no
Cleanup: provided
View: no

RESTRICTIONS:

Alcohol: provided, or BYO with corkage fee
Smoking: outside only
Music: amplified OK indoors with restrictions

Wheelchair Access: yes
Insurance: not required

UC Botanical Garden

Botanical Garden

200 Centennial Drive, Berkeley
510/642-3352
botanicalgarden.berkeley.edu/rentals/sites.shtml
mdrich@berkeley.edu

● Rehearsal Dinners	● Corp. Events/Mtgs.	
● Ceremonies	● Private Parties	
● Wedding Receptions	Accommodations	

In the hills above UC Berkeley resides a garden of earthly delights: a spectacular 34-acre site nestled in Strawberry Canyon and overlooking the San Francisco Bay. The Botanical Garden is home to over 12,000 different kinds of plants, including many rare and endangered species. The Garden feels like a horticultural wonderland, with plants grouped by geographical region, showcasing the world's rich botanical diversity. A stroll through these varied environments takes you from a cloud forest to a New World Desert, past a Japanese pool with waterfalls, and a Chinese Medicinal Herb Garden—there's even an orchid and carnivorous plant house! First established in 1890, the Garden's mission is research, education and conservation. The Botanical Garden is more than just a place with pretty flowers: it's a living museum. Amidst this natural splendor are several lovely sites to celebrate life's momentous occasions.

Imagine pledging your love in a grove of majestic redwood trees. Your guests are seated in a demi-amphitheater, atop benches built into the very earth itself. Expectant yet relaxed, they catch teasing glimpses of flowing white as you make your way up a forest path between majestic trees stretching their branches heavenward. The air is crisp, fresh, tinged with the scent of moist bark and leaves, and you're filled with the enormity of the moment. At last you reach the amphitheater, and your groom takes your hand as the ceremony begins.

Or perhaps you had something more intimate in mind? Then make your way to the Garden of Old Roses, a storybook bower high on the Garden's eastern slope with all the visual allure of Monet's garden at Giverny. Rough-hewn steps climb down a terraced knoll, resplendent with a mix of lavender, blooming annuals and antique roses. The steps lead to a site where your family and friends wait. Opposite, masses of climbing roses cascade over the beams of a quaint wooden pergola. Completing the romantic vignette, a panorama of the bay unfolds beyond acres of sprawling foliage, like a blue ribbon edging a flowery chintz gown.

Still another option is to wed and have your reception at the Conference Center, set in the middle of the Palm and Cycad Garden above lush Strawberry Creek. Surrounded by luxuriant palms, rare cycads and tree ferns, the Center's broad tiled Terrace makes a sunny place for a ceremony, with the palms defining a natural aisle. Or put a bar and food stations on the Terrace where guests can enjoy pre-reception mingling. Meanwhile, you and your photographer can take advantage of the many scenic backdrops. One particularly appealing spot is just beyond the Terrace: a footbridge poised between the lushly green banks of the creek. Here in the forest's dewy coolness, brightly colored dragonflies dart from delicate ferns to lily pads, and the silhouette of you and your groom is faintly mirrored in the water below.

Inside the Conference Center are two adjoining rooms, the Mirov and the smaller Ornduff. Each has greenhouse windows that let the sunshine in, as well as showcase the surrounding greenery. You might host your banquet in the Mirov, then do the cake cutting in the Ornduff and dance on the Terrace. Or during the cooler months, begin in the Ornduff for cocktails, then move into Mirov for your reception.

Whichever sites you choose at the Botanical Garden, you can be sure of one thing: You're taking the concept of "a simple garden wedding" to a whole new level!

CEREMONY CAPACITY: Outdoor garden spaces seat up to 100 guests; indoors the site accommodates up to 60–100 seated guests.

EVENT/RECEPTION CAPACITY: Outdoor spaces hold up to 40–60 guests; indoors, the site accommodates up to 100 seated or standing guests.

MEETING CAPACITY: Two spaces hold 10–70 guests seated theater-style or at tables.

FEES & DEPOSITS: Rental fees range from $75–400/hour depending on site(s) chosen, number of hours rented and day of event.

AVAILABILITY: Various UC Botanical Garden sites are available year-round, 9am–midnight.

SERVICES/AMENITIES:
Catering: select from list
Kitchen Facilities: kitchenette
Tables & Chairs: yes
Linens, Silver, etc.: BYO or through caterer
Restrooms: wheelchair accessible
Dance Floor: CBA, extra fee
Bride's Dressing Area: yes
Meeting Equipment: internet access, more equipment CBA

Parking: University lot, fees paid in advance
Accommodations: no guestrooms
Telephone: house phone/local and card calls
Outdoor Night Lighting: yes
Outdoor Cooking Facilities: no
Cleanup: caterer or renter
View: botanical garden, creek, SF Bay, city, Golden Gate Bridge

RESTRICTIONS:
Alcohol: BYO, permit required
Smoking: not allowed
Music: amplified OK with restrictions

Wheelchair Access: limited
Insurance: liability required

Trilogy at The Vineyards - Club Los Meganos

Private Club

1700 Trilogy Parkway, Brentwood
925/809-7191
www.vineyardsweddings.com
vineyardsweddings@trilogyresortliving.com

● Rehearsal Dinners	● Corp. Events/Mtgs.
● Ceremonies	● Private Parties
● Wedding Receptions	Accommodations

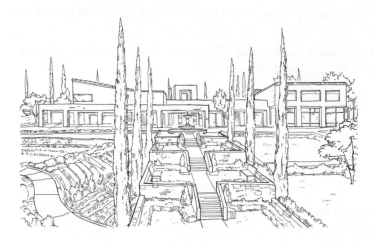

Club Los Meganos at Trilogy at The Vineyards, which debuted in the summer of 2010, is, quite simply, spectacular. Even the drive up to the venue is a pleasure, as you pass olive groves, stately Italian cypress trees and a profusion of white roses and bright flowers. When you arrive at the club, situated just above a series of gentle hills neatly planted with grapevines, you sense that this place is something special.

The 34,000-square-foot club devotes an entire wing specifically to events: the Mount Diablo Events Center, named for the well-known peak visible from almost everywhere on the property. Interior spaces throughout are beautifully designed, incorporating rich woods, natural stone and sweeping expanses of glass in a way that's reminiscent of Frank Lloyd Wright. Outdoors, there's a nod to Mediterranean influences like the circular stone plaza, the tiered terracotta fountain and, of course, the surrounding landscape itself.

Two separate and equally idyllic ceremony sites take full advantage of that landscape. The Vineyard Setting, located in the midst of the vineyards, presents a rare chance to enjoy breathtaking, 360-degree panoramas. The Event Promenade, a sprawling, lush lawn, features unobstructed views of the nearby hills in the foreground and Mount Diablo in the distance.

Serve cocktails and hors d'oeuvres on the Promenade, or indoors in the Reception Foyer. Here, as throughout the club, there's a masterful blend of contemporary design with an underlying homage to the Miwok tribe who once called this area home. A display case with Native American artifacts sits on one wall of this bright, airy space, while a modern painting of an Indian and vibrant turquoise pottery also capture your attention. Glass "NanaWalls," which reveal a spacious patio overlooking the gardens and water features, quickly fold away creating seamless access to the outdoors.

Dinner and dancing take place in the event center's versatile ballroom. Designed with a high, coffered ceiling and decorated in soothing shades of cocoa, cream and muted sky blue, the room has a sophisticated look. There's a view of Mount Diablo through more folding glass doors that open to the Promenade, creating a wonderful indoor-outdoor flow. A state-of-the-art AV system with drop-down screens and a gleaming wooden dance floor set the stage for a lively party.

For a unique rehearsal dinner or bridal shower, check out the Culinary Studio, a dream kitchen/dining room where your guests have an opportunity to observe the chef in action, perhaps whipping up a special menu using ingredients from local orchards. Or, they can relax outside on the adjoining private patio/herb garden with a glass of vino from the on-site wine cellar.

As if all this weren't enticing enough, both the bride and groom get to prepare for the day in the Hii/Kome Room, outfitted with full-length mirrors, a poker table, Wii games and movies.

CEREMONY CAPACITY: The site holds 200 seated guests indoors and 300 seated outdoors.

EVENT/RECEPTION CAPACITY: The facility can accommodate 200 seated indoors and 300 seated or outdoors.

MEETING CAPACITY: Meeting spaces hold 200 seated guests.

FEES & DEPOSITS: A $1,000 deposit is required to reserve your date and the balance of the estimated event total is due 30 days prior to the event. Rental fees range $750–7,000 depending on the guest count, time of year and day of the week.

AVAILABILITY: Year-round, daily, afternoons and evenings, only one event per day and only 25 weddings per year.

SERVICES/AMENITIES:

Catering: select from preferred list
Kitchen Facilities: limited
Tables & Chairs: provided
Linens, Silver, etc.: provided
Restrooms: wheelchair accessible
Dance Floor: provided
Bride's Dressing Area: yes
Meeting Equipment: provided

Parking: large lot
Accommodations: no guestrooms
Telephone: office and guest phones
Outdoor Night Lighting: provided
Outdoor Cooking Facilities: BBQ CBA
Cleanup: provided
View: garden, meadow, mountains, vineyards
Other: baby grand piano, spa services, AV equipment, event coordination

RESTRICTIONS:

Alcohol: provided
Smoking: outdoors only
Music: amplified OK

Wheelchair Access: yes
Insurance: liability required

Overwhelmed? Use the search criteria on www.HereComesTheGuide.com to narrow down your choices.

441

Wedgewood Wedding and Banquet Center
at Brentwood Golf Club

Golf Club

100 Summerset Drive, Brentwood
866/966-3009
www.wedgewoodbanquet.com/brentwood
sales@wedgewoodbanquet.com

● Rehearsal Dinners	● Corp. Events/Mtgs.
● Ceremonies	● Private Parties
● Wedding Receptions	Accommodations

First impressions mean a lot, and the lovely drive up to the Brentwood Golf Club along a wide concourse lined with stately royal palms really sets a grand tone. The clubhouse itself, with its sloping, shingle roof and mix of pale earth tones and natural stone, has the look of a relaxed, upscale country retreat surrounded by acres and acres of lushly landscaped grounds.

Private events have their own entrance via a shaded pathway that leads around the side of the building. Follow it and you come to the Ceremony Pavilion Patio, overlooking the first tee of the golf course. Front and center is the pavilion itself, a classical Italian-style rotunda with six white columns topped with an ornate wrought-iron dome. It's an elegant stage for exchanging vows, backed by a dense screen of graceful olive and Japanese maple trees mixed with vivid red and white oleanders.

Just around the corner, behind the clubhouse, is the trellised Terrace where guests can raise a congratulatory glass of bubbly and mingle during the cocktail reception. Dappled sunlight filters through the overhead beams, which create a natural awning above a row of stone pillars. This peaceful spot enjoys views of the fairway, a pond that overflows into a rushing waterfall, and a nearby bridge spanning a profusion of pastel flowers. Naturally all of these scenes make very picturesque backdrops for your wedding photos.

The Ballroom, decorated in soothing hues of sandstone and adobe, has tall windows along two walls that look out over the ceremony site and terrace to the verdant vistas beyond. As the sun sets and everyone is seated for dinner, create just the right mood by dimming the wrought-iron chandeliers and spotlights. Large enough to seat 200 with a permanent dance floor, this high-ceilinged space can accommodate an additional 100 by simply removing a dividing wall and expanding into the adjoining club restaurant. This also gives you access to the restaurant's large bar and the four LCD flat screens behind it to display home movies, photos or even a real-time video of the wedding itself.

Wedgewood Banquet Centers, which oversees special events at numerous locations throughout California, prides itself on service. With their experienced staff you can count on guidance, flexibility and attention to your specific needs. Customization is welcome, so if there's something special you'd like, just ask. You'll have a dedicated wedding planner who will work with you throughout the entire process, from the first consultation until the last guest says goodbye. They've designed a whole array of packages, many of which are all-inclusive and cover not only the menu, linens and setup, but everything from invitations and flowers to photographer and band. This is a boon for all you busy brides who just want to relax and enjoy your own wedding.

CEREMONY CAPACITY: The site holds 250 seated guests outside.

EVENT/RECEPTION CAPACITY: The facility can accommodate 300 seated or 500 standing outdoors.

MEETING CAPACITY: Meetings do not take place at this facility.

FEES & DEPOSITS: 25% of the estimated event total is required to reserve your date and the balance is due 10 days prior to the event. Meals range $19–40/person. Tax, alcohol and a 20% service charge are additional.

AVAILABILITY: Year-round, daily, in 5-hour time blocks depending on the day.

SERVICES/AMENITIES:

Catering: provided
Kitchen Facilities: n/a
Tables & Chairs: provided
Linens, Silver, etc.: provided
Restrooms: wheelchair accessible
Dance Floor: provided
Bride's Dressing Area: yes
Meeting Equipment: provided

Parking: large lot
Accommodations: no guestrooms
Telephone: emergency use only
Outdoor Night Lighting: access only
Outdoor Cooking Facilities: no
Cleanup: caterer or renter
View: fountain, fairways, landscaped grounds mountains
Other: picnic area, event coordination

RESTRICTIONS:

Alcohol: provided
Smoking: outdoors only
Music: amplified OK

Wheelchair Access: yes
Insurance: not required

Oakhurst Country Club

1001 Peacock Creek Drive, Clayton
925/672-9737 X217
www.countryclubreceptions.com
events@oakhurstcc.com

Country Club

● Rehearsal Dinners	● Corp. Events/Mtgs.
● Ceremonies	● Private Parties
● Wedding Receptions	Accommodations

Located on a bench of land just above Ygnacio Valley and the growing city of Clayton, Oakhurst Country Club sits near the base of Mt. Diablo's steep and wild eastern rampart.

The vistas from its two event spaces, the west-facing Heritage and Diablo View rooms, are impressive. The larger Heritage Room takes in a sweeping panorama of the Diablo Valley, from Pleasant Hill to the Carquinez Strait. The smaller Diablo View Room scans the vividly chiseled profiles of Mt. Diablo's precipitous lesser-known side. A wide terrace that zigzags across the clubhouse's west side connects both rooms from the outside and is a highly popular feature with wedding parties. Besides its unfettered view of distant landscapes, the terrace provides a closer-in look at the club's azure-watered swimming pool, putting green and golf course.

Because it's surrounded by a visually arresting landscape, it's no surprise that Oakhurst hosts many outdoor wedding ceremonies. But exchanging vows outside also gets a boost from the club's attractive appearance. The clubhouse is fronted by a majestic porte-cochère, whose twin support pillars are clad in large flagstones and whose steeply angled roof rests atop big, bold wooden trusses. Couples often enjoy getting married next to this structure, which provides a dramatic architectural backdrop to the club's landscaped front.

When celebrants move indoors to the banquet rooms, they pass through an airy window-lined lobby that opens out to a 40-foot-high atrium. Those striking trusses you first see under the porte-cochère continue inside, adding yet another eye-catching element to the clubhouse's design.

Over the past decade Oakhurst has assembled an unflappable, well-organized, people-oriented staff, and developed a wide range of packages. Naturally, the many brides who've enjoyed worry-free weddings here have generated enthusiastic word of mouth about this site. To them, Oakhurst seems blessed with everything in just the right proportion: a savvy wedding team, plenty of options and flexibility, a memorable setting and fine architecture. That's a pretty nice combination to bring to your wedding day.

CEREMONY CAPACITY: Indoors, this location seats up to 100 guests; outdoors, up to 150 seated guests.

EVENT/RECEPTION & MEETING CAPACITY: Indoors, the Diablo View Room seats up to 68 guests with additional open terrace seating for 50. Heritage room seats up to 190 with a covered terrace that seats up to an aditional 72 guests.

FEES & DEPOSITS: A nonrefundable deposit, which is applied to your food and beverage total, is required to reserve your date. The amount of the deposit is equal to 25% of the event minimum. 50% is due 6 months prior, and 100% of the final estimated balance is due 10 days prior to the event date. Rental fees range $200–1,000 depending on the space reserved and day rented. Wedding packages, including room rental, start at $50/person. Meals range $23–45/person. Tax, alcohol and a 20% service charge are additional.

AVAILABILITY: Year-round, daily, 6am–11pm.

SERVICES/AMENITIES:

Catering: provided
Kitchen Facilities: n/a
Tables & Chairs: provided
Linens, Silver, etc.: provided
Restrooms: wheelchair accessible
Dance Floor: CBA, extra fee
Bride's Dressing Area: yes
Meeting Equipment: CBA or BYO

Parking: large lot
Accommodations: no guestrooms
Telephone: emergency use only
Outdoor Night Lighting: CBA
Outdoor Cooking Facilities: BBQ CBA
Cleanup: provided
View: mountains, hills, fairways

RESTRICTIONS:

Alcohol: provided, or BYO with corkage fee
Smoking: outdoors only
Music: amplified OK

Wheelchair Access: yes
Insurance: not required
Other: no rice, birdseed or glitter

Blackhawk Museum

Museum

3700 Blackhawk Plaza Circle, Danville
925/934-0598
www.blackhawkmuseum.org
bjbarnette@scottswc.com

● Rehearsal Dinners	● Corp. Events/Mtgs.
● Ceremonies	● Private Parties
● Wedding Receptions	Accommodations

The Blackhawk Museum is an exciting place for private events. Overlooking Blackhawk Plaza, the building is a study in glass, granite and stainless steel—a multi-million-dollar facility that showcases rare classic automobiles and automotive fine art and artifacts in elegant, sumptuous surroundings. The foyer is awesome with its soaring skylights and dusty rose Italian granite floors and walls. The juxtaposition of metal and stone with soft rich colors creates a vivid impression. As the sun sets through the tinted glass façade, the entire space is bathed in a warm glow.

The dining area presents a striking contrast—black from its granite floor to unadorned ceiling. Beautiful vintage cars border the dining area and are highlighted by a network of computerized lights. Here guests are dazzled by colorful fender curves, gleaming surfaces and sparkling brass and chrome.

And what's particularly nice about this 65,000-square-foot facility is that you have so many options from which to choose. The facility's numerous event spaces include the automobile galleries, lobbies, mezzanine, terraces, classroom, executive room, outdoor plaza with fountain, and more. If you're seeking a smashing venue in the East Bay for a personal celebration or a company soirée, this is the place to have an unforgettable event.

CEREMONY/EVENT & RECEPTION CAPACITY: The site holds 40–500 seated or 75–1,000+ standing guests indoors, and 40–400 seated or 70–600 standing outdoors.

MEETING CAPACITY: Event spaces hold 22–500 seated guests.

FEES & DEPOSITS: The Museum is rented through *Scott's Catering* of Walnut Creek. Rental fees start at $1,500 and vary depending on the day of week, date of the event, and the time of day. Per person prices are flexible and menus are customizable for almost any budget. Meals start at $35/person and range depending on your event needs. For information contact *Scott's Catering* at 925/934-0598 or bjbarnette@scottswc.com.

AVAILABILITY: Year-round, except Thanksgiving and Christmas Days. During operating hours (Wednesday–Sunday, 10am–5pm), functions with catered meals may be scheduled in the event areas 7:30am–5pm, and the entire facility is available from 6pm–11:30pm. On Mondays and Tuesdays, when the museum is closed to the public, the entire facility is available for events 7:30am–11:30pm.

SERVICES/AMENITIES:

Catering: provided, no BYO

Kitchen Facilities: n/a

Tables & Chairs: provided

Linens, Silver, etc.: provided

Restrooms: wheelchair accessible

Dance Floor: provided

Bride's Dressing Area: yes

Meeting Equipment: AV, podium, TV, portable and adjustable stage, screen, zoned speaker system

Parking: large lots

Accommodations: no guestrooms

Telephone: no

Outdoor Night Lighting: access only

Outdoor Cooking Facilities: no

Cleanup: provided

View: East Bay hills; Blackhawk Plaza's ponds, fountains and waterfalls

Other: piano

RESTRICTIONS:

Alcohol: provided, service until 11:30pm

Smoking: outside only

Music: amplified limited, must end by 11:30pm

Wheelchair Access: yes

Insurance: liability required

The professionals in the back of this book are the best in the business. How do we know? Read page 701.

Crow Canyon Country Club

Country Club

711 Silver Lake Drive, Danville
925/735-5700
www.crow-canyon.com
stacy.manzo@ourclub.com

- Rehearsal Dinners
- Ceremonies
- Wedding Receptions
- Corp. Events/Mtgs.
- Private Parties
- Accommodations

Nestled against the foothills of Mt. Diablo, Crow Canyon Country Club offers both challenging recreational facilities and tastefully designed spaces for rehearsal dinners, wedding receptions, parties and business events.

All functions take place in the Clubhouse, a versatile group of rooms surrounded by a championship 18-hole golf course, swimming pool and tennis courts. Large parties can be accommodated in the Mark Twain Room, the Country Club's main dining area. The windowed east side of this room overlooks the golf course and a spectacular view of Mt. Diablo. For added flexibility, a stage and hardwood dance floor are located in the center of the room.

Smaller groups are comfortably accommodated in the Jack London Lounge, a section of the Mark Twain Room. And for more intimate functions, such as a bridal shower, rehearsal dinner or corporate meeting, the Eugene O'Neill Room provides a private and sophisticated retreat. It, too, has a dramatic view of the Diablo Valley.

Among Danville's handful of special event venues, the Crow Canyon Country Club stands out because it offers a wide range of services. Whether you have an informal affair or a sophisticated soirée in mind, this is one facility that can handle it from start to finish.

CEREMONY CAPACITY: The Club holds up to 250 guests outdoors and up to approximately 300 guests indoors. Many options are available, including larger capacities. Call for details.

EVENT/RECEPTION & MEETING CAPACITY: The club can accommodate 10–300 seated or 15–500 standing guests indoors.

FEES & DEPOSITS: Room rental fees range $300–1,800 and food and beverage minimums range $7,000–13,000 depending on the day and time of the event, and space rented. Food service is provided; catered events require 7 days advance confirmation of guest count. Approximate per person rates: breakfast $11–18, luncheon $18–26, dinner $28–42, and buffet stations $34–42. Customized menus are available. Alcohol, tax and a 20% service charge are additional.

AVAILABILITY: Year-round, daily, 7am–midnight.

SERVICES/AMENITIES:

Catering: provided
Kitchen Facilities: n/a
Tables & Chairs: provided
Linens, Silver, etc.: provided
Restrooms: wheelchair accessible
Dance Floor: yes
Bride's Dressing Room: yes
Meeting Equipment: overhead screen, VCR and monitor, LCD and slide projectors, phone lines, flip charts, wireless internet; all equipment extra charge

Parking: large lot, valet available
Accommodations: no guestrooms
Telephone: emergency use only
Outdoor Night Lighting: yes
Outdoor Cooking Facilities: BBQ
Cleanup: provided
View: Mt. Diablo and golf course
Other: baby grand and upright pianos

RESTRICTIONS:

Alcohol: provided; wine corkage $15/bottle
Smoking: outdoors only
Music: amplified OK indoors

Wheelchair Access: yes
Insurance: not required

Discovery Bay Golf and Country Club

Golf and Country Club

1475 Clubhouse Drive, Discovery Bay
925/634-0700

www.dbgcc.com
banquets@dbgcc.com

● Rehearsal Dinners	● Corp. Events/Mtgs.
● Ceremonies	● Private Parties
● Wedding Receptions	Accommodations

Down the long and winding road that leads through the tawny East Bay hills to where rivers gather to form the Sacramento Delta, you'll find a little Eden in the newly minted township of Discovery Bay. Set like an emerald at the heart of this gated community, the Discovery Bay Country Club offers a perfect slice of paradise at a highly affordable price.

Broad lawns, clouds of colorful flowers, grand old pepper trees, willows, poplars, and ash greet guests as they approach the handsome Members Only clubhouse. Ceremonies and gatherings are often held on the exquisitely manicured front lawn, where a gentle slope provides a natural dais. Serene and sophisticated, surrounded by shade trees and tickled by breezes and birdsong, both lawn and clubhouse are brilliant environments for any affair.

Inside the bisque-colored Mediterranean-style building, sunlight waterfalls through the skylights and down the tall white columns of the property's atrium-style lobby. Just ahead, the spacious lounge with its broad bar, floor-to-ceiling windows and elegant baby grand Disklavier (it's like having a concert pianist on call!) offers gorgeous golf course views and comfortable seating. This is a spectacular place to greet guests or to entertain them with cocktails and hors d'oeuvres. The lounge also has its own stone patio screened by tall hedges and trees where partygoers can step into the sunshine. The facility's on-site coordinator and well-trained staff will ensure that everyone feels quite at home.

But the lawns, lobby and lounge are merely an introduction. The welcome extends to the property's beautiful dining room. You won't need to bring anything into this glamorous setting, with its softly colored carpets and walls, classic furnishings, and breathtaking views of the rolling fairways and lakes. Multiple levels of indoor lighting, including chandeliers, spots and recessed illumination in the handsomely coved ceiling will spotlight your event to perfection. Or you can shower your guests in sunlight on the outdoor veranda. Framed by the country club's verdant, meticulously groomed gardens and greens, this is a picturesque place for a wedding ceremony or *plein air* gathering or reception. The north- and west-facing panorama takes in Mt. Diablo and rarely fades to black without an extravagant sunset and its finale of twinkling stars.

Two smaller dining rooms make excellent choices for more intimate events—for showers and pre- or post-wedding celebrations—and there is a Bridal Suite Meeting Room that can be reserved for the bride and her entourage. Also available off the lobby, down a wide, mirrored hall, are the club's carpeted, spa-quality locker rooms equipped with personal lockers, granite countertops, showers, hair dryers and sundries, all of which allow the bridal party to relax and enjoy in the midst of the wedding day whirl.

CEREMONY & EVENT/RECEPTION CAPACITY: The site holds a maximum of 200 guests, seated or standing, indoors or outdoors.

MEETING CAPACITY: Spaces hold up to 160 seated guests.

FEES & DEPOSITS: A $1,000 deposit is required to reserve your date. Rental fees range $0–500 depending on your guest count. Wedding prices range $42–52/person. Tax, alcohol and an 18% service charge are additional.

AVAILABILITY: Year-round. Weddings take place on Saturdays only.

SERVICES/AMENITIES:

Catering: provided
Kitchen Facilities: n/a
Tables & Chairs: provided
Linens, Silver, etc.: provided
Restrooms: wheelchair accessible
Dance Floor: provided
Bride's & Groom's Dressing Area: yes
Meeting Equipment: some provided

Parking: large lot, valet optional
Accommodations: no guestrooms
Telephone: office phone
Outdoor Night Lighting: CBA
Outdoor Cooking Facilities: BBQ CBA
Cleanup: provided
View: golf course, mountains, lake, garden
Other: event coordination, bridal suite

RESTRICTIONS:

Alcohol: provided or BYO wine with corkage fee
Smoking: outdoors only
Music: amplified OK indoors only

Wheelchair Access: yes
Insurance: not required

Hilton Garden Inn San Francisco/Oakland Bay Bridge

Hotel

1800 Powell Street, Emeryville
510/658-9300
www.sanfranciscooakland.stayhgi.com
sfobb-salesadm@hilton.com

- Rehearsal Dinners
- Ceremonies
- Wedding Receptions
- Corp. Events/Mtgs.
- Private Parties
- Accommodations

A recent multimillion-dollar remodel has transformed this Hilton into an extremely appealing East Bay venue for special events. Conveniently located just minutes from the Bay Bridge, yet eons away from the urban hustle, it has easy access to every Bay Area attraction. But it's unlikely you or your guests will want to venture too far afield: The hotel presides over some of the region's most spectacular protected shoreline (think romantic walk along the water at sunset), and there are plenty of topnotch amenities and entertainment options at the hotel and in its surroundings to keep you happily occupied.

Greet your guests in the hotel's attractive new lobby. The sophisticated, residential-style environment makes it a great place for family, friends and colleagues to congregate and relax. The roomy, lobby-level lounge and the Great American Grill, with its airy indoor and outdoor seating, make for cheery meetings and reunions. A 4,000-square-foot, ballroom-capacity Conference Center on the ground floor can be divided into four separate sections, and is easily adapted to suit any number of social or corporate events. French doors off the lobby lead to an elegant cloistered space for more intimate private gatherings.

Want to set your sights higher? Let the elevators whisk you up 14 stories to the top floor of the hotel. Here you'll find the jewel in the crown of this handsome Hilton Garden Inn. Step into a spacious foyer carpeted in rich shades of rust and green. Registration can be set up here for events held in the Placer Room, with its wall of windows and view of the Berkeley hills. Or ascend the four granite-banistered steps at the end of the foyer to the Top Of The Bay Ballroom. On the other side of the double doors you'll be welcomed with eye-popping, jaw-dropping, bridge-to-bridge views of the sparkling bay and the cities around it. Emeryville, Berkeley, Oakland, San Francisco, bridges, parklands, mountaintops, and marinas—you'll feel as if the entire Bay Area is within your grasp. This grand ballroom, which can be divided into two smaller salons, will turn any event into a gala.

Hilton Garden Inns get high ratings in customer satisfaction, and for good reason. They provide expert on-site wedding planning and catering staff, custom menu options and competitive pricing. They'll help you arrange a bridal shower or rehearsal dinner along with your reception, and take good care of all of your overnight guests. When the sun sets exquisitely upon your extravaganza, don't give up the glamour. Let the hotel staff shower you with that celebrated Hilton hospitality in the Premier Bridal Suite (with a parlor and two bedrooms!) or one of their other newly decorated, gorgeously appointed guestrooms.

CEREMONY, EVENT/RECEPTION & MEETING CAPACITY: The hotel accommodates 360 guests in the Top of the Bay Ballroom and can hold a total of 900 guests throughout the location.

FEES & DEPOSITS: A deposit is required to reserve your date. The balance is due 5 business days prior to the event. Rental fees range $500–5,000 depending on the space rented, the day and time of the event and your guest count. Meals range $25–150/person. Tax, alcohol and a service charge are additional.

AVAILABILITY: Year-round, daily, anytime.

SERVICES/AMENITIES:

Catering: provided
Kitchen Facilities: n/a
Tables & Chairs: provided
Linens, Silver, etc.: provided
Restrooms: wheelchair accessible
Dance Floor: CBA
Bride's Dressing Room: yes
Meeting Equipment: on-site AV specialist
Other: event coordination; AV equipment

Parking: large lot
Accommodations: 279 guestrooms
Telephone: house phones
Outdoor Night Lighting: CBA
Outdoor Cooking Facilities: no
Cleanup: provided
View: panorama of San Francisco skyline, Bay Bridge and Berkeley hills

RESTRICTIONS:

Alcohol: provided
Smoking: outdoors only
Music: amplified OK indoors with restrictions

Wheelchair Access: yes
Insurance: required

Want to know WHAT TO ASK a potential location or vendor? Check out our Questions to Ask on page 17.

Palmdale Estates

Historic Estate

159 Washington Boulevard, Fremont
925/462-1783

www.palmdaleestates.com
veenaatpalmdale@mac.com

- Rehearsal Dinners
- Ceremonies
- Wedding Receptions
- Corp. Events/Mtgs.
- Private Parties
- Accommodations

Originally part of the Old Mission San Jose garden, Palmdale Estates is a beautifully landscaped site, featuring dozens of stately palms and native California trees, verdant lawns, gardens and even a pond. In the midst of this lovely setting is Best House, a Tudor-style mansion whose delightful interior and grounds create a storybook backdrop for weddings any time of year.

Built in 1915, the house reflects much of the elegant and ornate detailing of the period: graceful arched doorways, bas-relief ceiling moldings, crystal chandeliers, hand-painted murals and gleaming hardwood floors. Moiré silk draperies add a rich, old-fashioned quality to the décor. The Ballroom, though the largest space in the house, still has an intimate feeling with its cream-colored walls, oversize decorative marble fireplace and huge leaded-glass window overlooking the garden. At one end of the Ballroom, a few steps take you up to the Music Room, a glitzy alcove with gold leaf walls and a colorful stained-glass window. At the other end are the formal Dining Room and Solarium, two light and airy rooms with an abundance of leaded-glass windows and views of the "backyard."

When you get married here, you have exclusive use of the main floor of the house as well as the adjacent lawns, and can orchestrate your wedding any way you like. During warm months, most couples tie the knot in the white gazebo on the rear lawn, which is bordered by pines and redwoods and dotted with palms and fruit trees. They have their reception outdoors as well, setting up tables on the grassy expanse next to the gazebo. Afterwards, guests are invited inside for dancing and cake cutting. In winter, receptions are generally held in the Ballroom, with the other spaces used according to the couple's preferences; a fluid floor plan offers plenty of flexibility. (The Starr Garden, behind the adjacent Peach Mansion, is also available for ceremonies and receptions.)

Indian weddings are quite popular at this location: There are two permanent Mandaps on the property and the on-site caterer specializes in North Indian, South Indian and Gujarati cuisine.

Whether you celebrate under the magnificent palms or in the gracious surroundings of Best House, you can't help but enjoy the quiet beauty of Palmdale Estates.

CEREMONY CAPACITY: The Best House Garden with gazebo accommodates 500 seated; the Starr Garden, 200 seated guests.

EVENT/RECEPTION CAPACITY: Best House holds 200 seated indoors and, combined with outdoor spaces, up to 500 guests. Starr Garden holds 200 seated guests.

MEETING CAPACITY: The Ballroom holds 100 seated conference-style or 75 theater-style.

FEES & DEPOSITS: To rent the mansion and garden, a $1,600 security deposit is required when the rental agreement is submitted. The rental balance is payable 9 months prior to the event. The facility provides catering; however, during certain time periods, you can make arrangements for your own caterer; call to get specific dates. Rental fees range $500–3,500 depending on space selected and date and time rented. Meals start at $26.95/person. Tax, alcohol and service charge are additional.

AVAILABILITY: Year-round, daily, except Thanksgiving and Christmas Days.

SERVICES/AMENITIES:
Catering: provided or BYO (call for specifics)
Kitchen Facilities: minimal
Tables & Chairs: provided for 200 guests
Linens, Silver, etc.: provided with catering
Restrooms: wheelchair accessible
Dance Floor: Ballroom or Solarium
Bride's Dressing Area: yes
Meeting Equipment: PA system, flip charts, VCR, and overhead projector

Parking: large lot
Accommodations: no guestrooms
Telephone: lounge phone
Outdoor Night Lighting: CBA
Outdoor Cooking Facilities: no
Cleanup: caterer or CBA
View: East Bay hills
Other: event coordination

RESTRICTIONS:
Alcohol: BYO
Smoking: outside only
Music: amplified OK within limits

Wheelchair Access: yes
Insurance: not required

Unitarian Universalist Church of Berkeley

Unitarian Church

1 Lawson Road, Kensington
510/525-0391 X302
www.uucb.org
events@uucb.org

- Rehearsal Dinners
- Ceremonies
- Wedding Receptions
- Corp. Events/Mtgs.
- Private Parties

Accommodations

Although the Unitarian Universalist Church of Berkeley is not actually in Berkeley, it's right next door in neighboring Kensington, high in the hills overlooking an expansive view of Berkeley, El Cerrito, Kensington and beyond. Several elements make this 1960s church popular for weddings: a large central atrium, an adjacent sanctuary with a magnificent Aeolian-Skinner pipe organ, and an outdoor brick terrace with a sweeping vista of the San Francisco Bay.

Larger ceremonies usually take place in the Sanctuary, whose one-of-a-kind, 2,752-pipe organ will make your walk down the aisle a memorable one. Nineteen rows of wooden pews face a recessed chancel area which functions as an altar. The chancel is dominated by a huge oak table with two bronze candelabras resting on its surface. To one side is a portable lectern, and to the other a wooden pulpit, decorated with fiery orange ceramic tiles. Smaller weddings use the Terrace or the Atrium with spectacular views of the bay and the Golden Gate Bridge.

When the ceremony's over, the Atrium can be used for the reception or for champagne and hors d'oeuvres. Four towering rubber trees create a leafy canopy, and light from skylights filters in through the branches. In the room's center, a black marble fountain lined with azure tiles bubbles softly while guests mingle. If you need more space or you'd like an outdoor reception, tables can also be set up on the Terrace. On a clear day, it's one of the few places in the East Bay where you can dine while admiring vistas of the Golden Gate and Bay bridges or a divine sunset.

Two additional reception options are the Social Hall, which has room for more guests and a stage for a band, and the Fireside Room, whose cozy ambiance and magnificent views make it suitable for small gatherings. You don't have to be a Unitarian or a member of the congregation to be married here, and you may bring in your own officiant. LGBT couples welcomed.

CEREMONY CAPACITY: The Sanctuary holds 400 seated, the Atrium 175 seated, the Terrace 150 seated, and the Fireside Room up to 75 seated, theater-style.

EVENT/RECEPTION CAPACITY: Depending on the room, the facility can accommodate 50–300 seated at tables or 100–500 standing guests indoors, and 80 seated at tables or 175 standing outdoors.

MEETING CAPACITY: Primarily nonprofit organizations hold business functions and fundraisers here. Meeting spaces hold 25–400 seated guests.

FEES & DEPOSITS: A $100 nonrefundable booking deposit is required to secure your date. Half of the total fees are due when the room reservation agreement is signed; the event balance is payable 1 month prior to the event. All events must provide a certificate of insurance.

Room rental fees for ceremonies range $480–1,500; fees for ceremonies with receptions range $1,200–3,500. There is a refundable security deposit; organist/pianist charges are additional.

AVAILABILITY: Year-round, daily. Events are scheduled around the Church's programmed functions. Events on Saturdays take place 10am–10pm and on Sundays 3pm–10pm. Fees increase sharply after 10pm.

SERVICES/AMENITIES:

Catering: BYO, must be approved
Kitchen Facilities: fully equipped, no utensils
Tables & Chairs: CBA, extra fee
Linens, Silver, etc.: BYO
Restrooms: wheelchair accessible
Dance Floor: in Social Hall, Atrium or Terrace
Bride's & Groom's Dressing Area: yes
Meeting Equipment: PA, VCR, DVD projector (laptop compatible) and large screen

Parking: large lot, 200 spaces
Accommodations: no guestrooms
Telephone: emergency use only
Outdoor Night Lighting: access only
Outdoor Cooking Facilities: no
Cleanup: caterer or renter
View: panorama of SF Bay and region

RESTRICTIONS:

Alcohol: BYO; beer, wine and champagne only
Smoking: outside, designated areas
Music: amplified OK indoors only until 10pm

Wheelchair Access: yes
Insurance: certificate of insurance required
Other: no hard alcohol, rice, glitter, birdseed or confetti; no open flames

Want to find more locations and services? Check out our informative website, www.HereComesTheGuide.com.

457

Lafayette Park Hotel & Spa

Boutique Hotel

3287 Mount Diablo Boulevard, Lafayette
925/283-3700, 800/368-2468
www.lafayetteparkhotel.com
baramayo@lafayetteparkhotel.com

- Rehearsal Dinners
- Ceremonies
- Wedding Receptions
- Corp. Events/Mtgs.
- Private Parties
- Accommodations

Few hotels are given any kind of special recognition, so the fact that the Lafayette Park Hotel & Spa is one of the few in the East Bay to have received a Four Diamond Award should tell you something: Namely, that they maintain an impeccable standard of comfort, ambiance and service. With its distinctive architecture—dormers, shuttered French windows, and peaked roofline—this local landmark looks like a French chateau. Behind its high walls, European charm abounds in lovely courtyards, a variety of event spaces, and a luxurious full-service health spa.

Just by walking around the hotel, you're struck by how its design and décor make you feel welcome. In the atrium-like lobby, sunlight streams in through windows 60 feet overhead, illuminating the sweeping oak staircase and white marble floor. On cool days, the couches in front of the oversize fireplace are the obvious place to relax. The warmth of wood is everywhere—even in the intricate inlaid floors in front of the elevators.

Step outside into the sunny Fountain Courtyard, and you quickly realize how idyllic this spot is for a ceremony or champagne reception. Enclosed by the golden walls of the hotel, the space becomes an Old World plaza with a trickling limestone fountain in its center, ringed by potted rose bushes, manicured trees and flowers.

From the Fountain Courtyard, it's a short walk inside to the Independence Ballroom where larger receptions and parties are held. The coffered ceiling is outfitted with handmade crystal chandeliers and spot lighting, which can be adjusted to create any mood.

Smaller ceremonies take place upstairs in the Wishing Well Courtyard. Named for the rose-entwined stone wishing well in its center, this petite patio is also embraced by the hotel's walls. As you gaze up at the shuttered windows, wrought-iron balconies and clinging ivy, you once again feel like you're in the middle of a French countryside inn. That European flavor carries over into the nearby George Washington Room, a more intimate reception space. Here, the Early American/French décor features gilt-framed mirrors, marble-topped consoles and a deep green carpet set off by fleur de lis border designs.

The Diderot Library, with its oak paneling, 18th-century marble fireplace mantel and hardwood floor, is custom-made for rehearsal dinners, bridal showers, brunches and executive meetings.

A wonderful Lafayette Park amenity is their European Day Spa. In addition to providing an appealing selection of face and body treatments, the Spa features a fitness pavilion, a pool and poolside café, an outdoor fireplace and a Jacuzzi. The bride and her attendants will not be able to pass up an opportunity to indulge here before and even after (why not!) the Big Day. Everyone staying overnight will appreciate the nicely appointed rooms, many of which have their own wood-burning fireplaces. The hotel also offers a complimentary premium room for the honeymoon couple, and special rates for wedding guests.

Melding European elegance with California comfort, the Lafayette Park Hotel is indisputably one of the East Bay's favorite locations for weddings and special events.

CEREMONY CAPACITY: For seated groups, the Fountain Courtyard accommodates 200, the Wishing Well Courtyard 64, and the George Washington Room accommodates 130.

EVENT/RECEPTION CAPACITY: The hotel can accommodate 24–150 seated or 30–200 standing guests indoors, and 60–220 seated or 50–230 standing outdoors. The Independence Ballroom and Courtyard combined hold 300 seated or 450 standing guests.

MEETING CAPACITY: A variety of spaces accommodate 15–200 theater-style, or 8–45 conference-style.

FEES & DEPOSITS: A $2,000 nonrefundable, nontransferable deposit is required to reserve your date. The hotel's wedding packages include butler service hors d'oeuvres, beverages, linens, champagne toast, candle centerpieces and a premium guestroom. The rental fee for the Independence Ballroom and the Fountain Courtyard is $1,950. The ceremony fee is $1,550. Special wedding menus range $88–125/person. Tax and service charges are additional. Fees for business functions vary depending on overnight rooms, services and menus selected.

AVAILABILITY: Year-round, daily. Business functions, 8am–5pm or 6pm–11pm; weddings, 11am–4pm or 6pm–11pm.

SERVICES/AMENITIES:

Catering: provided
Kitchen Facilities: n/a
Tables & Chairs: provided
Linens, Silver, etc.: provided
Restrooms: wheelchair accessible
Dance Floor: yes
Bride's Dressing Area: CBA
Meeting Equipment: full range, AV company
Other: event coordination

Parking: complimentary self-parking, valet available
Accommodations: 138 guestrooms
Telephone: guestrooms
Outdoor Night Lighting: yes
Outdoor Cooking Facilities: CBA
Cleanup: provided
View: courtyard and pool

RESTRICTIONS:

Alcohol: provided, no corkage fee
Smoking: outdoors only
Music: amplified within limits

Wheelchair Access: yes
Insurance: not required

Wildwood Acres

Special Event Facility

1055 Hunsaker Canyon Road, Lafayette
925/283-2600

www.wildwoodacres.com
events@wildwoodacres.com

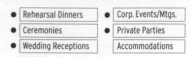

●	Rehearsal Dinners	●	Corp. Events/Mtgs.
●	Ceremonies	●	Private Parties
●	Wedding Receptions		Accommodations

It's hard to believe, as you drive through the suburban sprawl that makes up most of Contra Costa County, that a rustic jewel like Wildwood Acres could exist here. Nestled in a wooded canyon only five miles from downtown Lafayette, it's suitable for a wide variety of events. Whether you're planning a country-style reception, family reunion, or frothy Victorian wedding with picture hats and parasols, Wildwood Acres can magically transform itself into the ideal venue.

The indoor facility is a 2,000-square-foot lodge with warm decorative flooring and a 60-foot garden mural. Open-beamed ceilings, Oriental rugs, and a stone fireplace with benches on either side make the room cozy. And, there's even a full-service bar. This would be an especially nice area for a Christmas party, an intimate wedding or other winter event.

The outdoor facilities, however, are what make Wildwood Acres so special. If you're getting married here, there's a lovely ceremony site up on a hill in a fern grotto, deep in a grove of towering bay trees and bigleaf maples. Exchange vows on a stone platform in one corner while your guests, seated in the adjacent open area, savor their surroundings. Afterwards, have your reception on two terraces, shaded by a natural canopy of alder and maple trees. A redwood gazebo houses the band, and there's plenty of room to kick up your heels on the sunken dance floor. All around, pottery urns overflowing with impatiens and ferns add spots of color, and winding paths lead to shady nooks containing wrought-iron or wooden benches.

CEREMONY, EVENT/RECEPTION & MEETING CAPACITY: The Lodge holds 165 seated or 250 standing guests; the Outdoor Area holds up to 400 guests seated or standing.

FEES & DEPOSITS: The site rental fee ranges $100–350/hour with catering. To reserve your date, a nonrefundable $1,000 booking fee is required. For weddings, ceremony and reception charges include the rental fee and ceremony setup fee, plus in-house catering, starting at $49/person, with champagne, beer, wine and soft drinks.

Midweek business functions start at $36/person, including breakfast, lunch and nonalcoholic beverages. Tax and service charge is additional.

AVAILABILITY: Year-round, daily, 7:30am–midnight.

SERVICES/AMENITIES:

Catering: provided
Kitchen Facilities: n/a
Tables & Chairs: provided
Linens, Silver, etc.: provided
Restrooms: wheelchair accessible
Dance Floor: indoor and outdoor provided
Bride's & Groom's Dressing Area: yes
Meeting Equipment: full range

Parking: ample
Accommodations: no guestrooms
Telephone: calling cards OK
Outdoor Night Lighting: yes
Outdoor Cooking Facilities: n/a
Cleanup: provided
View: canyon, gardens
Other: event coordination

RESTRICTIONS:

Alcohol: provided, no BYO
Smoking: designated areas only
Music: amplified OK

Wheelchair Access: yes
Insurance: not required
Other: no rice or glitter

Hacienda de las Flores

2100 Donald Drive, Moraga
925/888-7045
www.moragahacienda.com
rents@moraga.ca.us

Historic Home & Garden

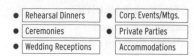

- Rehearsal Dinners
- Ceremonies
- Wedding Receptions
- Corp. Events/Mtgs.
- Private Parties
- Accommodations

An authentic Spanish-style mansion, the Hacienda de las Flores sits on land that was once the hunting ground for Miwok Indians. The historic town-owned structure is painted white with blue trim, and is surrounded by well-maintained park grounds. Inside the Hacienda, hardwood floors, beamed ceilings and a fireplace create a warm and inviting setting. Outdoors, a large lawn spreads out behind the building, enhanced by blue spruce trees, pines, weeping willows, palms and flowers. A circular flowerbed and fountain in the middle of the patio serve as the focal point for large parties or wedding receptions.

From the upper Hacienda lawn, flagstone stairs lead down to the Pavilion, a semicircular building with huge Corinthian columns overlooking a walled garden with lawn and patio. A set of large wrought-iron gates leads guests into the enclosure, where small seated functions or ceremonies can take place. Tranquil and secluded, the Hacienda offers one of the prettiest garden environments for special events in the East Bay.

CEREMONY CAPACITY: The Hacienda holds 50 seated or 75 standing guests indoors, and the adjacent lawn up to 200 seated or standing. The Pavilion holds 50 seated or 60 standing indoors, and the Pavilion lawn 150 seated or standing.

EVENT/RECEPTION CAPACITY: The Hacienda accommodates 200 guests outdoors or 100 for a seated meal indoors, throughout a few rooms. The Pavilion seats 50 inside and has an outdoor capacity of 150.

MEETING CAPACITY: There are 9 rooms which can accommodate 12–60 seated guests.

FEES & DEPOSITS: Event rental fees range $1,800–3,650 depending on the space selected and time of year. To reserve your date, half of the rental fee, a $500 refundable security deposit and a $250 nonrefundable application fee are required. Remaining fees are due 6 months prior to the event. A deposit is required if you plan to use a nonpreferred caterer or musicians. The security deposit will be refunded within 60 days after the event provided all conditions have been met.

For weekday business meetings, fees vary depending on room(s) selected, and include room setup. There is an additional fee for use of the Hacienda kitchen.

AVAILABILITY: For special events, Friday 3pm–10pm and Saturday and Sunday 8 consecutive hours between 9am–10pm; additional hours are not available. For weekday business meetings, the facility is available 8am–9pm.

SERVICES/AMENITIES:

Catering: select from preferred list

Kitchen Facilities: ample

Tables & Chairs: provided

Linens, Silver, etc.: through caterer

Restrooms: wheelchair accessible

Dance Floor: yes

Bride's Dressing Area: yes

Meeting Equipment: no

Parking: lot and on street

Accommodations: no guestrooms

Telephone: no

Outdoor Night Lighting: access only

Outdoor Cooking Facilities: no

Cleanup: provided

View: fountain, lawns, flowerbeds and trees

RESTRICTIONS:

Alcohol: BYO, WCB only

Smoking: outside only

Music: amplified OK with restrictions on speaker location

Wheelchair Access: yes

Insurance: included in fees

Other: decorations restricted; no birdseed, rice, confetti, flower petals or mylar balloons

---

This is important! Tell locations you're reading HERE COMES THE GUIDE and ask if our information is still current.

Bellevue Club

Private Lakeside Club

525 Bellevue Avenue, Oakland
510/451-1000, Catering
www.bellevueclub.org
asaldana@bellevueclub.org

- Rehearsal Dinners
- Ceremonies
- Wedding Receptions
- Corp. Events/Mtgs.
- Private Parties
- Accommodations

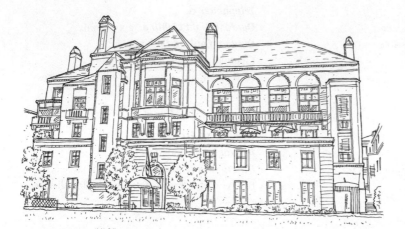

A romantic, Old World setting in Oakland? We found one! It's the Bellevue Club, a gem from a bygone era located on the edge of Lake Merritt. Opened as the Women's Athletic Club in 1929, today it's a private coed club, available for nonmember functions with member sponsorship.

Designed by architects Roeth and Bangs, this six-story building is more of a grand, Louis XIV-style French manor than a clubhouse. You enter a spacious, elegantly furnished lobby and take an elevator to the fourth floor for your celebration. You have your choice of four lovely rooms which, depending on the size of your party and budget, may be used in a number of combinations.

The Mural Lounge and the Main Dining Room (the two largest rooms) have billowing draperies, gilded moldings, marble fireplaces and two-story-high ceilings, all reminiscent of a European castle. In fact, a 1949 book about the Club's history describes the interior decoration as "inspired by Marie Antoinette's Petit Trianon." The Mural Lounge, a picturesque place for a ceremony, is named for the pastoral scenes painted over the fireplace and entryway. Other treasures fill the room: a whimsically hand-painted Mason Hamlin grand piano (that works), delicate porcelain figurines and a pair of bronze cherubs who sit atop a marble mantle clock. Rose-colored walls are punctuated with gilded moldings and decorative flower baskets done in gold relief. An additional benefit is that both the Main Dining Room and Mural Lounge have sweeping views of Lake Merritt.

Newly refurbished in February 2010, the Main Dining Room is the Bellevue Club's *pièce de résistance.* Hand-carved ornamentations, including small reliefs of women's faces, grace the walls between enormous arched windows framed by flowering draperies. A crystal chandelier and wall sconces cast a soft glow over evening parties. And if you want to give your wedding a truly regal flair, conduct your toasting or bouquet-throwing from the fifth floor interior balcony, a lofty perch from which to survey your "kingdom" below. It's also a wonderful vantage point for a photographer to capture aerial photos of your event.

Two smaller spaces, connected by a sunny enclosed terrace, are also highly detailed. The Wisteria Room is named for the flowered pattern on the hand-blocked linen drapery that frames two large brass windows with lake views; the Terrace Room is distinguished by a hand-painted mural above a black marble fireplace. And if you and some of your guests want to extend your stay, five guestrooms with full baths and some with private lakeside balconies provide pleasant and convenient overnight accommodations.

CEREMONY CAPACITY: The Mural Lounge seats 100 guests theater-style, and the Main Dining Room 150 with a dance floor.

EVENT/RECEPTION & MEETING CAPACITY: The club can accommodate from 16–150 seated with dance floor or 90–200 standing guests indoors.

FEES & DEPOSITS: A nonrefundable room rental deposit is due when reservations are confirmed. The estimated food and beverage total is payable 60 days prior to the event. Room rental fees range $150–1,500 depending on space selected. Meals range $25–65/person. Alcohol, tax and a 20% service charge are extra. For ceremonies, there's a $250 setup fee. There is also a beverage sales minimum and a bartender fee applies. For events with more than 50 guests, there's an additional parking and security fee.

AVAILABILITY: Year-round, daily, 11am–11pm. Weekend events are in 5-hour blocks and include 2 complimentary additional hours for setup.

SERVICES/AMENITIES:

Catering: provided

Kitchen Facilities: n/a

Tables & Chairs: provided

Linens, Silver, etc.: provided

Restroom: wheelchair accessible

Dance Floor: wood floor in Main Dining Room

Bride's & Groom's Dressing Area: yes

Meeting Equipment: AV and other CBA, extra charge

Parking: Club lot with attendant and on street

Accommodations: 10 guestrooms

Telephone: office phone

Outdoor Night Lighting: access only

Outdoor Cooking Facilities: no

Cleanup: provided

View: Lake Merritt and Oakland city skyline

Other: event coordination, grand pianos

RESTRICTIONS:

Alcohol: provided, or BYO with corkage fee

Smoking: outside building only

Music: amplified OK until 11pm

Wheelchair Access: yes

Insurance: not required

Other: no rice, birdseed or flower petals

Caffè Verbena

Restaurant

1111 Broadway, Lobby Level, Oakland
510/465-9300
www.caffeverbena.com
events@caffeverbena.com

- Rehearsal Dinners
- Ceremonies
- Wedding Receptions
- Corp. Events/Mtgs.
- Private Parties
- Accommodations

Caffè Verbena is what most urban restaurants long to be: a place that provides respite from the big bad city while simultaneously playing up the glamour of metropolitan life. Inside this upscale eatery, buttery walls, deep leather booths and a handsome bar envelop guests in comfort and calm; yet, thanks to vertical windows and an adjacent atrium and garden, the impressive Oakland skyline—and the excitement of the city—is never far away.

Right in the heart of Oakland's newly revitalized downtown, Caffè Verbena occupies a portion of the towering Shorenstein APL Building's lobby level. Businesses may inhabit the upper floors, but Caffè Verbena and its immediate environs are all about pleasure. You can limit your celebration to the restaurant itself, but it's great fun to expand into the light-filled atrium, gleaming marble lobby, and Zen garden just beyond the establishment's wide-open doors.

The atmosphere changes depending on where you are. In Caffè Verbena's paneled cherrywood dining room, low lighting, dark fabrics and mahogany wood accents set the tone, with an open kitchen and long, well-stocked bar completing the picture. These details provide a sophisticated backdrop for a seated meal or cocktail reception.

Just outside the restaurant proper, an atrium with floor-to-ceiling windows affords views of the garden and the nearby Federal and City Center buildings. This space can be used for just about anything: drinks and hors d'oeuvres, a delightful lunch or supper, or as a dance floor with room for a DJ booth.

Beyond the atrium, the sparkling but spare rear lobby of the building boasts a high ceiling and a rotating selection of contemporary abstract sculpture from the Oakland Museum. There's ample room for a cocktail hour, sit-down dinner or even a wedding ceremony. With plenty of advance notice, Caffè Verbena's management can remove the sculpture—but why bother? These artworks are an added bonus, enhancing the ambiance of the place.

Stepping into the great outdoors from the lobby, guests encounter a grassy courtyard surrounded by a waterfall, stone benches and more sculpture, known as the Zen garden. Some couples get married on the grass, while others exchange vows on the wide cement path that wraps around the courtyard. This open area can also accommodate larger groups, for both seated and standing receptions.

For smaller get-togethers, Verbena sports a petite patio that overlooks 11th Street. Amidst city views, a bride and groom can tie the knot, ply guests with champagne or sit down with an intimate group of family and friends for an al fresco party.

At Caffè Verbena, you can design your event using any or all of these spaces. In fact, this property's main draw might be the diversity of its event-friendly areas and the different moods they provide. Open since 2001, Caffè Verbena has become increasingly popular for weddings, wine tastings, private parties and corporate functions as people have discovered its enchanting urban setting.

CEREMONY CAPACITY: The Lobby holds 300 seated guests, and the Zen Garden holds 150 seated.

EVENT/RECEPTION & MEETING CAPACITY: The facility holds 50–350 seated or 100–400 standing indoors, and 40–250 seated or 75–400 standing outdoors.

FEES & DEPOSITS: 50% of the food and beverage minimum is required to reserve your date; the balance is due at the end of the event. Facility fees may apply depending on space rented. Luncheons range $18–35/person, dinners $35–55/person. Tax, alcohol and a 20% service charge are additional, as is a $3/person cake-cutting fee. A ceremony setup fee may apply.

AVAILABILITY: Year-round, daily, 9am–2am.

SERVICES/AMENITIES:

Catering: provided or BYO CBA
Kitchen Facilities: CBA for BYO catering
Tables & Chairs: provided or CBA
Linens, Silver, etc.: provided or CBA
Restrooms: wheelchair accessible
Dance Floor: yes
Bride's Dressing Area: CBA
Meeting Equipment: CBA, extra charge

Parking: on-site garage, extra fee; or on-street
Accommodations: no guestrooms
Telephone: pay phone
Outdoor Night Lighting: yes
Outdoor Cooking Facilities: no
Cleanup: provided, extra charge
View: cityscape, garden
Other: event coordination

RESTRICTIONS:

Alcohol: provided, or wine corkage $10/bottle
Smoking: outdoors only
Music: amplified OK, with restrictions

Wheelchair Access: yes
Insurance: required for outside vendors

California Ballroom

1736 Franklin Street, Oakland
510/834-7761
www.californiaballroom.com
info@californiaballroom.com

Historic Ballroom

● Rehearsal Dinners	● Corp. Events/Mtgs.
● Ceremonies	● Private Parties
● Wedding Receptions	Accommodations

During the Roaring Twenties, everyone loved a party. These were the days when folks dressed to the nines for "dinner and dancing." If you lived in the East Bay during those rollicking times, the highlight of your night on the town would probably have been doing the Charleston at the Leamington Hotel's elegant grand ballroom. Though the Leamington is no longer in business, its Ballroom is still going strong, rechristened as the California Ballroom. Thanks to a loving renovation in 1986, an invitation to this impressive landmark—just a few blocks from picturesque Lake Merritt—is still an occasion to look forward to.

When you arrive at the Ballroom, pass through a pair of wrought-iron gates that open to a walkway shaded by a burgundy awning. Once inside, stand back and take in the authentic Art Deco styling of this appealing space. The cream-colored walls contrast nicely with carpeting the color of fine claret, which gives way to a 700-square-foot hardwood dance floor polished to a gleam. In fact, the Ballroom is quite spacious, and even if you leave plenty of room for dancing, you can still comfortably seat 250 guests for dinner. Have more guests than that? Put tables on the dance floor, and have them cleared when folks are ready to kick up their heels.

The Ballroom feels even more expansive thanks to the lofty ceiling, which also sports a classic balcony reminiscent of a vintage playhouse. The ceiling itself is an art piece, lined with gold-leaf cornices and boasting gold-leaf panels in traditional Deco style. Ornate chandeliers bear complementary detailing, echoed throughout the décor. For example, along the walls you'll find several beveled-glass mirrors topped with elaborate gold carvings of heraldic emblems and cherubim. The more time you spend in the Ballroom, the more grace notes you discover, such as the antique-style light sconces that help set the mood with their subtle glow. Potted greenery illumined with twinkle lights accents the walls, and there's even a built-in bar in one corner, with a mirrored backsplash for a jazzy touch.

Perhaps the fanciest ornamentation is reserved for the proscenium of the large stage, which focuses all eyes up front towards its intricate design. A polished wood apron extends beyond burgundy velvet curtains and a scalloped valance. Many couples are so taken with the stage's innate drama that they hold their wedding ceremonies here, with guests seated below. Afterwards, the crowd heads for the bar and the dance floor is quickly cleared or set with more tables. You may decide to put the head table on the stage so everyone can admire the happy couple; alternatively, you might let your band or DJ be front and center, so they can best assist in coordinating each phase of your event.

The Ballroom includes a coat room (don't you wish more places offered this old-fashioned amenity?), as well as ample parking. There's an on-site kitchen, and you can bring in the caterer of your choice to serve the latest haute cuisine, or some retro favorites (think Veal Oscar and Cherries Jubilee). Completely private and reasonably priced, the California Ballroom brings a nostalgic glamour to your wedding or other momentous celebration.

CEREMONY, EVENT/RECEPTION & MEETING CAPACITY: The Ballroom holds 200 seated classroom-style, 300 seated at round tables, 400 seated theater-style or 600 standing guests.

FEES & DEPOSITS: Half of the rental fee (as a nonrefundable deposit) is required to reserve your date. The balance is due 90 days prior to the event. A cleaning deposit, along with security and other fees are due 30 days prior to the event. Rental fees range $1,000–2,500 depending on the day and time rented and the type of event. A $75/hour rehearsal charge is additional.

There is a discount for 501(c)(3) nonprofit groups on weekdays. For weekday business meetings and functions, fees vary depending on the day and time of the event; call for specific rates.

AVAILABILITY: Year-round, daily, until midnight on weekdays and until 2am on weekends.

SERVICES/AMENITIES:

Catering: BYO
Kitchen Facilities: moderately equipped
Tables & Chairs: provided
Linens, Silver, etc.: CBA, BYO or through caterer
Restrooms: wheelchair accessible
Dance Floor: hardwood floor
Bride's Dressing Area: yes
Meeting Equipment: CBA, extra charge

Parking: on-site lot and on-street
Accommodations: no guestrooms
Telephone: no
Outdoor Night Lighting: access only
Outdoor Cooking Facilities: no
Cleanup: renter or caterer
View: no
Other: stage, wetbar, event coordination CBA

RESTRICTIONS:

Alcohol: BYO, must have controlled bar
Smoking: outdoors only
Music: amplified OK indoors

Wheelchair Access: yes
Insurance: certificate required
Other: no tape, tacks or nails; no open flames; no rice or birdseed

---

Overwhelmed? Use the search criteria on www.HereComesTheGuide.com to narrow down your choices.

469

Camron-Stanford House

Lakeside Victorian Mansion

1418 Lakeside Drive, Oakland
510/444-1876, Special Events
www.cshouse.org
rentals@cshouse.org

● Rehearsal Dinners	● Corp. Events/Mtgs.	
● Ceremonies	● Private Parties	
● Wedding Receptions	Accommodations	

Gracing the shore of Lake Merritt, the Camron-Stanford House is the last of the grand Victorian homes that once ringed the lake. Constructed in 1876, it derives its name from the Camrons who built it and the Stanfords who occupied it for the longest period. When the building was scheduled for demolition in the late 1960s, concerned citizens formed the Camron-Stanford House Preservation Association and spent the intervening years raising funds to return the home to its former splendor.

Elaborate molding and authentic wallpaper patterns and fabrics have all been used to match the originals as closely as possible. Rooms filled with period artifacts, antiques and photos take you back to the late 1800s. The only operational gas chandelier in Northern California is located here. Outside, a large rear veranda overlooks Lake Merritt. Receptions can take place in the house, on the veranda or on the expansive lawn that extends to the lake. An iron fence enclosing the site ensures privacy, while allowing guests to appreciate the colorful tapestry of boats, birds and joggers that surrounds them.

CEREMONY CAPACITY: The Veranda alone holds up to 90 seated guests; the veranda and lawn combined (facing the lake) hold 450 seated.

EVENT/RECEPTION & MEETING CAPACITY: The facility accommodates 125 guests inside or 300 outside. The maximum seated in one room is 75 (or 60 if seated classroom-style).

FEES & DEPOSITS: Half the rental fee and a refundable $500 cleaning deposit are required when the facility is booked. Rental fees start at $950 for 100 guests and include staffing. Fees vary depending on space(s) selected and length of time rented. Additional hours are available at the rate of $150/hour.

AVAILABILITY: Year-round, weekdays until 10pm; Saturdays until 11pm.

SERVICES/AMENITIES:

Catering: BYO licensed

Kitchen Facilities: moderate

Tables & Chairs: BYO

Linens, Silver, etc.: BYO

Restroom: wheelchair accessible (ground level only)

Dance Floor: CBA

Bride's Dressing Area: CBA

Meeting Equipment: BYO

Parking: on-street, lot

Accommodations: no guestrooms

Telephone: emergencies only

Outdoor Night Lighting: BYO

Outdoor Cooking Facilities: BYO

Cleanup: caterer

View: Lake Merritt and Oakland city skyline

RESTRICTIONS:

Alcohol: BYO

Smoking: not allowed

Music: amplified OK outside only

Wheelchair Access: limited

Insurance: proof required

Other: no tacks or tape; no candles, no flame-heated chafing dishes; no confetti or rice

Chabot Space & Science Center

10000 Skyline Boulevard, Oakland
510/336-7421
www.chabotspace.org
rentals@chabotspace.org

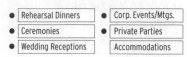

● Rehearsal Dinners	● Corp. Events/Mtgs.
● Ceremonies	● Private Parties
● Wedding Receptions	Accommodations

Looking for an out-of-this-world location to celebrate your wedding? Let the stars smile on you at Chabot Space and Science Center. In the evenings, this state-of-the-art science education center perched high in the Oakland hills makes a unique setting for private events.

The Center is surrounded by thirteen wooded acres in Joaquin Miller Park, and its architecture takes full advantage of that fact: Numerous floor-to-ceiling windows, a glass skyway, and a catwalk-like loggia hugging the exterior really make you feel like you're up in the trees. The two main buildings, the Spees and Dellums Buildings, are linked at the second floor by the skyway, and at ground level by an amphitheater and a courtyard with gardens. Exposed ceilings, black floors, and architectural details in green glass, aluminum and blond wood create a smart, polished look throughout the Center.

Event spaces in the Spees Building include the Tien MegaDome Theater, where you can project your own slides, DVD, VHS, or PowerPoint presentations; a café, which provides a handy reception site; and a surround-sound planetarium featuring one of the world's most advanced immersive visualization systems. This allows them to take their audience on real-time jouneys to the edge of the known universe and back again. We were particularly taken with the idea of a celestial ceremony in the planetarium: Imagine getting married on a spot-lit stage beneath a 70-foot dome of gorgeous night sky thick with stars, while your guests sit spellbound in comfortable tiered seats. If you want to go all out, you can even make arrangements with the projectionist to create a sky that changes throughout the event.

Another appealing ceremony option—and one that will give every guest a great vantage point—is the semicircular amphitheater surrounded by trees. This is a particularly appropriate place to mark an important moment in time, as the amphitheater also functions as a nifty clock. At the top level of the amphitheater, the Pleiades Courtyard stretches back to the Spees Building café. Together, the two spaces make a convenient indoor/outdoor spot for serving post-ceremony refreshments. After dining, guests will enjoy strolling through the adjacent EnviroGarden, designed to showcase native plants.

You'll also want to consider serving cocktails in the sleek open spaces of the Spees Building. Although the Spees is a two-story structure, there are several areas where you can stand on the ground floor and gaze up unobstructedly to the top of the building. The most striking of these is the Rotunda, an atrium-like space capped by a huge octagonal skylight. During the day, light flowing in from the skylight illuminates a decorative green glass compass inlaid on the first floor.

If you set up musicians or a DJ on the Rotunda's circular "balcony," the music floats down to your guests mingling below.

Indoor receptions can take place in the exhibit spaces of the three-level Dellums Building, but the size and configuration of your event will depend on the current exhibits. The top floor of the Dellums opens to the outdoor plaza of the observatory complex. This is the highest point of the center, and from here the sweeping bay views over the treetops are sure to wow your guests. The three domes house telescopes named Leah, Rachel and Nellie. You can arrange for access to the domes, and can actually hold a small sit-down dinner inside the larger of the two.

Chabot Space and Science Center is a stellar (sorry, we couldn't resist) location, not just for weddings, but for private and corporate events, too. And even if you aren't an astronomy buff, you'll delight in the sunset over the bay and the dazzling nighttime panorama of city lights twinkling below.

CEREMONY CAPACITY: The Obsevatory Complex and the Amphitheater each seat 150 guests, the Ask Jeeves Planetarium holds up to 241 seated guests and the Dellums Building accommodates up to 200 guests.

EVENT/RECEPTION CAPACITY: The facility can accommodate 150–500 seated or 200–1,000 standing guests indoors, and 100–150 seated outdoors.

MEETING CAPACITY: Galileo, Kepler and Copernicus can each hold up to 45 seated guests. The Ask Jeeves Planetarium holds up to 241 guests seated theater-style, and the Tien MegaDome holds up to 205 guests seated theater-style.

FEES & DEPOSITS: 50% of the rental fee is required to reserve your date. A $1,000 refundable cleaning deposit, along with the balance of the rental fee, is due 30 days prior to the event. Rental fees range $1,500–15,000 depending on space rented. There is a discount for 501(c)(3) nonprofit groups.

AVAILABILITY: Year-round, Mondays and Tuesdays, 6am–midnight, or Wednesday–Sundays, 5pm–midnight. Some seasonal restrictions apply, call for details.

SERVICES/AMENITIES:

Catering: select from preferred list
Kitchen Facilities: full kitchen
Tables & Chairs: BYO
Linens, Silver, etc.: BYO
Restrooms: wheelchair accessible
Dance Floor: built in or BYO
Bride's Dressing Area: no
Meeting Equipment: some provided

Parking: ample free parking on site
Accommodations: no guestrooms
Telephone: emergency use only
Outdoor Night Lighting: yes
Outdoor Cooking Facilities: no
Cleanup: some provided
View: panoramic and bay views
Other: use of exhibits, some event coordination provided

RESTRICTIONS:

Alcohol: BYO
Smoking: not allowed
Music: amplified OK

Wheelchair Access: yes
Insurance: extra liability required
Other: no balloons or confetti

Dunsmuir Hellman Historic Estate

2960 Peralta Oaks Court, Oakland
510/615-5562
www.oaklandnet.com/parks/rental
rmathews@oaklandnet.com

Historic Mansion and Grounds

- Rehearsal Dinners
- Ceremonies
- Wedding Receptions
- Corp. Events/Mtgs.
- Private Parties
- Accommodations

Nestled in the East Bay hills, the Dunsmuir Hellman Historic Estate offers a lovely and secluded setting. Featuring a turn-of-the-century white mansion and a 50-acre expanse of lawn and trees, it evokes the serenity of a bygone era. The mansion was a romantic wedding gift from Alexander Dunsmuir to his bride on the occasion of their marriage in 1899. Its foyer is a formal, softly lit space for an intimate ceremony: The bride can make an impressive entrance as she descends the staircase, and a baby grand piano is always available to provide musical accompaniment.

The nearby Pond Area, with its weeping elms and delicate white gazebo, is the most popular site for ceremonies. Following the service, guests walk through the picturesque grounds to one of the various venues available for receptions.

Indoor receptions are often hosted in the unique and rustic Carriage House. Its quaint seating nooks and mahogany paneling add an old-fashioned quality, and whether you're planning a wedding banquet, a conference of corporate executives or a western theme party, this place will bring out your creativity. Light cascades into the Garden Pavilion, whose large picture windows look out onto a treelined terrace. It's a versatile space for ceremonies or receptions, and is particularly well suited for company parties, meetings and seminars. The Open-Air Canopy is an elegant, white canvas-roofed structure that enjoys views of the historic mansion and surrounding landscape in the distance. Designed with a carpeted floor, subdued lighting and a patio area, it's perfect for receptions or gala events.

The grounds here are private, peaceful and beautiful throughout the year. Although this is one of the most exceptional sites in the Bay Area for a wedding celebration, Dunsmuir Historic Estate is also an excellent choice for other special events, daytime retreats, picnics and business functions.

Note: The City of Oakland has additional event venues for rental, including the Garden Center, Joaquin Miller Community Center and Morcom Rose Garden. For information on these and other facilities, please go to www.oaklandnet.com/parks/rental.

CEREMONY CAPACITY: Several spaces hold 20–150 indoors or 220–4,500 outdoors.

EVENT/RECEPTION & MEETING CAPACITY: The estate can accommodate 100–275 seated or 200–550 standing guests indoors, and up to 4,500 seated or standing outdoors for concerts and large events. The Carriage House holds 75 seated theater-style or 75 seated for dining. The Pavilion accommodates 275 seated theater-style, 275 seated for dining or 550 standing guests. Tent space available.

FEES & DEPOSITS: For weddings, a nonrefundable $1,200 deposit reserves your date. Half of the rental balance is payable 6 months prior, the other half is due 30 days prior to the event. Use fees range $2,500–8,500 (depending on guest count) for an 8-hour time block and include a choice of 2 separate sites for the wedding or reception, use of some tables and chairs as well as setup and breakdown. Any additional equipment must be rented through Dunsmuir.

Fees for business functions and meetings vary depending on group size, room setup and equipment; call for specific rates.

AVAILABILITY: Year-round, daily, 8am–midnight.

SERVICES/AMENITIES:

Catering: select from exclusive list
Kitchen Facilities: prep kitchen in Pavilion
Tables & Chairs: some provided
Linens, Silver, etc.: through caterer
Restrooms: wheelchair accessible
Dance Floor: CBA, extra fee
Bride's Dressing Area: yes
Meeting Equipment: CBA

Parking: on-street or adjacent lot
Accommodations: no guestrooms
Telephone: emergency use only
Outdoor Night Lighting: access only
Outdoor Cooking Facilities: CBA
Cleanup: provided
View: mansion and grounds, pond
Other: mansion photos, $200/hour; mansion tours, $300/hour

RESTRICTIONS:

Alcohol: BWC, through caterer only
Smoking: not allowed
Music: amplified OK

Wheelchair Access: yes
Insurance: required
Other: decorations limited; no rice, food or drink in the mansion

---

The professionals in the back of this book are the best in the business. How do we know? Read page 701.

Highlands Country Club

Country Club

110 Hiller Drive, Oakland
510/849-0743
highlandscc@aol.com

- Rehearsal Dinners
- Ceremonies
- Wedding Receptions
- Corp. Events/Mtgs.
- Private Parties
- Accommodations

Suppose you wanted a place for your event that had a genuine "country club" ambiance, but you only had a limited budget. Where could you go? Well, you might want to take a little drive over to the Highlands Country Club.

Embraced by a sloping green sweep of lawn, and overlooking tennis courts and crystal-blue swimming pools, this architectural phoenix has literally risen from its ashes (the original club was destroyed in the 1991 Berkeley-Oakland Hills fire). The community surrounding the club has also been rebuilt, and few, if any, traces of the previous devastation are visible from the club itself.

What is visible from the club's Fireside Room is a panoramic view of the San Francisco Bay and adjacent communities that is so spectacular it almost makes additional decoration redundant. Hardwood floors, a neutral color scheme and large windows showcase the magnificent vista, while the soaring stone fireplace and antique brass chandeliers add a touch of friendly rusticity. There's even a small balcony that affords you the luxury of watching the sun set over the Golden Gate or the fog pour over the Berkeley hills as you sip champagne and enjoy the breeze. In front of the clubhouse, a sunny patio surrounded by verdant lawns and small trees is available for outdoor receptions. Although it's high up on a hill, this country club is fresh, unpretentious and quite down to earth.

CEREMONY CAPACITY: The Fireside Room, patio or gazebo accommodate up to 100 guests, maximum.

EVENT/RECEPTION CAPACITY: The Fireside Room and Patio, combined, hold up to 100 guests.

MEETING CAPACITY: The Club holds 100 guests, maximum.

FEES & DEPOSITS: The rental fee is $1,200, and includes use of the Fireside Room, deck and patio areas for 4 hours; extra hours can be arranged. To secure your date, all of the nonrefundable rental fee plus a refundable $1,200 security deposit are required.

AVAILABILITY: Year-round, daily, 8am–11pm. Use of the deck and patio is seasonal. Only 1 event is booked per day.

SERVICES/AMENITIES:

Catering: BYO
Kitchen Facilities: moderately equipped
Tables & Chairs: provided
Linens, Silver, etc.: CBA or BYO
Restrooms: wheelchair accessible
Dance Floor: dining room or patio
Bride's Dressing Area: no
Meeting Equipment: microphones, screen

Parking: on-street
Accommodations: no guestrooms
Telephone: pay phones
Outdoor Night Lighting: access only
Outdoor Cooking Facilities: BBQ
Cleanup: caterer or renter
View: East Bay hills and San Francisco Bay
Other: bar

RESTRICTIONS:

Alcohol: BYO
Smoking: outdoors only
Music: amplified OK indoors with volume limits

Wheelchair Access: yes
Insurance: certificate required
Other: no rice, birdseed, petals or glitter

Jack London Aquatic Center

Banquet and Special Event Center

115 Embarcadero, Oakland
510/208-6066

www.jlac.org
facilityrentals@jlac.org

● Rehearsal Dinners	● Corp. Events/Mtgs.
● Ceremonies	● Private Parties
● Wedding Receptions	Accommodations

At Oakland's Jack London Aquatic Center, the pleasures of being on the waterfront take center stage. Situated at the water's edge across an inlet from the Alameda Marina, it gives guests an intimate view of the slowly drifting estuary and the ships, tugboats and sailboats floating by—one might even catch a glimpse of champion rowing crews and scullers as they train. The rhythmic clanking of boat lines and distant calls of seagulls provide the aural ambiance.

From the outside, this maritime-themed building cuts a crisp white silhouette against the surrounding blue of water and sky. Estuary Park, run by the Oakland Parks and Recreation Department, encircles the property with walkways along the water, outdoor sculpture and abundant trees. The Aquatic Center itself is dual purpose: The ground floor houses boats and sculls used for youth and adult water sports; upstairs on the second floor you'll encounter clean, uncluttered event spaces that capitalize on the dramatic waterfront vantage point.

The Regatta Pavilion is a sizable banquet room with blond wood trim on white walls, exposed beams, and a 22-foot-high peaked ceiling. Light pours in from everywhere: Two walls of the room boast tall windows that face the park and estuary beyond. There's ample space for sit-down dinners, buffets, receptions, a DJ and dancing—and some couples have tied the knot here, too.

Off this main room, two decks expand the Regatta Pavilion into the great outdoors. The Marina View Terrace faces east toward the Alameda Marina, and can accommodate a small seated ceremony, outdoor dining, or a bar and passed hors d'oeuvres. A more diminutive deck, just right for escaping for a few moments of solitude, opens south to views of Estuary Park's foliage and San Francisco in the distance. The Sunset and Horizon Wings, two small rooms also adjacent to the Regatta Pavilion, boast high coffered ceilings and, of course, views. They're great for a bar or buffet, and some brides have used them as private dressing rooms.

The Jack London Aquatic Center's greatest asset is undoubtedly its waterfront setting, but its well-kept interior, variety of rooms and plentiful free on-site parking (a valet can be arranged) add to its appeal. For those who love the water and are drawn to the maritime life, this is a winning venue for weddings, but anyone planning a private party, meeting or conference should consider it, too.

CEREMONY CAPACITY: The Regatta Pavilion holds 185 seated guests.

EVENT/RECEPTION CAPACITY: The site holds up to 185 guests seated or standing.

MEETING CAPACITY: The Regatta Pavilion accommodates up to 185 seated theater-style.

FEES & DEPOSITS: For weddings, a nonrefundable $500 deposit is required to reserve your date. Rental fees ($500–1,600 depending on the rooms rented) and equipment fees are payable 60 days prior to the event. For meeting and nonprofit rates, call for specifics. For caterers not on the preferred list, there is a $400 outside catering fee.

AVAILABILITY: Year-round, daily, 7am–midnight except major holidays.

SERVICES/AMENITIES:

Catering: select from list
Kitchen Facilities: prep only
Tables & Chairs: provided up to 185
Linens, Silver, etc.: through caterer
Restrooms: wheelchair accessible
Dance Floor: provided, extra fee
Bride's & Groom's Dressing Area: yes
Meeting Equipment: some provided, extra fee

Parking: complimentary large lot, valet CBA
Accommodations: no guestrooms
Telephone: emergency use only
Outdoor Night Lighting: for access only
Outdoor Cooking Facilities: through caterer
Cleanup: caterer
View: Oakland estuary, city skyline and Oakland hills
Other: event coordination

RESTRICTIONS:

Alcohol: through caterer
Smoking: outdoors only
Music: amplified music indoors only until midnight

Wheelchair Access: yes
Insurance: extra liability required

Lake Chalet Seafood Bar & Grill

Waterfront Restaurant

1520 Lakeside Drive, Oakland
510/653-8282
www.thelakechalet.com
events@thelakechalet.com

- Rehearsal Dinners
- Ceremonies
- Wedding Receptions
- Corp. Events/Mtgs.
- Private Parties
- Accommodations

Ringed by a delicate necklace of lights and comprised of parkland, gardens, and historic civic structures, Lake Merritt and its environs is not only the vibrant heart of Oakland, it's a thriving urban wildlife sanctuary (the first official refuge in the U.S). A multiyear project to upgrade the lakeshore's landscaping and buildings was completed in 2010, and the city's "crown jewel" now has a waterfront restaurant worthy of its surroundings: the Lake Chalet Seafood Bar & Grill.

Stepping down past colorful flowerbeds, you enter the handsomely restored edifice that was once the Lake Merritt Boathouse. It has never looked this grand. Materials throughout include water-inspired themes. Blue-painted curved wood panels reminiscent of a ship's hull, charcoal-colored floors, blackened steel, lacquer-red metal and mahogany accents surround you in comfort and luster. A magnificent white marble bar, running nearly the length of what used to be the Pump House, faces a long window view of the lake that extends all the way to the opposite shore. To the right, on the south side of the Lake Chalet, a 30-seat Executive Dining room with fireplace, big screen TV, wine library, garden views and separate entrance for red carpet arrivals is ideal for small mixers, meetings, rehearsal dinners or a hideaway for the bride.

Breezes blowing in through the restaurant's many windows draw you outside to the well-appointed patios, where a dock broad enough to accommodate a wedding ceremony, cocktail reception, or dinner reaches out into the placid lake waters. Outfitted with stylish furniture, heat lamps, palm trees, umbrellas and its own bar, this unique site has a resort-like feel. Wild ducks, snowy egrets, crested night herons and pelicans are among the protected birds that are at home here, as are the gondolas that glide gracefully by. That's right—a taste of Venice has come to Lake Merritt! Gondola Servicio and its genial gondoliers are available for pickup and delivery during an event. Picture the bride's dramatic arrival or the newlyweds' departure in one of those slender black vessels. Better yet, capture the moment in photos.

The romance will linger in the Gondola Room, named after that charming conveyance. Three walls of windows frame panoramic views, and European-style balconies look out over the dock and lake. Private restrooms, kitchen, and bar; light and lustrous earth colors; hardwood floors and an atmosphere of ease and serenity make it an excellent setting for fabulous wedding receptions, as well as corporate events, fundraisers and cocktail parties. The bar here, like all the others indoors and out, has fine beers on tap. And yes, the food is also amazing. This place is, after all, run by the talented restaurateurs responsible for the Beach Chalet Brewery & Restaurant and the Park Chalet Garden Restaurant in San Francisco.

If your guests want to stay in town, there are lakeside, downtown and bayside hotels just a short ride away. Many of the city's most popular attractions—the Oakland Museum, Jack London Square, City Hall and the transbay ferries—are also nearby, but remember, Lake Merritt is home to some of the best of them: Children's Fairyland, the Rotary Nature Center, and of course, the marvelous Lake Chalet.

CEREMONY CAPACITY: The restaurant holds 150 seated guests indoors or outoors.

EVENT/RECEPTION & MEETING CAPACITY: The facility can accommodate 130 seated or 175 standing indoors and 150 seated or 200 standing outdoors.

FEES & DEPOSITS: 50% of the food and beverage minimum is required to reserve your date and the balance is due 2 weeks prior to the event. Rental fees range $150–5,000 depending on the items needed. Meals range $30–60/person. Tax, alcohol and a 20% service charge are additional.

AVAILABILITY: Year-round.

SERVICES/AMENITIES:

Catering: provided
Kitchen Facilities: n/a
Tables & Chairs: provided
Linens, Silver, etc.: provided
Restrooms: wheelchair accessible
Dance Floor: provided
Bride's Dressing Area: CBA
Meeting Equipment: some provided, CBA

Parking: large lot, valet required, garage nearby
Accommodations: no guestrooms
Telephone: office and guest phones
Outdoor Night Lighting: provided
Outdoor Cooking Facilities: BBQ on site
Cleanup: provided
View: park, garden, landscaped grounds cityscape, lake

RESTRICTIONS:

Alcohol: provided or BYO with corkage fee
Smoking: designated areas only
Music: amplified OK

Wheelchair Access: yes
Insurance: not required

Want to know WHAT TO ASK a potential location or vendor? Check out our Questions to Ask on page 17.

Lake Merritt United Methodist Church

Lakefront Church

1330 Lakeshore Avenue, Oakland
510/465-4793
www.lakemerrittumc.org
info@lakemerrittumc.org

- Rehearsal Dinners
- Ceremonies
- Wedding Receptions
- Corp. Events/Mtgs.
- Private Parties
- Accommodations

Are you and your fiancé Buddhist? Jewish? Nondenominational Christian? Are you an interfaith couple, or a couple with no defined spiritual persuasion? Perhaps you're a lesbian or gay couple. If so, you've come to the right place, because the Lake Merritt United Methodist Church invites any and all of you to celebrate your wedding or holy union ceremony. "We are an open and welcoming congregation," their literature declares, and the church truly reflects a relaxed, progressive philosophy (despite their no-alcohol policy). After all, there aren't many religious establishments that allow you to hire the officiant of your choice to conduct your ceremony. It's spirituality for the new millennium!

Built in 1991, this contemporary church takes advantage of its scenic location overlooking the lovely Lake Merritt. A grand staircase trimmed in marble leads up to the main entrance, and brides often decorate the banisters with flowers or tulle. At the top of the stairs, there's also a spacious outdoor terrace that's a fun place for pre-event mingling or for serving refreshments during the social hour. From here, guests can watch the resident geese (and sometimes adorable goslings!) playing along the lakeshore, and greet the bride after she makes her arrival in a stylish limo, vintage auto or even a horse and carriage.

Just inside the entryway, the foyer leads to the Worship Center, where the atmosphere is bright and airy, thanks to a wall of floor-to-ceiling and clerestory windows that curves outward as if to embrace the lake below. In the evening hours, a circular inset ceiling dotted with small lights creates the illusion of a star-filled sky. The rest of the décor is simple—oak-trimmed walls, hunter green chairs and carpet, and a low altar. In contrast, behind the altar is a stunning work of art: a triptych of mosaic murals, commissioned from the studio of Louis Tiffany in 1923. The panels, called the *Te Deum Laudamus,* were a gift from a church in Los Angeles, where they were originally displayed. The flow of light in the Worship Center illuminates the outstanding beauty of the panels, composed of two million pieces of iridescent glass. Whether you're moved by the portrayals of the Biblical characters, or just appreciate the amazing detail of opalescent flowers, vines and blue skies, you'll likely experience the breathtaking power of Tiffany's masterpiece. The chairs and the altar are portable, so you can stage your ceremony in front of either the Tiffany Panels or the windows facing the lake; both backdrops inspire an exalted spiritual connection. Another mood enhancer is music, and the church has both a grand piano and a pipe organ; if you like, the staff will help you locate a qualified organist.

The Franklin Stark Room next door has a high ceiling and a row of tall windows looking out to a small courtyard that gives receptions an expansive feeling. Missing the view from the Worship Center? Simply slide back the movable wall that separates the Stark Room and the Worship Center, and voila! Guests dine and dance while admiring views of the lake and the Tiffany panels. There's a treat for the kiddies, too—a playground in the courtyard that will keep them occupied for hours, so nothing will disturb your own enjoyment of the day.

CEREMONY CAPACITY: The Worship Center accommodates up to 250 seated guests, maximum.

EVENT/RECEPTION & MEETING CAPACITY: The Stark Room holds up to 200 seated or 250 standing guests indoors; outdoors up to 50 seated or 75 standing guests. Smaller meeting rooms are also available.

FEES & DEPOSITS: For weddings and receptions a $500 refundable security deposit plus 50% of the total rental fee are required to secure your reservation. The balance is due 60 days prior to the event. Rental fees range $1,050–1,750 depending on space rented and guest count. Discounted wedding and reception package is available.

Other events or meetings require a $250 refundable security deposit. Nonprofit rates are available.

AVAILABILITY: Year-round, daily, 9am–11pm, excluding Sunday mornings and early afternoons. Amplified music ends by 10pm. Facilities must be empty by 11pm.

SERVICES/AMENITIES:

Catering: BYO
Kitchen Facilities: CBA
Tables & Chairs: provided
Linens, Silver, etc.: BYO
Restrooms: wheelchair accessible
Dance Floor: CBA
Bride's Dressing Area: yes
Meeting Equipment: WiFi internet access available

Parking: small lot and on street
Accommodations: no guestrooms
Telephone: house phone
Outdoor Night Lighting: yes
Outdoor Cooking Facilities: no
Cleanup: caterer or renter
View: Lake Merritt and cityscape
Other: pipe organ, grand piano available; officiant, musicians CBA

RESTRICTIONS:

Alcohol: not allowed
Smoking: not alowed
Music: amplified OK with restrictions

Wheelchair Access: yes
Insurance: may be required

Lake Temescal Beach House

Lakefront Event Facility

Temescal Regional Recreation Area, Oakland
510/544-3164
www.brazilianroom.org
brazil@ebparks.org

- Rehearsal Dinners
- Ceremonies
- Wedding Receptions
- Corp. Events/Mtgs.
- Private Parties
- Accommodations

A beach in the middle of Oakland? With water and sand and everything? Yes! And so much more, thanks to the East Bay Regional Park District, who developed this scenic gem as one of its first three parks back in 1938. Today, the 48 acres is a neighborhood oasis where busy urbanites can experience nature's rejuvenating powers. Lake Temescal can even become your own private getaway when you rent the handsome Beach House for your wedding or special event.

It's a leisurely stroll from the parking area down to the Beach House, picnic lawns and lake, and your guests will find it a rewarding nature walk. The East Shore Trail gently curves through stands of oak, willow and laurel, revealing sensory surprises: A flicker of ginger turns out to be a red squirrel; native songbirds cast their melodies from the treetops; the air is scented with tangy citrus and the spicy aroma of oak. Water lilies grace the shoreline, while butterflies pirouette amongst the bulrushes.

As the path slopes downward, the trees part to reveal the Beach House set against a forested knoll, overlooking a sweep of sandy shore and the blue lake. The two-story building has a cut-stone foundation accented with sea-green tiles that forms a trio of arches on the lower floor. The upper story (which is the rental space) is all windows, promising a spectacular view. Constructed by Works Project Administration crews in 1940, the historic Beach House has the quality craftsmanship and relaxed, unpretentious style typical of the era. Two wide flights of stone steps lead you to the rear of the building, where a terraced garden provides a lush backdrop to a charming flagstone patio. Fragrant roses in creamy white, lipstick pink and deep scarlet bloom from spring to fall, a romantic addition to any wedding ceremony. The sound of rushing water beckons you to a nearby footbridge spanning a waterfall that cascades down from a rocky outcropping to the lake. Boughs of oak, dewy fern and colorful rhododendron encircle a small clearing just beyond the bridge. A stone bench lets you survey the waterscape below, where snowy egrets and cormorants cavort in the lake, and majestic blue herons pose regally on the mossy bank.

As the evening grows cool, your guests can still enjoy the lakeside panorama as they retreat inside the Beach House, thanks to the long row of picture windows in the Lakeview Room and adjoining Fireside Room. Both spaces evoke an Americana theme, with gleaming hardwood floors, log cabin walls awash in an oh-so-pale mint green, and polished copper wall sconces. The Fireside Room also boasts dark rough-hewn open beams accenting its high ceiling. A grand flagstone hearth at the far end crackles and glows with a gas-burning fire, keeping everyone snug and toasty. Double

French doors give a glimpse of the garden, and add to the rooms' natural light. Leave these doors open during your event, and you'll let in the soothing harmony of the waterfall and the songbirds.

The Beach House and its peaceful surroundings capture the easy, gentle simplicity of the past, and when you come here for a visit, you might find yourself daydreaming about the possibilities...*an intimate garden fête, complete with breezy broad-brimmed hats and elegant china...the nostalgic warmth of a holiday gathering around the fireplace...a picnic on the patio, while lake trout jump for dragonflies in the lazy summer twilight...or stealing a kiss from your sweetheart on the shore of the moonlit lake.* Be creative—whatever celebration you imagine, Lake Temescal Beach House will make it wonderful.

CEREMONY CAPACITY: The Patio holds up to 130 seated guests.

EVENT/RECEPTION & MEETING CAPACITY: This location holds up to 80 seated guests.

FEES & DEPOSITS: A $100 deposit is required to secure your date. If cancelled more than 120 days prior to the event, $50 of this deposit is refundable. Signed contracts are required 2 weeks after the initial deposit at the Reservations Office at the East Bay Regional Park District Office in Oakland.

Weekend rates for Friday night, Saturday, Sunday and holidays (min. 8 hours) range $1,050–1,500 depending on the day and time frame reserved. Each additional hour is $150. Weekday rates range $250–675 depending on day and length of time rented. If you opt to bring your own food without a caterer, there is an additional fee. Evening noncatered events are prohibited. For nonresidents of Alameda and Contra Costa Counties, there is a surcharge that equals 20% of the room rental fee.

AVAILABILITY: Year-round, daily, 8am–midnight.

SERVICES/AMENITIES:

Catering: select from preferred list
Kitchen Facilities: prep only
Tables & Chairs: provided
Linens, Silver, etc.: BYO
Restrooms: wheelchair accessible
Dance Floor: yes
Bride's Dressing Room: yes
Meeting Equipment: BYO

Parking: large lot, fee charged April–Sept.
Accommodations: no guestrooms
Telephone: pay phone
Outdoor Night Lighting: patio only
Outdoor Cooking Facilities: no
Cleanup: through caterer
View: hills, lake, park
Other: fireplace available, extra fee

RESTRICTIONS:

Alcohol: BYO, BWC
Smoking: outside only
Music: amplified OK indoors, outdoors with restrictions

Wheelchair Access: yes
Insurance: extra liability is required

Oakland Marriott City Center

Hotel

1001 Broadway, Oakland
510/466-6455
www.marriott.com/oakdt
sales@oaklandmarriott.com

- Rehearsal Dinners
- Ceremonies
- Wedding Receptions
- Corp. Events/Mtgs.
- Private Parties
- Accommodations

With it's recent $17 million renovation, the Oakland Marriott City Center wanted to jazz things up and they certainly succeeded. From the entryway and lobby to the event spaces, restaurants and guestrooms, the hotel has been completely reinvented. The sophisticated new interior design features contemporary décor accented by natural elements including wood, glass and metal. A warm autumn color palette is used throughout, ranging from shades of gold and sunset orange to light tan and rich, deep brown.

The grand upgrade has added yet another layer of appeal to a venue that has always been a popular choice for a destination wedding or special event. Conveniently located between historic Old Oakland and Uptown (Oakland's Arts and Entertainment District), the hotel is close to the trendy new restaurants, businesses and residential spaces that are adding an incredible vitality to the city. The Paramount and Fox Theaters, the Oakland Museum, Chinatown, and the Housewives Market are mere blocks away, as is Jack London Square, Oakland's colorful waterfront district, and picturesque Lake Merritt.

But a lot of what's best about this party-perfect site can be found inside its walls. There are two huge ballrooms; a presidential suite (great for the wedding night!); a stunning 21st-floor banquet room with drop-dead views of the Bay, San Francisco, the Oakland Hills; 484 stylish, well appointed guestrooms and suites…plus much more.

Hold your gala in the 10,000-square-foot Grand Ballroom on the ground floor. It's adjacent to the sleek lobby, an impressive entrance for your affair be it a romantic wedding, fundraising blowout or stylish corporate gathering. This ballroom can be divided into as many as seven chambers if your requirements aren't quite as lavish, or you can book the somewhat smaller Junior Ballroom on the second floor, which can be partitioned into three salons. Both ballrooms have high ceilings, mood lighting, audiovisual capabilities and graceful prefunction foyers that are ideal for everything from registration and intermission to pre-event mixers with cocktails and passed hors d'oeuvres.

More intimate affairs of up to 150 can be hosted in the Skyline Room, the hotel's rooftop ballroom where a spectacular bird's-eye view of the bridges, San Francisco and the surrounding cities will make spirits soar.

Food for all events is prepared by the hotel's caring and experienced banquet staff, and no matter what size your celebration you'll receive the same award-winning Marriott service.

Our guess is that you and your guests will love this location. The Twelve Bars Lounge and LEVEL TWO Restaurant, with their dramatic atrium views, are congenial places for family and friends to mingle. Additional amenities—like the fitness facilities, business center and pool—might tempt them to stay put, but there's a lot to entice them beyond the hotel, too. Trains, planes, buses, and rental cars are all readily available, so it's easy to explore the many attractions the region has to offer.

CEREMONY CAPACITY: The hotel seats 900 guests indoors.

RECEPTION CAPACITY: The hotel can accommodate 600 seated or 1,000 standing indoors.

MEETING CAPACITY: The Convention Center holds 3,500 seated guests.

FEES & DEPOSITS: 30% of the total event cost is required to reserve your date. A portion is due 90 days prior to the event and the balance is due 30 days prior. Rental fees range $500–1,500 depending on the space rented. Meals range $49–69/person. Tax, alcohol and a 21% service charge are additional.

AVAILABILITY: Year-round, daily, anytime.

SERVICES/AMENITIES:

Catering: provided
Kitchen Facilities: n/a
Tables & Chairs: provided
Linens, Silver, etc.: provided
Restrooms: wheelchair accessible
Dance Floor: portable provided
Bride's & Groom's Dressing Area: yes
Meeting Equipment: provided
Other: grand piano, AV equipment

Parking: large lot, valet available
Accommodations: 484 guestrooms
Telephone: pay or guest phones
Outdoor Night Lighting: access only
Outdoor Cooking Facilities: no
Cleanup: provided
View: panorama of hills and San Francisco Bay, Lake Merritt, pool area

RESTRICTIONS:

Alcohol: provided or BYO with corkage fee
Smoking: not allowed
Music: amplified OK indoors

Wheelchair Access: yes
Insurance: liability required

Want to find more locations and services? Check out our informative website, www.HereComesTheGuide.com.

487

Oakland Museum of California

Art, History and Natural Science Museum

1000 Oak Street, Oakland
510/238-3009
www.museumca.org
awilbourn@museumca.org

- Rehearsal Dinners
- Ceremonies
- Wedding Receptions
- Corp. Events/Mtgs.
- Private Parties
- Accommodations

Since it opened in 1969, the Oakland Museum of California has been one of the city's most distinctive landmarks. Its dramatic tiered architecture and exhibits highlighting the rich diversity of California's geography and culture make it obvious that this is no stuffy, antiquated museum fit only for elementary school field trips.

The Oakland Museum of California is built on three levels, with stairs and walkways leading the visitor through the building's intriguing maze of courtyards, terraces and gardens. A koi pond full of well-fed fish, water lilies and papyrus plants graces the first level. Sculptures and artifacts, such as a replica of an Early California wagon and giant contemporary metal artworks, dot the grounds. The Great Court Gardens, a spacious lawn shaded by deodar cedars, sweet gum and alder trees, is a lovely setting for a wedding, reception, corporate picnic or similar event. Just beyond the Gardens is Rishell Court, an intimate space for smaller gatherings. Concrete pillars topped by planters form two sides of the courtyard; creeping-fig-covered walls form the other two sides. The air is perfumed by swags of Japanese honeysuckle interspersed with mounds of blue cape plumbago and purple lantana. Sunlight pours through the open roof, and a stately blue Atlas cedar provides shade.

Other outdoor venues include the Terraces, which look out on the Gardens, and the Patio, a sunny space that's enclosed by red and yellow lantana and overlooks the koi pond. Another terrace has a view of Lake Merritt and the Oakland hills. If you happen to be wandering around the Museum grounds and see a perfect spot but don't find it listed for rent, ask about it. The Oakland Museum will let you reserve almost any of its exterior spaces.

For indoor functions, consider the Museum's dining area, which forms a "bridge" over one of the main stairways. Two floor-to-ceiling windows allow you to view the koi pond from one side or the bustling Museum patrons from the other; rotating art exhibitions add a homey touch to the walls. The James Moore Theater and the Lecture Hall are suitable for business meetings and seminars. The theater is used for a multitude of events, such as concerts, theatrical performances and movie screenings.

Most people don't think of a museum as a potential wedding site, but where the Oakland Museum is concerned, they should. Here, you really can have a garden wedding: Exchange vows under a shady tree canopy surrounded by blooming flowers, and dine al fresco on a terrace with Lake Merritt views. The lake also makes a wonderful backdrop for photos, especially at sunset when the sky is painted with color. As you can see, the Oakland Museum of California offers all sorts of unexpected possibilities.

CEREMONY CAPACITY: The Great Court Gardens accommodate up to 750 seated or 2,000 standing guests. The Terrace and Patio areas combined hold 200 seated or 500 standing.

EVENT/RECEPTION CAPACITY: For the Gardens, Terrace and Patio areas, see figures above. The museum restaurant holds 150 seated guests, or 120 with a dance floor and small stage.

MEETING CAPACITY: The James Moore Theater accommodates 275 seated theater-style; the Lecture Hall holds 100.

FEES & DEPOSITS: 50% of both the facility rental and the anticipated food and beverage cost is payable 180 days prior to the event. The balance, along with a confirmed guest count, is due 5 working days prior to the event. Rental fees for a 6-hour block range from $1,160 for a meeting space to $11,500 for renting the entire museum. Contact the Special Events Department for the rental rates of specific areas. Security and other services are an additional charge. The museum garage, with a 170 car capacity, can be rented after regular hours.

Seated meals start at $45/person, not including hors d'oeuvres or beverages. Alcohol, tax and an 18.5% service charge are additional.

AVAILABILITY: Year-round, daily, 8am–11pm. The museum café is available all day Monday and Tuesday, and after 5pm on Wednesday, Saturday and Sunday. The outdoor Terraces and Garden are seasonal areas, available May–October as weather permits.

SERVICES/AMENITIES:
Catering: provided
Kitchen Facilities: fully equipped
Tables & Chairs: provided
Linens, Silver, etc.: through caterer
Restrooms: wheelchair accessible
Dance Floor: CBA, extra fee
Bride's Dressing Area: CBA
Meeting Equipment: full range
Other: some event coordination provided

Parking: museum garage, extra fee
Accommodations: no guestrooms
Telephone: emergency use only
Outdoor Night Lighting: CBA or BYO
in gardens
Outdoor Cooking Facilities: no
Cleanup: provided or caterer
View: Lake Merritt from upper level

RESTRICTIONS:
Alcohol: provided, no BYO
Smoking: not allowed
Music: amplified OK

Wheelchair Access: yes
Insurance: required
Other: no rice or birdseed

Preservation Park

Victorian Homes

660 & 668 13th St. at Martin Luther King Jr. Way, Oakland
510/874-7580
www.preservationpark.com
events@preservationpark.com

- Rehearsal Dinners
- Ceremonies
- Wedding Receptions
- Corp. Events/Mtgs.
- Private Parties
- Accommodations

Occupying two blocks just a heartbeat away from Oakland's City Center, Preservation Park is an eye-catching re-creation of a Victorian neighborhood. Sixteen Victorian homes have been beautifully restored and colorfully painted. The setting has been further enhanced with period park benches, ornate wrought-iron fences, old-fashioned streetlamps and a bronze fountain from Paris.

The Park's social center is the Pavilion, a graceful bandstand where ceremonies usually take place. While the bride and groom exchange vows on stage, their guests, seated on the lawn just below them, can appreciate the lovely landscaping and vintage architecture that surrounds them. Outdoor receptions are held in the adjacent Fountain Circle, a circular plaza with a large two-tiered fountain topped by the moon goddess Diana at its center. There's plenty of room for a band, or you could have an outdoor buffet on either side of the Pavilion.

If you're planning an indoor reception, two houses just off the Fountain Circle are available. The Ginn House, circa 1890, features two delightful light and airy parlors reminiscent of those in an English country home. Nile Hall, circa 1911, is a craftsman-style building with a sensational space for a grand and elegant party. It has a 30-foot-high ceiling, skylights, multiple windows, a stage and a theatrical lighting and sound system. This room is well designed, with soft colors, nice detailing and attractive appointments—and enough space to accommodate an extensive guest list. You can reserve one or both houses, as they're connected by a spacious interior hallway.

The Park is not only popular for weddings, it's hosted a wide range of events. When you reserve the outdoor spaces, the entrance gates are closed to cars so you and your guests can savor the feeling of having this charming "town" all to yourselves. For a remarkable glimpse of old-time Oakland, pay a visit to Preservation Park—it's well worth the trip.

CEREMONY CAPACITY: Ginn House holds 80 seated, Nile Hall 200 seated and the Pavilion Area 150–300 seated or 300–1,000 standing guests.

RECEPTION & MEETING CAPACITY: Various rooms hold 10–150 seated or 20–200 standing guests indoors. The Pavilion Area accommodates up to 300 seated and 1,000 standing.

FEES & DEPOSITS: A $500 deposit is required to secure your date. The rental fee is payable 120 days prior to the event. The fee for Nile Hall is $1,200; for Nile Hall plus the Ginn House, the fee is $1,875. The rental fee for the outdoor Pavilion Area is $950–1,450 without setup. If you rent the Pavilion Area in conjunction with Ginn House and Nile Hall, the fee is $625 without setup.

AVAILABILITY: Year-round, daily, 8am–11pm. The outdoor Pavilion, May to mid-October.

SERVICES/AMENITIES:

Catering: select from preferred list, or BYO-licensed, extra charge
Kitchen Facilities: setup only
Tables & Chairs: provided, extra fee outdoors
Linens, Silver, etc.: provided by caterer
Restrooms: wheelchair accessible
Dance Floor: CBA
Bride's Dressing Area: CBA
Meeting Equipment: sound equipment, VCR, DVD, DSL, microphones, flip charts

Parking: on-street or city garage nearby
Accommodations: no guestrooms
Telephone: no
Outdoor Night Lighting: yes
Outdoor Cooking Facilities: no
Cleanup: caterer
View: gardens and fountain

RESTRICTIONS:

Alcohol: provided, no BYO
Smoking: outside only
Music: amplified OK

Wheelchair Access: yes
Insurance: may be required

Skyline Community Church

Church

12540 Skyline Boulevard, Oakland
510/531-8212
www.skylineucc.org
office@skylineucc.org

Rehearsal Dinners	● Corp. Events/Mtgs.
● Ceremonies	● Private Parties
● Wedding Receptions	Accommodations

High in the Oakland hills, past handsome hillside residences, past woodsy Joaquin Miller Park and the Chabot Space & Science Center, you'll find a pleasant surprise. Follow the signs, make a U-turn on Skyline Boulevard, and when you see the sign for Skyline Community Church, turn into the drive. Let it lead you up past the two lower parking lots on a sun-splashed, flower-flanked climb to the white wooden bell tower that signals your arrival at the church. Set on the crest of a hill that borders the East Bay Regional Park District, this quiet sanctuary sits under an expanse of blue sky and sunlight. Birds sing in the treetops. Gentle breezes stir the pines. Noise and commotion seem far, far away.

It's a charming place for a wedding, a retreat, or any other event where a welcoming, open and affirming environment fits the bill. Receptions are generally held in the picturesque circular courtyard. Large terracotta planters further brighten the area with ferns and cheerful blooms, and if you look closely you might notice a subtle design in the rose and gray pavers—the stones have been set in the shape of an enormous Greek cross.

On one side of the courtyard a little path that winds through the well-kept lawn ends in a heart-shaped pattern just in front of an old-fashioned gazebo with a peaked roof and weather vane that spins with the cooling winds. From here you can look down on a hillside lovingly planted and tended, like the other nicely landscaped parts of the property, by church members. The gazebo is an attractive place to tie the knot, but you might want to save it for the cake cutting and photos and opt instead for a ceremony in the chapel on the opposite side of the courtyard.

Accessed by four large doors, the fan-shaped sanctuary has a beamed ceiling, parquet floor and a stunning wall of glass behind the altar that offers uninterrupted views of regional parkland and the hills that roll toward Mt. Diablo and the distant horizon. Acoustics in this hall are ethereal, making solo, a cappella, choir, instrument and pipe organ (yes, this church has one!) performances sublime. Sea-blue carpeting leads down the stairs to a choir room. It's a great place for the groom and his guys to meet with the pastor and shake off any pre-wedding jitters.

The Friendship Room off the courtyard, which is used for fellowship and community gatherings, has big windows and a compact adjacent kitchen. It's also a wonderful place for the bride and her attendants to get ready: Double-mirrored cabinets with stage lighting encourage plenty of primping.

Safe, private, relaxed and family-friendly, Skyline Community Church has much to offer children, too. Kids are encouraged to ring the church bell as the newlyweds leave the grounds. It's all so sweet and embracing; you and your guests will feel like you've found your own little piece of heaven.

CEREMONY CAPACITY: The Chapel holds 250 seated guests; the Courtyard, 300 seated guests.

EVENT/RECEPTION & MEETING CAPACITY: The Courtyard holds up to 300 seated guests.

FEES & DEPOSITS: A $500 deposit is required to reserve your date. The balance is due 4 weeks prior to the event. Rental fees range $950–2,600 depending on the space rented.

AVAILABILITY: Year-round, daily 9am–11pm, excluding Sunday mornings.

SERVICES/AMENITIES:

Catering: BYO
Kitchen Facilities: limited
Tables & Chairs: through caterer
Linens, Silver, etc.: through caterer
Restrooms: wheelchair accessible CBA
Dance Floor: through caterer
Bride's & Groom's Dressing Areas: yes
Meeting Equipment: digital projector and motorized screen with remote

Parking: large lot, on-street
Accommodations: no guestrooms
Telephone: emergency use only
Outdoor Night Lighting: yes
Outdoor Cooking Facilities: BBQ on site
Cleanup: caterer or renter
View: forest, mountains, valley, garden
Other: event coordination

RESTRICTIONS:

Alcohol: BYO BWC through licensed & insured caterer
Smoking: outside only
Music: amplified OK with restrictions

Wheelchair Access: limited
Insurance: liability required

This is important! Tell locations you're reading HERE COMES THE GUIDE and ask if our information is still current.

The Terrace Room
at the Lake Merritt Hotel

1800 Madison Street at Lakeside, Oakland
510/903-3580, Catering Department
www.theterraceroom.com
elizabeth@theterraceroom.com

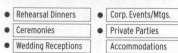

Hotel and Conference Facility

- Rehearsal Dinners
- Ceremonies
- Wedding Receptions
- Corp. Events/Mtgs.
- Private Parties
- Accommodations

Time has been good to the Lake Merritt Hotel. After three renovations in ten years, this classic 1927 Art Deco landmark is now filled with furnishings and accessories that enhance the building's striking architectural features.

The décor includes plush axminster carpeting, the design of which was inspired by a vintage fabric containing both a geometric pattern and exotic flowers in chestnut, gold, red and green; walls painted in a rich terracotta color; wrought-iron chandeliers; overstuffed Art Deco furniture covered in jewel-tone mohair fabric; and Lloyd Loom wicker chairs and cocktail tables.

The restoration extends to The Terrace Room, the hotel's restaurant and one of Oakland's premier entertainment sites. Twenty-foot, floor-to-ceiling windows along the entire front of this grand space offer an enchanting panorama of Lake Merritt, Lakeside Park and the Oakland hills. During the day the multilevel restaurant is bathed in light. At night, it has an intimate, almost cabaret feeling, and the view of the lake is spectacular: The dark surface of the water perfectly reflects the glittering Necklace of Lights gracing its perimeter.

The Terrace Room features a semicircular hardwood dance floor, and a sizable mural along one wall depicting Lake Merritt as it appeared over 40 years ago. A shiny black grand piano and Art Deco fixtures are nice finishing touches. In addition to its great location along Lake Merritt, the hotel provides a wide range of services, many of which can be specifically tailored to your special event.

CEREMONY CAPACITY: The Terrace Room holds 50–160 standing and/or seated guests.

EVENT/RECEPTION CAPACITY: The Terrace Room accommodates 230 seated or 350 standing guests.

MEETING CAPACITY: The Terrace Room holds 230 seated.

FEES & DEPOSITS: A $1,500 nonrefundable security deposit is required to reserve your date. An estimated 50% payment is required 2 months prior and the balance is due 1 month prior to your event. Full seated service, including food and beverage, starts at $38/person. Tax and a 20% service charge are additional. Any menu can be customized.

AVAILABILITY: For special events, year-round, Saturdays and Sundays 4pm–1am (call for details). Note that The Terrace Room and Lounge are also open to the public for dining: The Terrace Room hours Monday–Friday are 11am–2pm for lunch and 5–8pm for dinner (9:30pm on Thursday and Friday); Lounge hours Monday–Friday are 5–8:30pm. Additionally, The Terrace Room serves brunch from 10am–3pm on Saturday and Sunday.

SERVICES/AMENITIES:

Catering: provided, no BYO

Kitchen Facilities: n/a

Tables & Chairs: provided

Linens, Silver, etc.: provided

Restrooms: wheelchair accessible

Dance Floor: yes

Bride's Dressing Area: no

Meeting Equipment: podium, screen and microphone available

Parking: on-street

Accommodations: no guestrooms

Telephone: emergency only

Outdoor Night Lighting: access only

Outdoor Cooking Facilities: no

Cleanup: provided

View: Lake Merritt, Oakland hills, cityscape

Other: event coordinator on site

RESTRICTIONS:

Alcohol: provided, or BYO WC only with corkage fee

Smoking: outdoors only

Other: no food or beverages in lobby; no rice or confetti

Wheelchair Access: yes

Insurance: required for vendors

Music: amplified OK with volume limits

Wedgewood Wedding & Banquet Center
at Metropolitan Golf Links

Golf Course Clubhouse

10051 Doolittle Drive, Oakland
866/966-3009

www.wedgewoodbanquet.com
sales@wedgewoodbanquet.com

● Rehearsal Dinners	● Corp. Events/Mtgs.
● Ceremonies	● Private Parties
● Wedding Receptions	Accommodations

For red carpet treatment alongside the greens and fairways of a beautiful 18-hole golf course—just minutes from downtown Oakland and the Oakland Airport—book your special event at the Wedgewood Banquet Center at the Metropolitan Golf Links. This great value and year-round course (designed by American Society of Golf Course Architects member, Fred Bliss, and long-time Bay Area resident and World Golf Hall of Famer, Johnny Miller) is a terrific venue for weddings, golf events, corporate or other social functions and holiday parties. It was also awarded sanctuary status by Audubon International. Its spacious feel, plus long views to the Oakland hills, the bay, downtown Oakland and San Francisco lend it an uplifting outlook and unhurried charm.

To better accommodate weddings and special events, this facility has recently invested in an extensive renovation that includes a major banquet room expansion, additional ceremony space alongside the golf course, and attractive landscaping around the new event areas. The sizeable banquet room, with its two windowed walls, now opens onto a matching, 3,000-square-foot tent with amenities such as a built-in bar, state-of-the-art sound system, permanent dance floor, carpeting, and cooling Casablanca fans. Also new is an expansive lawn, complete with gazebo and rose garden, that's custom-made for ceremonies. Guests reach the banquet center via a breezeway that leads to the patio of the golf course's Sweet Spot Café. The patio can also be used as additional space for large celebrations, and features uninterrupted views of the course and the bayside surroundings.

Of course, one of the most reassuring aspects of booking an event at this appealing East Bay location is the professionalism and service you'll experience at the hands of the expert planning staff. Five lavish wedding packages include invitations, flowers, cake, and music, as well as the DJ, minister and menu—all of which are carefully sampled, screened and priced to ensure top quality, affordability and maximum satisfaction. Menu options are varied and generous with room for customization.

Will you choose the cream-white dendrobium orchids and bar grass in tall cylinder vases or the big bowls of floating roses, gerberas or gardenias? The stacked whipped cream cake with fresh flowers or the white-chocolate cake shaped like a gift box with a cascading ribbon? We can't list all of your options, but we can promise you this: You won't have to do any legwork, you'll know just what you're getting—and you won't lose track of the cost. Your only worry will be what to do after the party is over.

CEREMONY CAPACITY: The Center accommodates 250 indoors or outdoors.

EVENT/RECEPTION CAPACITY: The Center holds 250 seated and 300 standing indoors or outdoors.

MEETING CAPACITY: Wedgewood accommodates 200 seated.

FEES & DEPOSITS: A 25% deposit is required to reserve your date. The next 25% is due 90 days prior and the balance is due 10 days prior to the event. Meals range $20–30/person. Tax, alcohol and a 20% service charge are additional.

AVAILABILITY: Year-round, daily, 6am–midnight.

SERVICES/AMENITIES:

Catering: provided
Kitchen Facilities: n/a
Tables & Chairs: provided
Linens, Silver, etc.: provided
Restrooms: wheelchair accessible
Dance Floor: provided
Bride's & Groom's Dressing Areas: CBA
Meeting Equipment: full range CBA, extra charge

Parking: large lot
Accommodations: no guestrooms
Telephone: emergency only
Outdoor Night Lighting: access only
Outdoor Cooking Facilities: no
Cleanup: provided
View: fairways, landscaped grounds, SF skyline
Other: event coordination

RESTRICTIONS:

Alcohol: provided
Smoking: outside only
Music: amplified OK

Wheelchair Access: yes
Insurance: not required
Other: no rice, confetti or glitter; no open flames

Brownstone Gardens

Garden

91 Brownstone Road, Oakley
925/418-4532

www.brownstonegardens.com
info@brownstonegardens.com

● Rehearsal Dinners	● Corp. Events/Mtgs.
● Ceremonies	● Private Parties
● Wedding Receptions	Accommodations

For years, Bob and Karen Wiemholt talked of re-landscaping the old orchard around their Oakley property. Finally, they had an incentive: home weddings for all three of their daughters. Over several years they tackled the grounds one section at a time, and their mix of planning, passion and serendipity created an outdoor tapestry of color and texture that formed an increasingly beautiful backdrop for each event. Soon, friends and neighbors began asking if they, too, could get married here. Now, a decade later, what started as a labor of love for one family has blossomed into a popular garden spot where couples seeking an intriguing location can celebrate their own love.

Brownstone Gardens has three very distinct areas, all linked with winding walkways. Completely shielding you from the outside world are a profusion of mulberry and sycamore trees, variegated shrubbery, lilies and a fragrant, multicolored Rose Garden. Welcome breezes rustle the foliage overhead as your friends and family stroll down a shaded path towards one part of the Front Lawn where they can mingle until the ceremony begins. A gazebo, koi pond and wooden footbridge with waterfall are just a few of the visual highlights that will appeal to guests of all ages.

While the bride and her attendants prepare to make their entrance, everyone else is led down another path to the secluded ceremony site, guarded by two Doric columns and a pair of stone lions. The perimeter is fringed with towering pines interspersed with miniature roses and crepe myrtles, which put on a showy display of white flowers during the peak wedding months. Instead of a standard altar, couples exchange vows in the classically designed Temple Pavilion, an impressive structure supported by eight sandstone columns.

Cocktail receptions are usually hosted on the Front Lawn and utilize the entire area, which includes lots of nooks and crannies, trees encircled by brick pavers and an old-fashioned wooden swing in the corner. As your event continues, the garden has still more delights to share as you move towards the back of the property and the Reception Area, where a canopy of trees covers the multilevel dining space. Whimsical lighting, such as iron lanterns cast to resemble flowers and old grapevines and fitted with twinkling bulbs, adds sparkle to the surroundings. A large rock waterfall contributes a soothing backdrop to this romantic setting, while tables placed around the upper patio enjoy a sense of privacy as well as a great view of the dancing on the stone-floored lower level.

Although it's conveniently located off a main road, Brownstone Gardens will make you feel like you've traveled a bit off the beaten path to spend the day at a friend's country hideaway.

CEREMONY & MEETING CAPACITY: The site can accommodate 300 seated guests.

EVENT/RECEPTION CAPACITY: The site holds 250 seated and 300 standing guests.

FEES & DEPOSITS: A $1,000 deposit is required to reserve your date, and the balance is paid in monthly installments with the last payment due 30 days before the event. Packages range $5,000–35,000 depending on the day of the event and the space rented. Meals range $29–45/person. Tax, alcohol and a 22% service charge are additional.

AVAILABILITY: April–October, daily.

SERVICES/AMENITIES:

Catering: provided
Kitchen Facilities: n/a
Tables & Chairs: provided
Linens, Silver, etc.: provided
Restrooms: wheelchair accessible
Dance Area: yes
Bride's & Groom's Dressing Area: yes
Meeting Equipment: BYO

Parking: large lot
Accommodations: no guestrooms
Telephone: emergency use only
Outdoor Night Lighting: yes
Outdoor Cooking Facilities: none
Cleanup: provided
View: garden patio, waterfall, fountain, garden, landscaped grounds
Other: event coordination

RESTRICTIONS:

Alcohol: BYO
Smoking: designated areas only
Music: amplified OK outdoors with restrictions

Wheelchair Access: yes
Insurance: liability required

Overwhelmed? Use the search criteria on www.HereComesTheGuide.com to narrow down your choices.

Orinda Country Club

Country Club

315 Camino Sobrante, Orinda
925/254-4313
www.orindacc.org
catering@orindacc.org

● Rehearsal Dinners	● Corp. Events/Mtgs.	
● Ceremonies	● Private Parties	
● Wedding Receptions	Accommodations	

In the early 1920s, Orinda pioneer E.I. deLaveaga had a grand idea: to build a luxurious subdivision, centered around a country club that would provide its residents with "…family recreation, wholesome, happy country life…and something for every member of the family to do—golf, swimming, tennis, dancing…." He hired the finest architects, engineers and landscapers, and in 1925 the Orinda Country Club first opened its doors, bringing deLaveaga's joyful vision to life. Now, almost a century later, this spectacular club continues to offer its members and guests a host of recreational and social activities, all in a setting of unparalled natural beauty.

Designed by noted San Francisco architect Hamilton Murdock, the Orinda Country Club is a classic example of the the Spanish Mediterranean style that reached its pinnacle in the 1920s and '30s. Design elements such as a red-tile roof, balconies, archways, and a textured stucco exterior create a building that is in complete harmony with its woodland environment. Though it has been renovated many times since its opening, the clubhouse still evokes the glamour of those bygone days. You wouldn't be at all surprised to see Katherine Hepburn strolling off the tennis court or Clark Gable teeing up on the golf course (and that isn't just a fantasy—Bing Crosby, Bob Hope, Joe DiMaggio and Jack Benny are among the celebrities who have played golf here).

The clubhouse's interior reflects the handsome Spanish influence of its exterior. The main event space is the Grand Ballroom, which lives up to its name in every way. Upon entering, your eye travels upwards, past ornate metal chandeliers to the arched balcony supported by spiral columns, finally taking in the coffered ceiling and elaborately painted molding edged with copper. Large mirrors reflect the soft gold of the walls and the shining hardwood floors, and plush area rugs add touches of color. Fireplaces at both ends of the room can be lit in cool weather, heightening the room's warm, sumptuous ambiance.

Arched French doors lead from the ballroom to the Terrace Room. Here, one wall of windows opens onto fabulous views of the golf course and surrounding hillsides, so thickly covered in oaks, bays and alders that it must look much the same as when E.I. deLaveaga first set eyes on the property. A balcony runs the length of the terrace, perfect for contemplating the wooded vistas surrounding you. Large parties can use the terrace and the Grand Ballroom. There's even a "semiprivate" room just off the terrace that's popular with anyone looking for a place to relax and enjoy the festivities without feeling overwhelmed.

As befits such an exclusive, upscale establishment, the service here is "above par." The expert staff can assist you in every detail of your event, from choosing linen colors to selecting wines that will complement your customized menu. Everything is included in the price: bartenders, servers, insurance, and an on-site coordinator. And since only one event is scheduled per day, you and your guests can relax and savor every moment you spend at this unique facility. When you book your event at the Orinda Country Club, you're not just a customer, but a "member in spirit," participating in a tradition of gracious hospitality that's sure to continue for another hundred years.

CEREMONY CAPACITY: The Grand Ballroom holds 144 seated guests.

EVENT/RECEPTION CAPACITY: The Grand Ballroom accommodates up to 350 seated or 600 standing guests.

MEETING CAPACITY: Meetings do take place at this location. Call the Sales Department for details.

FEES & DEPOSITS: A $2,000 deposit is required to reserve your date. 50% of the estimated charges are due 3 months prior and the balance is due 7 days prior to the event. Rental fees range $250–3,000 depending on type of event and space rented. Meals range $31.95–51.95/person. Tax, alcohol and a 20% service charge are additional.

AVAILABILITY: Tuesday–Sunday, 7am–midnight.

SERVICES/AMENITIES:

Catering: provided
Kitchen Facilities: n/a
Tables & Chairs: provided
Linens, Silver, etc.: provided
Restrooms: wheelchair accessible
Dance Floor: provided
Bride's Dressing Area: CBA
Meeting Equipment: some provided, more CBA

Parking: large lot, valet optional
Accommodations: no guestrooms
Telephone: house phone
Outdoor Night Lighting: yes
Outdoor Cooking Facilities: no
Cleanup: provided
View: golf course, hills, forest, canyon
Other: event coordination, grand piano, on-site florals, AV equipment

RESTRICTIONS:

Alcohol: provided
Smoking: outside only
Music: amplified OK

Wheelchair Access: yes
Insurance: not required

Guild Hall at Piedmont Community Church

Community Hall

400 Highland Avenue, Piedmont
510/547-5700
www.piedmontchurch.org
jean@piedmontchurch.org

● Rehearsal Dinners	Corp. Events/Mtgs.
● Ceremonies	● Private Parties
● Wedding Receptions	Accommodations

You'll see the landmark bell tower of the beautiful Piedmont Community Church long before you arrive. Gleaming in the sunlight, the ivory-colored Mission-style building looks a bit like a wedding cake, set atop an ivy- and flower-covered rise overlooking the prosperous community that gives the venue its name.

An extensive renovation prior to the church's 100th-year anniversary added numerous features, making the facilities here even more guest-friendly. You can enter through a number of private and public stairways, ramps and drives, all of which lead to an expansive, landscaped inner courtyard that radiates around a colorful central fountain. This is, of course, the perfect place for an outdoor ceremony roofed in blue sky and skirted in blossoms. But you might want to use this area and the upper courtyard that surrounds it for music and cocktails, and instead get married in the church itself.

Nothing will prepare those attending for the regal ambiance within. Plush royal-blue carpet, dark pews cushioned in velvet, a lustrous, carved-beam ceiling, and two walls of stained-glass windows with floral motifs in brilliant, jewel colors evoke an Old World opulence. Couples tie the knot at an altar fit for a king and queen, beneath a rotunda brightened with lofty stained-glass windows. The church comes with a fabulous pipe organ hidden behind one altar wall, an organist, and acoustics that will naturally amplify even a whispered "I do." There are also separate spaces for the couple to get ready: the lounge-like Altar Guild Room for the groom; and a comfortable salon with mirrors, bathroom, vanity, private entrance and more for the bride and her retinue.

Across the courtyard, the welcoming Guild Hall provides a perfectly grand setting for a celebration of any kind. The beamed ceiling soars overhead, hardwood floors gleam golden, and pale sage-colored walls exude an embracing calm. Enormous windows can be left open on sunny days, and there's a generous stage for musicians. Another plus: a spacious commercial-quality kitchen that will surely please your caterer. Like the other structures on the property, Guild Hall has a private entrance, landscaped outdoor seating areas, and is flanked by graceful colonnades.

If your party is very large or very small, you may want to use the Clara Barton and Doris Murdock Rooms. Both open to the upper courtyard and provide parlor-like space for a guest lounge, additional buffet tables or a quieter, more intimate gathering. Panel doors separate the two rooms so that they can be used individually or together.

Sound heavenly? It is—especially when glasses are raised, toasts are made and the church bells chime for you.

CEREMONY CAPACITY: The sanctuary holds 300 seated guests. The outdoor area holds 100 seated.

EVENT/RECEPTION CAPACITY: Guild Hall can accommodate up to 200 seated guests.

MEETING CAPACITY: Meetings do not take place at this facility.

FEES & DEPOSITS: A deposit is required to reserve your date. The balance is due 30 days prior. Rental fees range $1,750–3,950 depending on the space rented, the length of your rental, and whether or not you are a Piedmont Community Church member. Fees include clergy on staff, organist, complimentary event coordination for the rehearsal and ceremony, fireplace, grand piano, tables and chairs.

AVAILABILITY: Year-round, daily, call for details.

SERVICES/AMENITIES:

Catering: BYO
Kitchen Facilities: fully equipped
Tables & Chairs: provided
Linens, Silver, etc.: CBA or through caterer
Restrooms: wheelchair accessible
Dance Floor: provided
Bride's Dressing Area: yes
Meeting Equipment: n/a

Parking: on street
Accommodations: no guestrooms
Telephone: house phone
Outdoor Night Lighting: provided
Outdoor Cooking Facilities: none
Cleanup: provided
View: fountain, garden, landscaped grounds
Other: grand piano, clergy on staff, complimentary event coordination

RESTRICTIONS:

Alcohol: BYO
Smoking: not allowed anywhere on the premises
Music: amplified OK indoors with restrictions

Wheelchair Access: yes
Insurance: liability required

Piedmont Community Hall

Community Park Building

711 Highland Avenue, Piedmont
510/420-3081, 510/420-3075
probb@ci.piedmont.ca.us

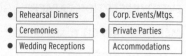

● Rehearsal Dinners	● Corp. Events/Mtgs.
● Ceremonies	● Private Parties
● Wedding Receptions	Accommodations

This facility is one of the most popular event venues in Northern California—and for good reason. The building is not only very attractive inside and out, but it has the added benefit of being situated in a lovely park setting.

Azaleas and camellias provide splashes of color near the circular landscaped plaza in front of the Hall. Redwoods and flowering cherry trees shade portions of the plaza, and behind the building a stream and more trees complete the circle of greenery.

The garden is home to another structure, a minisized Japanese Tea House which was relocated here after it was donated to the City of Piedmont. Couples can have a small ceremony in the Tea House, or brides can spend some quiet time here before the wedding or use it as a private place to dress and get ready for the big event. Two side walls of the Tea House are removable, so when the weather is mild, it's a terrific spot for an extra bar or hors d'oeuvres station.

Receptions take place in the Piedmont Community Hall, a splendid structure, Mediterranean in style with light taupe walls and terracotta tile roof. The Hall's interior looks so chic you'd never believe this is a city-owned facility. The main event space is a great party room, with a high, beamed ceiling, shining herringbone hardwood floors and chandeliers. Floor-to-ceiling windows allow lots of natural light and ensure that the "outdoor" feeling of the adjacent park carries over to your reception. This is a refined, nicely designed space, suitable for an elegant wedding, company party or corporate retreat. As we said, it's a popular spot, so remember to reserve early.

CEREMONY CAPACITY: The site holds up to 200 seated or standing guests indoors or outdoors.

EVENT/RECEPTION & MEETING CAPACITY: The site maximum is 200 guests. The Hall accommodates 200 standing or 120 seated guests. The patio area holds 150–200 guests.

FEES & DEPOSITS: For events on Friday, Saturday, Sunday or holidays, a $1,000 security deposit is due 2 weeks after booking and is refundable 6 weeks after the event. May–October weekend rates range $2,200–3,700 for a 7-hour block on Friday, or an 8-hour block on Saturday or Sunday. Piedmont residents receive a discounted rate. Additional hours available at $250/hour. Payment is due 60 days prior to the event. For Monday–Friday and off-season rates, please call for specifics.

Weekday rates for business functions vary depending on guest count and event duration; call for more information.

AVAILABILITY: Year-round, daily, 8am–midnight (1 event per day). Call early—the summer months are booked quickly.

SERVICES/AMENITIES:
Catering: BYO
Kitchen Facilities: fully equipped
Tables & Chairs: provided
Linens, Silver, etc.: BYO
Restrooms: wheelchair accessible
Dance Floor: hardwood floor
Bride's and Groom's Dressing Area: restrooms
Meeting Equipment: screen, TV, VCR, microphones, PA system

Parking: on- and off-street
Accommodations: no guestrooms
Telephone: pay phone
Outdoor Night Lighting: yes
Outdoor Cooking Facilities: BYO
Cleanup: caterer or renter
View: park setting

RESTRICTIONS:
Alcohol: BYO, must have controlled bar
Smoking: not allowed
Music: amplified OK

Wheelchair Access: yes
Insurance: included in weekend rates; for weekday use, BYO or purchase from Hall

---

The professionals in the back of this book are the best in the business. How do we know? Read page 701.

Piedmont Veterans' Memorial Building

Special Events Facility

401 Highland Avenue, Piedmont
510/420-3081, 510/420-3075
probb@ci.piedmont.ca.us

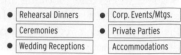

- Rehearsal Dinners
- Ceremonies
- Wedding Receptions
- Corp. Events/Mtgs.
- Private Parties
- Accommodations

There's nothing stuffy about the Piedmont Veterans' Memorial Building, a fixture of stately well-groomed Piedmont at the foot of the Oakland hills. Newly remodeled in 2008, this California modern structure built in 1953 is a favorite of civic organizations, private clubs, school groups and families. Far from fragile, it's the action-packed center of Piedmont community life and a popular place for family-friendly events.

The Piedmont police are the downstairs neighbors, and the Fire Department and City Hall are right next door. There's always something in bloom out back in meticulously landscaped Piedmont Park, with its wide walks, lush lawns and seasonal plantings. The Piedmont Public Works Department keeps the area neat and clean.

Behind the double glass doors of the balcony entrance, the airy vestibule opens up to a large community room with a light wood floor, high beamed ceiling and a big stage. Floor-to-ceiling windows on the north side of the room let in abundant light, and a small patio just beyond them allows guests an opportunity to step outside for a bit of fresh air and private conversation. The acoustics and sound system are first rate—good enough for the Piedmont Jazz Festival—and banquet tables can be arranged, leaving plenty of room for waltzes, cha-chas and tangos (which puts this venue at the top of the list for local dinner dances).

On the other side of the vestibule, a smaller room with a white iron balcony and filtered views of city and bay is a great spot for cocktails or a buffet. Adjacent, the big well-lit kitchen is a real caterer's delight, with an ice machine, coffee makers, two sink stations and an enormous fridge.

All of this makes for a very flexible space and an accommodating canvas for creative types. Fundraisers here have included everything from vivacious cabaret-style evenings to Polynesian-themed events replete with carved tikis and elaborate luau fare. Decorative touches like accent lighting and fancy flora are easily added. All in all, it's a marvelous value. East Bay and San Francisco hostelries are mere minutes away and Recreation Department staff—experienced hands at everything from weddings to pancake breakfasts to birdcalling contests to the Fourth of July Parade—know just what to do to ensure that the vibes are good and the good times vibrant at your very special event.

CEREMONY CAPACITY: The main room holds 200 seated. Ceremonies can take place across the street at the Exedra Plaza in Piedmont Park, which accommodates up to 150 seated guests.

EVENT/RECEPTION CAPACITY: The main room holds 200 seated with dancing, or 250 standing guests.

MEETING CAPACITY: The main room holds 300 seated theater-style or 125 seated classroom-style.

FEES & DEPOSITS: To reserve your date, a $1,000 refundable security deposit is required. The total rental fee is payable 3 months prior to the event. The weekend 7-hour rental fee ranges $1,295–1,650 depending on residency; call for weekday fees. Extra hours run $250/hour.

AVAILABILITY: Year-round, daily, 8am–midnight, including holidays.

SERVICES/AMENITIES:

Catering: BYO
Kitchen Facilities: fully equipped, but no dishwasher
Tables & Chairs: provided
Linens, Silver, etc.: BYO or caterer
Restrooms: wheelchair accessible
Dance Floor: hardwood floor
Bride's & Groom's Dressing Area: restrooms
Meeting Equipment: screen, microphones, sound system

Parking: on-street
Accommodations: no guestrooms
Telephone: pay phones
Outdoor Night Lighting: access only
Outdoor Cooking Facilities: no
Cleanup: renter or caterer
View: view of San Francisco from deck
Other: staff person provided during events

RESTRICTIONS:

Alcohol: BYO, bartender required
Smoking: outside only
Music: amplified OK

Wheelchair Access: yes
Insurance: included in weekend rates; required for weekday use
Other: no confetti, rice or birdseed

Rockefeller Lodge

Historic Lodge

Address withheld to ensure privacy. San Pablo
510/235-7344, Deborah, Event Coordinators
www.rockefellerlodge.com
rocklodge1@gmail.com

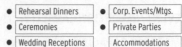

- Rehearsal Dinners
- Ceremonies
- Wedding Receptions
- Corp. Events/Mtgs.
- Private Parties
- Accommodations

Have you always wanted to do something a bit different? Maybe have a Victorian theme in one room and French lace and balloons in another? Or maybe treat your guests to milk and cookies baked on the spot? Whatever your fantasy, the owner and staff of the Rockefeller Lodge love the challenge of making your special event a reality. And with its variety of rooms and outdoor areas, the Lodge can accommodate a wide range of creativity.

Once a Japanese Buddhist temple, the Rockefeller Lodge still offers a fragrant, woodsy serenity. The brown-shingled building derives its secluded feeling from the surrounding trees and quiet neighborhood. Winding brick paths and wisteria-covered arbors invite leisurely relaxed strolls through the grounds. Outdoor ceremonies are often held in the gazebo area. You can have your reception or company party in the spacious interior rooms, featuring hardwood floors, hand-hewn ceiling beams and a noteworthy fireplace constructed of burnt bricks from the 1906 earthquake.

CEREMONY & EVENT/RECEPTION CAPACITY: The Lodge and grounds accommodate 410 seated guests; the Lodge alone holds 150 seated. The entire site holds 410 for a reception.

MEETING CAPACITY: The Lodge holds up to 150 seated guests.

FEES & DEPOSITS: A $600 security deposit is required to secure your date. The facility rental fee is complimentary for a 5-hour block Monday–Friday; it's $1,200 on Saturday and Sunday (day or evening). A 1-hour rehearsal can be arranged on Thursday evenings for $100. For events taking place November–March, except holidays, the rental fee is reduced by $600. Additional hours are $200/hour.

Buffets for over 100 guests range $13–29/person. Catering for 50 people, minimum, starts at $17/person; tax and an 18% service charge are additional. Full payment is required 14 days prior to the event. There is a $4.50/person beverage service charge which includes labor, glasses and nonalcoholic beverages. Any menu can be customized.

AVAILABILITY: Year-round, daily, 10am–4pm or 5pm–11pm. Available for any 6-hour block of time on Sunday.

SERVICES/AMENITIES:

Catering: provided, no BYO
Kitchen Facilities: n/a
Tables & Chairs: provided
Linens, Silver, etc.: provided
Restrooms: wheelchair accessible
Dance Floor: yes
Bride's Dressing Area: yes
Meeting Equipment: BYO

Parking: 2 lots
Accommodations: no guestrooms
Telephone: emergency use only
Outdoor Night Lighting: yes
Outdoor Cooking Facilities: no
Cleanup: provided
View: landscaped grounds and waterfalls
Other: full event planning

RESTRICTIONS:

Alcohol: BYO, service fee required
Smoking: outside only
Music: amplified OK inside only, 4-piece band limit

Wheelchair Access: yes
Insurance: certificate required
Other: no rice or birdseed

Want to know WHAT TO ASK a potential location or vendor? Check out our Questions to Ask on page 17.

Alcosta Senior and Community Center
Park and Gardens

Senior Center

9300 Alcosta Boulevard, San Ramon
925/973-3250
www.sanramon.ca.gov/parks/parks_facilities/rental.htm
pcstechniciansfacilities@sanramon.ca.gov

●	Rehearsal Dinners	●	Corp. Events/Mtgs.
●	Ceremonies	●	Private Parties
●	Wedding Receptions		Accommodations

The Alcosta Senior and Community Center not only has something for everyone, it offers a number of wonderful features you don't always find in a community center.

We love the fact that this venue has both indoor and outdoor event spaces, and comes with a fully equipped commercial kitchen. The center's banquet facility, the upscale Vista Grande Room, is well suited for wedding receptions, large meetings and other special events. The walls are painted a pleasant dusky peach, and the light oak floor is great for dancing. A high vaulted ceiling and windows with views of rolling hills add to its charm.

Sophisticated lighting and sound systems let you create the mood and music you want: Use lighting to highlight an area in a festive or sultry way; plug in your iPod (or any audio device) to listen to your own playlist.

Multiple doors open to an adjoining terrace, which extends your seating—and your celebration— outside. Shaded by a vine-covered arbor, the terrace is a lovely spot for dining, socializing and simply enjoying the fresh air and view of the hills. When the weather is warm, leave the Vista Grande Room doors open so that guests can flow easily between the two spaces.

Ceremonies here are held in the Gazebo, a Victorian-style confection with a white picket railing and peaked shake roof. Standing in the middle of a park-like setting, it's encircled by rose bushes and flowering trees and overlooks a broad lawn where family and friends are seated.

Throughout your event, the "park" provides a relaxing place for guests to stroll along brick paths, have a quiet conversation under a tree and even play bocce ball. As you sit on a bench soaking up the sun, you can't help but appreciate the unexpected beauty and serenity of this private little haven.

We think the Alcosta Senior and Community Center is a real find, and for those on a budget, very easy on the pocketbook.

CEREMONY CAPACITY: The Vista Grande Room seats 115 banquet-style or 200 seated theater-style.

EVENT/RECEPTION CAPACITY: The facility can accommodate up to 115 seated banquet-style.

MEETING CAPACITY: Several spaces accommodate 20–200 seated guests.

FEES & DEPOSITS: A $50–200 security deposit is due when you book the facility (depending on spaces rented). The rental fee ranges $45–165/hour on weekends (6pm Friday to 6pm Sunday) and $20–90/hour weekdays (6pm Sunday to 6pm Friday) and is due 90 days prior to the event. If the booking occurs less than 90 days prior to the event, the rental fee is due at the time of the booking along with the security deposit. San Ramon residents receive a discounted rate. The Vista Grande Room can be partitioned in half, and may be rented as a half space. There is an additional fee for use of the kitchen.

AVAILABILITY: Year-round. Monday–Thursday, 5pm–10pm; Friday, 5pm–1am; Saturday, 8:30am–1am; and Sunday, 8:30am–10pm.

SERVICES/AMENITIES:

Catering: pre-approved list or BYO with approval
Kitchen Facilities: fully equipped, extra fee
Tables & Chairs: provided
Linens, Silver, etc.: BYO
Restrooms: wheelchair accessible
Dance Floor: yes
Bride's Dressing Area: CBA, extra fee
Meeting Equipment: easel, LCD projector, screen; all are extra charge

Parking: ample lot
Accommodations: no guestrooms
Telephone: emergency use only
Outdoor Night Lighting: yes
Outdoor Cooking Facilities: BBQ
Cleanup: renter or caterer
View: Las Trampas Regional Park hills, landscaped surroundings
Other: piano, extra fee

RESTRICTIONS:

Alcohol: BYO, insurance required
Smoking: outside only
Music: amplified OK inside only

Wheelchair Access: yes
Insurance: sometimes required
Other: decorating restrictions; no birdseed, candles, confetti, rice, glitter, petals or bubbles; red wine and punch discouraged

The Bridges Golf Club

Golf Club

9000 South Gale Ridge Road, San Ramon
925/735-4253, Special Events
www.thebridgesgolf.com
events@thebridgesgolf.com

● Rehearsal Dinners	● Corp. Events/Mtgs.
● Ceremonies	● Private Parties
● Wedding Receptions	○ Accommodations

Perched on a gentle rise in the foothills of Mt. Diablo, the Bridges Golf Clubhouse looks every bit the Mediterranean villa, with its tiled roof, white walls and Moorish turrets. The interior has the feel of an exclusive country club, and from almost every window the view is a vision in green: acres of velvety fairways, rolling away into the distance. The setting is so lovely, you might easily forget that this place was built primarily for golf.

When you enter the clubhouse lobby, a pair of elaborate wrought-iron gates to your left opens into a swanky bar inside one of those exotic towers you noticed out front. The magnificent double-high coved ceiling boasts a massive chandelier that would seem at home in a Medici castle! The bar adjoins the Golfer's Patio, where guests can quaff cocktails under the shade of a sycamore while surveying the players on the links.

French doors and windows make up one wall of The Bridges' main dining area, appropriately christened the "View Room." Wall sconces and an antique-style chandelier produce a romantic candelabra effect, and together with the sunlight enhance the warm glow of the room's earth tones. A crosshatch of wooden ceiling beams harmonizes with the wood trim of the richly upholstered chairs and oak tables.

A veranda runs along the greens-side of the club, accessed by both the View Room and the adjacent Fireplace Room. Used separately, these two spaces are divided by a tasteful partition of wooden shutters topped with glass cutaways; to combine the rooms for a larger event, the partition is simply folded away. The ambiance of richness and comfort in the View Room also pervades the Fireside Room, a cozy space for a rehearsal dinner. Your focus here is drawn to a grand stone hearth with a novel design: The fireplace is actually double-sided, and doors lead to a curved patio that surrounds the hearth's outdoor face. They call this the "Back Fireplace," and if there's a chill in the evening air, simply snuggle up by the hearth and behold the picturesque panorama.

Bridges' most dramatic room is the Garden Pavilion, just a few steps from the Clubhouse. It's a grand space, with a 25-foot ceiling, antique wrought-iron chandeliers and a wall of huge archways overlooking the fairways. Guests love to step through the center arch onto the "Looking Terrace," where they have a panoramic view of the greens, Mt. Diablo and the color-streaked sky as the sun sets behind the hills. The archways have tall French doors and windows, and the facility is climate controlled for year-round comfort. When the weather is perfect, however, you are still able to open the windows and let in the afternoon breeze. Set for an elegant reception, the Pavilion is breathtaking: Tables are covered with linens, flowers and votive candles; silver and crystal sparkle in the candlelight, and the whole room is filled with a warm glow. If you'd like a more informal ambiance, however, the Pavilion's flexibility can accommodate your creativity. Some couples have brought in lion or dragon dancers for entertainment, and one even hosted a luau with hula dancers. During the holiday season, Bridges transforms the Pavilion with festive decorations, but if you have a different look in mind, the club's event coordinators will be happy to help you achieve it.

The Bridges Golf Club encourages "proper etiquette and the highest standards" on the golf course. This emphasis on quality and tradition is also reflected in the Clubhouse and Pavilion, so whether you host a customized golf tournament, a conference or the most sophisticated wedding reception, your event will be first class all the way.

CEREMONY CAPACITY: The outdoor ceremony site on the First Fairway holds up to 300 seated guests. Ceremonies only take place at Bridges in combination with a reception.

EVENT/RECEPTION CAPACITY: The Clubhouse accommodates 120 seated or 150 standing guests. The Garden Pavilion holds up to 300 seated or 400 standing guests.

MEETING CAPACITY: The Fireside and the View Rooms, combined, hold 80 guests seated theater-style. The Garden Pavilion holds 300 guests seated theater-style.

FEES & DEPOSITS: A $2,000 nonrefundable deposit is required to secure your date. 50% of the food and beverage minimum is due 6 months prior to the event, and the balance is due 2 weeks prior to the event. Room rental fees range $300–2,500 depending on space rented. Meals run $26–50/person; tax, alcohol and a 20% service charge are additional. A $1.50/person cake-cutting fee is additional. Food and beverage minimums apply and range $750–20,000 depending on space and time rented. Specials are available for Friday and Sunday bookings.

AVAILABILITY: Year-round, daily, 7am–2am.

SERVICES/AMENITIES:
Catering: provided, no BYO
Kitchen Facilities: n/a
Tables & Chairs: provided up to 300 guests
Linens, Silver, etc.: provided
Restrooms: wheelchair accessible
Dance Floor: yes
Bride's Dressing Area: CBA
Meeting Equipment: CBA, extra fee

Parking: large lot
Accommodations: no guestrooms
Telephone: emergency use only
Outdoor Night Lighting: yes
Outdoor Cooking Facilities: CBA
Cleanup: provided
View: fairways, East Bay Hills, Mt. Diablo
Other: event coordination

RESTRICTIONS:
Alcohol: provided, or corkage $14/bottle
Smoking: outside only
Music: amplified OK

Wheelchair Access: yes
Insurance: not required

The Ranch at Little Hills

Ranch

18013 Bollinger Canyon Road, San Ramon
925/426-3066
www.theranchatlittlehills.com
weddings@theranchatlittlehills.com

● Rehearsal Dinners	● Corp. Events/Mtgs.
● Ceremonies	● Private Parties
● Wedding Receptions	Accommodations

For a joyous celebration in the great outdoors few places can top The Ranch at Little Hills. This 25-acre oasis nestled in the East Bay hills next to the vast Las Trampas Regional Wilderness is mere minutes from the freeway, but you and your guests will feel like you've managed to get completely away from it all.

The well-equipped property, part of the East Bay Regional parks system, is perfect for anything from a corporate gathering or family fun to a wedding on the grass—all framed in oaks and canopied by the sky. Events here are run by *The California Parks Company,* which has successfully catered to over a million guests in their two decades of operation.

A secluded path leads from the parking lot to the Pergola Deck, where wedding parties of all sizes can witness a romantic ceremony. Afterwards, it's just a few steps to Oak Knoll for the reception. Here, a natural wood fence and enormous live oaks seclude the large white pavilion and patio. Twinkle lights, lanterns, uplights and spots can augment moonlight and stars when night falls. There's a pretty little bride's room close at hand with vanity and mirrors, white wicker furniture and a closet for gowns and accessories. Another plus: an on-site coordinator to take care of all the details.

If Oak Knoll is too formal, kick back in Moonshine Heaven or Buckeye Flat, where picnic tables amid parkland trees set the scene for relaxed al fresco dining. Host a fabulous high-end picnic or a quaint wedding in the woods, and feel free to bring in hay bales and live musicians to add flair to your ranch-style affair. The venue's outdoor concession stand serves as a beverage and snack bar for these spots and for High Falutin' Hill on the opposite side of the rise.

No matter where your wedding takes place, you'll find a plethora of photo opportunities throughout the park. There are also numerous places where you and your new spouse can take a break from the festivities and steal a few moments alone.

Most of the areas in the park work equally well for corporate events, especially at the large Buffet Pavilion and grill in front of the California Park Company offices.

More than likely if you've opted for a natural environment, outdoor activities will be part of the mix. The Ranch at Little Hills has a wealth of options. You can party poolside near the Pergola

Deck and lawn, or take your celebration over to Lowlander's Holler and entertain guests in a shady pavilion surrounded by two softball fields, basketball hoops, a rock climbing area, dunk tank, trout pond and more.

From corporate and school groups to wedding celebrants, everyone seems to enjoy themselves here. So why not prolong the party? Out-of-towners who wish to extend their stay in the sunny East Bay will find a wide range of accommodations nearby, as well as a variety of great things to see and do.

CEREMONY, EVENT/RECEPTION & MEETING CAPACITY: The facility holds 250 seated or standing guests outdoors.

FEES & DEPOSITS: The rental fee is required to reserve your date, and the balance is due 2 weeks prior to the event. The rental fee ranges $1,850–2,850 depending on the number of people attending. Catering packages range $18–$27/person and beverage packages range $8–$15/person.

AVAILABILITY: May–October, flexible hours.

SERVICES/AMENITIES:

Catering: provided
Kitchen Facilities: n/a
Tables & Chairs: provided
Linens, Silver, etc.: provided
Restrooms: wheelchair accessible
Dance Area: provided
Bride's Dressing Area: yes
Meeting Equipment: provided

Parking: large lot
Accommodations: no guestrooms
Telephone: emergency use only
Outdoor Night Lighting: provided
Outdoor Cooking Facilities: BBQ on site
Cleanup: provided
View: canyon, hills, landscaped grounds
Other: picnic area, event coordination

RESTRICTIONS:

Alcohol: provided
Smoking: designated areas only
Music: amplified OK outdoors with restrictions

Wheelchair Access: yes
Insurance: not required

Want to find more locations and services? Check out our informative website, www.HereComesTheGuide.com.

515

San Ramon Community Center

Community Center

12501 Alcosta Boulevard, San Ramon
925/973-3200
www.sanramon.ca.gov/parks/parks_facilities/rental.htm
pcstechniciansfacilities@sanramon.ca.gov

●	Rehearsal Dinners	●	Corp. Events/Mtgs.
●	Ceremonies	●	Private Parties
●	Wedding Receptions		Accommodations

We'd like to introduce you to a sophisticated facility whose spaces can compete with those of the best event sites. There's even a rose garden for ceremonies! Would you believe that this beautifully designed venue is a community center?

Built in 1989, this outstanding rose-colored granite-and-glass structure features pools, fountains and lush landscaping. Inside, the Fountain Room is the most popular area for receptions. Curved laminated beams radiate from a center point, creating a domed ceiling 40 feet high. This sizable room, decorated in subtle plums and lavenders, is equally suitable for black-tie affairs, casual parties and large meetings.

For smaller events we like the cool, gray Terrace Room, which is perfect for intimate dinners or cocktail mixers. Guests are welcomed into the space through a wonderful gallery that features different works of art each month. Warmed by light filtering through a 40-foot wall of windows, it also overlooks the center's fountain courtyard.

If you're interested in a site in this area, come take a look. We think that the San Ramon Community Center is a real find—the price and the ambiance are both sure to please.

CEREMONY CAPACITY: Outdoors, the Rose Garden holds 75 seated guests. Indoors, the Fountain Room seats 250 banquet-style, and 300 theater-style; the Terrace Room seats 80 banquet-style and 150 theater-style.

EVENT/RECEPTION CAPACITY: The Fountain Room holds 250 seated guests. The Terrace Room accommodates 80 seated or 150 for a standing reception. Outdoors, the Rose Garden holds 75 seated or 100 standing guests.

MEETING CAPACITY: Several spaces accommodate 20–250 seated guests.

FEES & DEPOSITS: A $100–1,000 security deposit (depending on the room rented) is required when you book the facility. The rental fee is due 90 days prior to the event. If the booking occurs less than 90 days prior, the rental fees are due at the time of the booking along with the security deposit. Rental fees range $20–320/hour depending on the day and spaces rented. Sunday evening events as well as San Ramon residents will receive a discounted rate. A 4-hour minimum is required for the Fountain and Terrace Rooms.

AVAILABILITY: Year-round, daily: Sunday–Thursday, 8:30am–10pm; Friday and Saturday, 8:30am–1am.

SERVICES/AMENITIES:

Catering: pre-approved list, BYO with approval
Kitchen Facilities: fully equipped, extra fee
Tables & Chairs: provided
Linens, Silver, etc.: BYO
Restrooms: wheelchair accessible
Dance Floor: yes, extra fee
Bride's Dressing Area: CBA, extra fee
Meeting Equipment: full range, extra charge

Parking: ample lot
Accommodations: no guestrooms
Telephone: emergency use only
Outdoor Night Lighting: yes
Outdoor Cooking Facilities: no
Cleanup: renter or caterer
View: San Ramon Valley hills, landscaped gardens, fountains

RESTRICTIONS:

Alcohol: BYO, insurance required
Smoking: outside only
Music: amplified OK inside only

Wheelchair Access: yes
Insurance: sometimes required
Other: decorating restrictions; no candles, birdseed, confetti, glitter, rice, petals or bubbles; red wine and punch discouraged

Wedgewood Wedding & Banquet Center
at the San Ramon Golf Club

Golf Club and Banquet Facility

9430 Fircrest Lane, San Ramon
866/966-3009
www.wedgewoodbanquet.com
sales@wedgewoodbanquet.com

- Rehearsal Dinners
- Ceremonies
- Wedding Receptions
- Corp. Events/Mtgs.
- Private Parties
- Accommodations

Waterfowl often swim with their offspring in the small lake between the wedding gazebo and the 9th-island green. A 50-year-old weeping willow growing at the water's edge frames the tranquil scene. At San Ramon Golf Club, romantic settings like this are as much a part of the landscape as the fairways and surrounding foothills.

Over the years the ranch-style clubhouse has transformed into a popular banquet and wedding facility. A recent renovation has given this property a fresh look, with new paint and décor throughout, recessed lighting and a completely refurbished bar. Of special interest to brides are the floor-to-ceiling mirrors in what the club boasts is "the largest bridal dressing room in Contra Costa County." Cherubic angels adorn the vanity and an antique French armoire, while potted plants and a Goddess of Love water fountain add to the charming atmosphere of the space.

Almost all wedding ceremonies at the club take place on the lawn outside the reception hall. On a sunny day the weeping willow casts a cooling shadow across the grass, providing plenty of shade for your guests. Evening affairs are even more enchanting, with the lights from the white gazebo reflecting off the lake. When the ceremony begins, the bride appears at the French double doors of the Wedgewood Room and then walks along the curving path to her groom. Because weddings are held year-round, the club is always ready with an alternative indoor site. Should rain clouds appear at the last minute, the staff will open a room adjoining the reception hall. With a fire crackling in the brick fireplace the setting becomes quite cozy.

Receptions take place in the Wedgewood Room, brightened by a bank of windows overlooking the lake and golf course. The tinted windows afford complete privacy while allowing everyone to enjoy the view. The patio between the building and lawn is a lovely spot to serve appetizers—guests can sit at umbrella-shaded tables or stroll along the bank to watch the swans, herons, turtles and other wildlife.

Wedgewood Wedding and Banquet Center operates many facilities throughout the state, and is known for their all-inclusive wedding packages. When you book your wedding here almost everything can be covered: food, beverages, DJ, cake, flowers and invitations. The folks at Wedgewood focus on delivering value and service, and pride themselves on taking care of all your needs. The club also offers conveniences you might not expect to find at a privately owned facility, such as an 18-hole golf course open to the public, plenty of parking, and an entire building reserved just for your event. And, with 25 years of wedding planning experience, the Wedgewood Banquet Center staff will help make your celebration one you'll always remember.

CEREMONY CAPACITY: Outdoors, the lawn area holds 400 seated guests. Indoors, the Wedgewood Room holds 400 seated guests.

EVENT/RECEPTION CAPACITY: The Wedgewood Room holds 400 seated guests or 500 for a cocktail reception. The lawn area accommodates 500 seated or 700 for a standing reception.

MEETING CAPACITY: Several spaces accommodate 50–300 seated guests.

FEES & DEPOSITS: 25% of the estimated event total is required to reserve your date, another 25% is due 90 days prior and the balance is due 10 days prior to the event. Meals range $25–40/person. Tax, alcohol and a 20% service charge are additional. There are no room rental fees as long as certain food and beverage minimums are met.

AVAILABILITY: Year-round, daily, 6am–midnight.

SERVICES/AMENITIES:

Catering: provided
Kitchen Facilities: n/a
Tables & Chairs: provided
Linens, Silver, etc.: provided
Restrooms: wheelchair accessible
Dance Floor: yes
Bride's Dressing Area: yes
Meeting Equipment: full range, extra charge

Parking: ample lot
Accommodations: no guestrooms
Telephone: emergency use only
Outdoor Night Lighting: yes
Outdoor Cooking Facilities: no
Cleanup: provided
View: lake, hills, fairways, waterfall, swans and ducks
Other: event coordination

RESTRICTIONS:

Alcohol: provided
Smoking: outside only
Music: amplified OK

Wheelchair Access: yes
Insurance: not required
Other: no rice, confetti or glitter; no open flames

Civic Park Community Center

Community Center

1375 Civic Drive. Walnut Creek
925/256-3575
www.walnut-creek.org/rentals
rentals@walnut-creek.org

- Rehearsal Dinners
- Ceremonies
- Wedding Receptions
- Corp. Events/Mtgs.
- Private Parties
- Accommodations

Romance is in the air at Civic Park Community Center. It blossoms in the rose gardens and flutters about the shade trees growing in this tranquil urban hideaway. It also resides in the Center's wedding gazebo, an inspiration not only for ceremonies, but for marriage proposals as well. Recently, a young man was so taken with the pretty structure he hung twinkle lights around it and hired a caterer to serve dinner for two beneath its canopy. Then, after he and his girlfriend toasted their love for each other with glasses of champagne, he popped the question—and she accepted!

Located at the edge of Walnut Creek's busy downtown, the park and buildings that make up the Community Center feel surprisingly secluded. Mature sycamores and redwoods help screen out the sights and sounds of passing traffic. In many places the trees are so tall and thick you can barely see their tops. As you walk beneath their wide boughs or perhaps picnic on the lawn in their long, cool shadows, you have the pleasant impression you've stepped through the looking glass into the countryside.

Weddings have become so popular here they often have to be scheduled a year in advance. Along with the ceremony and reception sites, you can also reserve the Center's Social Hall or Conference Room for a casual rehearsal dinner. These two small, unadorned rooms in the main building can be decorated in any style that suits you, and both of them open to a large commercial kitchen available for your use. On the day of the wedding, the carpeted lounge in the back of the building can be rented as a changing room for the bridal party. A big plus for many brides is the fact that all of the important wedding areas are just steps apart, making the transition from the changing room to the ceremony in the gazebo to the reception in the Assembly Hall easy and convenient.

Another plus is the simple architecture of the spacious Assembly Hall. The building's uncomplicated interior is a blank canvas awaiting your personal vision. The six-foot banquet tables and metal-and-resin chairs provided by the Center can be set up in any arrangement you choose. Many couples like to dress them up by renting special chair covers, tablecloths and table settings. The neutral tones of the well-lit room blend easily with almost any décor, and the overhead lights can be dimmed or brightened to accent the changing mood of the occasion. A full Bose sound system, with speakers on all the overhead trestle beams, will have your guests swaying to the music wherever you place the dance floor.

With the exception of a fog machine or nails in the wall, the transformation of the Assembly Hall is only limited by your imagination. One bride and groom expanded their reception outside the building by opening the room's ten-foot sliding glass door that leads to a small patio and the park beyond. Connecting the nearby trees with colorful ribbons they created a large grassy "courtyard." Another couple arrived early to reserve the first-come-first-served picnic tables and barbecue grills beside the hall for their guests to enjoy during the reception.

However you celebrate at the Center, you'll love the flexibility of the spaces, and the park setting is sure to provide a beautiful backdrop.

CEREMONY, EVENT/RECEPTION & MEETING CAPACITY: Various indoor areas hold up to 225 seated banquet-style or 250 theater-style. Smaller events can also be accommodated. The gazebo and park area holds up to 300 guests seated or standing. (Chairs not provided outdoors.)

FEES & DEPOSITS: A $500 nonrefundable deposit is required to reserve your date. The balance and security deposit are due in full 90 days prior to your event. Rental fees range $45–150/hour depending on the day and the room rented.

AVAILABILITY: Year-round: Monday–Thursday, 8am–10pm; Friday and Saturday, 8am–1am; Sunday, 8am–midnight.

Weekend reservations may be made up to 1 year in advance. Weekday evenings may be scheduled on a limited basis depending on availability. Rental hours must include setup and cleanup time.

SERVICES/AMENITIES:

Catering: BYO
Kitchen Facilities: large, commercial kitchen
Tables & Chairs: provided for indoor use
Linens, Silver, etc.: BYO or through caterer
Restrooms: wheelchair accessible
Dance Floor: yes
Bride's & Groom's Dressing Area: no
Meeting Equipment: BYO

Parking: limited on-site
Accommodations: no guestrooms
Telephone: emergency use only
Outdoor Night Lighting: yes
Outdoor Cooking Facilities: BYO BBQ
Cleanup: caterer or renter
View: park, garden, landscaped grounds

RESTRICTIONS:

Alcohol: BYO WB only, permits required, not allowed at youth events
Smoking: outdoors only
Music: amplified OK indoors with restrictions

Wheelchair Access: yes
Insurance: not required
Other: no birdseed, confetti, rice, rose petals, aerosol streamers, hay, sand or glitter; security required at all youth events

---

The Clubhouse at Boundary Oak

Restaurant

3800 Valley Vista Road, Walnut Creek
925/934-3600 X21
www.playboundaryoak.com

● Rehearsal Dinners	● Corp. Events/Mtgs.
● Ceremonies	● Private Parties
● Wedding Receptions	Accommodations

Nature abounds at this premier Walnut Creek venue, known for its wonderful views. Sitting on acres of manicured greens, it's bordered by open space and ringed by an extensive network of rustic, ridgeline trails.

The Clubhouse at Boundary Oak, named for a particularly majestic and artfully gnarled 350-year-old tree on the grounds, is just moments from town yet feels worlds away. From its hilltop perch it offers a front row seat to the location's expansive vistas.

Perhaps the best way to start off your momentous day in this city/country setting is to opt for an outdoor ceremony at one of two terrific sites. For peaceful panoramas that include the surrounding fairways, a towering stand of eucalyptus trees and a glimpse of Concord in the distance, exchange vows at the Lake View, set on a knoll beside the 9th-hole water feature and its impressive center fountain. If you prefer a more intimate alternative, get married on the Patio, which overlooks the putting green with the lake and fountain in the background.

You may be tempted to enjoy hors d'oeuvres and a glass of bubbly al fresco as well, but there are also several inviting spots inside the Clubhouse. For example, the multilevel Mira Room adjoining the Patio has a long bar, wooden floors and great sunset views. Then, when you're ready for dinner, just step through the arched entryway into the Vista Room. This architecturally interesting space is cantilevered above the walkway below with three walls of windows that angle outwards, making the outdoors feel like part of the room. A pyramid-style ceiling completes the whole "mid-century modernist" feel.

If, however, your dream reception (or the size of your guest list) calls for something larger, take a short stroll through the Main Entrance Foyer—which doubles as a gallery displaying works by local artists—and start your festivities in the Atrium. In this bright space, anchored by a large permanent bar and rows of slanted skylights running the length of the ceiling, friends and family can mingle over cocktails. At dinnertime, three sets of double doors open to reveal the beautifully decorated Celebration Ballroom, which easily hosts 275 for dinner and dancing. And if you want to dance late and crank up the music, you don't have to worry—there are no neighbors nearby.

Be sure to take advantage of the photo opportunities on this 160-acre property, named "Best Golf Course of the East Bay" by *Diablo Magazine*. That great oak, with its spreading branches, as well as the lake, waterfall, and colorful floral displays around the building, all make picturesque backdrops that will add immeasurably to your album of memories from the day.

CEREMONY CAPACITY: The site holds 300 seated indoors or outdoors.

EVENT/RECEPTION CAPACITY: The clubhouse accommodates 300 seated or 500 standing guests indoors.

MEETING CAPACITY: Meeting rooms hold 200 seated guests.

FEES & DEPOSITS: An initial deposit is required to confirm your date. The event balance and final guest count is due 7 business days prior to the event. All events must meet a food and beverage minimum that varies depending on the date and time booked. Flexible wedding packages start at $35/person. Tax, alcohol and service charge are additional.

AVAILABILITY: Year-round, daily.

SERVICES/AMENITIES:

Catering: provided
Kitchen Facilities: n/a
Tables & Chairs: provided
Linens, Silver, etc.: provided
Restrooms: wheelchair accessible
Dance Floor: yes
Bride's Dressing Area: yes
Meeting Equipment: CBA

Parking: large lot
Accommodations: partner hotels nearby
Telephone: house phone, extra fee
Outdoor Night Lighting: access only
Outdoor Cooking Facilities: BBQ CBA
Cleanup: provided
View: garden, landscaped grounds, fountain, fairways, hills, lagoon, lake, mountains, valley

RESTRICTIONS:

Alcohol: provided
Smoking: outdoors only
Music: amplified OK indoors with restrictions

Wheelchair Access: yes
Insurance: may be required

The Gardens at Heather Farm

Garden Education Center

1540 Marchbanks Drive, Walnut Creek
925/947-1678
www.gardenshf.org
rentals@gardenshf.org

● Rehearsal Dinners	● Corp. Events/Mtgs.
● Ceremonies	● Private Parties
● Wedding Receptions	Accommodations

Something is always in bloom at this nonprofit garden education center. Covering six landscaped acres, it features a series of paved footpaths that wind their way through a colorful variety of flowerbeds, herb and rock gardens and water features. Off in the distance there's a pond with two fountains, and beyond that a view of Mt. Diablo.

Anyone who equates romance with roses will want to tie the knot beneath the fragrant, rose-covered gazebo, surrounded by rose bushes that bloom continuously from spring through fall. Afterwards you and your guests can stroll through the gardens, admiring the wide range of floral and herbal displays on your way to the patio. This large terrace, like the rest of the garden center, offers an abundance of olfactory and visual treats. Concrete-and-tile planters border the patio and are filled with a horticultural riot of textures, scents and hues. A caterer-friendly pavilion—complete with sink, electrical outlets, lighting and four easy-access tiled counters—is great for a buffet setup or as a serving station for a cocktail party.

Receptions are usually held upstairs in the Camellia Room. Light and airy, it has a high, beamed ceiling and floor-to-ceiling windows that afford a commanding view of Mt. Diablo and the gardens. With its neutral walls and light-colored floor, this pleasant space is easy to decorate.

A spacious wraparound deck gives guests access to the outdoors; to explore the gardens they simply take the ramp or stairs from the deck to the patio and pavilion below. The nearby Meadow Garden, with its expansive lawn, is also available for outdoor receptions.

Since they were first established in 1968, the Gardens at Heather Farm have become one of Walnut Creek's most popular venues. When you have your event here, you not only get to enjoy this delightful (and educational!) garden setting, you're supporting a living museum and wildlife habitat.

CEREMONY CAPACITY: The site holds 300 seated guests indoors or outdoors.

EVENT/RECEPTION & MEETING CAPACITY: The facility accommodates 175 seated guests for dining or 300 standing indoors, and 300 seated or standing outdoors on the patio or in the garden.

They offer customized floor plans that include dining, dancing and auditorium styles as well as standing formats for cocktail receptions, special events or company mixers.

FEES & DEPOSITS: A nonrefundable deposit of 50% of the rental fee is required to reserve your date; a $500–800 security deposit and the balance of the rental fee are due 6 months prior to the event. A garden ceremony setup is an additional $300 charge. Weekday rental fees, Monday 9am–Friday 2pm, range $75–200/hour with a 2-hour minimum. Rental fees Friday 2pm–Sunday 10pm and holidays range $800–2,200 depending on the space rented and time of year. Extra hours are available.

AVAILABILITY: Year-round, daily. Weekdays, 9am–10pm; weekend times vary.

SERVICES/AMENITIES:

Catering: select from list, additional fee for off-list catering, by approval
Kitchen Facilities: moderately equipped
Tables & Chairs: provided, including chairs for a gazebo ceremony
Linens, Silver, etc.: BYO
Restrooms: wheelchair accessible
Dance Floor: yes
Bride's Dressing Area: yes

Parking: lot and on-street
Accommodations: no guestrooms
Telephone: emergency use only
Outdoor Night Lighting: yes
Outdoor Cooking Facilities: BYO BBQ
Cleanup: caterer or renter
View: Mt. Diablo, gardens and pond
Meeting Equipment: podium, PA, projection screen

RESTRICTIONS:

Alcohol: BYO
Smoking: outside only
Music: amplified OK indoors only

Wheelchair Access: yes
Insurance: proof of liability insurance required
Other: no confetti, rice, birdseed, flower petals, butterfly or balloon releases

Heather Farm Community Center

Community Center

301 North San Carlos Drive, Walnut Creek
925/256-3575
www.walnut-creek.org/rentals
rentals@walnut-creek.org

● Rehearsal Dinners	● Corp. Events/Mtgs.
● Ceremonies	● Private Parties
● Wedding Receptions	☐ Accommodations

Clark Gable was on the brink of becoming a major movie star when he came to Heather Farm in 1931 to make the motion picture *Sporting Blood*. Of course that was during the park's former life as a horse ranch and racetrack. The actor was so taken with the place he stabled his thoroughbreds there. Today Heather Farm shows little evidence of its equestrian past, but it retains a country-like atmosphere that draws visitors from all around the East Bay.

Tucked behind a hill on the outskirts of Walnut Creek, the 102-acre park is an oasis of shade trees, green grass and flower gardens. Meandering paths connect the picnic and nature areas with the swim center, tennis courts and athletic fields. With groves of trees and meadows separating the facilities from one another, it's almost as if each site is a park unto itself. And nestled in one of the most picturesque of these spots is Heather Farm Community Center.

Wedding receptions at the Center are held in the Lakeside Room overlooking a large pond. One of our favorite features of this venue is its wraparound deck, which extends over the water. Guests who stroll out here are treated to an unobstructed view of ducks and geese swimming between the two large fountains that aerate the man-made lagoon. On the opposite shore, sycamores, oaks and pepper trees shade the extensive lawns and create a protective screen around the Center. Some couples are so charmed by the scenery they hold their wedding ceremony on the deck followed by the reception inside.

The pond and fountains are also visible from the Lakeside Room through the wide windows along two walls. Although the hall is spacious, the dark wood interior and coffered ceiling add a coziness to the ambiance. More warmth comes from the fireplace nook, where friends and family can gather to toast the bride and groom. Pretty and unpretentious, the room requires very little decorating for those who want to keep their reception simple. Banquet and round tables, along with folding chairs, are provided with the reservation—the atmosphere, be it casual or elegant, is totally up to you.

And you won't have to worry about keeping your reception private in the middle of a park. Tall bushes and trees mask the entrance to the Lakeside Room from the rest of the park and the Community Center is closed to the public while you celebrate the day or night away.

CEREMONY CAPACITY: The Deck accommodates up to 140; the Lakeside Room holds up to 200 guests.

EVENT/RECEPTION & MEETING CAPACITY: The Lakeside Room accommodates 200 guests.

FEES & DEPOSITS: A $500 nonrefundable deposit is required to reserve your date. The balance and security deposit are due in full 90 days prior to your event. Rental fees range $45–150/hour depending on room, day and time rented.

AVAILABILITY: Year-round: Monday–Thursday, 8am–10pm; Friday and Saturday, 8am–1am; Sunday, 8am–midnight.

Weekend reservations may be made up to 1 year in advance. Weekday evenings may be scheduled on a limited basis depending on availability. Rental hours must include setup and cleanup time.

SERVICES/AMENITIES:
Catering: BYO
Kitchen Facilities: moderately equipped
Tables & Chairs: provided
Linens, Silver: through caterer
Restrooms: wheelchair accessible
Dance Floor: yes
Bride's Dressing Area: no
Meeting Equipment: BYO

Parking: ample on-site
Accommodations: no guestrooms
Telephone: pay phone
Outdoor Night Lighting: yes
Outdoor Cooking Facilities: BYO BBQ
Cleanup: caterer or renter
View: pond, trees, garden, park, fountains

RESTRICTIONS:
Alcohol: BYO WB only, permits required, not allowed at youth events
Smoking: outside only
Music: amplified OK indoors only

Wheelchair Access: yes
Insurance: not required
Other: no confetti, rice, birdseed, rose petals, aerosol streamers, hay, sand or glitter; security required at all youth events; fountains cannot be guaranteed to function at all times

---

Overwhelmed? Use the search criteria on www.HereComesTheGuide.com to narrow down your choices.

Scott's Gardens

Restaurant & Gardens

1333 North California Boulevard, Walnut Creek
925/934-0598
www.scottseastbay.com
bjbarnette@scottswc.com

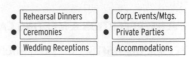

- Rehearsal Dinners
- Corp. Events/Mtgs.
- Ceremonies
- Private Parties
- Wedding Receptions
- Accommodations

Take note! If you're looking for an exceptional East Bay outdoor wedding spot, you must see this facility. Scott's Gardens is a site that could be aptly described as an urban oasis. Situated in the heart of Walnut Creek's retail district, Scott's has spared no expense to transform a small hillside into a brick-walled, multi-terraced courtyard garden with a conservatory cover. If you're worried about the weather, don't fret—during November through April, the garden is totally glass-enclosed and heated to keep your guests comfortable.

Under the broad canopy of a 400-year-old oak tree (the site's centerpiece) you'll find amenities such as designer wood benches and sizable free-standing umbrellas, in addition to lush landscaping. Of special interest are a green lattice aviary, several fountains and an antique water wheel. Observe the details here. All of the terraces are paved with slate, and even the outdoor bar and indoor dressing room feature marble counters. The latter is one of the best bride's dressing rooms we've seen, with floor-to-ceiling mirrors and a well-lit makeup area. At the topmost terrace, you'll find a back stairway leading to Scott's restaurant, where there's another outdoor patio for evening rehearsal dinners and small weekend receptions. Inside the restaurant, additional private and semiprivate rooms are available for parties.

CEREMONY CAPACITY: The Garden holds up to 150 seated or 200 standing guests.

EVENT/RECEPTION CAPACITY: The Garden accommodates a maximum of 200 seated guests, or 300 for a standing reception.

MEETING CAPACITY: Several spaces hold 32–150 seated guests.

FEES & DEPOSITS: A $2,000 nonrefundable deposit is required when the event date is booked. The rental fee on Saturday ranges $500–1,250; Sunday–Friday, $350–500. Rental includes tables, chairs, linens, silverware, setup and cleanup. Hors d'oeuvre receptions start at $35/person, buffets at $49/person, and seated luncheons or dinners at $35/person. Alcohol, tax and service fees are additional. The estimated food and beverage total is due 7 days prior to the event; the remaining portion is payable at the event's conclusion. The ceremony setup fee ranges $250–500.

For Monday–Friday business functions in private rooms, the fee is $75–500.

AVAILABILITY: Year-round, daily, 8am–4pm or 6pm–midnight.

SERVICES/AMENITIES:

Catering: provided, no BYO
Kitchen Facilities: n/a
Tables & Chairs: provided
Linens, Silver, etc.: provided
Restrooms: wheelchair accessible
Dance Floor: yes
Bride's Dressing Area: yes
Meeting Equipment: full range audiovisual

Parking: complimentary valet
Accommodations: no guestrooms
Telephone: no
Outdoor Night Lighting: yes
Outdoor Cooking Facilities: CBA
Cleanup: provided
View: landscaped garden
Other: event coordination, flowers, wedding cakes, invitations, music, transportation, favors

RESTRICTIONS:

Alcohol: provided, no BYO
Smoking: outside only
Music: DJ or small combos only

Wheelchair Access: yes
Insurance: not required

Shadelands Arts Center

Arts and Education Center

111 North Wiget Lane, Walnut Creek
925/256-3575
www.walnut-creek.org/rentals
rentals@walnut-creek.org

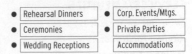

● Rehearsal Dinners	● Corp. Events/Mtgs.
● Ceremonies	● Private Parties
● Wedding Receptions	Accommodations

There are quite a few reasons why Shadelands Arts Center has become a local favorite. Not only is it a great value for those looking for an affordable event venue, it's also one of the largest facilities in the East Bay (accommodating up to 300!) where you can bring the caterer of your choice.

Another plus is the building itself, which is easy to work with thanks to its neutral décor. The white interior is amenable to virtually any kind of decorating, and the high, open-beamed ceiling—often draped for weddings—gives the space a lofty feeling.

State-of-the-art sound and lighting systems (and an AV staff person on site during your event) enable you to create whatever ambiance you like. Whether you're having a live band or planning to listen to your own playlist through your iPod, the music will sound great because the room was designed for music or theater performances and the acoustics are excellent. You can also entertain your guests with a slideshow or video on the large projection screen. Use lighting in a variety of colors to create a particular mood or to highlight the ceiling or dance floor. Custom gobos with your initials or scenes that you've selected can be projected on the walls. Add to all these features a gleaming hardwood floor, a bride's room, and a full catering kitchen and you have an event site that will satisfy all your needs.

Shadelands is perfectly suited for large weddings, because the entire event can be held in the main hall. If you require more space, the hall opens onto an expansive, enclosed patio that can be used for a ceremony, cocktail party or additional reception seating. It works well as a place for supervised activities for children, too. An indoor option for kids is a room next to the hall where they can do art projects or watch TV.

For corporate functions, Shadelands supplies most of the equipment required for presentations: an LCD projector (extra fee), large projection screen, sound and lighting equipment—and complimentary Wi-Fi. The venue is also popular for fundraisers, as it provides different rooms for a silent auction and banking.

The center's staff are very accommodating, going out of their way to help you create the event you want while staying within your budget. And access to the fully equipped professional kitchen—with the option of bringing in your own caterer—are real benefits for couples planning a casual wedding or rehearsal dinner.

With its flexibility, ample parking and reasonable prices, Shadelands Arts Center is in demand. Its convenient location is also appreciated by guests coming from all over the Bay Area. If you want to host a wedding, private party or corporate event that's very much your own, this is definitely a location to consider.

CEREMONY CAPACITY: The Banquet Room holds 350 seated guests.

EVENT/RECEPTION CAPACITY: The Banquet Room can accommodate 300 seated at round tables.

MEETING CAPACITY: The Banquet Room holds 350 seated theater-style or 150 guests seated conference-style.

FEES & DEPOSITS: A $500 nonrefundable deposit is required to secure your date. The event balance is due 90 days prior to the function. An additional $75 fee is charged if alcohol is served. Rental fees include tables, chairs, microphone, use of the kitchen and attendant, and range $65–175/hour depending on the time frame of the event.

AVAILABILITY: Year-round, daily until 1am. Youth events until midnight.

SERVICES/AMENITIES:

Catering: BYO
Kitchen Facilities: fully equipped, commercial
Tables & Chairs: provided
Linens, Silver, etc.: BYO or caterer
Restrooms: wheelchair accessible
Dance Floor: provided
Bride's & Groom's Dressing Area: yes
Meeting Equipment: full range

Parking: large lots, ample parking
Accommodations: no guestrooms
Telephone: emergency use only
Outdoor Night Lighting: access only
Outdoor Cooking Facilities: BYO
Cleanup: renter or caterer
View: no

RESTRICTIONS:

Alcohol: BYO, permits required; not allowed at youth events
Smoking: outside only
Music: amplified OK, indoors only

Wheelchair Access: yes
Insurance: not required
Other: security required at all youth events; no rice, birdseed, confetti, glitter, fog machines, bubbles, hay, sand, rose petals or aerosol streamers.

Shadelands Ranch Museum

Museum

2660 Ygnacio Valley Road, Walnut Creek
925/935-7871
www.walnutcreekhistory.info
wcshadelands@sbcglobal.net

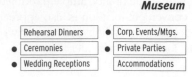

Rehearsal Dinners	● Corp. Events/Mtgs.
● Ceremonies	● Private Parties
● Wedding Receptions	Accommodations

Stately shade trees tower above the lawn, gardens and terrace surrounding the former Penniman home at Shadelands Ranch Museum. From its curved glass bay windows to its classical white columns and wraparound veranda, the 1903 Colonial Revival house reflects the refinement and elegance of a bygone era when the handsome two-story home was the heart of a large fruit ranch in the Ygnacio Valley.

Today Shadelands is lovingly maintained by the Walnut Creek Historical Society and the City of Walnut Creek. Citrus, pomegranate, walnut and quince still grow among the sycamores and redwoods shading the aptly named property. The fruit trees, along with the herb and vegetable gardens planted on the site, also serve as a reminder of Shadelands' rural past. While strolling the paths leading toward the patio and garden at the back of the house, it's easy to imagine the gracious hospitality that was once extended to guests of the ranch over 100 years ago. These days, events at Shadelands are held outdoors with the carefully restored house providing a charming backdrop.

On the spacious lawn at the back of the house, couples exchange vows in a gazebo encircled by roses. The garden setting is lovely on its own, or can be easily decorated to suit your taste. Recently a father escorted his daughter between two rows of flagstones placed along the grassy aisle. Another couple added an iron arch covered with tulle for the bride to pass through on her way to meet her groom. For an evening wedding, tiny lights woven through the trees add an enchanting ambiance to the occasion.

After the ceremony, the celebration continues on the adjoining patio. The terrace is large enough to accommodate tables for the reception and a DJ. Or, in keeping with the turn-of-the-(last)-century atmosphere, you might want to hire a band to play in the gazebo and have your guests dance on the patio.

Access to the inside of the house is limited to the kitchen, which is available as a bridal changing room or as a preparation site for the caterer. As committed as Shadelands is to keeping the ranch authentic to its early 20th-century style, the "old-fashioned" kitchen comes with a new gas range masquerading as a black wood-burning stove and a refrigerator camouflaged with wood paneling. Modern restrooms are adjacent to the new barn, just behind the circa 1902 water tank house and worker's cabin that border the garden.

Of the many reasons to hold your wedding and reception at the nonprofit Shadelands Ranch Museum, the most satisfying may be that the money you spend here goes toward preserving the history of Walnut Creek for future generations. Of course, at the same time, you and your betrothed will be making a little history of your own.

CEREMONY CAPACITY: The lawn area holds 250 seated guests.

EVENT/RECEPTION CAPACITY: The lawn area accommodates 250 seated or 400 standing guests.

MEETING CAPACITY: The location holds up to 250 seated guests for outdoor parties and meetings.

FEES & DEPOSITS: A $500 nonrefundable deposit is required to secure your date, and is applied toward the rental fee. An additional $500 refundable damage deposit is also required, and due 30 days before your event. Rental fees range $585–2,700 depending on number of hours rented.

AVAILABILITY: April–October.

SERVICES/AMENITIES:

Catering: BYO
Kitchen Facilities: fully equipped
Tables & Chairs: 250 provided
Linens, Silver, etc.: BYO or caterer
Restrooms: wheelchair accessible
Dance Floor: patio available
Bride's Dressing Area: yes, in kitchen
Meeting Equipment: tables and chairs

Parking: ample
Accommodations: no guestrooms
Telephone: use cell phones
Outdoor Night Lighting: yes
Outdoor Cooking Facilities: BYO or caterer
Cleanup: renter or caterer, trashcans provided
View: landscaped grounds, garden, gazebo

RESTRICTIONS:

Alcohol: BYO, beer and wine only
Smoking: outside only
Music: amplified OK with volume limits, no amplifiers after 11pm

Wheelchair Access: yes
Insurance: proof of insurance required
Other: no rice, birdseed or confetti

The professionals in the back of this book are the best in the business. How do we know? Read page 701.

Solano County

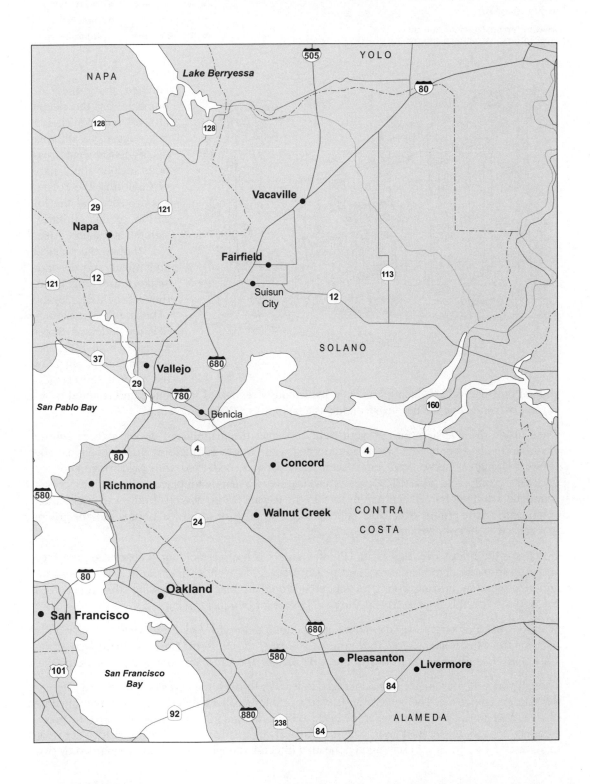

Jefferson Street Mansion

Historic Mansion

1063 Jefferson Street, Benicia
707/746-0684
www.jeffersonstreetmansion.com
info@jeffersonstreetmansion.com

● Rehearsal Dinners	● Corp. Events/Mtgs.	
● Ceremonies	● Private Parties	
● Wedding Receptions	☐ Accommodations	

Perched above the Carquinez Strait, the sleepy little town of Benicia is a rich nugget of California history. Its former incarnations include the capitol of California, the Solano County seat and the location of the militarily significant Benicia Arsenal. Though the political and military movers-and-shakers are long gone, they left behind a legacy of beautiful old structures like the Jefferson Street Mansion. Built in 1861 for a commanding officer of the Arsenal, this classical Federal Italianate-style building has been meticulously renovated, retrofitted and restored by its current owner, giving it a new lease on life as a fabulous special event venue.

Once inside the mansion, turn to your right and enter the magnificent double parlors, whose cream-and-pale green-washed walls are adorned with custom gilt molding and medallions. The twelve-foot-high windows have plush wine velvet drapes, bedecked with gold fringe and tied back with plump gold tassels. The parlors also feature two marble fireplaces, oil paintings, crystal chandeliers and gilt-framed antique mirrors. In the elegant Salon, nervous brides can regain their composure on the primrose brocade "fainting couch" or pose for whimsical photos with the groom in a carved wooden "courting chair."

Upstairs is the bride's dressing room. Like the parlors, it has gilt molding, a chandelier, fireplace and custom-made drapes in cream and peach brocade, as well as practical items like a white-and-gold wooden dressing screen, an antique mirrored armoire and a dressing table. A generous balcony, also on this floor, serves as the perfect spot for bouquet tossing.

With its wealth of sumptuous appointments, it's quite clear why *Bay Area Backroads* called the mansion the "Most Romantic Spot in Northern California," the California Heritage Council gave it the 2004 "Preservation of the Year Award" and CBS *Eye On The Bay* featured it as a top wedding site.

Though you and your guests are encouraged to wander through the mansion, the primary festivities take place outside. The new Veranda works well for smaller events and ceremonies anytime of year. And it's the perfect place for the bride to begin her grand entrance, descending the porch steps on her way to the west lawn where a classical colonnaded wisteria arbor shades her waiting guests. Here, vows are exchanged beneath a fifteen-foot-high trellised "arch" guarded by two majestic palm trees. Receptions are held on the mansion's opposite side among fountains, statues and flowerbeds, or in the two elegant fabric-draped pavilions (each with its own chandeliers). The buffet is set up in front of two exquisite antique back-bars, fashioned with intricate carving and spoolwork.

No matter how beautiful the surroundings, your event isn't going to be much of a success without a competent staff working hard behind the scenes, and that's exactly what you'll get at the Jefferson Street Mansion. A concierge captain/coordinator, provided at no charge, considers it her personal mission to keep each bride calm, elegant, and relaxed. Another plus: The "one event per day" policy means you can celebrate as long (and as enthusiastically) as you want. And although we've described the mansion in terms of weddings, the entertainment possibilities at this topnotch facility are practically endless. So if you're seeking a venue with the romance of the past and the convenience of the present, take a trip to Benicia and the Jefferson Street Mansion. Your event is sure to be a day you and your guests will never forget.

CEREMONY CAPACITY: West Lawn holds 250 seated guests. The East Tent holds 250 seated guests.

EVENT/RECEPTION CAPACITY: The East Patio accommodates 250 seated or 350 standing. The Mansion holds 50 seated or 100 standing.

MEETING CAPACITY: The Mansion holds up to 40 guests seated theater-style.

FEES & DEPOSITS: A $2,500 deposit is required to reserve your Saturday date, or a $1,500 deposit to reserve your Friday or Sunday date. The balance is due 2 weeks prior to the event. Rental fees range $1,750–3,000 depending on guest count. For weddings, meals range $33–43/person; tax, alcohol and an 18% service charge are additional.

For business functions, see their website for fee information. Meals range $50–200/person; tax, alcohol and an 18% service charge are additional.

AVAILABILITY: Year-round, daily, 7am–midnight.

SERVICES/AMENITIES:

Catering: provided or BYO
Kitchen Facilities: use fee required
Tables & Chairs: provided, extra charge
Linens, Silver, etc.: provided, extra charge
Restrooms: wheelchair accessible
Dance Floor: yes
Bride's Dressing Area: yes
Meeting Equipment: some provided, other CBA, extra fee

Parking: large lot
Accommodations: no guestrooms
Telephone: house phone
Outdoor Night Lighting: yes
Outdoor Cooking Facilities: no
Cleanup: provided
View: panorama of SF Bay, Carquinez Strait, rolling hills
Other: full range of decorations and florals

RESTRICTIONS:

Alcohol: provided, or corkage $10/bottle
Smoking: outside only
Music: amplified OK

Wheelchair Access: yes
Insurance: liability required

Admiral's Mansions at Mare Island
and St. Peter's Chapel & the Mare Island Museum

Mansions, Historic Chapel & Park

Walnut Avenue, Mare Island, Vallejo
707/643-1711 Catering, 707/557-1538 Chapel/Mansions
www.alexscatering.com
info@alexscatering.com

- Rehearsal Dinners
- Ceremonies
- Wedding Receptions
- Corp. Events/Mtgs.
- Private Parties
- Accommodations

With the 1996 closure of Mare Island Naval Installation, four landmark buildings are now available for special events. These venues are operated by the Mare Island Historic Park Foundation, so you no longer need military connections. And since they're located in the island's quaint historic district, (which dates back to the mid 1800s) you feel like you have an entire small town all to yourself.

Set in its own grassy park with a eucalyptus grove, St. Peter's is a picturesque interdenominational chapel. Built in 1901, it's the oldest naval chapel in the United States. A classic example of Victorian Gothic architecture, this tidy brown shingle, with cream-colored trim, steep pitched roof and a soaring octagonal spire, has as much charm and history inside as out. The largest collection of Tiffany glass under one roof is displayed in the chapel's 29 exquisite stained-glass windows, and they fill the intimate interior with a soft rosy light. One window depicts Sir Galahad who, when illuminated, becomes the ultimate knight in shining armor. Rich wood paneling complements the creamy plaster walls, and open beams accentuate the vaulted ceiling. The chapel also displays a collection of memorial plaques. Some are set into the ceiling and others (one dates back to the Civil War), hang on the walls, making intriguing reading.

Naturally there's a pipe organ (it's the original one from 1926!) to fill the sanctuary with strains of "Here Comes The Bride." After the ceremony, take advantage of the lovely setting for formal photos while your guests make the short trip back down Walnut Avenue to Officer's Row.

Receptions and business retreats are held in the Admiral's and the Captain's former quarters, two of the thirteen white Colonial Revival mansions lining Officer's Row. As you enter the Admiral's Quarters, it's easy to imagine the social galas of a century ago. The brass nautical lamps that lit the entryway then still hang on either side of the massive oak front door; the wide front veranda graced with Corinthian columns still invites guests to stroll outside for a leisurely chat. The gracious feel of the place continues inside in the vestibule, a large U-shaped entry hall complete with an inviting fireplace and built-in seating. Your guests can enjoy cocktails and hors d'oeuvres in here and as they explore the first- and second-floor rooms, all furnished in period pieces. The

Captain's Quarters, similar in style to the Admiral's, are often reserved for smaller functions. The 1855 Mare Island Museum building also has several spacious rooms available.

For an al fresco treat, set up a buffet and umbrella-shaded tables in the Victorian gardens adjacent to both of these mansions: It's an acre of lawns interspersed with low hedges, flowerbeds, and a variety of trees brought back from the far corners of the world by sea captains.

If you really want to make a splash, depart via ferry or yacht—the ferry terminal and marina are just a short distance from the island. But no matter which mode of transportation you choose, an event here is a trip back in time and a chance to relive a little of the grace and gentility of another era.

CEREMONY CAPACITY: The Chapel holds 200 seated guests. The Admiral's Mansion seats up to 160 guests using all available rooms. The Captain's Mansion holds up to 140 guests. The Garden area is about 1 acre and holds up to 800 seated guests. The Main Hall in the Museum will seat up to 700 guests.

EVENT/RECEPTION CAPACITY: The facility can accommodate 125–700 seated or 200–1,000 standing guests indoors, and 1,000 seated or 2,000 standing outdoors.

MEETING CAPACITY: The Mansion seats 150–160 using all rooms, with 40 maximum in any one room. The Museum Main Room holds 325 seated or 550 standing guests. The Musuem can seat 60 to 300 depending on which room is selected.

FEES & DEPOSITS: For weddings, a nonrefundable 50% rental deposit plus a $200 refundable security deposit are required to secure your date. Reception rental fees range $850–1,400 depending on the space selected. Ceremony rental fees range $200–700 depending on space rented. Organ in Chapel is available for $75 and use of the pianos is $35/event. Catering is provided by *Alex's Catering.* Fees for business meetings vary; call for more information.

AVAILABILITY: Year-round, daily, 8am–10pm.

SERVICES/AMENITIES:

Catering: provided or BYO upon approval
Kitchen Facilities: moderately equipped
Tables & Chairs: BYO
Linens, Silver, etc.: caterer
Restrooms: wheelchair access CBA
Dance Floor: patio, or CBA, extra charge
Bride's & Groom's Dressing Area: yes
Meeting Equipment: video player and projector

Parking: large lot and private street parking
Accommodations: no guestrooms
Telephone: emergency use only
Outdoor Night Lighting: CBA
Outdoor Cooking Facilities: through caterer
Cleanup: caterer, renter or CBA, extra fee
View: historic Alden Park
Other: grand piano, event coordination, tours of Mare Island's historic locations

RESTRICTIONS:

Alcohol: CBA or BYO, licensed and insured server
Smoking: designated outdoor areas
Music: amplified OK with volume limits

Wheelchair Access: Chapel and Mansions have ramps; gardens have full access
Insurance: certificate required
Other: no rice, food or alcohol in Chapel

Sacramento, Central Valley and Chico

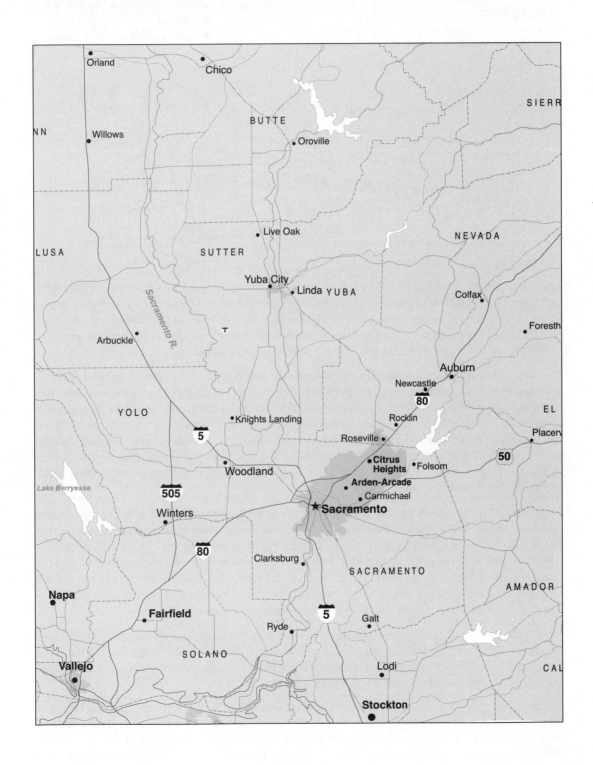

Orland
Chico
BUTTE
Willows
Oroville
NN
Live Oak
NEVADA
LUSA
SUTTER
Sacramento R.
Yuba City
Linda Y U B A
Colfax
Foresth
Arbuckle
5
Auburn
Newcastle
80
YOLO
Knights Landing
Rocklin
E L
Placer
5
Roseville
Citrus
Heights
Folsom
50
Lake Berryessa
Woodland
Arden-Arcade
505
Carmichael
Winters
★ Sacramento
80
Clarksburg
SACRAMENTO
AMADOR
Napa
Fairfield
Ryde
Galt
5
SOLANO
Lodi
Vallejo
C A L
Stockton

Canyon Oaks Country Club

Golf Club

999 Yosemite Drive, Chico
530/343-2582
www.countryclubreceptions.com
catering@canyonoakscc.com

● Rehearsal Dinners	● Corp. Events/Mtgs.
● Ceremonies	● Private Parties
● Wedding Receptions	Accommodations

The Sierra Nevada foothills provide some of Northern California's most beautiful outdoor scenery, including Chico's Bidwell Park, a nearly 4,000-acre state treasure. The Upper Park, highly prized for its rugged canyon terrain, hiking trails and abundant wildlife, is an ode to nature in the wild. It's also the next door neighbor of Canyon Oaks Country Club, whose rolling hills and profuse greenery provide a tamer version of nature and a lovely setting for your wedding.

To reach this lush property, located in the upscale community of Canyon Oaks, you drive through a wrought-iron gate past pine and oak trees to the clean-lined, contemporary clubhouse. The surrounding golf course is one of the most prestigious in Northern California, and is the key factor in an enticing incentive to hold your festivities here: a complimentary golf package. As part of your rehearsal day, four lucky members of your group can enjoy a full round of pre-wedding play or, for an additional fee, you can have a tournament arranged for all your guests. Even if you're not a golfer, you'll appreciate the verdant, well-maintained landscaping that often draws visiting quail, rabbits and even the occasional deer.

Canyon Oaks prides itself on anticipating your every need, and their staff will help guide you through your event. When it's time to get ready, you and your bridesmaids can retreat to the spacious, fully mirrored Bridal Room while the groom and his attendants relax in their own space—complete with TV and poker table. From here it's just a short walk to the picture-perfect gazebo, bordered by flowers. Set between the 1st and 18th fairways, this outdoor ceremony site affords fantastic, unobstructed golf course views. You can heighten the drama of your entrance by arriving in a golf cart or, as one recent bride did, in a horse-drawn carriage.

After tying the knot, you and your photographer can take full advantage of several nearby scenic backdrops, including romantic bridges and a waterfall made of natural rock. Meanwhile, your friends and family start the festivities with a lovely al fresco cocktail hour by sampling an array of hors d'oeuvres to the accompaniment of live music or a DJ.

For the main reception, move inside to the second-story Vista Room, so named for the banks of large windows that frame those expansive exterior views. Muted earth tones, wainscoted walls, a large stone fireplace and crystal chandeliers help set a tone of low-key elegance. A variety of menu options, ranging from tri-tip to sushi, are available for your menu. After dining, some guests will gravitate to the central dance floor while others might drift out to the large private terrace. Here they can bask in the night air, gaze up at the stars, and take a quiet moment to savor nature's gifts one more time.

CEREMONY CAPACITY: The facility holds 200 seated guests outdoors.

EVENT/RECEPTION CAPACITY: The club can accommodate 175 seated or 225 standing guests indoors.

MEETING CAPACITY: Meeting spaces hold up to 150 seated guests.

FEES & DEPOSITS: A nonrefundable deposit, which is applied to your food and beverage total, is required to reserve your date. The amount of the deposit is equal to 25% of the estimated event total. 50% is due 6 months prior, and 100% of the final estimated balance is due 10 days prior to the event date. Rental fees range $400–2,000 depending on the day of the event and the space rented. Meals range $32–68/person. Tax, alcohol and a 20% service charge are additional.

AVAILABILITY: Year-around, daily, 7am–midnight.

SERVICES/AMENITIES:

Catering: provided
Kitchen Facilities: n/a
Tables & Chairs: provided
Linens, Silver, etc.: provided
Restrooms: wheelchair accessible
Dance Floor: portable provided
Bride's & Groom's Dressing Area: yes
Meeting Equipment: some provided, CBA

Parking: large lot
Accommodations: no guestrooms
Telephone: house phone
Outdoor Night Lighting: CBA
Outdoor Cooking Facilities: BBQ on site
Cleanup: provided
View: fairways, hills, lagoon, fountain, landscaped grounds
Other: event coordination

RESTRICTIONS:

Alcohol: provided
Smoking: not allowed
Music: amplified OK

Wheelchair Access: yes
Insurance: not required

Want to know WHAT TO ASK a potential location or vendor? Check out our Questions to Ask on page 17.

Doubletree Hotel Sacramento

Hotel

2001 Point West Way, Sacramento
916/924-4902
www.sacramento.doubletree.com
RLSA_DS@hilton.com

- Rehearsal Dinners
- Ceremonies
- Wedding Receptions

- Corp. Events/Mtgs.
- Private Parties
- Accommodations

Few hotels offer as warm a welcome as the Doubletree Hotel Sacramento, where you're greeted with a fresh-baked chocolate chip cookie upon arrival. It's a sweet introduction, and sets the friendly tone you'll experience for your entire stay. From valet parking to the experienced catering team, the entire staff at the Doubletree could not be nicer. They pay attention to the little things, like pointing out the best places for photos. When you add this kind of personal attention to the venue's flexible event spaces and other amenities, it's obvious why the Doubletree is an excellent choice for a destination wedding or special event.

The hotel can accommodate almost any size group or function: each of its three ballrooms has a unique style, as well as its own entrance, foyer and convenient parking for easy access; two ballrooms are divisible into four salons for smaller events. In the versatile Capital Ballroom, the high, coffered ceiling and natural light flowing in through walls of windows create an expansive feeling. Glass doors open to the Capital Patio, an ideal spot for a wedding ceremony. Bordered by a gentle creek, it overlooks a lush garden and rolling lawn. The bride makes her grand entrance through the garden, arriving via a quaint footbridge that spans the creek. A petal-strewn aisle leads to the wooden arbor where vows are exchanged in the shade of sheltering trees. Both the bridge and arbor can be decorated with flowers, fabric or garlands coordinated with your color scheme. In the evening, twinkle lights or hanging candles on the arbor add a magical quality to the setting.

The California and Grand Ballrooms are also quite spacious. Both feature crystal chandeliers and softly draped windows framing garden views. The Grand Ballroom, which is the largest, also boasts an 18-foot ceiling inset with reflective mirrors that add extra sparkle at night.

A favorite option for intimate receptions or rehearsal dinners is the white, tented Event Pavilion and patio on the opposite side of the garden, a semi-private site secluded by a tall screen of white oleander bushes. In spring and summer the pavilion is normally left open-sided, but even during cooler weather when its "walls" are drawn down, you still feel warm, comfortable and connected to the surrounding greenery through clear acrylic windows. Couples who choose to host their entire wedding here can tie the knot beneath the delicate wrought-iron gazebo next to the pavilion.

If you select one of the Doubletree's catering packages, their certified wedding professionals will help orchestrate your event, from offering vendor recommendations to day-of coordination. You have several packages to choose from, and customized menus are also available. Certain ethnic cuisines, such as Indian or Middle Eastern, may be prepared and brought in by a licensed caterer.

The hotel has 448 oversized guestrooms with balconies, which means all your friends and family can stay in one place. And whether they're lounging by the hotel pool, shopping in the nearby mall or taking in the historic attractions of Old Sacramento, your guests will enjoy their free time almost as much as attending your wedding.

CEREMONY CAPACITY: The site holds 1,300 seated guests indoors and 200 seated outdoors.

EVENT/RECEPTION CAPACITY: The facility can accommodate 830 seated or 1,500 standing indoors and 150 seated or 250 standing outdoors.

MEETING CAPACITY: Meeting spaces hold 1,300 seated guests.

FEES & DEPOSITS: 25% of the total event cost is required to reserve your date and the balance is due 10 days prior to the event. Rental fees range $0–5,000 depending on the space needed and food and beverage commitment. Meals range $30–56/person. Tax, alcohol and a 21% service charge are additional.

AVAILABILITY: Year-round, daily.

SERVICES/AMENITIES:

Catering: provided, or BYO (ethnic cuisine only)
Kitchen Facilities: limited
Tables & Chairs: provided
Linens, Silver, etc.: provided
Restrooms: wheelchair accessible
Dance Floor: provided, portable CBA
Bride's Dressing Area: CBA
Meeting Equipment: CBA
Other: grand piano, AV equipment, event coordination

Parking: large lot, valet/self-parking
Accommodations: 448 guestrooms
Telephone: house phone
Outdoor Night Lighting: provided
Outdoor Cooking Facilities: BBQ CBA
Cleanup: provided
View: fountain, garden, landscaped grounds, pool area, waterfall

RESTRICTIONS:

Alcohol: provided or BYO with corkage fee
Smoking: outside only
Music: amplified OK with restrictions

Wheelchair Access: yes
Insurance: liability required

The Firehouse

Historic Restaurant

1112 Second Street, Old Sacramento
916/442-4772
www.firehouseoldsac.com
info@firehouseoldsac.com

- Rehearsal Dinners
- Ceremonies
- Wedding Receptions

- Corp. Events/Mtgs.
- Private Parties
- Accommodations

When those scorching Valley days begin—along about May—everyone heads for a favorite oasis. None is cooler, greener, or leafier than the sprawling brick patio at the back of The Firehouse, the Gold Rush era landmark restaurant where Sacramentans have dined, politicked and gotten married for over 50 years.

Built in 1853, it's located in the heart of the old riverfront historic district and really did house Engine Company No. 3, which stabled its horses in what is now the wine cellar. The Firehouse opened as a restaurant in 1960, with the owners scouring the Central Valley and Sierra foothills for antique furnishings. Recently renovated, it offers seven cool Gilded Era dining and reception areas with twelve-foot ceilings, mahogany wainscoting, ornate mirrors, and massive paintings of grande dames and friskier ladies.

Most popular for weddings is the Courtyard, the al fresco dining area that's won local awards for "best special occasion" and "best outdoor" dining. Enter through the narrow 19th-century alley at the back of The Firehouse and you really do feel transported to another place and time: The wrought-iron balconies, ivy-covered brick walls, fountains, and canopy of mulberry and Chinese elm trees feel more like New Orleans than Sacramento. With lights laced through the overhanging branches, it's magic on summer nights.

Guests seated in the Courtyard dine on California nouveau continental cuisine accompanied by selections from the 25,000-bottle wine cellars, the largest in the Valley. Decoration here is simple—perhaps just some flowers. "If you didn't add anything extra, it'd still be spectacular," says Mario Ortiz, General Manager, Sommelier and 38-year employee of The Firehouse, though he recalls one outside event planner who created a "Wedding in Paris" theme with a canvas Eiffel Tower. Bring in a band, orchestra or DJ, and you can dance out here, too.

Larger wedding parties spill over into the adjacent Courtyard Grill, a garden-like room under a Tiffany-style glass dome with a long bar, floor-to-ceiling windows, and a massive fireplace used on cool harvest nights. This space can also be used by itself for small events.

Some weddings and the ubiquitous Capitol fundraisers, receptions and banquets are held in the Golden Eagle Room and adjoining Salon. Or, guests can thread their way past an iron grille door and down a narrow staircase into a pair of small, immaculate banquet rooms known as Wine Cellars I and II.

The Firehouse has long been a draw for politicos and celebrities, with Ronald Reagan holding both of his inaugural dinners here, and Arnold Schwarzenegger a recent guest. It's become a pilgrimage site for tourists who wander through with cameras, trying to capture the rich mélange of Gold Rush memorabilia, rococo chandeliers, bare brick walls and long, gleaming bars.

Out-of-town visitors will enjoy the ambiance of the building itself, as well as the bustling boardwalks and horse-drawn carriages out front. And its location in the heart of downtown Sacramento makes it easy for everyone to find. So if you want to combine Old World elegance with a rambunctious history lesson and a magical walled garden, The Firehouse has it all.

CEREMONY CAPACITY: The Courtyard holds up to 300 seated guests. Indoors, the Firehouse holds up to 120 seated guests.

EVENT/RECEPTION CAPACITY: The Courtyard holds up to 300 seated or 400 standing guests. Indoors, 7 banquet rooms hold up to 120 seated or 175 standing guests. Several configurations are available; call for details.

MEETING CAPACITY: The Firehouse can accommodate up to 200 guests seated theater-style.

FEES & DEPOSITS: A $750–1,500 deposit is required to reserve your date. A second payment of 50% of the food and beverage minimum is due 90 days prior to the event date, and the remaining 50% is due 30 days prior. The balance is due upon completion of the event. Rental fees range $0–1,500 depending on room rented and day and time rented. Meals range $23–58/person for the dinner menu and weekend day events. Tax, alcohol and a 20% service charge are additional.

AVAILABILITY: Year-round, daily. Weekend hours for courtyard use only are 11am–4pm and 6:30pm–midnight.

SERVICES/AMENITIES:

Catering: provided, no BYO
Kitchen Facilities: n/a
Tables & Chairs: provided
Linens, Silver, etc.: provided
Restrooms: wheelchair accessible
Dance Floor: CBA
Bride's Dressing Area: CBA
Meeting Equipment: CBA, extra charge

Parking: large lots, valet CBA
Accommodations: no guestrooms
Telephone: no
Outdoor Night Lighting: yes
Outdoor Cooking Facilities: BBQ CBA
Cleanup: provided
View: fountain, garden, landscaped grounds
Other: event coordination

RESTRICTIONS:

Alcohol: provided
Smoking: outside only
Music: amplified OK with restrictions

Wheelchair Access: yes
Insurance: not required

The Reserve at Spanos Park

Golf Course and Clubhouse

6301 West Eight Mile Road, Stockton
209/477-4653
www.countryclubreceptions.com
catering@reserveatspanospark.com

● Rehearsal Dinners	● Corp. Events/Mtgs.
● Ceremonies	● Private Parties
● Wedding Receptions	Accommodations

Bordered by the maze of rivers and tributaries that make up California's Delta and positioned amid the rapidly developing region between North Stockton and Lodi, The Reserve at Spanos Park is a golfer's sanctuary. Designed to blend in with the surrounding environment, the Reserve's tranquility lies in its offering of wide-open space and stunning sunset views of Mt. Diablo. Golfers are not the only ones seeking asylum at this "Reserve." Blue herons and egrets make occasional appearances among the 18 holes and eight lakes of its 7,000-yard championship course. And although the Reserve has the look and feel of an exclusive country club, fear not—this semiprivate club is affordably priced and does not require membership for facilities usage.

The main event space, the Mount Diablo Room, opened its doors in September of 2004. This versatile 3,200-square-foot venue can accommodate large receptions, rehearsal dinners, bar/ bat mitzvahs or corporate events. Whatever celebration you're planning, you can be assured of eating well: The skilled catering team's creations feature the region's bounty of fruits, vegetables (Stockton is home to the Asparagus Festival) and Lodi Appelation wines. Beyond the tiled foyer lies the spacious banquet area, brightened by a wall of windows and a large skylight. The interior is attractively designed with a high ceiling, earth-toned tile and carpet, granite countertops and brick wainscoting. Glass doors open to the western-facing terrace, an ideal place for saying your vows or hosting a rehearsal dinner. Couples also have the option of holding their ceremony on the first tee, overlooking a small lake.

At the adjacent clubhouse, a porte-cochère offers arriving guests shelter from the heat or rain. Inside, two meeting rooms are available as dressing areas for the bride, groom and wedding parties. The relaxed atmosphere at the Clubhouse Bar makes it a perfect spot for friends and family to unwind before or after the ceremony. Out back, a wraparound patio overlooks the fairways and can be used for smaller weddings or informal dinners.

Easy to find and conveniently located, The Reserve at Spanos Park is a little more than a mile west of Interstate 5 between Stockton and Sacramento. Lodging is just minutes away, and shopping is close by for those last minute gifts.

While you don't have to be a golfer to hold your event at the Reserve, golf enthusiasts will certainly appreciate their state-of-the-art indoor learning center, first-rate practice facility, and complete short game area. Whether you choose to link up at the first tee or incorporate a round of golf into your next event, the experienced staff at the Reserve will provide superb customer service and assist you in every aspect of your special celebration.

CEREMONY, EVENT/RECEPTION & MEETING CAPACITY: The Reserve holds up to 200 seated or 250 standing guests, both indoors and outdoors.

FEES & DEPOSITS: A nonrefundable deposit, which is applied to your food and beverage total, is required to reserve your date. The amount of the deposit is equal to 25% of the estimated event total. 50% is due 6 months prior, and 100% of the final estimated balance is due 10 days prior to the event date. Rental fees range $50–1,200 depending on space rented, day and time of the event and guest count. Meals range $20–70/person. Tax, alcohol and a 20% service charge are additional.

AVAILABILITY: Year-round, daily, 6am–1am.

SERVICES/AMENITIES:

Catering: provided, no BYO

Kitchen Facilities: n/a

Tables & Chairs: provided

Linens, Silver, etc.: provided

Restrooms: wheelchair accessible

Dance Floor: yes

Bride's & Groom's Dressing Area: CBA

Meeting Equipment: CBA, extra fee

Parking: medium-sized lot

Accommodations: hotels nearby

Telephone: pay phone

Outdoor Night Lighting: yes

Outdoor Cooking Facilities: BBQ CBA

Cleanup: provided

View: fairways, lake, mountains, meadow

RESTRICTIONS:

Alcohol: provided or BYO wine with corkage fee

Smoking: outdoors only

Music: amplified OK

Wheelchair Access: yes

Insurance: not required

Want to find more locations and services? Check out our informative website, www.HereComesTheGuide.com.

549

Bear Flag Farm

Winery, Organic Farm & Private Estate

Address withheld to ensure privacy. Winters

530/753-9494

www.bearflagfarm.com
info@bearflagfarm.com

- Rehearsal Dinners
- Ceremonies
- Wedding Receptions

- Corp. Events/Mtgs.
- Private Parties
- Accommodations

Just an hour from San Francisco and twenty minutes from Sacramento lies an exquisite organic farm and winery. Surrounded by peach and apricot orchards, lavender fields, grapevines and seasonal row crops, Bear Flag Farm looks as if it was plucked straight from the French countryside. The winery, main house, guest cottage and barn are like a tiny village, with orange tile roofs and golden stucco walls that seem to glow in the sunlight.

As guests arrive, they drive onto the farm past a wrought-iron gate that opens onto a winding driveway divided by a row of flowering crepe myrtles. At the end of the drive, their cars are whisked away by a valet to a parking area hidden from view.

The bridal party has its own changing rooms in the guest cottage, which also includes a room equipped with salon chairs for hair and makeup preparation.

By now, the couple has already decided which of the farm's wonderful ceremony and reception sites are best suited for their special day. Some brides like to glide through the French doors of the cottage onto a small terrace, and then walk down the steps to exchange vows on the soft lawn below. Or, the couple might say "I do" on the 3,000-square-foot lavender lawn, nestled in the lavender field. Yet another option is a ceremony next to the vineyard, where guests are seated after being treated to fresh lemonade or minty iced tea and a stroll through the almond orchard.

Formal dinners, buffets, champagne receptions, cake-cutting ceremonies and dancing can be staged on the grand terrace, in the grassy amphitheater guarded by sycamore trees, or under a sprawling tent shading the vineyard lawn. Parasols are available for daytime events, and as the sun sets, silk lanterns or even chandeliers can be used to cast a romantic glow over the evening's festivities.

Bear Flag Farm provides a tremendous amount of flexibility for its guests. Since only one daylong event is allowed per weekend, couples have the time and space to fully prepare for their celebration. The preferred list of caterers includes some of the best Bay Area and Sacramento chefs, and early in the year Bear Flag Farm works with each chef to select specific crops that will be harvested fresh from the farm for seasonal menus. In this way, Bear Flag Farm's goal of providing a true field-to-table experience is fulfilled, and guests reap the rewards of flavors only available to those who come to the farm. Live music is not only allowed, but encouraged—the one restriction being that is has to end at a reasonable hour out of consideration for neighboring farmers.

In addition to weddings, Bear Flag Farm hosts other events such as private and corporate parties, and a farm dinner series that features Northern California's most extraordinary chefs and winemakers. Part of Bear Flag Farm's mission is to expand people's awareness of organic and sustainable farming. That shouldn't be hard—its benefits and delights are easy for anyone to appreciate as they linger amid this abundance of fruit trees, grapevines and rows of lavender.

CEREMONY, EVENT/RECEPTION & MEETING CAPACITY: The location accommodates up to 200 seated guests outdoors.

FEES & DEPOSITS: A $5,000 nonrefundable deposit is required to reserve your date. The remaining balance is due 6 months prior to the event. The rental fee for exclusive use of the farm is $8,500 for up to 200 guests.

AVAILABILITY: The regular season begins in April and ends in October. Smaller, off-season events can be arranged. All events must end by 10pm.

SERVICES/AMENITIES:

Catering: select from list
Kitchen Facilities: prep only
Tables & Chairs: through facility or planner
Linens, Silver, etc.: through facility or planner
Restrooms: partially wheelchair accessible
Dance Floor: terrace or BYO
Bride's & Groom's Dressing Area: yes
Meeting Equipment: BYO

Parking: valet required
Accommodations: no guestrooms
Telephone: house phone
Outdoor Night Lighting: CBA
Outdoor Cooking Facilities: BBQ CBA
Cleanup: through caterer
View: vineyards, mountains, meadows, garden, lavender fields

RESTRICTIONS:

Alcohol: provided or BYO with no corkage fee
Smoking: designated area only
Music: amplified OK with time & volume restrictions

Wheelchair Access: limited
Insurance: liability required

Wine Country

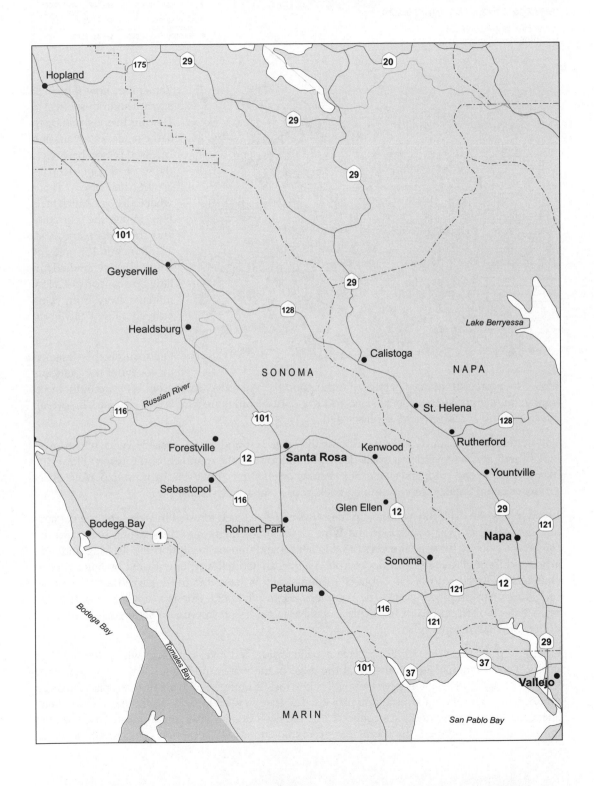

Calistoga Ranch

Resort & Spa

580 Lommel Road, Calistoga
707/254-2817 or 800/942-4220
www.calistogaranch.com
weddings@calistogaranch.com

● Rehearsal Dinners	● Corp. Events/Mtgs.
● Ceremonies	● Private Parties
● Wedding Receptions	● Accommodations

Remember how it feels to stay at a luxurious retreat in Hawaii? Every space open to the outdoors… your skin caressed by soft breezes… the sense of bone-deep relaxation and ease…. That's what Calistoga Ranch feels like, minus the humidity and the long plane ride. The Ranch is 157 acres of natural beauty, cradled in a little box canyon just a few minutes away from Napa Valley's famed Silverado Trail.

Calistoga Ranch is designed for lovers of the outdoors who also appreciate quality, privacy and the good life. All lodges and event sites are indoor/outdoor venues, constructed of local stone and wood; furnishings are simple and elegant. The overall effect is rustic and serene, yet sophisticated.

The perfect Wine Country ambiance for small events is found at the Poolside Patio, which overlooks the Sotero vineyard that spills down the hill toward the entrance of the resort. Flowering oleander trees lend color and shade. For evening celebrations, not even the most expensive event producer could create a more stunning backdrop: a Napa Valley sunset.

If you follow the driveway winding up the canyon, past rugged forested hillsides and the cottage-like guest lodges, you come upon the Wine Cave. Dug straight into the existing rock, and designed specifically for special events, it's a beautiful and unusual reception site. Passing under an arbor and through massive oak doors, you enter an arched hallway, illuminated by huge circular chandeliers. At the end of this room is a dramatically lit bas-relief frieze carved into the stone, providing a striking focal point. The Founder's Room off to one side is a smaller version of the main hall: Vaulted and furnished with a massive table, it's an impressive setting for a rehearsal dinner or small reception.

Emerging from the Wine Cave, you face a petite spring-fed lake, complete with a few resident ducks. The Lakehouse Restaurant sits at the edge of the water and has a scenic view, especially from its decks. The Lakehouse Restaurant Deck, which is outfitted with a pair of fireplaces plus an outdoor bar, is reserved for restaurant patrons. The Lakeview Patio Deck is where events are held. Sheltered by a covered trellis, it's connected by tall glass doors to two small private rooms within the restaurant. Combined, the rooms can accommodate a cozy reception of up to 40; however, they generally serve as places for a bar setup, cake or cheese display, or an espresso bar. When the glass doors are open, there's an easy flow indoors and out.

As the bride and groom must be guests of Calistoga Ranch to hold a wedding at the resort, it's worth describing a typical guest lodge. At a minimum, each one has a generously proportioned bedroom with his-and-her bathrooms, connected by a covered deck to a living room with a cheery fireplace. An outdoor bath garden is attached to each, and some lodges also have hot tubs. Cathedral ceilings, modern furnishings and a wet bar complete the picture of a habitat that's in harmony with nature, yet profoundly luxurious. Guests can take advantage of the resort spa amenities, which include healing baths and a variety of massages and skin treatments.

Calistoga Ranch is an intimate setting for the couple who treasures the region's native splendor. Though it's close to the Bay Area—and even closer to the delights of the Napa Wine Country—the Ranch is a remarkable place where, as they say here, the passage of time is measured by the growing grapes, and every day is blessed with spirituality, peace and a touch of magic.

CEREMONY & EVENT/RECEPTION CAPACITY: The resort holds up to 84 seated or 110 standing guests, indoors or outdoors.

MEETING CAPACITY: Up to 60 seated guests can be accommodated for a meeting at Calistoga Ranch.

FEES & DEPOSITS: 100% of the facility fee and 100% of the room rate is the deposit required to reserve your date. 100% of the food and beverage minimum is due 60 days prior to the event and at 7 days prior, final estimated cost of event is due. Rental fees range $3,500–10,000 depending on space, day and time rented. Meals range $85–125/person. Tax, alcohol and a 20% service charge are additional.

AVAILABILITY: Year-round, daily.

SERVICES/AMENITIES:
Catering: provided
Kitchen Facilities: n/a
Tables & Chairs: provided
Linens, Silver, etc.: provided
Restrooms: wheelchair accessible
Dance Floor: CBA
Bride's Dressing Area: guest lodge
Meeting Equipment: BYO or CBA

Parking: valet
Accommodations: 48 guest lodges
Telephone: house phone
Outdoor Night Lighting: yes
Outdoor Cooking Facilities: CBA
Cleanup: provided
View: mountains, vineyards, lake, grounds
Other: event coordination, full spa services

RESTRICTIONS:
Alcohol: provided
Smoking: designated areas only
Music: amplified OK indoors only

Wheelchair Access: yes
Insurance: not required
Other: no confetti, rice or birdseed

Hans Fahden Vineyards

Winery

4855 Petrified Forest Road, Calistoga
707/942-6760
www.hansfahden.com
mary@hansfahden.com

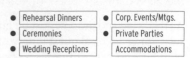

- Rehearsal Dinners
- Corp. Events/Mtgs.
- Ceremonies
- Private Parties
- Wedding Receptions
- Accommodations

High in the mountains between Santa Rosa and Calistoga, the Hans Fahden family has created an incredible place with outdoor sites elegant enough for satin gowns and tuxedos, and a marvelous indoor facility with some of the most extraordinary features we've ever seen.

Even at first glance, the winery's gardens and event facilities are quite lovely, but like a Fabergé egg, their outward beauty is only a prelude to a wealth of creativity, craftsmanship and aesthetic richness within.

Your special event may start in the Teahouse, a quaint wooden structure covered with wisteria, grapevines and red climbing roses. Small gatherings can use the Teahouse for ceremonies or receptions, but larger groups mingle there before descending into the gardens below. The gardens are an exquisite combination of French country style and wildlife habitat, and if they remind you of an Impressionist painting, it's no coincidence. Winery owners and landscapers Antone and Lyall Fahden relied heavily on Monet's paintings of the gardens at Giverny when they designed their own. As you travel the path down to the pond, your senses are tantalized by the sights and smells of roses, irises, petunias, pansies, cornflowers, poppies, ornamental grasses and native shrubs. The garden has been cleverly planted so that something different blooms each month, creating one wave of color after another. In late spring, roses take center stage; other floral "coming attractions" include matilija poppies, oleander, zinnias, sunflowers and blue pitcher sage. Midway between the Teahouse and pond, a terraced lawn bordered by a volcanic-ash rock wall and beds of pink evening primroses, lavender, roses and California poppies serves as a ceremony site for large weddings. The covered bridge spanning the lily pond can also be used for weddings, and brings you close to a variety of wildlife—thanks to the ducks, egrets, quail and mourning doves that call the gardens home.

After exchanging vows, join your guests in the winery building, a long graceful structure whose mellow wood exterior and peaked, sage-green roof blend with the rugged mountainside behind it. Inside, a gray slate floor, a high, beamed ceiling of grooved pine and redwood, and cream walls give the room a simple beauty that complements the glory of the gardens viewed through French doors. In one corner, a grand piano provides background music as your guests nibble appetizers and sip champagne. Just when everyone thinks that their eyes simply couldn't take in any more beauty, the 400-pound Douglas fir doors at one end of the room are thrown open to reveal a wine cave containing candlelit tables set for dinner. This amazing cave is like the jewel within a Fabergé egg: gorgeous, surprising and utterly unique. Formed of volcanic ash rock, the T-shaped cave's walls are lined with wine barrels; metal fixtures with grape-leaf cutouts and twinkle-light-wrapped poles provide subtle lighting. At the T's apex, two wine barrels support a massive arrangement of fresh flowers; above, gold candle sconces in floral designs await lighting. When these sconces are lit, along with the candelabras on the tables and the twinkle lights, Ali Baba's cave itself could not be more enchanting. Magical doesn't even begin to describe an event here—as you sit down to dinner, surrounded by flowers, flickering shadows and the piquant smell of aging wine, you'll feel as if you're part of a breathtaking fairy tale. And, unlike limestone caves, this cave's volcanic-ash rock adjusts to body temperature when occupied, so you can wear the most daring *décolleté* gown and never have to throw a jacket over your shoulders.

If you're thinking that Hans Fahden sounds like a wonderful place, but you're not planning to get married anytime soon, keep in mind that the winery can accommodate all types of events, from a gala celebration to a business seminar. But we can't help feeling that the site's stunning visual appeal may be most appreciated at a wedding. So, brides, if your fantasy includes a vision of you in a magnificent Vera Wang gown against a backdrop of pristine natural beauty, you owe yourself a visit to Hans Fahden Winery. They can make your dream wedding a beautiful reality!

CEREMONY CAPACITY: The Teahouse holds up to 50 guests; the Amphitheater 120 guests.

EVENT/RECEPTION CAPACITY: The Main Hall holds 120 seated guests; the Wine Cave holds 120 seated guests. The facility accommodates up to 85 guests December–March, or 100 guests outdoors, May–October.

MEETING CAPACITY: The Main Hall holds 120 seated theater-style; the Wine Cave 120 guests.

FEES & DEPOSITS: For events, a $2,500 deposit is required to reserve your date; the balance is due 10 days prior to the event. The rental fee is $4,500 on weekdays including Friday, $5,500 on Sunday, and $6,500 on Saturday.

AVAILABILITY: Year-round, daily, 10am–10pm.

SERVICES/AMENITIES:

Catering: select from preferred list
Kitchen Facilities: prep only
Tables & Chairs: provided through caterer
Linens, Silver, etc.: BYO
Restrooms: wheelchair accessible
Dance Floor: textured cement floor
Bride's Dressing Area: yes
Meeting Equipment: BYO

Parking: on-site lot
Accommodations: no guestrooms
Telephone: emergency use only
Outdoor Night Lighting: yes
Outdoor Cooking Facilities: BBQ
Cleanup: caterer
View: vineyards, Mayacamas Mountains
Other: day-of coordinator, baby grand piano; rentals valued at $5,000+ included with rental fee

RESTRICTIONS:

Alcohol: full bar available, wine provided or BYO no corkage fee with 1 case minimum purchase
Smoking: outdoors only
Music: amplified OK until 9:30pm, an extra hour CBA

Wheelchair Access: limited
Insurance: certificate required
Other: no rice, birdseed, confetti, sparklers or butterfly release

---

This is important! Tell locations you're reading HERE COMES THE GUIDE and ask if our information is still current.

The Geyserville Inn
& Hoffman House Restaurant

21714 Geyserville Avenue, Geyserville
877/857-4343
www.geyservilleinn.com
terry@geyservilleinn.com

- Rehearsal Dinners
- Ceremonies
- Wedding Receptions
- Corp. Events/Mtgs.
- Private Parties
- Accommodations

This wine country destination is a rare "triple threat" venue that offers a lovely outdoor wedding site, full-scale dinner and reception facilities, and inviting accommodations for family and guests. The inn provides all of this at a terrific price point—and that's even before you add in other amenities, such as an excellent restaurant, the Hoffman House right next door (where many newlyweds eat their first breakfast together as a married couple), a swimming pool and plenty of parking. Catering is done on site by the Hoffman House, and the kitchen uses ingredients from all over Sonoma County's great breadbasket, an agricultural wonderland that consistently produces many of the country's finest vegetables, meats and dairy products. This award-winning restaurant has won six gold medals for its food at the regional Harvest Fair.

The inn offers a pair of lawns for ceremonies and receptions. Each is partially covered by shade cloth so that tents aren't needed during summer months. The smaller lawn is bordered by low hedges and ornamental trees. The larger one is a long, wide expanse of beautifully tended grass that sidles right up to a vineyard on two sides. Bordered by three white wooden arbors, it looks lovely when set with tables for an afternoon or evening meal. The main arbor, which is surrounded by wild roses and decorated with iron railings and Japanese-style lamps, is a superb spot for a head table or exchanging vows. A ceremonial gateway at the opposite end of the lawn lends an element of drama—brides often use it to make their entrance, then begin a stately march the length of the lawn. And we can't overlook the view from here: a green panorama of the tree-covered Mayacamas Hills in the distance.

We doubt you'll need any additional enticements to stay at the inn, but there is one more: a choice of three luxury suites for the bridal couple, set apart from the main building and next to the lawns. All of them feature a private entrance and patio or deck, along with sweeping views of the vineyards. Each also has HDTV and a Jacuzzi, and two have a fireplace and wetbar. The main building also offers junior suites with patios or decks.

Geyserville Inn is the only facility in the area that can easily combine so many services and conveniences under one roof. But the inn's attractive amenities are not the only reason to come here; there's also the powerful appeal of the wine country itself, with its earthy, romantic cachet.

The small town of Geyserville adds considerably to the allure: It has a rural look and feel, with no cookie-cutter homes, large developments or chain stores. Slick hasn't arrived here yet, and the locals are proud that so many out-of-towners feel drawn to this rustic setting.

Geyserville Inn is the kind of place you look for when you want a simple, no-hassle wedding. All of its components work so well together that it's easy to imagine settling in and letting capable hands take care of you, from your rehearsal dinner to that wonderful first bite of post-wedding brunch.

Note: This property is owned by the Christensen Family.

CEREMONY, EVENT/RECEPTION & MEETING CAPACITY: Indoor spaces hold up to 65 seated or 75 standing guests. The Lawns hold up to 250 seated guests.

FEES & DEPOSITS: 50% of the rental fee is required to reserve your date. The balance is due 20 days prior to the event. Rental fees range $100–4,750 depending on the space selected. Dinner banquet prices range $40–60/person. Tax, alcohol and an 19.5% service charge are additional.

AVAILABILITY: Year-round, daily until 3pm for events. The Hoffman House Restaurant is also open daily from 7:30am for breakfast and lunch.

SERVICES/AMENITIES:

Catering: provided
Kitchen Facilities: fully equipped
Tables & Chairs: provided
Linens, Silver, etc.: provided
Restrooms: wheelchair accessible
Dance Floor: CBA
Bride's Dressing Area: CBA
Meeting Equipment: CBA, extra fee
Other: event coordination, wedding suites, picnic area, Hoffman House Restaurant next door

Parking: large lot or on street
Accommodations: 41 guestrooms including 5 suites
Telephone: guest phone
Outdoor Night Lighting: yes
Outdoor Cooking Facilities: no
Cleanup: provided
View: panorama of vineyards, mountains

RESTRICTIONS:

Alcohol: provided or BYO WBC with $15 corkage fee
Smoking: outdoors only
Music: amplified OK with restrictions

Wheelchair Access: yes
Insurance: liability required

Trentadue Winery

Winery

19170 Geyserville Avenue, Geyserville
707/433-3104 X107
www.trentadue.com
events@trentadue.com

● Rehearsal Dinners		● Corp. Events/Mtgs.
● Ceremonies		● Private Parties
● Wedding Receptions		Accommodations

Italians are famous for their warm hospitality and zest for living. They may not have invented *la dolce vita* ("the sweet life"), but they perfected the recipe for it: good friends, good food and good wine, plus a generous splash of lively music. If this sounds like your idea of a good time, you'll be happy to know that Trentadue Winery can provide all the ingredients for a really smashing special event.

The winery entrance is marked by stone pillars topped with crouching lions; from here it's a short drive through the vineyards to the tasting room and event facilities. A bubbling lion-head fountain marks the entrance to the Garden Area, which consists of a quaint lattice arbor with stage, dance floor, room for tables, and a sunny lawn area. At one end of the lawn, a smaller Tuscan-style arbor, its columns and trellis wrapped in leafy vines, makes a romantic spot for exchanging vows. Along the west side of the entire space, a windbreak of sweet gum and redwood trees casts a shade as cool and refreshing as a drink of spring water on a hot afternoon. Standing here in the sun, it's hard to imagine anything lovelier, but at night, with twinkle lights covering fences, trees and both arbors, everything sparkles like a miniature Milky Way. Additional lighting, thoughtfully equipped with dimmers, means your guests will be able to see the festivities without being blinded.

A second, more dramatic, ceremony site is the vast North Lawn on the opposite side of the Event Center. Getting married here is like getting married in a vineyard: There are grapevines all around you with views of redwoods and mountains beyond.

But what if your event is planned for the cooler months? Never fear—the Trentadue family has built an indoor facility, the Sala del Leone ("Hall of the Lion"). This expansive space has a white, peaked, beamed ceiling, hand-sponged golden walls, and intriguing glass and wrought-iron light fixtures and sconces. Plenty of arched French doors all around the building allow your guests to feel connected to the natural beauty that surrounds them, yet protected from the elements. Potted olive trees (yes, they are strung with twinkle lights) create a "Mediterranean" look, but this versatile room blends with any décor. Recently, a corporate event featured a Morrocan theme, draping the walls to resemble a Bedouin tent. Should your guests wish to wander over to the arbor area, they are free to do so, because when you host your event at Trentadue, all the facilities are included in the rental price. And though the panoramic views of spreading vineyards and distant wooded mountains may make you think you're far from the madding crowd, the bustling town of Santa Rosa is a mere twenty minutes away!

So if you like to party "Italian style," the folks at Trentadue Winery would be happy to help you out. They can provide everything from award-winning wines to topnotch coordination services. All you need to do is add friends and stir!

CEREMONY, EVENT/RECEPTION & MEETING CAPACITY: The Sala del Leone Events Center holds 250 seated. The lawn and garden areas can accommodate up to 500 guests, seated or standing.

FEES & DEPOSITS: A $4,000 partially refundable rental deposit and signed contract are required to reserve your date. The remaining rental fee, plus a $750 refundable security deposit are required 30 days before the event. Fees are based on guest count and time of year. Overtime is available at $500/hour and extra setup time runs $100/hour. A ceremony fee is an additional $500. Rental fees range $5,500–9,500 depending on guest count and date of event. There are discounts available for events taking place on weekdays and Sundays.

AVAILABILITY: Year-round, daily, 11am–10pm, excluding holidays.

SERVICES/AMENITIES:

Catering: select from approved list
Kitchen Facilities: ample
Tables & Chairs: provided
Linens, Silver, etc.: through caterer
Restrooms: wheelchair accessible
Dance Floor: indoor and outdoor provided
Bride's & Groom's Dressing Area: yes
Meeting Equipment: BYO

Parking: ample on-site
Accommodations: no guestrooms
Telephone: emergency use only
Outdoor Night Lighting: garden arbors and lawn
Outdoor Cooking Facilities: BBQ, extra fee
Cleanup: provided
View: mountains and vineyards
Other: event coordination

RESTRICTIONS:

Alcohol: provided
Smoking: outdoors only
Music: amplified OK with volume restrictions, music until 10pm

Wheelchair Access: yes
Insurance: extra liability required
Other: no confetti, rice, birdseed or glitter; no tacks or nails; children must be supervised

Beltane Ranch

Private Estate and Ranch

11775 Sonoma Highway, Glen Ellen
707/833-4233
www.beltaneranch.com
anne@beltaneranch.com

Rehearsal Dinners	Corp. Events/Mtgs.
● Ceremonies	Private Parties
● Wedding Receptions	● Accommodations

The story goes that in 1892, Mary Ellen Pleasant, a black woman from New Orleans, built this house in Sonoma's fabled Valley of the Moon. It was both a refuge from and celebration of the great business success she had enjoyed in San Francisco. She created a wooden confection, graced with delicate lathed railings and Victorian-style wood trim, as well as grand verandas strewn with wicker furnishings. The handsome new home was called "Beltane," a likely reference to the ancient Celtic festival of spring and Thomas Bell, her long-time big-city business partner.

It's easy to see what drew her to erect this two-story, five-room structure on this spot. Beltane nestles beneath venerable oaks atop a gentle slope that rises from the valley's main highway. To reach it, you turn onto a narrow drive flanked by old trees, vineyards, grassy fields and beautiful hand-built stone walls. The front of the house is bordered by a flower garden that's enclosed by a classic white picket fence.

Next to the house are two lawns used for ceremonies. The larger one is edged with flowerbeds, low stone walls and towering oaks. A stage for the DJ in one corner is festooned with strings of lights that create a festive glow, day or night. The smaller lawn right behind the house is a bit more intimate. It's especially appealing when a musician, positioned in one corner of the adjacent upstairs veranda, provides soft music during the ceremony. Another lawn near the trellised entrance to the main house often hosts small receptions.

When brides who've wed here talk about what they liked, the first thing they cite is Beltane's authenticity. A still-working ranch that raises cattle and grows grapes and olives, Beltane evokes Old Sonoma from the days before the county became an upscale destination. The lovingly maintained old house has nothing slick about it. Its vibrant gardens have evolved over the years and seem part of the landscape, not something designed on a drafting table. Bridal party members often enjoy breakfast fruit harvested from raspberry bushes planted decades ago by the owner's grand aunt. Another attractive feature is the stand-alone cottage, a Berber-carpeted hideaway that has a firebox, sitting area, private bath, and a small garden and deck overlooking the main lawn.

Brides also like Beltane's seasoned staff, many of whom have been on site at least fifteen years. One dividend of the ranch's reputation for great service is that quite a few newlyweds return for their anniversaries. (The ranch has even welcomed the children of couples who have been married here.)

Beltane remains one of the most beautiful old ranch houses in California. Owned by the same family since the 1930s, and surrounded by 1,000 acres of open-space preserve, the ranch's 100 acres are the place to hold a true Sonoma County country wedding. Everything here—site and surroundings—blends seamlessly to create a perfect pastoral stage.

CEREMONY & EVENT/RECEPTION CAPACITY: Beltane Ranch can accommodate up to 150 guests, seated or standing.

FEES & DEPOSITS: One third of the rental fee is required to reserve your date. The next third is due 3 months prior to the event and the final third is due 2 weeks prior. The rental fee is $14,400. This includes 5 bed and breakfast rooms and a garden cottage for Friday and Saturday nights, and exclusive use of the ranch. There is a full breakfast for all B&B guests included.

AVAILABILITY: Outdoor events held from the first weekend in June through the first weekend in October. Events may be held from 4pm–10pm.

SERVICES/AMENITIES:

Catering: select from list

Kitchen Facilities: prep only

Tables & Chairs: provided

Linens, Silver, etc.: through caterer

Restrooms: not wheelchair accessible

Dance Floor: provided

Bride's Dressing Area: CBA

Meeting Equipment: CBA

Parking: large lot

Accommodations: 6 guestrooms

Telephone: office phone

Outdoor Night Lighting: garden arbors and lawn

Outdoor Cooking Facilities: caterers only

Cleanup: provided

View: mountains, vineyards, forest, garden

RESTRICTIONS:

Alcohol: BYO

Smoking: outdoors only

Music: amplified OK outdoors with restrictions

Wheelchair Access: limited

Insurance: extra liability required

Overwhelmed? Use the search criteria on www.HereComesTheGuide.com to narrow down your choices.

B.R. Cohn Winery

Winery

15000 Sonoma Highway, Glen Ellen
707/931-7930, 800/330-4064 x130
www.brcohn.com
paula@brcohn.com

● Rehearsal Dinners	● Corp. Events/Mtgs.
● Ceremonies	● Private Parties
● Wedding Receptions	Accommodations

Just 45 minutes north of the Golden Gate Bridge in the heart of Sonoma Valley, B.R. Cohn Winery offers a multitude of possibilities in a romantic Wine Country atmosphere. Olive trees, whose graceful branches shade the road leading up to the winery, are a fitting introduction to this pastoral location.

From the top of the hill, it's a short walk down to the outdoor Amphitheater, a spectacular ceremony site with a large stage and terraced lawn. Couples exchange vows on the stage beneath an enormous oak tree. Behind them is a stunning natural backdrop: acres of lush Cabernet vineyards and a full view of the Sonoma Mountains. Guests seated on the stage or lawn have the perfect vantage from which to enjoy the lovely panorama.

Nearby is another gorgeous venue to tie the knot: Fox Hill. Set in the middle of a vineyard, this rustic spot is shaded by 300-year-old oaks and manzanita trees and so private that all you hear is the occasional chirping of birds. Guests have a 360-degree view of the surrounding grapevines, and on hot days a soft breeze keeps them comfortable. Nature provides ample "decoration" so you don't need to add anything—except perhaps some rose petals for the aisle.

A third choice is the Poolside Arbor. Ideal for smaller ceremonies and cocktail receptions, it features landscaped gardens and fruit trees and has a view of the olive grove, vineyards and mountains in the distance.

When it's time to dine, most couples invite their guests to the Olive Grove for an al fresco celebration. Partially enclosed by a white split-rail fence, this expansive lawn is shaded by more than a dozen 140-year-old French Picholine olive trees. Flowers make a colorful border, while tiny lights woven throughout every other tree create nighttime sparkle. Although this grove is usually used for receptions, it's equally beautiful for ceremonies.

A new indoor ceremony/reception option, due to be completed in 2011, is the Barrel Room. Lined with wooden wine casks, it will provide a cool alternative during those hot summer months, and a wonderful venue in winter, too. The aroma of aging wine, soft lighting and flickering candles will make dinners here both fragrant and romantic.

In addition to its numerous event spaces, B.R Cohn provides a charming cobblestone cottage for the bride, her entourage and her family. Outfitted with an antique vanity, full-length mirror and couches, it's a cozy place to primp and relax.

Nestled between the Mayacamas and Sonoma Mountains, B.R. Cohn Winery's 90 acres possess a wealth of beauty, tranquility and options. Add to that fine wines and a friendly, experienced event coordinator and you have everything you need for an outstanding event.

CEREMONY & EVENT/RECEPTION CAPACITY: The winery holds up to 250 seated guests in the tented terrace area outdoors.

FEES & DEPOSITS: A deposit in the amount of 50% of the site fee is required to secure your date; the balance is due 6 months prior to the event. Site fees range $4,500–8,000 depending on the day of your event and the guest count. Fees include use of the site for ceremony and reception, event coordinator services on the day-of, and time necessary for ceremony rehearsal.

AVAILABILITY: Year-round, daily, flexible hours. Outdoor spaces available April–November, weather permitting.

SERVICES/AMENITIES:

Catering: select from list or BYO with approval
Kitchen Facilities: prep area only
Tables & Chairs: BYO or through caterer
Linens, Silver, etc.: BYO or through caterer
Restrooms: wheelchair accessible
Dance Floor: CBA, extra fee
Bride's Dressing Area: yes
Meeting Equipment: n/a
Other: event coordination

Parking: ample, complimentary, attendant required, shuttles or valet for over 150 guests
Accommodations: no guestrooms
Telephone: office phone
Outdoor Night Lighting: yes
Outdoor Cooking Facilities: no
Cleanup: caterer
View: vineyards, olive trees, Sonoma Mountains, landscaped grounds

RESTRICTIONS:

Alcohol: wine provided; BYO BC, no hard alcohol
Smoking: designated areas
Music: amplified OK until 10pm

Wheelchair Access: yes
Insurance: certificate of liability required

Jack London Lodge

13740 Arnold Drive, Glen Ellen
707/938-8510
www.jacklondonlodge.com
info@jacklondonlodge.com

Lodge, Restaurant & Historic Tavern

- Rehearsal Dinners
- Ceremonies
- Wedding Receptions
- Corp. Events/Mtgs.
- Private Parties
- Accommodations

Located in the quaint village of Glen Ellen, the Jack London Lodge is a perennial favorite for wine-country celebrations. Named for the famous writer who lived nearby until his death, the Lodge includes the historic 1905 brick building that houses the saloon, the adjoining Wolf House Dining Room and Creekside Patio where special events are held, and a 22-unit lodge.

Couples getting married here have a number of choices. For more traditional ceremonies, there are several churches just minutes away, including a historic church within walking distance of the Lodge. But many brides and grooms prefer to exchange vows outdoors on the Lodge's Creekside Lawn, a lovely grass area adjacent to the patio, pool and the treelined Sonoma Creek. The bride and groom can stand next to the creek with a tapestry of trees as a backdrop, or under a rose-covered arbor at the entrance to the patio.

Wedding receptions, rehearsal dinners and other special events are hosted on the Creekside Patio, which is shaded by the branches of towering trees and overlooks Sonoma Creek. With its bubbling stone fountain and outdoor serving bar, it's an al fresco setting adaptable for all types of gatherings, from casual barbecues to candlelit suppers. Flowerbeds filled with perennials provide an abundance of color, eliminating the need for any additional decoration.

The Patio connects to the Saloon, which is also a great place for socializing. Your guests can wander in for a change of scene during or after your event. Its period décor, Jack London memorabilia, Tiffany lamps and antique oak bar will give them a taste of another era.

For smaller gatherings, the elegant Wolf House Dining Room offers a warm and intimate ambiance, with its honey-gold walls, rustic brick fireplace, and beautiful view of the creek along with two creekside decks. This space is a perfect year-round option for rehearsal dinners, receptions and parties for all occasions.

One reason the Jack London Lodge is so popular is that it's one of the few facilities in the Wine Country where you can have your event and house many of your out-of-town guests all at the same location. The Lodge's 22 antique-filled guestrooms are set off in a secluded area that has a swimming pool and in-ground spa. Colorful seasonal flowers surround the pool and grace the front of the Lodge, affording guests a garden experience. A very private three-bedroom, three-bath house just a few minutes from the Lodge is a convenient retreat for wedding parties. The woodsy setting, full of oak and pine trees, makes this a tranquil place for brides who need their own dressing room or a quiet getaway. It's also wonderful for families who want to spend some quality time together.

The garden setting, historic atmosphere and excellent food and lodging attract celebrants from all over the country. And the location is ideal: just minutes from the City of Sonoma, Jack London State Park, wineries, golf, horseback riding, balloon rides and a long list of other activities. So if this Valley of the Moon facility is the right place for you, we suggest you reserve it as early as possible. Your family and friends will be extremely grateful.

CEREMONY CAPACITY: Ceremonies can be arranged on the patio or lawn for up to 150 guests.

EVENT/RECEPTION CAPACITY: The Creekside Patio holds 40–150 guests. The Wolf House dining room holds 20–60 seated or 20–80 standing guests

FEES & DEPOSITS: Fees and deposits vary depending on the type of event and will be quoted accordingly. Meals start at $25/person for lunch, $41/per person for dinner. Alcohol, tax and a 20% service charge are additional.

AVAILABILITY: Daily, 10am–10pm. The Wolf House Dining Room is available year-round, and the Creekside Patio May–October.

SERVICES/AMENITIES:
Catering: provided by *Wolf House Restaurant*
Kitchen Facilities: n/a
Tables & Chairs: some provided
Linens, Silver, etc.: provided
Restrooms: wheelchair accessible
Dance Floor: deck or patio
Bride's Dressing Area: guestroom CBA
Meeting Equipment: n/a

Parking: on-street and lot
Accommodations: 22 guestrooms
Telephone: no
Outdoor Night Lighting: yes
Outdoor Cooking Facilities: no
Cleanup: provided
View: treelined Sonoma Creek

RESTRICTIONS:
Alcohol: provided, WC corkage $13/bottle
Smoking: outdoors only
Music: OK with restrictions

Wheelchair Access: yes
Insurance: not required
Other: no rice, birdseed, confetti, tape or staples

Vineyard Ranch & Barn

Private Ranch Estate

Address withheld to ensure privacy. Glen Ellen
707/935-0621 X2
www.sonomacatering.com
info@julieatwoodevents.com

- Rehearsal Dinners
- Ceremonies
- Wedding Receptions
- Corp. Events/Mtgs.
- Private Parties
- Accommodations

Cabernet grapes hang heavy on rows of vines disappearing towards the eastern mountains, and a long view of Sonoma Valley stretches before you. This is only one of the lovely scenes you see as you survey Vineyard Ranch's idyllic surroundings and consider all the possibilities.

The 140-year-old ranch is spread out over 70 acres, with horses roaming the property amidst olive trees, vineyards and organic gardens. Numerous areas on the estate lend themselves to events, especially the contemporary barn and gardens. Included with this stunning setting are the services of one of the Bay Area's most elite planners, Julie Atwood Events (JAE). Their team offers complete wedding planning from start to finish, as well as site tours of other exclusive properties for rehearsal parties, brunches, and other events.

By handling the coordination, design and staging for all events at this private estate, JAE ensures that every wedding has a distinctive, totally personal feeling. To help you realize your vision, they'll provide you with a select cadre of Wine Country resources, including florists, musicians, lighting designers and lodging. They'll also assist you in choosing a caterer from their exclusive list who will create a menu just for you using only the freshest and best regional foods, highlighted by seasonal vegetables, herbs and olive oil from the ranch's own garden. Your feast will be paired with wines that you have chosen from fabulous Sonoma County wineries.

Couples getting married here usually exchange vows in a meadow or on an expansive lawn, with vineyards and the Sonoma Mountains as a backdrop. From their ceremony site, a path spilling over with roses and lavender guides them to the oak-shaded flagstone patio where the festivities begin.

Cocktails may be served on the patio in the dappled shade of an oak canopy. Dinner and dancing follow on the lawn or in the barn, depending on the size of your group. Evening receptions look spectacular with colored lanterns strung overhead and candles flickering on tables. After dinner, the barn becomes the uber-Wine Country lounge. It can completely change its look to suit your event: Considering an Old California atmosphere? Bring in handmade textiles and a Latin orchestra. Rich metallics and a state-of-the-art DJ turn the space into an edgy SOMA loft. Or, to create a classic, romantic backdrop for a swinging Big Band, just add chandeliers, crystal and silk.

And so…newlyweds, friends, family and barn swallows party into the night. Barn swallows? You bet! Bluebirds, owls and other creatures of nature are what keep the ranch fly- and chemical-free.

This is an estate that supports sustainable farming and artisan producers, and all the vendors who work here share the same philosophy. The venue also contributes a portion of the coordination fees to local charities.

In addition to weddings, the ranch specializes in out-of-the-box corporate events, ranging from winemaker dinners and fly-fishing seminars to horse-drawn wagon rides to the vineyard for al fresco cocktails. Whatever your celebration at Vineyard Ranch, you can be assured of several things: You'll see beauty everywhere you look; you're going to enjoy yourself immensely; and every detail will be handled for you.

CEREMONY CAPACITY: The Meadow holds up to 200 seated guests and the Garden up to 100 seated guests. The Vineyard Lawn holds up to 200 seated guests.

EVENT/RECEPTION CAPACITY: The barn holds up to 175 seated or 250 standing guests and the patio up to 150 standing guests.

MEETING CAPACITY: The barn holds up to 100 seated guests.

FEES & DEPOSITS: A 50% deposit is required to reserve your date. The balance is due 30 days prior to the event. The fee ranges $10,000–20,000 depending on guest count, site usage and event type. Meals range $90–250/person. Alcohol is additional. Liability insurance, equipment rentals and parking/shuttle services are required and additional to the fee. The fee includes all wedding coordination, site staffing and vendor supervision.

AVAILABILITY: Year-round, daily, 9am–11pm. One event per weekend. The maximum guest count is 250 guests, June–October; 100, November–May.

SERVICES/AMENITIES:
Catering: preferred list
Kitchen Facilities: through coordinator
Tables & Chairs: through coordinator
Linens, Silver, etc.: through coordinator
Restrooms: not wheelchair accessible, portables
Dance Floor: provided, extra fee
Bride's Dressing Area: yes
Meeting Equipment: CBA

Parking: shuttle required, extra charge
Accommodations: no guestrooms
Telephone: available
Outdoor Night Lighting: yes, minimal
Outdoor Cooking Facilities: CBA
Cleanup: caterer
View: vineyards, pond, hills, gardens
Other: event coordination and management included

RESTRICTIONS:
Alcohol: BYO wine, liquor by licensed provider
Smoking: very restricted
Music: OK with restrictions

Wheelchair Access: limited
Insurance: liability required
Other: no rice, birdseed, confetti, sparklers or fireworks

The professionals in the back of this book are the best in the business. How do we know? Read page 701.

Healdsburg Country Gardens

Private Country Estate & Vineyards

Address withheld to ensure privacy. Healdsburg
707/431-8630

www.hcgweddings.com
info@hcgweddings.com

Rehearsal Dinners	Corp. Events/Mtgs.
● Ceremonies	Private Parties
● Wedding Receptions	● Accommodations

As you walk through the "tunnel" of rose-covered arches at the entrance of Healdsburg Country Gardens, you're completely enveloped by its fragrant beauty. And when you emerge from this magical walkway, the scenery only gets better.

What greets you is a lush rose garden, dotted with flowers, ancient oaks and towering redwoods. Walkways wind through lawns bordered by beds of brightly colored lavender, lilacs, roses and wisteria, past a bubbling fountain and two aviaries filled with cockatiels and singing canaries. Framing this gorgeous tableau are sweeping views of estate vineyards, which are visible from almost everywhere in the garden.

Four spacious event areas flow together seamlessly, so guests can easily mix and mingle. The site's focal point is the historic four-story redwood barn. Built in 1902, it has huge doors on two sides that open to vistas of the gardens and vineyards. Walls are decorated with bouquets of dried flowers, and a grapevine-covered terrace wraps around the building. At night, tiny white lights in the arbor and soft lighting inside the barn and throughout the gardens add a romantic glow while your friends and family dine, dance or just stroll through the grounds. The barn's perfect acoustics will also enhance whatever music your band or DJ is playing.

Some of the best photo opportunities are in front of the 1920s cottage, which faces the barn from the other side of the garden. This adorable little house is the epitome of charming: Constructed in the wood-slat fashion of the time and enclosed by a picket fence, it beckons you to sit on the covered front porch and watch the grapes grow. Flowering vines creep up the support posts, while a colorful array of blossoms peek through the railings. The side deck and arbor offer yet more views of vineyards and garden. Brides use the interior of the cottage as a dressing room.

Couples get married under a majestic oak, while guests seated on a large shady lawn admire the vineyards in the background. Following the ceremony, champagne and hors d'oeuvres are served near the oak tree or on the barn's wraparound terrace. The party then moves to a large adjoining lawn, where guests dine at tables beneath market umbrellas. Afterwards, everyone has an opportunity to dance in the barn, stroll through the gardens, and simply enjoy the irresistible setting of this Wine Country estate.

Owners Barbara and Walt Gruber specialize in just one kind of event: beautiful Wine Country weddings. So come and walk through the tunnel of roses; what you'll find on the other side is a private haven that can be exclusively yours for a day and it's only one and a half miles from Healdsburg Plaza!

Shown by appointment only. Not open to the public.

CEREMONY CAPACITY: The large lawn with the oak tree holds 150 seated guests.

EVENT/RECEPTION CAPACITY: The terrace, lawns and garden can accommodate 150 seated.

FEES & DEPOSITS: For weddings, half the rental fee is the deposit that holds your date. Rental fees for up to 150 guests are $11,500 for Saturdays ($10,500 for other days). The rental balance and a $500 refundable cleaning/security deposit are payable 90 days prior to the event. The fee covers a 6-hour block plus guest arrival, setup and cleanup times.

AVAILABILITY: May–October, 11am–9pm.

SERVICES/AMENITIES:

Catering: BYO, licensed and insured
Kitchen Facilities: prep only
Tables & Chairs: provided; market umbrellas provided
Linens, Silver, etc.: BYO
Restrooms: wheelchair accessible
Dance Floor: on terrace, or barn's cement floor
Bride's & Groom's Dressing Area: yes
Meeting Equipment: no

Parking: ample lot, attendants provided
Accommodations: cottage for 2, guesthouse for 6
Telephone: guest phone CBA
Outdoor Night Lighting: yes
Outdoor Cooking Facilities: yes
Cleanup: caterer and renter
View: panorama of vineyards, rolling hills and gorgeous gardens

RESTRICTIONS:

Alcohol: caterer or BYO
Smoking: designated area only
Music: amplified OK until 9pm

Wheelchair Access: yes
Insurance: extra insurance required
Other: no pets, children must be supervised, decorations are restricted

Madrona Manor

1001 Westside Road, Healdsburg
707/433-1542 X111
www.madronamanor.com
emily@madronamanor.com

Historic Inn

- Rehearsal Dinners
- Ceremonies
- Wedding Receptions
- Corp. Events/Mtgs.
- Private Parties
- Accommodations

"Madrona Manor"...the very name sounds like something out of a romantic novel, and if romance is what you're looking for, you've come to the right place. Built in 1881 by Sonoma County businessman John Paxton as a family residence, it became an inn during the 1980s and earned a spot in the National Register of Historic Places. Current owners Bill and Trudi Konrad worked diligently to restore this landmark to its former splendor, and they've succeeded admirably.

This elegant boutique hotel is a classic example of Victorian architecture with period scrollwork, a mansard roof, dormer windows and columned verandas. The property occupies eight acres of prime Sonoma County real estate, whose tangled woodlands have been lovingly coaxed into a garden showplace with fountains, rolling lawns, herb gardens, a citrus grove and a rainbow of seasonal flowers.

The Manor's interior shows the same attention to detail and eye for authenticity as the grounds. The first-floor rooms all have fireplaces, crystal chandeliers, carved sideboards and turn-of-the-century art. The Palm Terrace is a large covered veranda, whose wicker furniture, potted palms and cheerful upholstery make it reminiscent of a Victorian conservatory.

Madrona Manor offers four types of wedding packages, and each one makes ample use of the Manor's felicitous environs. The favored ceremony site is the capacious Wedding Lawn, bordered by masses of flowers and towering sycamores.

The Victorians were known for their elaborate multicourse repasts, and Madrona Manor is as authentic in this as it is in everything else. Thanks to Chef Jesse Mallgren, the venue has a prestigious one-star Michelin rating. Chef Mallgren's considerable talents and renowned seasonal menus are at your disposal. Another talented staff member is director of special events Emily Rowan, who is adept at creating breathtakingly romantic destination weddings.

Madrona Manor is also available during the week and in the off-season. Of course, nonwedding events such as celebratory dinners or corporate functions are also welcome. If your love life could use a jump-start, you don't have to wait for Valentine's Day—just take a trip to Madrona Manor, where romance is in the air all year round.

CEREMONY & EVENT/RECEPTION CAPACITY: The facility can accommodate 150 guests.

MEETING CAPACITY: The Manor has various rooms which can hold 15–28 seated conference-style or theater-style.

FEES & DEPOSITS: For weddings, 50% of the facility fee is required upon booking to reserve your date. The facility fee ranges $2,500–13,000. Meals range $52–65/person. Tax, alcohol and a 20% service charge are additional.

AVAILABILITY: Year-round.

SERVICES/AMENITIES:

Catering: provided, no BYO

Kitchen Facilities: n/a

Tables & Chairs: provided

Linens, Silver, etc.: provided

Restrooms: wheelchair accessible

Dance Floor: Amber Room and Rose Room

Bride's Dressing Area: yes, during the day

Meeting Equipment: projector, screen, conference phone and broadband

Parking: complimentary

Accommodations: 22 guestrooms

Telephone: guest or house phones

Outdoor Night Lighting: yes

Outdoor Cooking Facilities: no

Cleanup: provided

View: estate gardens, Dry Creek Valley

Other: personal coordinator provided

RESTRICTIONS:

Alcohol: provided

Smoking: designated areas outside

Music: amplified OK indoors only

Wheelchair Access: yes

Insurance: not required

Other: no rice, birdseed, confetti or bubbles

Villa Chanticleer

Historic Lodge

1248 North Fitch Mountain Road, Healdsburg

707/431-3303

www.villachanticleer.com
villainfo@ci.healdsburg.ca.us

● Rehearsal Dinners	● Corp. Events/Mtgs.
● Ceremonies	● Private Parties
● Wedding Receptions	Accommodations

Among the trees and manicured lawns of a seventeen-acre park owned by the City of Healdsburg you'll find Villa Chanticleer, a charming venue that will put you in mind of a gentler, more graceful time.

Built in 1910 as a country resort, the Villa has a rich history of hosting weddings, receptions, parties and community events. And thanks to functional upgrades over the years, guests appreciate not only the peace and beauty of the lovely surroundings, but the facility's modern amenities as well.

When you arrive on the Villa grounds, take a moment to enjoy the many large trees, the fresh air and the birdsong. As you cross the stone steps to enter the Villa Main Building, notice the wide veranda shaded by a handsome, wisteria-draped arbor. Inside, you're welcomed by an open, gracious lobby. The bar area directly ahead is conveniently U-shaped and surrounded by eight large booths, perfect for a quiet drink or conversation.

The doors to your right lead to the Dining Room; those on your left open to the Ballroom. Each 3,000-square-foot room features redwood paneling, light-toned hardwood floors and bucolic views. In the Dining Room, generous picture windows frame panoramic vistas of the Alexander Valley below and Geyser Peak in the distance. From the Ballroom, you can see the veranda, the lawn, and the hillside covered in oaks, maples and bay laurel trees. A centrally located, modern commercial kitchen is easily accessible from both spaces, adding to their versatility.

A short walk from the Villa is the casual yet elegant Wedding Garden. Wrought-iron gates invite you into the two-level secluded lawn bordered by terraced flowerbeds and redwood trees. A quaint gazebo may serve as either a backdrop or the focal point for your ceremony.

The Villa Chanticleer Annex and the Picnic/Barbecue area are available for more informal events.

This multifaceted facility provides a memorable setting for large or intimate gatherings, and the price is quite attractive. No wonder Villa Chanticleer has been a favorite of wedding couples and their guests for generations.

CEREMONY CAPACITY: The Ballroom and Dining Room each accommodate 300 seated guests; the Wedding Garden holds up to 250 guests.

EVENT/RECEPTION CAPACITY: The Dining Room and Ballroom each hold 300 seated or standing guests, or 250 seated banquet-style. The Annex (which is a smaller building located next to the Main Villa) accommodates 150 seated guests or 200 for a standing reception. Outdoor picnic facilities hold 200 people and the bar area up to 100 guests.

MEETING CAPACITY: For corporate functions, the entire building holds up to 600 seated guests.

FEES & DEPOSITS: The Villa's 12-hour rental fee ranges $795–4,995 depending on day of the event. Fees for the Wedding Garden range $875–1,200 depending on day of the week. The rental fee for the Villa Annex is approximately half that of the Villa. An hourly rate is also available for both buildings; call for details. Rental fees are due when reservations are confirmed. A security/damage deposit is required: $1,000 for the Wedding Garden, or the Villa and $600 for the Annex. These are due 60 days prior to your event and will be refunded 30 days after the event. There is a rental fee for use of the picnic area; a $200 security/damage deposit is required.

AVAILABILITY: Year-round, daily, including some holidays.

SERVICES/AMENITIES:

Catering: BYO licensed caterer

Kitchen Facilities: commercial

Tables & Chairs: provided

Linens, Silver, etc.: silver provided, BYO linens

Restrooms: wheelchair accessible

Dance Floor: yes

Bride's Dressing Area: yes

Meeting Equipment: PA, easels, screen, podium, stage

Parking: large lot, 185 spaces

Accommodations: no guestrooms

Telephone: pay phone

Outdoor Night Lighting: no

Outdoor Cooking Facilities: BBQ

Cleanup: caterer or provided, extra fee

View: nearby mountain range

RESTRICTIONS:

Alcohol: service only through the American Legion

Smoking: outdoors only

Music: amplified OK indoors only

Wheelchair Access: yes

Insurance: extra required

Other: no rice, birdseed, metallic balloons, streamers or confetti

---

Want to know WHAT TO ASK a potential location or vendor? Check out our Questions to Ask on page 17.

The Carneros Inn

Inn and Spa

4048 Sonoma Highway, Napa
707/299-4967, Wedding Department
www.thecarnerosinn.com
bbaglietto@thecarnerosinn.com

- Rehearsal Dinners
- Ceremonies
- Wedding Receptions
- Corp. Events/Mtgs.
- Private Parties
- Accommodations

The Carneros Inn, 4:00 Thursday afternoon:

The in-laws have landed, your adoring fans arrive tomorrow for the rehearsal dinner, and the wedding whirlwind is about to begin, but you two are already having the time of your lives....

After a leisurely morning you brunched al fresco at the Hilltop Restaurant, had a full-body massage at The Spa, and then melted away any remaining tension in the poolside hot tub, which has one of the best vineyard views in Napa. Tonight you're going to play "spot the celeb," while sipping a cult Cabernet by one of the inn's wood-burning fireplaces, followed by dinner at Farm Restaurant, where the cuisine celebrates the bounty of Carneros and its neighboring farmers and ranches. As the sun sets behind lavender hills, you'll be able to relax knowing that everything will be expertly taken care of.

The Carneros Inn is the area's only resort, nestled among 27 acres of rolling hills, grapevines, unspoiled farmland, and scenic apple orchards. Its architectural style is based on cues from the local countryside—barns, silos and ranchers' cottages—but rendered with a shot of industrial soul. The resulting look has a clean, modernist aesthetic softened by a hip, "farm-shui" vibe—true luxury without any pretense.

Beautifully landscaped walking paths meander from the apple orchard—their premier ceremony location—through flowering gardens with fountains to all the facilities on the property. A wide range of inspiring event locations can accommodate the size and style of almost any celebration. The Napa and Sonoma Ballrooms showcase the resort's rustic-luxe design with their soaring peaked roofs, hand-crafted barn-board walls, and state-of-the-art lighting and sound. Both light-filled ballrooms are divisible into smaller sections for more intimate events, and each opens onto the Carneros Courtyard through multiple sets of French doors.

The trellised Carneros Courtyard is custom-made for outdoor gatherings. Along with its spacious lawn, apple trees and stone wood-burning fireplace, it's wired for sound and has festival lighting. It's a dream setting for an open-air cocktail reception or post-dinner cigars and cognac by a roaring fire.

For rehearsal dinners or smaller weddings and private events, reserve the Hilltop Restaurant. Its patios flank the signature infinity-edged pool, and whether you're entertaining inside the restaurant or out, you'll enjoy a breathtaking view of the hills and surrounding vineyards.

Wine tasting is a favorite pastime in the valley, but the resort offers a long list of other tempting activities. Get the blood moving with a yoga class, a round of bocce ball or a swim in the "infinity" lap pool (which is lined with cabanas, outfitted with phone and internet). The Fitness Barn (overlooking the pool) provides plenty of equipment, and features retractable walls to take advantage of the Napa weather.

At the end of a thoroughly satisfying day, your own little hideaway awaits. Indulge in an outdoor shower for two on your private patio with a view of bucolic vineyards and rolling hills. Then luxuriate in the heated slate floors, 800-thread-count sheets, and a match-ready fireplace. Although The Carneros Inn is only an hour from San Francisco, you'll feel like you've traveled to another world, a place where beauty and serenity reign and every one of your sophisticated desires is catered to.

CEREMONY, EVENT/RECEPTION & MEETING CAPACITY: The Inn holds up to 175 guests, indoor or outdoor, seated or standing.

FEES & DEPOSITS: 50% of the estimated event total is required to reserve your date. The balance is due 14 days prior to the event. Rental fees range $7,000–12,000 depending on the space rented. Food and beverage minimums begin at $130/person. Tax and a 20% service charge are additional.

AVAILABILITY: Year-round, daily, anytime.

SERVICES/AMENITIES:

Catering: provided
Kitchen Facilities: n/a
Tables & Chairs: provided
Linens, Silver, etc.: provided
Restrooms: wheelchair accessible
Dance Floor: provided
Bride's Dressing Area: CBA
Meeting Equipment: CBA
Other: spa services, AV equipment

Parking: large lot
Accommodations: 86 guestrooms and homes
Telephone: office and house phones
Outdoor Night Lighting: yes
Outdoor Cooking Facilities: BBQ CBA
Cleanup: provided
View: garden, meadow, mountains, vineyards, hills, pool

RESTRICTIONS:

Alcohol: provided
Smoking: outdoors only
Music: amplified OK indoors; outdoors, acoustic only with volume restrictions

Wheelchair Access: yes
Insurance: not required

Meritage Resort and Spa

Resort and Spa

875 Bordeaux Way, Napa
707/251-1900
www.themeritageresort.com
sthomas@themeritageresort.com

- Rehearsal Dinners
- Ceremonies
- Wedding Receptions
- Corp. Events/Mtgs.
- Private Parties
- Accommodations

Launched to great acclaim in 2006, this elegant three-story complex has the look of an opulent Tuscan Villa thanks to sienna- and umber-colored buildings, a dazzling cedar loggia and a flagstone-faced porte-cochère. Yet Meritage Resort and Spa is unlike any other venue in Northern California. With its innovative approach to luxury and epicurean delights, the resort may be the quintessential embodiment of the Wine Country lifestyle.

The buzz in Napa is all about Meritage's Estate Wine Cave, a manmade marvel carved 128 feet into a hillside. Situated beneath Meritage's vineyards and gardens, the vast 22,000-square-foot cave is home to Spa Terra, the world's only underground four-star spa. Lavished with natural stone and copper water features, this richly hued, gently lit haven offers a long list of indulgences, including nurturing couples' treatments and bridal beauty services. The Estate Wine Cave also boasts wine barrel-lined walls, the Trinitas Tasting Room, and novel reception areas that evoke the warm glow and dramatic ambiance of Old World Florentine wine caves.

The grounds of the Meritage are equally alluring. Laced with walking paths, the hilltop's lush landscape provides the perfect backdrop for slow, romantic strolls. Weddings take full advantage of the stunning scenery at the Vineyard Terrace, an oak-fringed plaza that overlooks eight acres of grapevines. If you prefer an intimate indoor ceremony, then tie the knot at one of Napa's only private chapels, Our Lady of the Grapes. With a soaring wood-beamed ceiling and windows that let in natural light, the chapel casts an ethereal radiance over the proceedings.

The resort has another unique asset: the Meritage Grand Salon, the largest ballroom in Napa Valley (divisible into up to ten sections). With dark wood trim against cream-colored walls and imposing chandeliers decorated with stylized grapes, it has an appealing Italian flair. The ballroom's simple and studied stylishness makes it easy to imagine gliding onto the dance floor, swept up in good cheer and joyful music. The ballroom is bracketed by a long loggia that bathes it in soft northern light, and an inviting lobby that faces the resort's inner courtyard through a bank of French doors. Both spaces, which are lovely for mingling and wine tasting, create a sense of expectation before you make your way into the ballroom.

Superior hospitality and plush accommodations are other keys to Meritage's success. Many of the guestrooms have private balconies and vineyard views, and you can reserve private wings for the wedding party and family members. As the VIP couple, why not stay in one of the luxury suites?

Spacious and up-to-the-minute, the suites are decked out with marble baths, granite counters and a chef's kitchen where meals can be prepared and served just for the two of you.

Speaking of food, Meritage's award-winning restaurant, Siena, has a stellar wine list and Tuscan-influenced menus that are available for your event. Artfully incorporating ingredients from local organic farms, the rustic and naturally flavorful cuisine promises to be as inspiring as the setting.

If it all sounds a little overwhelming, don't worry. Meritage's accomplished wedding coordinator will personally arrange all the details, from floor plans to flowers, so you'll be free to enjoy every moment of your celebration. Meritage's developers wanted to fashion a deluxe, one-stop resort where guests are utterly pampered. Mission accomplished.

CEREMONY CAPACITY: The outdoor space holds up to 300 seated guests, the Chapel holds up to 50 seated guests.

EVENT/RECEPTION CAPACITY: The Ballroom holds up to 800 seated or 900 standing guests. Outdoor spaces hold up to 300 seated or 400 standing guests.

MEETNG CAPACITY: Event spaces accommodate 12–900 seated guests indoors.

FEES & DEPOSITS: Rental fees range $3,000–12,000 depending on season and space rented. Meals range $45–85/person. Tax, alcohol and a 21% service charge are additional.

AVAILABILITY: Year-round, daily, call for details.

SERVICES/AMENITIES:

Catering: provided
Kitchen Facilities: n/a
Tables & Chairs: provided
Linens, Silver, etc.: provided
Restrooms: wheelchair accessible
Dance Floor: yes
Bride's Dressing Area: provided
Meeting Equipment: CBA

Parking: large lot, valet optional
Accommodations: 158 guestrooms and suites
Telephone: house phone, guestroom phones
Outdoor Night Lighting: yes
Outdoor Cooking Facilities: CBA
Cleanup: provided
View: vineyards, valley, garden, hills, fairways
Other: event coordination, spa services

RESTRICTIONS:

Alcohol: BYO with corkage fee
Smoking: outside only
Music: amplified OK indoors and outdoors

Wheelchair Access: yes
Insurance: not required

Wedgewood Wedding & Banquet Center
at Foxtail Golf Club

100 Golf Course Drive, Rohnert Park
866/966-3009

www.wedgewoodbanquet.com
sales@wedgewoodbanquet.com

Event Center at Golf Club

● Rehearsal Dinners	● Corp. Events/Mtgs.
● Ceremonies	● Private Parties
● Wedding Receptions	Accommodations

The Wedgewood at Foxtail Golf Club is one of the Wine Country's newest wedding locations, offering both class and outstanding value. The 36-hole municipal golf course sits in the middle of Rohnert Park, a friendly community just south of Santa Rosa and an hour north of San Francisco. With trees blocking out most of the surrounding suburbs, all you see from the Banquet Center's 125 feet of floor-to-ceiling windows are velvety greens, the occasional golfer, and a duck or two heading for the pond just off the 9th hole.

Yes, only a short stroll from the center lies a calm green pond looking newly transplanted from the English countryside. Complete with weeping willows, waterfowl, and a lacy white gazebo bordered by roses, it's an idyllic setting for exchanging vows. In addition to being very pretty, this waterside spot accommodates almost 300 seated guests, all comfortably facing away from the sun.

Weddings are held year-round in either an afternoon or an evening time slot, but they never overlap. In winter, couples get married inside before an arch and floral displays that the facility sets up. During the warmer months, the bride changes in a room off the Banquet Center, then comes out through double doors along a curving walkway to the gazebo for the service. While the couple poses for pictures afterwards, guests walk up a red carpet into the center, a 3,300-square-foot, airy white hall filled with natural light from the expanse of windows. Everyone enjoys appetizers and drinks in the bar area until the newlyweds are announced and take their place at the head table. Since there are no noise restrictions, you can party until midnight.

With five all-inclusive packages available, your only concern is transportation and, of course, the dress. Catering runs the gamut from a buffet with BBQ chicken and a no-host bar to a sit-down dinner with "duet" entrées like filet mignon and salmon bearnaise accompanied by a hosted full bar. You can add extras like a cappuccino bar with petit fours and chocolate-covered strawberries, but all packages include a DJ and music, a dance floor, invitations, a choice of linen colors and help with planning the affair. In some cases, a wedding night room at a premium local hotel is part of the package.

Wedgewood Banquet Centers, a family-run company with venues throughout California, oversees hundreds of weddings a year. Their experienced and extremely flexible staff is happy to customize their all-inclusive packages to suit your particular needs. For example, they added borscht to a Russian couple's reception menu, and assisted a Vietnamese pair in holding a tea ceremony.

Some couples have released butterflies during the ceremony, while one even rolled their Harley out to the gazebo for photos.

Although Wedgewood Foxtail is popular for weddings, they also host golf tournaments, fundraisers, retirement parties, and civic luncheons. Whatever event you have in mind, you can be confident it will turn out just the way you envisioned it.

CEREMONY CAPACITY: The ceremony area accommodates up to 300 guests; indoors, the Center holds up to 300 seated guests.

EVENT/RECEPTION CAPACITY: The Center holds up to 300 seated or 400 standing guests.

MEETING CAPACITY: The Center accommodates up to 200 guests seated theater-style.

FEES & DEPOSITS: 25% of the estimated event total is required to reserve your date. The next 25% is due 90 days prior to the event and the balance is due 10 days prior. Meals range $19–40/person. Tax, alcohol and a 20% service charge are additional.

AVAILABILITY: Year-round, daily, anytime.

SERVICES/AMENITIES:

Catering: provided, no BYO

Kitchen Facilities: n/a

Tables & Chairs: provided

Linens, Silver, etc.: provided

Restrooms: wheelchair accessible

Dance Floor: yes

Bride's Dressing Area: yes

Meeting Equipment: full range CBA, extra charge

Parking: ample on-site

Accommodations: hotels nearby

Telephone: emergency use only

Outdoor Night Lighting: yes

Outdoor Cooking Facilities: no

Cleanup: provided

View: fairways, pond, mountains

Other: event coordination

RESTRICTIONS:

Alcohol: provided

Smoking: outdoors only

Music: amplified OK

Wheelchair Access: yes

Insurance: not required

Other: no rice, confetti or glitter; no open flames

Want to find more locations and services? Check out our informative website, www.HereComesTheGuide.com.

581

Auberge du Soleil

Luxury Inn & Restaurant

180 Rutherford Hill Road, Rutherford
707/963-1211

www.aubergedusoleil.com
lazimi@aubergedusoleil.com

- Rehearsal Dinners
- Ceremonies
- Wedding Receptions
- Corp. Events/Mtgs.
- Private Parties
- Accommodations

On a Napa hillside, near the Silverado Trail, you'll find the lovely and highly acclaimed Auberge du Soleil. The Mediterranean-style building welcomes guests through a simple, yet refined, garden courtyard, shaded by a canopy of gray olive trees. The beautifully appointed, understated lobby is refreshing in warm earth tones, and gives you a sense of what's to come.

The inn's private dining rooms are at the base of a curved staircase that descends from the lobby. The Cedar Room is the smaller of the two. It's circular, and right in its center, seemingly supporting the ceiling, is a cedar tree trunk which acts as the room's focal point. Light sand-colored walls frame the many French doors and windows that overlook the valley below; original artwork and cozy furnishings lend a fresh contemporary flavor to the room. The wood ceiling and a large stone fireplace make this a very comfortable spot, one where guests can chat or just curl up in front of the fire. The Cedar Room is terrific for smaller gatherings and dinners, and also serves as a cocktail area or bridal suite.

The adjacent Vista Rooms offer valley view dining for larger groups. Everything here is designed to be soothing to the eye: An olive-hued carpet inscribed with an olive branch pattern, stone wall sconces, natural cedar ceiling and soft sand-colored walls combine to make an inviting environment. No matter where you sit, you'll be able to take in glorious panoramic views of the Napa Valley. One mirrored wall is strategically placed to reflect acres of vineyards into the room, and multiple French doors invite diners to amble outside onto the adjacent decks. The Terrace and ceremony deck have unparalleled vistas, and on warm days or evenings can be set up for outdoor receptions with tables and umbrellas. A stone-sculpted fountain is set off to one side of the Terrace, and terracotta pots filled with brilliantly colored annuals are placed around its periphery. A wisteria-entwined trellis at one end of the Terrace offers guests a sheltered spot where they can enjoy hors d'oeuvres and watch a sunset or wedding ceremony. The ceremony deck, which extends out from the Terrace, offers the bride and groom a special spot to take their vows while their lucky guests get to see them, framed by the panorama beyond.

The ambiance here is both warm and *très chic*. For an upscale California-style wedding, the Auberge has few peers.

CEREMONY CAPACITY: The Terrace and Ceremony Deck hold 120 guests.

EVENT/RECEPTION CAPACITY: The Cedar Room holds up to 40 seated guests or 75 standing; the Vista Room I and II, combined, hold 120 seated or standing.

MEETING CAPACITY: There are 4 rooms which hold 10–60 seated guests.

FEES & DEPOSITS: A deposit and signed contract are required to confirm your date. Half the estimated event total is due 60 days prior to the event; the estimated balance is due 7 days prior; any remaining balance is payable upon departure. The facility fee ranges $500–4,000 based on guest count and rooms selected. There is a $500 ceremony fee. Luncheons start at $60/person and dinners at $105/person. Beverages, tax and a 20% service charge are additional.

For business meetings or conferences, a $15/person conference fee applies, which includes coffee and tea service.

AVAILABILITY: Year-round, daily, 6am–midnight. Weddings take place 10am–3pm or 5pm–11pm.

SERVICES/AMENITIES:

Catering: provided, no BYO
Kitchen Facilities: n/a
Tables & Chairs: provided
Linens, Silver, etc.: provided
Restrooms: wheelchair accessible
Dance Floor: yes
Bride's & Groom's Dressing Area: CBA
Meeting Equipment: CBA

Parking: valet
Accommodations: 52 guestrooms and suites
Telephone: pay phone
Outdoor Night Lighting: yes
Outdoor Cooking Facilities: no
Cleanup: provided
View: panorama of Napa Valley and vineyards

RESTRICTIONS:

Alcohol: provided, no BYO
Smoking: area CBA
Music: amplified OK with approval

Wheelchair Access: elevator
Insurance: not required

Fountaingrove Golf and Athletic Club

Private Country Club

1525 Fountaingrove Parkway, Santa Rosa
707/521-3224
www.fountaingrovegolf.com
jthomas@fountaingrovegolf.com

● Rehearsal Dinners	● Corp. Events/Mtgs.
● Ceremonies	● Private Parties
● Wedding Receptions	Accommodations

More than a century ago, the mystic theologian and poet Thomas Lake Harris and his disciple, Kanaya Nagasawa, arrived in the beautiful Santa Rosa Valley and proclaimed it the perfect place to create an ideal society. Amidst the fertile, unspoiled countryside, the pair of dreamers founded one of the first communal settlements and successful wineries in California, and named it Fountaingrove Ranch.

Nagasawa eventually inherited the ranch and winery and became an expert vintner. He answered to the title of "Baron" or "Prince," and lived at the ranch until he died in 1934 at the ripe age of 82. During his colorful life Nagasawa gained recognition from both the Japanese and American governments for his contributions to the community and the art of viticulture.

From its roots as a utopian commune, Fountaingrove Ranch evolved into its current incarnation—an upscale planned community, where a few traces of Harris's quixotic experiment still remain, such as the circa-1899 Round Barn that was built at Kanaya Nagasawa's behest.

Another place that bears testament to Nagasawa's importance in the Sonoma County wine country is the Fountaingrove Golf and Athletic Club, a primary locale for special events. The three-story clubhouse features a sloped tile roof atop off-white walls trimmed in wood and stone. The timeless grace of this simple façade is complemented by a contemporary American interior. Celebrations are held in the ballroom on the second floor. A high ceiling creates an open, airy feeling; walls of windows bring in lots of sunlight and a terrific view of the club's green fairways and rolling, oak-covered hills both near and far. A wraparound terrace lets guests step outside for a closer look. Another plus: a classically trained and award-winning chef who'll customize your event menu, focusing on the freshest local ingredients.

With its bucolic setting, outdoor wedding ceremonies are the norm at Fountaingrove (although during inclement weather, they can be held in one half of the ballroom). The most popular site is the Wedding Deck, an oak-shaded terrace with a wooden gazebo, conveniently situated across from the clubhouse. From here, you have a magnificent vista of Fountaingrove's 170 picturesque acres, strewn with ponds, streams and granite boulders that create a natural haven for the native wildlife. It's not unusual to spy deer and wild turkeys come to feed, a flock of geese taking flight, and spectacular sunsets bursting forth across the mountainous horizon.

If you've invited just a handful of guests to witness your ceremony, then pledge your vows in the garden at the front of the clubhouse. Nestled in its own grove of trees, this is an enchanting spot and a lovely tribute to a man who believed that humans could create their own heaven on earth. When you're standing in this little piece of paradise, you just might believe it, too.

CEREMONY CAPACITY: The site accommodates 200 seated guests indoors or outdoors.

EVENT/RECEPTION & MEETING CAPACITY: Fountaingrove holds 250 seated and 350 standing.

FEES & DEPOSITS: A $2,500 deposit is required to reserve your date. The balance is due 3 days prior to the event. Rental fees for weddings range $1,000–5,000 depending on the space rented. Meals range $35–50/person and up. Tax, alcohol and a 20% service charge are additional.

AVAILABILITY: Year-round, Tuesday–Sunday.

SERVICES/AMENITIES:

Catering: provided
Kitchen Facilities: n/a
Tables & Chairs: provided
Linens, Silver, etc.: provided
Restrooms: wheelchair accessible
Dance Floor: patio or deck, rental CBA
Bride's Dressing Area: yes
Meeting Equipment: some provided, CBA

Parking: spacious lot
Accommodations: no guestrooms
Telephone: guest phone
Outdoor Night Lighting: yes
Outdoor Cooking Facilities: no
Cleanup: provided
View: forest, fairways, pond
Other: event coordination

RESTRICTIONS:

Alcohol: provided or BYO wine with corkage fee
Smoking: outdoors only
Music: amplified OK

Wheelchair Access: yes
Insurance: not required

Hilton Sonoma Wine Country

Hotel

3555 Round Barn Boulevard, Santa Rosa
707/569-5529
www.hiltonsonomahotel.com
salesadmin@hiltonsonoma.com

- Rehearsal Dinners
- Ceremonies
- Wedding Receptions
- Corp. Events/Mtgs.
- Private Parties
- Accommodations

Set on a knoll above Santa Rosa, this hotel has the best view in town. The vista takes in the city's landmark red Round Barn, as well as much of Santa Rosa to the south and the high hills that form its eastern limits. Although it's a 250-room facility with several wings, the Hilton's architecture successfully evokes a more intimate feeling. The low-key design of wooden buildings, spread out over a series of terraces and connected by staircases and arcades, creates a casual, resort-like ambiance.

Because the hotel is also centrally located in the Wine Country—only minutes away from Dry Creek's famous Zinfandels or the Russian River's sparkling champagnes—it's a great place for an extended stay with family and friends. Rooms have either king or double-queen beds and charming bay windows. When your guests aren't off wine tasting or sightseeing, they'll probably spend most of their time at the large swimming pool, surrounded by lawns and shade trees. (Also, the bar here is very sleek and sophisticated, and is often itself a destination for Santa Rosans out for a night on the town.)

As you would expect, the Hilton offers a variety of event spaces, including three ballrooms: the 3,000-square-foot Golden Gate; the 2,600-square-foot Nagasawa (which has a lobby); and the Sonoma, easily the most popular with its steeply sloping ceiling of dark knotty pine and adjoining terrace.

The terrace, sheltered under an elaborate trellis of crisscrossing fir beams, is available year-round thanks to outdoor heaters and windshields. A multitude of chairs and curtained couches encourages socializing, and the indoor/outdoor combination of terrace and ballroom creates an easy flow. Right next to the terrace is a lawn that can host a small wedding and looks out over the hotel's sweeping city view. A second al fresco ceremony site is on a sloping lawn near the swimming pool.

The Hilton's pricing is very competitive, so the high caliber of their food comes as a nice surprise. Couples who have their reception here are invariably impressed with the cuisine and the service, and give both excellent reviews. Some brides have reported that their guests raved about their dining experience for months after the wedding.

With thirteen acres of redwood and eucalyptus-dotted grounds, the Hilton Sonoma has created an oasis-like setting. You and your guests will appreciate the refreshing feeling of being a bit above and away from it all, even in the midst of Wine Country's biggest city.

CEREMONY & EVENT/RECEPTION CAPACITY: Both indoor and outdoor spaces hold up to 250 seated or 350 standing guests in one area.

MEETING CAPACITY: Several spaces are available which hold 20–250 seated guests.

FEES & DEPOSITS: A $1,500 deposit is required to reserve your date. The balance is due 10 working days prior to the event. Rental fees range $250–2,500 depending on day, time and season of the event. Meals range $25–85/person. Tax, alcohol and a 21% service charge are additional.

AVAILABILITY: Year-round, daily, anytime.

SERVICES/AMENITIES:

Catering: provided
Kitchen Facilities: n/a
Tables & Chairs: provided
Linens, Silver, etc.: provided
Restrooms: wheelchair accessible
Dance Floor: yes
Bride's Dressing Area: yes
Meeting Equipment: provided

Parking: large lot, complimentary self-parking
Accommodations: 250 guestrooms
Telephone: house phone
Outdoor Night Lighting: CBA
Outdoor Cooking Facilities: BBQ CBA
Cleanup: provided
View: hills, forest, cityscape, grounds
Other: event coordination, AV equipment, assistance with rentals

RESTRICTIONS:

Alcohol: provided
Smoking: outdoors only
Music: amplified OK

Wheelchair Access: yes
Insurance: required

This is important! Tell locations you're reading HERE COMES THE GUIDE and ask if our information is still current.

Oakmont Golf Club

Golf Course and Clubhouse

7035 Oakmont Drive, Santa Rosa
707/537-3671
www.oakmontgc.com
tina@oakmontgc.com

● Rehearsal Dinners	● Corp. Events/Mtgs.
● Ceremonies	● Private Parties
● Wedding Receptions	Accommodations

Located in the heart of the Wine Country, the Oakmont Golf Club is just one hour north of San Francisco and ten minutes from downtown Santa Rosa. Nestled under weeping willows and majestic oaks, it offers panoramic views of the Mayacama Mountains and the entire Sonoma Valley.

This restaurant and banquet facility has developed a dedicated clientele that appreciates not just the lovely setting, but the event spaces and affordable cuisine as well. The large, brightly lit banquet room can be used in its entirety or divided into a series of smaller rooms. Floor-to-ceiling windows frame expansive views of Oakmont's award-winning golf course and the surrounding mountains. Just outside, a spacious terrace overlooking the 18th green is a refreshing spot for a summer cocktail reception.

The venue's two ceremony sites take advantage of the beautiful scenery. The first is the banquet room terrace, which is accessed by three double doors. On a sunny day you can sit beneath umbrellas and just enjoy the view of Mt. Hood and the Mayacamas Mountains, as well as the golf course's groves of mature firs, sycamores, maples and redwoods.

The second option is a tree-and-grass-fringed pond about 250 yards from the clubhouse. Guests are seated under shade trees facing the pond and waterfall, which serve as a marvelous backdrop during the ceremony. A storybook bridge beneath a canopy of tall willows spans the pond and invites post-ceremony photos.

The club's impressive bar is right down the hallway from the banquet room, and rewards with huge picture windows that look out onto the fairways and peaks.

Like the neighborhood around it, the Oakmont Golf Club has a mellow, reassured feel to it. Years of experience in dealing ably and amiably with people's expectations have made it a local favorite.

CEREMONY & MEETING CAPACITY: The site accommodates 300 guests indoors or outdoors.

EVENT/RECEPTION CAPACITY: The site holds up to 250 seated or 300 standing guests indoors or outdoors.

FEES & DEPOSITS: A $1,500 deposit is required to reserve your date. Rental fees start at $250, and vary depending on the day and time of year. Meals range $29–59/person. Tax, alcohol and a 20% service charge are additional.

AVAILABILITY: Year-round, daily, 6am–midnight (or later with special arrangements).

SERVICES/AMENITIES:

Catering: provided
Kitchen Facilities: n/a
Tables & Chairs: provided
Linens, Silver, etc.: provided
Restrooms: wheelchair accessible
Dance Floor: yes
Bride's Dressing Area: yes
Meeting Equipment: some provided, more CBA

Parking: ample on-site
Accommodations: no guestrooms
Telephone: guest phone
Outdoor Night Lighting: yes
Outdoor Cooking Facilities: BBQ on site
Cleanup: provided
View: mountains, fairways, hills, fountain, lake
Other: event coordination

RESTRICTIONS:

Alcohol: provided or BYO with corkage fee
Smoking: outdoors only
Music: amplified OK with volume restrictions

Wheelchair Access: yes
Insurance: not required

Paradise Ridge Winery

Winery

4545 Thomas Lake Harris Drive, Santa Rosa
707/528-9463
www.prwinery.com
events@prwinery.com

●	Rehearsal Dinners	●	Corp. Events/Mtgs.
●	Ceremonies	●	Private Parties
●	Wedding Receptions		Accommodations

So sweeping is the view from the western veranda at the Paradise Ridge Winery that a bride can get an inkling of what it's like to be an eagle, suspended above hillside vineyards and oak groves, gazing for miles over the Russian River Valley. Yet the winery is just minutes from downtown Santa Rosa in the heart of Sonoma County wine country. Its proximity to the city, as well as its spectacular scenery, draws locals who flock here for sunset wine tasting on the veranda. Wedding parties come to the 156-acre family-run estate, too, and not just for the view. Owners Walter Byck and the late Marijke Byck-Hoenselaars combined the European traditions of Marijke's Dutch homeland with their own artistic tastes to create a unique setting for celebrations.

The centerpiece of the winery is a spacious, newly remodeled two-story building whose stucco walls, loggia, and mahogany veranda echo early California architecture. Built for special events, it houses the Vineroom (the estate's tasting room), the champagne cellar, and a professional catering kitchen. Guests drive up to the winery through pastures, vineyards, and the unique four-acre "Marijke's Grove" of artwork set among the oaks (also a potential ceremony site). They then gather on the covered veranda before being seated for the ceremony on the Poetry Terrace, a terracotta patio with two bridal stages—and a spectacular wine country vista.

A separate deluxe changing room is reserved for the bride and her entourage, so they can relax and sip champagne before the big moment. The bride makes her grand entry through the Vineroom's double doors onto the veranda, and then descends eight steps to the Poetry Terrace, which is partially shaded by colorful crepe myrtle trees. The groom makes his own entrance from the loggia, because the owners feel it's his special day, too.

After the ceremony, guests mingle on the Poetry Terrace and enjoy estate-bottled wines, champagne and hors d'oeuvres. As dusk descends, twinkle lights add a romantic touch. When it's time for the reception, the doors to the Vineroom are thrown open. An oversized wood-burning fireplace and dramatic Italian chandeliers evoke Old World charm, and floor-to-ceiling windows capture magnificent sunsets over a vineyard panorama. At night, ambient lighting casts a honeyed glow over the room. If you're hosting a large gala, additional tables can be placed on the wraparound veranda, which shares an indoor/outdoor bar with the Vineroom. Wedding parties usually dance on the Vineroom's oak floor, but you can also set up a band on the Poetry Terrace. With the city lights winking in the distance and the moon cresting over the hillside, it's absolutely glorious.

While most couples prefer a sunset wedding during the warmer months, winter weddings here are also lovely. The Champagne Cellar is a novel option for an intimate ceremony in front of the grand, wood-burning fireplace. Your caterer, selected from the winery's preferred list, will help you create delicious pairings from the estate's vintages.

At the close of the festivities, friends and family gather in the winery's European-style courtyard for a traditional send-off of the newlyweds, whose marriage has been magnificently launched at this sophisticated venue.

CEREMONY CAPACITY: The Poetry Terrace holds 250 seated; the Champagne Cellar, 175.

EVENT/RECEPTION CAPACITY: The winery holds 250 seated or 250 standing guests indoors, and 110–250 seated or 250 standing outdoors.

MEETING CAPACITY: Several spaces accommodate 40–250 seated guests.

FEES & DEPOSITS: Half of the rental fee is required to confirm your date. The rental balance is due 4 months prior to the event; a beverage deposit and a refundable $500 security deposit are due 30 days prior. The rental fee ranges $3,500–9,500 depending on guest count and day and time of event. Wine, champagne and beer are charged on consumption, with the estimated total payable 30 days in advance. Note that on Friday and Sunday, and January–April, the facility offers lower pricing. For business meetings or seminars on other days, the rental fee varies depending on guest count, day of week and time of day. Weekday minimums start at $700, call for details.

AVAILABILITY: Year-round, daily. Special events and business functions, 8am–midnight.

SERVICES/AMENITIES:

Catering: select from list
Kitchen Facilities: fully equipped
Tables & Chairs: provided
Linens, Silver, etc.: through caterer and winery
Restrooms: wheelchair accessible
Dance Floor: wood floor/terrace
Bride's Dressing Area: yes
Meeting Equipment: podium, microphone, full audio system, screen

Parking: ample on-site, complimentary
Accommodations: no guestrooms
Telephone: courtesy phone
Outdoor Night Lighting: yes
Outdoor Cooking Facilities: no
Cleanup: caterer and facility
View: vineyards and Russian River Valley, panoramic west-facing sunset views

RESTRICTIONS:

Alcohol: wine, beer and champagne provided
Smoking: designated area outdoors
Music: amplified OK with volume limits, outside until 10:30pm

Wheelchair Access: yes
Insurance: additional liability required
Other: no confetti, glitter, rice, birdseed, fresh flower petals or bubbles; children must be supervised

Vintners Inn

Restaurant and Hotel

4350 Barnes Road, Santa Rosa
707/566-2619

www.vintnersinn.com
creynolds@vintnersinn.com

- Rehearsal Dinners
- Ceremonies
- Wedding Receptions
- Corp. Events/Mtgs.
- Private Parties
- Accommodations

Stepping onto the grounds of this 92-acre estate is a little like going through the proverbial looking glass—you're just a few minutes north of bustling Santa Rosa, but you appear to have entered a small village in Tuscany. Suddenly you're enveloped by vineyards, flowerbeds, courtyards, and fountains in a tranquil setting artfully designed to enhance peace of mind.

A grand bell tower and French fountain mark the entrance to Vintners Inn Event Center, created especially with weddings in mind. The interior features a beautifully detailed ceiling, an abundance of windows, wood and stone surfaces, vibrant wall coverings and rich fabric furnishings. Outdoor terraces are surrounded by rows of grapevines, gardens, orchards and a multitude of flowers. An expansive prefunction area doubles as a wedding chapel for indoor ceremonies. Mirrored stone alcoves on either side of the room are filled with candles and flowers, adding warmth and beauty to the space. When the weather is balmy, however, most couples prefer to tie the knot under the Wedding Pavilion, a gorgeous ceremony spot at the edge of a vineyard. A simple structure of four tall white columns topped by a wooden trellis frames the leafy vineyard backdrop and provides shade as you say your vows. Guests enjoy this quintessential Wine Country tableau from their seats on the adjacent lawn.

The *pièce de résistance* of the center is the Rose Ballroom, a 3,200-square-foot space with walls of windows overlooking the gardens. The richly decorated room features a fifteen-foot ceiling, impressive iron chandeliers and plush Axminster carpeting thoughout. It's also equipped with state-of-the-art audiovisual systems, including theater-sized screens that automatically drop down for a DVD or video presentation. The Ballroom opens onto a trellised veranda and stone fireplace, flanked by gardens and lawn.

The estate is also home to the nationally renowned restaurant, John Ash & Co., and the deluxe, Four-Diamond Vintners Inn, a 44-room boutique hotel housed in three separate villas. A short stroll across manicured lawns and tile pathways takes you from restaurant to hotel, and gives you a sense of just how close you are to some of the most important things in life: good food and wine, a soft (and elegant) place to lay your head at night, and a tangible connection to nature. Walk out of your guestroom and in one minute you can be standing in the vineyards or sitting on the restaurant's wisteria-draped rear terrace, touching the tendrils of grapevines just inches away.

The restaurant, which receives the *Wine Spectator's* Best of Award of Excellence year after year, showcases California cuisine. Its menu changes seasonally to take advantage of fresh, locally grown foods, and dishes are paired with an award-winning wine list featuring some 600 wines. Because the cuisine is such an integral part of this venue's appeal, bridal couples work with the chef to select a multicourse menu and design their own wedding cake. Hors d'oeuvre choices might include Sonoma Liberty Duck Spring Rolls and Housemade Porcini Ravioli, while entrées range from Grilled Filet of Beef in Zinfandel reduction sauce to California Sea Bass in raspberry beurre blanc.

Many guests want to fully experience the Wine Country, and plan an overnight stay at the inn. Nearby attractions include more than 100 Sonoma County wineries, hot-air balloon tours, golf, tennis, fishing, and even whale-watching and kayaking on the coast. In addition, a day spa and pool are opening on site in Fall 2012, making a visit here profoundly satisfying to all the senses.

CEREMONY & EVENT/RECEPTION CAPACITY: The Event Center holds up to 300 seated or 500 standing guests, indoors or outdoors.

MEETING CAPACITY: The Event Center holds up to 240 guests, seated conference-style.

FEES & DEPOSITS: 50% of the estimated event total is required to reserve your date. The balance is due 60 days prior to the event. Any remaining balance is due at the conclusion of the event. Rental fees range $3,500–8,500 depending on space rented and guest count. Meals start at $85/person. Tax, alcohol and a 20% service charge are additional. Wedding cake is included in the per-person price.

AVAILABILITY: Year-round, daily, 9am–midnight.

SERVICES/AMENITIES:

Catering: provided
Kitchen Facilities: full kitchen
Tables & Chairs: provided
Linens, Silver, etc.: provided
Restrooms: wheelchair accessible
Dance Floor: provided
Bride's Dressing Area: yes
Meeting Equipment: full range CBA

Parking: large lot, valet available
Accommodations: 44 guestrooms
Telephone: house phone
Outdoor Night Lighting: yes
Outdoor Cooking Facilities: BBQ CBA
Cleanup: provided
View: vineyards, gardens, landscaped grounds

RESTRICTIONS:

Alcohol: provided or BYO with corkage fee
Smoking: outdoors only
Music: amplified OK with restrictions

Wheelchair Access: yes
Insurance: not required

Overwhelmed? Use the search criteria on www.HereComesTheGuide.com to narrow down your choices.

593

Sova Gardens

Garden and Event Facility

5186 South Gravenstein Highway, Sebastopol
707/795-4747
www.sovagardens.com
information@sovagardens.com

● Rehearsal Dinners	● Corp. Events/Mtgs.
● Ceremonies	● Private Parties
● Wedding Receptions	Accommodations

It would take a pleasurable lifetime to discover all of the treasures hidden alongside Sonoma County's country lanes—the tucked away redwood groves, the small farms growing heirloom vegetables, the quiet studios of hardworking artists. One of those gems is Sova Gardens, a wedding venue that combines the best of indoor and outdoor amenities. Although it's located just yards off the highway to Sebastopol, you'd be hard pressed to spot it along the road. When you do find it, you'll be pleased you did.

Sova's wide lawns and rustic-style structures create a relaxed country feel. The first buildings that catch your eye are the water tower and the yellow-shingled, two-story 1906 farmhouse beside it. Faithfully and beautifully restored, the four-bedroom house—right next to the ceremony site—is a lovely backdrop for photos.

Sova's long main facility and the place where most people enter the venue is called the Tavern Building. Converted from an early 20th-century chicken coop, it's a combination banquet and reception hall, club, lounge and bar (featuring an early 1900s bar from the old Santa Rosa Hotel). With its many windows, hardwood floors, red curtains, goldenrod walls and dark furniture, the Tavern is both an excellent stand-alone indoor space for winter ceremonies, and a welcoming retreat where guests can mingle and rest on warm days. (The commercial kitchen here is like catnip to local caterers—all they have to bring is the food!)

An arbor festooned with small lights extends from one end of the Tavern Building and looks out over the smaller of the site's two lawns as well as a grove of fragrant redwoods. Beyond, Sova's 10,000-square-foot lawn seems to extend forever, sloping gently from the Tavern Building toward a line of ornamental trees and rose-garlanded wooden fences. The lawn is intensely green—almost emerald—and its spaciousness makes it easy for guests to circulate and socialize. A three-tiered fountain splashes at its exact center, and potted flowers and ornamental palms flank it almost everywhere. The view extends to distant pastures, farm buildings and houses, adding to the very bucolic ambiance.

Photographers love Sova. One great photo op is the waterwheel at the base of the tower. With its lush pond, filled with reeds and blooming plants, the site is like a grand wishing well. Other choice spots for photos are under the redwoods, next to a rose garden, by the centerpiece fountain, in a rustic barn or at the edge of the smaller lawn overlooking a dance pavilion. The pavilion, easily accessed by a ramp or stairway, is bounded by ornamental trees, and blooms including dazzling sunflowers and colorful vines.

Sova Gardens has an easygoing rural vibe, with all of the openness, informality and charm a bride might want as she imagines her perfect country wedding day.

CEREMONY & EVENT/RECEPTION CAPACITY: The site holds 100 seated or 150 standing guests indoors and 250 seated or 400 standing outdoors.

MEETING CAPACITY: Meeting spaces accommodate 250 seated guests.

FEES & DEPOSITS: 50% of the total event cost is a nonrefundable deposit required to reserve your date. The balance is due 90 days prior to the event. Rental fees range $500–4,500 and vary depending on the time and date of the event and the space selected. Meals start at $50/person. Tax, alcohol and a 21% service charge are additional. All-inclusive wedding packages are available, call or email for details.

AVAILABILITY: Year-round, daily. Outdoor events must conclude by 9pm.

SERVICES/AMENITIES:

Catering: provided or BYO
Kitchen Facilities: fully equipped
Tables & Chairs: provided
Linens, Silver, etc.: through caterer
Restrooms: not wheelchair accessible
Dance Floor: provided
Bride's Dressing Area: yes
Meeting Equipment: CBA
Other: picnic area, complimentary event coordination

Parking: large lot
Accommodations: no guestrooms
Telephone: emergency use only
Outdoor Night Lighting: provided
Outdoor Cooking Facilities: BBQ on site
Cleanup: provided
View: gardens, landscaped grounds, pond, fountain, meadow

RESTRICTIONS:

Alcohol: provided or BYO
Smoking: allowed outdoors only
Music: amplified OK

Wheelchair Access: yes
Insurance: liability required

Vine Hill House

Private Guest House and Gardens

3601 Vine Hill Road. Sebastopol
888/889-0929

www.vinehillhouse.com
info@vinehillhouse.com

- Rehearsal Dinners
- Ceremonies
- Wedding Receptions
- Corp. Events/Mtgs.
- Private Parties
- Accommodations

It takes practically no time at all for Vine Hill House to rejuvenate the flagging spirit and lower the blood pressure of anyone beleaguered by city stresses. As you head through the Russian River Valley on a picturesque two-lane, country highway, and up the hill through apple orchards and vineyards, you can't help but wonder what awaits you. By the time you've reached the guest house and gardens, the fragrant air and country quiet have already begun to smooth your rough edges.

Enter through a small gate to the left of the guest house and into the garden, and any remaining tenseness melts away. What you see before you is a landscape of uncommon beauty. Set on a slight rise, the garden has an almost 360-degree view of the surrounding hills, covered with apple orchards and row upon perfect row of premium-quality grapevines. You can see distant Mount St. Helena to the north and the coastal mountain range stretching south.

Fortunately for you, this breathtaking setting can be the backdrop for your celebration. You won't need much in the way of decoration, since nature's already done such a great job. And what nature hasn't done, owners Dan and Jan O'Connell have. The handsomely landscaped grounds are tidy and well-groomed: One part of the garden is covered with plush lawns bordered by flowerbeds, densely planted with brightly hued blooms; another section is planted with a small grove of firs, redwoods, oaks and madrones.

Weddings in this little bit of heaven are particularly sweet. The bride makes her entrance either from the guest house or through the entry gate, and walks along the garden path to a peaceful ceremonial lawn. Seated guests have the dual pleasure of watching the ceremony and taking in the spectacular view. For receptions, the manicured lawn is turned into an al fresco dining room, filled with linen-clad tables shaded by market umbrellas. No matter where you sit, you're treated to an eyeful of rolling hills, vineyards and endless sky. Later on, dance under stars and stately oak trees, where there's ample room for a band or DJ. And if the weather becomes uncooperative, tents or canopies are provided so that you don't have to worry about the elements.

Vine Hill House sits in the center of the gardens, and is a real charmer. Built in the late 1800s, the house was originally a two-story stagecoach stop, located further down the hill. Restored as a classic single-story, 1920s-style cottage around 80 years ago, it was relocated up the hill in 1957 to its present-day setting. The updated, fully furnished house is perfect for overnight stays, with a large sunny kitchen, living room, and two bedrooms with private bathrooms. Each sunlit room has windows overlooking gardens, vineyards or orchards. For those who really want to unwind, there's even an outdoor spa. During events the bridal party has exclusive use of the guesthouse to get ready, or to just relax. The house and gardens are also great for corporate meetings, picnics, nonprofit events, company seminars or retreats.

This is a place where you and your guests can slow down, relax and take in the changing landscape: blossoming apple trees and fields of mustard flowers in the spring; warm breezes and the sounds of frogs and crickets in summer; a blaze of color and the excitement of the annual harvest and crush in the fall. The beauty here is compelling, and we think you'll be more than a little tempted to stay overnight to prolong your experience.

CEREMONY, EVENT/RECEPTION & MEETING CAPACITY: Outdoors, the site accommodates up to 225 guests; indoors, 20 guests.

FEES & DEPOSITS: A nonrefundable deposit of $2,800 and the signed contract are required to reserve your date. The balance is required 3 months prior to the event. For a 6-hour wedding, fees range $4,495–7,995 April–November. Overtime is $600/hour. Overnight stays in the guest house run $340–385/night. Elopement, intimate and complete event packages are available; call for more detailed information.

For meetings and nonprofit events, call for more detailed information.

AVAILABILITY: Outdoor events, April 1–November 30, 10am–10pm.

SERVICES/AMENITIES:

Catering: select from list
Kitchen Facilities: fully equipped and prep area
Tables & Chairs: provided, plus market umbrellas
Linens, Silver, etc.: CBA, extra charge
Restrooms: wheelchair accessible
Dance Floor: yes
Bride's Dressing Area: yes
Meeting Equipment: provided
Other: tents/canopies can be arranged; heaters provided

Parking: ample on-site
Accommodations: guesthouse, sleeps 6
Telephone: house phone, internet access
Outdoor Night Lighting: yes
Outdoor Cooking Facilities: BBQ, caterer's kitchen facility
Cleanup: caterer
View: vineyards, apple orchards, Sonoma hills

RESTRICTIONS:

Alcohol: BYO, no corkage fees
Smoking: outdoors, designated areas only
Music: amplified OK with volume restrictions

Wheelchair Access: yes
Insurance: certificate required

Gloria Ferrer Caves & Vineyards

Winery

23555 Highway 121, Sonoma
707/996-7256 x1939
www.gloriaferrer.com
weddings@gloriaferrer.com

- Rehearsal Dinners
- Ceremonies
- Wedding Receptions
- Corp. Events/Mtgs.
- Private Parties
- Accommodations

You can find this winery atop a gentle slope in the Sonoma Carneros area by driving up the long private entry road through picturesque rolling hills dotted with vineyards. At the crest, you'll spy Gloria Ferrer Caves & Vineyards, a Spanish-style hacienda offering Old World hospitality. The main building is large and impressive, with a red-tile roof and wide entry steps.

Inside, the tasting room—called the Sala de Catadores—is a warm and inviting space highlighted by an attractive mahogany bar and fireplace of matching wood and tile. Adjoining the Sala is the aptly named Vista Terrace, a versatile and serene locale that takes full advantage of the panoramic view of Sonoma Valley and the Gloria Ferrer vineyards below. Refreshed by balmy breezes, this is a lovely place for wine tasting, mingling during your social hour, or staging a wedding ceremony.

Another sublime spot for saying "I Do" is beneath a long arbor in front of the stairs at the winery entrance. Imposing Mediterranean-inspired columns support a wooden trellis entwined with Pinot grapevines. The couple weds at one end of the arbor, with the cultivated hills and fields in the background, while guests lounge comfortably beneath the arbor's dappled shade. Alternatively, dress up the arbor with banquet tables laden with hearty local fare and Gloria Ferrer bubbly, and enjoy a delightful al fresco luncheon.

If you prefer a more traditional setting for a rehearsal dinner or corporate party, then consider the Executive Dining Room. Rich mahogany wood accents add elegance to the intimate space and windows look out onto a colorfully landscaped promenade. Doors open from the dining room onto the Cave Overlook, a broad balcony that offers an up-close look into the winery's Main Cave. Gloria Ferrer is famous for their man-made underground caves, where their sparkling and still wines are kept naturally cool without the need for mechanical refrigeration. This provocative peek into the subterranean world of bottles and barrels lends an authentic wine-country atmosphere to your celebration.

The Gloria Ferrer portfolio has been praised by many, including *Wine Spectator* magazine who called their sparkling wines "some of California's best." Getting to sample this renowned bubbly is just one more benefit of getting married here. With winemaking traditions that stretch back to

18th-century Spain, the Ferrer family expanded their offerings in 1991 to include premium quality estate Pinot Noir and Chardonnay varietal wines. The knowledgeable staff will guide you in selecting just the right pairings for your private event.

This winery is an off-the-beaten-path, very private getaway for any special occasion.

CEREMONY CAPACITY: The Vista Terrace or Tasting Room (Sala de Catadores) can accommodate up to 120 seated or standing guests.

EVENT/RECEPTION CAPACITY: The Tasting Room (Sala de Catadores) holds up to 120 for a reception.

MEETING CAPACITY: The Executive Dining Room seats up to 45 guests for lunch or meetings and the outdoor arbor seats up to 120.

FEES & DEPOSITS: 50% of the rental fee is required as a nonrefundable deposit to reserve your date; the balance is due 60 days prior to the event. Wine fees are payable the day of the event. Rental fees range $3,500–5,500 depending on guest count. The wine fee is a required 1–4-case minimum purchase (based on guest count). Additional wine may be purchased by the bottle; call for current prices. Tax is additional.

AVAILABILITY: Year-round. Weddings held Saturday and Sunday evenings. Private parties held daily, daytime and evenings.

SERVICES/AMENITIES:

Catering: select from preferred list
Kitchen Facilities: ample
Tables & Chairs: up to 120 provided
Linens, Silver, etc.: BYO
Restrooms: wheelchair accessible
Dance Floor: provided
Bride's Dressing Area: yes
Meeting Equipment: CBA

Parking: large lot
Accommodations: no guestrooms
Telephone: house phone
Outdoor Night Lighting: limited
Outdoor Cooking Facilities: no
Cleanup: caterer
View: vineyards and surrounding foothills
Other: event coordinator

RESTRICTIONS:

Alcohol: wine and champagne provided
Smoking: designated outdoor areas only
Music: amplified OK inside only

Wheelchair Access: yes
Insurance: liability certificate required

The professionals in the back of this book are the best in the business. How do we know? Read page 701.

Nicholson Ranch Winery

Winery

Address withheld to ensure privacy. Sonoma
707/793-9645, Park Avenue Catering
www.parkavecater.com
sales@parkavecater.com

- Rehearsal Dinners
- Ceremonies
- Wedding Receptions
- Corp. Events/Mtgs.
- Private Parties
- Accommodations

A wedding is about to begin at Nicholson Ranch. Guests arriving at the hilltop winery assemble in its Fountain Courtyard. Off to their left, a lily-speckled pond and distant waterfall glitter in the afternoon sun. While everyone waits in anticipation, the bride and her bridesmaids are upstairs in the winery's Bombay Room, putting the finishing flourishes on their ensembles. Theirs is a calming view of the valley's ancient live oaks, as they fan out over the tawny grasses. The groom and his men, gathered on the Fireside Terrace (around the corner and out of view of the Courtyard), are perhaps contemplating how nice it will be to sample the product of the grapevines that trace the contours of nearby hills.

When it's time for the ceremony, guests are escorted to their seats, facing the courtyard's ten-foot-wide, hand-carved stone fountain. The band strikes up the wedding march, while the bride joins her groom in front of the fountain. After the knot is tied, guests are invited to the wine caves below the winery for preliminary toasts and tasty hors d'oeuvres. Cool stone walls and oak wine barrels line the two long caves, one of which ends at the Great Room. Bejeweled by four stained-glass windows, framed by stone pillars, this space is well suited for serving wine and mingling. Returning to the courtyard, guests find it all set for dinner and dancing.

At some point, the bridal party might steal away for a photo op at Soc's Dock—a small Grecian-columned platform that overlooks the pond. The "Soc" of the dock is Socrates Nicholson, a first-generation Greek-American who bought this 160-acre ranch in 1962.

His daughter, Ramona Nicholson, is the winery's mastermind and visionary. She designed the buildings to be reminiscent of early-California architecture and to fit into the landscape: Thick adobe-like walls are finished with a French lime technique that creates subtle earthen tones, which blend in with the surrounding hills. The variegated slate roof has a deep overhang for afternoon shade, and also tends to fade into the background. Salvaged first-growth redwood was used for the lintels, shutters and trellises—like the trellis that covers the Fireside Terrace.

The Terrace is a wonderful gathering place, even during the cooler months, thanks to a double-sided fireplace. One side warms those enjoying the crisp outdoor air; the other side warms the Vintner's Room, where a soaring tongue-and-groove fir ceiling steals the show. Simple, elegant wrought-iron chandeliers light the room, and glass doors galore let in the views. The Vintner's Room would be our choice for a smaller wedding or the cake cutting. When not in use for the crush, the winery's tank room is available for large indoor receptions. With the stainless steel wine tanks moved to the side, the space is nearly 100 feet long. A balcony along one end is perfect for a live band and wine-enhanced toasts.

When all's said and done, the newlyweds can slip back upstairs to the Bombay Room and spend their wedding night in its cushy four-poster bed. Awakening the next morning, with a glorious wedding behind them and the beauty of Nicholson Ranch all around, they know their marriage is off to an auspicious beginning.

CEREMONY & MEETING CAPACITY: The Fountain Courtyard or Lakeside Meadow can accommodate up to 150 seated guests. The Great Room seats up to 18 guests, the Vintner's Room accommodates up to 70 seated guests.

EVENT/RECEPTION CAPACITY: The Fountain Courtyard holds up to 175 seated or 250 standing guests. Indoors, the Winery seats up to 85 guests in the Vintner's Room and 18 guests in the Great Room.

FEES & DEPOSITS: A 50% deposit is required to reserve your date. The balance is due 30 days prior to the event. Rental fees range $1,000–10,000 depending on space rented. Meals range $30–75/person. Tax, wine and service charges are additional. Setup and breakdown fees apply. Security and liability insurance are additional. Call for details.

AVAILABILITY: Year-round, daily, 10am–midnight.

SERVICES/AMENITIES:
Catering: provided by *Park Avenue Catering*
Kitchen Facilities: n/a
Tables & Chairs: provided for up to 135 guests
Linens, Silver, etc.: through caterer
Restrooms: wheelchair accessible
Dance Floor: n/a
Bride's Dressing Area: yes
Meeting Equipment: CBA, extra charge

Parking: ample on-site
Accommodations: honeymoon suite
Telephone: house phone
Outdoor Night Lighting: some
Outdoor Cooking Facilities: CBA
Cleanup: caterer
View: vineyards, lake and surrounding foothills
Other: event coordination, wireless internet access

RESTRICTIONS:
Alcohol: wine, sparkling wine and beer only
Smoking: not allowed
Music: amplified OK

Wheelchair Access: yes
Insurance: liability required

Viansa Winery & Vineyards

Winery

25200 Arnold Drive, Sonoma
707/935-2728
www.viansa.com
events@viansa.com

Rehearsal Dinners	● Corp. Events/Mtgs.
● Ceremonies	● Private Parties
● Wedding Receptions	Accommodations

If you've ever gone wine tasting in Sonoma, you probably noticed Viansa as you drove into the county, or maybe you caught a glimpse of it on your way back home. If, however, you actually stopped to visit the winery, chances are you didn't get much further. This place is so wonderful, it's easy to spend hours here—sampling the wines, having lunch, shopping in the Italian Marketplace and just strolling the grounds. Set atop a hill overlooking the Valley of the Moon and resembling a Tuscan villa, Viansa embraces you with Italian hospitality and satisfies all your senses.

The Villa (aka the winery building), with its tiled roof, terracotta walls and shuttered windows, is your first taste of Tuscany. A series of French doors along the left wing opens onto a circular courtyard, flanked by olive trees and grapevines; colorful flowerpots encircle the fountain in the center and mark the perimeter.

To the right of the Villa a stone-walled staircase takes you past the thriving grapevines on either side up to a huge bronze door at the top. As you pass through the doorway, you enter a thoroughly enchanting hilltop "village." To one side is an intimate fountain courtyard, enclosed by ivy-clad walls and shaded by silvery olive trees; to the other is Le Mura, the fully enclosed, tented reception pavilion. A few steps further is the expansive Main Lawn, a picnic area beneath a trellis laced with grapevines, and the Italian Marketplace. Everywhere you look you'll see bright red geraniums spilling out of planters, wrought-iron benches and, of course, the delicate presence of olive trees shimmering in the sun.

Once the winery closes to the public, Viansa is yours to enjoy. Get married in the circular courtyard or candlelit wine cellar. If you like the festive ambiance of the Marketplace, serve sparkling wine here while your guests mingle amongst vibrant displays of wines, mustards, olive oils, pestos and other gourmet delicacies. For a gorgeous finale, hold your reception in Le Mura: Linen-draped tables set with crystal and flowers are an elegant complement to the flagstone floor and soaring white canopy overhead. If you like, you can add candelabras festooned with flowers for a romantic glow.

Before the sun sets completely, take a walk up to Alto Piano, the highest point of the property. From the edge of the plateau you have a fantastic view of Viansa's 91 acres of restored wetlands far below. This seasonal home to one million ducks, shorebirds and golden eagles also attracts avid birdwatchers during peak migrations every spring.

The people at Viansa have long felt that Americans should be able to enjoy wine and food together, just as Italians have done for centuries. Guests who dine here appreciate the extraordinary amount of care that goes into the cuisine and service, and they have responded with their patronage: 80% of the winery's event business is word of mouth. At Viansa, they've not only created an exquisite environment for celebrating, they've made it possible for each guest to have an unforgettably delicious Italian experience.

CEREMONY CAPACITY: The Courtyard and the Lawn accommodate up to 220 seated guests.

EVENT/RECEPTION & MEETING CAPACITY: Le Mura, the tented pavilion, holds 220 seated guests. Outside, the facility holds 500 standing.

FEES & DEPOSITS: A nonrefundable deposit is required to reserve your date; the final balance is due 2 weeks prior to the event. Facility rental fees, including rehearsal time, start at $3,000 and can range up to $9,000 depending on the date selected for your event. Meals start at $75/person; tax, alcohol and a 20% service charge are additional.

AVAILABILITY: The winery is open year-round. Weddings take place in the evenings only; call for details.

SERVICES/AMENITIES:
Catering: provided, no BYO
Kitchen Facilities: n/a
Tables & Chairs: provided
Linens, Silver, etc.: provided
Restrooms: wheelchair accessible
Dance Floor: area provided
Bride's Dressing Area: yes
Meeting Equipment: CBA, extra fee
Other: event coordination

Parking: large lot
Accommodations: no guestrooms
Telephone: pay phones
Outdoor Night Lighting: yes
Outdoor Cooking Facilities: no
Cleanup: provided
View: Sonoma Valley, mountains, vineyards, wetlands preserve

RESTRICTIONS:
Alcohol: WB only provided, no BYO
Smoking: outside only
Music: amplified OK

Wheelchair Access: yes
Insurance: certificate required
Other: no rice or birdseed

Harvest Inn

Hotel

One Main Street, St. Helena
707/963-9463, 800/950-8466
www.harvestinn.com
weddings@harvestinn.com

- Rehearsal Dinners
- Ceremonies
- Wedding Receptions
- Corp. Events/Mtgs.
- Private Parties
- Accommodations

If an elegant, classic wedding is what you have your heart set on, well, we've found a place that every bride should put on her A-list. Whether your dream is an English country-style wedding, a sophisticated black-tie affair, or an intimate ceremony amid roses and grapevines, the fabulous Harvest Inn can make your vision a reality.

Stroll along the inn's curving brick pathways to the Manor House Lawn. Encircled by mature redwoods, birches and flowerbeds, this sunny verdant expanse is perfect for large events. Behind you the Manor House, with its spiral chimney, dormer windows and authentic Tudor architecture, is a majestic backdrop for your festivities and will convince anyone viewing your wedding photos that you got married in an old English village.

From the house it's a short walk via a quaint stone Wishing Bridge to the Vineyard Terrace, where you'll exchange vows, fanned by breezes redolent of ripening grapes. Guests can admire the terrace's fountain, fragrant plantings of roses and lavender, and panoramic vineyard and mountain views. (By the way, the Harvest Inn is one of the few facilities in the Napa Valley where you can get married right next to a vineyard.)

Afterwards, everyone walks back to the Manor House lawn for photos and champagne while the terrace is set for the reception. When dinner is over, guests simply step into the adjacent Vineyard View Room for dancing and cocktails. In keeping with the inn's Tudor motif, this space boasts white walls, exposed wood beams, plenty of windows and a massive stone fireplace. Though we saw the Vineyard View Room in the summer, it would be equally lovely for winter events, with a crackling fire casting a warm glow. For more intimate weddings, the Vin Rose Lawn, with its rose border and shady trees, is a delightful spot.

Within Harvest Inn's eight acres of landscaped grounds, several guest cottages are hidden among trees, flowers, lawns, fountains, ponds and statues—a combination that creates a secluded, romantic ambiance. The structures all display the design elements that make Tudor architecture so appealing: exposed beams, plaster walls, dormer windows, stained glass and unique arched or spiral chimneys. Inside, the guestrooms feature such deluxe amenities as fireplaces, down featherbeds and comforters, and private terraces.

St. Helena, with its shops, restaurants and Wine Country charm, is only a short drive away. And, if you're a wine aficionado, there are dozens of nearby wineries where you can sample the fruit of the vine to your heart's content. Whether you're an Anglophile, a garden lover, or just looking for a place that will have your guests marveling at your party-planning prowess, the Harvest Inn is likely to be the perfect choice. And if your beloved is reluctant to pop the question, why not book a weekend at Harvest Inn? The romantic atmosphere (helped along by a glass of premium Napa Valley wine) will have him proposing in no time at all!

CEREMONY CAPACITY: The Vin Rose Lawn holds 40 seated guests and the Vineyard View Terrace holds 120 seated guests. Indoors, the Mountain View Room and the Vineyard View Room each hold 60 seated guests.

EVENT/RECEPTION & MEETING CAPACITY: The inn's rooms each hold 60 seated or 80 standing guests indoors; outdoors the lawn and terrace accommodate 50–120 seated or 120–150 standing.

FEES & DEPOSITS: 50% of the site rental fee is the nonrefundable deposit that reserves your date. Site fees range $4,000–14,500 depending on venue selected. The estimated event balance is due 60 days prior to the event. The site fee includes guestrooms (which are required), as well as all sales & occupancy taxes; call for details. For weddings, a professional event or wedding coordinator is required to be on site on the day of the event.

AVAILABILITY: Year-round, daily, 11am–11pm.

SERVICES/AMENITIES:

Catering: select from preferred list
Kitchen Facilities: prep only
Tables & Chairs: provided
Linens, Silver, etc.: provided
Restrooms: wheelchair accessible
Dance Floor: yes
Bride's Dressing Area: CBA, extra charge
Meeting Equipment: CBA, extra charge

Parking: some on-site; valet required
Accommodations: 74 guestrooms
Telephone: guest phones
Outdoor Night Lighting: CBA, extra charge
Outdoor Cooking Facilities: CBA
Cleanup: caterer and facility
View: vineyards, mountains, gardens

RESTRICTIONS:

Alcohol: Wine or beer provided, or BYO or through licensed caterer
Smoking: outside only
Music: amplified OK indoors only

Wheelchair Access: yes
Insurance: required for all vendors
Other: no rice, confetti, rose petals or birdseed

Want to know WHAT TO ASK a potential location or vendor? Check out our Questions to Ask on page 17.

Meadowood Napa Valley

Resort

900 Meadowood Lane, St. Helena
707/963-3646
www.meadowood.com
lwickersham@meadowood.com

- Rehearsal Dinners
- Ceremonies
- Wedding Receptions
- Corp. Events/Mtgs.
- Private Parties
- Accommodations

Driving into the exclusive Meadowood Napa Valley property is indeed a pleasure. You follow a narrow tree-shaded lane, flanked by forested hillsides, to the sophisticated estate, which includes a wine education program, executive conference center and first-rate recreational facilities. The superbly designed buildings are reminiscent of New England during the early 1900s, with white balconies, gabled roofs and gray clapboard siding. All is secluded on 250 acres of densely wooded Napa Valley countryside.

The sprawling, multitiered clubhouse accommodates private parties. It's set high, overlooking lush green fairways and manicured lawns. The large Vintners' Room and Woodside Room are available for indoor meetings or receptions. The Vintners' Room is fabulous, with high ceilings and a stone fireplace, decks with umbrella-shaded tables and outstanding views. The nearby lawn slopes down to steps adjacent to a dry creek bed planted with willows, leading to a footbridge that crosses over to golf fairways.

For outdoor celebrations, Meadowood arranges tables and tents on the lawns next to the Vintners' Room. There is something very special about this facility. It provides award-winning cuisine, deluxe accommodations and an environment to match. It ranks high on our list of special event locations.

CEREMONY CAPACITY: The resort can accommodate 20–250 seated or 80–400 standing guests outdoors.

EVENT/RECEPTION CAPACITY: The Vintners' Room seats 120 guests indoors, and with the lawn area, up to 250 seated guests. The Woodside Room seats 60 guests, 80 in conjunction with an adjacent lawn area.

MEETING CAPACITY: There are several rooms which hold 12–140 seated guests.

FEES & DEPOSITS: For weddings, the $2,500–7,500 facility fee also serves as the deposit required to secure your date. The facility fee includes ceremony coordination, rehearsal and setup, a white aisle runner, china, glassware and floor-length white table linens with overlays and napkins. Votive candles and Japanese lanterns are provided for evening events. Catering services are provided: Lunch buffets and barbecues range $64–70/person, 3-course luncheons range $52–70/person, and 4-course dinners range $110–130/person. Tax and a 20% service charge are applied to the final total.

For business functions or other events, fees vary depending on room(s) selected and services required; call for more specific information.

AVAILABILITY: For special events and business functions, year-round, daily, anytime. Weddings take place Sunday, 10am–3pm or 5pm–10pm; Friday–Saturday, 11am–4pm or 6pm–11pm.

SERVICES/AMENITIES:

Catering: provided, no BYO

Kitchen Facilities: n/a

Tables & Chairs: provided

Linens, Silver, etc.: provided

Restrooms: wheelchair accessible

Dance Floor: CBA in Vintners and Woodside rooms

Bride's Dressing Area: CBA

Meeting Equipment: CBA

Parking: multiple lots, valet CBA

Accommodations: 99 guestrooms and suites

Telephone: guest phones

Outdoor Night Lighting: yes

Outdoor Cooking Facilities: provided

Cleanup: provided

View: fairways, Napa hills

Other: spa and fitness facilities, golf, croquet, tennis, wine education

RESTRICTIONS:

Alcohol: provided, or BYO

Smoking: outside only

Music: amplified OK indoors only

Wheelchair Access: yes

Insurance: not required

V. Sattui Winery

Winery

1111 White Lane, St. Helena
707/286-7273
www.vsattui.com
orders@vsattui.com

- Rehearsal Dinners
- Ceremonies
- Wedding Receptions
- Corp. Events/Mtgs.
- Private Parties
- Accommodations

The scenic Napa Valley abounds with grand wineries, many of them doing big business these days. With so many players vying for a visitor's attention, the "little gems" may go unnoticed. It would be a shame to miss out on V. Sattui, a small family winery run by the fourth generation of Sattuis, who demonstrate both pride in their winemaking traditions and warm hospitality. Even the marketing of their award-winning wines is a personal affair—all vintages are sold directly to their customers via mail-order or at the winery itself. This is the sort of authentic quality and old-fashioned charm that sets just the right note for heartfelt special occasions.

Founded back in 1885, V. Sattui occupies a massive vine-covered stone building in the classic manner of Early California. The surrounding landscape is quintessential Napa: a backdrop of magnificent hillsides covered with chaparral and live oaks; acres of lush, green lawns; and row upon row of grapevines.

Like the grapes themselves, wedding ceremonies flourish in such a bucolic environment. A stone patio in front of the winery has several small terraces that make a dramatic descent down to a courtyard hugged by the two-story winery. A path sprinkled with rose petals marks the wedding aisle, and flowering shrubs, saplings, a gnarled oak, and garlands draped on the balconies create a lovely garden atmosphere. Evening ceremonies in the courtyard are magical, with luminarias flickering along the aisle and twinkle lights illuminating the balconies. For larger weddings, say "I do" under the ivy-covered tower that overlooks an expanse of emerald lawn bordered by colorful flowerbeds, with the magnificent vista of the Napa Valley in the distance.

While the bridal party takes photographs in the many picturesque settings on the property, guests soak up the vineyard ambiance on the front patio, where water splashing from a large Mediterranean-style fountain contributes to the festive mood.

Have one of the outdoor areas set for an al fresco reception, or invite guests to dine in a castle-like wine cellar, where hand-hewn stone walls, heavy ceiling timbers and wine barrels evoke an Old World atmosphere. A pleasant, piquant aroma wafts from the aging wines, kept behind wrought-iron gates in four caves reached through a stone archway. The cellar takes on a haunting beauty by candlelight, so go ahead and lavish the room with votives—in wall ledges, atop rows of oaken barrels, on the tables. Fancy candelabras are an elegant effect, and draping the barrels with Tivoli and icicle lights add even more sparkle.

At V. Sattui, the wine you serve will be as appreciated as the scenery. Among their many accolades, V. Sattui was awarded the 2006 Golden Winery Award, the California State Fair's top honor. They can even personalize wine bottles with gold foil labels commemorating your celebration. When their fine varietals are paired with the exquisite cuisine served up by the event pros at *Wine Valley Catering,* you and your guests will savor every detail of your culinary experience. In fact, everything at this historic venue will make your celebration a landmark event.

CEREMONY CAPACITY: The Tower Lawn holds 250 seated or standing; the Cellar holds 250 seated or standing; the Stone Courtyard accommodates 180 seated or 250 standing.

EVENT/RECEPTION CAPACITY: The Barrel Cellar holds 250 seated guests; the tri-level stone courtyard holds 180 seated; and the Tower Lawn holds 250 seated or standing guests.

MEETING CAPACITY: The Barrel Cellar holds 300 seated theater-style or classroom-style and 250 seated conference-style.

FEES & DEPOSITS: Half of the site rental fee is a nonrefundable deposit required to secure your date. Rental fees plus a final guest count are due 2 weeks prior to the event. Site rental fees range $4,000–9,000 depending on the date of the event.

AVAILABILITY: Year-round, daily 6pm–11pm.

SERVICES/AMENITIES:

Catering: provided or select from list
Kitchen Facilities: prep only
Tables: provided
Linens, Silver, etc.: through caterer
Restrooms: wheelchair accessible
Dance Floor: yes
Bride's Dressing Area: yes
Meeting Equipment: CBA, extra fee

Parking: large lot
Accommodations: no guestrooms
Telephone: emergency use only
Outdoor Night Lighting: yes
Outdoor Cooking Facilities: no
Cleanup: caterer
View: vineyards, hills, garden, valley, fountain
Other: tents/canopies CBA; barrel room heaters provided

RESTRICTIONS:

Alcohol: provided
Smoking: outdoors only
Music: amplified OK indoors, acoustic outdoors

Wheelchair Access: yes
Insurance: certificate required

Brix

Restaurant

7377 St. Helena Highway, Yountville
707/944-2547
www.brix.com
matt@brix.com

- Rehearsal Dinners
- Ceremonies
- Wedding Receptions
- Corp. Events/Mtgs.
- Private Parties
- Accommodations

Brix may sit right on Napa Valley's main highway, but once you're inside you're in some sort of Wine Country Dreamtime, where nothing matters but good food, good wine and the sharing of both with family and friends. (By the way, "Brix" is a term used by wine growers that refers to the percentage of sugar in ripening grapes.)

Brix is surrounded by vineyards, but behind the restaurant is a huge kitchen garden, formally laid out in the European style. Many of the fruits, vegetables and herbs used in Brix's cuisine are grown here—you frequently see a white-garbed sous-chef in the garden, gathering ingredients for an order. Here, too, you can hold a ceremony amid the flowers and fruit, with a vista of the vineyards stretching out across the valley to the foot of the western mountains.

Intimate receptions often take place in the Oakville Room, which succeeds in being both elegant and informal. Sunflower-yellow walls and an abundance of wood details create a warm, deliciously inviting atmosphere. At the far end, a *trompe l'oeil* mural makes you think you're looking out a large picture window at a quintessential Wine Country landscape. Along one side of the room, a grand mirror reflects the lovely scene on the opposite side: tall windows framing a serene view of the adjacent tree-filled patio.

The largest reception site is the Flower Garden Dining Area. Set around a fountain and bordered by an ever-changing mix of flowers, plantings and grasses that reflect the colors of the season, this al fresco space enjoys sweeping views of nearby vineyards and the Mayacamas Mountains beyond. Here you're seated on Chiavari chairs at tables regally set with Riedel stemware, St. Andrea silverware and Villeroy & Boch bone china. The food, the service and the ambiance will make you feel totally pampered.

Smaller events find a cozy nest in the (literally!) rose-covered Cottage, which has its own private patio. Inside, pale wainscoting rises up to meet mellow ochre walls, with glass sconces providing soft illumination. The western wall, which is almost all glass, overlooks the covered patio with its garden view. As your gaze rests on the long dining table, it's easy to visualize the toasts, the laughter, and the easy conviviality of an intimate reception or rehearsal dinner in this cheerful room.

In addition to growing a significant percentage of the produce used in the restaurant, Brix bakes its own bread and smokes its own salmon. Other ingredients are procured in season, and as fresh as possible. The wine list is graced by some of Napa's most prestigious vintages—in 2004 it won the *Wine Spectator* Best of Award of Excellence and the International Restaurant & Hospitality Diamond Award. (Really, if their wine list were a movie, it would star Denzel Washington, Julia Roberts and 52 others of the same star caliber.)

Warm, low-key, relaxed and intimate: If these words describe the wedding your heart desires, Brix awaits you.

CEREMONY CAPACITY: 100 indoors; 150 outdoors at the vineyard site.

EVENT/RECEPTION CAPACITY: The Flower Garden Dining Area holds up to 150 guests. Indoors, the Oakville Room holds up to 60 guests, the Cottage holds up to 30 and the Reserve Cellar up to 12 guests.

MEETING CAPACITY: The Oakville Room holds up to 80 guests seated conference-style.

FEES & DEPOSITS: A $50/person deposit is required to reserve your date. 50% of site fees due at booking, the balance is due at the close of your event. Meals range $38–68/person. Tax, alcohol and a 20% service charge are additional.

AVAILABILITY: Year-round, during lunch and dinner Monday–Saturday and brunch and dinner on Sunday.

SERVICES/AMENITIES:

Catering: provided
Kitchen Facilities: n/a
Tables & Chairs: provided
Linens, Silver, etc.: provided
Restrooms: wheelchair accessible
Dance Floor: patio or CBA, extra fee
Bride's Dressing Area: yes
Meeting Equipment: BYO

Parking: ample on site
Accommodations: no guestrooms
Telephone: pay phone
Outdoor Night Lighting: terrace
Outdoor Cooking Facilities: yes
Cleanup: provided
View: vineyards, garden, mountains

RESTRICTIONS:

Alcohol: provided
Smoking: outside only
Music: amplified OK

Wheelchair Access: yes
Insurance: not required

Want to find more locations and services? Check out our informative website, www.HereComesTheGuide.com.

The Vintage Estate-Napa Valley

Resort & Spa

6525 Washington Street, Yountville
707/945-4549 or **707/945-4545**
www.vintageestate.com
sfiscus@villagio.com

● Rehearsal Dinners	● Corp. Events/Mtgs.
● Ceremonies	● Private Parties
● Wedding Receptions	● Accommodations

As you drive through California's most fabled wine region, Yountville is the first town you reach heading north from the city of Napa on Highway 29. Almost as well known as St. Helena up the road, it shares many of the same amenities but moves at a slower, more relaxed pace. At the southern end of Yountville's main street is the 23-acre Vintage Estate, a multifaceted destination for anyone planning a Wine Country wedding or special event. If you want to experience a seamless melding of country casual and uptown elegance, this is the place to come.

The estate includes two AAA Four Diamond Award-winning hotels, Villagio Inn & Spa and the Vintage Inn; V Marketplace, a collection of specialty shops and galleries; and the property's newest addition, the glorious Pavilion at the Vintage Estate.

Unquestionably the star of the estate, The Pavilion is a stunning, 16,000-square-foot outdoor space designed expressly for weddings. As you watch people enter it, you see them respond instinctively to its fine proportions and materials. Your eyes will dance about in appreciation, too, imagining just how beautiful your wedding day will look here.

The Pavilion is basically a pair of large lawns, one terraced above the other, bounded by fountains, arbors, and flagstone-faced and ivy-covered walls. The lower west lawn is the larger of the two, and its well-tended grass is almost as luxurious as a putting green. Criss-crossing brick paths divide the lawn into four quarters. The main path—the bridal aisle—ends at a tall wooden arbor set atop a stepped brick base and backed by a sinuous stone wall. This is The Pavilion's primary ceremony space. Photographers often use the steps for photos, posing bridesmaids and groomsmen on them ascending toward the wedding couple. (The surrounding vineyards offer plenty of other photogenic spots, too.)

On one side of the lower west lawn area, two wall fountains gush glassy panes of water, while on the opposite side a long flowing fountain forms the retaining wall of the upper lawn. This smaller east lawn spreads toward a large arbor on The Pavilion's east edge. The arbor, enclosed by large stone walls, is where most couples place their head table or softly playing musicians, while using the upper lawn for the reception. Another option is to use the arbor and upper lawn as the ceremony site and have guests dine on the lower lawn—the choice is entirely yours. After the meal, dance the evening away in the nearby Historic Barrel Room, entered through a garden populated with whimsical sculptures and flowerbeds.

Guests planning to extend their stay can simply walk over to either of the estate's two hotels. The landscaping and range of flora at Villagio are magnificent, as is the inn's very successful attempt at creating a bit of Tuscany and old Rome in the Napa Valley. The adjacent Vintage Inn is French Country in style. Both provide a lovely ending to a memorable Wine Country wedding. The Vintage Estate is a place given over to romance and pleasure, two things we think every bride deserves to expect in abundance.

CEREMONY CAPACITY: Outdoors, the site accommodates 700 guests; indoors, 220 guests.

EVENT/RECEPTION & MEETING CAPACITY: The facility holds 220 seated or 250 standing indoors; 700 seated or 1,200 standing outdoors.

FEES & DEPOSITS: Meals start at $175/person. Site fees range $3,500–12,000.

AVAILABILITY: Year-round, 9am–midnight.

SERVICES/AMENITIES:

Catering: provided, no BYO
Kitchen Facilities: n/a
Tables & Chairs: provided
Linens, Silver, etc.: provided
Restrooms: wheelchair accessible
Dance Floor: CBA
Bride's Dressing Area: yes
Meeting Equipment: provided
Other: event coordination, full spa services and florals, picnic area, AV equipment, PA sound system, CD music system

Parking: large lot, valet and shuttle required for large events
Accommodations: 192 guestrooms
Telephone: guest phones
Outdoor Night Lighting: yes
Outdoor Cooking Facilities: no
Cleanup: provided
View: vineyards, hills, gardens, meadow

RESTRICTIONS:

Alcohol: provided, no BYO
Smoking: outdoors only
Music: amplified OK indoors until midnight, outdoors until 9pm

Wheelchair Access: yes
Insurance: not required

Santa Cruz Area

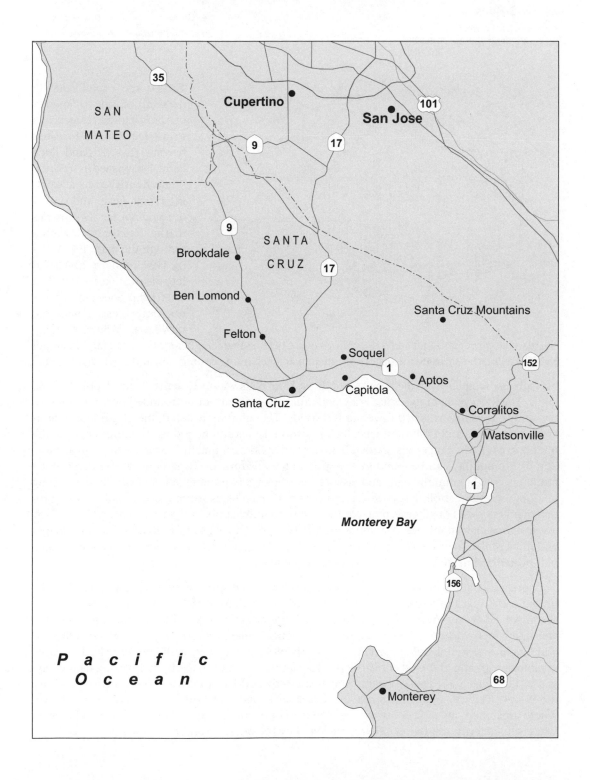

Historic Sand Rock Farm

Historic Country Inn

Address withheld to ensure privacy. Aptos
831/688-8005
www.sandrockfarm.com
reservations@sandrockfarm.com

- Rehearsal Dinners
- Ceremonies
- Wedding Receptions
- Corp. Events/Mtgs.
- Private Parties
- Accommodations

Tucked into a rural valley in the pretty seaside community of Aptos, a former stagecoach route leads to a forested haven—Historic Sand Rock Farm. Established in 1885, the estate flourished as a working ranch, farm, and one of the original family wineries in the Monterey Bay Area through the early 1900s. But by 1999, the farm had fallen into disuse. Enter world-class Chef Lynn Sheehan, who is not only blessed with the proverbial "golden spatula," she also has a green thumb and a decorator's eye. Chef Sheehan and her mother, veteran innkeeper Kris Sheehan, transformed the historic estate into an enchanting country inn and celebration venue.

Though just minutes from the beach, Sand Rock Farm rests within 10 acres of sun-dappled woodlands. The focal point of the estate is a wonderful shingled mansion surrounded by acres of meadows, trails, twisting oaks and towering redwoods. Thoughtfully restored, the elegant inn retains an authentic Arts and Crafts aesthetic. Rich redwood details and period light fixtures enhance the interiors, while rocking chairs, garden benches and trickling fountains inspire outdoor relaxation. Zen-like tranquility can be found in any of Sand Rock Farm's lovely gardens, where tiered stone fountains delight hummingbirds and visitors alike. Enjoy a fragrant ramble in Eva's Garden among heirloom roses, or stroll the Spiral Garden, where vintage lilacs adorn hidden nooks inviting romantic interludes. Equally romantic are the five beautifully appointed guestrooms, which convey a warm, nostalgic ambiance. Amenities include two-person Jacuzzi tubs, hand-printed wallpaper and flower-filled views. Luxurious furnishings like a French hand-carved armoire and an antique half-poster bed make you feel like the Lady of the Manor!

This private country estate also offers an array of wonderful event sites. Elaborate ceremonies unfold in the spacious Redwood Grove, where couples pledge their love among mature redwoods, accompanied by the melodious splashing of a wine-barrel fountain. Beyond the Grove lies the versatile Winery Meadow, 5,000 square feet of level field ringed with soaring trees. Whether dressed with linens and stunning floral centerpieces or styled California-casual, the Winery Meadow easily combines with any of the other nearby party areas: the rustic Carriage Barn, boasting high white-washed ceilings and exposed beams; the Heart Redwood Pavilion, with wisteria-covered trellis; the Winery Terrace, an alcoved space that has stone walls and broad stairs; and the Barrel Cellar, where an arched, ivy-clad doorway opens into an open-air dining or dancing space. Aglow with white silk lanterns, the Barrel Cellar is sheltered by the original sand rock walls.

Intimate celebrations often feature the reception rooms of the inn itself. The central redwood staircase affords the bride a graceful entrance into the parlor for an old-fashioned wedding ceremony. Afterwards, French doors swing open onto the expansive dining decks where guests enjoy champagne and delicious appetizers overlooking a lush shade garden.

Sand Rock Farm, located in the heart of organic farming on the Central Coast, works closely with local caterers who partner with neighboring farmers and winemakers to create tantalizing and sustainable local cuisine. In addition, Sand Rock Farm is officially a "Green Hotel."

Considering avoiding the wedding hoopla altogether? Sand Rock Farm's romantic Elopement Package makes it easy. So whether you're planning a lavish gala, a spontaneous getaway or a honeymoon to remember, let Historic Sand Rock Farm introduce you to "the Art of the Good Life," the well-chosen motto of this gracious retreat.

CEREMONY, EVENT/RECEPTION & MEETING CAPACITY: Indoors, Sand Rock Farm holds up to 150 seated or 200 standing guests; outdoors, up to 250 seated or 300 standing guests. Several spaces are available; please call for configuration details.

FEES & DEPOSITS: A $1,500 deposit is required to reserve your date and the balance is due 4 weeks prior to your event. Rental fees range $1,000–4,000 depending on space rented. Meals range $35–100/person. Tax, alcohol and a 20% service charge are additional. A $3.50/person cake-cutting fee may apply.

AVAILABILITY: Year-round, daily, 9am–9pm.

SERVICES/AMENITIES:

Catering: select from list of approved caterers
Kitchen Facilities: n/a
Tables & Chairs: CBA
Linens, Silver, etc.: CBA
Restrooms: wheelchair accessible
Dance Floor: CBA
Bride's & Groom's Dressing Area: CBA
Meeting Equipment: CBA, extra charge

Parking: available, CBA
Accommodations: 5 guestrooms
Telephone: emergency use only
Outdoor Night Lighting: CBA
Outdoor Cooking Facilities: CBA
Cleanup: provided
View: garden, grounds, fountains, hills, forest
Other: event coordination CBA

RESTRICTIONS:

Alcohol: provided or BYO with corkage fee
Smoking: outdoors only with restrictions
Music: amplified OK with restrictions

Wheelchair Access: yes
Insurance: liability required

Seascape Beach Resort

Oceanfront Resort

1 Seascape Resort Drive, Aptos
800/929-7727
www.seascaperesort.com
weddings@seascaperesort.com

- Rehearsal Dinners
- Ceremonies
- Wedding Receptions
- Corp. Events/Mtgs.
- Private Parties
- Accommodations

Spread out along the bluffs overlooking Monterey Bay, this resort definitely lives up to its name. From almost any vantage point, inside or out, you have sweeping ocean vistas, and if you're one of those people who comes alive in the sea air (and who isn't?), you'll find the surroundings here quite rejuvenating.

Take the ceremony spot, for example: It's an expanse of lawn on top of a bluff, set against a postcard-beautiful backdrop of cypress trees and shimmering sea. The miniforest at the edge of the property is a favorite place for the bride and groom to have their pictures taken, and a short path leads down to the beach for a walk along the sand.

Receptions are held indoors in a variety of banquet rooms. The largest, the Seascape Room, has a light, airy feel and fabulous ocean views. Smaller weddings take place in the Riviera Room, which has one wall of windows that face the bay and another that overlooks the treetops. A skylight adds to the natural light in the space. Probably the most popular room for intimate gatherings is the Bayview Room. It not only faces the ocean, but has its own terrace. For a very small party or rehearsal dinner, reserve the Peninsula Room. It, too, benefits from an abundance of windows as well as views of the bay and tree-studded bluff.

All of these spaces, along with additional rooms, are also available for meetings. Each one has state-of-the-art audio, video, computer, high-speed internet and modem connections. Another huge benefit are the in-house professional meeting, wedding and special event planners who will assist you with the planning and execution of your event.

Whether you're getting married or hosting a meeting, conference or retreat here, Seascape is a great place to bring your guests for an extended stay. All of the accommodations (from suites to two-bedroom beach villas) have decks or patios, kitchenettes and fireplaces, and many have direct ocean views. You can go for a dip in one of three heated pools and hot spas, or take advantage of the tennis courts, gym and Olympic-size pool at the Seascape Sports Club. Sanderlings, the on-site restaurant, offers dining with sweeping ocean vistas. Nearby there are award-winning golf courses, and, of course, the Santa Cruz/Monterey/Carmel coastline is one of the most spectacular stretches of coast in the country. So, if you're tempted to turn your event into a vacation, go ahead—Seascape makes it easy.

CEREMONY CAPACITY: The Wedding Bluff accommodates 250 seated guests.

EVENT/RECEPTION & MEETING CAPACITY: The resort holds 50–250 seated indoors.

MEETING CAPACITY: 8 rooms accommodate 35–400 guests.

FEES & DEPOSITS: For weddings or special events, a nonrefundable $2,000 deposit is required to reserve your date. Ceremony site fees start at $600. Wedding packages start at $85/person including catering and room rental. Seated meals for nonwedding special events or business functions start at $30/person; alcohol, tax and a 20% service charge are additional.

For special events or day meetings, the banquet room rental fees range $400–800/day, with catering à la carte. Meeting packages are available which include meals, refreshment breaks, banquet/meeting room rentals and basic audiovisual.

AVAILABILITY: Year-round, daily, 7am–11pm. Wedding receptions are held on Saturdays and Sundays in the Seascape Room, 4pm–9:30pm; or in the Riviera or Bayview Rooms, 1pm–6:30pm. For meetings or conferences, please call the sales department.

SERVICES/AMENITIES:
Catering: provided, no BYO
Kitchen Facilities: n/a
Tables & Chairs: provided
Linens, Silver, etc.: provided
Restrooms: wheelchair accessible
Dance Floor: provided
Bride's & Groom's Dressing Area: rentable suites
Meeting Equipment: fully equipped

Parking: on-site for 500 guests
Accommodations: 285 suites and villas
Telephone: pay phones
Outdoor Night Lighting: yes
Outdoor Cooking Facilities: no
Cleanup: provided
View: Pacific Ocean panorama
Other: coordination, theme and beach events

RESTRICTIONS:
Alcohol: provided, no BYO
Smoking: outdoors only
Music: amplified OK with limits

Wheelchair Access: yes
Insurance: not required
Other: no rice, confetti, birdseed or uncontained candles

This is important! Tell locations you're reading HERE COMES THE GUIDE and ask if our information is still current.

Seascape Golf Club

Golf Club

610 Clubhouse Drive, Aptos
831/688-3213 x217
www.countryclubreceptions.com
sales@seascapegc.com

● Rehearsal Dinners	● Corp. Events/Mtgs.
● Ceremonies	● Private Parties
● Wedding Receptions	Accommodations

Santa Cruz and its environs have long been re-nowned for spectacular scenery. Clusters of forested hillsides hug a shoreline that teems with marine life and rainbow-hued flora, and the favorite pastime of locals seems to be watching for that twilight moment when the setting sun kisses the blue surf. Santa Cruz's quaint suburbs boast small-town charm aplenty, attracting artisans, tourists and nature-seekers by the thousands. Yet, like the monarch butterflies that flutter among the region's many eucalyptus groves, Santa Cruz has undergone a transformation during the last decade or so, shedding its Bohemian persona in favor of a laid-back sophistication. You'll want to take advantage of the area's attributes for your special celebration, and one of the nicest spots to do this lies in the beachside village of Aptos.

From Highway 1, head shoreward into a quiet residential neighborhood tucked away in the Coastal highlands. Here you'll find the appropriately named Seascape Golf Club, perched on a bluff facing the Pacific. The cream-colored building has an arched colonnade running along the front, accented with flowering herbs and shrubs; a towering pine stands at one end, while a willow spills its languid boughs over the other, contributing to Seascape's lush allure.

Seascape is known for its "Weddings on the Green," ceremonies on the manicured grass of the 10th tee. To reach this magic spot from the parking lot, follow a flight of mariner-style stairs with ropes for banisters down to a delightful garden hollow. Landscaped slopes dotted with cheery surprises of color cradle a swath of lawn, ample enough for an enchanting ceremony for 240 guests. Set an archway, gazebo or columns just so, and your friends and family will enjoy a sweeping vista of the redwood-studded fairways. Then, while you newlyweds pose for scenic wedding photos, guests enjoy an open-air cocktail hour on an adjacent lawn, set up with umbrella-shaded tables.

For the dinner and dancing phase of your event, Seascape brings the party inside to the Monarch Room. This breezy, sun-washed space comes with a high ceiling and clerestory windows; ornate bronze chandeliers lend a dash of formality. The airy mood is enhanced by a neutral palette and a ribbon of windows that wraps around the room's outer edge, embracing a view that extends over swaying treetops and gently rolling fairways. Those reluctant to forsake the outdoors simply walk out to the terrace where garden benches invite a quiet respite, the better to watch the stars illuminate the sky.

A short walkway connects the Monarch Room to the Clubhouse, another attractive space for smaller events (or as a foul-weather backup for the ceremony and cocktail hour.) The Clubhouse's natural wood ceiling and a cool-blue color scheme convey a relaxed-yet-refined quality. Windows frame the pretty golf course panorama, with the blue expanse of the Pacific just beyond; set café tables and chairs on the Clubhouse's adjoining terrace, and guests can delight in the salty tang of the sea air.

Also delightful are Seascape's "package deals," which let you mix and match your event options. Seascape even offers "A Little Tyke's Reception," which provides a party room, buffet and entertainment for the kids—all you bring is the babysitter.

CEREMONY, EVENT/RECEPTION & MEETING CAPACITY: The Club hosts up to 240 seated or 300 standing guests.

FEES & DEPOSITS: A nonrefundable deposit, which is applied to your food and beverage total, is required to reserve your date. The amount of the deposit is equal to 25% of the estimated event total. 50% is due 6 months prior, and 100% of the final estimated balance is due 10 days prior to the event date. Rental fees range $150–1,200 depending on space rented. Meals range $10–46/person. Tax, alcohol and a 20% service charge are additional.

AVAILABILITY: Year-round, daily, 6am–midnight.

SERVICES/AMENITIES:

Catering: provided, no BYO

Kitchen Facilities: n/a

Tables & Chairs: provided

Linens, Silver, etc.: provided

Restrooms: wheelchair accessible

Dance Floor: yes

Bride's & Groom's Dressing Area: yes

Meeting Equipment: CBA, extra charge

Parking: large lot

Accommodations: no guestrooms

Telephone: emergency use only

Outdoor Night Lighting: yes

Outdoor Cooking Facilities: no

Cleanup: provided

View: Pacific Ocean, fairways

Other: event coordination

RESTRICTIONS:

Alcohol: provided, or BYO wine with corkage fee

Smoking: outdoors only

Music: amplified OK

Wheelchair Access: yes

Insurance: not required

Monarch Cove Inn

Inn

620 El Salto Drive, Capitola
831/464-1295
www.monarch-cove-inn.com
monarchcoveinn@charter.net

- Rehearsal Dinners
- Ceremonies
- Wedding Receptions
- Corp. Events/Mtgs.
- Private Parties
- Accommodations

We're going to ask you to participate in a guided meditation: Relax, breathe deep, and envision your private sanctuary…a place of perfect beauty, peace, and contentment…. Did you conjure up an image of the seashore? Then slow your breathing to the rhythm of the waves…. Or perhaps you see yourself in a pretty garden, filled with butterflies, songbirds and delicate blossoms? Then let the sweetly fragrant air fill your senses…. Now, imagine combining these two idyllic havens into one spectacular seaside garden venue…. Can you picture a romantic wedding at such a divine spot? Wake up! Your dream has come true—at the Monarch Cove Inn.

Poised on an ocean bluff, the Monarch Cove Inn looks out onto a breathtaking curve of forested shoreline, home to flocks of pelicans and the bright butterflies that inspired the inn's name. Yet the enviable location of this dove-colored Victorian is only part of its allure. The delightfully understated architecture has just enough period features—gabled roof, angled bay windows—to evoke the grace of the past, yet is not so ornate as to make modernists uncomfortable. Originally built in 1883 as a private retreat for two wealthy British families, in the '20s the property passed to an oil magnate who added quaint cottages for his celebrity visitors, like silent film star Mary Pickford (it is even rumored that Al Capone once spent the night!). Today, the Monarch Cove Inn offers a variety of genial accommodations—as well as an enchanting site for an oceanview wedding.

The inn's vintage façade is framed against a backdrop of swaying treetops and flowering greenery. Listen closely and you can hear the rush of the tide just beyond. Off to one side, a serpentine path meanders through an informal English garden, where a parade of fluffy hydrangeas, wild lavender and California poppies charms the eye. Here, a winsome statue peeks out from behind a hedge; there, a canopy of climbing heirloom roses makes an inviting hideaway. Finally, the path comes to a large clearing, and you find yourself face to face with the sea; when the sun dispels the morning mist, the breathtaking azure panorama stretches all the way to Monterey.

The clearing comprises a carpet of green lawn that sweeps along the cliffs, and an expansive wooden deck that takes center stage. Couples say their vows on the deck or the lawn, with the splashing surf just below. A hidden path leads down to an area called The Terrace (really a swath of grass perched below the gardens) where guests sip cocktails and savor the refreshing sea breeze.

Next, everyone moves to the deck for the reception. Whether styled elegant, casual or somewhere in between, the picture-postcard setting will have everyone wearing an "I'm-in-Heaven" smile.

The wedding party usually takes over the inn for the weekend, and though continental breakfast is brought to each room, you can arrange for an al fresco brunch the next morning out on the deck. To experience the inn's nighttime ambiance, host a rehearsal dinner beginning with a blazing sunset, followed by a candlelight soirée. Lodging includes spacious suites and private cottages, some with Jacuzzi and fireplace, all with dynamic views. One thing is certain: Whatever room is yours for the night, the inn will make you feel at home.

CEREMONY, EVENT/RECEPTION CAPACITY: The site holds 150 guests outdoors.

MEETING CAPACITY: The Inn accommodates up to 40 guests seated theater-style.

FEES & DEPOSITS: A $2,500 deposit is required to reserve your date. The balance is due 60 days prior to the event. Rental fees range $4,000–10,000 depending on the date of the event.

AVAILABILITY: Year-round, daily, 10am–6pm.

SERVICES/AMENITIES:

Catering: BYO
Kitchen Facilities: prep only
Tables & Chairs: BYO
Linens, Silver, etc.: BYO
Restrooms: wheelchair accessible
Dance Floor: on deck
Bride's Dressing Area: CBA
Meeting Equipment: BYO

Parking: limited on-site, off-site lot provided, shuttle recommended
Accommodations: 11 guestrooms
Telephone: emergency use only
Outdoor Night Lighting: access only, BYO
Outdoor Cooking Facilities: BYO
Cleanup: caterer or renter
View: ocean panorama, garden, hills
Other: wedding planner/coordinator available

RESTRICTIONS:

Alcohol: BYO
Smoking: outside only
Music: amplified OK outside with volume restrictions

Wheelchair Access: limited
Insurance: not required

Shadowbrook

Restaurant & Gardens

1750 Wharf Road, Capitola
831/475-1222 or toll free 888/475-1222
www.shadowbrook-capitola.com
office@shadowbrook-capitola.com

- Rehearsal Dinners
- Ceremonies
- Wedding Receptions
- Corp. Events/Mtgs.
- Private Parties
- Accommodations

Shadowbrook is unlike any place we've ever seen and, truth be told, you can't really see it until you're actually in it. Almost completely hidden at the base of a steep, beautifully landscaped hillside, the site has a tantalizing aura of mystery and romance. We were intrigued. Instead of descending via the cable car, we walked down one of the winding garden paths through a riot of palms, ferns, colorful flowers, waterfalls and koi-filled ponds.

When we finally reached the restaurant, it proved to be quite remarkable. The building—originally built in the 1920s as a log cabin summer home—now consists of six distinctly different rooms and three patios in tiers above Soquel Creek. Shadowbrook continues to be named "Most Romantic Restaurant" by various Bay Area publications year after year, and it's easy to see why. The garden theme, so meticulously executed outside, is carried throughout the interior. Greenery is visible everywhere, from vines clinging to the ceilings in the Main Dining Room to the almost-100-year-old cypress growing through the ceiling of the Garden Room. And then there's your choice of views: gardens, woods, the quietly flowing creek or all of the above.

Weddings have been held at Shadowbrook since the early 1950s, and the recently remodeled Rock Room Lounge is a sublime spot for a ceremony. While its massive wooden beams, impressive stone fireplace and stone walls convey a comforting sense of history, it's the partially glass ceiling and wall that make ceremonies here truly magical. Through the glass everyone can watch the bride's entrance as she walks down a garden path, framed by the gorgeous landscape. Outdoor ceremonies on the private Creekside Patio are also blessed by nature: Held at the water's edge, they're enveloped in a lush mix of ferns, flowers and coastal redwoods. At dusk, the surrounding treescape comes alive with twinkle lights that mirror the stars in the evening sky.

Every room at Shadowbrook has its own individual charms. The Fireside Room dates back to 1947, and the original stone fireplace, redwood walls, and Craftsman-style lighting fixtures preserve its rustic feel. A lovely choice for an intimate event is the Redwood Room, featuring redwood beams and wainscoting, and a sun-drenched brick patio next to the chef's herb garden. The Owner's Private Reserve Room will make you feel like you have the restaurant all to yourself, as a fire blazes in the river rock fireplace. Larger groups who still want a sense of privacy will appreciate the Wine Cellar Room, a redwood and brick room with a brick fireplace and a collection of fine wines on display. Last, but certainly not least, is the Greenhouse Room, which delights the senses with an abundance of plants and light. Windows along the entire length of the room afford a view of the creek, and open to let in fresh coastal breezes.

For decades people have been drawn to Shadowbrook for its incomparable ambiance, and now they have another reason to come: the food. Chef de Cuisine Ashley Hosmer utilizes regional products, organics and hormone-free meats to provide diners with consistently high-quality cuisine. Each menu is tailored to your tastes, and thanks to a talented on-site pastry chef, you can even order custom wedding and celebration cakes. It's clear to us that the restaurant's popularity has only increased its emphasis on customer service. As the Banquet and Events Manager says, "We're more interested in having you tell us what you want, rather than us telling you what you can have."

CEREMONY CAPACITY: The Creekside Patio and the Rock Room Lounge each accommodate up to 100 guests.

EVENT/RECEPTION & MEETING CAPACITY: For large events, wedding receptions or personal preference, you may reserve the entire restaurant (which accommodates up to 225 seated guests) when it is not open to the public. For rehearsal dinners and smaller social or business functions, you may reserve private areas or rooms within the restaurant. The Greenhouse Room holds 60 guests, the Wine Cellar Room 46, the Redwood Room 26, and the Owner's Private Reserve Room 18.

FEES & DEPOSITS: For weddings and larger events, there is a facility fee of $2,500 for exclusive use and $500–1,250 for semiprivate use. For smaller social or business events during regular operating hours, private room rental fees range $100–200 depending upon the size of the room. The deposit required to book most events is equal to the food and beverage minimum or the facility fee/room rental fee, whichever is higher. Three-course meals start at $35/person. Alcohol, tax and service charges are additional.

AVAILABILITY: Daily, 9am–10pm. Earlier hours for business meetings can be arranged.

SERVICES/AMENITIES:
Catering: provided, no BYO (except for cake)
Kitchen Facilities: n/a
Tables & Chairs: provided
Linens, Silver, etc.: provided
Restrooms: wheelchair accessible
Dance Floor: in lounge area
Bride's & Groom's Dressing Area: yes
Meeting Equipment: PA, microphones, projection screen, other CBA

Parking: ample, complimentary
Accommodations: no guestrooms
Telephone: complimentary
Outdoor Night Lighting: on patio and paths
Outdoor Cooking Facilities: no
Cleanup: provided
View: Soquel Creek and gardens
Other: event coordination

RESTRICTIONS:
Alcohol: provided, or BYO with corkage fee
Smoking: patio only
Music: amplified OK indoors with volume limits; outdoors, acoustic only

Wheelchair Access: yes
Insurance: not required
Other: no rice or birdseed

Overwhelmed? Use the search criteria on www.HereComesTheGuide.com to narrow down your choices.

Chaminade Resort & Spa

Resort & Spa

One Chaminade Lane, Santa Cruz
831/475-5600
www.chaminade.com
snorfleet@benchmarkmanagement.com

- Rehearsal Dinners
- Ceremonies
- Wedding Receptions
- Corp. Events/Mtgs.
- Private Parties
- Accommodations

Set high on a mountain bluff overlooking forested hills, Chaminade Resort & Spa is a sublime Mediterranean-style retreat blessed with a stunning view of Monterey Bay and the Santa Cruz Mountains. A recent $11 million renovation has added a refreshing, contemporary flair to this historic estate, mingling the best of Old World elegance and modern luxury. The original Mission-style buildings, constructed in the 1930s, have been expanded into a gracious resort set in the midst of meticulously tended gardens and embraced by 300 acres of native oak, redwood and madrone.

Naturally, such romantic surroundings make Chaminade a prime spot for weddings. Have your ceremony on the Courtyard Terrace, an intimate setting reminiscent of a Spanish plaza thanks to planter walls brimming with flowers and the tranquil splashing of a tiered fountain. Couples recite their vows atop a slightly elevated stage, canopied by an arbor laced with climbing roses and seasonal wisteria. In the background, a sweeping vista of native woodland and the brilliant blue bay accents the photo-worthy moment. Another pretty possibility is the Sunset Patio, which guests enter through an archway of bougainvillea. Ornamental grasses, lavender and blooming perennials create a fragrant garden atmosphere, and as the bride and groom recite their vows they're framed by a dramatic panorama of rolling hills and the Pacific on the horizon.

Large receptions are held in the Santa Cruz Ballroom. A high, soffited ceiling arches overhead, while windows on three sides overlook the wooded valley and the sea in the distance. The ballroom has a generous dance floor and access to its own balcony. Smaller celebrations gather in the Sunset Room, with arched floor-to-ceiling windows that bring the outside in; another choice is the Seascape Room, which adjoins the Fireside Patio and shares the same spectacular views of the forest and ocean.

Lavish and varied wedding packages offer a number of bride-pleasing amenities, such as complimentary valet parking for all your guests and custom wedding cakes.

After the festivities wind down, you and your guests will discover that the accommodations here are as enticing as the scenery. Guestrooms have been stylishly updated with granite counters, Spanish-inspired dark wood furnishings and a bold color palette that reflects the rich beauty of the California coast. Newlyweds will also appreciate the lush views from their private patio, and dreamy featherbeds that invite late-morning lingering.

Another feel-good feature: Chaminade Resort is a certified "Green Business." This commitment extends to their spa, which has a holistic approach to relaxation and rejuvenation, and only uses natural products. Throw a private spa party for your bachelorette gathering, or choose the "Time for Two Package" and indulge in some pampering for you and your groom; the spa also has special bridal options, including makeup consultation and application.

With an on-site pool, tennis courts and, of course, miles of beautiful hiking trails, there's plenty to keep everyone entertained. And let's not forget dinner in the Sunset Restaurant, the resort's award-winning fine dining establishment. Off property, you can stroll on a beach, go wine tasting, rock climb or board a yacht for a sunset cruise.

You'll be able to relax and truly enjoy yourself, knowing you've entrusted your celebration to experienced professionals, dedicated to providing world-class hospitality down to the tiniest detail. Along with the outstanding facilities and gorgeous location, a "dream come true" wedding at Chaminade Resort & Spa is virtually a sure thing.

CEREMONY CAPACITY: The Courtyard Terrace holds 250 seated and the Sunset Patio up to 200 seated guests.

EVENT/RECEPTION & MEETING CAPACITY: The facility can accommodate 250 seated or 300 standing, indoors or outdoors.

FEES & DEPOSITS: For weddings, a $1,000–5,000 nonrefundable deposit is required (based on guest count); the estimated balance is due 5 working days prior to the event. For Saturday evening Ballroom events, there is a guest minimum. Other spaces also have guest minimums, call for details.

Wedding packages are available that include site rentals, setup, cleanup, all furniture and linens, professional event coordination, generous hors d'oeuvres, buffet or sit-down meal, deluxe wedding cake, discounted guestrooms and complimentary valet parking. Packages range $94–154/person; beverages, tax and service charges are additional. Wedding package price varies depending on day of week and time of year. Special rates are available for overnight accommodations for the wedding couple, call for details.

For other types of events, call for details.

AVAILABILITY: Year-round, weekends. Saturday wedding reception luncheons 11am–4pm, dinners 5pm–midnight. Friday and Sunday events, please call for hours of availability.

SERVICES/AMENITIES:

Catering: provided, no BYO
Kitchen Facilities: n/a
Tables & Chairs: provided
Linens, Silver, etc.: provided
Restrooms: wheelchair accessible
Dance Floor: included in package
Bride's Dressing Area: yes
Meeting Equipment: provided
Other: on-site wedding cake, spa services, tennis courts, AV equipment, hiking trails, event coordination

Parking: complimentary valet
Accommodations: 156 guestrooms
Telephone: house phone
Outdoor Night Lighting: provided
Outdoor Cooking Facilities: BBQ CBA
Cleanup: provided
View: garden patio, pool area, fountain, landscaped grounds; panorama of forest, valley, Pacific Ocean and rolling hills

RESTRICTIONS:

Alcohol: provided, no BYO
Smoking: outdoors only
Music: amplified OK indoors, acoustic only outdoors

Wheelchair Access: yes
Insurance: not required
Other: no rice or birdseed

Hollins House at Pasatiempo

Banquet Facility

20 Clubhouse Road, Santa Cruz

831/459-9177

www.thehollinshouse.com
mseifert@pasatiempo.com

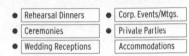

- Rehearsal Dinners
- Ceremonies
- Wedding Receptions
- Corp. Events/Mtgs.
- Private Parties
- Accommodations

The Hollins House, built in 1929 by championship golfer Marion Hollins, is located above the Pasatiempo Golf Club in the Santa Cruz Mountains, not far from Highway 17. Approached through acres of green fairways, the house is situated atop a knoll and offers panoramic views of Monterey Bay. You can reserve either the entire facility or just the Hollins Room and patio.

The main dining room is very long, with high ceilings, big mirrors and picture windows with views of the garden and ocean beyond. There's also a fireplace and hardwood parquet dance floor. The Tap Room is a more informal space, a cocktail lounge with a long brass bar, fireplace and windows overlooking garden and ocean. The adjacent garden is narrow, with a lawn bordered by profusely blooming impatiens. A medium-sized patio, surrounded by wisteria and situated next to the Hollins Room, is a picturesque place for an outdoor reception. The Hollins Room is an intimate private dining room with a big mirror, fireplace, chandelier, rounded bay windows with bench seat and a vista of the Pacific Ocean framed by nearby oak trees. The banquet coordinator will assist you with all of your event arrangements, from flowers to specialized menus.

CEREMONY CAPACITY: The Garden with gazebo holds 200 seated guests.

EVENT/RECEPTION CAPACITY: The entire facility accommodates 80–250 seated or standing guests in the summer and fall and 175 guests during cooler months. The Hollins Room and Patio, combined, hold 30 seated guests.

MEETING CAPACITY: The Hollins Room accommodates 10–30 seated conference-style; the Dining Room holds 50 seated conference- or theater-style.

FEES & DEPOSITS: A nonrefundable $2,500 deposit for the entire Hollins House or $500 deposit for the Hollins Room is required to secure your date. The total balance is due 7 days prior to the event, along with the final guest count. The facility fee for the entire Hollins House ranges $3,500–5,500. For the Hollins Room and Patio, it's $500. The ceremony setup fee is $900.

Hors d'oeuvres/buffets run approximately $40/person and seated meals for up to 100 guests run $40–53/person. You may customize your menu with help from the chef and in-house event coordinator. For parties of 50 or more, a $300 security guard is required. Alcohol, tax and a 19% service charge are additional. There's also a $2/person cake-cutting charge.

For meetings, Hollins House offers customized packages that may include continental breakfast, full lunch and dinner, plus tee times when available.

AVAILABILITY: For weddings, the entire Hollins House is available Saturday 11am–4pm and 4pm–11pm with a buyout, or Sunday 4pm–9pm. For the Main Dining Room and Patio only, 6pm–11pm Saturday. Meeting availability is 8am–4pm Monday–Friday, and Tuesday–Saturday evenings from 6pm–11pm.

SERVICES/AMENITIES:

Catering: provided, no BYO

Kitchen Facilities: n/a

Tables & Chairs: provided

Linens, Silver, etc.: provided

Restrooms: wheelchair accessible

Dance Floor: yes

Bride's Dressing Area: yes

Meeting Equipment: AV, extra charge

Other: meetings with golf

Parking: large lots

Accommodations: no guestrooms

Telephone: emergency use only

Outdoor Night Lighting: yes

Outdoor Cooking Facilities: BBQ CBA

Cleanup: provided

View: Monterey Bay and Pasatiempo Golf Course

RESTRICTIONS:

Alcohol: provided

Smoking: outside only

Music: amplified OK

Wheelchair Access: yes, ramp

Insurance: not required

Amphitheatre of the Redwoods
at Pema Osel Ling

2013 Eureka Canyon Road, Santa Cruz Mountains
831/761-6270

www.polmountainretreat.com
info@polmountainretreat.com

Retreat & Conference Center

● Rehearsal Dinners	● Corp. Events/Mtgs.
● Ceremonies	● Private Parties
● Wedding Receptions	● Accommodations

The Amphitheatre of the Redwoods is part of the Pema Osel Ling Retreat Center, a name that means "Lotus Land of Clear Light." The phrase conjures up images of a mystical mountain paradise, and it's an apt vision: Sequestered on over 102 acres of redwood forests, open meadows and gardens, this natural haven provides a sense of tranquility that's often missing from the frenzy surrounding a wedding. That peaceful easy feeling begins as you start the drive up Eureka Canyon into the wilds of the Santa Cruz Mountains. Dense woods with mist-shrouded treetops, fern grottoes and an occasional deer prepare you for the center's rustic yet welcoming ambiance.

With a variety of on-site accommodations ranging from large family homes to cozy cabins and campsites, you might want to take over the entire center for your own destination wedding weekend. Guests often meet up first at the Orchard House, a two-story lodge with a fireplace and a towering redwood growing right up through the front deck. Greet everyone with the center's signature mint iced tea, hand out maps and itineraries, and let the fun begin.

The retreat center has several extraordinary locations for ceremonies. The Amphitheatre of the Redwoods offers an intimate forest experience. The wind whistles through the branches, and the cry of blue jays and chattering squirrels make you feel like you're in the middle of nowhere. A soaring canopy of magnificent redwoods stretches heavenward, the boughs weaving patterns against the blue sky. You can also wed amidst another awe-inspiring natural phenomenon: a real-life "fairy ring"—a circle of redwoods, born from one "grandmother" tree that survived a storm. Underground, all the trees' roots intertwine for added strength—just as you and your groom will support each other during your marriage. What an inspired place to say "I do"! The most spacious ceremony site is Bayview Meadow and Terrace. With guests seated on the treelined meadow, bride and groom wed on a redwood deck at the edge of a hillside. Behind them, green thickets soften the view, while the distant blue waters of Monterey Bay wink in the sunlight.

Receptions are celebrated in the Gallery Meadow, which overlooks an Asian fountain courtyard and art gallery. Choose whatever type of tenting and configuration you want, and the center's event pros will make it happen. The Dining Hall, a ranch-style A-frame that opens to a garden, is an indoor/outdoor option. Several more benefits are worth noting. One is the knowledgeable staff, who'll assist you in structuring your agenda to include yoga, massage, hikes, bonfires, pool parties or whatever you can dream up. Then there's the award-winning gourmet catering. From vegan to prime rib, the on-site culinary team will not only whip up a delicious wedding feast, but will handle brunches, rehearsal dinners and barbecues, too.

There is no curfew here so you can party as late as you like, and there's no corkage fee so you can bring your own libations. What there is at this retreat is beautiful scenery, friendly banquet staff and a refuge of freedom and renewal to call your own.

The Pema Ling Osel Retreat Center is a nonprofit run by the Vajrayana Foundation that preserves the spiritual, cultural and artistic traditions of Tibetan Buddhism. Couples who choose Amphitheatre of the Redwoods or any other of the retreat center's event venues have the added pleasure of supporting the foundation's mission to cultivate the Buddhist ideals of peace and compassion in the world.

CEREMONY CAPACITY: The Center holds 150 seated guests indoors and 400 seated outdoors.

EVENT/RECEPTION CAPACITY: The Center accommodates 135 seated or 300 standing indoors and 400 seated or standing outdoors.

MEETING CAPACITY: Meeting spaces hold 175 seated guests indoors and 400 seated outdoors.

FEES & DEPOSITS: A $1,000 deposit is required to reserve your date. 40% of the estimated event total is due within 2 weeks of initial deposit, and the balance is due upon check-in. Rental fees range $1,950–7,950 depending on the day of the event, the length of your stay and the time of year, among other factors. Meals range $15–120/person. A 20% service charge is additional.

AVAILABILITY: Year-round, daily, anytime.

SERVICES/AMENITIES:

Catering: provided
Kitchen Facilities: fully equipped
Tables & Chairs: some provided, CBA
Linens, Silver, etc.: some provided, CBA
Restrooms: wheelchair accessible
Dance Floor: portable provided, CBA
Bride's Dressing Area: yes
Meeting Equipment: some provided, CBA
Other: event coordination

Parking: large lot
Accommodations: 60 beds in various cabins and houses, camping space for 350 tents
Telephone: house phones (local only)
Outdoor Night Lighting: provided
Outdoor Cooking Facilities: BBQ on site
Cleanup: provided
View: courtyard, landscaped grounds, garden, pond, forest, fountain, valley, canyon; panorama of hills, coastline and ocean

RESTRICTIONS:

Alcohol: BYO
Smoking: in designated areas only
Music: amplified OK

Wheelchair Access: yes
Insurance: liability required

The professionals in the back of this book are the best in the business. How do we know? Read page 701.

Kennolyn
Hilltop Hacienda & Stone Creek Village

Address withheld to ensure privacy. Soquel

831/479-6700

www.kennolyn.com
weddings@kennolyn.com

Special Event & Retreat Center

- Rehearsal Dinners
- Ceremonies
- Wedding Receptions
- Corp. Events/Mtgs.
- Private Parties
- Accommodations

The first event venue in Santa Cruz County to earn the prestigious Diamond Certified Award, Kennolyn offers a variety of facilities with their own personality, unique features and considerable charm. The Hilltop Hacienda, set literally on top of one of the Santa Cruz Mountains, overlooks redwood forests and Monterey Bay. It not only has a fabulous view, but it's so quiet up here you can truly hear yourself think (or not think, as the case may be). You enter this Spanish-style building through a sun-drenched courtyard, with a four-tiered fountain bubbling in its center and pots of vibrant flowers all around. Step into the banquet room and you'll find it equally welcoming. Spacious and unpretentious in design, it has a wood-beamed ceiling with wrought-iron chandeliers that convey elegant simplicity. At one end of the room, a lofty fireplace mantel of rich chocolate brown provides a striking contrast to the light tan walls. Sets of white French doors along two sides open onto either the courtyard or a heavenly patio that faces the bay. When the sun goes down, you can extend the day's warmth by lighting a fire in the fireplace. As you might imagine, weddings here are delightful, and for corporate seminars or retreats you'd be hard pressed to find a more restful spot.

Located in another part of this 300-acre redwood paradise is Stone Creek Village, a miniature "town" reminiscent of a bygone era when logging and mining were going concerns. It contains a terrific lodge, sports facilities and Kennolyn's overnight accommodations. While this area is most often used for weekend reunions and retreats, it has become very popular for wedding weekends. This is a wonderful arrangement, where over the course of a weekend, the bridal families and wedding party spend quality time together in the Village, and join their extended family and friends at the Hilltop Hacienda for the wedding reception itself. Some couples and their overnight guests start off the wedding day with a ropes course, then join the rest of the wedding guests for a ceremony on the Hacienda lawn followed by the reception. Afterwards, they can all go back to Stone Creek Village and relax.

The old-fashioned Lodge, with its great river rock fireplace, is Stone Creek Village's main space. Your guests can stay in cabin cottages appointed with antiques, down comforters and old-fashioned stoves.

Kennolyn's gorgeous surroundings will bring beauty and serenity to any event.

CEREMONY CAPACITY: The site holds up to 50 seated indoors or 300 seated outdoors.

EVENT/RECEPTION CAPACITY: The site can accommodate 120 seated or standing indoors and 300 seated or standing outdoors.

MEETING CAPACITY: Meeting spaces hold up to 100 seated guests.

FEES & DEPOSITS: To reserve your date, 25% of your anticipated event total is required as a non-refundable deposit. Another 25% payment is required 90 days prior to the event date. The balance plus a refundable $500 damage deposit are payable 10 days prior to the event. Wedding packages start at $55.95/person and include a private consultation with Kennolyn's professional wedding coordinator, event coordination on the wedding day, hors d'oeuvres, buffet or plated meal, setup and cleanup, tables, chairs and linens, plus an invitation to Kennolyn's Wedding Day Overview. Beverages, facility fee, tax and a 20% service charge are additional.

AVAILABILITY: May–October, Friday–Sunday or by arrangement.

SERVICES/AMENITIES:

Catering: provided, no BYO

Kitchen Facilities: n/a

Tables & Chairs: provided

Linens, Silver, etc.: provided

Restrooms: wheelchair accessible

Dance Floor: courtyard or CBA, extra fee

Bride's & Groom's Dressing Area: yes

Meeting Equipment: CBA

Parking: ample, several lots

Accommodations: 30 cabin cottages and suites

Telephone: house phones

Outdoor Night Lighting: yes

Outdoor Cooking Facilities: BBQ

Cleanup: provided, renter cleans decorations

View: vistas of Monterey Bay and Santa Cruz

Other: event coordination, carriage rides, full range of sports activities

RESTRICTIONS:

Alcohol: provided, no BYO

Smoking: courtyard or patio only

Music: amplified OK until 9pm

Wheelchair Access: most areas, not all

Insurance: not required

Other: no pets, glitter, rice or birdseed; decorations with approval

Monterey and Carmel

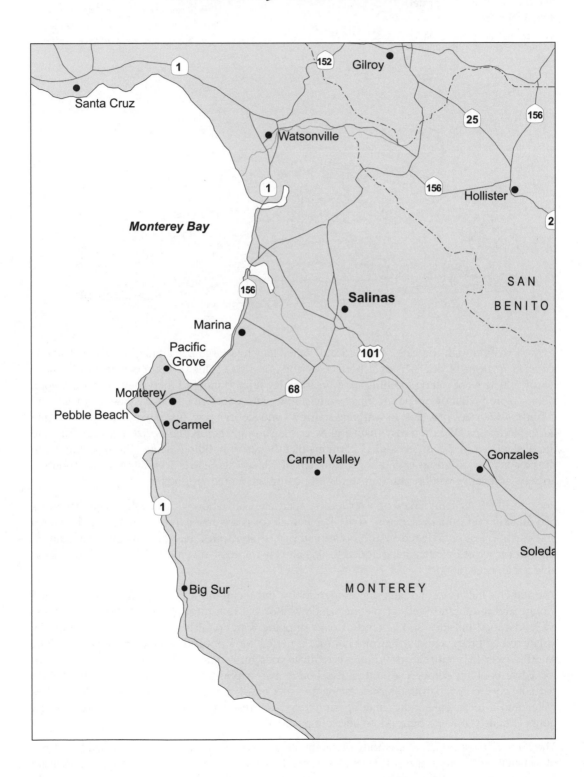

Santa Cruz

152
Gilroy

25
156

Watsonville

156
Hollister

2

Monterey Bay

SAN

BENITO

156

Salinas

Marina

101

Pacific
Grove

68

Monterey

Pebble Beach

Carmel

Gonzales

Carmel Valley

1

Soleda

Big Sur

MONTEREY

Carmel Valley Ranch Resort

Resort

One Old Ranch Road, Carmel
831/626-2579

www.carmelvalleyranch.com
weddings@carmelvalleyranch.com

- Rehearsal Dinners
- Ceremonies
- Wedding Receptions
- Corp. Events/Mtgs.
- Private Parties
- Accommodations

As we drive through the gate of the Carmel Valley Ranch, a large black-tailed deer nonchalantly saunters in front of our car. It's a perfect welcome to this exclusive country hideaway, whose nearly 500 acres of rolling foothills are a breathtaking embodiment of the valley's timeless allure. Neon-colored wildflowers pop from green meadows, rare California condors glide overhead, and countless oak trees play host to warbling sparrows and Steller's jays. Just beyond, the tawny Santa Lucia Mountains take on a rosy-mauve glow as the sun dips below the horizon. So careful were the designers to maintain ecological harmony that the resort buildings seem almost sculpted into the pastoral surroundings by Mother Nature herself. The golf course is accredited by the Audubon Society, and native wildlife wanders undisturbed throughout the grounds.

Recently, the Ranch embarked on a spare-no-expense revitalization with a fresh design that puts a playful spin on Carmel's signature style. The new décor is a warm expression of natural textures and earth tones, punctuated by the occasional rich, fruit-inspired hue or contemporary pattern. An extra layer of luxe has been added to this already impressive venue, making it keenly desirable for any celebration.

The Ranch's hub is the Lodge, where open lobby and reception areas flow into the view-filled lounge and restaurant: Walls of picture windows look out to a turquoise pool and deck, framed by landscaped hillsides and a stand of oaks dripping with Spanish moss. The attractive locale, enhanced by fire pits and an Infinity hot tub, is perfect for a poolside soirée or rehearsal dinner. Another twist for your rehearsal dinner is to invite your guests into the Ranch's Adventure Kitchen for a live cooking demo. The Lodge also houses two sophisticated ballrooms, which adjoin a partially covered wraparound terrace facing the oak canopy. A tall stacked-stone fountain splashes water into a rectangular pool, making the terrace a refreshing place for cocktail mixers. Social hours can also convene beneath an adjacent pavilion.

The Ranch's most popular ceremony site is the River Lawn, a sweep of grass crowned by a froth of seashell-pink climbing roses. Lavender-spiked hedgerows along the perimeter cast a delicate perfume on the air, and a backdrop of forested hills completes the pretty tableau. And since we're in the heart of Carmel Valley Wine Country, why not wed on the resort's new Vineyard Lawn, surrounded by over four acres of Pinot Noir grapevines?

For a reception with an indoor-outdoor flow, reserve the Golf Clubhouse. It boasts its own terrace next to the Valley Lawn (another ceremony site with lush mountain and canyon views). Wherever you celebrate on the property, you'll appreciate the staff's personalized, unobtrusive service and expertise in organizing your destination event weekend.

After the festivities, savor some alone time in your spacious luxury suite; actually, ALL the accommodations are suites with cathedral ceilings, cozy fireplaces and balconies for soaking up the valley vista. Though the rooms convey a soothing understated elegance, they include up-to-the-minute amenities embodying the latest technological advances.

If this isn't enough pampering, the resort's Spa Aiyana, a new 10,000-square-foot facility, offers an exhilarating menu of services and includes a salon, fireplace suites and treetop fitness center. Ahhh, what a sublime way to round out your extraordinary Carmel Valley Ranch experience!

CEREMONY CAPACITY: The resort accommodates up to 250 seated guests indoors and 400 outdoors.

EVENT/RECEPTION CAPACITY: The resort holds 220 seated indoors and 300 outdoors; 300 standing indoors and 400 outdoors.

MEETING CAPACITY: The resort accommodates 250 seated guests.

FEES & DEPOSITS: A deposit equal to the site fee plus 10% of the estimated food and beverage cost is required to reserve your date. The balance is due according to your customized deposit schedule as agreed upon in your contract. Site fees start at $5,000, depending on venue selection. Dinners start at $80/person. Tax, alcohol and a 21% service charge are additional.

AVAILABILITY: Year-round, daily, 6am-11pm.

SERVICES/AMENITIES:

Catering: provided
Kitchen Facilities: yes
Tables & Chairs: provided
Linens, Silver, etc.: provided
Restrooms: wheelchair accessible
Dance Floor: provided, portable CBA
Bride's & Groom's Dressing Area: CBA
Meeting Equipment: provided
Other: spa services, AV equipment

Parking: large lot, self-parking, valet parking
Accommodations: 139 guest suites
Telephone: house and office phones
Outdoor Night Lighting: CBA
Outdoor Cooking Facilities: BBQ CBA
Cleanup: provided
View: landscaped grounds, garden, forest, mountains, golf course, vineyards

RESTRICTIONS:

Alcohol: provided
Smoking: outside only
Music: amplified OK with restrictions

Wheelchair Access: yes
Insurance: not required

The Highlands Inn, A Hyatt Hotel

Oceanside Inn

120 Highlands Drive, Carmel
831/622-5457
www.highlandsinn.hyatt.com
WeddingHIGPH@hyatt.com

- Rehearsal Dinners
- Ceremonies
- Wedding Receptions
- Corp. Events/Mtgs.
- Private Parties
- Accommodations

Built in 1916 in the Carmel Highlands just south of Carmel, the Highlands Inn, A Hyatt Hotel, is one of the most sought-after event locations in California. Noted for its panoramic views and extraordinary cliffside setting, the inn provides an idyllic environment for a special celebration.

After its multimillion-dollar award-winning renovation, this venue is more stunning than ever. Commanding one of the world's most spectacular vistas, with exploding waves crashing 200 feet below, the inn offers a variety of first-class facilities for either business functions or weddings. For outdoor ceremonies, a redwood deck complete with contemporary gazebo is perched just above the rocky cliffs overlooking the Pacific.

After the ceremony, guests are escorted into a variety of reception areas—each is elegant, with comfortable furnishings and outstanding views. The inn's chefs are renowned for culinary excellence, and the extensive wine and champagne list frequently garners the Grand Award from *Wine Spectator*. The staff can organize a traditional party or a more creative event for the adventuresome. If you are looking for a very special place for one of life's great moments, the incomparable Highlands Inn should be high on your list.

CEREMONY CAPACITY: The outdoor gazebo accommodates 100 seated guests. If the weather is uncooperative, the Fireside Room can be used.

EVENT/RECEPTION CAPACITY: The inn can accommodate 12–120 seated guests indoors. The Gazebo and Deck hold up to 100 seated outdoors.

FEES & DEPOSITS: Site fees range $1,000–5,000. Luncheons start at $85/person, dinners at $105/person; alcohol, tax and an 18% service charge are additional. Half the estimated total is due 4 weeks prior to the event, and the balance is due 10 working days prior. A final confirmed guest count is required 3 working days in advance of the event.

AVAILABILITY: Year-round, daily, anytime.

SERVICES/AMENITIES:

Catering: provided, no BYO
Kitchen Facilities: n/a
Tables & Chairs: provided
Linens, Silver, etc.: provided
Restrooms: wheelchair accessible
Dance Floor: CBA, extra charge
Bride's Dressing Area: CBA
Meeting Equipment: full range CBA, extra fee
Other: off-premise catering also available

Parking: complimentary valet
Accommodations: 48 guestrooms, including 10 spa suites
Telephone: house, guestroom or pay phone
Outdoor Night Lighting: limited
Outdoor Cooking Facilities: n/a
Cleanup: provided
View: coastline panorama at the gateway to Big Sur

RESTRICTIONS:

Alcohol: provided
Smoking: outdoors only
Music: amplified restricted

Wheelchair Access: limited
Insurance: may be required

Want to know WHAT TO ASK a potential location or vendor? Check out our Questions to Ask on page 17.

The Holly Farm

Private Estate & Garden

9200 Carmel Valley Road, Carmel
831/625-1926
www.hollyfarm.com
info@hollyfarm.com

● Rehearsal Dinners	● Corp. Events/Mtgs.
● Ceremonies	● Private Parties
● Wedding Receptions	● Accommodations

Here's a gem of a location that offers something rare—not only exclusive use, but the option to house up to 24 of your event guests for two to six days. Doyle and Mary Moses, The Holly Farm's owners, have fashioned their chic tropical hideaway in Carmel with destination weddings, special events and corporate retreats in mind, so you can treat your closest friends and family to a fun-filled getaway in a lush fantasy world of comfort and ease.

First established over 100 years ago, The Holly Farm is a private six-and-a-half-acre estate located in a sunny inland valley only five miles from the coast. The property contains the last holly "farm" in the state: 49 enormous holly trees that flank both sides of the entrance drive to the property. Doyle, himself a noted artist, expanded the original 4-bedroom, 3-bath adobe hacienda, and now it could easily grace the pages of *Architectural Digest*. Inside you'll find a pleasing mix of California-style architecture and contemporary furnishings; walls are a warm apricot, floors are oak and Mexican tile. Guests can mingle in front of the fireplace in the spacious, fully stocked kitchen, and then sit down for a rehearsal dinner or other intimate gathering in the sun-filled sunken dining room. The living room is kept cozy by a second fireplace, and there's a beautiful view of the Santa Lucia Mountains beyond the private fountain patio.

At the end of a nearby tropical garden path lies the Banana Cabana. This whimsical redwood bungalow features "island wild" décor, with bamboo curtains, futons, murals, eclectic artifacts and a wraparound redwood deck. Meanwhile, the newlyweds can play "Tarzan and Jane" in the Paraiso Suite, sheltered from the rest of the grounds by a low vine-covered adobe wall. This exotic getaway has a rustic service area for champagne and strawberries, a private bath and dressing room with potted orchids, and a Carmel flagstone fireplace.

Outdoors, the romance continues in the picturesque and colorful landscape. The Holly Farm's immaculately tended tropical gardens are complemented by hundreds of sweet-scented blossoms spilling over flowerbeds and pots; a small pond and sparkling waterfall next to a majestic oak tree make a lovely setting for wedding photos and ceremonies of up to 200 guests. A sweeping lawn with a classic farm windmill is perfect for larger weddings, while al fresco receptions in the Carriage House enjoy an impressive stone bar and an entertainment space for cocktails and dancing.

To top it all off, The Holly Farm also has a versatile chef who insists on using only the finest ingredients, including organic produce. The Moses family is passionate about food, and loves to create artfully presented dishes inspired by your personal favorites—whether they're gourmet vegan or hearty barbecue fare.

Up to 24 guests can actually lodge at The Holly Farm, but others staying nearby can still attend the wedding, the reception, Sunday Garden Brunch or an afternoon game of bocce ball. Past guests have dubbed this unique experience a "Wedding-Moon," so relaaax, and turn over all the details to The Holly Farm's expert and devoted care. We've sampled their hospitality firsthand, and can't decide what we enjoyed most—the delicious offerings the chef brought to our doorstep or being lulled to sleep by the tranquil melody of splashing fountains.

The staff here will lavish you with personal attention, and can arrange for the cream of local vendors to assist at your event. Their reputation for quiet efficiency and fine taste has earned them the patronage of an elite clientele. You too can join the privileged, when you "slow down and settle in" at the delightful Holly Farm.

CEREMONY CAPACITY: The Waterfall Pond Area holds up to 200 seated or standing guests; the Windmill Lawn Area accommodates up to 300 seated guests.

EVENT/RECEPTION & MEETING CAPACITY: The Carriage House seats 70 comfortably; the Banquet Lawn Area holds 300 seated guests. The Adobe Hacienda's Dining Room holds 32 seated guests.

FEES & DEPOSITS: The Holly Farm offers three different wedding packages that start at $15,000. The fees include exclusive use of the estate and all its facilities, sleeping accommodations for up to 24 people, daily maid service, assisted parking and event planning guidance. A $5,000 deposit plus a refundable $500 security deposit are required when reservations are confirmed. Catered meals are not included in the package, and start at $40/person. Alcohol, tax and a 15% service charge (on food only) are additional.

Fees for corporate retreats or business meetings vary; call for more information.

AVAILABILITY: Larger weddings, late April–November. Smaller, off-season weddings can be arranged. Corporate retreats or business meetings, daily, year-round.

SERVICES/AMENITIES:

Catering: provided, no BYO
Kitchen Facilities: available in guest cottages
Tables & Chairs: provided
Linens, Silver, etc.: provided
Restrooms: most are wheelchair accessible
Dance Floor: in Carriage House
Bride's & Groom's Dressing Area: yes
Meeting Equipment: microphone, screen

Parking: on-site, with attendant
Accommodations: up to 24 guests
Telephone: yes
Outdoor Night Lighting: yes
Outdoor Cooking Facilities: BBQs
Cleanup: provided
View: Carmel hills, valley and Santa Lucia Mtns.
Other: wireless internet, ping pong, darts, volleyball, bocce ball, croquet; massage, ceremonial music, bride's hair/makeup/nails

RESTRICTIONS:

Alcohol: BYO, no corkage fees
Smoking: outside only
Music: provided or BYO, amplified OK, with volume restrictions

Wheelchair Access: yes
Insurance: certificate required

La Playa Hotel

Historic Hotel

Camino Real and 8th Street, Carmel
800/582-8900, 831/624-6476

www.laplayahotel.com
rwood@laplayahotel.com

- Rehearsal Dinners
- Ceremonies
- Wedding Receptions
- Corp. Events/Mtgs.
- Private Parties
- Accommodations

Occupying several acres in the heart of residential Carmel, just two blocks from the beach, La Playa remains one of the loveliest and most inviting places we've had the pleasure to write about. Originally built in 1904 as a private residence, La Playa was converted and expanded into a hotel in 1916. Standing in front of the building, you feel a bit like you've been transported to Europe. The distinctly Mediterranean style, with earthy terracotta-tile roofs, soft pastel walls and a bright green formal garden are reminiscent of Italy. Even though there's a lovely patina about La Playa, make no mistake—this is a full-service resort hotel offering a contemporary freshness as well as a romantic Old World appeal.

For outdoor celebrations, the wrought-iron gazebo is the spot, set amid brick patios, a fountain, technicolor annuals, manicured lawns and climbing bougainvillea. The entire setting is lush and private. Inside are rooms of various size for private functions, with antiques, lithographs and memorabilia of early Carmel. The hotel is a refreshing destination for a personal or business retreat—here tasteful furnishings, French doors and magnificent views are standard amenities. We can't help but love this place. And if you can't drag yourself away, feel free to stay overnight, or have your honeymoon here, too.

CEREMONY CAPACITY: The gazebo area seats 120 guests.

EVENT/RECEPTION CAPACITY: The hotel can accommodate 12–150 seated guests.

MEETING CAPACITY: There are several rooms which hold 12–120 seated guests.

FEES & DEPOSITS: For weddings, a $2,500 nonrefundable deposit is required to confirm your date and banquet space. Half the estimated event total is due 6 weeks prior to the function; the remaining balance is due 3 weeks prior to the event. Rental fees range $250–1,900 depending upon the space rented. Reception buffets and plated meals range $34–60/person. Room rental fees, beverages, wedding cakes, tax and a 20% gratuity are additional. For meeting or corporate event information, contact the sales and catering department.

AVAILABILITY: Year-round, daily.

SERVICES/AMENITIES:

Catering: provided, no BYO

Kitchen Facilities: n/a

Tables & Chairs: provided

Linens, Silver, etc.: provided

Restrooms: wheelchair accessible

Dance Floor: portable

Bride's Dressing Area: CBA

Meeting Equipment: CBA, extra fee

Parking: on-street, valet

Accommodations: 75 guestrooms, 5 cottages

Telephone: guest phones

Outdoor Night Lighting: limited

Outdoor Cooking Facilities: no

Cleanup: provided

View: ocean and gardens

RESTRICTIONS:

Alcohol: provided, no BYO

Smoking: not allowed

Music: amplified OK until 10pm with restrictions

Wheelchair Access: yes

Insurance: not required

Mission Ranch

26270 Dolores Street, Carmel
831/624-3824
www.missionranchcarmel.com
banquet@missionranchcarmel.com

Historic Retreat

- Rehearsal Dinners
- Ceremonies
- Wedding Receptions
- Corp. Events/Mtgs.
- Private Parties
- Accommodations

Mission Ranch has been a Carmel tradition for over 50 years. Once a working dairy, the Ranch is a delightful and rustic retreat, extensively renovated in 1992. Situated on the grounds are a turn-of-the-century farmhouse, a bunkhouse, hotel rooms and triplex cottages with spectacular views of Carmel Beach and rugged Point Lobos. These historic buildings, surrounded by 100-year-old cypress trees and natural landscaping, offer the kind of quiet and peaceful ambiance not found in nearby bustling downtown Carmel.

Outdoor celebrations and ceremonies are often held on the brick patio of the Patio Barn or on the 4-plex lawn adjoining the meadow. The Patio Barn is known for its friendly bar and great dance floor, and it features a stage for live music. It has a wall of full-length glass doors opening onto a brick patio with a restful view of meadows and wetlands rolling down to Carmel River Beach. The Large Barn is also used as an adjunct to the Patio Barn for larger parties with its lofty three-story-high ceiling. The Catering Department prides itself on the uncompromising quality of its food and creative menus for any occasion. If you're looking for a place to hold a relaxed event in a classic country setting, this is it.

CEREMONY CAPACITY: The Patio accommodates 96 seated guests, the 4-Plex Lawn accommodates 168 seated guests.

EVENT/RECEPTION CAPACITY: The Patio Barn can accommodate up to 96 seated guests and the Large Barn up to 168 seated guests. There is a 50-guest minimum for rental of the barns.

MEETING CAPACITY: There are 3 different facilities which hold 12–168 seated guests.

FEES & DEPOSITS: The rental fee is required to reserve a date. A deposit in the amount of 60% of all estimated services is due 60 days prior to the event, with the remaining estimated balance due 10 days prior. The rental fee is $3,500–4,000 on Saturday and $2,500–3,500 on Friday or Sunday. The Barn rental fees cover a 5-hour maximum period. Entrée prices start at $48/person. Alcohol, tax and an 18% gratuity are additional. Call for meeting room rates.

AVAILABILITY: Year-round, daily, 8am–10pm.

SERVICES/AMENITIES:

Catering: provided, no BYO

Kitchen Facilities: n/a

Tables & Chairs: provided

Linens, Silver, etc.: provided

Restrooms: wheelchair accessible

Dance Floor: yes

Bride's Dressing Area: no

Meeting Equipment: BYO

Parking: large lot

Accommodations: 31 guestrooms

Telephone: guest phones

Outdoor Night Lighting: CBA

Outdoor Cooking Facilities: CBA

Cleanup: provided

View: meadow with sheep, Pt. Lobos & ocean

Other: full event planning services

RESTRICTIONS:

Alcohol: provided, no BYO

Smoking: not allowed in barns

Music: volume restrictions; no amplified outdoors

Wheelchair Access: yes

Insurance: required for entertainment

Want to find more locations and services? Check out our informative website, www.HereComesTheGuide.com.

645

Rancho Cañada Golf Club

Public Golf Club

4860 Carmel Valley Road, Carmel
831/622-2454
www.countryclubcaterers.com
info@countryclubcaterers.com

- Rehearsal Dinners
- Ceremonies
- Wedding Receptions
- Corp. Events/Mtgs.
- Private Parties
- Accommodations

The lovely green fairways and Spanish Colonial buildings of Rancho Cañada Golf Club are spread out on a spacious plateau in beautiful Carmel Valley. The road into the club winds through nicely landscaped grounds, past a small pond fringed with bamboo and golden poppies bathed in sunshine. Forested hillsides form a picturesque backdrop, and by the time you park your car, you're already surrendering to Rancho Cañada's serene, relaxed mood.

There are no pretensions here, just friendly professional service and appealing event spaces. Resting on land that was once part of a Spanish rancho, this historic facility pays homage to its heritage with classic Iberian architecture and décor that hints at the romantic days of Spanish grandees and exotic beauties in lace mantillas. The beige-toned buildings sport red-tile roofs, dark wood trim and arched doorways; tall oaks and fragrant pine trees, manicured hedges and flowerpots provide color.

Most gatherings begin in the heart of the golf club: the Fountain Courtyard. Guests enter a covered patio with wooden beams, ginger-colored wall tiles, and a stone wood-burning fireplace. The rest of the courtyard is under open sky, with a splashing fountain at the center providing a tranquil vision and hacienda flair. Garden beds in the corners spill over with blooms in a cheerful rhapsody of scarlet, yellow and magenta, while graceful saplings look on from the sidelines. In this clement section of Carmel Valley, guests enjoy hors d'oeuvres and champagne in this pretty plaza or mingle in the tastefully appointed foyer just inside before retiring to one of the adjacent banquet rooms for the reception.

The Fiesta Ballroom is a commodious event space with wood-beam ceiling and skylights contributing to an open, airy quality. Elaborate Mission-style chandeliers capture Old World elegance, and expansive picture windows make it seem as if your reception is set among the oak groves and camellia bushes, with everything cradled by the hilly vistas. Smaller gatherings enjoy the Merienda Room. It also features a vaulted open-beam ceiling and rustic fixtures. Creative accents include an alcove that showcases a framed watercolor and stone sculpture, and a series of beveled mirrors that add sparkle to a corner of the room. A wall of picture windows captures the cascading green fairways, adorned with clusters of trees and flowers and surrounded by the majestic hills. You can admire the view up close on the Merienda's outdoor patio, which is also suitable for cocktails or even a wedding ceremony.

The setting at Rancho Cañada is not this venue's only inviting attribute—so is the very reasonable price tag. The Club offers several packages of savory sit-down dinners or lavish buffets that take you from champagne toast to after-dinner coffee for a modest charge and no hidden extras (would you believe buffet luncheons starting at just $27.95 per person?!). And if you want to make golf part of your weekend, you'll get discounted rates for that as well. The Club's award-winning Executive Chef is adaptable, too, and he'll happily adjust the menu to suit your taste.

Though this facility is open to the public, the welcoming ambiance and quality service is on par with that of an exclusive country club. And the prestigious Carmel Valley location, just a few minutes from the fabled Carmel Mission and legendary beaches, will make your guests feel even more privileged to attend your special event at the Rancho Cañada Golf Club.

CEREMONY CAPACITY: The Merienda Patio holds up to 95 seated guests, and the Clubhouse Lawn up to 300 seated guests.

EVENT/RECEPTION & MEETING CAPACITY: The Fiesta Ballroom accommodates up to 400 seated or 550 standing guests, and the Merienda Ballroom up to 200 seated or 300 standing. These spaces can be divided into smaller sections for meetings or intimate events.

FEES & DEPOSITS: A $1,000 nonrefundable deposit is required to reserve your date; the balance is due 72 hours prior to the event. Rental fees for the Fiesta Room range $750–1,500 and for the Merienda Room range $500–1,000 depending on the space required and the day of the event. Lunches range $17–25/person, dinners $29–45/person. Or ask about their all-inclusive affordable wedding packages. Tax, alcohol and a 17% service charge are additional, as is a $500 ceremony setup fee.

AVAILABILITY: Year-round, daily, 7am–midnight.

SERVICES/AMENITIES:

Catering: provided, no BYO
Kitchen Facilities: n/a
Tables & Chairs: provided
Linens, Silver, etc.: provided
Restrooms: wheelchair accessible
Dance Floor: yes
Bride's Dressing Area: yes
Meeting Equipment: some, more CBA, extra fee

Parking: large lot
Accommodations: no guestrooms
Telephone: pay phones
Outdoor Night Lighting: limited
Outdoor Cooking Facilities: CBA
Cleanup: provided
View: golf fairways, valley, mountains
Other: event coordination

RESTRICTIONS:

Alcohol: provided or wine corkage $10/bottle
Smoking: outside only
Music: amplified OK

Wheelchair Access: yes
Insurance: not required

Bernardus Lodge

Lodge & Resort

415 Carmel Valley Road, Carmel Valley
831/658-3504

www.bernardus.com
reservations@bernardus.com

- Rehearsal Dinners
- Ceremonies
- Wedding Receptions
- Corp. Events/Mtgs.
- Private Parties
- Accommodations

You have to love a resort where the Concierge greets you by name and hands you a glass of fine wine as soon as you cross the threshold. This is just the beginning of the personalized services you'll receive at Bernardus Lodge.

Serenity and natural beauty are hallmarks of Carmel Valley, and the lodge's tasteful Old World-meets-Monterey styling harmonizes with the surrounding wilderness. The young resort has already garnered a collection of prestigious accolades, and may soon surpass the fame of the winery for which it was named. Bernardus vintages strive to "transcend the ordinary," and this idyllic retreat accomplishes the feat superbly.

The warm and inviting lobby has a pastoral European flavor with rich woods and textures softened by fresh-cut flowers and the glow from a stone hearth. A vaulted ceiling crowns the expansive space, and a glass door at the far end offers a tantalizing glimpse of what lies beyond. Set along a terraced hillside, the boutique resort's 57 sumptuous suites occupy several adobe buildings, spread out among acres of gardens, stately oak and pine trees, and a working vineyard.

The centerpiece of the grounds is the Croquet Lawn, a carpet of manicured grass. Overlooking the green is Wicket's Terrace, a delightful patio with a limestone fireplace and a trellis to shelter your intimate al fresco gathering. Adjoining the terrace is Wicket's Proper, a casual bistro with a built-in bar, hardwood floors, and plenty of windows facing the terrace. Small rehearsal dinners feel right at home in Marinus, the lodge's award-winning and decidedly sophisticated gourmet restaurant. A stunning 12-foot-wide limestone fireplace with a raised hearth lends distinction, and a sweep of windows brings in a magnificent mountain vista. Marinus also opens onto a peaceful terrace, complete with a meditation pool and water garden.

Lavish receptions come alive in the Meritage Ballroom, a discreetly elegant banquet space with 22-foot vaulted ceilings and wrought-iron chandeliers. Arched windows above French doors are hugged by velvet draperies, pulled back to capture a lush garden view. Several more cozy rooms at the lodge offer their own unique charms.

Perhaps what makes most brides fall in love with Bernardus is the spectacular Wedding Garden, a vast cornucopia of floral and herbal delights. A splashing fountain encircled with fragrant rosebushes welcomes the wedding guests, who take their seats on the lawn facing an elevated flagstone pavilion.

With the bridal party posed on the pavilion's broad steps, the bride and groom exchange vows under a classic stone pergola adorned with flowering vines. If you get married as evening falls, the setting sun paints a luminous panorama of cotton-candy pink and dusky orange over the Santa Lucia Mountains.

The romance continues in private guest suites that define sensual splendor: a complimentary wine grotto, limestone fireplace, two-person tub, and a featherbed dressed in imported linens that enfold you in a dreamy embrace. For more pampering, the on-site spa offers a tempting array of signature treatments, and the salon attends to all your styling needs. With its outstanding amenities and superb cuisine, Bernardus Lodge is an epicurean paradise that alternately nurtures and titillates the senses. Any event here is sure to be sensational.

CEREMONY CAPACITY: The Wedding Garden accommodates up to 150 seated guests.

EVENT/RECEPTION CAPACITY: The resort can accommodate 12–150 seated or 12–200 standing guests indoors.

MEETING CAPACITY: Meeting spaces hold up to 150 seated guests.

FEES & DEPOSITS: For special events, a deposit equal to the banquet space rental fee is required to reserve your date. Half of the estimated event total is payable 45 days prior, the balance 7 days prior to the event. In-house catering is provided: Luncheons start at $55/person, dinners at $95/person. Alcohol, tax and a 20% service charge are additional. The rental fee is $1,500 for the Wedding Garden and $2,500 for the Meritage Ballroom. Other rooms range $750-$4000.

AVAILABILITY: Year-round, daily until 11pm, including holidays.

SERVICES/AMENITIES:

Catering: provided, no BYO
Kitchen Facilities: n/a
Tables & Chairs: provided
Linens, Silver, etc.: provided
Restrooms: wheelchair accessible
Dance Floor: portable floor
Bride's Dressing Area: guestroom CBA
Meeting Equipment: full range, extra fee

Parking: complimentary valet and self-parking
Accommodations: 57 guestrooms
Telephone: pay phones or in guestrooms
Outdoor Night Lighting: access only
Outdoor Cooking Facilities: no
Cleanup: provided
View: Santa Lucia Mountains, vineyard
Other: spa package, croquet and bocce ball, tennis, lap pool, lawn, wedding cakes

RESTRICTIONS:

Alcohol: provided or wine corkage $30/bottle
Smoking: not allowed
Music: amplified OK indoors, curfew 11pm, acoustic only outdoors

Wheelchair Access: yes
Insurance: not required
Other: no confetti

Holman Ranch and Vineyard

Historic Private Residence

Address withheld to ensure privacy. Carmel Valley
831/659-2640

www.holmanranch.com
events@holmanranch.com

- Rehearsal Dinners
- Ceremonies
- Wedding Receptions
- Corp. Events/Mtgs.
- Private Parties
- Accommodations

High atop the sunny hills of Carmel Valley rests Holman Ranch and Vineyard, a historic private residence available for your one-of-a-kind event. Blessed with a treasure chest of scenic jewels, the ranch has a rich legacy of hosting society's elite. In 1928 as a gentlemen's retreat, the secluded location was a favorite hideaway for Hollywood celebrities like Charlie Chaplin. When the Holmans purchased the property in 1943, their improvements helped make the ranch the center of the Carmel Valley social scene. Recently, the 392-acre spread was adopted by the Lowder family, who've completed a loving restoration that retains the ranch's Old World character while adding up-to-the-minute luxuries. This 21st-century renaissance features enhanced interiors and lavish outdoor spaces that make the most of the spectacular view-filled grounds.

A private road climbs to the ranch's pond and stables, where golf carts shuttle guests to the hilltop entrance. Arriving at the Main Plaza, visitors get a captivating first impression: a mélange of red-tile roofs, landscaped walkways, shade trees and glimpses of grapevines against a mountainous panorama. Finally eyes rest on the Hacienda itself, an architectural gem crafted of Carmel stone and oak, with tile and metal details. This easy blend of grand Spanish style and relaxed Western attitude evokes an aura of rustic elegance.

Both varied and flexible, Holman Ranch holds so many possibilities…so why not stage each phase of your event in a different spot? Ceremonies are gorgeous on the Hacienda Lawn, which sweeps to the edge of a hillside studded with Pinot Noir grapevines. Wedding guests have an endless view of the Carmel Valley, alive with chaparral, oak trees and hawks soaring overhead. As the sunset burnishes the Santa Lucia Mountains, the scene becomes even more postcard-perfect. Against this breathtaking backdrop, couples say their vows atop the Ceremony Veranda, a demilune stone platform that seems suspended above the valley floor.

After "I dos," serve cocktails on the nearby Stone Terrace, which is ringed with olive trees. Everyone is free to relax in the adjoining Great Room, where a vaulted ceiling, fireplace and player piano contribute to a comfortable, homey ambiance.

Receptions bask in the warm valley twilight out on the Rose Patio, dressed with rose bushes and potted citrus trees. Family-style rehearsal dinners might prefer the Arbor, a magnificent wooden promenade at the plaza's center, where olive trees and young grapevines lend a Mediterranean flair. Afterwards, move the party to the barn-style Carriage House, where an explosion of twinkle lights along whitewashed rafters creates the illusion dancing beneath a star-filled sky.

When it's time to cut the wedding cake, gather friends and loved ones in the Hacienda's Inner Courtyard. Here high stone walls surround an enclave built of moss-fringed tiles and graced with an old oak tree at the center. Some couples hang paper lanterns or fairy lights from its spreading boughs, while the cake is showcased beneath a white gauze canopy.

And let yourself think outside the wedding: Host a casual welcome dinner or barbecue that includes bocce ball, croquet or trail rides, so the families can get acquainted before the main event. You can even throw a pool party, complete with umbrella drinks and beach balls. Weekend event packages include use of eight recently restored guestrooms which can accommodate up to 32 overnight guests. The cozy, home-away-from-home experience comes with a deluxe Continental-plus breakfast, and access to a full kitchen and the Ranch's recreation facilities. From refined entertainment to laid-back fun, Holman Ranch and Vineyard can arrange it all, and oh so well.

Holman Ranch is shown by appointment only. Please call to schedule a visit.

CEREMONY CAPACITY: The site can accommodate 200+ seated guests.

EVENT/RECEPTION CAPACITY: Outdoors, the Rose Patio holds 200 seated and the Main Plaza holds 200+ seated. Indoors, the Carriage House holds 100 seated guests.

MEETING CAPACITY: The Conference Room holds 10 seated around a boardroom table with executive chairs, the Carriage House holds 150 seated.

FEES & DEPOSITS: A nonrefundable deposit of one third of the site fee and room rental fee is required to reserve your date. A second nonrefundable deposit totaling 50% of the balance is due 6 months before the event. The final balance is due 1 month before the event. The site rental fee ranges $5,000–15,000 depending on the time of year, day of the week and hours of usage for the event. Rental of the 8 overnight guestrooms is required for weekend events, starting at $6,000 plus tax for 3-day/2-night packages, including daily breakfast and access to pool and fitness center.

AVAILABILITY: Year-round, anytime. Off-season rates apply November 15–April 15.

SERVICES/AMENITIES:

Catering: select from preferred list or BYO, licensed
Kitchen Facilities: prep only for caterer use, full kitchen for overnight guests
Tables & Chairs: provided for up to 200 guests
Linens, Silver, etc.: through caterer
Restrooms: 5 are wheelchair accessible, 6 total
Dance Floor: provided
Bride's Dressing Area: yes
Meeting Equipment: some provided

Parking: large lot, limited to 100 cars
Accommodations: 8 guestrooms
Telephone: emergency use only
Outdoor Night Lighting: provided
Outdoor Cooking Facilities: through caterer
Cleanup: caterer and renter
View: panoramic views of Carmel Valley and the Santa Lucia Mountains
Other: player piano, AV equipment, pool, trail rides, pony rides, vineyard tours, games, heaters and market umbrellas

RESTRICTIONS:

Alcohol: through licensed caterer or bartending service
Smoking: designated areas only
Music: amplified OK with restrictions

Wheelchair Access: yes
Insurance: required

This is important! Tell locations you're reading HERE COMES THE GUIDE and ask if our information is still current.

Quail Lodge Golf Club

Golf Club

8000 Valley Greens Drive, Carmel Valley
831/620-8866

www.quaillodge.com
info@quaillodge.com

◆ Rehearsal Dinners	◆ Corp. Events/Mtgs.
◆ Ceremonies	◆ Private Parties
◆ Wedding Receptions	Accommodations

With 850 acres of lush gardens, tree-shaded lakes, rolling meadows and a beautifully designed golf course, Quail Lodge Golf Club has been a favorite Carmel Valley venue for over 40 years and a premier destination for weddings and other special events.

Located on the sunny side of the Monterey Peninsula in the scenic Carmel Valley, the golf club offers a wonderful selection of indoor and outdoor settings, including a ceremony site that takes advantage of the glorious weather. Picturesque Quail Meadows is just the thing for supersized weddings and receptions—its verdant lawns can hold as many as 600 of your nearest and dearest. It's especially popular for ceremonies: A peaceful lake plays host to the occasional blue heron or covey of resident quail, and tree-covered hillsides form a gentle wave along the horizon. Whether you add a flower-laden bridal arch or let the scenery form the backdrop, this splendid spot will take your breath away. For an extra romantic touch, you can arrange for a horse-drawn carriage to bring you to the wedding site, which also boasts the Barn Loft, a cozy, rustic retreat.

The property and clubhouse provide a variety of spaces for receptions, parties and rehearsal dinners. Intimate private rooms and an outdoor terrace enjoy garden and poolside views; receptions for larger groups are held in the elegant Peninsula Ballroom, which boasts cathedral ceilings and three walls of windows that showcase the spectacular natural surroundings.

As you would expect at such a high-caliber club, dining here is a pleasurable experience. Edgar's, a casual bistro with expansive golf course views, serves up fresh, local California cuisine and is the perfect place for a relaxed gathering with family and friends. And if your guests would like to unwind with a round of golf the day before or after your festivities, the challenging 18-hole course is one of the most walkable courses on the Monterey Peninsula.

Quail Lodge Golf Club possesses all the elements for a stellar event, but it's their professional planners who weave these elements together in a way that matches your vision. Combining attention to detail with creative sparkle, they'll transform your special occasion into something truly memorable.

CEREMONY CAPACITY: Outdoors, the Quail Meadows area holds up to 600 seated. Indoors, the Peninsula Ballroom holds 300 seated theater style, and 5 other rooms accommodate up to 100 seated guests.

EVENT/RECEPTION CAPACITY: Indoors, the Peninsula Ballroom holds 200 seated or 300 standing, the Oak Room 30 seated or 50 standing, the Garden Room 50 seated or 70 standing guests.

MEETING CAPACITY: There are 3 rooms that can accommodate 30–300 theater-style, 26–60 boardroom-style or 24–200 seated classroom-style.

FEES & DEPOSITS: For special events, a $500–5,000 nonrefundable site fee plus a 10% deposit on the estimated food and beverage total is required as a deposit. A customized payment schedule is developed with all charges due 30 days prior to the event. Luncheons start $38/person, dinners at $45/person, and buffets at $42/person; alcohol, tax and a 19% service charge are additional. Wedding packages can be arranged.

AVAILABILITY: Year-round, daily, including holidays.

SERVICES/AMENITIES:

Catering: provided, no BYO

Kitchen Facilities: n/a

Tables & Chairs: provided

Linens, Silver, etc.: provided

Restrooms: wheelchair accessible

Dance Floor: provided

Bride's & Groom's Dressing Area: CBA

Meeting Equipment: full range, extra fee

Parking: large, ample lots

Accommodations: no guestrooms

Telephone: pay phones

Outdoor Night Lighting: CBA

Outdoor Cooking Facilities: no

Cleanup: provided

View: fairways, lakes, ponds, valley, hills

Other: baby grand piano

RESTRICTIONS:

Alcohol: provided, or corkage $25/bottle

Smoking: designated areas

Music: amplified OK indoors only

Wheelchair Access: yes

Insurance: not required

Beach Resort Monterey

Waterfront Hotel

2600 Sand Dunes Drive, Monterey
831/655-7650
www.montereybeachresort.com
weddings@montereybeachresort.com

● Rehearsal Dinners	● Corp. Events/Mtgs.
● Ceremonies	● Private Parties
● Wedding Receptions	● Accommodations

For the couple who dream of exchanging vows in full view of rolling waves, an endless blue horizon, and the dynamic Monterey skyline, this is your place. It also has the delightful distinction of being the only resort in the area that's located directly on the beach and can accommodate beach ceremonies. Miles of pristine white sand stretch in either direction; during the day sailboats dot the white-capped waters of the bay, and at night the lights of Monterey glitter on the far shore.

Of course, it takes more than a beautiful beach to make a first-class event facility, and Beach Resort Monterey has a variety of newly renovated venues, thanks to its $6 million makeover in 2008. A wedding reception, corporate event, or any type of large gathering can be held in one of two ballrooms on the fourth floor. The Points Ballroom has plenty of windows with a sweeping vista of Monterey Bay. Air walls allow the ballroom to be divided if desired. The La Grande Room is smaller than the Points Ballroom, but virtually identical to it in all other respects, including the panoramic view.

With all this stunning scenery, you'd expect outdoor events at Beach Resort Monterey to be popular and they are. Adventurous couples can be married on the resort's ocean deck or the South Terrace, and the resort will provide a wedding arch, white chairs and an aisle runner.

If you'd like to be married outdoors but still crave a bit of formality, there's the Wedding Garden, a secluded, lushly planted lawn area set up with a chairs and a classic arch.

As evening descends, retire indoors to one of the elegant ballrooms for dinner and dancing. Or have your reception outdoors—why not go for something casual and fun, like a luau or clambake? The staff can even customize your package with specialty menu items to enhance your wedding theme.

For an intimate rehearsal dinner or post-wedding brunch, the Captain's Table Ballroom on the hotel's top floor serves up panoramic views of the ocean and Monterey skyline along with its California coastal cuisine.

The resort is a great place for a destination wedding, because in addition to its flexible event spaces it boasts upgraded guestrooms that make staying here a pleasure. Amenities include 42" flat panel HD TVs, motorized shades, iPod clock radios, and platform beds.

At the Beach Resort Monterey you and your guests not only have access to your very own "back-yard" beach, you can take a little vacation and enjoy all that this famous coastal region has to offer.

CEREMONY CAPACITY: The resort can accommodate 10–300 seated or standing, indoors or outdoors.

EVENT/RECEPTION CAPACITY: The resort accommodates 10–300 seated or standing guests.

MEETING CAPACITY: Several banquet rooms hold 5–400 seated guests.

FEES & DEPOSITS: For weddings, 25% of the estimated total is required to reserve your date. Reception packages range $70–100/person excluding beverages. Ceremony only and reception only packages are also available.

AVAILABILITY: Year-round, daily, 7am–10pm. All events must conclude at 10pm. An after-party location is available from 10pm–2am at an additional cost.

SERVICES/AMENITIES:

Catering: provided
Kitchen Facilities: n/a
Tables & Chairs: provided
Linens, Silver, etc.: provided
Restrooms: wheelchair accessible
Dance Floor: provided
Bride's & Groom's Dressing Area: CBA
Meeting Equipment: CBA, extra charge

Parking: self-parking; valet CBA
Accommodations: 196 guestrooms, 2 suites
Telephone: pay phones
Outdoor Night Lighting: yes, more CBA
Outdoor Cooking Facilities: n/a
Cleanup: provided
View: Pacific Ocean and Monterey coastline
Other: event coordination, decorations

RESTRICTIONS:

Alcohol: provided
Smoking: designated areas
Music: amplified OK until 10pm

Wheelchair Access: yes, except to beach
Insurance: required for vendors
Other: no rice, birdseed or glitter; rose petals must be real outdoors and artificial indoors; only preferred vendors may be used

Casa Munras Hotel & Spa
A Larkspur Collection

Hotel

700 Munras Avenue, Monterey
831/375-2411
www.hotelcasamunras.com
svillani@hotelcasamunras.com

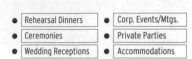

● Rehearsal Dinners	● Corp. Events/Mtgs.
● Ceremonies	● Private Parties
● Wedding Receptions	● Accommodations

Remember the old friend of yours, who returned from her European vacation sporting a smart wardrobe, a cool attitude and witty foreign expressions? She's still the same warm and sweet person you always loved…but boy, she sure is a lot more hip! The same can be said of Casa Munras Hotel & Spa, a beloved Monterey landmark that's recently undergone a stylish transformation. Constructed in 1824, the original Casa Munras was the hacienda of Don Esteban Munras, the last Spanish diplomat to California.

The recent renovation pays a nod to the Casa's Early California influence, particularly in the guest buildings and landscaping. But the lobby, new restaurant and banquet rooms, done in warm woods, stone textures and mellow earth tones, have a decidedly contemporary flair and polish that place the hotel squarely in the "now." Modern upgrades include hi-speed wireless internet, a sleek new business center, and a fitness room—all complimentary. So is the ample parking, proving that even though the Casa has gone upscale, it's still a friendly and welcoming event destination.

With 171 tastefully appointed guestrooms (51 with fireplaces), the hotel can accommodate your overnight wedding guests, who'll appreciate the FeatherBorne bed, an oasis of plush comfort. For you, there's an exclusive bridal floor in the main building, providing privacy and a convenient place to prep. The hotel's 11 two-story buildings are spread out over the property, connected by red brick paths that meander past flowering shrubs, lofty pines and palms, and vibrant fuchsia. The whitewashed brick façades of the cottage-like buildings are laced with lipstick-pink bougainvillea. Colorful hanging flower baskets are sweet surprises in many of the first-floor colonnades.

The crowning glory of Casa Munras is its central garden, which flourishes around a swimming pool and patio. A medley of rose bushes is especially enticing in spring, when the unfurling blossoms cast their perfume on the breeze. Just outside the pool patio's gate, willow, maple and oak trees provide dappled shade for a triangle of lawn. Here, graceful tree boughs frame the bridal couple against a backdrop of roses and the shimmering aqua pool. On a pleasant afternoon, serve cocktails poolside and savor the garden view.

Another option for the cocktail hour is Esteban, the hotel's indoor-outdoor restaurant that's been dubbed by local papers "a classy gem," and "Monterey's Best New Restaurant." The interior has a stone fireplace and built-in bar, but most guests will prefer to relax on Esteban's stone patio, with its intriguing metal sculptures, fire pit and garden view.

Receptions are usually held in the 2,250-square-foot Andalucia Ballroom, a warm and inviting space trimmed in wood and done in simple, understated hues that adapt to your own color scheme. A more intimate option is the Antonia, a great spot for a rehearsal dinner since it opens up to Esteban's bar. Another choice for small events is the Marbella Room, which includes a window-lined, bricked enclave called the Adobe that was part of the Casa's original structure.

Brides and their girlfriends will also appreciate Sano, the hotel's spa that launched in June 2008. It features Zen-like relaxation alcoves, an outdoor fountain lounge and a "his-and-her" treatment room—and Sano can provide manicures and up-dos as well.

A short walk from downtown Monterey, Fisherman's Wharf and the Monterey Bay Aquarium, the reborn Casa Munras has much to offer out-of-town guests, family weddings or simply a pair of lovebirds spending a mini-honeymoon on the fabulous Central Coast.

CEREMONY CAPACITY: The hotel seats 80–100 guests indoors or outdoors.

EVENT/RECEPTION CAPACITY: Casa Munras holds 140 seated and 200 standing indoors.

MEETING CAPACITY: The site accommodates 200 seated guests.

FEES & DEPOSITS: A deposit is required to reserve your date. The balance is due 10 days prior to the event. Wedding packages range $50–65/person. Tax, alcohol and a 20% service charge are additional.

AVAILABILITY: Year-round, daily, anytime.

SERVICES/AMENITIES:

Catering: provided, no BYO

Kitchen Facilities: n/a

Tables & Chairs: provided

Linens, Silver, etc.: provided

Restrooms: wheelchair accessible

Dance Floor: provided

Bride's & Groom's Dressing Area: yes

Meeting Equipment: some provided, more CBA

Parking: limited on-street

Accommodations: 171 guestrooms

Telephone: guest phones

Outdoor Night Lighting: CBA

Outdoor Cooking Facilities: BBQ CBA

Cleanup: provided

View: garden, pool area, landscaped grounds

Other: event coordination, AV equipment

RESTRICTIONS:

Alcohol: provided or BYO wine with corkage fee

Smoking: not allowed

Music: amplified OK with restrictions

Wheelchair Access: yes

Insurance: not required

Overwhelmed? Use the search criteria on www.HereComesTheGuide.com to narrow down your choices.

Club Del Monte
at Monterey Naval Postgraduate School

1 University Circle, Building 220, Monterey
831/656-1049

www.nps.edu/services/mwr/services/diningservices/clubdelmonte.html
mwrcatering@nps.edu

Historic Landmark

- Rehearsal Dinners
- Ceremonies
- Wedding Receptions
- Corp. Events/Mtgs.
- Private Parties
- Accommodations

Club Del Monte is an Art Deco jewel set amongst 25 acres of sprawling lawns dotted with oak, cypress, and pine. Originally built in 1880 as the grand Hotel del Monte, it was destroyed twice by fire and rebuilt. The present imposing structure (which is the 1926 incarnation) resembles a Spanish-Moorish fortress. It remained an elegant hotel until 1951, when it was acquired for the Navy's Naval Postgraduate School. As you can see, this facility's history is long and illustrious.

Your guests will step back in time and feel like royalty, when welcomed with cocktails in the Quarterdeck Lounge. This majestic lobby was built on the scale of a castle foyer, with soaring 30-foot ceilings which are crosshatched with hand-painted wooden beams. Two stately rows of stone columns grace both sides of the room, framing a towering floor-to-ceiling window that overlooks the estate-like grounds.

Proceed to the ballroom for a formal dinner-dance; you'll be transported back to the era when Jean Harlow, Clark Gable and Carole Lombard danced here, and when water cascaded down the room's main attraction: an ornately tiled fountain that dominates one wall. The fountain and the elaborate tilework bordering the floor-to-ceiling arched windows at either end of the room bring the Moorish influence inside, and give the space a spicy, exotic ambiance. Other Art Deco details include the lacy plasterwork ceiling, huge wrought-iron chandeliers, and matching wall sconces. French doors opening onto the terrace and overlooking the European-style rose gardens are the finishing touch.

For a buffet luncheon or catered business meeting, La Novia Room, with plaster walls and rich wood trim, offers the elegance of the ballroom but on a more intimate scale. It opens onto La Novia Terrace, an atrium with a rustic brick fireplace, window benches and a brick floor. There are outdoor settings, too. The lawn works well for a romantic Victorian wedding. Club Del Monte offers a treasure-trove of site options, and as you'd expect from a Naval facility, everything here is top rank.

CEREMONY CAPACITY: The facility accommodates up to 400 seated or standing guests on the lawn.

EVENT/RECEPTION CAPACITY: Indoors, several rooms hold from 25–600 seated or 25–1,000 standing guests.

MEETING CAPACITY: The Ballroom holds 600 seated in rounds of 10, 500 seated theater-style or 150 conference-style; the La Novia Room holds 90 in rounds of 10, 75 theater-style or 40 conference-style; and the La Novia Terrace holds 40 in rounds of 10.

FEES & DEPOSITS: For weddings and receptions, a $550–1,600 nonrefundable deposit, depending on the room reserved, is required to book the facility. 75% of the estimated event total is payable 4 weeks prior to the function, and the balance is due 1 week prior.

Catering is provided starting at $22/person, with a $1/person cake-cutting fee. Wine, champagne and a 19% service charge are additional.

Weekday meeting fees vary depending on catering services required.

AVAILABILITY: Year-round, daily. Weddings can be booked 11am–4pm or 6pm–11pm; conferences or other special events, 7am–4pm or 6pm–11pm. Extra hours are available for an additional charge.

SERVICES/AMENITIES:
Catering: provided, no BYO
Kitchen Facilities: n/a
Tables & Chairs: provided for indoor events
Linens, Silver, etc.: provided
Restrooms: wheelchair accessible
Dance Floor: yes
Bride's Dressing Area: yes, additional fee
Meeting Equipment: CBA

Parking: on-base lot; weekday carpooling recommended for large events
Accommodations: military or Department of Defense cardholders only
Telephone: no
Outdoor Night Lighting: no
Outdoor Cooking Facilities: no
Cleanup: provided
View: of lawns and gardens

RESTRICTIONS:
Alcohol: provided, no BYO
Smoking: outside only, 20 feet away from building
Music: amplified OK

Wheelchair Access: yes
Insurance: not required
Other: no rice, birdseed, glitter, confetti, bubbles or wall decorations

InterContinental The Clement Monterey

Waterfront Hotel

750 Cannery Row, Monterey
831/375-4500

www.intercontinental.com/montereyic
ggrammatico@pahotel.com

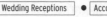

- Rehearsal Dinners
- Ceremonies
- Wedding Receptions
- Corp. Events/Mtgs.
- Private Parties
- Accommodations

Throughout the years, Monterey's timeless natural beauty has been the inspiration for artists, poets and novelists alike. Recently, a downtown renaissance has put a glamorous polish on historic districts like Cannery Row, and author John Steinbeck would be amazed to see these formerly rough-and-tumble dockside streets dramatically transformed into a thoroughly modern boulevard. Today's Cannery Row is alive with fashionable boutiques, delectable eateries, upscale galleries and a vibrant street scene that attracts visitors from all over the world. And right next door, at the heart of the action, sits the celebrated Monterey Bay Aquarium.

Can this quaint yet oh-so-now slice of paradise get any better? Yes, it can. InterContinental The Clement Monterey was designed as a serene coastal retreat for personal rejuvenation and spectacular private celebrations.

Wedding ceremonies are staged on an expansive landscaped courtyard facing the sapphire-blue waters of the bay. Two fire pits provide an ambient glow, particularly romantic at sunset. Couples say their vows with the bay in the background, while seabirds trace graceful curves on the horizon, and otters and sea lions perch atop the rocky shore.

With such a picturesque setting, have your social hour out in the fresh ocean air as well. While the bridal party poses for pictures, guests enjoy the hotel's boardwalk and pier, which extends out over the bay. Cut-outs along the wooden pier reveal tantalizing peeks directly down at the teeming underwater world of the Monterey Bay Sanctuary.

As twilight descends, retire indoors to admire the vista from another perspective. The Pacific Ballroom is a refined setting for a bayside gala, replete with picture windows that capture a panorama of the moonlit ocean and the star-filled heavens. Bring the sparkle indoors by decorating with luminarias and fairy lights—the banquet staff can customize your event according to your wishes. The view will be even more impressive from the Ocean Terrace Ballroom, located upstairs. It's an intimate space that boasts a huge bayview terrace.

The resort's equally impressive public spaces are tranquil and welcoming, thanks to the stylish use of wood and other natural materials, along with décor in soothing shades of green and blue, evocative of the sea and sky. One of the most notable spaces is the Reading Room, warmed by a contemporary stone-faced fireplace. Adjacent to the Reading Room, the Library serves as a private dining salon that's perfect for formal rehearsal dinners.

One of the benefits of a destination event at InterContinental The Clement Monterey is that friends and family can have a mini-vacation, because there's simply no end to the area's fun-filled activities. Hotel accommodations feature up-to-the-minute amenities, and many have fireplaces, ocean views and balconies. Energia Spa, located on site, pampers with the latest in beautification and wellness treatments.

The hotel's VIP Kid's Club provides entertaining and innovative recreational programs for kids from four to thirteen years old. VIP babysitting is also available for younger children, enabling parents to enjoy the wedding celebration.

Rich with promise, this magnificent hotel opened in May 2008. Reserve your event space now to take advantage of Monterey's legendary allure.

CEREMONY CAPACITY: The resort holds 220 seated indoors or outdoors.

EVENT/RECEPTION & MEETING CAPACITY: The facility accommodates 220 seated or 350 standing indoors or outdoors.

FEES & DEPOSITS: A nonrefundable deposit of 25% of the estimated food and beverage total and 100% of the facility fee is required to confirm your event, and is due within 14 days of contract signing. Facility fees range $2,000–5,000 depending on the space(s) rented. Wedding packages range $79–159/person. Tax and a 20% service charge are additional.

AVAILABILITY: Year-round, daily, 6am–midnight.

SERVICES/AMENITIES:

Catering: provided
Kitchen Facilities: n/a
Tables & Chairs: provided
Linens, Silver, etc.: provided
Restrooms: wheelchair accessible
Dance Floor: provided
Bride's Dressing Area: yes
Meeting Equipment: provided

Parking: valet and self-parking
Accommodations: 208 guestrooms
Telephone: house phone
Outdoor Night Lighting: provided
Outdoor Cooking Facilities: BBQ CBA
Cleanup: provided
View: ocean
Other: spa, 24-hour fitness center, pool, Jacuzzi, babysitting, kid's club

RESTRICTIONS:

Alcohol: provided
Smoking: designated areas only
Music: amplified OK with restrictions

Wheelchair Access: yes
Insurance: not required

Memory Garden

Garden

20 Custom House Plaza, Monterey
831/649-3445, Grapes of Wrath Catering
www.grapesofwrath.com
grapes@grapesofwrath.com

● Rehearsal Dinners	● Corp. Events/Mtgs.
● Ceremonies	● Private Parties
● Wedding Receptions	Accommodations

Stroll through Monterey's downtown historic district, and you'll find it studded with secret gardens. Each of them is private and within walking distance of hotels ranging from bed & breakfast to 4-star. Memory Garden, in the Monterey State Historic Park is perhaps the most intriguing of them all.

Framed on three sides by tall adobe walls with graceful arched cutouts and on the fourth by the Pacific House, an elegant 1847 Spanish-Colonial style building, it's a grand plaza suitable for all kinds of events. Four 75-year-old magnolias shade the plaza, their branches casting an intricate web of shadows on the ground. In spring and summer the trees also provide a gorgeous floral display, along with the other flowers planted along the perimeter. A fountain burbling in the courtyard's center soothes the ear, while sea breezes supply natural air-conditioning.

Corporate picnics, luncheons and dinners are popular here, but the Garden is especially lovely for weddings. The site can accommodate a formal dinner for 300 guests, yet it's warm and intimate enough for a casual gathering of 50.

If you're getting married in the Garden, you may choose as your backdrop the massive arched wooden gate at the entrance, the wisteria-covered pergola along the southwest wall or the towering cedar opposite the pergola.

Afterwards, the open configuration of the Garden lends itself to lively hors d'oeuvre stations followed by either a seated dinner or a buffet beneath the trees. And you don't need a lot of decorations—a simple thread of color can pull together the surrounding foliage and architecture, creating a beautiful setting with little effort. Floral arrangements on the tables can be as elaborate as exotic blooms in a wrought-iron centerpiece or as understated as a terracotta pot with greenery. For evening events, permanent subtle lighting in the trees makes it easy to create a fairy-tale or Old California atmosphere.

To get just the right food for your celebration, turn to *Grapes of Wrath Catering*. They have lots of experience orchestrating events in the Garden, and will cook up a California Cuisine-style feast to satisfy your taste (and that of all your guests!). You might want to start off with an hors d'oeuvre griddle, featuring crab cakes, towers of layered polenta, and pesto risotto cakes, or indulge in the ultimate California treat—a sushi boat filled with assorted maki! Bright, fresh flavors are the hallmark of their main dishes, too. Choices from Monterey Bay include grilled salmon with a Mediterranean tapenade, fresh albacore with a mango salsa or maybe braised halibut in ginger and orange. These are often paired with a medium rare sirloin with rich Cabernet mushrooms, or perhaps Castroville chicken, perfectly seasoned with artichokes, wine and herbs.

After checking out the local seasonal produce, *Grapes of Wrath* might serve up grilled vegetables, a crunchy sugar snap pea salad, or heirloom tomatoes with fresh mozzarella and basil...all colorful reminders that Monterey is in California's premium growing region.

Two more elements for a successful event are great music and good wine, and *Grapes of Wrath* staff can help you with both. As full-service caterers, they'll match you up with musicians and other vendors that best fit your vision, provide excellent (and affordable) wines, and coordinate the day of your event.

We don't know how this garden got its name, but it was an inspired choice—when your party is over, you'll walk away with a wedding's worth of wonderful memories.

CEREMONY, EVENT/RECEPTION & MEETING CAPACITY: The garden holds 300 seated or 250 standing guests for a cocktail reception.

FEES & DEPOSITS: A $1,000 deposit is required to reserve your date. 50% of the estimated event total is due 30 days in advance and the balance is due 3 days prior to the event. Rental fees range $500–1,500 depending on length of event.

Grapes of Wrath Catering has been hosting events at the Memory Garden for years; however, you may bring in the caterer of your choice. All menus created by *Grapes of Wrath Catering* are custom-designed; for menus and pricing go to www.grapesofwrath.com. There is no cake-cutting fee and beverages are provided at retail cost.

AVAILABILITY: Year-round, daily, 9am–10pm, weather permitting. Closed major holidays. Setup must be done within the time stated on your permit.

SERVICES/AMENITIES:

Catering: *Grapes of Wrath* or BYO
Kitchen Facilities: no
Tables & Chairs: through caterer
Linens, Silver, etc.: through caterer
Restrooms: wheelchair accessible
Dance Floor: through caterer
Bride's Dressing Area: nearby hotels, none on site
Meeting Equipment: through caterer

Parking: covered garage within 2 blocks
Accommodations: hotels nearby
Telephone: office phones
Outdoor Night Lighting: some provided
Outdoor Cooking Facilities: no
Cleanup: caterer
View: garden
Other: walking distance to Wharf, downtown and hotels; event coordination available through caterer

RESTRICTIONS:

Alcohol: provided, or BYO
Smoking: designated areas only
Music: amplified OK with limits

Wheelchair Access: yes
Insurance: required, CBA through caterer or arrange your own
Other: no rice, picking flowers, etc.

The professionals in the back of this book are the best in the business. How do we know? Read page 701.

Monterey Beach Party
at Del Monte Beach House

Historic Beach House

285 Figueroa Avenue, Monterey
831/648-7240
www.montereybeachparty.com
info@montereybeachparty.com

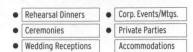

- Rehearsal Dinners
- Ceremonies
- Wedding Receptions
- Corp. Events/Mtgs.
- Private Parties
- Accommodations

If you love the sea, you've probably fantasized about spending time at a quaint beach house, with the sand right outside your door and seals and pelicans as your only neighbors. You've envisioned admiring ocean views and spectacular sunsets from your front porch, and gathering friends and family around an evening bonfire, with the sublime setting putting everyone in a summertime state-of-mind no matter what the time of year.

Well, the event professionals at Monterey Beach Party (MBP) can cheerfully make your fantasy a reality, at least for your wedding day. They've been arranging festivities-to-remember for years, and many of the most memorable have happened at the historic Del Monte Beach House.

Located next to a waterfront park and wharf, and within walking distance to Monterey hotels and activities, the beach house is a simple cloud-colored building trimmed in sailor blue. Steps from its broad front deck descend onto the sand, and since Monterey Beach Party lays claim to its own stretch of this pristine shoreline, they'll set up your event right at the water's edge.

Ceremonies come with a palm tree-lined wedding aisle, a white wedding arch and the blue Pacific. Drinks and appetizers are served on the deck, and while the bridal party poses for scenic photos the staff sets up the outdoor reception. The usual motif includes frond huts, tiki torches, a bonfire and beach furniture, and the beach site can accommodate up to 1,000 guests. Want fire and hula dancers? Ask, and Monterey Beach Party will make it happen. This is also one of the only local beaches that allow cocktails—so bring on the paper umbrellas!

Inside the beach house, social hours and receptions are anything but dull, thanks to a myriad of novelty attractions: Ping pong, pool, shuffleboard, a vintage juke box and a "surf's up" photo backdrop are all sure-fire icebreakers, and an old-fashioned popcorn machine is a homey touch. If you prefer a more elegant ambiance, the staff will remove the games and have everything looking fancy as you please. The newly renovated interior features light, faux-finished floors, open-beamed ceilings and pillars clad in bamboo. Most couples like to play up the beachy theme by choosing tropical colors from a wide array of linens and other vibrant décor. Just ask the staff for help and ideas!

A stage at one end of the room is outfitted with a rear projection screen and state-of-the art light and sound system. Amp up the entertainment by booking the house DJ or band, who will "wow" your guests with cool tunes and a light show.

MBP also takes care of the food, which is both hearty and delicious: Entrées are grilled fresh during your event, and whether you opt for the Luau Feast, Lobster Bash or Clam Bake, your guests are sure to be satisfied.

And here's a thought: If you're planning a formal affair at another Monterey venue, why not change things up by reserving the Del Monte Beach House for your rehearsal dinner? Their inclusive event packages and high-caliber service are not only a tremendous value, but they practically guarantee good times. Lots of venues can host a wedding…but if you want a party, then this is the place.

CEREMONY & MEETING CAPACITY: The site holds 100 seated guests indoors and 300+ seated outdoors.

EVENT/RECEPTION CAPACITY: The facility can accommodate 297 seated or 570 standing indoors and 400 seated or 600 standing outdoors.

FEES & DEPOSITS: A $1,500 nonrefundable deposit is due at time of booking. 90% of the estimated total is due 30 days prior to the event and the balance is due by the business day following the event.

Their all-inclusive wedding package is $100/person which includes site fee, beach ceremony with palm tree aisle, white chairs and white arch; beach party reception setup with beach huts, palm trees, bonfire, beach chairs and tiki torches. This package also includes choice of 2 menu options, cake-cutting fee, assorted sodas and water, ice cups and bar setup. Tax and service charge are included in the package price, alcohol is additional.

AVAILABILITY: Year-round, daily, 10am–3pm or 5pm–10pm.

SERVICES/AMENITIES:

Catering: provided
Kitchen Facilities: on-site
Tables & Chairs: provided
Linens, Silver, etc.: provided or CBA
Restrooms: wheelchair accessible
Dance Floor: provided
Bride's Dressing Area: CBA
Meeting Equipment: some provided

Parking: large lot
Accommodations: no guestrooms
Telephone: emergency use only
Outdoor Night Lighting: provided
Outdoor Cooking Facilities: BBQ on site
Cleanup: provided
View: ocean/bay
Other: clergy on staff, AV equipment, event coordination

RESTRICTIONS:

Alcohol: provided, or BYO with corkage fee
Smoking: outdoors only
Music: amplified OK with restrictions

Wheelchair Access: yes
Insurance: not required
Other: no rice, birdseed or fake petals on beach

Monterey Museum of Art - La Mirada

Historic Estate, Museum & Gardens

720 Via Mirada, Monterey
831/372-3689
www.montereyart.org
events@montereyart.org

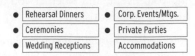

- Rehearsal Dinners
- Ceremonies
- Wedding Receptions
- Corp. Events/Mtgs.
- Private Parties

Accommodations

The Monterey Museum of Art - La Mirada is one part historic home, one part gardens, and one part art gallery...all adding up to one incredible and unique event location!

Resting on a picturesque mesa above Monterey Bay, La Mirada, as the museum is most commonly known, began as a Mexican adobe that once housed pioneer John C. Fremont. At the dawn of the Jazz Age, new owner Gouverneur Morris, a silent movie mogul, embarked on a dizzying era of expansion and lavish decoration: Artists created hand-painted murals, and Hollywood designers transformed the estate into a graceful retreat, suitable for distinguished luminaries like Rudolf Valentino and Charlie Chaplin. In 1936, Morris sold La Mirada to the Work family, and doyenne Maud Porter Work renovated the Rose Garden, which still bears her name. In 1983 Frank Work donated the entire estate—including the priceless art and furnishings—to the Monterey Museum of Art so that the public might enjoy its grounds and eclectic treasures. More recently, the museum added the Dart Wing, which encompasses four modern galleries with views of the gardens.

Today, visitors enter the museum via a cozy courtyard that recalls La Mirada's Early California heritage. Colorful European tiles embellish thick adobe walls, and potted citrus trees give a cheerful greeting. Through the lobby is the bi-level Rose Garden and Patio, a sweet site for wedding ceremonies. An Art Deco tiled fountain is the focal point of the upper patio, which overlooks the showy blossoms just below. A pair of bay and fig trees stretch their boughs wide, as if embracing the wedding couple as they say their vows. A brick path descends to the garden, where more than 125 species of flora are ablaze in vibrant springtime hues. A view out to neighboring Estero Lake with a thin slice of the bay in the distance completes the idyllic milieu.

Prefer a modern twist? Then hold your social hour on the Drawing Room Patio, where an avant-garde fountain, a large bronze horse, and a Buddha statue peeking out from lush landscaping are conversational ice-breakers. Tall glass doors slide open to the Drawing Room, a glamorous scene of retro opulence. At one end stands a 17th-century lacquered panel, a relic of China's Forbidden City; in the window casement, a pair of brass peacocks catches the sunlight. Crystal chandeliers, gilded mirrors, a grand piano and intriguing objets d'art let you party in the lap of luxury.

For after-dinner fun, adjourn to the Courtyard Gallery. Crisp and contemporary, the Gallery has lofty ceilings and polished wood floors perfect for dancing. With windows that look out to the Rose Garden, it's also a sophisticated setting for fine dining.

La Mirada has several other options to make your day memorable: For a culture-filled social hour, invite guests to tour the Dart Wing galleries. Meanwhile, bride and groom pose for photos in the estate's former living quarters, still festooned with extravagant trappings of the past—silk wallpaper, opulent canopy beds and antique rarities that convey a timeless air of romance. Another photogenic environment is the Rhododendron Garden, a sheltered dell awash with violet-hued blooms flourishing beneath flowering trees.

Whether your wedding vision is nostalgic or fashion-forward, quaint or bold, Gatsbyesque or exotic, La Mirada can make it happen with grace and style.

CEREMONY, EVENT/RECEPTION & MEETING CAPACITY: The museum holds 100 seated or 150 standing guests indoors, and 150 seated or 300 standing outdoors.

FEES & DEPOSITS: A nonrefundable deposit of 50% of the total event cost is required to reserve your date. The balance is due 30 days prior to the event. There are two wedding packages priced at $2,500 and $5,000.

AVAILABILITY: Year-round, daily, call for details.

SERVICES/AMENITIES:

Catering: select from approved list
Kitchen Facilities: fully equipped
Tables & Chairs: some provided, CBA or through caterer
Linens, Silver, etc.: CBA or through caterer
Restrooms: wheelchair accessible
Dance Floor: CBA
Bride's Dressing Area: yes
Meeting Equipment: some provided, CBA
Other: grand piano, picnic area, docent tours, galleries open for guests, event coordination, AV equipment, wireless internet, stereo/CD

Parking: large lot, valet, shuttle service available
Accommodations: no guestrooms
Telephone: office phone
Outdoor Night Lighting: provided
Outdoor Cooking Facilities: CBA
Cleanup: provided
View: courtyard, garden, cityscape, ocean/bay, coastline, forest, lake, fountain, landscaped grounds

RESTRICTIONS:

Alcohol: BYO
Smoking: not allowed
Music: amplified OK with restrictions

Wheelchair Access: yes
Insurance: liability required

Monterey Plaza Hotel & Spa

Oceanfront Resort

400 Cannery Row, Monterey
831/646-1700

www.montereyplazahotel.com
weddings@montereyplazahotel.com

- Rehearsal Dinners
- Ceremonies
- Wedding Receptions
- Corp. Events/Mtgs.
- Private Parties
- Accommodations

There's something about being next to the ocean that most of us find irresistible. Maybe it's the bracing aroma of sea air, or the way the light glints off the waves. Whatever it is, you experience that special "something" here at the Monterey Plaza Hotel & Spa. Built right at the water's edge, the Plaza takes advantage of a spectacular bayside setting that's just a heartbeat away from the world-renowned Monterey Bay Aquarium and Cannery Row.

The Plaza's 17,000 square feet of event space encompasses an array of sophisticated banquet rooms enhanced by Mediterranean-inspired furnishings. A recent $3 million renovation has brought fresh polish to the décor, and ensured that all the amenities are state-of-the-art—including advanced audiovisual and wireless capabilities. Aesthetic upgrades, like decorative crown moldings and Villeroy & Boch plateware and silver, add extra elegance to your affair.

Ceremonies at the resort are held on either of two sun-splashed terraces, both embracing panoramic vistas of the Pacific. On the Lower Terrace, the bride captures every eye as she descends the main staircase to a broad, tiled deck; on the sprawling Upper Plaza, the wedding processional walks beneath a white trellis, set off by terracotta planters brimming with flowers. Then vows are exchanged under a simple arch with the ocean and sky as a blue-on-blue backdrop.

Afterwards, most receptions take place in the Monterey Bay Room or the Dolphins Room. The latter is so close to the water you can see otters floating by and hear the gentle lapping of the waves. Both rooms mirror the earthy palette of the coastal milieu—deep marine blues and greens, terracotta reds, and warm, sun-kissed golds. Scenic artwork adorns the walls, complementing the gorgeous floor-to-ceiling bay view. For a more formal gala, the Cypress Ballroom has teakwood paneling, new custom chandeliers and its own terrace overlooking the seascape.

Rich with history and diverse activities, Monterey is a sightseer's paradise; and with the Plaza's exceptional hospitality, your guests will appreciate the fact that you've chosen it as their home base—especially when they experience the hotel's rooftop spa! This is the place to relax before the big celebration (or unwind after), by indulging in a massage, facial, or one of the spa's signature treatments. The spa even boasts an outdoor sundeck complete with fireplace and whirlpool tubs, where you can enjoy a light lunch along with the invigorating salt-laced breezes.

Newlyweds often opt to stay in a spacious luxury suite, featuring a fireplace and oceanview deck. The accommodating staff can even transform your suite into a celebratory setting for a cocktail party or a post-wedding brunch. However, we highly recommend a romantic candlelight dinner for two on your private deck, where you can raise your glasses to the glorious sunset coloring the horizon, the boundless sea, and each other.

CEREMONY CAPACITY: The Lower Terrace accommodates 120 guests seated in rows and a few more standing guests; the Upper Plaza holds 300 guests seated in rows.

EVENT/RECEPTION CAPACITY: Various rooms seat 20–300 without dancing or 20–250 with dancing.

MEETING CAPACITY: There are 11 conference rooms (17,000 square feet of meeting space) which accommodate up to 250 guests.

FEES & DEPOSITS: The rental fee for a 5-hour event ranges $850–2,500, depending on the banquet room reserved. It is payable, along with the $2,000–2,500 ceremony site fee (if applicable), when reservations are confirmed. The event balance (based on the estimated food and beverage total) is due 10 working days prior to the function. Luncheons start at $40/person, dinners at $65/person. Additional evening hours may be purchased at $300/hour. Wedding cake, alcohol, tax and a 19% service charge are additional. Note that overnight accommodations for the bride and groom can be arranged at a special rate for up to two nights.

AVAILABILITY: Year-round, daily, until 10pm.

SERVICES/AMENITIES:

Catering: provided, no BYO

Kitchen Facilities: n/a

Tables & Chairs: provided

Linens, Silver, etc.: provided

Restrooms: wheelchair accessible

Dance Floor: provided

Bride's & Groom's Dressing Area: CBA

Meeting Equipment: some provided, other CBA extra fee

Parking: valet, extra fee

Accommodations: 290 guestrooms

Telephone: emergency use only

Outdoor Night Lighting: additional CBA

Outdoor Cooking Facilities: CBA

Cleanup: provided

View: Monterey Bay and Pacific Ocean

RESTRICTIONS:

Alcohol: provided, no BYO

Smoking: outside only

Music: amplified OK with volume restrictions

Wheelchair Access: yes

Insurance: required for outside vendors only

Other: no glitter, birdseed or rice

Want to know WHAT TO ASK a potential location or vendor? Check out our Questions to Ask on page 17.

Tarpy's Roadhouse & Monterey Stone Chapel   *Restaurant and Chapel*

2999 Monterey-Salinas Highway, Monterey
831/655-2999
www.tarpys.com/weddings.html
banquet@tarpys.com

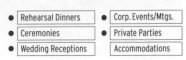

- Rehearsal Dinners
- Ceremonies
- Wedding Receptions
- Corp. Events/Mtgs.
- Private Parties
- Accommodations

We know what you're thinking: How appealing can a place be with the word "roadhouse" in its name? Well, in this case, very appealing indeed. Though this historic stone building and its five landscaped acres boast a slightly raffish past (it's the site where Matt Tarpy was lynched for the murder of his neighbor in 1873), it's now known for delicious food, eclectic atmosphere and an enticing array of both indoor and outdoor event spaces.

The most popular spot for a garden ceremony is on the Chapel Lawn, a velvety carpet of green surrounded by redwoods, pines and blossoming greenery. While guests look on from white chairs, couples say "I do" in front of an old-fashioned white gazebo. Continue to savor this scenic milieu during your cocktail hour, and invite your guests to meander onto an adjoining lawn, where a pond with a spouting fountain provides a mini-ecosystem for turtles and all sorts of fish.

For a quaint, intimate ceremony, who can resist the Monterey Stone Marriage Chapel? A picture window looks out to the garden, and whisper-pink walls, white-lace curtains and angel-themed décor lend an air of ethereal romance. Guest chairs are arranged facing a stone fireplace, whose mantel is embellished with candles, floral wreaths and garlands. Against this pretty backdrop, the bride and groom declare their love. During evening weddings, luminarias cast a dreamy glow over the charming tableau. The Chapel comes with a private changing room and sound system, as well as three on-site nondenominational ministers, should you choose to have one of them conduct your ceremony.

A sunset gathering or reception dinner lit by Craftsman-style lanterns and twinkling stars is nothing short of sensational in the courtyard. A vine-covered stone arch leads to an enchanting enclave with a honeysuckle-draped grotto and a stone-and-wood arbor laced with passionflower vines. The walls of the restaurant building rise on two sides, sporting more flowering vines, as well as a bronze frieze of dancing figures. Wooden tables and metal chairs are complemented by market umbrellas and heat lamps for all-weather comfort.

The restaurant itself has a variety of pleasing rooms for receptions and rehearsal dinners. In the Shell Room, soft cream walls and crisp white linens impart a relaxed elegance, while a fireplace constructed entirely of seashells provides a whimsical counterpoint. The Vintner's Room displays award-winning local wines, contemporary art and views of the restaurant's lush gardens. Upstairs, the Library is a spacious, private room with a large hearth, chandeliers and distinctive metal-and-leather chairs. Adjoining the Library is a private patio, where the bold hues of fuchsias and nasturtiums vie for attention. One side of the patio is a wall, ingeniously built into the hillside, with nooks and crannies abloom with flowers and aromatic herbs. A delightful mélange of textures, colors and scents, this terracotta-paved terrace is a lovely option for pre-dinner cocktails or post-dinner dancing.

Whatever your special occasion, Tarpy's is sure to fill the bill. And don't worry, you won't find any shady characters drinking bathtub gin at this roadhouse—just delighted diners enjoying the congenial ambiance.

CEREMONY CAPACITY: The site seats 50 indoors and 70 outdoors.

EVENT/RECEPTION CAPACITY: Tarpy's accommodates 80 seated and 110 standing indoors; 110 seated or standing, outdoors.

MEETING CAPACITY: The facility seats 80 guests.

FEES & DEPOSITS: A $50 minimum deposit is required to reserve your date; deposit rates vary depending on the size of the event. The balance is due on the day of the event. Rental fees may apply depending on event specifications. Meals start at $12/person. Tax, alcohol and a 20% service charge are additional.

AVAILABILITY: Year-round, daily, 8:30am–midnight.

SERVICES/AMENITIES:

Catering: provided, no BYO
Kitchen Facilities: n/a
Tables & Chairs: provided
Linens, Silver, etc.: provided
Restrooms: wheelchair accessible
Dance Floor: CBA
Bride's & Groom's Dressing Area: CBA
Meeting Equipment: some provided

Parking: large lot
Accommodations: no guestrooms
Telephone: emergency use only
Outdoor Night Lighting: yes
Outdoor Cooking Facilities: BBQ CBA
Cleanup: provided
View: forest, garden, pond
Other: clergy on staff; AV equipment

RESTRICTIONS:

Alcohol: provided, or BYO with corkage fee
Smoking: outside only
Music: amplified OK with volume restrictions

Wheelchair Access: yes
Insurance: not required
Other: no glitter, birdseed or rice

Gatherings, a Private Venue
and Monterey Beach Weddings

Private Wedding Venue

157 15th Street, Pacific Grove
831/647-0114
www.montereyweddingsites.com
debbie@montereycatering.com

● Rehearsal Dinners	● Corp. Events/Mtgs.
● Ceremonies	● Private Parties
● Wedding Receptions	Accommodations

Gatherings is an all-inclusive event venue that offers the perfect wedding trifecta: a homey, vintage-style setting; superb, made-to-order cuisine; and beach wedding ceremonies. This clever combo is the brainchild of *Classic Catering,* a family-run culinary team that's been pleasing local palates for years. The venue itself is a fetching Victorian in Pacific Grove, a historic Monterey suburb known for its simple charm. When we first drove up the treelined street to Gatherings, a mother goose and her fuzzy goslings were waddling along the roadside, an appropriately quaint welcome to this cozy home.

Built in 1907, the recently restored moss-colored house now has modern amenities, but still retains its original Art Deco flair. The home makes the most of its petite size, with votives and fresh flowers spread throughout the rooms. Events here are warm, relaxed affairs, and doors are left open so that there's a natural flow from one area to the next. The foyer introduces Gatherings' inviting aesthetic: cherry and gold brocade wallpaper, Deco fixtures, and soft impressionist masterpieces that convey the elegance of a bygone era.

The three adjoining event rooms are similarly arrayed. In the Parlor, period furnishings are clustered around a fireplace; a plasma TV above a rose marble mantle often plays a photographic montage of the wedding couple. A leaded-glass transom frames the passageway to the Dining Room, whose gleaming wood floors make a perfect dance floor. Ceiling speakers and adjustable lights let you set the desired mood, and a bay window showcases the wedding cake. Finally, the Music Room boasts a player piano that can also be played by hand. A viewing window peers into a state-of-the-art chef's kitchen, and guests are welcome to wander in and check out the culinary action up close.

Mingling also extends to the home's wooden deck, part of which is tented, twinkle-lit and dotted with cocktail tables; the rest is open to the refreshing sea air, and comes with a wood bar and an outdoor fireplace. As evening descends, firelight, candlelight and moonlight create a romantic glow.

And if your romantic vision includes a beach wedding ceremony, then Gatherings will stage yours on one of the local beaches. Lover's Point, a lovely coastal enclave, is just a couple of blocks away, so afterwards it's easy to return to Gatherings for the reception.

In keeping with the personable theme, Gatherings offers butlered receptions that allow friends and family to roam freely. Committed to five-star service, the impeccably turned-out staff is both friendly and well trained. All food is cooked or grilled during the event—which is not only tastier, but more fun, too. Gatherings has several event packages that offer terrific value. All of them allow you to bring your own alcohol, for example, and they'll provide the bartender at no extra cost.

Classic Catering recently acquired The Perry House, a historic property that's divine for garden weddings with a view of the Monterey Bay—and capacity for up to 150. So if your celebration won't quite fit at Gatherings, then check out The Perry House! At either venue, the congenial proprietors will give their all to exceed your expectations.

CEREMONY CAPACITY: The site holds 100 seated guests outdoors.

EVENT/RECEPTION & MEETING CAPACITY: The venue can accommodate 75 seated or standing indoors and outdoors.

FEES & DEPOSITS: A $1,500 deposit is required to reserve your date and the balance is due 2 weeks prior to the event. Wedding packages range $3,545–7,950 depending on the day of the week, the number of guests and the menu selection.

AVAILABILITY: Year-round, daily, until 10pm.

SERVICES/AMENITIES:

Catering: provided
Kitchen Facilities: n/a
Tables & Chairs: provided
Linens, Silver, etc.: provided
Restrooms: wheelchair accessible
Dance Floor: provided
Bride's Dressing Area: no
Meeting Equipment: CBA

Parking: on street, valet required
Accommodations: no guestrooms
Telephone: emergency use only
Outdoor Night Lighting: provided
Outdoor Cooking Facilities: no
Cleanup: provided
View: garden courtyard
Other: grand piano, on-site florals, AV equipment, complimentary event coordination

RESTRICTIONS:

Alcohol: BYO
Smoking: outdoors only
Music: amplified OK with restrictions

Wheelchair Access: yes
Insurance: not required

Gold Country and Yosemite

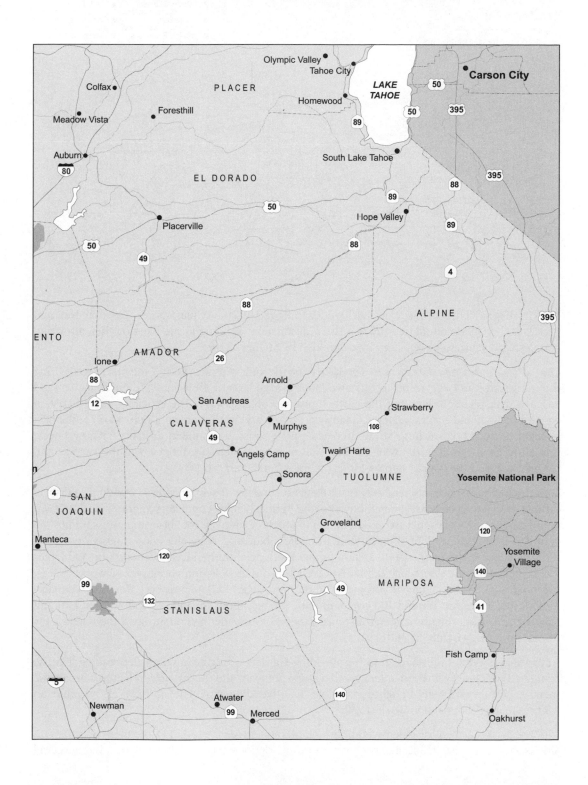

Colfax

Olympic Valley
Tahoe City
Carson City

PLACER

LAKE
TAHOE

Foresthill

Homewood

50

Meadow Vista

50

395

Auburn

80

EL DORADO

South Lake Tahoe

88

50

89

395

89

Placerville

Hope Valley

49

89

88

4

88

ALPINE

395

SACRAMENTO

AMADOR

26

Ione

Arnold

88

4

12

San Andreas

Strawberry

CALAVERAS

Murphys

108

49

Twain Harte

Yosemite National Park

Angels Camp

Sonora

TUOLUMNE

4

4

SAN

Groveland

120

JOAQUIN

Yosemite
Village

Manteca

140

120

99

MARIPOSA

41

132

STANISLAUS

Fish Camp

5

140

Newman

Atwater

99

Merced

Oakhurst

Tenaya Lodge at Yosemite

Mountain Resort

1122 Highway 41, Fish Camp

877/247-9249

www.tenayalodge.com

TenayaWeddings@dncinc.com

- Rehearsal Dinners
- Ceremonies
- Wedding Receptions
- Corp. Events/Mtgs.
- Private Parties
- Accommodations

With its magnificent soaring peaks, backwoods trails and legendary panoramas, Yosemite National Park is a cherished natural treasure. It's also a destination wedding locale like no other, attracting couples who yearn to pledge their love enfolded by Mother Nature.

One of the most congenial places in Yosemite to tie the knot is Tenaya Lodge, the first hotel to bring the luxuries of a classic resort to this awe-inspiring wilderness. Built in 1990, the four-diamond lodge is a resplendent blend of the earthy and the contemporary. The spacious lobby boasts a vaulted ceiling, and natural materials like wood, stone and leather create a rich, warm ambiance. A cut-slate floor holds a huge stone fireplace, and whimsical mountain artifacts (a snowshoe, a miniature cabin) enliven the walls. Native American influences are reflected in the carpets and furnishings, and the overall impression is one of refined comfort.

Tenaya's banquet spaces also embody rustic elegance, and put Yosemite's scenic wonders on display during your fête. The newest ceremony site, the Terrace, is a second-story outdoor deck fringed with feathery pine trees that are close enough to touch. A simple wrought-iron pergola frames the couple against this verdant expanse and an endless blue sky. After the vows, guests descend a flight of stairs to the open-sided Pavilion for another angle on the lovely scenery. Cocktail tables are clustered on one side, while dinner is served beneath the Pavilion's honey-hued wood ceiling, trimmed with twinkle lights. If you prefer an indoor celebration, then reserve the 10,000-square-foot Grand Ballroom. Tasteful and contemporary, it boasts floor-to-ceiling windows that look out to the stunning mountains carpeted in Sugar Pines. For a smaller reception, book the Forest View Room, affording equally beautiful vistas.

Intimate ceremonies are magical in the Wedding Garden, a private lawn nestled among a copse of trees. Enclosed by a wooden fence and a stone archway, the quaint garden features an artistic metal sculpture of a leafy bough that doubles as a wedding arch. The staff can also arrange an off-the-beaten-path ceremony—just ask.

The Lodge is a haven for green weddings—the banquet rooms are LEED-certified, and the cuisine is local and sustainable. Tenaya has four dining options: the casual Jackalope's Bar and Grill for fun after-parties; the family-friendly Timberloft Pizzeria; the Sierra Restaurant, which includes an outdoor patio with fire pit; and the upscale Embers for romantic fireside dining and exquisite organic seasonal menus. Any of these can be reserved for your rehearsal dinner, depending on your desired atmosphere.

Yosemite's rugged grandeur, made famous by photographer Ansel Adams' indelible images, will enhance your own wedding photos, too. Tenaya's knowledgeable event planning professionals can point out the best backdrops, as well as arrange activities for your guests. Nature Lovers can feed their souls with spectacular sunsets and scintillating starscapes. The more adventurous might like to golf, bike, ice skate, ride horses or hike to a waterfall. Meanwhile, the bride will probably want to unwind at ASCENT, Tenaya's expansive, pampering Spa, so that when it's time for her spotlight moment she'll be as serene as the surrounding landscape.

Well-appointed accommodations include spa suites, but we recommend the newlyweds cuddle up in one of the secluded cottage-style rooms with fireplaces for quality alone-time. Think of Tenaya Lodge at Yosemite as "Happiness in the High Sierras!"

CEREMONY CAPACITY: The site holds 400 seated guests indoors and 350 seated outdoors.

EVENT/RECEPTION CAPACITY: The facility can accommodate 850 seated or 1,000 standing indoors and 275 seated or 350 standing outdoors.

MEETING CAPACITY: Meeting spaces hold up to 1,200 seated guests.

FEES & DEPOSITS: A $2,500 deposit is required to reserve your date and the balance is due 30 days prior to the event. Rental fees range $500–2,500 depending on the day and time of the event and the space rented. Meals range $50–75/person. Tax, alcohol and a 20% service charge are additional.

AVAILABILITY: Year-round, daily, 6am–1:30am.

SERVICES/AMENITIES:

Catering: provided
Kitchen Facilities: n/a
Tables & Chairs: provided
Linens, Silver, etc.: provided
Restrooms: wheelchair accessible
Dance Floor: portable provided
Bride's Dressing Area: yes
Meeting Equipment: some provided
Other: grand piano, spa services, clergy on staff, AV equipment, event coordination

Parking: large lot, complimentary valet
Accommodations: 294 guestrooms, suites and cottages
Telephone: house phone
Outdoor Night Lighting: yes
Outdoor Cooking Facilities: none
Cleanup: provided
View: garden, landscaped grounds, panorama of forest and mountains

RESTRICTIONS:

Alcohol: provided or BYO wine or champagne with corkage fee
Smoking: designated areas only
Music: amplified OK with restrictions

Wheelchair Access: yes
Insurance: not required

Want to find more locations and services? Check out our informative website, www.HereComesTheGuide.com.

677

Monte Verde Inn

Inn & Garden

18841 Foresthill Road, Foresthill

530/888-8123

www.monteverdeinn.net
monteverde@foothill.net

- Rehearsal Dinners
- Ceremonies
- Wedding Receptions
- Corp. Events/Mtgs.
- Private Parties
- Accommodations

If you're looking for a very special place, it's in Foresthill, a small hamlet about 40 minutes northeast of Sacramento. Here you'll find the historic Monte Verde Inn, which is, in a word, wonderful.

The property was originally a gathering spot for Native Americans, and after gold was discovered in 1849, it became a toll station and respite for travelers. A private residence was built on the site in 1936, and today this stately Georgian-style manor is a gracious reminder of the past. A glassed-in sun porch covers the front of the manor house, and makes a sparkling backdrop for photos of the bridal party.

The landscaped grounds have the feel of an English country estate: A long entry drive, lined with flowering plum trees, draws you back in time. Manicured lawns, 100-year-old quince trees and a veritable tapestry of flowers (changed seasonally according to the whim of the owners) invite you to celebrate amid a garden of earthly delights. For ceremonies try the patios—they're surrounded by tall cedars that form an informal outdoor cathedral. At night, "fairy lights" and turn-of-the-century streetlights create a glittering halo around dancing couples.

Guests can also enjoy the inn's inviting interior, whose large open rooms feature an array of architectural embellishments and antiques. Spacious, newly refurbished guestrooms occupy the second floor. They're prettily decorated and have high ceilings, hardwood floors and Oriental carpets. The inn offers a wedding package that accommodates up to sixteen overnight guests, and includes champagne and snacks, plus a full breakfast. For a nominal charge, you can invite other friends or family staying nearby to join you for this "morning after" get-together.

Your congenial proprietors, Douglas and Kelly Dalisa, have a very personal connection to the Monte Verde Inn. They fell in love with the beautiful inn and gardens and were actually married here. Someday, they thought, they would like to own and operate this place.... Years passed and at last their dream came true: In early 2006, they purchased the inn and have already made substantial upgrades. Thrilled by their new venture, Doug and Kelly go out of their way to ensure that your event will be all you imagined and more.

As innkeepers, your hosts are eminently qualified. Doug, a professional chef and graduate of the California Culinary Academy, personally prepares all the inn's meals using only the freshest, highest-quality ingredients. With his extensive knowledge of wines, he is more than happy to suggest perfect pairings for your bright California menu. The warm and friendly Kelly has a bachelor's degree in Hotel & Restaurant Management. She's worked in the catering industry for years, and was even an award-winning instructor in Culinary Arts and Hospitality Management! Now she lavishes her expertise upon the inn's lucky guests.

All these elements combined—the enchanting grounds, delicious cuisine, quaint accommodations, and enthusiastic service—create the Monte Verde Inn's successful mix of country charm and elegance.

CEREMONY CAPACITY: The patio accommodates 225 seated or standing guests; indoors, the inn holds 100.

EVENT/RECEPTION CAPACITY: Inside, 100 guests maximum; outdoors, up to 225 seated.

MEETING CAPACITY: The inn holds up to 100 seated guests.

FEES & DEPOSITS: A $1,000 deposit is required to secure your date. Rates start at $79/person, which includes rental of the inn for 5 hours, rehearsal, all setups for ceremony and reception, color-coordinated, fresh floral centerpieces for all tables, wedding cake, hors d'oeuvres, full buffet and nonalcoholic beverages. Note that all food is prepared from fresh ingredients on the premises. Alcoholic beverages, tax and a 21% service charge are additional.

AVAILABILITY: Year-round, daily.

SERVICES/AMENITIES:

Catering: provided, no BYO
Kitchen Facilities: n/a
Tables & Chairs: provided
Linens, Silver, etc.: provided
Restrooms: wheelchair accessible
Dance Floor: patio
Bride's Dressing Area: yes; also CBA for bridal party
Meeting Equipment: BYO

Parking: 2 large lots
Accommodations: 6 guestrooms
Telephone: house phone
Outdoor Night Lighting: yes
Outdoor Cooking Facilities: no
Cleanup: provided
View: garden and forests
Other: event coordination included

RESTRICTIONS:

Alcohol: provided, BWC only
Smoking: outside only
Music: amplified OK

Wheelchair Access: outdoor access only, limited indoor access
Insurance: not required

Winchester Country Club

Private Golf Club

3030 Legends Drive, Meadow Vista
530/878-3015

www.winchestercountryclub.com
dcarrier@winchestercountryclub.com

- Rehearsal Dinners
- Ceremonies
- Wedding Receptions
- Corp. Events/Mtgs.
- Private Parties
- Accommodations

As you make the scenic drive towards Meadow Vista, less than an hour north of Sacramento, you're invigorated by the crisp, clean air of the Sierra Nevadas. Your destination, the Winchester Country Club, lies at the top of a majestic ascent lined with towering evergreens. This meticulously maintained venue boasts a rustic-meets-modern aesthetic, evoking both the homey warmth of the country and contemporary elegance.

The award-winning Clubhouse is situated on its own promontory, and at 32,000 square feet is spacious and impressive. Fashioned of dark wood and cut stone, its exterior resembles a forest lodge; yet, within you'll find a sophisticated lobby, decked in marble and intricate wood inlays that echo the forested environs. Constructed in 2004 with large events in mind, Winchester offers a view-filled ceremony site and three reception options. At the rear of the Clubhouse, a broad stone deck features a ramp that sweeps down onto a velvety lawn called the Ceremony Green. Guests seated in white chairs can easily follow your graceful descent as you make your grand entrance. They'll be even more captivated as they witness your exchange of vows against a breathtaking panorama of nature: thickets of pine trees and rolling hills silhouetted against a vast blue sky.

After the ceremony, explore the grounds for memorable photo ops while your guests retreat inside to the Clubhouse Lounge for the cocktail hour. Traditional wood paneling and a stately bar lend a sense of occasion, and the views—fit for a coffee-table book—put everyone at ease. The Lounge adjoins the beautiful Main Dining Room, where a wall of windows takes in the treelined fairways and the stunning Sierra foothills. Patios on either side of the Dining Room invite guests to mingle in the mountain air and watch the stars as they fill the evening sky.

If you're looking to imprint your own style on a space, opt for the Upstairs Banquet Room. Here, coffered ceilings and a neutral palette will harmonize with whatever décor you choose. For an ethereal, romantic effect, simply drape tulle and fairy lights across the high ceilings. Lofty multi-paned windows look out across feathery treetops, adding to the banquet room's allure.

Prefer to party in the great outdoors? Celebrate on the Clubhouse Deck overlooking the picturesque Ceremony Green. It'll accommodate up to 400 of your nearest and dearest, and all or part of the deck can be elegantly tented, complete with chandeliers and canopy-style ceiling swags. A short path leads to a sheltered dance floor patio that's visible from the deck so guests can watch the dancing without leaving their seats.

Winchester is the kind of place that encourages you to indulge your wedding fantasies: As a grand finale, one adventurous couple led their surprised guests to the driving range and made their getaway by helicopter!

This facility's event professionals take pride in their wedding packages, which include separate dressing suites for the bride and groom, the ceremony site, and complimentary amenities like the cake cutting and champagne toast. The on-site coordinator will also gladly assist with vendor referrals and your day-of needs.

Truly a diamond in the rough, Winchester Country Club is a Gold Country bridal bonanza!

CEREMONY CAPACITY: The site holds 200 seated guests indoors, and 400 seated outdoors.

EVENT/RECEPTION & MEETING CAPACITY: The facility accomodates 150 seated or 200 standing indoors and 375 seated or 500 standing outdoors..

FEES & DEPOSITS: 25% of the estimated event cost is required to reserve your date, and the balance is due 10 days prior to the event. Customizable packages start at $105/person and include the facility fee, tax and service charge.

AVAILABILITY: Year-round, 8am–11pm, Mondays, Wednesdays–Sundays.

SERVICES/AMENITIES:

Catering: provided
Kitchen Facilities: n/a
Tables & Chairs: provided
Linens, Silver, etc.: provided
Restrooms: wheelchair accessible
Dance Floor: provided
Bride's Dressing Area: yes
Meeting Equipment: provided

Parking: large lot
Accommodations: no guestrooms
Telephone: emergency use only
Outdoor Night Lighting: provided
Outdoor Cooking Facilities: BBQ CBA
Cleanup: provided
View: landscaped grounds, panorama of fairways, cityscape, mountains, and valley
Other: AV equipment, event coordination

RESTRICTIONS:

Alcohol: provided
Smoking: designated areas only
Music: OK with restrictions

Wheelchair Access: yes
Insurance: not required

The Ahwahnee

Historic Lodge in National Park

One Ahwahnee Drive, Yosemite National Park

801/559-5019

www.yosemitepark.com/weddings
yosevent@dncinc.com

- Rehearsal Dinners
- Ceremonies
- Wedding Receptions
- Corp. Events/Mtgs.
- Private Parties
- Accommodations

Yosemite National Park's beauty is so vast and sublime that Ansel Adams' photos could hardly contain it. In his famous black & white images, impossibly high granite domes buttress the sky and giant redwoods brush the clouds with their pine-needled tops. Nature on this scale is extraordinary, and a photo simply can't compare with the experience of being there. To camp, hike, and canoe in the majesty of Yosemite's High Sierra landscape is fairly inspiring. To get married here is downright magical.

Within the park proper, four hotels take full advantage of the stunning surroundings—and two of them offer first-rate accommodations for weddings of all kinds. Right in Yosemite Valley is The Ahwahnee, a 1920s-era lodge that strikes the perfect balance between rustic and elegant. A veritable log-and-stone castle in the woods, The Ahwahnee features cathedral ceilings and enormous hearths alongside rich wood details and Native American motifs. The grand, Early American atmosphere is complemented by expansive windows throughout, which frame views of the Valley's most prized natural treasures: Half Dome, Glacier Point, and Yosemite Falls in the distance.

Not far from The Ahwahnee, Curry Village provides a historic and charming setting more than 100 years in the making. You can tie the knot nearby in the impressive Yosemite chapel, followed by a reception in the Curry Pavilion. A high-beamed ceiling and roaring fireplace make the venue inviting, but it's also spacious enough for 500 guests.

You'll find two more wonderful options for your celebration at Yosemite Lodge at the Falls, located near the tallest waterfall in North America. The seasonally available Cliff/Falls Room holds up to 160, and The Mountain Room Restaurant treats diners to a spectacular view of the cascading falls through twenty-foot, floor-to-ceiling windows.

Just a little further south, another wedding-friendly spot awaits—the Wawona Hotel. Built in 1879, it's not only one of California's oldest mountain hotels, it possesses an irresistible Victorian-era appeal. This landmark building, cradled between the Mariposa Grove of Giant Sequoias and Yosemite Valley, boasts verandas off nearly every room. Inside, period antiques, delicate floral ornamentation, and exquisite hanging light fixtures create an old-fashioned ambiance.

When it comes to weddings here, couples often marry outdoors in the spring, summer and fall. The Wawona's large lawn overlooks mountain peaks and thick groves of pines, an excellent backdrop for a formal seated ceremony or a casual outdoor barbecue/reception. Inside, the hotel's Sun

Room easily hosts cocktails and seated dinners. Walls of French doors open onto the veranda and showcase the lush, scenic vistas beyond.

At all of these wedding venues and in every season of the year, Yosemite National Park captivates: A winter moon over a snow-dusted valley is every bit as romantic as fields of wild flowers in summer. When you get married here, the overall magnificence of Yosemite—along with the moment you say "I do," dance that first dance, and cut the cake—will sparkle in your memory for years to come.

Most of the information below applies to The Ahwahnee. For details on the other venues go to www.yosemitepark.com/weddings.

CEREMONY CAPACITY: The Ahwahnee accommodates 200 seated guests outdoors. Indoor ceremonies also available in various locations.

EVENT/RECEPTION CAPACITY: The Ahwahnee holds 80 seated or 100 standing guests indoors; Yosemite Lodge accommodates 160 seated or 185 standing; the Wawona Hotel holds 100 seated or 130 standing indoors in spring and fall, and 200 seated or 300 standing guests outdoors in summer.

MEETING CAPACITY: Meeting spaces accommodate up to 400 seated guests, depending on the facility used.

FEES & DEPOSITS: A nonrefundable deposit is required at the time of booking. Deposits range $500–4,000 depending on the type of event, venue(s) selected and number of guests. Average total reception costs range $150–200/person, which include hors d'oeuvres, bar, wine/champagne, plated dinner or buffet, wedding cake, room rental fees including setup/cleanup, linens, china/crystal; and tax and service charges. Alcohol and lodging are additional.

AVAILABILITY: Year-round, daily, 8am–10pm. Certain holiday blackout dates may apply. Call for availability.

SERVICES/AMENITIES:

Catering: provided, no BYO
Kitchen Facilities: n/a
Tables & Chairs: provided
Linens, Silver, etc.: provided
Restrooms: wheelchair accessible
Dance Floor: yes
Bride's & Groom's Dressing Area: guestroom CBA
Meeting Equipment: CBA, extra fee

Parking: medium-sized lot
Accommodations: 123 guestrooms and cottages
Telephone: pay phone and in guestrooms
Outdoor Night Lighting: access only
Outdoor Cooking Facilities: BBQ CBA
Cleanup: provided
View: Yosemite Park, mountains, forest, waterfalls

RESTRICTIONS:

Alcohol: provided
Smoking: not allowed
Music: acoustic only

Wheelchair Access: limited
Insurance: not required
Other: no rice, petals or birdseed

This is important! Tell locations you're reading HERE COMES THE GUIDE and ask if our information is still current.

Tahoe Area

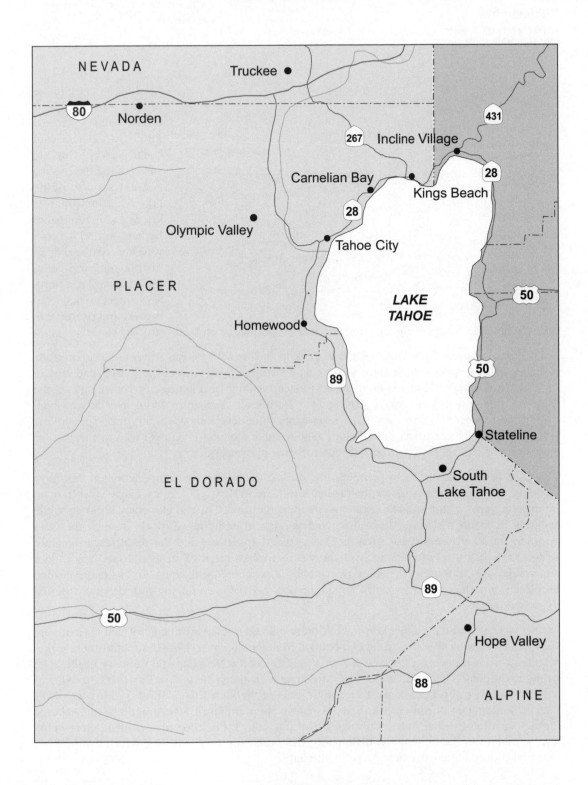

Big Water Grille

341 Ski Way, Incline Village
775/833-0606

www.bigwatergrille.com
john@bigwatergrille.com

Restaurant

● Rehearsal Dinners	● Corp. Events/Mtgs.
● Ceremonies	● Private Parties
● Wedding Receptions	Accommodations

Catching just a glimpse of Lake Tahoe, with its brilliant color and amazing clarity, can take your breath away. But big views of Big Blue, as the country's only alpine lake is affectionately known, can sometimes be hard to find for your wedding day festivities. That is, until you get to Big Water Grille, a North Shore mecca where your nearest and dearest can revel for hours in what are arguably the area's most spectacular and unobstructed vistas.

Located just a quarter mile from Diamond Peak in Incline Village, Big Water Grille masterfully balances being a special destination with being a favorite dining spot of the locals. Clad in river rock, the residential building is on a slope just steep enough and jutting just far enough off the shoreline that you feel like you're getting away from it all. A clean, modern interior with high ceilings and recessed lighting gives the restaurant's three levels an open, airy feel. The striking artwork is by top local artists, but fabulous as they are, it's tough to compete with that irresistible view of the lake, visible everywhere through soaring glass walls.

There's enormous flexibility in planning how to use the facility for your celebration, but most wedding parties are drawn first to the inviting outside deck. Here, you can exchange vows, framed by majestic pines as the sparkling water is tinted by the sunset, or you can enjoy cocktails while drinking in nature's beauty. Afterwards, your guests can easily move inside through the glass doors to the lounge-styled Bar Area for butler-passed appetizers and the restaurant's signature seafood raw bar, a spectacular array of the week's freshest catch. With its polished wood floor and comfy sofas, this area provides a great clubby atmosphere for dancing, and its massive stone fireplace is a perfect photo backdrop for cutting your cake or even staging your ceremony during the winter months.

Dinner is served in the Dining Room, built on two levels to take advantage of that ever-present view, which now faces some strong competition from the highly acclaimed, mouth-watering presentations from Executive Chef Jayson Poe. A graduate of the New England Culinary Institute, he worked with famed chef Daniel Boulud at Restaurant Daniel in New York City before moving to Lake Tahoe. He's also been a guest chef with some of the West Coast's most well-known chefs: Richard Reddington at Auberge du Soleil, Gregory Short at Masa's, Walter Manzke at L'Auberge Carmel and Ron Boyd at Aqua. Although classically trained, Chef Poe uses contemporary cooking techniques in the preparation his Modern California cuisine. His dishes, which feature fresh seasonal produce, are extremely flavorful and light.

To complement your meal, Big Water Grille's wine list offers more than 200 wines from around the world in a range of prices. In fact, if you're planning an intimate reception or rehearsal dinner, wine lovers in your party will appreciate the Wine Cellar, a sophisticated private setting separate from the Main Dining Room.

And since this is Nevada, where there are no restrictions on when to end your music or have last call, if you buy out the restaurant they will let you set your own hours so you can start later in summer to catch the sunset and then party the night away.

CEREMONY CAPACITY: The restaurant holds 100 standing guests indoors in front of the fireplace and 30 seated or 100 standing outdoors.

EVENT/RECEPTION CAPACITY: The restaurant accommodates 120 seated or 135 standing indoors and 30 seated or standing outdoors on the deck.

MEETING CAPACITY: Meeting spaces hold 100 seated guests.

FEES & DEPOSITS: 50% of the food and beverage minimum is required to reserve your date. The balance is due at the end of the event. Rental fees range $0–750 depending on your event needs. Meals range $48–100/person. Tax, alcohol and a 20% service charge are additional.

AVAILABILITY: Year-round, daily, anytime. Call for details.

SERVICES/AMENITIES:

Catering: provided
Kitchen Facilities: n/a
Tables & Chairs: provided
Linens, Silver, etc.: provided
Restrooms: wheelchair accessible
Dance Floor: provided
Bride's Dressing Rooms: CBA
Meeting Equipment: some provided

Parking: large lot
Accommodations: no guestrooms
Telephone: emergency use only
Outdoor Night Lighting: provided
Outdoor Cooking Facilities: no
Cleanup: provided
View: panorama of Lake Tahoe and mountains
Other: event coordination

RESTRICTIONS:

Alcohol: provided
Smoking: not allowed
Music: amplified OK

Wheelchair Access: yes
Insurance: not required

North Tahoe Event Center

Lakeside Conference Center

8318 North Lake Boulevard, Kings Beach
530/546-7249
www.northtahoeevents.com
sales@northtahoeevents.com

- Rehearsal Dinners
- Ceremonies
- Wedding Receptions
- Corp. Events/Mtgs.
- Private Parties

Accommodations

The North Tahoe Event Center, located in an enviable spot on the lake's North Shore, is a modern facility with nothing between it and the deep blue waters of the lake except a wide stretch of pristine beach. Both large and small events are invited to take advantage of this exceptional setting.

During those glorious months from late spring to early fall, have your entire celebration on the center's expansive Lakeview Deck, right next to the sand. The serene, azure lake and jagged mountain silhouettes form a stunning backdrop, highlighting the importance of the moment. No matter where you are, gentle breezes flow off the water, and you feel like a part of the breathtaking panorama all around you. After, why not stroll along the shore with your new spouse, wriggle your toes in the sand, and let your photographer capture candid moments for you to look back on in the years to come? For your reception, continue to embrace the great outdoors, and dine on the spacious deck, a premium spot to savor a romantic sunset or watch as the moon rises above the Eastern Sierras, casting a golden shimmer upon the lake.

The center also has several options for indoor gatherings year-round. The contemporary Lakeview Suite overlooks the deck through floor-to-ceiling windows, and the neutral décor doesn't distract from the mesmerizing view of the lake and surrounding peaks dusted with snow. The 4,800-square-foot Timberline Room, with its hardwood stage and audiovisual equipment, is perfect for an elaborate gala. Other nice features include a large bride's room, roomy commercial kitchen and in-house catering. You're also free to bring your own alcohol, and use your own caterer.

Both you and your guests will love the chance to experience Tahoe's year-round recreation—skiing, fishing, golf and hiking—as well as less strenuous but equally satisfying activities like fine dining, shopping and visiting art galleries.

With its prime location, flexibility, and glorious view, the North Tahoe Event Center has developed quite a following for those who wish to celebrate in one of the country's most desirable destinations.

CEREMONY CAPACITY: Several rooms accommodate up to 350 seated or standing guests indoors. The Lakeview Deck holds 350 seated or standing outdoors.

EVENT/RECEPTION CAPACITY: Various rooms hold up to 350 seated or 500 standing guests indoors. The Lakeview Deck can seat 250 and accommodate 350 standing guests outdoors.

FEES & DEPOSITS: A 50% deposit is required to confirm your date. The balance is due 2 weeks prior to the event. Rental fees range $1,100–9,000 depending on guest count and space reserved. If you bring your own caterer, there is a $3–8/person kitchen use fee. Use of the in-house caterer requires a deposit (applied to the final catering invoice) to retain those services. In-house catering starts at $30/person. Tax, alcohol and service charges are additional.

AVAILABILITY: Year-round, daily, 9am–2am.

SERVICES/AMENITIES:
Catering: provided or BYO
Kitchen Facilities: commercial
Tables & Chairs: provided
Linens, Silver, etc.: BYO linens, silver and glassware provided with in-house caterer
Restrooms: wheelchair accessible
Dance Floor: portable provided
Bride's Dressing Area: yes (large or small available)
Meeting Equipment: large screens, LCD projectors, easels, AV, WiFi, conference calls, high speed internet available

Parking: large lot, extra fee
Accommodations: available nearby
Telephone: house phones
Outdoor Night Lighting: yes
Outdoor Cooking Facilities: BBQ grill
Cleanup: provided
View: Lake Tahoe and Sierras
Other: wedding and event coordination, vendor referral list available

RESTRICTIONS:
Alcohol: provided or BYO
Smoking: designated areas
Music: amplified OK indoors

Wheelchair Access: yes
Insurance: required
Other: no rice, confetti or artificial flower petals

Sugar Bowl Resort

Sugar Bowl Ski Area, Norden
530/426-6769

www.sugarbowl.com
mshrewsbury@sugarbowl.com

Tahoe Area Ski Resort

- Rehearsal Dinners
- Ceremonies
- Wedding Receptions
- Corp. Events/Mtgs.
- Private Parties
- Accommodations

Sugar Bowl Resort leads a double life. In the winter, thousands of skiers descend upon its well-groomed slopes, anxious to make the most of the ample snowfall. In summer, however, visitors discover a quiet, awe-inspiring, high-alpine resort that's custom-made for an exclusive mountain wedding, retreat or family reunion.

Built in 1939 at the base of Mt. Disney, the original Lodge at Sugar Bowl is still the resort's focal point and the site of most special events. When you host your celebration here, you have exclusive use of the entire venue, including bar, lounge, dining room, decks and lawn. You also get the 27 guestrooms, which are quite cozy—especially the spacious suite where the newlyweds usually spend their wedding night.

The Lodge's décor is steeped in Old Tahoe charm with a European flair. A large stone fireplace and oak Craftsman-style furniture welcome you into the lounge, where creamy white board-and-batten walls are covered with vintage prints depicting Donner Summit's rich history and storied past. Most rooms have a wall of windows overlooking scenic Mt. Disney.

While the lounge and dining room are often used for rehearsal dinners and indoor receptions, the Lodge's expansive wooden deck is the standout site. Facing majestic mountains and a flower-studded hillside, it offers plenty of space for dining and dancing. It can also be partially covered with a white canopy or set with umbrella-shaded tables. Below the deck is a manicured lawn bordered by tall trees, a custom-built fire pit ringed by Adirondack chairs, and a gently flowing stream. It's a lovely spot for exchanging vows and taking photos.

The secluded Lake Mary Cabin offers a different but equally stunning setting. Built at the water's edge, the peaked cabin has its own generous deck facing a quintessential alpine vista of the sparkling lake and Mt. Disney. This is a wonderful place for a Friday night rehearsal dinner, an intimate ceremony on the adjacent lawn, or a relaxing afternoon spent on the private beach.

If you want to get married at Sugar Bowl but don't plan to stay over, reserve the Judah Day Lodge, a large, contemporary venue featuring wraparound windows that provide mountain views from every table. You can tie the knot outside on the vast brick patio that runs along the front of the room, with the ever-present mountains as a backdrop.

And don't miss the opportunity to invite your guests to the top of Mt. Disney for champagne and appetizers. As family and friends gather on the deck of the mountaintop station and take in the spectacular panoramas all around, they'll be thanking you for bringing them to such a magical place.

It's true, weddings simply shine here. Sugar Bowl's natural assets, Old Tahoe charm and impeccable service impress everyone who visits, no matter what time of year.

CEREMONY, EVENT/RECEPTION & MEETING CAPACITY: The Village Lodge can accommodate up to 300 guests outdoors and 150 guests indoors, the Judah Lodge up to 400 guests indoors or outdoors, and the Village Hall up to 110–125 guests, indoors only. The Lake Mary venue holds up to 100 guests outdoors.

FEES & DEPOSITS: For weddings, a $1,000 nonrefundable deposit is required when the event is booked. Half of the estimated food and beverage cost is due 30 days prior to the event; the balance is payable at the event's conclusion. Catering costs start at $42/person. Tax and an 18% service charge are additional.

AVAILABILITY: June through October.

SERVICES/AMENITIES:

Catering: provided, no BYO
Kitchen Facilities: n/a
Tables & Chairs: provided, extra fee
Linens, Silver, etc.: provided, extra fee
Restrooms: wheelchair access limited
Dance Floor: deck or lounge
Bride's Dressing Area: yes
Meeting Equipment: TVs and VCRs
Other: event coordination and referrals

Parking: ample
Accommodations: 27 guestrooms for Village Lodge functions only
Telephone: pay phone
Outdoor Night Lighting: limited
Outdoor Cooking Facilities: BBQs, no BYO
Cleanup: provided
View: mountain peaks

RESTRICTIONS:

Alcohol: provided
Smoking: designated areas
Music: amplified OK

Wheelchair Access: limited
Insurance: not required

Overwhelmed? Use the search criteria on www.HereComesTheGuide.com to narrow down your choices.

PlumpJack Squaw Valley Inn

1920 Squaw Valley Road, Olympic Valley
800/323-7666, 530/583-4158
www.plumpjack.com
ldugan@plumpjack.com

Inn & Event Facility

- Rehearsal Dinners
- Ceremonies
- Wedding Receptions
- Corp. Events/Mtgs.
- Private Parties
- Accommodations

Tucked in a quiet valley at the base of the majestic Sierra Nevada Mountains is a world-class hotel with all the charm of a mountain lodge. The PlumpJack Squaw Valley Inn boasts a truly original look—one you won't find anywhere else in Tahoe. The Lobby and guestrooms are done in muted earth tones and sumptuous fabrics, and display an exceptional melding of decorative elements: innovative metal sculpture, eye-catching furnishings and striking light fixtures that combine whimsy with copper, glass and chrome.

The ambiance of the main building continues through the adjacent event facility. Here a split-level ballroom features huge natural wood beams that crisscross beneath a high peaked ceiling, giving the entire space the feeling of an elegant cabin in the woods. Natural light, rich hues on the walls, and blond wood wainscoting create an understated sophistication. The highlight of the ballroom is the floor-to-ceiling views: snow-dusted mountains that seem close enough to touch, and a garden landscape bursting with springtime colors. The lower level holds the dining tables, while the upper level is often used for dancing or cake cutting. If you're planning an intimate get-together, the ballroom can be divided into four sections by luxurious tapestry panels.

During the warmer months, as the snow melts and the wildflowers and waterfalls regain their glory, the inn becomes a haven for outdoor celebrations, held on the sun-splashed pool patio. Bordered by the event facility, the PlumpJack Cafe, and lofty aspens and pines, the patio has the rustic appeal of a village courtyard. Wedding ceremonies are staged against the dramatic backdrop of trees, rugged peaks and open sky. After the vows, have a cocktail hour and reception next to the pool on the patio's raised level. Adjacent to the pool deck is a more secluded site for intimate ceremonies: Couples can wed atop a cut-stone deck on the bank of Squaw Creek, where pine trees, boulders and a mountain slope create a natural milieu.

Wherever you hold your event at the inn, it will be handled by a professional staff, known for their dedication and attention to detail. All event catering is provided exclusively by the inn's renowned restaurant, the PlumpJack Cafe. Their menu focuses on innovative California cuisine, incorporating locally sourced, organic and seasonal ingredients. The Cafe also boasts an extensive wine list, which has received Wine Spectator's Award of Excellence for the past five years.

Your destination wedding at the inn treats your guests to luxuriously appointed accommodations, complete with complimentary gourmet breakfast buffet. And the inn makes a perfect base camp for exploring the breathtaking surroundings, including a jewel of a lake just a few minutes away. Recreational activities abound—biking, hiking, fishing and more.

PlumpJack's designers have conceived something unique: a mountain inn, banquet facility and restaurant with both the avant-garde distinction of a cosmopolitan city and the fresh simplicity of a mountain retreat. Whether you dream of a winter wonderland wedding or exchanging vows in the pine-scented summer air, PlumpJack Squaw Valley Inn lets you celebrate in the lap of nature any time of year.

CEREMONY CAPACITY: Each of the 2 banquet rooms accommodates 235 seated or 400 standing guests; the pool patio holds 300 guests.

EVENT/RECEPTION CAPACITY: Receptions can be held in any of the above areas.

MEETING CAPACITY: Each conference room holds 300 seated theater-style or 200 conference-style.

FEES & DEPOSITS: For weddings and special events, a deposit is required to reserve your date. Catering fees for weddings and special events start at $50/person for dinners or buffets. Tax, alcohol and a 20% service charge are additional.

AVAILABILITY: Year-round, daily.

SERVICES/AMENITIES:

Catering: provided
Kitchen Facilities: n/a
Tables & Chairs: provided
Linens, Silver, etc.: provided
Restrooms: wheelchair accessible
Dance Floor: provided
Bride's Dressing Area: Penthouse Suite
Meeting Equipment: fully equipped

Parking: large lot, complimentary
Accommodations: 55 guestrooms, 5 suites including penthouse
Outdoor Night Lighting: no
Outdoor Cooking Facilities: n/a
Cleanup: provided
View: Sierra Nevada Mountains
Other: event coordination; activities such as tram rides, hikes, horsebackriding, skiing, sledding, golf, mountain biking, etc.

RESTRICTIONS:

Alcohol: provided, corkage $25/750 ml bottle or $50/magnum
Smoking: outdoors only
Music: amplified OK

Wheelchair Access: yes
Insurance: not required
Other: no rice or balloon releases

Edgewood Tahoe Golf Course

Golf Course & Clubhouse

100 Lake Parkway, Stateline/Lake Tahoe

775/588-2787

www.EdgewoodTahoe.com/weddings
events@EdgewoodTahoe.com

●	Rehearsal Dinners	●	Corp. Events/Mtgs.
●	Ceremonies	●	Private Parties
●	Wedding Receptions		Accommodations

Sometimes you encounter a place so completely unexpected it takes your breath away. Edgewood Tahoe is certain to do just that. As you drive through the pine forest along Lake Parkway, only the occasional glimpse of green fairway hints at what lays ahead. Suddenly the trees part and there, spread out before you, is a gorgeous scene: A striking timber-and-glass clubhouse rises from a small hill, while the sparkling blue water of the nation's deepest alpine lake and the soaring peaks of the Sierra Nevadas frame the building like a living photograph.

After parking the car you may be tempted to linger beside the lake to take in the view and listen to the waves lap against the shore. When you're ready to move on, low rock walls usher you along the steps and pathways leading up to the clubhouse. Everything about the building feels as immense and majestic as its surroundings. Granite boulders rest on the sloping lawns. Tall windows reflect the passing clouds. And the multiple gables of the gray roof alternately soar skyward and slant close to the ground, mimicking the mountains in the background.

The interior of the clubhouse is equally dramatic: Massive beams support the expansive vaulted ceilings throughout the building; sunlight streams through the floor-to-ceiling windows that grace nearly every room; and, in the center of the long entrance hall, granite rock pillars draped with ferns mark the way up the steps to the spacious bar and lounge.

The best views of Lake Tahoe can be seen from the nearly identical North and South Rooms, located on either side of the lounge. Both of these banquet spaces have their own patios and adjoining decks, which create a wonderful indoor-outdoor flow. In each room, peaked windows along three walls bring the scenery inside, creating a mountain cathedral atmosphere. Guests are treated to the sight of whitecaps racing across the lake in the afternoon, and panoramic views of the Sierras, where snow sometimes clings to the uppermost ridges far into June.

The patios were specifically designed for wedding ceremonies, with the lake and mountains providing a glorious backdrop. After the ceremony, appetizers are served in the banquet room you've chosen for your reception. During the summer, guests often enjoy their champagne and hors d'oeuvres at tables on the adjoining deck before moving inside for a sit-down dinner or buffet. In the winter, the entire wedding can be held in the larger North Room. Vows are exchanged in front of the picture window overlooking the snow-covered landscape. Family and friends then follow the newlyweds into the lobby for cocktails, while Edgewood quickly rearranges the hall for the reception.

Afternoon and evening weddings held on weekends book quickly at Edgewood, especially in the summer and fall. You will often find it easier to make a reservation for a weekend morning or for a weekday. Not only is the clubhouse much more available, but the breeze off the lake is calmest before noon, and nearby lodging is less expensive Monday through Friday. No matter what season or time of day you choose for your wedding, one thing is a given: The scenery will never be anything less than beautiful.

CEREMONY CAPACITY: The North Patio accommodates 130 seated guests; the South Patio holds 100 seated guests.

EVENT/RECEPTION CAPACITY: Indoors, the South Room holds 60–100 seated guests. The North Room holds 100–250 seated guests. The entire facility accommodates a total of 400 seated guests.

FEES & DEPOSITS: A nonrefundable deposit ranging $4,000–5,000 is required to reserve your date. The balance is due 3 weeks prior to the event. Rental fees range $1,750–5,500 depending on the day of week and space rented. Meals range $38–76/person. Tax, alcohol and a 19% service charge are additional.

Ceremony fees or chair covers are an additional charge. There are no cake-cutting, parking or other rental fees.

AVAILABILITY: Year-round, daily.

SERVICES/AMENITIES:

Catering: provided
Kitchen Facilities: n/a
Tables & Chairs: provided
Linens, Silver, etc.: provided
Restrooms: wheelchair accessible
Dance Floor: provided
Bride's Dressing Area: yes
Meeting Equipment: no

Parking: ample lot
Accommodations: no guestrooms
Telephone: pay phones
Outdoor Night Lighting: limited
Outdoor Cooking Facilities: n/a
Cleanup: provided
View: mountains, lake
Other: event coordination

RESTRICTIONS:

Alcohol: provided
Smoking: outdoors only
Music: amplified OK with restrictions

Wheelchair Access: yes
Insurance: not required

The Lodge

12850 Northwoods Boulevard, Truckee
530/587-9458
www.thelodge-tahoe.com
ckammerer@TahoeDonner.com

Restaurant & Banquet Facility

- ● Rehearsal Dinners
- ● Ceremonies
- ● Wedding Receptions
- ● Corp. Events/Mtgs.
- ● Private Parties
- Accommodations

Set in the Sierra Mountains near Donner Lake, The Lodge is a wonderful place to celebrate your destination special event amid breathtaking pastoral beauty. This popular restaurant and banquet center is the cornerstone of Tahoe Donner, an exclusive planned community with its own golf course and access to a wealth of outdoor recreation. Many of these activities, such as the equestrian center, tennis, skiing, camping, golf and more, are also open to the public.

The Lodge is designed with floor-to-ceiling windows overlooking emerald fairways, towering pines and the rugged sierras. A proud member of the Audubon Cooperative Sanctuary program, it puts both the glories of the natural world and Classic Tahoe-style amenities at your disposal.

Spring through fall, wedding ceremonies can be held at one of The Lodge's picturesque sites. The Pavilion Area, just outside the restaurant, offers a beautiful arbor overlooking the wooded mountains. Say "I do" right on the grass, then enjoy cocktails and appetizers al fresco followed by your reception in the adjacent tiled Pavilion. This spacious peaked tent, luxuriously draped in pleated white fabric, is compatible with any style of décor and the clear sides all around let the outside in.

For a more intimate ceremony, cocktail party or dinner, host it in the landscaped Grotto, which features a waterfall and also provides some lovely photo opportunities.

In the winter months, all of The Lodge's interior spaces are warm and inviting, with alderwood trim and high, open-beamed ceilings. Huge picture windows capture the dynamic view, which is especially compelling in winter when the trees and mountains wear a dusting of snow, creating a magnificent panoramic landscape.

The Sage and Aspen Rooms on the second story are cozy settings for rehearsal dinners, family reunions, or birthday parties. Both overlook the 18th green and the Aspen Room has a fireplace. The attractive downstairs banquet room is a private reception option in any season. And last but not least, The Lodge's pub is available, too, as a fun spot for the after-party.

With the rustic splendor of its environs, pleasing architecture and gracious hospitality, The Lodge at Tahoe Donner is a standout venue for any event.

CEREMONY CAPACITY: The Lodge accommodates 90 seated indoors and 200 seated outdoors.

EVENT/RECEPTION & MEETING CAPACITY: The facility holds 94 seated and 120 standing indoors; 200 seated and 350 standing outdoors.

FEES & DEPOSITS: 20% of the estimated event total is required to reserve your date. The balance is due on the day of the event. Rental fees range $500–2,500 depending on the space rented. Meals range $28–75/person. Tax, alcohol and a 20% service charge are additional.

AVAILABILITY: The outdoor space is available June through October (weather permitting), 8am–10pm. Indoor spaces are available year-round, 6am–10pm.

SERVICES/AMENITIES:

Catering: provided

Kitchen Facilities: n/a

Tables & Chairs: provided

Linens, Silver, etc.: some provided

Restrooms: wheelchair accessible

Dance Floor: CBA

Bride's & Groom's Dressing Areas: CBA

Meeting Equipment: some provided

Parking: large lot, on-street

Accommodations: no guestrooms

Telephone: emergency use only

Outdoor Night Lighting: CBA

Outdoor Cooking Facilities: BBQ CBA

Cleanup: provided

View: river, forest, mountains, fairways

RESTRICTIONS:

Alcohol: provided

Smoking: outside only

Music: amplified OK indoors or outdoors with restrictions

Wheelchair Access: yes

Insurance: not required

The professionals in the back of this book are the best in the business. How do we know? Read page 701.

Part Two: Event Services

All our Event Services have been

1. We only represent the best professionals in the biz.

The professionals featured in our Service Directory aren't plucked from the *Yellow Pages*. They're a carefully selected group of vendors who we'd recommend to our friends and business associates without hesitation.

2. Because we're picky, you don't have to worry about who to hire for your event.

We've thoroughly checked the professional track record of our advertisers so you can be as confident about their abilities as we are. The companies we highlight have passed our reference check with flying colors, and we're honored to represent each of them. They've all been *Certified By The Guide*.

3. Getting into Here Comes The Guide is tough.

The service providers we represent are topnotch. We put each one through a rigorous reference check, which involves interviewing up to 30 other event professionals and brides. We call every single reference and ask about the professionalism, technical competency and service orientation of the advertiser in question.

When you invest 7–10 hours talking to that many professionals, you get a crystal clear picture of who's doing a superb job and who isn't. Those candidates who received consistent, rave reviews made it into *The Guide*. Those who didn't were (nicely) turned down.

Working With Professionals

Hiring a Caterer: Get References and Look for Professionalism

If you're selecting your own caterer, don't just pick one at random. Get references from friends and acquaintances or, better yet, call the caterers listed in the *Here Comes The Guide* Service Directory. We've thoroughly screened these companies and can assure you that they're in the top 5% of the industry in terms of quality and service. We keep all of their references on file, so you can call us and ask questions about them.

Every caterer is different. Some offer only preset menus while others will help you create your own. Menus and prices vary enormously, so know what you want and what you can spend. After you've talked to several caterers and have decided which ones to seriously consider, get references for each one and call them. Ask not only about the quality of the food, but about the ease of working with a given caterer. You'll want to know if the caterer is professional—fully prepared and equipped, punctual and organized. You may also want to know if the caterer is licensed, prepares food in a kitchen approved by the Department of Health, or carries workmen's compensation and liability insurance. Although this level of inquiry may seem unnecessary, responses to these questions will give you a more complete picture of how a caterer runs his or her business, and will help you determine which caterer is best suited for your event.

Facility Requirements for Caterers

Facilities often have specific requirements regarding caterers—they may have to be licensed and bonded, out by 11pm or fastidiously clean. Before you hire a caterer, make sure that he or she is compatible with your site. In fact, even if the facility does not require it, it's a good idea to have your caterer visit the place in advance to become familiar with any special circumstances or problems that might come up. You'll notice throughout *Here Comes The Guide* the words "provided" or "select from list" after the word *Catering*. Sites that have an exclusive caterer or only permit you to select from a preferred list do so because each wants to eliminate most of the risks involved in having a caterer on the premises who is not accustomed to working in that environment. Exclusive or preferred caterers have achieved their exalted status because they either provide consistently good services or they won the catering contract when it went out to bid. Whether you're working with one of your facility's choices or your own, make sure that your contract includes everything you have agreed on before you sign it.

Working with an Event Planner, Wedding Coordinator or Consultant

Opting to hire a professional planner may be a wise choice. A good consultant will ask all the right questions, determine exactly what you need, and take care of as much or as little of your affair as you want. If you'd like to feel like a guest at your own event, have the consultant manage everything, including orchestrating the day of the event. If you only want some advice and structure, hire a planner on a meeting-by-meeting basis.

Most of the principles used in selecting a caterer apply to hiring an event coordinator. Try to get suggestions from friends or facilities, follow up on references the consultants give you, compare service fees and make sure you and the consultant are compatible. The range of professionalism and experience varies greatly, so it really is to your advantage to investigate each consultant's track record. Again, once you've found someone who can accommodate you, get everything in writing so that there won't be any misunderstandings down the road. Although engaging someone to "manage" your event can be a godsend, it can also be problematic if you turn the entire decision-making process over to them. Don't forget that it's your party, and no one else should decide what's right for you.

Event Services by Category

Marriage Preparation Workshop

Officiants

Photo Booths

Photographers

Videographers

Caterers

...planning our wedding was so easy and our big day was perfect!

- Helen and Nells Godfredsen

GREEN BUSINESS

Serving the Bay Area since 1993

149 West Hendy Avenue
Sunnyvale, CA 94086

408.245.4712

www.savoryandsweet.com

Caterers

le papillon

DINING & SPECIAL EVENTS

410 Saratoga Avenue | San Jose | 408.296.3730 | www.lepapillon.com

The Day was perfect

"your planning and expertise made everything go smoothly."

Email or request a proposal for your event today

PREMIER CATERING & EVENTS

- Full Service Catering and Event Design & Coordination Since 1994
- Old World Classical and New World Cuisine
- Creativity, Flexibility, and Peace of Mind

Laura Parente
415.986.4710
events@premiercatering.com
www.premiercatering.com

PREMIER
CATERING & EVENTS

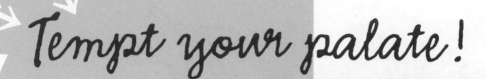

California Rose

catering & special events

- ~ Complimentary Tastings
- ~ Exclusive Menu Selections
- ~ Full Equipment & Rental Coordination
- ~ Wedding Coordinators

- ~ Venue Selection
- ~ Design and Décor
- ~ Florist
- ~ Cakes and Desserts

1012 B Grayson Street • Berkeley, CA 94710 • tel: 510-644-4473 • fax: 510-644-4430 • www.californiarose.com • info@californiarose.com

ELAINE BELL 🌰 CATERING

www.elainebellcatering.com   707-603-1400
San Francisco | Wine Country
Certified Bay Area Green Business

THE OTHER WOMAN

EVENT PLANNING & CATERING

425 El Camino Real, Menlo Park, CA 94025
T: 650.326.6911   F: 650.326.6457

To Request an Estimate Contact: Tami Perez - tami@cateringbytow.com

www.cateringbytow.com

A Moveable Feast

Fine Catering on the Monterey Peninsula
Fresh, local, organic foods & innovative menus.

831.659.5100

www.a-moveable-feast.com
movrmike@montereybay.com

* ANY SIZE *   * SINCE 1949 *

FULL SERVICE OR DELIVERY * WINE COUNTRY SPECIALISTS

BUSINESS OR SOCIAL * FULLY INSURED * ABC LICENSED

THE ART OF GOOD FOOD

ALEX'S CATERING

SERVING THE BAY AREA AND BEYOND
CHEF RAY VARGELLA

707-643-1711

* IMAGINATIVE MENUS * CREATIVE PRESENTATION *

COASTSIDECOUTURE

EST. 2004

MONTEREY BAY'S PREMIER EVENT PLANNERS

Offering full-service planning to day-of coordination

Home of

THE COUTURE HOUSE

Northern California's only wedding lounge and library
A one-stop resource for planning fabulous and affordable events

831.600.8206

COASTSIDECOUTURE.COM

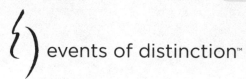

Photos courtesy of TGO Photography

ALLISON WEDDINGS

Entertainment

Musicians

- Ceremony

- Cocktails/Dinner

- Dance

www.Siliconvalleymusic.com

Email: calmeida@sbcglobal.net

408.927.0854

TAPESTRY
INNOVATIVE FUN ROMANTIC

www.tapestryflowers.com
415 550 1015

featured in:
ELEGANT BRIDE, BRIDE'S, INSIDE WEDDINGS, BETTER HOMES AND GARDENS, THE KNOT, GRACE ORMONDE, AND MORE

PAT GIBBONS
FLORAL DESIGNS

510.527.3197   www.patgibbonsfloral.com

STYLE . DESIGN . BEAUTY

Floral & Event Designers

ELEGANT MODERN WEDDING DESIGN

PAUL ROBERTSON
FLORAL DESIGN

WWW.PRFLORALDESIGN.COM
415 412 3374

Perfect Harmony

WEDDING & EVENT DESIGNS

Penny Basso, *Designer*

707-746-4824
www.perfectharmonydesigns.com

Floral & Event Designers

Vanda
FLORAL DESIGN

Beautiful Wine Country Weddings
Sonoma | Napa | Marin

tel: (707) 763-9271
www.vandafloral.com

abcdefghijklmnopqrstuvwxyzabcdefgh

· thank yous · monograms · stationery · moving cards · marriage vows ·

· invitation design · envelopes · placecards · announcements · menus ·

Calligraphy

english · עברית

Adrienne D. Keats

(415) 956·5006
navarac53@aol.com

GORGEOUS GOLD

Combined with understated gray hues, gold provides the perfect hint of luxurious style.

Being Stylish Has Never Been So Simple.

SAVE 10% on orders of $50 or more, visit weddingpaperdivas.com/hctg or call us at 866.594.1226

WEDDING ✱ PAPER *divas*
simply perfect. perfectly simple.

WEDDING INVITATIONS   SAVE THE DATES   SHOWER INVITATIONS   THANK YOU CARDS

Marriage Preparation Workshop

"This workshop was one of the best time and money investments we've made for our relationship...it should be on every couple's wedding to-do list." JULIE & PAUL

fun

Marriage Prep 101

informative

"It was amazing to see how certain assumptions that we had about each other's feelings and perceptions got totally turned on their head, just by learning to communicate in a new way." VICTORIA & CHRIS

Marriage Prep 101 is an award-winning workshop for engaged, seriously dating and newlywed couples. Taught by Drs. Patrick and Michelle Gannon—husband-and-wife psychologists/relationship experts—the class will help you:

- Focus on the strengths of your relationship.
- Learn positive communication.
- Develop conflict resolution and intimacy enhancement skills.
- Lay the foundation for a successful, satisfying marriage.

proactive

The Gannons have conducted over 90 workshops for more than 1400 couples. They welcome people of all backgrounds, ages and faiths.

Featured on the CBS Early Show *and* Evening Magazine TV, *as well as in the* SF Chronicle, Huffington Post, Time, *and many more publications. Great reviews on* Yelp.com.

practical

Drs. Michelle & Patrick Gannon

"The Gannons' sense of humor, honesty, and experiences from fifteen years of marriage made it seem like we were learning from good friends." KRISTA & JEREMY

MarriagePrep101.com · drmichellegannon@gmail.com · 415.905.8830
Facebook.com/MarriagePrep101 · Twitter.com/DrMichellexo

Officiants

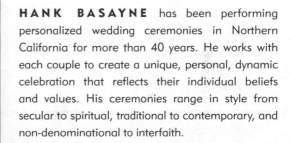

JEN WOOD PHOTOGRAPHY

THE REVEREND TIMOTHY MILLS

Putting Couples at Ease...

- 25 years of wedding experience
- strong dignity, great humor
- accommodating, versatile, creative
- a sense for the sacred
- friendly, positive, reassuring

- never late, lost or long-winded
- attentive to detail, sees the big picture
- adjusts easily, naturally, in the moment
- deep voice, rich quality, easily heard
- professional demeanor, emotionally present

"Your wonderful sense of humor made us feel at ease. My guests and family kept commenting 'This guy is great! Where did you find him?'" —Jen and Armando

"The ceremony was uplifting and fun—we cannot thank you enough." —Parisa and Nicolas

"The way you remembered my dad in the ceremony was perfect, just what the family needed. Thank you." —Akiko and Mike

Reverend Tim Mills is non-denominational and ordained, having spent many years as a church pastor, addiction counselor, jail chaplain and college professor. He has broad experience with Christian and Jewish ceremonies (fluent in Hebrew), also Persian and Indian, but most couples he serves are non-religious. In addition to creating and personalizing your ceremony according to your style, Reverend Tim works well with other wedding professionals at your ceremony and family members you choose to involve.

Free consultation. Pre-marital counseling upon request. 5-Star YELP reviews. Serves the entire Bay Area and beyond.

REV. TIMOTHY MILLS, PH.D.
901 Waterford Place, Pinole CA 94564

OFFICE 510-724-5250 CELL 510-334-5308
WEB timothymills.weebly.com
EMAIL timmills2005@sbcglobal.net

Photo Booths Designed for Weddings

- The Modern Photo Booth
- The Vintage Photo Booth
- The APM™

- Green Screen
- Red Carpet Photos
- Get Flipped™

- Custom Backdrops
- Designer Graphics
- SO MUCH MORE

1.800.944.9585

www.SanFranciscoPhotoBooth.com

shanti duprez
fine portrait photography

650 726 7773

portraitsbyshanti.com

Julie Mikos photographer

www.juliemikos.com

Photographers

www.darcyweddings.com

www.LionPhotography.com
415.215.2579
707.766.6955

Photographers

- One of Bride's Magazine's "Top Shots" for the 2008 and 2009 Photojournalism Competitions.
- Named one of the top wedding photojournalists in the world in 2006 and 2008 by WPJA.
- Published in Grace Ormonde Wedding Style, the Knot, Brides Magazine and others.

- Named the snuggliest mama in the world by her 5-year old (her 30-something husband agrees).

rhee bevere
PHOTOGRAPHY

www.rheebevere.com

a smile. a teardrop. a kiss. an instant.

www.kiphotography.com

Claudia Akers
photography with passion

www.claudiaakersphotography.com
408.497.5050

Photographers

DEBORAH COLEMAN PHOTOGRAPHY

Professional photojournalist Deborah Coleman shoots weddings with an eye for detail and a non-intrusive style. She's comfortable in both intimate and high-intensity situations, and expertly uses natural light and great camera angles to capture the best moments of your day.

www.colemanfoto.com

tu
photography

when photography means everything…

Photographers

Liz Edlund
PHOTOGRAPHS
elegantly fun wedding photojournalism

www.lizedlund.com

Photographers

415.543.3100 • KARINA@KARINAMARIEDIAZ.COM

WEDDINGS • BAR/BAT MITZVAH • FAMILY   WWW.KARINAMARIEDIAZ.COM

BOUDOIR • MATERNITY WWW.COLETTEPHOTOGRAPHY.COM

Videographers

Photo © Todd Rafalovich

Alpha Mae & Scott in 1939

On their 50th anniversary

1938. Scott met Alpha Mae at a party that neither was in a mood to attend. They left the party together and talked for hours. Scott learned she was a pianist, so he began singing lessons in hopes of impressing her. It worked, and they were married in 1939. 71 years of marriage, five children, fifteen grandchildren and seven great-grandchildren later, Scott still can't carry a tune. But that doesn't stop him from singing to her every morning. Loudly.

EVERY COUPLE HAS A STORY...

How will *your* story be told?

METMEDIA

"Stories don't have a middle or an end anymore. They usually have a beginning...that never stops beginning." — Steven Spielberg

MetMediaVideo.com

Indexes

Event Locations

C

j

k

l

m

t

u

Event Services

Bridal Salons

Here's a list of our favorite
bridal salons in Northern California.

Collectively, they offer a wide range of fabulous wedding attire to suit a variety of budgets. If you'd like a free copy of the Here Comes The Guide book for a friend or to give as a gift, just visit one of these salons and ask! (Free books available while supplies last.)

Don't forget to check out our website **www.HereComesTheGuide.com,** which includes listings of *local Trunk Shows & Sample Sales!*

SAN FRANCISCO

Amy Kuschel Bride
23 Grant Avenue, Fifth Floor
San Francisco, CA 94108
415/956-5657
www.AmyKuschel.com

Bridal Galleria
3 Embarcadero Ctr., Lobby Level
San Francisco, CA 94111
415/362-2277
www.BridalGalleria.com

Glamour Closet
114 Columbus Avenue
San Francisco, CA 94133
415/505-4138
www.GlamourCloset.com

Haute Bride Couture Bridal
1954 Union Street
San Francisco, CA 94123
415/923-5900
www.HauteBride.com

JinWang
111 Maiden Lane, 3rd Floor
San Francisco, CA 94108
415/397-9111
www.JinWang.net

Joan Gilbert Bride, European Collection
3866 Clay Street
San Francisco, CA 94118
415/752-1808
www.JoanGilbertBride.com

Marina Morrison
30 Maiden Lane, 4th floor
San Francisco, CA 94108
415/984-9360
www.MarinaMorrison.com

Siri Boutique
540 D Barneveld Avenue
San Francisco, CA 94124
415/431-8873
www.SiriInc.com

SOUTH BAY

Gabrielle's Bridal Atelier
422 East Campbell Avenue
Campbell, CA 95008
408/370-4999
www.GabriellesBridal.com

SWATI Couture
2321 Farmcrest Street
Milpitas, CA 95035
510/610 5990
www.SwatiCouture.com

TRUDYS Brides & Special Occasions
1875 South Bascom Ave., Suite 134
Campbell, CA 95008
408/377-1987
www.TrudysBrides.com

Vastra by Namrita Chettiar
714 Valley Way
Santa Clara, CA 95051
408/761-8678
By appointment only.
www.NamritaChettiar.com

SACRAMENTO

Bella Donna Bride
2663 Town & Country Place
Sacramento, CA 95821
916/481-5065
www.BellaDonnaBride.com

PENINSULA

Nouvelle Vogue
132 E. 3rd Avenue
San Mateo, CA 94401
650/347-3444
www.NouvelleVogue.com

Perfect Details
851 Burlway, Suite #301
Burlingame CA 94010
650/576-4927
By appointment only,
or buy online at:
www.PerfectDetails.com

Notes

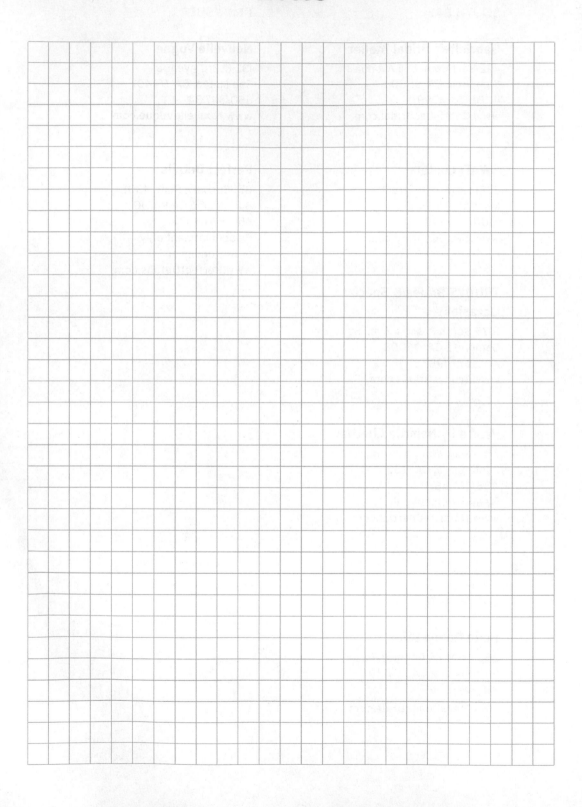

Notes

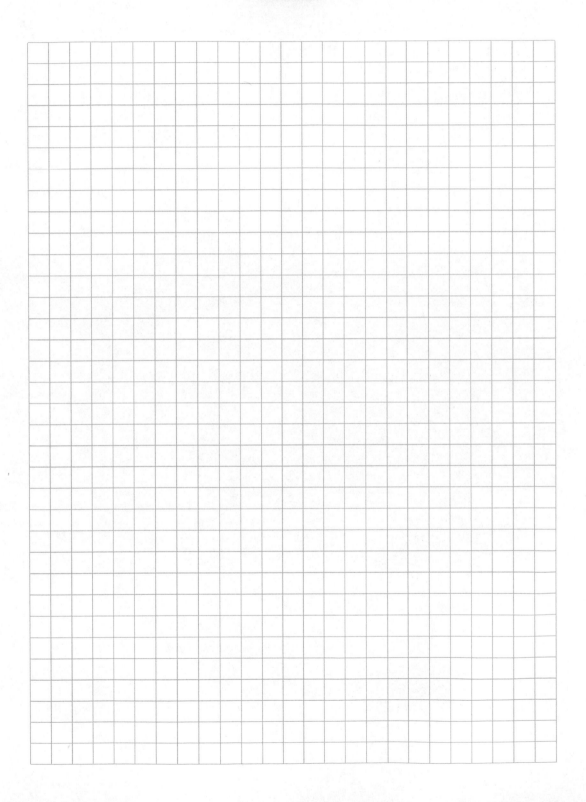

Notes

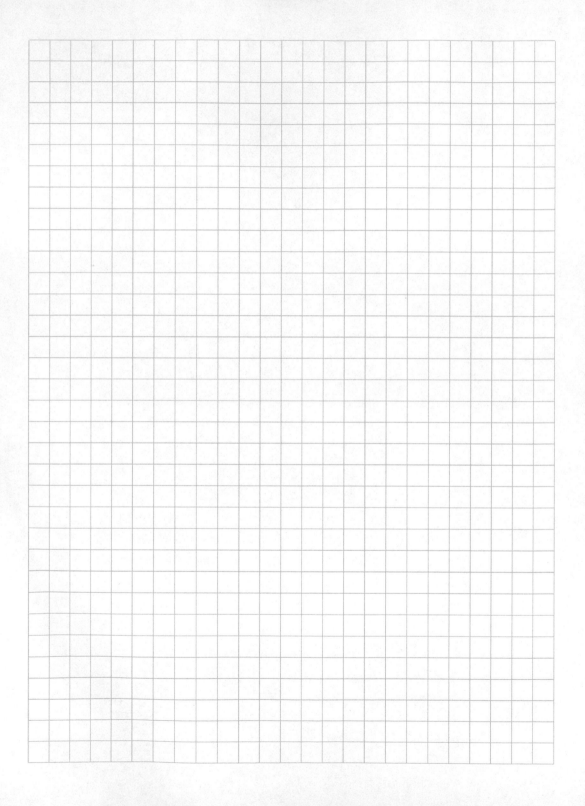

Notes

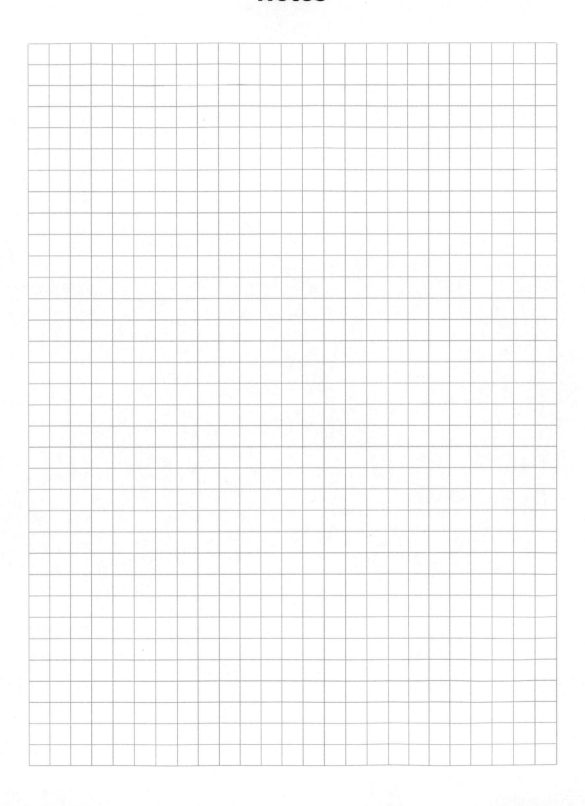

Notes

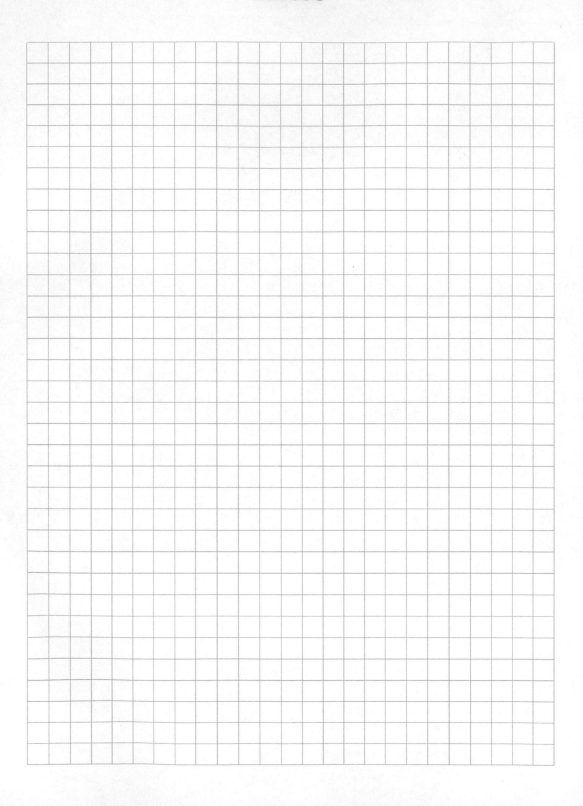

Notes

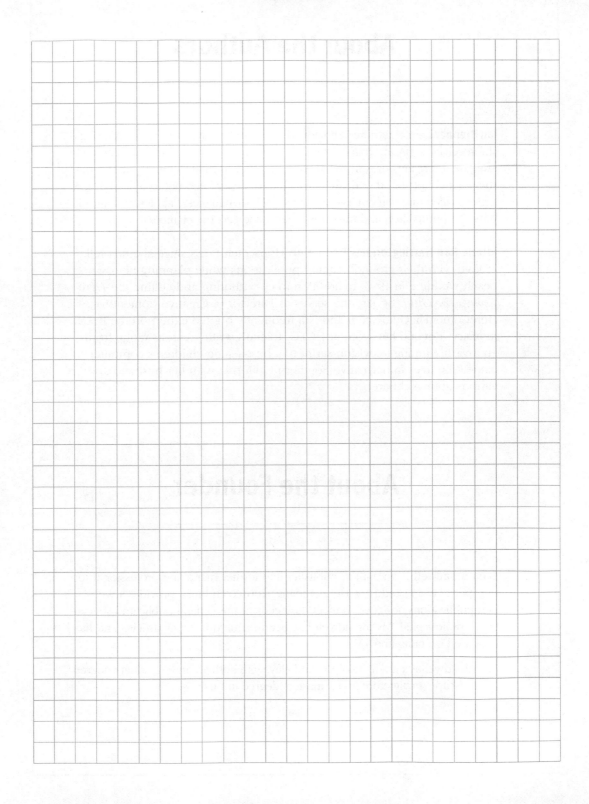

About the Authors

Jan Brenner has co-authored and edited all of Hopscotch Press' books. Although she received a BA in English from UC Berkeley, she backed into writing only after spending ten years in social work and four in publishing. Along the way she got a couple of other degrees which have never been put to official use. A lifelong dilettante, she's quasi-conversant in 3.1 languages, dabbles in domestic pursuits, pumps iron and travels whenever she gets the chance.

Jolene Rae Harrington has been with Hopscotch Press since she first fell in love with their groundbreaking publications while planning her own beach wedding in 1995. In addition to co-authoring and editing the *Here Comes The Guide* books, she serves as Director of Creative Content for HereComesTheGuide.com and is a frequently quoted expert on the bridal industry. Beyond her work at HCTG, Jolene's writing credits range from an award-winning television script to a best-selling children's computer game. She lives in her native Southern California with her husband and various animal children.

About the Founder

Lynn Broadwell is an author, publisher and former marketing professional for the special events industry. Her company, Hopscotch Press, provides a website and publications designed to meet the needs of the general public and special event professional. Ms. Broadwell has been featured in many articles and has appeared on radio and TV.

Ms. Broadwell is a graduate of UC Berkeley, with both an undergraduate degree in landscape architecture and a masters degree in business.